Abstract

Data

Types

Abstract

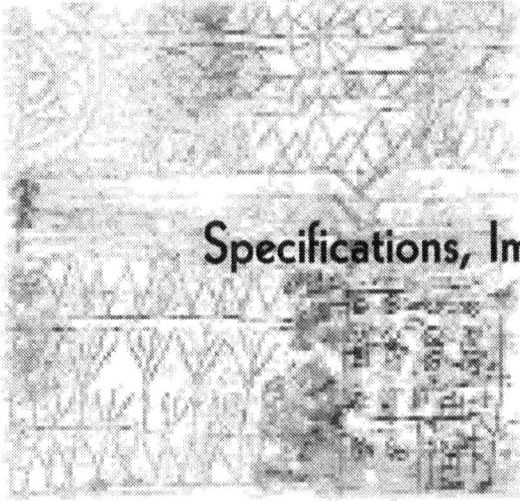

Specifications, Implementations, and Applications

Data

Nell Dale
The University of Texas at Austin

Henry M. Walker
Grinnell College

Types

D. C. Heath and Company
Lexington, Massachusetts   Toronto

Address editorial correspondence to
D. C. Heath and Company
125 Spring Street
Lexington, MA 02173

Acquisitions: Walter Cunningham
Development: Rebecca Johnson, Karen H. Jolie
Editorial Production: Heather Garrison, Anne Starr
Design: Henry Rachlin
Production Coordination: Charles Dutton

Published simultaneously in Canada.

Printed in the United States of America.

International Standard Book Number: 978-0-669-40000-7

Library of Congress Catalog Number: 95-68945

10 9 8 7 6 5 4 3 2 1

To Al, my husband and best friend

N. D.

To my family:
my wife, Terry
my daughters, Donna and Barbara
my parents, Alice and Benjamin

H. M. W.

Preface

Fresh, Modern Approach

This book takes a fresh, modern approach to the organization and manipulation of data by computer systems. This approach is innovative in several important ways:

1. Abstract data types (ADTs) are organized following a top-down perspective, based upon a user's view of data.

2. As the book's title suggests, each ADT is explored from three perspectives: specification, implementation, and application.

3. ADTs are defined precisely and formally through the use of axiomatic specifications.

4. Several implementations of most ADTs are presented and the strengths and weaknesses of each are reviewed. Further, we regularly tie an implementation to the ADT's specifications, arguing why a particular implementation is correct.

5. Implementations include both single-processor algorithms and parallel algorithms.

6. The book includes a very broad range of applications, from standard coding algorithms (e.g., Huffman coding) to new contexts (e.g., the use of tables within Internet communication).

Data Types and Data Structures

Data structures have been a fundamental subject in computer science curricula beginning with the ACM's Curriculum '68. However, the focus has broadened considerably in the last few years. Data structures refers to the study of data and how to represent data objects within a program: the *implementation* of structured relationships. We are now interested in the study of the abstract properties of classes of objects in addition to how these objects might be represented in a program. Johannes J. Martin puts it very succinctly: ". . . depending on the point of view, a data object is characterized by its type (for the user) or by its structure (for the implementer)."[1]

---

[1] Johannes J. Martin, *Data Types and Data Structures*, Prentice-Hall International Series in Computer Science, C. A. R. Hoare, Series Editor, 1986.

The subjects of this broader topic are abstract data types (ADTs): classes of objects whose logical behavior is defined by a set of values and a set of operations. The object-oriented programming (OOP) approach to problem solving has contributed considerably to this change of focus. OOP is often described as the use of abstract data types in an environment with inheritance and polymorphism. However, this book is about abstract data types; we do not consider inheritance and polymorphism, but we do discuss generic data types.

Top-Down Organization of Abstract Data Types

In response to this new focus, the authors proposed a changed paradigm for classifying data types.[2] This book follows the new paradigm. More specifically, we classify ADTs according to their logical operations, as shown in Figure 1. Beyond simple scalar types, ADTs may be viewed as being unstructured, semistructured, or structured. For example, unstructured ADTs include sets, keyed tables, and records in which data are stored and retrieved, but the user is unaware of any relationships among these data. Internally, of course, the data may be stored in a bit vector, hash table, or other data structure, but the external user does not care about such details.

Similarly a semistructured ADT provides the user with limited access to data; such ADTs include stacks, FIFO queues, and priority queues. Internally, data may be stored in an array or a linked list, but externally a user may access information with only a constrained collection of operations.

Structured ADTs organize data in particular ways, so that various relationships may exist among the data. Structured ADTs may be subdivided into nondimensional data types, linear data types, and multidimensional data types. Relationships among data in nondimensional data types are defined by a hierarchy of information or by explicit edge relationships. Data in multidimensional structures are accessed through two or more subscripts. Data in linear structures are organized through either explicit subscripts or an implicit ordering where each data item (except the last) has an explicit successor.

This classification of data types begins at a high level of abstraction. Then, as shown in Figure 1, each subsequent level in the hierarchy is obtained by adding logical properties to the operations available within the ADT. The nature of these properties is explained through the book as each kind of data type is examined in detail.

ADT: Specification, Implementation, Application

The text presents the various ADTs in Figure 1 in three stages, again following a top-down methodology. First, we consider an ADT from the user's perspective; that is, we consider the ADT's specifications. In this discussion, we are particularly

---

[2] Nell Dale and Henry M. Walker, "A Classification of Data Types," *Journal of Computer Science Education*, 1994.

Data Types

Scalar

Composite

Ordinal
Enumerated
Subrange
Integer
Character
Boolean
Finite Group

Continuous
Rational
Real
Complex

Structured

Semi-Structured
Stack
Queue
Priority Queue

Unstructured
Set
Keyed Table
Record

Nondimensional
Tree
Binary Search Tree
Multi-Way Search Tree
Heap
Graph

Linear

Multi-Dimensional
Array

Nonindexed

Indexed
Array
Sequence

Homogeneous

Nonhomogeneous
Generalized List

Unsorted
List

Sorted
Sorted List

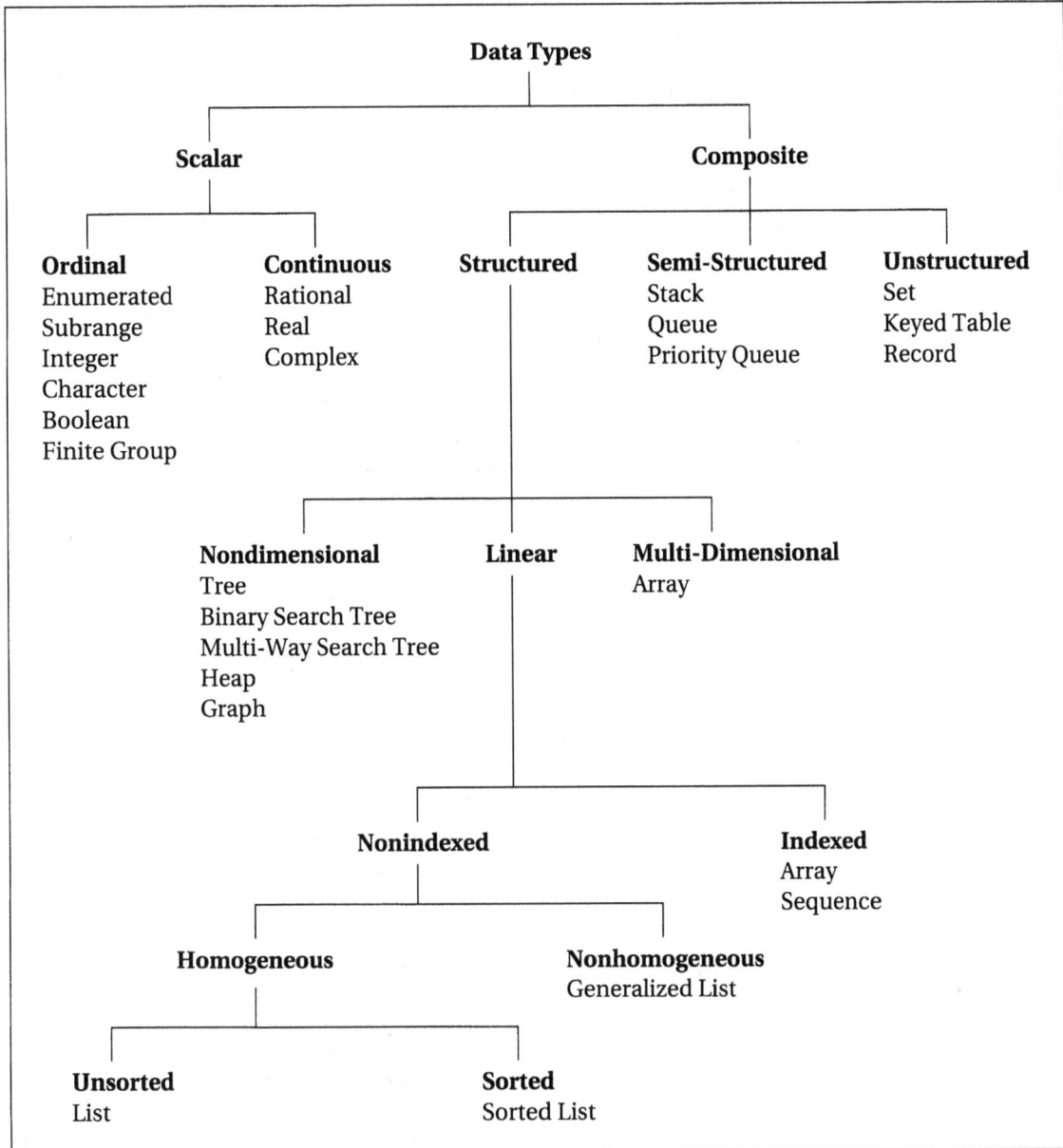

Figure 1   A Classification of Data Types

careful not to bias the user's needs by anticipating how the ADT might be implemented. From a user's perspective, an ADT is useful if it provides needed operations for data storage, retrieval, and processing. Applications do not start with the notion that data are stored in arrays, records, or lists; rather, applications begin by identifying needs for problem solving. We approach the specification of ADTs from this same user's perspective.

Next, for each ADT, we consider one or more implementations. This work includes the presentation of many classical algorithms, and we often examine several implementation alternatives. In each case, the algorithms are written in an easily understood pseudocode based on the Pascal, Modula-2, Ada model of programming languages.

As part of this presentation of algorithms, we provide detailed descriptions of algorithm construction. Many texts suffer from the "We leave the coding of this algorithm as an exercise" syndrome. All too often algorithms are handled in one of two ways. In the first approach the structures are pictured with boxes and arrows, followed by a brief verbal description of the algorithm, leaving the student with a feeling that the algorithm is trivial. The second approach jumps from pictures to code, leaving the student feeling at a loss because he or she does not follow the translation from pictures to code, which the author seems to imply is trivial. In fact, it is a complex process to move from an understanding of a structure or algorithm through diagrams, converting the boxes and arrows to nodes and pointers, specifying the algorithm, and finally writing the detailed algorithm. We attempt to clarify this problem-solving process by working through detailed examples.

Each ADT then is used in one or more applications. Such applications include discussions of some classical algorithms, alternative implementations of previously defined ADTs, and problems that arise in a real-world context. Such real-world applications include the use of the Huffman coding algorithm for file compression and data transmission, the storage of addresses in hash tables and other tables for Internet communication, and the use of multiway trees for searching within files and files directories. Such applications are presented because specifying and implementing ADTs without using them would be like planning a menu, cooking a meal, and never getting to taste any of the food. Students need to see these ADTs used in solving problems. We have chosen to introduce classic computing algorithms as applications for many of the ADTs.

Axiomatic Specification

In defining the operations within ADTs, users and implementers must be able to agree upon capabilities in clear, precise, and unambiguous terms. Students learning about ADTs, therefore, need to gain experience in reading and writing formal specifications.

This book takes a reasonably simple, but rigorous, approach to defining ADTs through the use of axiomatic specifications. Such specifications are self contained, precise, unambiguous, and mathematically formal. Axiomatic specifications also allow students to determine exactly what information must be obtained as the result of a sequence of operations; students can experiment with operations formally before considering details of implementation or coding. This approach, therefore, is particularly helpful in emphasizing to students that specifications need not rely upon underlying implementation details.

Axiomatic specifications have the further advantage that they can be translated naturally into symbolic-algebra packages, where sequences of operations can be applied and results can be verified. The use of Mathematica to directly execute specifications is discussed further in Appendix B.

Analysis and Correctness of Algorithms

We are careful that our discussion of an implementation does not stop with just the description of an algorithm. In particular, an implementation is helpful only if it satisfies an ADT's specifications and if it is reasonably efficient. Therefore, throughout the book we regularly compare implementations with specifications, and we frequently argue explicitly why an implementation is correct. Also, we consistently analyze the efficiency of each algorithm. We frequently examine code at a detailed level, giving a micro-analysis of an algorithm, and we almost always determine the Big-O complexity of each implementation at a macro level.

Uniprocessor and Parallel Algorithms

In recent years, technological developments in hardware and software have led to an increased emphasis on the use of parallelism to solve problems. Recent curricular recommendations[3] also have highlighted the need to include parallelism as part of the core of undergraduate computer science, not just as an advanced elective.

This book responds to these developments by including discussions of parallelism in many chapters. As early as Chapter 3, we provide a framework for later work, by providing a conceptual basis for understanding parallelism at both the hardware and the problem-solving (software) levels. In several later chapters, we include parallel algorithms as alternative means to solve problems and process data.

Throughout, our treatment supports the view that parallel algorithms should not be considered as unusual or different. Rather, algorithms and implementations should take advantage of the processing environment available to the user. When that environment contains only one processor, then classical uniprocessor algorithms are appropriate. When several processors are available, then parallel algorithms should be considered.

A single book, of course, cannot cover all types of algorithms for all types of processing environments. However, various approaches and ideas can and should be introduced at all levels of the curriculum, and this text provides some basic insights into algorithm development in both the uniprocessor and multiprocessor environments.

---

[3] For example, the following curricular recommendations include parallelism as an important theme:

ACM/IEEE-CS Joint Curriculum Task Force, *Computing Curriculum 1991*, IEEE Computer Society Press and ACM Press, 1991.

Henry M. Walker and G. Michael Schneider, "A Revised Model Curriculum for a Liberal Arts Degree in Computer Science," *Communications of the ACM*, to appear. This paper is the culmination of discussions by the Liberal Arts Computer Science Consortium.

Student Preconditions

This book assumes that students have had the material outlined in traditional introductory courses, commonly designated CS1 and CS2. Thus students should be capable of the following tasks:

1. Using built-in data types of a modern programming language to write a medium-sized program.
2. Implementing and using stacks, queues, and binary search trees.
3. Distinguishing between sorting algorithms, which are $O(n\log_2 n)$ and $O(n^2)$, and being able to implement several of them.
4. Designing and implementing recursive algorithms, at least for recursive structures (i.e., trees).
5. Developing and implementing algorithms following a clear, clean, readable style.

Choice of Programming Language

Because this book focuses upon data types and algorithms, students should have experience programming in a language that supports modularization and algorithmic thinking. Within this context, however, specific details of syntax are not particularly important to the discussion in this book. Traditionally, algorithms have been written in a structured, procedure-oriented language, such as Pascal, Modula-2, or Ada. Any of these languages (or other procedure-based languages that support pointers and recursion) should be quite adequate for implementing the algorithms that we present.

Such procedural languages share many common characteristics, so algorithms in this text are written in a composite language or pseudocode that combines many elements of Pascal, Modula-2, and Ada. We have tried to avoid idiosyncrasies of any of these languages, however. Moreover, because the algorithms are not tied to specific language details, the pseudocode also can be translated in a reasonably direct way to many other procedural languages, such as C, or to extensions of such languages, such as C++.

Because this book emphasizes ADTs and algorithms, not programming tricks, we leave the choice of a specific implementation language to the reader.

Book Organization

Chapter 1 sets the tone of the book by defining what an abstract data type is and how to formally specify one. Proofs of the state of an instance of a data type are presented to demonstrate how to reason formally about a data type.

Chapter 2 introduces the analysis of algorithms, including Big-O notation. A precondition to this book is that students are familiar with storing and retrieving items (both sorted and unsorted) in an array, in a linked list, and in a binary search tree. In Chapter 2, the order of inserting into and deleting from a list in each of these structures is discussed. These five implementations are called our *primitives*.

Chapter 3 discusses issues involved in making algorithms more general. The concept of language-independent algorithms is presented along with a discussion of information hiding, encapsulation, visibility and access, and generic structures. Parallelism is defined and examined from both a hardware and a software perspective.

The rest of the book is organized in a spiral fashion. **Chapter 4** covers unstructured data types (sets, records, and keyed tables). The implementation alternatives are the structures that have been defined previously: the list implementation primitives. Hashing, a technique that some students may have seen already, is reviewed and presented as another way of implementing keyed tables. When a more complex data type is defined, its use in implementing a previously defined data type is discussed in the applications section for the more complex data type.

Chapter 5 focuses on stacks, queues, and priority queues. These three ADTs are called semistructured data types. Their common characteristic is that each has a designed item: the last item put in (stack), the first item put in (queue), the item with the highest priority (priority queue). These ADTs have been considered restricted versions of linear lists in the literature, but that classification reflects how they are traditionally implemented, not their logical structure.

Chapter 6 covers linear structures. As illustrated in Figure 1, a distinction is made between indexed linear structures (arrays and sequences) and nonindexed linear structures (sorted and unsorted lists). **Chapters 7** through **11** introduces the nonlinear data types. **Chapter 7** discusses binary trees and heaps; **Chapter 8** features binary search trees; **Chapter 9** describes multiway search trees; **Chapters 10** and **11** present digraphs and graphs respectively; and **Chapter 12** covers generalized lists. **Chapter 13** pulls together all the principles of memory management, some of which have already been illustrated in earlier chapters.

Additional Features

Exercise Answers   Answers to a third of the exercises are included in the back of the text. The remaining noncoding exercises are answered in the *Instructor's Guide*.

Glossary   A glossary containing the terms introduced in the text is included.

Appendixes   The abstract model specifications for a sample of the ADTs presented in the text are included in Appendix A. Appendix B contains an unsolicited paper written by a student in one of the author's classes. This paper demonstrates how the axiomatic specifications used in the book can be coded directly in *Mathematica* to prove the state of an abstract data type after a series of operations.

Instructor's Guide   Prepared by the authors, the *Instructor's Guide* features sample syllabi, guided discussion exercises (with answers), sample quizzes and exams (with answers), programming assignments, answers to the noncoding exercises that are not included in the main text, and transparency masters.

Student Disk   This disk is divided into four directories: Pascal, Ada, C++, and Michael. At least one implementation of each abstract data type is included on the Student Disk. Many of the ADTs are implemented in several languages. Most applications are included in at least one language. Several of the programming assignments in the *Instructor's Guide* involve debugging or modifying programs that are on the Student Disk.

Acknowledgments

The authors first began discussing abstract data types, their classification, and implementation, while the second author was at The University of Texas at Austin on sabbatical leave from Grinnell College. In the subsequent years, both institutions have been very supportive of this collaborative work, and we gratefully acknowledge their help. In particular the authors wish to thank the Department of Computer Sciences at The University of Texas at Austin and Dean Charles Duke and the Grinnell College Grant Board for their help and support in this project.

Suggestions for improvements and clarifications for this text have come from many reviewers and students. The authors particular want to thank Jeff Brumfield (The University of Texas at Austin) and the other formal reviewers for their very helpful comments: Linda Elliott, La Salle University; Sue Crane Fitzgerald, Rockhurst College; Henry G. Gordon, Kutztown University of Pennsylvania; Harold C. Grossman, Clemson University; George C. Harrison, Norfolk State University; Judy Ann Hill, Purdue University Calumet; David L. Ranum, Luther College; and Stan Walljasper, University of Northern Iowa. The authors also have used various preliminary versions of this text in several classes at both The University of Texas at Austin and Grinnell College, and we express our appreciation to both our teaching assistants and our students for their insightful comments and suggestions.

Special thanks go to Randy Wang, who wrote many of the exercise answers while still an undergraduate at The University of Texas. Our special thanks go to Michael Vincent Stanton who became so intrigued with axiomatic specifications of ADTs that he wrote a paper about implementing the specifications in Mathematica. His paper is included in Appendix B. Michael also contributed C^{++} implementations in the Michael directory.

We wish to thank all the people at Heath who have participated in the production of this book: Lee Ripley, Randall Adams, Karen Jolie, Rebecca Johnson, Walter Cunningham, Mary Ned Fotis, Heather Garrison, Anne Starr, and Andrea Cava.

Finally, we especially want to thank our families for their encouragement and support throughout the writing of this book. The writing of a book spans many cycles of joy and frustration, elation and discouragement, and anticipation and concern, and our families have tolerated us through these many ups and downs. Special thanks to Al, Terry, Donna, and Barbara for your support.

N. D.

H. M. W.

Contents

5 Semi-Structured Data Types 151

6

Structured Linear Data Types   193

7 *Binary Trees* 251

8 *Binary Search Trees* 313

Undirected Graphs and Complexity   491

11

Abstract

Data

Types

Abstract Specification Techniques

In this chapter, we lay the groundwork for the rest of the book. We define exactly what we mean by an abstract data type, and we look at two formal methods of specifying precisely the logical behavior of each type. These two methods are axiomatic specifications and abstract models. We use the stack to demonstrate these methods, because its logical properties should be familiar to any reader.

We show how we can formally analyze the contents of an instance of an abstract data type using the axioms that define its behavior within the axiomatic specification technique. Finally, we define the axioms for the UnsortedList ADT (abstract data type) and show how to prove an implementation meets its specification.

What Are Abstract Data Types?

This book, as its title indicates, discusses abstract data types—three words with common, everyday, informal meanings:

abstract: conceptual, not concrete

data: information that has been put into a form a computer can use

type: a category of objects sharing common characteristics

As a computer science student, you know that "data" and "type" also combine to form the technical term "data type," which can be formally defined as the shared characteristics of a category of data objects. This description includes a set of values (the domain) that a variable or constant of that data type can have and the set of operations that can be applied to values of that data type.

A computer often is considered concrete and literal, so where does "abstract" or "conceptual" fit into the picture? An abstract, or conceptual, data type is one whose set of operations is defined at a formal, logical level, without being restricted by the operational details. This formal definition or specification becomes the sole interface for both the people writing applications and the people who implement the abstract data type in a computer program.

We consider the type integer as an example of an abstract data type. Integer numbers seem very concrete because we are used to working with numbers. However, we do not know how they are represented in a particular computer, how multiplication or division is actually accomplished between two integer numbers, or if the integers are limited to a specific range and what that range might be. All we know is what the syntax and operations of a language tell us. For example, Modula-2 defines three formats for integers (octal, decimal, and hexadecimal), two unary operations (+ and −), and eleven binary operations (+, −, *, MOD, DIV, =, <>, <, >, <=, >=).

Typically, syntax is described in a formal manner to indicate what constructs are allowed. Sometimes, the meaning of these symbols also is specified explicitly through such advanced techniques as denotational or operational semantics. However, more frequently, arithmetic symbols are assumed to have the same meaning as the familiar mathematical operations defined on integer numbers; that is, the meaning of the operations of the data type INTEGER in Modula-2 are defined in terms of the corresponding mathematical concepts. The integer numbers of mathematics are a model upon which the data type INTEGER is based. In using this model, the language may or may not formally specify a restricted range for integers, and there may or may not be a careful statement of what happens if there is an attempt to process numbers outside that range.

While the term **abstract data type (ADT)** describes a comprehensive collection of data values and operations, the term **data structures** refers to the study of data and how to represent data objects within a program, that is, the implementation of structured relationships. Historically, a course on data structures was a mainstay of many Computer Science Departments. However, over the last 10 years, the focus has broadened considerably. We are now interested in the study of the abstract properties of classes of data objects in addition to how these objects might be represented in a program. Johannes J. Martin puts it very succinctly: ". . . depending on the point of view, a data object is characterized by its type (for the user) or by its structure (for the implementer)."[1]

The topic of data structures has now been subsumed under the broader topic of abstract data types (ADTs): the study of classes of objects whose logical behavior is defined by a set of operations.

> **Data Structures** The implementation of structured relationships.
>
> **ADTs (abstract data types)** Classes of objects whose logical behavior is defined by a set of values and a set of operations.

The traditional model for studying data structures is based on characteristics of the implementation of the structures. For example, a stack and a queue are classified as restricted versions of a linear list where access is limited to one or both ends of the list. The properties of a stack and a queue can certainly be represented this way. However, the *user* of the two abstract data types, stack and queue, does not care about ends and restricted access. In fact, the user does not care what happens when an item is stored in a stack or a queue; the user is only interested in what is returned on a pop or a dequeue. The item that is returned is the last one inserted in the case of a stack or the first one inserted in the case of a queue.

The study of ADTs requires that we step back and view data types from the *functional view of the user*. The classification used in this book is based on such a view.

The subtitle for this book describes the way in which each chapter is organized: from specification through implementation to application. Each abstract data type is defined using a formal specification technique. The formal properties of each abstract data type are examined. The formal specifications become the interface used for the implementation. Various implementations consistent with the interface are examined and compared using Big-O analysis. Some implementations use the built-in data types of modern programming languages. Other implementations use previously defined abstract data types. Each abstract data type is used in at least one application. As the data types get more complex, the application section for one abstract data type may describe the use of that type as a more efficient implementation for a type that is defined previously.

Throughout, this text emphasizes the fact that abstract data types and their implementations are not ends in themselves. Rather, abstract data types are some of the basic tools for building correct, efficient, modifiable, reusable software. Because such software is the goal of software engineering, we consider our treatment of abstract data types as a small-scale application of software engineering

---

[1]Johannes J. Martin, *Data Types and Data Structures*, Prentice-Hall International Series in Computer Science, C.A.R. Hoare, Series Editor, 1986.

techniques. That is, we are specifying and implementing correct, efficient, and modifiable abstract data types to be used and reused as building blocks in larger software systems.

We introduce two formal specification techniques for defining abstract data types: *axiomatic (or algebraic) specifications* and *abstract models*. In the following sections, we examine abstraction further and introduce the two specification techniques for describing abstract data types in detail.

Abstraction

Software Engineering was one of the key phrases of the eighties, and it continues to be a key topic in the nineties. Although there are more formal definitions, our working definition of software engineering is "the development and application of careful methodologies for the writing of software." One of the most important principles in accomplishing this is the use of abstraction. Abstraction allows us to organize the complexity of a task by focusing on the logical properties of data and actions rather than on the implementation details.

> **Software Engineering** The development and application of careful methodologies for the writing of software.

Two kinds of abstraction are of interest to computer scientists: *procedural abstraction* and *data abstraction*. Procedural abstraction is the separation of the logical properties of an action from the details of how the action is implemented. You can think of the logical properties as being the "what," and the implementation details as being the "how." Data abstraction is the separation of logical properties of data from the details of how the data are represented.

Procedural Abstraction

When developing an algorithm following a top-down approach, we are practicing **procedural abstraction**. We name a task at a high level and do not worry about how the task is to be accomplished until the module is expanded at a lower level. When we code our algorithm in a programming language, the name of a task becomes a call to the procedure or function that implements the task. Surely, the procedure does have to be coded; the details cannot be ignored forever. However, the part of the program that calls the procedure does not have to be bothered with the details of how it is to be implemented. This is procedural abstraction. In fact, if the code of the procedure is changed, the calling module need not be affected in any way as long as the interface between the calling module and the procedure remains the same.

> **Procedural Abstraction** Separation of the logical properties of an action from the implementation details.

The use of built-in procedures and functions in a programming language is another example of procedural abstraction. For example, we use the Abs, Ord, and

Trunc functions in Pascal or Modula-2 without giving a second thought as to how they are implemented. The same is true of the procedures New and Dispose. The details are handled by the respective run-time support systems. The implementation complexity is hidden behind a procedure or function name.

All we need to know is how to call the procedure or function. That is, we must know the proper parameters, their types and their order, and any assumptions that the procedures or functions make. The specification of the parameter list and the documentation stating any assumptions form the interface between the built-in procedure or function and us, the users. Preconditions are used to specify the state of the input parameters on entry to the procedure or function; postconditions are used to specify the state of the output parameters when the procedure or function completes execution.

Data Abstraction

A set of data values and a set of operations on the values are described by a **data abstraction**. Many data types are built directly into programming languages. For example, integer arithmetic is allowed in most, if not all, programming languages. We take integers for granted. We add, subtract, multiply, divide, and compare them. Are integers kept in binary or binary-coded decimal? Are negative numbers represented by two's complement or sign and magnitude notation? We neither know nor care. In fact, we do not even have to know what these words mean. A programming language provides a data type integer that does what the syntax and semantics of the language tell it to do. How the machine actually accomplishes this does not concern us. These messy implementation details are hidden from our view.

> **Data Abstraction** Separation of the logical properties of data from the implementation details.

Clearly, procedural abstraction and data abstraction are closely related: the operations within an abstract data type are procedural abstractions. An abstract data type encompasses both procedural and data abstraction; the set of operations are defined for any data type that might make up the set of values.

In the next section, we look at techniques for writing the formal specifications for abstract data types.

Specification Techniques

Have you ever been asked by someone to pick up an item at the store, only to bring back the wrong thing? For example, you may have had an experience similar to the following story described by one of the authors.

> *My daughter asked me to pick up some sugar on the way home from the office. When I got home with the sugar, she clutched her head and said, "You got granulated sugar! You knew I wanted powdered sugar. I want to dust the tops of the cookies I made."*

The moral is that the author made a choice different from what the daughter intended because the specifications were not complete. When specifications are incomplete, different people often make different assumptions.

This form of miscommunication happens all the time. No great damage was caused by buying the wrong sugar. The daughter simply had to go back to the store. If, however, one person is implementing an algorithm on another person's data and such a misunderstanding occurs, much time and money can be lost.

Software engineering tries to keep this sort of problem from occurring by formulating ways of precisely defining both procedural and data abstractions. These definitions (called *interface specifications*) describe the effect of these abstractions on the external environment, that is, on the rest of the program. The specification techniques vary from informal English descriptions to formal languages designed for this purpose.

Formal, precise specifications are preferable to informal ones for two reasons. First, formal specifications can be analyzed mathematically. Formal verification techniques can be used to determine if two specifications are equivalent or to detect certain inconsistencies. Second, two people are more likely to agree on the meaning of a formal specification than on the meaning of an informal, natural language specification. There are two common techniques for writing formal specifications: axiomatic (or algebraic) specifications and abstract models.

In both techniques, the syntax of each operation is specified in terms of the name of the operation and the associated domains and ranges (the types of its parameters or arguments). The difference between the two techniques lies in how the semantics (logical properties) of the operations are defined, that is, how we describe what each operation does. Axiomatic specifications are completely self-contained, specifying each object as a composition of functions. Abstract models describe the semantics of the operations in terms of another well-defined data type. *The key to these and all formal specification techniques is that the description of the semantics does not refer to any implementation.*

In the next sections, we describe both of these techniques. Throughout the rest of the text, we use axiomatic specifications to define each of the ADTs that we examine. Abstract model specifications for some of the ADTs are in the Appendix.

Specification of an Abstract Data Type

One of the first abstract data types that students encounter is the stack. (It may not always be called an abstract data type, but it is one.) A stack is a composite data type that captures the Last In First Out (LIFO) property. You probably have implemented a stack in several different ways. We use the stack to illustrate the concepts in this section. We formally define **the specification of an abstract data type** to be a triple (D, F, A).

D, the first set in the triple, contains the domains and ranges involved in the data type. The data type being defined is called the *designated domain* or the *carrier domain*. It is often represented by a lowercase letter d. The other domains involved in the data type are called *auxiliary domains*. In the case of the stack, D would be the set {Stack, ItemType, Boolean}, Stack would be the designated domain, and ItemType and Boolean would be auxiliary domains. ItemType is the type of what is put on the stack. Boolean is the range of the function that tests to see if a stack is empty. Note that we are defining an abstract data type stack, not the data type stack, because ItemType is undefined. ItemType can be any set of values.

F, the second set in the triple, contains the names of the allowable operations. In the case of the stack, the most common operations are Create, Push, Pop, Top, and IsEmpty. With these operations, F would be the set {Create, Push, Pop, Top, IsEmpty}. If we also wanted other operations, such as IsFull, then these too would be in the set F.

A, the third set in the triple, contains the axioms or rules that describe the semantics (the meaning) of the operations. In the case of the stack, the set of axioms must define the Last In First Out property of a stack. We define the form of these axioms in the next section.

> **Specification of an Abstract Data Type** An ADT is a triple (D, F, A) where
>
> D is the set of all domains involved (D identifies the data types)
>
> F is the set of operations (F specifies formal syntax)
>
> A is the set of axioms or rules that relate the operations to one another (A specifies semantics)

Axiomatic (Algebraic) Specifications

The first part of the algebraic specification of the abstract data type stack is given below.

```
structure   Stack (of ItemType)
interface   Create                    → Stack
            Push(Stack, ItemType) → Stack
            Pop(Stack)                → Stack
            Top(Stack)                → ItemType
            IsEmpty(Stack)            → Boolean
      end

d = Stack (of ItemType)
D = {Stack, ItemType, Boolean}
F = {Create, Push, Pop, Top, IsEmpty}
```

The *interface section* (sometimes called the *declaration section*) lists the functions, their parameter types (domains), and their result types (ranges). There is no indication of what the functions do, only their names and their domains and ranges. Push is a function that takes an instance of a Stack and a value of ItemType and returns an instance of a Stack. The relation between the input stack and the output stack is not specified. The meaning of the functions is given later in axioms.

Axiomatic specifications define the behavior of an abstract data type by giving axioms that relate these functions to one another. There are two types of functions: those that build, construct, or modify instances of the data type (called *constructors*) and those that provide some information about objects of the data type (called *observers*).[2]

> **Axiomatic (Algebraic) Specifications** A formal mechanism for *completely* specifying an abstract data type; the operations are defined in terms of themselves.

Each instance in the Stack data type can be represented by a sequence of function applications called a *stack expression*. For example, if ItemType is Character,

Push(Push(Push(Create, 'A'), 'B'), 'C')

specifies the stack containing the letters 'A', 'B', and 'C'. In this example, we started with an empty stack (Create), then pushed a first element ('A'), then a second ('B'), and then a third ('C'). The functional notation shows that the last operation was Push (. . . , 'C'), so 'C' is at the top of the stack.[3]

The observer (or query) functions are defined in terms of the constructor functions, but they do not become part of the stack expression. That is, they are applied to a stack expression returning a value of an auxiliary data type, rather than a stack. Thus, you should not think of these operations as changing the stack itself, because their result is not a stack at all. Create, Push, and Pop are constructor functions, and Top and IsEmpty are observer functions.

In writing expressions from these operations, note that we can only apply an operation to the types specified in the axioms. Thus, for the axioms defined above, we can write:

Top(Push(Create, 'A'))

because Create is a stack, we can Push 'A' onto a stack to get another Stack, and Top can be applied to such a stack. On the other hand, it is incorrect to write:

Push(Top(Push(Create, 'A')), 'B')

Here, Top returns a value (the value 'A'), not a stack, and it is incorrect to apply Push in the statement Push ('A', 'B'). Push can only be applied to a stack and an item.

The axioms form the third of the triple in the definition of an abstract data type. The axioms for the observer functions are written in terms of the constructor functions. The constructors that remove an item from the structure are defined in terms of the constructors that add an item to the structure. The constructor functions that create a new stack and put an item on the stack are not explicitly de-

---

[2]In Chapter 4 we introduce a third type of operation, called an *iterator*, which examines each item in the ADT in sequence. However, an iterator is not defined on a stack.

[3]When referring to any specific stack, we use lowercase letters; when referring to the Stack data type, we use uppercase letters.

fined. In fact, neither the function that creates a new structure nor the function that takes an item and a structure and returns a new structure with the item stored in it are explicitly defined using this technique. We talk more about that later. The axioms for the Stack are as follows:

axioms	**for all S in Stack, i in ItemType, let**	
	IsEmpty(Create) = True	(1)
	IsEmpty(Push(S, i)) = False	(2)
	Top(Create) = Error	(3)
	Top(Push(S, i)) = i	(4)
	Pop(Create) = Error	(5)
	Pop(Push(S, i)) = S	(6)
end		
end stack		

The axioms are interpreted in the following way: given any operation on a stack S, we look at the axioms and try to match the stack expression S to the stack expressions on the left-hand side of the rules. If we find a match, we return the right-hand side of the rule as the result. For example, given the operation IsEmpty(S), if S is the empty stack (represented by the function Create), True is returned. If S is not empty, it can be represented by the Push function that formed it, thus matching the second axiom.

Given the observations made earlier, let us examine these axioms and determine what they tell us about the behavior of the Stack ADT. IsEmpty takes a stack as an argument and returns a Boolean value. The first axiom says that if the stack that is the argument to IsEmpty is Create, IsEmpty returns True. What is Create? Create is the parameterless function that returns (creates) a new stack. Therefore, we can use the function name to represent a stack in its newly created (empty) form. Axiom 2 says that if the argument to IsEmpty is constructed using Push, then the function returns False.

In this discussion we use "=" rather than ":=" in the definition of the axioms. The literature is inconsistent on what symbol should be used. We use "=" to make clear the distinction between the value returned from a function call and the assignment operator of Pascal, Modula-2, and Ada.

Top is another observer function. As in the axioms for IsEmpty, the stack that is the formal argument to Top is written in two different ways representing the two different cases. If the stack is empty (as represented by the stack expression Create), trying to access the top element causes an error. If the stack is not empty, then we can rewrite the argument for Top into an equivalent stack expression: Push applied to the previous stack expression. It is the element that is pushed that we want. Therefore, Top(Push(S, i)) returns i.

Here it is important to realize that the axioms are written to be valid with S being a local variable representing any instance of a Stack and i being a local variable representing any value of ItemType. For example, suppose we want to evaluate the following expression:

Top(Push(Push(Push(Create, 'A'), 'B'), 'C'))

We can consider this expression to be the same as

Top(Push(S, 'C'))

where S is the stack Push(Push(Create, 'A'), 'B'). Then, if axiom (4)

Top(Push(S, i)) = i

is to be valid for any choice of S and i, the axiom must hold when S is Push(Push(Create, 'A'), 'B') and i is 'C'. Thus Top(Push(S, 'C')) must be 'C'. Because this general use of variables (on both sides of a rule) sometimes seems related to recursion, axioms in this form are called *recursive rewrite rules*.

We have the function Pop yet to interpret. Again, we have two cases for which Pop must be defined: one where the stack to which it is applied is empty and one where it is not. Trying to Pop an empty stack is an error; this is what axiom 5 states. Popping a nonempty stack returns the stack to the configuration it had before the last item was pushed; this is what axiom 6 states.

Axiomatic specifications are expressed in functional notation. Because a function maps values from the domain types into a single value of the range type, a function can have only one output for a given input. Notice that the domain and range of Pop are both stacks. That is, the function does not return a stack and an item, only a stack. We could, of course, have the range of Pop be a cross product (Stack $\times$ ItemType), but this seems unnecessarily complex. We do not need to let Pop return both an item and a smaller stack. Instead, if we need both item and the stack with the top item removed, we can apply Top and Pop to the same stack. For example, we can consider the pair of operations in the following sequence:

Top(Push(Push(Push(Create, 'A'), 'B'), 'C'))

and

Pop(Push(Push(Push(Create, 'A'), 'B'), 'C'))

Alternatively, if you are comfortable with the cross product of functions, you could even consider ((Top $\times$ Pop)(Push(Push(Create, 'A'), 'B'), 'C')), which returns ('C' $\times$ (Push (Push(Create, 'A'), 'B'))). In fact, if you have written a set of stack routines where Pop returned an item, your Pop is equivalent to this cross product operation!

Throughout, Error is used as both a stack (result of Pop) and an item (result of Top) in the specification of the Stack. Error can be thought of as an element common to all possible domains—a universal constant. Furthermore, any stack expression that contains an error reduces to Error. That is,

Push(Pop(Create), 'A')

is a stack expression whose value is Error. We could add the axioms

Pop(Error) = Error

Push(Error, i) = Error

but we have chosen to make the general assumption that any stack expression that contains Error reduces to Error.

Throughout, keep in mind that functional notation specifies only the procedural properties of a data type, the set of operations. Because our specification actually defines a collection of stacks, one for every type that ItemType can be, we are defining an abstract data type. Any instance of this abstract data type would be a stack of a specified ItemType. The interface of an abstract data type is always in terms of *types*, and the axioms are always in terms of *instances of these types*. It is this property that allows the specification to define an abstract data type.

Also, we must emphasize that there is nothing in this definition that gives a clue as to the implementation. In fact, you know yourself that a stack can be implemented in many ways. Once we agree upon a specific set of axioms, however, then any implementation is obliged to meet that specification. To reinforce this linkage between axioms and implementation, suppose that someone decided to add the operation IsFull in the context of trying to implement a stack using an array. While this implementation might be lovely in many ways, it could not be considered a valid implementation of our axioms, because it would define something beyond that which the axioms specified and because the stated axioms would not contain an explicit limitation on the size of a stack. In many applications, it still might be reasonable to consider this revised stack data type, but one would need to change the stack axioms first and then check that such a change would still yield a data type that would work in given applications. We discuss this further in Chapter 4.

Returning to the formal description of stack, any legal stack can be expressed as a composition of the constructor functions, that is, a stack expression. This sequence of functions is said to be in **reduced form** if it contains only the constructors Create and Push. Any stack expression containing Pop can be converted into its reduced form by applying the axioms.

Create and Push are called *basic constructors* because no stack can be expressed using Pop if it cannot be expressed with just Push and Create.[4] In an axiomatic specification, there rarely are axioms for the basic constructors. These constructors are the "givens"; all the other functions are defined in terms of the basic constructors and each other. The reason for this is simple: any attempt to define them depends on how they are implemented. The axioms state that, however they are defined, the relationships among the other functions must hold.[5]

---

[4]Liskov and Guttag call the basic constructors *generators* and add a section to the description that specifies the set of generators (*Abstraction and Specification in Program Development*, MIT Press, 1986).

[5]In later chapters, we see that axioms can be added for a basic constructor to ensure certain properties. For example, we might want to state that attempting to store an item in an array outside the bounds of the array is an error.

Reduced Form An expression consisting only of the basic constructors.

We can use these axioms to analyze stack expressions formally. We have numbered the axioms and use them to prove that 'b' is the value returned as a result of the following sequence of operations. (Top(S) is of type ItemType—Character in this example.) In what follows, we use (global) variables s1, s2, s3, s4, and x to describe the various structures and values that are created.

s1 ← Create

s2 ← Push(s1, 'b')

s3 ← Push(s2, 'c')

s4 ← Pop(s3)

x ← Top(s4)

One approach to analyzing a stack expression is to work backwards from the expression we wish to evaluate, writing each stack as a function of the previous stack. That is, we can rewrite the argument stack as a function of the previous stack. When the stack expression is in a form that can be reduced by one of the axioms, we apply the axiom. We use the symbol → to mean rewrite.

Top(s4)	→ Top(Pop(s3))	Step 1
	→ Top(Pop(Push(s2, 'c')))	Step 2
	= Top(s2)	Step 3 by axiom 6
Top(s2)	→ Top(Push(s1, 'b'))	Step 4
	= 'b'	Step 5 by axiom 4

At Step 1, s4 is rewritten as a function of the previous stack.[6] At Step 2, s3 is again rewritten as a function of the stack before it. The result of Step 2 leaves the expression in a form to which axiom 6 can be applied. Step 3 shows the result of applying axiom 6. At Step 4, s2 is rewritten as a function of the previous stack. At Step 5, the result of applying axiom 4 gives the answer we are looking for. Top(s4) has been proven to be 'b'. A second approach to evaluating an expression begins with the first statement and moves forward.

s1	=	Create	Step 1
s2	=	Push (s1, 'b')	Step 2
	=	Push (Create, 'b')	Step 2a—From Step 1

---

[6] Because a stack expression is a specification for a stack (a data structure), we tend to use "stack" and "stack expression" interchangeably.

s3	=	Push (s2, 'c')	Step 3
	=	Push (Push (Create, 'b'), 'c')	Step 3a—From Step 2a
s4	=	Pop (s3)	Step 4
	=	Pop (Push (s2, 'c'))	Step 4a—From Step 3
	=	s2	Step 4b—By axiom 6
	=	Push (Create, 'b')	Step 4c—From Step 2a
x	=	Top (s4)	Step 5
	=	Top (Push (Create, 'b'))	Step 5a—From Step 4c
	=	'b'	Step 5b—By axiom 4

In this approach, we simplify each expression as it is encountered, and we use earlier results when that allows further simplifications.

In the next section, we look at a different type of specification technique, one where the operations are defined in terms of another, well-defined data type. This technique is called abstract modeling.

Specifications Using Abstract Models

Abstract models use the operations of another abstract data type to describe the semantics of the abstract data type being defined. The underlying model can be a well-defined mathematical model or one that has been defined axiomatically. A different notation usually is used to express the axioms in this technique. The operations are defined as procedure or function headings, with the axioms stated as preconditions and postconditions for the procedure or function. Preconditions define what the procedure or function can assume on entry. Postconditions define what is true on exit from the procedure or function (assuming the preconditions hold at the start).

> **Abstract Model** A formal mechanism for specifying an abstract data type where the operations on the domain *d* are described in terms of operations on another data type.

We use the abstract data type *nonindexed, unsorted linear list* (list for short) as the underlying model to define the abstract data type stack. That is, a Stack ADT is being modeled as a list. (The axiomatic specification of a list is given in the Application section.) We need to define some notation.

Notation:	S	a stack (a list)
	S'	the stack S prior to the current operation
	i	element of the stack (list)
	(i)	list with i as its one item
	( )	empty list
	//	concatenation operator
	⊥	undefined

If the stack S is the formal parameter for the operation, S' refers to the stack on input to an operation and S refers to the stack on output from the operation.

Operations:
Create(VAR S : Stack)
Pre: True
Post: S = ( )

Push(VAR S : Stack; i : ItemType)
Pre: S' <> ⊥
Post: S = (i) // S'

Pop(VAR S : Stack; VAR i : ItemType)
Pre: (S' <> ⊥) AND NOT (S' = ( ))
Post: S' = (i)//S

IsEmpty(S : Stack) : Boolean
Pre: S' <> ⊥
Post: IsEmpty = (S = ( ))

The properties of a stack are defined here in terms of lists. The LIFO property is expressed in terms of concatenating the one-item list to the front of the list and removing an item from the front of the list. This in no way implies that the stack is implemented as a list, only that the behavior of the stack is defined in terms of the behavior of a list. In fact, we argue in Chapter 5 that the stack is not a list at all, but a semistructured data type.

The definition of the abstract data type INTEGER mentioned in the first part of this chapter is an abstract model. The mathematical data type integer is used to give meaning to the operations *, /, +, and − defined in Pascal, Modula-2, and Ada.

A Word About Notation

These two specification techniques provide alternative ways of specifying an abstract data type. Axiomatic specifications use functions and axioms, which define the semantics of the functions. Abstract models use procedure headings, with the semantics defined by preconditions and postconditions. The functional nature of axiomatic specifications allows a structure to be specified as a sequence of function applications. Then observer functions, such as Top, are necessary to retrieve values that are stored in the structure. The abstract model does not use expressions to specify the data type, so Pop can be a procedure that returns both the item that is removed and the changed stack. Technically, this makes the operation Top redundant. (To read the top of a stack without a Top operation, one could do a Pop to retrieve the top item and then a Push to return the stack to its previous form. Because specifications do not imply implementation details, there is no way to know from the specifications whether this use of Pop and Push is less efficient than a Top operation—after all, Top might actually be implemented as this Pop/Push combination!)

Returning to the notion of the formal specification of an abstract data type as a triple (D, F, A), it is important to note that each of these three pieces—the set of domains, the set of functions, and the set of axioms—are present in either specification technique. They are explicit in axiomatic specifications because the same words are used.

In the abstract model, these elements are implicit. The procedure or function headings are equivalent to the set of functions in an axiomatic specification: they form F. The preconditions and postconditions in an abstract model are equivalent to the axioms in an axiomatic specification: they form A. The set D is made up of all the domains and ranges used by the operations in F. In both forms, the set F defines the interface between the abstract data type and its implementation. The set A defines the semantics of the abstract data type. The set D defines the data types that are used in the interface. No reference to implementation is made in either technique.

Almost every book and article that you read concerning abstraction uses a slightly different notation. To a great extent, this is because Computer Science is still such a young discipline. The best we can promise is to try to be consistent within our own notation.

Application

In defining a Stack using the modeling approach, we used the underlying model of a nonindexed, unsorted linear list. What follows is the formal specification for the abstract data type that most people mean when they say a "list." We call it UnsortedList to be more precise and to distinguish this form of list from one where elements are ordered alphabetically, numerically, or in another predetermined way. As we see in Chapter 6, there is a collection of abstract data types that exhibit properties that we may associate with lists.

UnsortedList ADT

Now, to give you a little more experience with the axiomatic specification technique, we develop the specifications for the abstract data type UnsortedList. However, rather than just listing the axioms and discussing what they mean, we go the other way. We discuss what we want and write the axioms to reflect these semantics.

In fact, following the approach we used in defining stacks of a generic type, we now define a collection of UnsortedLists, one for every component type. ItemType is used as a generic component type. Also, the following discussion demonstrates the rationale behind some of our choices of operations. In practice, abstract data types almost never begin as formal, well-developed, rigid entities. Rather, they reflect ideas that developers have concerning what might be useful.

We begin with a small set of functions and expand the set later. What should the initial set of functions include?

Experience suggests that we need a function to create a new list, a function to add an item to an existing list, a function to remove a specific item from an existing list, functions to take a list apart, and a function to determine if a list is empty. The following interface lists these functions with meaningful identifiers.

structure	UnsortedList (of ItemType)	
interface	Create	$\rightarrow$ UnsortedList
	Make(UnsortedList, ItemType)	$\rightarrow$ UnsortedList
	IsEmpty(UnsortedList)	$\rightarrow$ Boolean
	Head(UnsortedList)	$\rightarrow$ ItemType
	Tail(UnsortedList)	$\rightarrow$ UnsortedList
	Delete(UnsortedList, ItemType)	$\rightarrow$ UnsortedList
end		

d = UnsortedList (of ItemType)
D = {UnsortedList, ItemType, Boolean}
F = {Create, Make, IsEmpty, Head, Tail, Delete}

In our definition of a stack based on an abstract model, we used the notation ( ) for the empty UnsortedList. In the current interface, we use the parameterless function Create to represent the empty UnsortedList. Our notation used (i) to represent a one-item UnsortedList containing i. Here we use the function Make(Create, i) to make a one-item UnsortedList. Concatenation, for which we used the notation //, is not one of our original functions because it is a binary operation. We add it to the set of functions later.

The functions are always defined in terms of *data types*. The axioms are always defined in terms of *instances of the data types*. Therefore, we need to add a clause to begin our axioms that states the formal parameters or (local) variable names to be used as instances in the axioms. We use the following clause:

axioms   **for i1, i2 in ItemType and L1, L2 in UnsortedList, let . . .**

The axioms are rules that relate the operations of our ADT. They are the semantics of our specification. We make no assumptions concerning the workings of the primitive constructor operations (Create and Make). Instead, we define the other operations in terms of these. Thus, an implementation is free to treat Create and Make in any way it wishes, provided the various operations interact with Create and Make according to the axioms. In what follows, we use "list" to refer to the abstract data type UnsortedList.

IsEmpty The observer function IsEmpty is an easy one to begin with, because it is the same in almost every abstract data type. IsEmpty(L1), where L1 is Create, is True; IsEmpty(L1), where L1 contains at least one item, is False. How do we represent a list that has at least one item? Any nonempty list must have at least one item in it, so it must look like a list expression containing Make. We state this in the following axioms:

IsEmpty(Create) = True

IsEmpty(Make(L1, i1)) = False

Head Head is an observer function that allows us to view the front of the list. It is analogous to Top in the Stack ADT. Head(L1) returns the front of L1. What is the front of L1? A simple choice would identify the item that was most recently inserted into the list (i1). While other definitions of Head are possible, we use this one, because it is particularly straightforward and easy-to-use.

We can express this element by rewriting L1 as Make applied to the previous list expression. Because L1 and i1 are formal parameters, this rewrite is always valid unless the original parameter is Create. We discuss this situation later. A simple definition for Head might read as follows:

Head(Make(L1, i1)) = i1

Tail The constructor function Tail returns the list without the first item. Following the discussion of Head, Tail should return the L1 in the previous expression.

Tail(Make(L1, i1)) = L1

We have defined the functions Head and Tail in the general case. What about the case where there is only one component in the list? Or the case where the list is empty? The case where there is only one component in the list is taken care of in the general case because L1 in the axioms could be Create.

Tail(Make(Create, i1)) = Create

The case where the list is empty must be taken care of with an explicit axiom. If a list is empty, there is no item for Head to return. Therefore, we must state that applying Head to the empty list is an error. Tail returns a list with an item removed. When there is no item to be removed, applying Tail to the empty list must also be an error. The following axioms reflect this where the word "Error" is used to indicate that this is an error condition. In Chapter 4, we review axiomatic specifications and discuss error conditions in more detail.

Head(Create) = Error

Tail(Create) = Error

As noted in our discussion of stack expressions, any list expression that contains Error reduces to Error.

Delete We have two tasks to express in the Delete axiom: searching for the item to be deleted and returning the list without it. A first approximation for an axiom that states this might be

```
Delete(Make(L1, i2), i1) =
    IF i1 = i2
        THEN L1
        ELSE   Delete(L1, i1)
    END IF                                   (* close but not right *)
```

If the item to be removed is the first in the list that we are searching, this axiom is correct. However, the ELSE branch has a logical error. The axiom tells us to keep looking in the rest of the list, but each item that is not the one we are searching for is discarded. We need to be sure that these items are replaced in the resulting list expression. We do so by putting such items back onto the resulting list, as follows:

Make(Delete(L1, i1), i2)

This expression handles the case where the component to be removed is in the list. What happens if the component is not part of the list? This situation must be defined by an axiom that has Delete(Create, i1) on the left-hand side. What goes on the right-hand side of the axiom depends on whether we consider attempting to delete a component that is not there to be an error condition. If we view this attempted deletion as an error, the following axiom is used.

Delete(Create, i1) = Error

If it is not an error to search for an item that is not there, the list should be returned unchanged. This is expressed in the following axiom.

Delete(Create, i1) = Create

While this defines a simple Delete operation, we also may want to consider some other variations. We have assumed that there is only one copy of the element to be removed. If there is more than one, the current axiom removes the first one encountered. (To demonstrate this for yourself, apply the axioms to various lists to see which element is removed. Based on this experience, you may prove that this axiom always removes only the first item.) If you want Delete to remove the last copy or all copies, then different axioms are needed. To delete all copies of an item in a list, Delete must be called again in the THEN branch as follows:

THEN   Delete(L1, i1)

The axioms that specify various assumptions are summarized in Table 1.1(a), (b), and (c). The fourth combination, (d), is listed, but it always returns Error. (Do you know why?) If you were asked to write the Delete function without being told which interpretation to use, you would have two ways to be wrong and only one way to be right.

We now evaluate the state of a list after the following series of operations. (We use version (a) of the Delete operation, which removes the most recent copy if there is one.) Again, we have given a unique name to each list expression in order to make the analysis easier to follow.

L1 ← Create

L2 ← Make(L1, 1)

L3 ← Make(L2, 2)

L4 ← Make(L3, 3)

L5 ← Delete(L4, 2)   (∗ version (a) ∗)

L6 ← Delete(L5, 2)

We work forward, expressing each list as an application of the function that constructed it. That is, we replace each named list with its expanded list expression and reduce the expression if we can apply one of our axioms.

Table 1.1 Four Delete Specifications

(a) Delete most recent copy (if there)	(b) Delete all copies
Delete(Create, i1) = Create	Delete(Create, i1) = Create
Delete(Make(L1, i2), i1) =	Delete(Make(L1, i2), i1) =
IF i1 = i2	IF i1 = i2
THEN L1	THEN Delete(L1, i1)
ELSE Make(Delete(L1, i1),i2)	ELSE Make(Delete(L1, i1),i2)
END IF	END IF

(c) Delete most recent copy (one must be there)	(d) Always causes Error
Delete(Create, i1) = Error	Delete(Create, i1) = Error
Delete(Make(L1, i2), i1) =	Delete(Make(L1, i2), i1) =
IF i1 = i2	IF i1 = i2
THEN L1	THEN Delete(L1, i1)
ELSE Make(Delete(L1, i1),i2)	ELSE Make(Delete(L1, i1),i2)
END IF	END IF

Operation	Rewritten list
Create	Create
Make(L1, 1)	Make(Create, 1)
Make(L2, 2)	Make(Make(Create, 1), 2)
Make(L3, 3)	Make(Make(Make(Create,1), 2), 3)
Delete(L4, 2)	Delete(Make(Make(Make(Create,1),2),3),2)
	2 <> 3:
	Make(<u>Delete(Make(Make(Create,1),2),2)</u>,3)
	2 = 2:
	Make(Make(Create, 1), 3)
Delete(L5, 2)	Delete(Make(Make(Create, 1), 3), 2)
	2 <> 3:
	Make(<u>Delete(Make(Create, 1), 2)</u>, 3)
	2 <> 1:
	Make(Make(Delete(Create, 2), 1), 3)
	Create:
	Make(Make(Create, 1), 3)

Now we can complete the specification of the abstract data type UnsortedList by stating the axioms for the functions we have defined using interpretation (a) of delete. In the exercises at the end of the chapter we ask you to specify an ADT UnsortedList using the alternative specifications for the Delete function.

axioms   **for i1, i2 in ItemType and L1, L2 in Unsorted List, let**

IsEmpty(Create) ≡ True	(1)
IsEmpty(Make(L1, i1)) ≡ False	(2)
Delete(Create, i1) ≡ Create	(3)
Delete(Make(L1, i2), i1) ≡	(4)

    IF i1 ≡ i2
        THEN   L1
        ELSE   Make(Delete(L1, i1), i2)
    END IF

Head(Create) ≡ Error	(5)
Head(Make(L1, i1)) ≡ i1	(6)
Tail(Create) ≡ Error	(7)
Tail(Make(L1, i1)) ≡ L1	(8)

    end
end UnsortedList

As a review, we reexamine each axiom to be sure that it does what we intend. We express the empty list as the parameterless function Create, so IsEmpty(Create) is True. IsEmpty(Make(L1, i1)) is False because the list that is a parameter to IsEmpty has at least one item in it: i1.

Axiom 3 states that deleting an item from an empty list returns an empty list. Axiom 4 states that if the item is found in the list, the list is returned without the item.

The functions Head and Tail each have two axioms that describe their behavior. These functions return the first item in the list (the front) and the rest of the list, respectively. The axioms also state that the first item in the list is the last item put on the list.

Axiom 5 states that trying to apply the function Head to an empty list is an error. Axiom 6 states that Head applied to a list with one or more items returns the first item. Axiom 7 states that trying to apply the function Tail to an empty list is an error. Axiom 8 states that applying the Tail function to a list with more than one item returns a list containing all but the last item added to the list. With these basic operations defined, we next consider several other useful operations that might be defined on our abstract data type UnsortedList.

Additional Functions

Binary Constructor Concat

Our abstract model specification of a stack used the operation concatenation. Concatenation is a binary operation that returns a list composed of the elements of the first list followed by the elements of the second list. In our definition of a stack, we used the symbol // as an infix symbol to represent concatenation. (We call this an *infix symbol*, because we put the symbol in between the two UnsortedLists to be concatenated.) Here we use the function Concat for concatenating two UnsortedLists.

Concat (UnsortedList, UnsortedList) → UnsortedList

Concatenation can be expressed in two different ways: (1) items are taken from the right end of the first list and appended to the front of the second list or (2) items are taken from the left end of the second list and appended to the back of the first list. Here, our approach is suggested by the primitive constructors, Make and Create. Because the Head axiom suggests that Make puts an item on the front of the list, our approach to concatenation uses strategy (1) that appends items from the right end of the first list to the front of the second list. Our challenge is to specify this unambiguously in our axiomatic notation.

As axiomatic specifications are recursive, we first identify a base case where the function is applied to an empty list. Next we consider the general case where the function is applied to a nonempty list. In the base case, the result of concatenating an empty list to another list is the other list. We can state this as follows:

Concat(Create, L2) = L2   (9)

The general case must state that the head of the concatenated list is the head of the first list L1, with the rest of L1 concatenated with L2. This requires that we express (rewrite) the first list as two parts: the first component and the rest of the list. While we could proceed by using either Make or Head and Tail, we base our approach here on the basic constructor. (Alternatively, in the exercises you are asked to rewrite the Concat axioms using Head and Tail.) Thus, the general case considers the following expression:

Concat (Make(L1, i1), L2)

We concatenate L1 with L2 and put i1 on to the front of it. This is expressed as follows:

$$\text{Concat (Make(L1, i1), L2)} = \text{Make(Concat(L1, L2), i1)} \quad (10)$$

Just to review this operation: The general axiom states that concatenating two lists is equivalent to taking the first item from the first list repeatedly, and making a list out of that item and the result of concatenating the second list with the first list minus the first item. Eventually, the base case is reached where the first list is empty.

In these definitions, note that we do not have to make separate axioms for when the second list is empty, because axioms 9 and 10 both allow L2 to be empty.

In case the concatenation axioms seem a little mysterious, we apply them to show the result of Concat(M, N) where

M $\leftarrow$ Make (Make (Make (Create, 'z'), 'y'), 'x')

N $\leftarrow$ Make (Make (Create, 'a'), .'b')

Initially, we have specified the list expression in its expanded form. In considering the expression Concat (M, N), we work directly from what is given toward a simplified form. As we apply the axioms, we assign appropriate values to the formal parameters in the axioms. In this process, remember that formal parameters may be regarded as local variables—that is, the values they have in one application of an axiom may be different from the values in another application. After all, the axioms are specified to hold for all values, so the same relationships hold regardless of what value is assigned to each axiom parameter.

For example, we may rewrite

Concat(M, N) $\rightarrow$ Concat(Make(L1, 'x'), N)

where L1 is a local variable representing Make(Make(Create, 'z'), 'y'). We now work backwards, rewriting the list as the function that constructed it, and whenever we apply an axiom, we identify the current values for the parameters (local variables) L1 and L2. To distinguish one local variable from another, we add primes (', '', etc.) to their names. The base case of Concat is axiom 9, and the general case is axiom 10. Under the Reason column, the justification for the transformation is listed. "rewrite" means that the list in the expression on the left-hand side is rewritten as the function that constructed it.

	Reason
Concat(M, N) → Concat(Make(L1', 'x'), N)	rewrite with
	L1'= Make(Make(Create, 'z'), 'y')
	L2'= N
Concat(Make(L1', 'x'), N) = Make(Concat(L1', N), 'x')	axiom 10
Make(Concat(L1', N), 'x') →	
Make(Concat(Make(L1'', 'y'), N), 'x')	rewrite with
	L1'' = Make(Create, 'z')
	L2'' = N
Make(Concat(Make(L1'', 'y'), N), 'x') =	
Make(Make(Concat(L1'', N), 'y'), 'x')	axiom 10
Make(Make(Concat(L1'', N), 'y'), 'x') →	
Make(Make(Concat(Make(L1''', 'z'),N), 'y'), 'x')	rewrite with
	L1''' = Create
	L2''' = N
Make(Make(Concat(Make(L1''', 'z'), 'y'), 'x') =	
Make(Make(Make(Concat(L1''', N), 'z'), 'y'), 'x')	axiom 10
Make(Make(Make(Concat(L1''', N), 'z'), 'y'), 'x') →	
Make(Make(Make(Concat(Create, N), 'z'), 'y'), 'x')	substitution for L1'''
Make(Make(Make(Concat(Create, N, 'z'), 'y'), 'x') =	
Make(Make(Make(N, 'z'), 'y'), 'x')	axiom 9
Make(Make(Make(N, 'z'), 'y'), 'x') →	substitution for N
Make(Make(Make(Make(Make(Create, 'a'), 'b'), 'z'), 'y'), 'x')	

Informally, this result says that if we concatenate the list ('x', 'y', 'z') with the list ('b', 'a'), we get the list ('x', 'y', 'z', 'b', 'a'). This agrees with our intuition of how concatenation should work.

Observer Function IsIn

What if we want to determine if a particular item is in the list? The set of functions does not include such a test. If we are using the meaning of delete as represented in (c) of Table 1.1, however, then the IsIn function is necessary. We now turn to a specification of such an observer function:

IsIn (UnsortedList, ItemType) → Boolean

This function must be defined by using one or more of the constructor functions. How would you look for an item in a list if you were going to do it by hand? You would compare the first item in the list with the one you are looking for. If they are the same, then IsIn is True. If they are not the same, then you would have to look in the rest of the list. You would know that the item is not there when the list is the empty list. This algorithm can be expressed as follows:

```
IsIn (Create, i1) = False      (11)
IsIn (Make(L1, i2), i1) =       (12)
    IF i1 = i2
        THEN   True
        ELSE   IsIn (L1, i1)
    END IF
```

Given the following list of alphabetic characters,

M ← Make(Make(Create, 'c'), 'a')

we evaluate the result of IsIn(M, 'c').

We begin by trying to apply the axioms. To do this, we must rewrite M in the form shown in the axioms. That is, M must be rewritten as the application of the operation that created it. Again, we use appropriate symbols to indicate appropriate formal parameters/local variables:

IsIn(M, 'c') → IsIn(Make(L1', 'a'), 'c')

where L1' = Make(Create, 'c'). We begin by trying to apply the axioms. Because the list expression Make(L1', 'a') is not empty, we apply the axiom for the general case (axiom 12). Because 'c' is not equal to 'a', we rewrite the problem as IsIn(L1', 'c'). Rewriting L1' as Make (L1'', 'c') for L1'' = Create, we get

IsIn(L1', 'c') → IsIn(Make(L1'', 'c'), 'c')

Applying axiom 12 again, we see that the item being put on the list is the one we are looking for. Therefore, True is returned. Note that we do not replace the items that we are not looking for because IsIn is an observer function—that is, it does not return a list expression.

If we had been looking for 'b', we would have taken the ELSE branch IsIn(L1'', 'b'). After rewriting L1'' = Create, we would apply axiom 11, thus returning False.

Observer Function Length

As another example of a function that we might want as part of our ADT UnsortedList, we define a function that counts the number of components on a list. Such a function might have the following form.

Length(UnsortedList) → Integer

Integer must now be added to D, the set of domains. In defining the axiom, we follow the same pattern that we have used before. We define a case where we know the answer directly (the list is empty), and then we define the general case in terms of the general constructor Make. Specifically, the length of the empty list is 0, and the length of any other list L1 is 1 (the first component) plus the length of the rest of the list. Note that Length is only defined on a reduced list expression, because any list expression can be simplified to such a form involving only the basic constructors.

Length(Create) = 0   (13)

Length(Make(L1, i1)) = 1 + Length(L1)   (14)

Let us use these axioms to demonstrate the length of M where M is (Make(Make(Make(Create, 1), 2), 3)). (We trust the result is 3.) We rewrite M and apply axiom 14 three times and axiom 13 once, as shown below. With each rewrite, we must introduce another formal parameter/local variable.

		Reason
Length(M) =		
Length(Make(L1', 3))		rewrite
=	1 + Length(L1')	axiom 14
→	1 + Length(Make(L1'', 2))	rewrite
=	1 + 1 + Length(L1'')	axiom 14
→	1 + 1 + Length(Make(L1''', 1))	rewrite
=	1 + 1 + 1 + Length(L1''')	axiom 14
→	1 + 1 + 1 + Length(Create)	rewrite
=	1 + 1 + 1 + 0	axiom 13
=	3	

Alternative Way of Decomposition

There is often more than one way to write the set of axioms. For example, all of the axioms in this chapter were based upon the basic constructors Create and Make.

Alternatively, we could base our axioms on Head and Tail. In the exercises, you are asked to write the axioms for Concat, IsIn, and Length using Head and Tail.

In another variation, we have chosen to write two axioms for each function: one where the list is empty (the base case) and one where the list is not empty (general case). We could write this as one axiom with conditionals. For example, the Delete and Length axioms could have been written as follows:

```
Delete(L1, i1) =
    IF IsEmpty(L1)
        THEN   Create
        ELSE
            IF i1 = Head(L1)
                THEN   Tail(L1)
                ELSE   Make(Delete(Tail(L1), i1), Head(L1))
            END IF
    END IF
Length(L1) =
    IF IsEmpty(L1)
        THEN   0
        ELSE   1 + Length(Tail(L1))
    END IF
```

We use the form of multiple axioms throughout this book, but either is correct.

Relating Axioms and Implementations

So far in our discussion, we have focused upon how specifications are written in a precise manner, and we have seen how such specifications can be used to evaluate what happens when a series of operations are applied to various structures. An equally important element of abstract data types involves relating the axioms to their implementations. Because axioms indicate how ADTs are supposed to behave, we must make sure that the implementations actually behave appropriately. Thus, we conclude this chapter by outlining a technique to verify that implementations are correct.

There are four steps involved in verifying the correctness of an implementation. This process is shown in Figure 1.1.

1. Specify a one-to-one mapping from logical expressions formed from basic constructors to the implementation structure. (These are the vertical arrows in Figure 1.1.)

2. Apply each operation to a reduced-form logical expression to get a second reduced-form logical expression. (This is the upper horizontal arrow in Figure 1.1.)

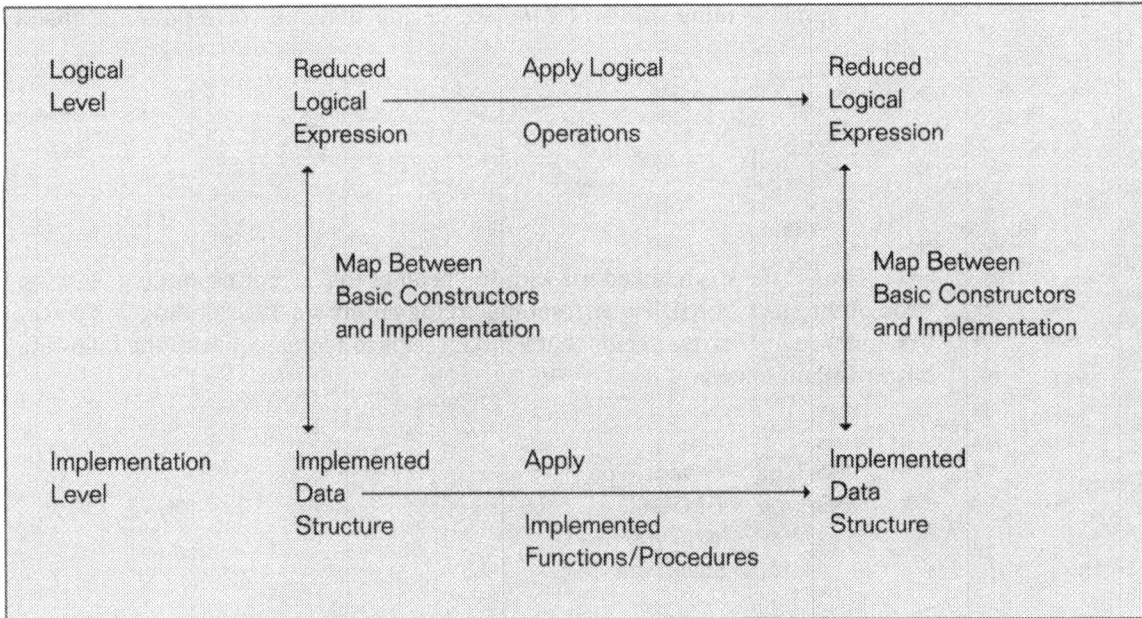

Figure 1.1 Outline of Verification of an Implementation

3. Apply the procedure or function implementing each operation to the implementation structure. (This is the lower horizontal arrow in Figure 1.1.)

4. Verify that the logical result of Step 2 corresponds to the implementation result of Step 3.

A general discussion of this topic may seem rather abstract, so we give an example that illustrates the general principles of verifying that an implementation meets a specification.

Linked List Implementation of a Stack (Using Pointers)

As a running example of a general approach to verifying correctness, consider an implementation of a Stack (of ItemType) involving a linked list using pointers. In the specification of a stack, the structure is constructed first by using the Create operation to give an empty stack and then by adding elements to the stack using Push operations. Thus, the reduced form for a typical stack expression with n items $(i_1, \ldots, i_n)$ is as follows:

$$\text{Push} \, (\text{Push} \, (\ldots \, (\text{Push} \, (\text{Push} \, (\text{Create}, i_1), i_2), \ldots), i_{n-1}), i_n)$$

where i_n is at the top of the stack.

In implementing this structure, we decide that the corresponding linked list is:

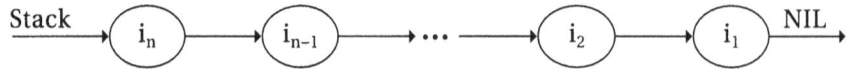

Thus, a stack is a linked list with the head of the list corresponding with the top of the stack. A NIL list corresponds to the empty stack. Extending this correspondence further, we decide that a linked list is implemented with the following type declarations:

```
TYPE
    StackType = ↑ NodeType
    NodeType = RECORD
        Data:    ItemType
        Next:    StackType
    END
```

Here, we store a data item on the stack in the Data field of a node, and we use the Next field of a node to specify the next item on the linked list.

This description provides a formal correspondence or mapping between a stack constructed in the formal specifications by Create and Push and a linked list constructed with pointers. Given a stack specified through Create and Push operations, we know precisely how to build the corresponding linked list (including which nodes to use, which data is in each field of each node, and how the nodes are related). Similarly, given a linked list structure, we can write out the corresponding axiomatic representation of the stack with Create and Push operations. In short, we now have an explicit, formal, one-to-one mapping between an axiomatic stack expression and a linked list. This correspondence completes the first step in verifying that an implementation meets its specifications. We have the mappings needed to go from the logical level to the implementation level and from the implementation level to the logical level.

The remaining steps in verifying an implementation involve examining the various operations and their relationships. In this example, we consider the following code for our implementation, where we assume Error sets an error flag. For simplicity, we have written each of these operations as functions. If we use procedures instead, then we need to identify which parameters are being used for input to the procedure and which parameters are being used as output. These functions are written in the pseudocode that we use throughout the book. This pseudocode is described in Chapter 3 but should be clear to anyone who knows Pascal, Module-2, or Ada.

```
FUNCTION Create: StackType
(* Function returns an empty stack.                          *)
BEGIN
```

```
        RETURN NIL
END;


FUNCTION Push (S: StackType; Item: ItemType): StackType
(* Function returns the stack obtained by inserting Item onto S.   *)
VAR
    Temp:   StackType
BEGIN
    New (Temp)
    Temp↑.Data ← Item
    Temp↑.Next ← S
    RETURN Temp
END;


FUNCTION IsEmpty (S: StackType): Boolean
(* Function returns True if and only if S contains no elements.   *)
BEGIN
    RETURN (S = NIL)
END;


FUNCTION Pop (S: StackType): StackType
(* Function returns the stack S with the top item removed.   *)
VAR
    Temp:   StackType
BEGIN
    IF IsEmpty (S)
        THEN   Error
        ELSE
            Temp ← S
            S←S↑.Next
            Dispose (Temp)
            RETURN S
    END IF
END;


FUNCTION Top (S: StackType): ItemType
(* Function returns the most recent item added to the stack.   *)
BEGIN
    IF IsEmpty (S)
        THEN   Error
        ELSE   RETURN S↑.Data
    END IF
END;
```

Functions Create and Push implement the mapping from the logical level to the implementation level. To verify that this implementation is correct, we now write out a proof that our implementation satisfies each axiom.

IsEmpty Axiom 1 requires that IsEmpty (Create) = True. From the above discussion, we know that Create maps to an empty list. Thus, in our implementation, S is NIL when it represents an empty list. Examining the code for IsEmpty when S is NIL, we conclude that IsEmpty returns True. Therefore, the implementation of IsEmpty is correct for the base case.

Axiom 2 requires that IsEmpty (Push (S, i)) = False for any stack S and any item i. Consulting our implementation structure, we know that Push (S, i) must correspond to the following structure:

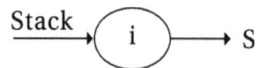

While we do not know the exact nature of S, we do know that the list corresponding to Push (S, i) begins with a pointer to a node that has i in its data field. We conclude that the pointer to this list cannot be NIL. Examining the code for IsEmpty, we conclude that IsEmpty returns False in this case, and the implementation is correct for the general case.

Top Axiom 3 requires that Top(Create) = Error. As noted above, an empty stack corresponds to a NIL list. Because the code for Top tests for an empty list and explicitly calls Error if the stack is empty, the implementation is correct for the base case.

Axiom 4 requires that Top(Push(S, i)) = i. In reviewing the expression Top (Push (S, i)), we first note that Push (S, i) yields the following list structure, as noted earlier:

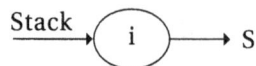

With this list structure, we next trace the code for Top. With this beginning structure for a list, IsEmpty reports False, and execution moves to the ELSE clause. Examining this code, we see that the value returned is the data in the head of the list. This value is i, so this implementation is correct for the general case; it meets axiom 4.

Pop The discussion of the axioms for the Pop operation is similar. In each case, we first identify the list structure that corresponds to the given stack created from Create (axiom 5) or Push (axiom 6). Next, we examine the code for Pop to check that the correct result or structure is obtained in each case. Furthermore, in reviewing axiom 6, we know that Pop returns the linked list S, and this linked list corresponds to the list given in the axioms. We conclude that Pop returns the correct result.

After checking each operation, we reach two conclusions:

1. We can reassert that there is a precise correspondence between an axiomatic stack constructed from Create and Push operations and the linked list used in our implementation.

2. We have established that our implementation produces the correct result for each operation, based upon this correspondence. IsEmpty produces the correct Boolean result in each case, Top generates an error or returns the correct item, and Pop generates an error or returns the correct stack structure (that is, linked list).

With this analysis, we conclude that our code correctly implements our specifications.

These same steps apply whenever we want to verify carefully that an implementation meets its specifications. The discussion here indicates how such a review can proceed, using commentary to establish that an implementation works correctly. At a still more rigorous level, one could use the formal techniques of program verification to prove mathematically that each procedure meets its preconditions and postconditions, as given by the axioms. However, because a discussion of formal program verification is beyond the scope of this book, we are content throughout the remainder of this book with a careful commentary, following the technique depicted in Figure 1.1, to establish correctness.

SUMMARY

A colloquial definition of **abstraction** might be "Remembering the what, ignoring the how." Applied to data abstraction, this means that a specification of an abstract data type must define what a data type is supposed to do for any set of values. In other words, a formal specification must tell a person writing code what an ADT does. As a user of the data type that is an instance of the ADT, you have no need to know how an implementation is being done. If you are implementing an instance of an abstract data type, you must be sure the implementation has the required properties.

> **Abstraction** Remembering the what, ignoring the how.

Procedural abstraction and data abstraction are very closely related. An abstract data type is a set of values and a set of operations. The operations are an example of procedural abstraction. The parameters of the operations indicate the set of values.

A formal way of defining procedural abstraction is to say that it performs a mapping from a set of input values (the domain) to a set of output values (the range). The domain and the range of the abstraction consist of abstract data types. Therefore, any discussion of abstract data types must include both procedural abstraction and data abstraction.

There are two common, formal specification techniques used to define abstract data types: *axiomatic specifications*, where the behavior of the functions is explicitly defined within the set of functions, and *abstract models*, where the axioms are defined in terms of the behavior of another, already defined, data type. Instances using axiomatic specifications are expressions made up of the functions. Instances in an abstract model are specified as behaving like instances of the underlying model.

There are a variety of ways in which to write the specifications within each technique. We have used functional notation in the axiomatic approach, and procedure and function headings with preconditions and postconditions in the modeling approach.

Once we have specifications and a proposed implementation, we must check that the implementation is correct. First, we identify a mapping for the basic constructors into an implementation structure. Then, we review the code for each operation for the base case and the general case, observing what is returned. These results are then mapped back into the logical level to see if they agree with the results of the axioms.

We continue to use axiomatic specifications throughout the body of this book and give abstract model specifications for some of the ADTs in Appendix A.

EXERCISES

1. Fill in the blanks in the following axiomatic specification for the ADT Stack.

    structure Stack (of ItemType)
    interface   Create $\rightarrow$ _____
                  Push(Stack, ItemType) $\rightarrow$ _____
                  Pop(Stack) $\rightarrow$ _____
                  Top(Stack) $\rightarrow$ _____
                  IsEmpty(Stack) $\rightarrow$ _____
    Axiom   **for all S in Stack, i1, i2 in ItemType, let**
                  IsEmpty(Create)   = _____
                  IsEmpty(_____)   = _____
                  Pop(Create)   = _____
                  Pop(_____)   = _____
                  Top(_____)   = _____
                  Top(_____)   = _____

2. Write a stack expression containing the letters a, b, d, q, r (a is in the top) as a legal stack. (ItemType is a character.)

3. The ADT Stack is augmented by the following function and axioms.

    Guess(Stack, Stack) $\rightarrow$ Stack
    Guess(Create, S2)   = S2
    Guess(Push(S1, i1), S2) = Push(Guess(S1, S2), i1)

    a. Say in words what Guess does.

b. Evaluate the state of the stack g1 after the following series of operations.

s1 ← Create
s2 ← Push(s1, 1)
s3 ← Push(s2, 2)
s4 ← Push(s3,3)
p1 ←Create
p2 ←Push(p1, 9)
p3 ←Push(p2, 8)
p4 ←Push(p3, 7)
p5 ←Pop(p4)
g1 ←Guess(s4, p5)

c. What is the result of the following pseudocode segment, when applied to stack g1 in (b)?

```
WHILE NOT IsEmpty(g1) DO
     Write(Top(g1));
     g1 ← Pop(g1)
END WHILE
```

4. Listed below are the functions for the ADT CookieJar. The Create, IsEmpty, PutIn, and IsIn functions operate as you would expect. The Eat operation eats only the desired cookie; at least one cookie of the desired type must be in the Jar. If there are more than one of the desired cookies, only one is eaten.

structure	CookieJar (of CookieType)	
interface	Create	→ CookieJar
	IsEmpty(CookieJar)	→ Boolean
	PutIn(CookieJar, CookieType)	→ CookieJar
	IsIn(CookieJar, CookieType)	→ Boolean
	Eat(CookieJar, CookieType)	→ CookieJar
axioms	**for all Cookie1 and Cookie2 in CookieType, Jar in CookieJar, let**	

(∗ fill in the axioms ∗)

5. The ADT CookieJar in Exercise 4 was specified using an axiomatic specification. Use an abstract model to specify the same ADT CookieJar. The underlying model should be a bag. A bag behaves like a set but may have duplicate copies of an item. Be sure the specifications are consistent with those in Exercise 4.

Jar' is the Jar on entry
Jar is the Jar on exit

PutIn(VAR Jar : JarType; Cookie : CookieType)
Eat(VAR Jar : JarType; VAR Cookie : CookieType)

6. Could the underlying model in Exercise 5 have been a Set? Explain your answer.

7. Consider the following abstract definition of a List.

structure	List (of ItemType)	
Interface	Create	→ List
	IsEmpty(List)	→ Boolean
	Add(List, ItemType)	→ List
	Join(List, List)	→ List
	Front(List)	→ ItemType
end		

axioms for L1, L2 in List, i1, i2 in ItemType, let

IsEmpty(Create)	= True	(1)
IsEmpty(Add(L1, i1))	= False	(2)
Front(Create)	= Error	(3)
Front(Add(L1, i1))	= i1	(4)
Front(Join(L1, L2))	= Front(L1)	(5)
Join(Add(L1, i1), L2)	= Add(Join(L1, L2), i1)	(6)
Join(Create, L1)	= L1	(7)

    end
    end List

a. Apply the axioms one at a time to evaluate the following expression. Indicate which axiom is being used at each step.

Front(Join(Add(Create, i1), Add(Create, i2)))

b. The axioms listed above are inconsistent, which means that the result depends on the order in which the rules are invoked. Evaluate the following expression in two different ways to get two different results:

Front(Join(Create, Add(Create, i1)))

c. To make the axioms consistent, it is necessary to modify the meaning of Front. Finish the following axiom:

Front(Join(L1, L2)) =

IF _____

    THEN _____

    ELSE _____

END IF

8. Explain why version (a) of the Delete axiom for the UnsortedList ADT, as described in the text, removes the most recent copy of the identified value.

9. Explain why version (d) of the Delete axiom for the UnsortedList ADT, as described in the text, always results in Error.

10. Rewrite the axioms for the Concat, IsIn, and Length functions of the ADT UnsortedList using Head and Tail to decompose the list.

11. Write the specification for the ADT UnsortedList using the other valid interpretations of the function Delete.

12. Write a pointer implementation for the simple, UnsortedList ADT and prove that your implementation is correct.

13. Suppose that you tried to implement the simple, UnsortedList ADT using an array to store the list values.

a. What troubles might you have in successfully writing this implementation?

b. How might you expand or change the axioms to permit a correct array implementation of the UnsortedList ADT?

c. Write an array implementation for your revised axioms and prove that your implementation is correct.

Analysis
of Algorithms

After a specification has been determined for an ADT, the next step is to develop an algorithm to implement the operations on the ADT. For any possible implementation, it is reasonable to ask, "How good is this implementation?" Furthermore, when several algorithms are possible, we might ask, "Which implementation is best?" In practice, the answer to these questions may involve many factors.

In this chapter, we look at the factors involved in comparing algorithms. We discuss micro and macro analysis of the running time for algorithms, and we introduce Big-O notation as a way of comparing the time complexity of algorithms at the macro level. We end the chapter by looking at five possible implementations of a list, which we call list primitives and use throughout the rest of the book.

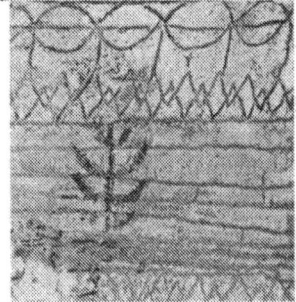

Factors Involved in Comparing Algorithms

There are many factors involved in comparing algorithms. We look at six of them in this section: accuracy, convenience of use, reliability, efficiency, use of memory, and ease of maintenance.

Accuracy Certainly, any program should produce correct answers. (If we were satisfied with wrong results, it is trivial to produce many such answers very quickly.) However, it may not be immediately clear just *how* accurate results should be in a specific instance. For example, one algorithm may be simple to program and may run relatively quickly, but it only may be accurate to 5 digits in a computation. A second algorithm may be more complex and much slower, but may give 15 digits of accuracy. If 5-digit accuracy is adequate for a specific problem, the first algorithm is the better choice. However, if 10 or 12 digits are required for an application, the slower algorithm must be used.

Convenience of Use When an ADT is used in specialized circumstances by highly trained personnel, intricate interfaces that allow fast data entry or parameter passing may be acceptable. When an ADT is used by a general audience, however, a relatively simple interface is extremely important. For example, in an airline reservation system used by thousands of ticket agents throughout the world, a highly complex interface could be a disaster. The processing might be fast, but the complexity would lead to a high error rate and, ultimately, many dissatisfied customers. Screen-oriented, easy-to-read, graphical input might require considerably more processing time, but the costs would be offset by fewer incorrect tickets and more happy customers.

Reliability Some algorithms yield results quickly *when* they work, but fail or slow down considerably in certain circumstances. For example, a Quicksort is a very efficient sorting algorithm for many types of data, but Quicksort is not quick when the data are already ordered—it slows down dramatically if the pivot is the first value in the partition. Similarly, if you have taken calculus, you know that Newton's method is an extremely efficient way in which to approximate solutions to equations f(x) = 0, but this approach fails completely in certain (relatively rare) circumstances. In contrast, other algorithms work consistently for all data sets, but are relatively slow.

Efficiency Efficiency can be measured in many ways: programmer time, algorithm execution time, memory used, ease of maintenance, and so on. For example, if you need to sort a short list of numbers quickly—say, within the next half hour—you would probably use selection sort, insertion sort, or bubble sort. These are all notoriously slow sorts, but they are so simple that you can code any one of them in a couple of minutes. If you need a sorting algorithm that is to become part of your personal library of routines that you use frequently, it is worth the time spent to implement a more complicated, but faster, sort.

If an algorithm is going to be run many times, then a more complex algorithm with a faster running time might be called for. If the algorithm is going to be run only once or twice on small data sets, the efficient algorithm is the one that can be coded and debugged most easily.

Use of Memory   Memory is another consideration. One algorithm may be faster than another but may require more computer memory in which to execute. If space is a scarce resource, then the amount of space an algorithm requires should be taken into consideration when comparing algorithms. For example, a fast matrix manipulation algorithm might require the entire matrix to be in main memory. This is not a problem if the matrix is a 10×10, or even a 100×100. But what about a 1000×1000 or a $10,000 \times 10,000$? If a slower algorithm can process the matrix one row or one column at a time, then it must be used with large matrices.

Ease of Maintenance   Another consideration is maintenance. Remember, old programs never die, they just get modified. A very obscure algorithm that is difficult to understand (and therefore maintain) is seldom justifiable, unless it runs dramatically faster than the next candidate.

For the most part, the rest of this book focuses upon time efficiency when analyzing algorithms. Most computer memories are large enough to accommodate an average algorithm's demands, so space is not usually as significant a factor as time. Other issues of accuracy, convenience of use, and reliability depend mostly upon particular applications, which cannot all be considered in a general book such as this one. Thus, as we compare one algorithm with another, we restrict our attention to time efficiency.

Difficulties of Time Analysis

Even when restricting ourselves to time as the measure, we face a dilemma. The time analysis of an algorithm depends on several major factors: the programming language being used, the compiler, the machine operations available on a particular machine, and how fast the machine executes its various instructions. How can we compare algorithms in general and not just specific implementations compiled on the same machine? Before we can answer this question, we must distinguish between micro and macro analysis.

Micro/Machine-Specific Analysis

If we are interested in specific times on a specific machine, we need to know what data movement operations are available and what (base and offset) instructions are needed for array access. Similarly, choices must be made concerning which data are stored where. Code executes faster if the variable I can be stored in a (high-speed) register rather than in (slower) main memory. Also, the machine code generated to implement a FOR loop can have a significant effect upon time efficiency.

All of these issues are part of a **micro analysis** of an algorithm. Such analysis allows very detailed conclusions concerning run time. For example, in his classic book, *The Art of Computer Programming*, Donald Knuth introduced a special assembly language (called MIX), translated a wide variety of algorithms to this language, and compared results. This work allowed considerable analysis and refinement of algorithms and advanced the theory of both general and specific algorithms.

> **Micro Analysis** An analysis based on the specific details of an implementation on a given machine.

Macro/Machine-Independent Analysis

Unfortunately, such a detailed analysis is both compiler- and machine-specific. Although MIX has many elements in common with instruction sets for many machines, details vary. Such variations may be magnified as algorithms are moved from traditional, complex-instruction-set (CISC) machines to a variety of newly developed, reduced-instruction-set (RISC) chips. Each machine has its own idiosyncrasies, but one might hope basic elements in an analysis would carry over from one machine to another.

This interest in analyzing algorithms in a machine-independent way gives rise to a **macro analysis** of algorithms. Such an analysis ignores machine details and compiler choices and considers broader issues. As a result, macro analysis cannot predict fine distinctions among algorithms on specific machines—what runs particularly fast on one machine due to specialized hardware or instructions may run more slowly on another. On the other hand, in many cases, even a macro analysis may be sufficient to distinguish among many algorithms.

In order to do a macro analysis, we find a variable or factor within a problem that we can use to measure the *size* of the problem. The number of data values that a program processes can be used as a measure of the size of the problem. If the task is to sort a file of items, the number of items in the file can be used as a measure of the size. If we are calculating the values in a series (the Fibonacci numbers, for example), the number of values to be calculated can be thought of as a measure of the size of the problem. If we are searching a list of items for a specific item, the number of items in the list is a measure of the size of the problem.

> **Macro Analysis** An analysis that ignores machine-dependent issues and focuses upon the processing of large data sets.

Because this book is concerned with abstract data types, the logical choice for the size factor is the number of items stored in an instance of the abstract data type. We use the size of the problem as a way of measuring the time efficiency of the algorithms proposed to solve the problem.

To clarify this discussion further, we now perform both a micro and a macro analysis of the following pseudocode segment that determines how many times a specific value appears within a list of N items, which are stored in the first N places in an array.

```
Reps ← 0;
FOR I ← 1 TO N DO
    IF A[I] = Value
        THEN   Reps ← Reps + 1
    END IF
END FOR
```

As we start a micro analysis of the time required for this code to execute, we must decide which activities are relevant and their relation to N. We might start by considering how this code is translated into machine instructions. However, even here, some questions arise. If the values within the array are characters or numbers, then a simple compare instruction may be adequate to implement A[I] = Value. On the other hand, if these values are strings of characters, this test may require a long sequence of comparisons.

In the first case, the comparison of numbers may take roughly the same amount of time as some other operations in the code, and our time analysis should consider all operations in the code as being important. In the case of strings, however, determining that two strings are equal may take dramatically more time than any of the other parts of the code. In the second case, therefore, we might focus our attention primarily on the test in the IF statement.

In considering this, let us consider all machine instructions as being important. Total time, therefore, is simply the sum of the times for each step, and an initial analysis of the code yields the following general conclusions:

Initialization At the start, a value is assigned to the variable Reps. In addition, some work may be needed to set up the FOR loop.

Loop Body Within the loop, one comparison is always made, and some overhead may be needed in preparation for the next time the loop executes. Also, one addition and one assignment may be made in some cases.

Even at a high level, this last statement requires some further discussion. The number of times the addition and assignment occur in the loop depends upon how many times the specific value appears within the array, and this number varies from one data set to another. Thus, we must make some assumptions concerning our data. Typically, three options are identified:

Best Case One might assume that the data required the least amount of work from the code. In the example, the value might not be in the array, in which case, the addition and assignment within the loop would never occur.

Worst Case One might assume that the data always required the most work possible. In the example, every array element might equal the specified value.

Average Case One might look for some middle ground between best and worst cases, and consider some average amount of work. The average, however, may depend upon some properties of the data. For example, if we are looking for a specific letter in a random array of letters, then we might expect each letter to appear 1/26 of the time. Thus, in n elements, the specified value would occur n/26 times.

On a practical level, a best-case situation may occur relatively rarely, and a best-case analysis is rarely performed (except by eternal optimists). Also, an average case analysis often requires very subtle modeling and analysis. Averages may involve probability distributions, sophisticated mathematics, and lengthy and complex reasoning. Average case analysis can be very worthwhile, but it also may be very difficult. As a result, such analysis often is omitted. (In the rest of the book, we examine average cases occasionally, but we frequently skip them.)

In contrast, a worst-case analysis often is relatively easy to perform, and frequently produces results that are adequate for many purposes. Thus, worst-case analyses are most common. Applying a worst-case analysis to the example, we assume that the THEN clause is always executed within the loop, so the machine always performs both the addition and the assignment. This yields the following:

— Outside loop

    1 assignment

    some overhead

— Within loop body

    1 comparison

    1 addition

    1 assignment

    some overhead

Quantitatively, we do not know just how much time is required for each of these tasks, but we let a be the time for initialization (assignment plus overhead) and b be the time to execute once within the loop body (comparison, addition, assignment, overhead). For an array of size n, the loop is executed n times, and the total time $T(n)$ would be

$$T(n) = bn + a$$

At this point, we do not know exactly what b and a are (they are machine-dependent), but we do have a general idea of the work involved. A micro analysis would look at various machines to obtain specific values for a and b. At a macro level, we are interested in what we can conclude without further analysis of a and b. Sometimes, even these micro-level results may be very illuminating. For example, consider Table 2.1, which shows the time algorithms might take for several different functions T(n) and several values of n.

Assuming a machine can perform 1 million steps per second (a reasonable speed for many machines if a step requires only a few machine instructions), an algorithm requiring

T(n) = n

steps finishes quickly. Even if one machine takes 10, 100, or 1000 times longer to execute than another, giving

T(n) = 1000n,

work up to 1000 items might be done within a second.
In contrast, if the amount of time is

T(n) = 2^n

Table 2.1* **Time Required to Perform Algorithms with Various Time Functions T(n) for Different Numbers n of Data**

Value of n	Time Function T(n)					
	n	*n²*	*n³*	*2ⁿ*	*n!*	*nⁿ*
1	0.000001 seconds	0.000001 seconds	0.000001 seconds	0.000002 seconds	0.000001 seconds	0.000001 seconds
5	0.000005 seconds	0.000025 seconds	0.000125 seconds	0.000032 seconds	0.000120 seconds	0.003125 seconds
10	0.00001 seconds	0.0001 seconds	0.001 seconds	0.001024 seconds	3.6288 seconds	2.778 hours
20	0.00002 seconds	0.0004 seconds	0.008 seconds	1.04858 seconds	78,218 years	3.37×10^{12} years
50	0.00005 seconds	0.0025 seconds	0.125 seconds	36.1979 years	9.77×10^{60} years	2.87×10^{70} years
75	0.000075 seconds	0.005625 seconds	0.421875 seconds	1.21×10^9 years	7.89×10^{97} years	1.38×10^{110} years
100	0.0001 seconds	0.01 seconds	1.00 second	4×10^{17} years	3×10^{143} years	3.2×10^{183} years

*Assumption: a computer executes 1 million steps of an algorithm per second.

with n being 75 or 100, then an algorithm may take millions of years to execute. Increasing machine speed or optimizing details of code to reduce the time to

$$T(n) = \frac{2^n}{1000}$$

still requires the algorithm to run far longer than a user's lifetime. Factorial functions (n!) and exponentials (n^n) are even worse.

We conclude that algorithms may finish in a reasonable amount of time when the time function T(n) has some forms (for example, polynomials or logarithms), but the algorithm may be completely impractical if T(n) is exponential or factorial.

Big-O Notation

The discussion up to this point suggests that a macro analysis of algorithms must ignore constants, because specific timings vary from one machine to another. If

$$T(n) = bn + a$$

both b and a may change dramatically from machine to machine.

Also, Table 2.1 indicates that efficiency may be relatively unimportant for small data sets (n small), as many approaches work well when processing only a few data. (Even $T(n) = 2^n$ is manageable if n is small enough.)

Suppose an algorithm A requires T(n) steps to process n pieces of data. Then we say *algorithm A (or function T(n)) has order g(n)*, written

$$T(n) \in O(g(n)),$$

if there are constants c and N_0 so that

$$|T(n)| \le c\,|g(n)|$$

whenever $n \ge N_0$. When $T(n) \in O(g(n))$, we say *T(n) has order g(n)*, or T(n) *is in Big-O of g(n)*, or *the complexity of T(n) is g(n)*. Similarly, we say *algorithm A has complexity g(n)*.

While the absolute value function within the definition allows functions T(n) and g(n) to take on both positive and negative values, in practice time functions are always nonnegative, and the absolute value notation may be omitted.

Saying that $T(n) \le c\,g(n)$ indicates that g(n) is a bound for T(n), if one ignores constants. The constants for T(n) and g(n) may differ, but if one juggles constants appropriately, then g(n) is bigger. Similarly, saying that

$$T(n) \le c\,g(n) \text{ for } n \ge N_0$$

specifies that g(n) is bigger when n is large enough; we do not care how T(n) and g(n) are related for small values of n. If n is 1, 3, 10, or 50, T(n) may be much larger, but *when n is large enough, g(n) dominates* (after juggling constants).

Because definitions sometimes may seem rather abstract, we now apply this definition to a variety of examples.

Example 1

$T(n) = 2n + 4$ has order n (or $2n + 4 \in O(n)$).

Proof: Clearly,

$2n = 2n$ for all n

$4 \leq n$ if $n \geq 4$

Adding,

$2n + 4 \leq 3n$ for all $n \geq 4$

Considering 3 as the constant c and 4 as N_0, we have

$2n + 4 \leq c\, n$ for all $n \geq N_0$

and by the above definition,

$2n + 4 \in O(n)$

Example 2

$T(n) = n$ has order $2n + 4$ (or $n \in O(2n + 4)$).

Proof:

$n \leq 2n \leq 2n + 4$ for all $n \geq 0$

Letting constant c be 1 in the definition, and letting $N_0 = 0$,

$n \leq 1 (2n + 4)$ for all $n \geq N_0$

and the result follows.

Together, Examples 1 and 2 prove that $2n + 4$ has order n and, conversely, n has order $2n + 4$.

Example 3

Proof:

$T(n) = 2n + 4$ also has order n^2.

From Example 1 above,

$2n + 4 \leq 3n$ for all $n \geq 4$

But

$n \leq n^2$ for all $n \geq 0$

Thus,

$2n + 4 \leq 3n \leq 3n^2$ for all $n \geq 4$

Letting $c = 3$ and $N_0 = 4$ in the definition of order, the result follows.

Example 4

Consider the following code segment (which is not in a loop):

```
IF A[1] = A[n]
    THEN X ← 2
    ELSE
        X ←3
        Y ← 4
END IF
```

Though n appears in the code, the execution time depends only on the two values A[1] and A[n], not on the processing of n array elements. Whenever this code is run, it always makes one comparison. In addition, sometimes one assignment is made and sometimes two.

Let T(n) be the time required to execute this code, let R be the time needed for a comparison, and let S be the time required for an assignment. Then

T(n) = R + (1 or 2) S has order 1.

Proof:

T(n) is not constant, but the code never executes more than two assignments, and $T(n) \leq R + 2S$. Considering $R + 2S$ as the constant c in the definition of order,

$T(n) \leq R + 2S = c = c * 1$

so T(n) has order 1.

More generally, O(1) applies to any algorithm that finishes in a bounded amount of time. This amount of time may vary from one data set to another, but the time never exceeds a specified amount (the constant c).

Example 5

Suppose an algorithm requires

$T(n) = 17n^2 + 45n + 46$

steps. Then $T(n) \in O(n^2)$. Also, $T(n) \in O(2n^2)$ and $T(n) \in O\left(\dfrac{n^2}{3}\right)$.

Proof:

$$17\,n^2 \quad \leq 17\,n^2 \quad \text{for all n}$$

$$45\,n \quad \leq n^2 \quad \text{for all n} \geq 45$$

$$46 \quad \leq n^2 \quad \text{for all n} \geq 7$$

Adding the three inequalities, we get

$$T(n) = 17\,n^2 + 45n + 46 \leq 19n^2 \quad \text{for all n} \geq 45$$

If we let $c = 19$ and $N_0 = 45$ in the definition,

$$T(n) \in O(n^2)$$

Also, the same equation gives

$$T(n) \leq \frac{19}{2} * 2n^2 \text{ for all n} \geq 45$$

Thus, if $c = 19/2$ in the definition,

$$T(n) \in O(2n^2)$$

Similarly, $c = 3*19$ gives

$$T(n) \in O\!\left(\frac{n^2}{3}\right)$$

This example illustrates three additional properties of the definition of order. First, the statement $f(n) \in O(g(n))$ states only that $f(n)$ is bounded by $g(n)$ (using appropriate constants). In this case, $17n^2 + 45n + 46$ is bounded by n^2, $2n^2$, and $n^2/3$ (again, with appropriate constants). Thus, a function can have many orders. Often, as a matter of simplicity, we choose a bound that seems easy to write. It looks simpler to write $17n^2 + 45n + 46 \in O(n^2)$ than it does to write $17n^2 + 45n + 46 \in O\!\left(\frac{n^2}{3}\right)$, but there is nothing unique about stating a bound or an order.

Second, in determining that $T(n)$ has a particular order, all computations and approximations can be very rough. The definition of order does not require that we find a small constant c. Similarly, it does not require that we find the "best" approximation for c or N_0. We simply must show that some c and N_0 exist.

Third, in determining order, only the fastest growing terms must be considered. In analyzing polynomials, for example, higher degree terms ($n^{(\text{big})}$) dominate lower-degree terms ($n^{(\text{small})}$) when n is large. Here, n^2 is larger than $45n$ or 46 when n is large. After adjusting constants, this suggests that we can ignore all but the largest degree terms in discussing the order or complexity of an algorithm.

Example 6

$T(n) = n^2$ does not have $O(n)$.

Proof: If we consider any possible constant c, then n^2 is not less than c*n if n > c. Thus, we can never find a constant c so that $n^2 \leq cn$ for all large n. In this case, n has order n^2, but the converse is not true.

Example 7

Consider the following simple pseudocode for a Bubble Sort.

```
FOR I ← N − 1 DOWNTO 1 DO
    FOR J ← 1 TO I DO
        IF A[J] > A[J + 1]
            THEN
                Temp ← A[J]
                A[J] ←A[J + 1]
                A[J + 1] ← Temp
        END IF
    END FOR
END FOR
```

In starting a worst-case analysis, one time through the innermost loop requires 1 comparison, 3 assignments, and some overhead for the FOR loop. Suppose the time for this work is k.

Next, consider the execution of the inner loop. In each case, J goes from one to I, so the amount of work depends on the value of I, as follows:

Value of I	Time Required
n − 1	(n − 1)k
n − 2	(n − 2)k
.	.
.	.
.	.
2	2 k
1	1 k

Thus, the total time is

$$T(n) = (n − 1)k + (n − 2)k + \ldots + 2k + 1k = [(n − 1) + (n − 2) + \ldots + 2 + 1] k$$

Analyzing this sum now may be done in any of several ways. You may already know the formula

$$(n − 1) + (n − 2) + \ldots + 2 + 1 = \frac{(n^2 − n)}{2} = \frac{n(n − 1)}{2}$$

from algebra, in which case you know $T(n) = [(n^2 − n)/2] k$. Because k and 2 are constants, you can conclude that $T(n)$ has $O(n^2)$, as in the previous example.

Alternatively, having been given this result, you may wish to use mathematical induction to prove that the formula above is correct. This handling of the analysis may not help you generate new formulas, but it does allow you to check other people's work.

As a third approach, informally, you may write the sum for T(n) both from left to right and from right to left:

$$T(n) = (n - 1)k + (n - 2)k + \ldots + 2\,k + 1\,k$$

$$T(n) = 1\,k + 2\,k + \ldots + (n - 2)k + (n - 1)k$$

Adding the terms vertically gives

$$2T(n) = nk + nk + \ldots + nk + nk$$

Because the right side has $n - 1$ terms of the form nk,

$$2T(n) = (n - 1)nk = (n^2 - n)k$$

Dividing by 2 gives the same formula found earlier. Even less formally, you might find an average term in the sum

$$T(n) = (n - 1)k + (n - 2)k + \ldots + 2\,k + 1\,k$$

Here, an average $(n/2)k$ seems about right (for example, average the first and last terms). Because this average would occur $(n - 1)$ times in the sum, $T(n) = (n - 1)(n/2)k$, as computed earlier. From any of these forms, the Bubble Sort has order n^2.

Some Common Orders

$O(1)$ represents *bounded order* or *bounded complexity*. As noted in Example 4, the amount of processing involved may vary from one data set to another, but we can state an upper limit on the amount of time, where the limit is independent of the size of the problem or data set. Although $O(1)$ is sometimes referred to as constant time, it is not constant; it is bounded by a constant.

$O(\log n)$ is called *logarithmic complexity*, where the amount of work depends upon the log of the size measure. Algorithms that successively cut the amount of data by a factor of p (for example, cut it in half) at each step typically fall into this category. For example, the binary search of an ordered list and the insertion into a balanced binary search tree are $\log_2 n$ algorithms, where $\log_2$ arises due to the halving of data at each step. More generally, reduction of data by a factor of p normally yields an algorithm of complexity $\log_p n$.

As a technical note, a common algebraic formula states that

$$\log_p n = \frac{(\log_2 n)}{(\log_2 p)}$$

If we consider p a constant, then $\log_2 p$ also is constant, and $\log_p n$ and $\log_2 n$ are equal (except for a constant factor). Because the notion of the order of a function ignores constants, this relationship of logs allows us to conclude that $O(\log_2 n)$ and $O(\log_p n)$ involve the same collection of functions—that is, logarithmic complexity does not depend upon the base of the logarithm, because all such logarithms are the same (within constants). Thus, throughout the rest of this book, we sometimes use log n to refer to $\log_2 n$, but any logarithmic base would do.

$O(n)$ is called *linear complexity*. The amount of work is bounded by a constant times the number of data items. Algorithms that process each input item a known number of times typically fall into this category.

$O(n \log n)$, often called *n log n complexity*, often arises in one of two contexts. Sometimes an algorithm contains n main steps, where each step requires log n operations. Alternatively, an algorithm may involve log n main steps, where each step requires n operations. For example, a heap sort follows the first approach, while a merge sort is based upon the second. The amount of work in each case is proportional to n log n.

$O(n^2)$ represents *quadratic complexity*, while $O(n^3)$ represents c*ubic complexity*. Such algorithms arise when a linear algorithm is executed n or n^2 times, respectively. For example, taking a list of n items and inserting each item into a linked list has complexity $O(n^2)$, while searching a linked list for every element in a two-dimensional table has complexity $O(n^3)$.

We could keep increasing the exponent on the size measure, but soon we would run out of pronounceable names. These categories all are part of a larger class of algorithms that have *polynomial complexity*. That is, their time can be measured by a function that is a polynomial in the size measure.

In contrast, $O(2^n)$, $O(3^n)$, and, more generally, $O(a^n)$ (for any a > 1), represent *exponential complexity*. From Table 2.1, we note that such exponential functions increase extremely fast, and algorithms requiring an exponential amount of work to complete a task are likely to take far too long to be of any value (except in the simplest cases). Thus, algorithms that require this amount of time are called *intractable*: they may be solvable in theory, but not in practice. While waiting for an answer, you would have time for a leisurely lunch with your grandchildren many years from now.[1] We return to issues of intractability in Chapter 11.

Families of Function

Examples 1 and 3 showed that $T(n) = 2n + 4$ is in both $O(n)$ and $O(n^2)$. In fact, the same argument used in Example 3 shows that any algorithm with order n also has $O(n^2)$. A similar argument shows that this $T(n)$ also has orders n^3, n^4, and so on.

---

[1] Complexity theory has proven that some problems cannot be solved at all. Some text definitions of "intractable" include those problems as well. Other texts reserve "intractable" for problems that are solvable, but whose solutions do not have polynomial complexity.

The definition of order indicates that O(n) actually consists of a family of functions, each of which are bounded by n (after constants are juggled). Similarly, $O(n^2)$ contains functions bounded by n^2, $O(n^3)$ contains functions bounded by n^3, and so on. We can extend the argument in Example 3 to show that families of functions have the following relationships:

$$O(n) \subseteq O(n^2) \subseteq O(n^3) \subseteq O(n^4) \subseteq \ldots$$

In analyzing a function, we often may want to know how small an order an algorithm might have—that is, we might want some notion of a *minimal order*. Sometimes, we may refer to an order that *best describes an algorithm*, but even here it is hard to distinguish between O(n) and O(2n), or between $O(\log_2 n)$ and $O(\log_p n)$. In any case, any notion of a minimal order or an order that best describes an algorithm is beyond the actual definition of order.

Application

Unsorted List [2]

To illustrate a more extensive analysis of algorithms, we implement the Unsorted List ADT defined in the last chapter and analyze insertions (using the Make operation) and deletions (using the Delete operation). Two common ways to keep a list are in an array and in a linked structure. We determine the macro analysis and complexity (order) for insertions and deletions in both of the implementations and compare them. (Here, we ignore that the specifications for the UnsortedList have no limit on the number of items, so that an array-based implementation does not meet the specifications. We examine this point in Chapter 4.) The algorithms for inserting and deleting are as follows:

Insertion (Make for UnsortedList ADT)

Find where item belongs Put item there

Deletion

Find item Remove item

---

[2] Throughout the rest of this chapter, we assume that you, the readers, have had some experience implementing array-based lists, linked lists, and binary search trees in a Pascal-like language. We realize that only the abstract data type Unsorted list has been defined formally, if briefly, in Chapter 1. While sorted lists and trees are not defined formally until later, please draw upon your informal experience with these concepts for now. We promise to look at these ADTs in great detail in coming chapters.

List Implemented in an Array

An array is fixed in size, but the size of the list stored in the array grows and shrinks. Therefore, a list kept in an array has two parts: the array (List.Data) and the length (List.Length). We refer to the two parts as Data and Length. The length of the list is the size factor of the algorithm. That is, the time required to insert and delete items in the list depends on the number of items in the list.

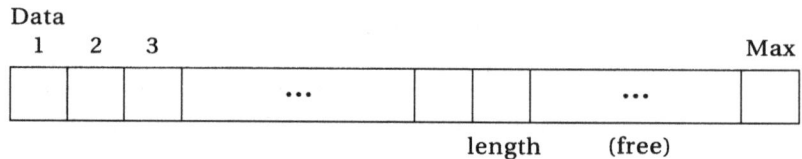

Data

1	2	3				Max

length   (free)

In the implementation we analyze here, Create maps to a Length of 0, and Make(L, i) maps to incrementing Length and storing i in Data[Length]. We could have mapped Make(L, i) to storing i in Data[1] and moving all of the other items up one place in the array. Exercise 14 at the end of the chapter asks you to analyze the complexity of insertions and deletions for this alternative mapping.

Insertions Our mapping explicitly gives the amount of work done; we increment Length and store the item in Data[Length]. Both incrementing and storing are constant time. Therefore, the complexity of inserting into an unsorted list kept in an array is $O(1)$.

Deletions To find an item in an unsorted list, we have to search the list. This requires a loop in which the item in each position is compared with the item we wish to remove until we find the item or until we reach the end of the list. The time it takes to search the list is clearly dependent on the number of items in the list. Therefore, the order of finding the item to delete is $O(Length)$. Once we have found the item, we must remove it by shifting all of the items below it up one place, and this operation also is $O(Length)$. Combining the searching and replacement phases, the amount of work involved is $c_1 Length$ plus $c_2 Length$ for constants c_1 and c_2, so deletion is $O(Length)$.

A programming technique that is often used to speed up the deletion of an item from an unsorted array-based list is to exchange the item in the Length position with the item being deleted and decrement Length. Although the complexity is the same $O(Length)$, the constant is certainly smaller. However, this technique leads to an unsorted list that does not meet the specifications given in Chapter 1. Exercise 15 asks you to consider this implementation and write a consistent delete axiom.

List Implemented in a Linked Structure

Because the list kept in the linked structure is unsorted, a simple linked list suffices. The size of the structure and the size of the list are identical, so there is no need to keep a length field. If we need to know the length of the list, we can count the elements. This does not mean that the list does not have a length, only that we do not need to keep it explicitly.

The mapping for this implementation is identical to the mapping shown for the Stack data type in Chapter 1. Create maps to NIL, and Make(L, i) maps to inserting i as the first item in the list.

Insertions Again, the mapping explicitly states the work that must be done. The processing requires getting a node, putting the item in the component field, and changing two pointers. Neither of these operations is dependent on how many items are in the list, so the operation is $O(1)$.

Deletions Finding the item to delete requires searching the list. Searching a linked structure is logically just like searching an array; the operation is dependent on the length of the list ($O(Length)$). Removing an item from a linked list is simpler than removing an item from an array-based implementation. All we have to do is change a pointer and dispose of the node. Combining the search and deletion phases as we did with the array-based implementation, we conclude that deletion has $O(Length)$.

Comparison of Implementations

Inserting in the array-based implementation and inserting in the linked implementation are both $O(1)$. Deletion in both implementations is $O(Length)$. However, we still can ask if one implementation might be faster than the other within the same equivalence class, so we look more closely at the micro analysis.

The constant for inserting an item in an unsorted array involves one incrementation and one store. The constant for inserting an item into a linked structure involves getting a node and moving two pointers. The array implementation has a very slight edge for insertions. Deletion in both implementations starts with finding the item to be deleted: $O(Length)$. Removing the item from an array-based implementation requires shifting all later elements down in the array. In contrast, removing the item from a linked structure requires moving a pointer and disposing of a node. The pointer implementation is clearly better here.

How can we determine which implementation is better if one has a smaller constant for one operation and the other has a smaller constant for another operation? If you do not know which operation is likely to be executed more often, you cannot determine which is better.

Sorted List

When analyzing the complexity of an abstract data type, we must know the underlying implementation. We have analyzed insertion and deletion in an unsorted list using both the array and the linked implementations. Sorted lists can also be kept in an array and in a linked list. In addition, a sorted list can be implemented in a balanced binary search tree. To make our analysis more complete, we include the operations Create, Length, and IsEmpty, as well as Insert and Delete. The mappings for the primitive constructors are the same as for the unsorted list.

Create Create is the operation that initializes the structure. For an array implementation, this involves setting the Length field to zero. For the linked implementations, this involves setting the external pointer to the structure to NIL. These operations are O(1).

IsEmpty IsEmpty for the array implementations is a simple comparison of the Length field with zero. For the linked implementations, a comparison of the external pointer to the structure with NIL gives the correct result. These operations are also O(1).

Insertions Just as in the unsorted case, inserting into a sorted list breaks down into two operations: finding the place and inserting the item. In an array implementation, we can use a binary search to find the insertion point because the list is sorted. Binary search is an O(log Length) algorithm. Inserting the item requires moving all the items in the array below the insertion point down one position. By the same argument used in from an unsorted list, this operation is O(Length).

Finding the insertion point in a linked list requires that each item be examined until the proper place is found or until the end of the list is reached (item is inserted as the last). To examine each item in a list of Length items is O(Length). Inserting the item once the insertion point has been found is not dependent on the number of items, so it is O(1).

Finding the insertion point in a balanced binary search tree is O(log Length) because each comparison sends you either right or left, cutting the remaining items to be searched in half.[3] Inserting the item once the place has been found is again O(1).

Deletions Deleting from a sorted array-based list is the mirror image of the insertion operation, that is, O(log Length) to find the item to be deleted and O(Length) to remove it. Deleting from a sorted linked list is the mirror image of the insert operation, that is, O(Length) to find the item and O(1) to remove it.

Simple deletion from a balanced binary search tree requires two searches: one for the item to be removed and one for the successor (or predecessor) to replace the item being removed if it has two children. However, the sum of these two searches is never more than O(log Length) because the search for the replacement item begins with the item being removed and progresses from there to a leaf node or a node with only one child. The replacement and

---

[3] While this analysis assumes that the initial tree is balanced, it should be noted that with simple insertion or deletion it may not be possible to maintain this balance in the resulting binary search tree. Instead, some additional work may be required if a reasonably balanced tree is to be retained. Chapter 8 discusses such algorithms in some detail.

removal of the extra node (or simple removal) is not dependent on the number of nodes; therefore, it is O(1).

Length Determining the number of items in a list (the Length) in an array implementation is bounded time, that is, the result is the value in the Length field. In the linked structures, the number of items can be counted because the logical list and the physical structure are the same size. The order of the Length operation is O(Length).

We could, of course, keep a Length field for the linked structures as well. This would require that we increment or decrement this field with each operation, but would give us O(1) for the Length operation. Is it worth it? We cannot say in the abstract. It depends on the relative use of the Length operation in relation to the number of insertions and deletions.

Before summarizing these orders in table form, we should point out that our analysis of insertion and deletion from a binary search tree holds for the balanced tree. The shape of a binary search tree is dependent on the order in which the items are entered. If the items are entered in order, the tree degenerates to a linked list. Therefore, the worst-case order of insertion and deletion in a binary search tree is the same as for the linked list. Both balanced case and worst case are shown in Table 2.2.[4]

Table 2.2   Complexity Comparison of Alternate Data Structures for List Operations

	Insert Operation			Delete Operation			Length Operation
	Find Place	Place Item	Total Insert	Find Item	Delete Item	Total Delete	
Array							
Sorted	O(logN)	O(N)	O(N)	O(logN)	O(N)	O(N)	O(1)
Unsorted	O(1)	O(1)	O(1)	O(N)	O(N)	O(N)	O(1)
Linked							
Sorted	O(N)	O(1)	O(N)	O(N)	O(1)	O(N)	O(N)
Unsorted	O(1)	O(1)	O(1)	O(N)	O(1)	O(N)	O(N)
Binary Search Tree							
Balanced	O(logN)	O(1)	O(logN)	O(logN)	O(1)	O(logN)	O(N)
Worst	O(N)	O(1)	O(N)	O(N)	O(1)	O(N)	O(N)

[4] Mathematicians usually use n (lowercase) as a limit in complexity analysis. When referring to a specific data set, computer scientists usually use N (uppercase) as a limit. Do not be confused; just consider n to be non–case-sensitive.

When we begin our examination of abstract data types, starting with unstructured data types in Chapter 4, we use the implementations of unsorted and sorted lists given here as our first implementation structures. We refer to these implementations as our *primitives*. We use the following interface for these list primitives. If the list is unsorted, we call the operation Make for the UnsortedList ADT. If we do not know if the list is sorted or unsorted, we call the operation Insert, a more generic identifier.

```
PROCEDURE Create(VAR List : ListType)
(* Post:    List is initialized.                             *)


FUNCTION IsEmpty(List : ListType) : Boolean;
(* Pre:     List has been created.                           *)
(* Post:    IsEmpty is False if List contains at least       *)
(*          one item, and True otherwise.                    *)


PROCEDURE Make(VAR List : ListType; Item : ItemType)
(* Pre:     List has been initialized; List is unsorted.     *)
(* Post:    Item is in List; List may contain duplicates.    *)


PROCEDURE Delete(VAR List : ListType; Item : ItemType)
(* Pre:     List has been initialized                        *)
(* Post:    If Item is in List, the first occurrence         *)
(*          is removed; otherwise, List is unchanged.        *)


PROCEDURE Head(List : ListType; VAR Item: ItemType)
(* Pre:     NOT IsEmpty(List)                                *)
(* Post:    If the list is ordered, Item is the first element in *)
(*          List; otherwise Item is the last element put on List. *)


FUNCTION IsIn(List: ListType; Item: ItemType) : Boolean
(* Pre:     List has been initialized.                       *)
(* Post:    Returns True if Item is in List; False, otherwise. *)


FUNCTION Length(List: ListType) : Integer
(* Pre:     List has been initialized.                       *)
(* Post:    Returns the number of items in List.             *)


PROCEDURE Tail(List: ListType; VAR Result : ListType)
(* Pre:     NOT IsEmpty(List)                                *)
(* Post:    If the list is ordered, Result is List without the *)
(*          first element; otherwise Result is List with the *)
(*          last element put on it removed.                  *)


PROCEDURE Insert(VAR List: ListType; Item: ItemType)
(* Pre:     List has been initialized.                       *)
(* Post:    Item is in List.                                 *)
```

SUMMARY

While many analyses of algorithms focus upon time efficiency, other measures of effectiveness may involve such factors as accuracy, ease of use, reliability, and space efficiency. Time considerations may be broken down further into best, average, or worst cases.

In considering an algorithm, a micro analysis reviews the specific details of an implementation on a given machine. Macro analysis ignores machine-dependent issues and focuses upon the processing of large data sets. (Small data sets frequently can be handled quickly with any algorithm.) These elements of macro analysis give rise to the definition of the order of an algorithm.

While Big-O notation and macro analysis ignore many details, in many cases they still allow us to determine if an algorithm might be a feasible solution to a problem. For example, if our algorithm requires exponential time, we know that it is impractical for even a moderate size data set. Conversely, even a rough macro analysis may be able to give us an idea of how large a problem we can solve with an algorithm in a given amount of time. In determining the complexity of an algorithm, we are trying to find upper bounds on the amount of work required. In such a setting, large-degree terms dominate terms of lower degree, and we often ignore all but the highest-degree term of a polynomial.

We have defined a set of primitive list data structures, which we use in subsequent chapters to implement our abstract data types. The complexity of the operations on an abstract data type depends on the complexity of the underlying data structure. Table 2.2 compares the complexity of operations for several primitive data structures.

EXERCISES

1. Distinguish between micro analysis and macro analysis.

2. Given the function

   $T(n) = 4x^2 + 5x = 23$

   prove that $T(n) \in O(n^2)$.

3. Explain why best-case analysis is not used very often, but worst-case analysis is.

4. Consider the following Pascal procedure:

```
PROCEDURE Search
   (List : ListType;          (* List.Data array to be searched *)
                              (* List.Length is number of items*)
    Item : ItemType;          (* Item being looked for *)
    VAR Found : Boolean;       (* Result of search      *)
    VAR Index : IndexType);    (* Where found or Length + 1 *)
```

```
BEGIN   (* Search *)
  Found  := False;
  Index  :=1;
  WHILE  (Index <=List.Length) AND NOT Found DO
    BEGIN
     IF Item = List.Data[Index]
         THEN Found := True
         ELSE Index := Index + 1
    END
END; (* Search *)
```

a. If you have studied some assembly language or machine organization, identify at least two reasonable choices that might be made by a compiler (or compiler writer) and that would yield different machine language code. (For example, you might consider the possible use of main memory versus registers.)

b. Assume Boolean operations can be done in time b, additions in time a, and assignments in time m. Assume further that b and a take one unit of time, while memory access (time m) takes two units of time. Determine an expression that gives the amount of time required to execute the code, considering the best case, average case, and worst case. Your answer involves Length, the number of items being processed.

c. Using your answer from part (b) and assuming that there are n data items in the array (that is, Length = n), determine whether this algorithm is $O(1)$, $O(100)$, $O(n)$, $O(n^2)$, and/or $O(3n^2)$ in its worst case.

d. Prove your conclusions in part (c), using the definition of order, involving constants c, N_0, and so on.

e. If you made different assumptions concerning the relative times for operations of addition, comparison, and assignment, would your conclusions in part (c) change? Explain.

5. Repeat the questions in Exercise 4 using the following Modula-2 code:

```
PROCEDURE Insert(VAR List : ListType;
                    (* List.Data : array to be searched *)
                    (* List.Length : length of list     *)
                         Item : ItemType);
(* Item is inserted into its proper place in List.  *)
(* Assumption:  Order is ascending.                 *)

VAR
 Place : IndexType;

(* ------------------------------------------------*)

PROCEDURE FindPlace;
(* Find where Item belongs in List. *)
VAR
   PlaceFound : BOOLEAN;

BEGIN  (* FindPlace *)
  PlaceFound := FALSE;
```

```
   Place := 1;
   WHILE (Place <= List.Length) AND NOT PlaceFound DO
     IF Item > List.Data[Place]
        THEN Place := Place + 1
        ELSE PlaceFound := TRUE
      END
    END
  END; (* FindPlace *)

(* ----------------------------------------------*)

PROCEDURE ShiftDown;
(* Shift the items from Place to Length down one. *)

VAR
 Index : IndexRange;

BEGIN  (* ShiftDown *)
  FOR Index := List.Length DOWNTO Place DO
    List.Data[Index + 1] := List.Data[Index]
END;  (* ShiftDown *)

(* ---------------------------------------------*)

BEGIN  (* Insert *)
 FindPlace;
 ShiftDown;
 List.Data[Place] := Item;
 List.Length := List.Length + 1
END;  (* Insert *)
```

6. Consider the following code Ada procedure:

```
PROCEDURE P (VAR N, Result: Integer) IS
I, Value : Integer;
BEGIN
    N := 0;
    Result := 0;
    WHILE NOT End_Of_File LOOP
      N := N + 1;
    Get(Value);
    FOR I IN 1 . . _____  LOOP
      Put(I*Value, Width => 5);
      Result := Result + I*Value
    END LOOP;
    New_Line;
  END LOOP;
END P;
```

Now consider filling in the blank above with 10,000, N, 5*N, and N*N (from the code, consider N to be the number of Values in the input files). Complete the following table, indicating whether the procedure has the order specified or not. (For example, in row 1 column 1 of the table, write "yes" if P has order 1 when 10,000 is filled in, and write "no" if P does not have order 1 when 10,000 is filled in.)

Blank	O(1)	O(N)	O(5N)	O(N²)	O(N³)
10,000					
N					
5∗N					
N²					

7. Determine whether each of the following pseudocode segments has O(1), O(n), O(n²), O(n³) and/or O(N⁴). In each case,

   a. Find a time function T(n) for the amount of work required to execute the code, and use constants as needed to represent the time for assignments, arithmetic, conditionals, and so forth.

   b. State the order of the algorithm.

   c. Prove your result in part (b), using the formal definition of order, involving constants c, N_0, and so on.

   Segment a:

```
    Count ← 0
    FOR I ← 1 TO N DO
      FOR J ← 1 TO N DO
       IF A[I] = A[J]
          THEN Count ← Count + 1
       END IF
      END FOR
    END FOR
```

   Segment b:

```
    Count ← 0
    FOR I ← 1 TO N DO
      FOR J ← 1 TO I-1 DO
        IF A[I] = A[J]
           THEN Count ← Count + 1
        END IF
      END FOR
    END FOR
```

```
Segment c:
    Count ← 0
    FOR I ← 1 TO N DO
      FOR J ← 1 TO 10 DO
        IF A[I] = A[J]
            THEN Count ← Count + 1
        END IF
      END FOR
    END FOR

Segment d:
    Count ← 0
    FOR I ← 1 TO N*N DO
      FOR J ← 1 TO I DO
        IF I ≤ A[J]
            THEN Count ← Count + 1
        END IF
      END FOR
    END FOR
```

8. Using the definition of order, show that $T(n) = [(n^2 - n)/2]k$ has order n^2 as claimed in Example 7.

9. Show that for any function $f(n)$, $f(n) \in O(f(n))$.

10. a. Some texts use the notation $f(n) = O(g(n))$ to mean that $f(n)$ has order $g(n)$. Explain why this use of the symbol $=$ is different from the usual meaning "is equal to."

    b. Why do you think the notation $f(n) \in O(g(n))$ is better?

11. a. Find a function $g(n)$, where $g(n) \in O(1)$ but $g(n)$ is not constant.

    b. Find two functions $f(n)$ and $g(n)$ where $f(n)$ does not have $O(g(n))$ and where $g(n)$ does not have $O(f(n))$.

    c. As an added challenge in part (b), see if you can find $f(n)$ and $g(n)$ that both have order 1.

12. Consider what might be meant by the statement, "An algorithm has $O(g(n))$ as its minimal order." How unique could $g(n)$ be in this definition? Be sure your description is not contradicted by your functions described in Exercise 11.

13. Justify the following rules involving the order of algorithms. In each case, your justification should refer to the definition of the order of an algorithm. Throughout, you should assume that code segment A has $O(f(n))$ and segment B has $O(g(n))$.

    a. *Rule of Sequences:* The code A followed by B

    ```
    BEGIN
      A;
      B
    END
    ```

    has $O(\text{Max}\,(f(n), g(n)))$. (*Hint:* $f(n) + g(n) \leq 2\text{Max}(f(n), g(n))$. Why?)

b. *Rule for Assignments, Read, and Write:* These operations have O(1).

c. *Rule for an IF Statement:* The code

```
IF (condition)
   THEN A
   ELSE B
END IF
```

has O(Max (f(n), g(n))), provided the condition being tested does not contain a function call and provided that both A and B are not null code segments.

d. Give counter examples to the Rule for an IF statement when any of the conditions are violated. This shows that each condition stated is necessary.

e. Formulate your own rule for loops.

14. As part of the discussion of the order of an algorithm, this chapter considers the example of implementing an unsorted list using an array Data, where Data[Length] represents the head of the list and Data[1] corresponds to the last element. Consider another mapping where Data[1] corresponds to the head of the list and Data[Length] is the last element.

a. Compare this implementation with the operations Make, Head, and Tail given in the specifications in Chapter 1.

b. Show how the specifications of an unsorted list could be changed so that the specifications would be consistent with this implementation.

c. Show that the complexity of this implementation of the insertion procedure is O(Length).

15. As in the previous problem, consider the array implementation of a list, with Data[1] being the head of the list and Data[Length] being the last element. Suppose the deletion operation were implemented as follows:

Find the item to be deleted by searching from the head until the desired item is obtained. Then move the last item in the list to this position and decrease the length of the list by one.

a. Compare the action of this delete operation to the specifications from Chapter 1. Give an example illustrating how this implementation does not meet the specifications for an unsorted list.

b. Show how the specification Delete could be changed, so that the specifications are consistent with this implementation.

c. Compare the efficiency of this implementation with the array implementation given in this chapter. Is one implementation faster than the other in the best case? in the worst case? in the average case?

d. Determine the order of each implementation in part (c) in the average and worst cases.

16. Another array-based implementation of the unsorted list specifications of Chapter 1 stores list items in array elements Data[Start] to Data[Max], where Max is the end of the array and Start specifies the head of the array.

Data
[1]   [2]   [3]   [Start]   [Max]

| | | | ... | | | | | ... | |

(free)   head   last

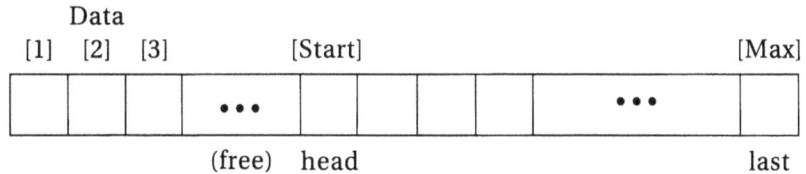

In this implementation, the insertion procedure is implemented by the following code:

Start ← Start − 1;
Data[Start] ← Item

a. Write code for the other unsorted list operations for this implementation.

b. Show that your implementation meets the specifications of Chapter 1.

c. Determine the best characterization of the complexity of each of these operations.

17. One algorithm for sorting an array A of n elements instructs the computer to generate all possible permutations of A and determine which one is sorted. For example, the Prolog code for such an algorithm is particularly elegant:

Sort (A, B) : − Perm (A, B), Ordered (B).

Briefly, this statement means that B is the result of sorting A if B is a permutation of A and if B is sorted. If one is lucky, a sorted permutation of A is found quickly, and this algorithm will finish quickly. However, if one is unlucky, all permutations of A may be generated before a sorted one is found.

Normally, checking n elements to determine if they are sorted requires n or n−1 operations, so Ordered (B) is O(n).

a. How many permutations of A might have to be generated in the worst case?

b. Based on your answer to part (a), which order best describes the complexity of this algorithm in the worst case?

c. Because the computer must generate permutations before checking if they are ordered, this algorithm takes some time to get started. On one system, this algorithm took about 0.199 seconds to sort 5 elements. How long would you expect the algorithm to take to sort 10 elements? 20 elements?

18. At the end of the chapter, we conclude that in determining the order of an algorithm, "larger-degree terms [of a polynomial] dominate lower-degree terms, and we often ignore all but the highest-degree term of a polynomial." Justify this practice of focusing on the highest-degree term by proving that if $p(n)$ is a polynomial of degree m, then $p(n) \in O(n^m)$. (*Hint*: Suppose $P(n) = a_0 + a_1 n + a_2 n^2 + \ldots + a_m n^m$, and use the definition of the order of a function, finding appropriate values for constants c and N_0.)

19. A list of items (< info, value > pairs) is to be implemented. Five ways of implementing this list are given in the chart on the following page. (Note: BST stands for Binary Search Tree.)

a. Fill in the Big-O notation for each of the operations on the list.

Create initializes the list.
Insert puts the item on the list.
Delete removes the item with the highest value.
IsEmpty returns True if the list is empty; False, otherwise.
Length returns the number of items in the list.

	Array		Linked List		
	Sorted*	*UnSorted*	*Sorted***	*Unsorted*	*Binary Search Tree*
Create	_____	_____	_____	_____	_____
Insert	_____	_____	_____	_____	_____
Delete	_____	_____	_____	_____	_____
IsEmpty	_____	_____	_____	_____	_____
Length***	_____	_____	_____	_____	_____

* List is maintained sorted in ascending order by value.
**List is maintained sorted in descending order by value.
***The array and binary search tree implementations have a length field; the linked list implementations do not.

b. In each operation, outline the algorithm you used.

Towards More Generality in Algorithms

3

This chapter is concerned with the following four issues related to the implementation of abstract data type: language-independent algorithm descriptions, general error handling, type-independent algorithms, and parallel hardware and algorithms. Although the four topics may seem only loosely related, they all identify ways of making the implementations of abstract data types more general through the use of one of the following: a language-independent pseudocode rather than a particular programming language, a standard approach to error handling, generic data types to specify the set of values for the data type rather than a specific type, and parallel rather than sequential algorithms if they improve the efficiency of the operations. The first three are solely concerned with software; the fourth is concerned with a new approach to software determined by new hardware advances.

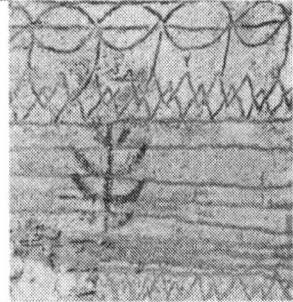

Writing More General Algorithms

We must be very careful to maintain the distinction between the specification and the implementation of an abstract data type. The specification states the logical behavior of the abstract data type, while the implementation states how the behavior is accomplished. We use axiomatic specifications to state the logical properties; we use a language-independent pseudocode to state the algorithms that implement the specifications.

Some programming languages, such as Ada, provide a rich set of constructs for handling error conditions, while some provide none at all. We briefly discuss the issues behind error handling and introduce a construct into our pseudocode to handle error conditions.

If our algorithms are going to be useful, they must be as general as possible. One of our goals is to provide a collection of implemented abstract data types that are useful in many applications. If we have to have a different implementation for our abstract data type for every type of item that might be in the structure, then our abstract data type is not very abstract!

Advances in hardware have always put pressure on software designers to come up with new ways in which to take advantage of new hardware features. Algorithms written assuming a one-processor system cannot take advantage of the parallel architectures being developed today. Here, we consider three conceptual approaches for designing parallel algorithms, in later chapters, we describe how algorithms that take advantage of parallel architectures can be written for some of our operations.

Language-Independent Algorithms

Pascal, Modula-2, and Ada are representatives of a class of languages called *procedural languages*. Their syntax varies, but their fundamental structures are quite similar. The algorithms given in this book are in a pseudocode that looks like constructs in these languages. Because Pascal is the simplest of these languages, and clearly understandable to users of either Modula-2 or Ada, the pseudocode is closer to the syntax of Pascal. However, we use 'END <construct>' rather than BEGIN/END pairs to terminate compound statements. The only control structure that we use that is not in Pascal is the LOOP with EXIT. Both Modula-2 and Ada have this construct. Pascal uses semicolons to separate statements, while Ada uses semicolons to terminate each statement. We use semicolons only to clarify relationships where confusion might otherwise arise. For simplicity, we often omit semicolons when the structure of a code segment is clear. Comments are enclosed in parenthesis/asterisk pairs: (* *). An example is given below.

```
LOOP
    Read(Data)
    IF Data = 0
        THEN  EXIT
    END IF
    (* process Data *)
END LOOP
```

The EXIT transfers control to the statement immediately below the END associated with the LOOP. Therefore, it is a structured statement even though the EXIT acts as a GoTo.

We use the word *procedure* for a subprogram used as a statement, and the word *function* for a subprogram that returns a single value and is used in an expression. We do not limit the type of a function; it can return either atomic or composite types. Value-returning parameters have their names prefaced by the word *VAR*; non–value-returning parameters have no prefacing word.

Pascal, Module-2, and Ada do not use the same symbols for structure operators. Here we again normally choose to stay with the Pascal symbols because they seem more descriptive. Note, however, that we use ← for the assignment operator.

Structure Operator	**Meaning**	**Use**
[ ]	Encloses array indexes	Data[Index], A[I,J]
.	Separates record variable and field	List.Length
↑ (prefix)	Defines pointer type	↑NodeType
↑ (postfix)	Dereferences pointer variable	NodePointer↑
←	Assignment operator	Data[Index] ←'C'
New	Allocates storage	New(Pointer)

If these operators are used together, they are interpreted left to right. For example, consider the following declarations.

```
TYPE
    NodePointer = ↑NodeType;      (* defining a pointer type *)

    NodeType = RECORD             (* defining a record containing a pointer type *)
        Data    : Integer;
        Next    : NodePointer
    END RECORD;

    ListType = RECORD             (* defining a record containing an array *)
        Length     : 0..10;
        Data       : ARRAY[1..10] OF Character   (* Character rather than Char *)
    END RECORD;

VAR
    LinkedList: NodePointer;
    ArrayList : ListType
```

With these declarations, variables, fields, and pointers are interpreted as follows:

LinkedList is a pointer variable that can point to a variable of NodeType.

New(LinkedList) stores a pointer into LinkedList that points to a newly allocated record variable of NodeType.

LinkedList↑ is the record to which LinkedList points.

LinkedList↑.Data is the integer field Data in the record variable LinkedList↑.

LinkedList↑.Next is the pointer field in the record variable LinkedList↑.

LinkedList↑.Next↑ is the record variable to which LinkedList↑.Next points.

ArrayList is a record variable with two fields: Length and Data.

ArrayList.Length is the integer field in the record variable ArrayList.

ArrayList.Data is the array field in the record variable ArrayList.

ArrayList.Data[1] is the character variable stored in the first place in the array variable ArrayList.Data.

In the next few sections, we expand our pseudocode with three additional constructs: exceptions (a general method of error handling), the module (a collection of declarations and code compiled separately), and generic data types (types where the operations are defined but the set of values is not).

Generalized Error Handling

There are three steps involved in handling errors in a program:

1. Determining what constitutes an error.
2. Detecting the error.
3. Performing appropriate processing when the error occurs.

In the context of an abstract data type, the specifications determine what constitutes an error. For example, in the Stack ADT, applying Push or Pop to an empty stack returns Error. In the discussion about deleting from an UnsortedList, we pointed out that there could be at least five interpretations for the Delete operation, one of which generated an error in certain cases and one of which always generated an error condition. Because the interpretation of all of the operations are clearly spelled out in the axioms, all logical error conditions are determined by the specifications.

Detection of an error condition in an abstract data type can occur in one of two places: in the user program before the operation is called or in the operation before any other code is executed.

When an error occurs, the processing that must be done can vary from skipping the operation that contains the error to trying to correct the error to writing out the contents of all related variables and halting. However, there is one important rule: *the processing required depends on the application, that is, upon the con-*

text of the problem that uses the ADT. Therefore, the determination of what must be done in an error situation should not lie with the abstract data type. It is, after all, abstract, or devoid of any context. The user supplies the context when the set of values is specified. Hence, the responsibility of handling errors lies with the user.

The question then becomes, How does the user know if an error occurs? One way is to have the user check for error conditions and not call the ADT operations if an error condition exists. Another way is to let the ADT operations check for the error condition, notify the user program, and return without doing any other processing if the error occurs. The user program then checks after each call to see if an error has occurred and acts appropriately. (Throughout this section and the rest of the book, we often refer to the *user* of an abstract data type. You may visualize the user as either the program that uses the ADT or the person writing the program.)

It is the responsibility of the module encapsulating the ADT to determine where the errors are detected. If the user is responsible for detecting error conditions, this is stated in the operations preconditions: the operation is not called if the error condition exists. If the ADT is responsible, the postconditions of an operation state what is done if the error is detected. Therefore, the preconditions and postconditions form a contract between the user and the ADT implementation.

One might argue that both the user and the ADT should check the validity of all preconditions at the start of every operation, and certainly this might add a measure of safety to a program. Such duplication of checking, however, can have a significant impact on efficiency, because the same work is repeated several times. On a practical level, the ADT cannot check some preconditions, such as the valid initialization of a variable. The storage location of an integer variable, for example, always contains some value, but the ADT may not be able to determine if that value has resulted from initialization or from a random event. With such difficulties, we view preconditions as requirements that user code must meet before calling an ADT operation, just as we view postconditions as requirements for the ADT operations (assuming preconditions have been met).

We use both methods of detecting errors: a precondition that the operation is not called when the error condition exists (user must check) or a postcondition stating what is checked and how the user is notified. In Pascal and Modula-2, communication from the module to the user must be done through parameters or nonlocal flags. In Ada, there is a built-in mechanism called an *exception.* This mechanism has constructs to define named errors, detect errors by name, and define code to handle named errors. We borrow the concept from Ada for our pseudocode. We use the word ERROR in capital letters to stand for employing a mechanism for letting the user know that an error has occurred. The user is then responsible for handling the error in any way deemed appropriate for the context in which the ADT is being used.

Type-Independent Algorithms

The goal of writing type-independent algorithms is to be able to implement an abstract data type where the set of operations is defined but the set of values is not defined until the ADT is actually used in a program. In addition, we must be able to implement the set of operations in such a way that the user cannot change the ADT's logical properties.

Information Hiding with Modules

Procedural abstraction can be implemented in any programming language that supports procedures. Data abstraction can be implemented by coding conventions in these same languages. An instance of an abstract data type can be defined in Pascal, for example, by defining the set of values in the type section and implementing the operations on the set of values as procedures. By convention, the only access to the ADT is through calls to these procedures. The use of programming techniques to hide the details of data or actions is called **information hiding**.

> **Information Hiding** Use of programming techniques to hide the implementation details of data or actions from other parts of a program.

In Standard Pascal, however, information hiding is only partially possible, because the details such as type definitions and code are visible to the user. Only convention keeps the user of the ADT from accessing the ADT directly. For example, if a stack of integers is implemented in an array with a variable storing the index of the stack top, there is nothing that prohibits the user from accessing the third element in the stack (the array).

We need the capability to *encapsulate* the implementation of an abstract data type; that is, we need a mechanism to do two things: (1) bundle definitions of the set of values and the set of operations together and (2) make this bundled information and code available for use while keeping the implementation details hidden and the structure inaccessible. Turbo Pascal, Modula-2, and Ada provide a mechanism for creating named collections of definitions, declarations, and code within their language structures, although Standard Pascal does not. In Turbo Pascal, the construct is called a *unit*; in Modula-2, the construct is called a *module*; and in Ada, the construct is called a *package*. This construct that allows the programmer to bundle together related data and operations on the data is a very important one, and we use it extensively. We use the general term **module** for this construct. The module provides the first part of the definition of encapsulation.

> **Module** A named collection of definitions, declarations, and code that are stored and compiled separately.

Information hiding is accomplished with modules by having each module defined in two parts: an interface section and an implementation section. The *interface* section of a module specifies what the module does from a user's perspective; it contains the interface between the module and the program using it. Any type or variable defined in the interface section of a module is available to any program using the module. The *implementation* section of a module contains the code that implements the operations specified in the interface section of the module. Types and/or variables defined or declared in an implementation section are not available to the program using the module.

In practice, this distinction between interface and implementation sections of a module may be somewhat blurred, because a particular language may require that some implementation details we wish to keep hidden must be part of an interface. In particular, in allocating space, a compiler must know the type of each constant and the space requirements for each variable. Turbo Pascal requires that all details of a *public type* (a type defined in the interface section of a unit) must be given, thus making all public types accessible to the user. Ada requires all details to be shown as well, but allows a type to be marked "private," protecting the structure it describes from access. Modula-2 requires either all details of a public type to be given (thus making the structure described accessible) or the type to be a pointer. In this way, either the compiler knows the size of any records or arrays or it knows that the type is a pointer variable, which also has a known size. The alternative to this declaration of details within an interface module is to postpone many allocation issues until link time, after all modules are compiled. This latter approach preserves a high level of information hiding, but makes the linking process rather complex. After an example involving an UnsortedList module, we return to this issue of visibility and information hiding and complete our definition of encapsulation.

The interface section includes the information that the user must have. We express this section as declarations and procedure and function headings. The implementation section includes the code for the procedures and functions listed in the interface section and any necessary auxiliary procedures and functions. In order to maintain our language independence, we show the implementation section as pseudocode algorithms.

We use no special syntax associated with the module construct, but every time we implement an abstract data type we assume that the implementation is encapsulated into a module with three parts: the module documentation, the interface section, and the implementation section. The module documentation consists of the specifications.

UnsortedList Module

We demonstrate the use of the module construct by writing the module UnsortedList, one of the list primitives. While we include all three parts here, for brevity we do not repeat the specifications in any of the later chapters. However, a complete module includes the specifications as part of the documentation.

Module UnsortedList;

```
(*
```
Specifications
structure UnsortedList (of ItemType)
interface Create   → UnsortedList
            Make(UnsortedList, ItemType)   → UnsortedList
            IsEmpty(UnsortedList)   → Boolean
            Head(UnsortedList)   → ItemType

    Tail(UnsortedList)   → UnsortedList
    Delete(UnsortedList, ItemType)   → UnsortedList
end
axioms   for i1, i2 in ItemType and L1, L2 in UnsortedList, let
    IsEmpty(Create) = True
    IsEmpty(Make(L1, i1)) = False
    Delete(Create, i1) = Create
    Delete(Make(L1, i2), i1) =
        IF i1 = i2
            THEN L1
            ELSE   Make(Delete(L1, i1), i2)
        END IF
    Head(Create) = Error
    Head(Make(L1, i1)) = i1
    Tail(Create) = Error
    Tail(Make(L1, i1)) = L1
end
end UnsortedList
*)

Interface Section UnsortedList;

(* A variable of ListType is defined in the user's program and passed   *)
(* to the operations defined in this module as a parameter.   *)
(* Items are not ordered by value.   *)
TYPE
    ItemType = Character;
    NodePointer = ↑NodeType;
    NodeType = RECORD
        Data   : ItemType;
        Next   : NodePointer;
    END RECORD;
    ListType = NodePointer;

PROCEDURE Create(VAR List : ListType)
(* Post: List is initialized.   *)
(* Pre: None   *)

FUNCTION IsEmpty(List : ListType) : Boolean
(* Pre: List has been created.   *)
(* Post: IsEmpty is False if List contains at least one *)
(*   item; True otherwise.   *)

PROCEDURE Make(VAR List : ListType; Item : ItemType)
(* Pre: List has been initialized.   *)
(* Post: Item is in List;   *)
(*   List may contain duplicates.   *)

PROCEDURE Delete(VAR List : ListType; Item : ItemType)
(* Pre: NOT IsEmpty(List)   *)

```
(* Post:     If Item is in List, the first occurrence      *)
(*           is removed; otherwise, List is unchanged.     *)
```

PROCEDURE Head(List : ListType; VAR Item: ItemType)
```
(* Pre:      NOT IsEmpty(List)                             *)
(* Post:     Item is the last element put on the list.     *)
```

PROCEDURE Tail(List: ListType; VAR Result : ListType)
```
(* Pre:      NOT IsEmpty(List)                             *)
(* Post:     Result is List with the last item removed.    *)
```

Implementation Section UnsortedList;

Create (List: ListType)

```
List ← NIL
```

IsEmpty (List: ListType): Boolean

```
RETURN (List = NIL)
```

Make (VAR List: ListType, Item: ItemType)

```
New(NewNode)
NewNode↑.Data ← Item
NewNode↑.Next ← List
List ← NewNode
```

Delete (VAR List: ListType, Item: ItemType)

```
IF (List <> NIL) AND (List↑.Data = Item)
    THEN   (* Remove first item on list. *)
        List ← List↑.Next
    ELSE  (* Check later in list. *)
        Ptr ← List
        TrailingPtr ← NIL
        WHILE (Ptr <> NIL) AND (Ptr↑.Data <> Item) DO
            TrailingPtr ← Ptr
            Ptr← Ptr↑.Next
        END WHILE
        IF Ptr <> NIL
        THEN   (* item is found *)
            TrailingPtr↑.Next← Ptr↑.Next
        END IF
END IF
```

Head(List: ListType, VAR Item: ItemType)

```
Item ← List↑.Data
```

Tail(List: ListType, VAR Result: ListType)

Result ← Copy(List↑.Next)

The example of the implementation section points out three features of our pseudocode algorithms:

1. We repeat the operation name and the parameter list with each algorithm for clarity, and we continue to do so.

2. The Delete algorithm does not dispose of the node being deleted. Pascal and Modula-2 require the user to determine when space is no longer needed and return it. On the other hand, Ada does not. The Ada run-time support system takes care of deallocating space when it is no longer needed. Our pseudocode assumes an Ada-like memory management system. We return to this subject in Chapter 13.

3. We assume short-circuit evaluation of Boolean expressions in our algorithms. That is, evaluation stops as soon as the result is known. For example, if an item is not found in the above list, then the first loop continues until Ptr is NIL. When Ptr reaches this value, (Ptr <> NIL) becomes False, and short-circuit evaluation infers that the entire Boolean expression, therefore, must be False—there is no need to evaluate the rest of the exit condition. In contrast, under full evaluation, the second expression would always be evaluated, raising the possibility that the evaluation of Ptr↑.Data could raise a "dereferencing nil pointer" error.

It is important to the notion of an abstract data type and to the concept of the module that previously defined modules can be left in a library for later use. Therefore, we need a way of telling the compiler that we intend to use a module that is in the library. Pascal, Modula-2, and Ada each have their own syntax for doing this. We choose to use the notation "USES <module name>". Depending on which language you are using, the modules may be compiled and saved in the library in object code or saved in the library in source code and recompiled each time they are used.

Visibility and Access

All types and variables defined and/or declared in an interface section of a module are visible to the program using the module. Because the structure of ListType is defined in the interface section of the UnsortedList module in the previous example, ListType is called a transparent data type, or simply a *transparent type*. A transparent data type is both *visible* and *accessible*. It is visible because the user can read the structure in the module listing, and it is accessible because the user can access parts of variables of that type. The structure of ListType can be hidden by the use of an **opaque type** (Modula-2), or a visible type may be made inaccessible by declaring it to be a **private type** (Ada).

An opaque data type is a data type whose name is listed in the interface section of a module but whose actual type is defined in the implementation section of the module. A private data type is a data type defined in the interface section of a module but marked as being private. The user of opaque or private data types can declare variables of that type *but cannot access parts of them*. Variables declared to be opaque or private can be passed as parameters and assigned to one another but cannot be accessed in any other way.[1]

> **Transparent Types** Data types whose description is visible. Component variables of that type can be accessed directly by the user.
>
> **Opaque Types** Data types whose name only is visible. Access to variables of opaque types must be through operations defined in the interface section that defines the type name.
>
> **Private Types** Data types whose description is visible but access to variables of the type must be through the operations defined in the interface module.

Opaque types and private types are language features that can be used with modules to provide true encapsulation. The user can declare variables of opaque or private types but cannot access them except through the interface provided.

Declaration of the Structure

In the UnsortedList example, the procedures that implement the operations take a variable of ListType as a parameter. Variables of ListType are declared in the program that uses the module. This technique allows a program to have several instances of an implementation of an abstract data type, and the operations defined in the module can be applied to each instance.

Another approach is to place the declaration of the ListType variable in the implementation section of the module itself. In this case, the user does not pass a list—only items to be inserted or deleted. The definition of ListType and the declaration of List are hidden within the implementation section of the module. That is, List is a local variable of the implementation section of the module. Module variables, unlike variables that are local to procedures, exist for the entire execution of the program. This technique allows the module structure to encapsulate the ADT and is effective when only one list is needed. If more than one list of the same type is needed by the program using the module, then the user should declare the variables of ListType and pass instances as parameters to the module encapsulating the UnsortedList ADT.

---

[1] In any specific language, a programmer should be advised that the assignment of opaque or private types may be risky. In particular, the statement A := B may cause both A and B to refer to the same structure, or it may copy B's structure to A. In the former case, a change in either A or B could change the other, while in the latter case, a change in one would not affect the other.

Now we can define encapsulation precisely. *Encapsulation* is the use of a programming language feature that provides mechanisms (1) to separately compile named collections of definitions, declarations, and code and (2) to make the structure described inaccessible and the details of the operations invisible while making the named collection available. An alternative, and simpler, definition of encapsulation is a programming mechanism that enforces information hiding.

Our pseudocode assumes that all definitions and declarations in the interface section are visible but not accessible.

Generic Data Types

Is the expression "implementation of an abstract data type" an oxymoron? In our discussion of abstract data types, we have said that the definition given using the axiomatic specifications defines a *family* of types, one for each type of data that ItemType can assume. Yet the implementation we have provided is not general. It is limited to the case where the items to be put on the list are characters. Although we defined the type of the items on the list as type ItemType, we assigned a specific type to ItemType. That is, we did not implement an abstract data type UnsortedList, but a data type UnsortedList of Characters. Is there a way of implementing an abstract data type UnsortedList where the items can be anything from characters to records of arrays of records? What we are asking is, Can we implement a **generic data type** UnsortedList where ItemType is left undefined?

> **Generic Data Types** Data types where the operations are defined but the types of the items being manipulated are not; that is, the set of operations is defined but the set of values is not.

The answer is both no and yes. Ada does have the facility to define a generic package, where the type of the items being manipulated (and other information such as constants and comparison operators) is unspecified. The source code for an Ada package states that certain parameters to the package are generic; that is, they are supplied by the user when the package is instantiated (accessed by the user program). Pascal and Modula-2 do not allow this directly, but Modula-2 does have some low-level features of the language that allow a programmer to simulate generic types. We choose not to demonstrate this technique because it breaks the concept of strong typing. Instead, we suggest an alternate technique that works in all of these languages: let the user of the UnsortedList module define the type of the items to be manipulated in an auxiliary module.

In this approach, the *source code* for the UnsortedList implementation does not depend upon the type of the items being manipulated. It is only the *object code* that varies. That is, the object code to access a record in an array varies according to the size of the record, but the source statement that specifies the access does not change. Therefore, rather than define an UnsortedList for each type of item, we specify in the interface section of the module that it USES a module that defines the type of the item. If the UnsortedList implementation is array-based, we could have that module define MaxList as well. The user of the UnsortedList module is responsible for defining a module where ItemType is defined. The user accesses the source code of the ADT module to enter the name of the auxiliary data-defining module. After all, it *is* the user of the ADT who knows the context in which the UnsortedList (or any implementation of an abstract data type) is to be used.

The implication here is that the interface section and implementation section must be recompiled, but the source code in the implementation section does not change. The documentation of the interface section of the UnsortedList module must instruct the user to prepare a module defining the data type ItemType. Here is an example.

Interface Section UnsortedList;
(* Module Preconditions: *)
(*   The user of this module must provide a module that defines   *)
(*   the type of item (ItemType) to be put on the UnsortedList.   *)

USES <user supplies the module name >
   (* Get access to ItemType *)

   (* Rest exactly the same *)

To review, suppose UserOfList is the program that is using the UnsortedList Module and suppose this ADT module defines ItemType. Then the following chart shows the communications between modules and the definition and access of various types.

Module UnsortedList (* defines *)	UserOfList (* accesses *)
ListType, ItemType,	ListType, ItemType,
Create, IsEmpty, Make, Delete,	Create, IsEmpty, Make, Delete,
Head, and Tail	Head, and Tail

The type of the item being manipulated is fixed. The interface and implementation sections of Module UnsortedList do not have to be recompiled each time they are used.

The communication among modules is more complex in the case where the user of the UnsortedList module is responsible for defining ItemType. A module defining ItemType must be written, compiled, and made available for use. The source code for UnsortedList is recompiled with the name of the auxiliary module in its USES clause. Because the user of the UnsortedList must also have access to the type defined in the auxiliary module, the name of this module must also be in a USES clause of the UserOfList program. The diagram on page 76 shows the UserOfList including both DataDefn and UnsortedList in its USES clause. Some languages allow indirect references in their equivalent of the USES clause; that is, if UnsortedList USES DataDefn and UserOfList USES UnsortedList, then UserOfList automatically has access to DataDefn. Other languages do not have this feature. Turbo Pascal, for example, does not allow indirect references, thus DataDefn must be included directly in UserOfList. Our pseudocode allows indirect references.

UserOfList
USES
   DataDefn to access ItemType

   UnsortedList to access
     Create, Make, Delete,
     IsEmpty, Head, Tail

Module DataDefn
(* auxiliary module *)
Defines:
   ItemType

Module Unsorted List
USES
   DataDefn to access ItemType
Defines:
   Create, Make, Delete,
   IsEmpty, Head, Tail

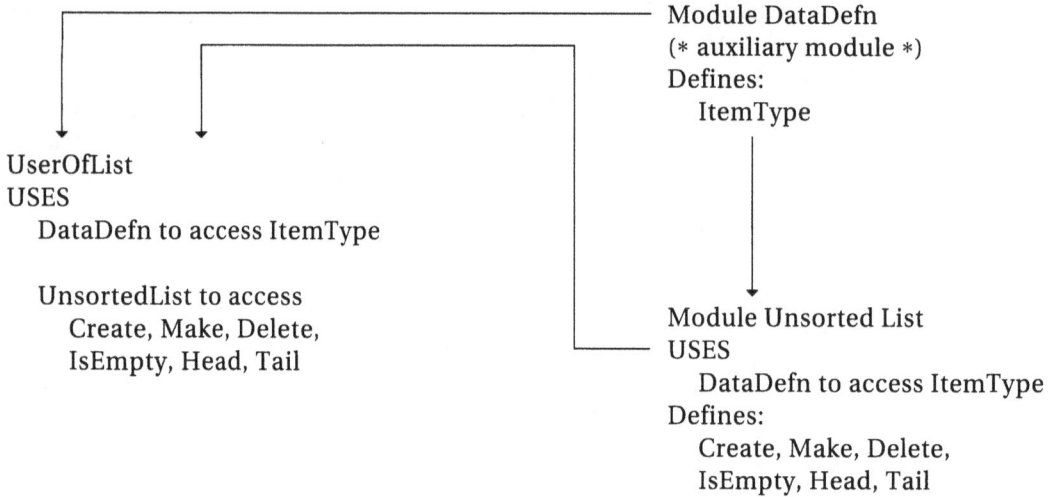

The list primitive that we have used to demonstrate the use of modules stores the item in the next available place on the list. What if the list is to be kept sorted? What if the items on the list are records and we want to keep the list sorted by a field in the record? We can continue to write very general modules by specifying that the user must define a comparison function in the auxiliary module. This comparison function (we call it Compare) takes two items of ItemType and returns a value of RelationType. Here is an example of the interface section of module DataDefn.

Interface Section DataDefn;
TYPE
   RelationType = (LessThan, EqualTo, GreaterThan);
   ItemType = <problem-related type defined here>

FUNCTION Compare(Item1, Item2 : ItemType) : RelationType;
(* Pre: None   *)
(* Post: Compare returns   *)
(*   LessThan   if Item1 is "less than" Item2   *)
(*   EqualTo   if Item1 is "equal to" Item2   *)
(*   GreaterThan   if Item1 is "greater than" Item2   *)

In the implementation section for this module, the user defines Compare to be whatever makes sense for the given ItemType. In a SortedList module, Compare would determine the relationship between two items of ItemType. This relationship might be based on one field of a record one time and another field of a record the next. Ada actually allows the relational operators to be redefined and used as parameters to a package. Our pseudocode does not make this assumption.

Back to the question posed at the beginning of this section: Is the expression "implementation of an abstract data type" an oxymoron? Our answer is no. Ada allows the user to write generic source code. The user supplies the missing pieces (constants, types, and operations) when the package is accessed using the syntax provided in the language. Thus, a generic Ada package is the implementation of an abstract data type. We have shown a way of accomplishing the same task using an auxiliary module. If an abstract data type is a set of values and a set of operations, we can supply the set of values at the time the ADT is compiled.

Can we have various instances of an ADT with different sets of values available at the same time? Yes, if we are using Ada, because Ada generics provide this facility. You can instantiate as many copies of a package as you wish, all with different information filling in the missing pieces. The technique we have outlined, however, allows for only one instance of the data type at a time. Fortunately, this is easy to fix: we can make as many copies of the source code for a module as we want and give each a different name.

Having discussed the issues involved in implementing an abstract data type in Pascal, Turbo Pascal, Modula-2, and Ada, we now assume the pseudocode expression USES <module name> is generic. That is, in the module encapsulating an ADT, USES <module name> provides the declarations, definitions, and code that are needed for an instantiation of the abstract data type being encapsulated, and more than one can be instantiated at the same time.

Parallel Algorithms

Once specifications are defined for an ADT, problem solving naturally turns to the design and implementation of algorithms. Historically, many algorithms have been developed in the context of a single process or processor to implement a specification. Modern hardware, however, may permit other approaches as well. Of course, the starting point for any algorithm is the specification of a problem, and we expect the statement of a specification or a logical ADT interface to be independent of how many processors we have available or the idiosyncrasies of our computing environment. Approaches to design and implementation, however, sometimes depend upon such factors.

When several processors are available, individual processors may work on separate, independent parts of an algorithm concurrently, or processors may apply the same algorithm to several independent pieces of data concurrently. In this setting, using several processors simultaneously often allows the work to proceed much more quickly. Single-processor algorithms are adequate for many purposes, but in some settings, newer approaches may be much better.

Overall, a multiple-processor environment provides many opportunities for writing efficient implementations of specifications, but such an environment also may require a rethinking of algorithm design and development. Furthermore, the effective development of parallel algorithms may require some knowledge of parallel hardware as well as approaches to algorithms and software. Thus, an introduction to parallel algorithms to implement specifications requires some discussion of both hardware and problem solving. We begin that discussion by identifying some general hardware configurations and some approaches to problem solving. Later chapters continue this discussion by examining specific algorithms to implement various ADT operations.

Example: Bank Account

A simple example illustrates several opportunities for using multiple processes in solving a problem, and it also indicates some pitfalls to avoid.

Suppose a bank has separate files for each savings or checking account. For each request to deposit or withdraw money, a process could run on a processor to update the balance on a file. To transfer money, a process would update two account files. Several processes could be allowed to run in parallel on multiple processors.

For the most part, this works well, and many transactions may proceed at the same time. We may deposit money in our account at the same time you are accessing your (separate) account. The following example, however, shows that this approach sometimes can lead to difficulties.

Two Transactions

You and your spouse both have the brainstorm of transferring money between accounts.

You want to transfer $50 from checking to savings.

Your spouse wants to transfer $50 from savings to checking.

A natural outline of steps follows:

Savings to Checking	**Checking to Savings**
Find old savings balance	Find old checking balance
Find old checking balance	Find old savings balance
Add $50 to checking balance	Add $50 to savings balance
Subtract $50 from savings balance	Subtract $50 from checking balance
Save new checking balance	Save new savings balance
Save new savings balance	Save new checking balance

This outline works fine unless both you and your spouse go to separate ATMs at the same time. For example, suppose the initial balances were $500 in savings and $200 in checking. Now, consider the following steps:

Read savings = $500	Read checking = $200
Read checking = $200	Read savings = $500
New checking = $250	New savings = $550
New savings = $450	New checking = $150
Write checking = $250	Write savings = $550
Write savings = $450	Write checking = $150

What balances are left in the accounts? Unfortunately, the answer depends upon the order in which the two files are updated. If one process saves its new balances and the other then does both of its updates, the results are $250, $450 or $150, $550. If the two processes do their last steps concurrently, however, the final values in the accounts are $450 and $150, and you and your spouse have lost $100 on these transfers.

This example leads to the following observations:

1. In parallel computing, coordination sometimes is needed among processes and/or data accesses.

2. Parallelism is possible only when computations are independent. Parallelism is not possible when one computation requires the result of another.

3. In operating systems, such issues arise regularly in allocating resources and in scheduling processes.

4. In developing solutions involving parallelism for applications, coordination may be built into data structures, algorithms, or programming languages.

Approaches to Parallelism

In considering how parallelism may help speed up processing, discussions often follow one of two common perspectives: the hardware perspective or the algorithm perspective.

A hardware perspective considers types of parallel architectures and ways of tying *processors* together. Here, one focuses first on the hardware, and then tries to tailor algorithms to that hardware. This might be called the bottom-up approach to parallel processing.

An algorithm/problem-solving perspective considers ways of approaching problems by focusing on *tasks or processors* to be done or data to be processed. Here, algorithms and approaches to problem solving are investigated first, and hardware considerations come later. Such a focus might be called a top-down approach to parallelism.

Hardware Approaches

While processors may be organized in many ways, some configurations have become reasonably common. Let us examine three of these approaches.

1. Multiple processors may apply the same program to multiple data sets. In this approach, processors often execute the same instructions at the same time; a common program is run at each processor. Such an approach, often called *synchronous processing*, is particularly effective in working on repeated computations that are applied to many data sets. As a variation of this approach, several processors may execute the same instructions in lock-step on different data sets. Such an approach is called *data-parallel programming*. For example, the same formulas for making weather forecasts may be applied to

each point on a weather map. In such a setting, each process or processor may compute the work for a specific place, and the computations for each point throughout the map may proceed in parallel. This can be visualized as shown in Figure 3.1.

2. Processors may be arranged in tandem, with each contributing one part to an overall computation. This approach, commonly called *pipelining*, is reminiscent of an assembly line. In manufacturing a table, for example, a first worker might handle the table top; a second worker might attach a leg; workers three, four, and five might attach the next three legs; the sixth worker might add crossing supports; a seventh worker might apply a first coat of varnish; after this dries, an eighth worker might smooth this primer coat; a ninth worker then might apply a second coat of varnish; and a tenth worker might package the table in a box. This approach can be visualized as shown in Figure 3.2.

In a common computing application, a processor often executes code by following a fetch-decode-execute cycle. Here a machine instruction first is obtained from main memory, this instruction then is decoded (in one or more steps), and the instruction is run. When several specialized hardware circuits are utilized, however, one circuit may perform the fetch operation, one or more

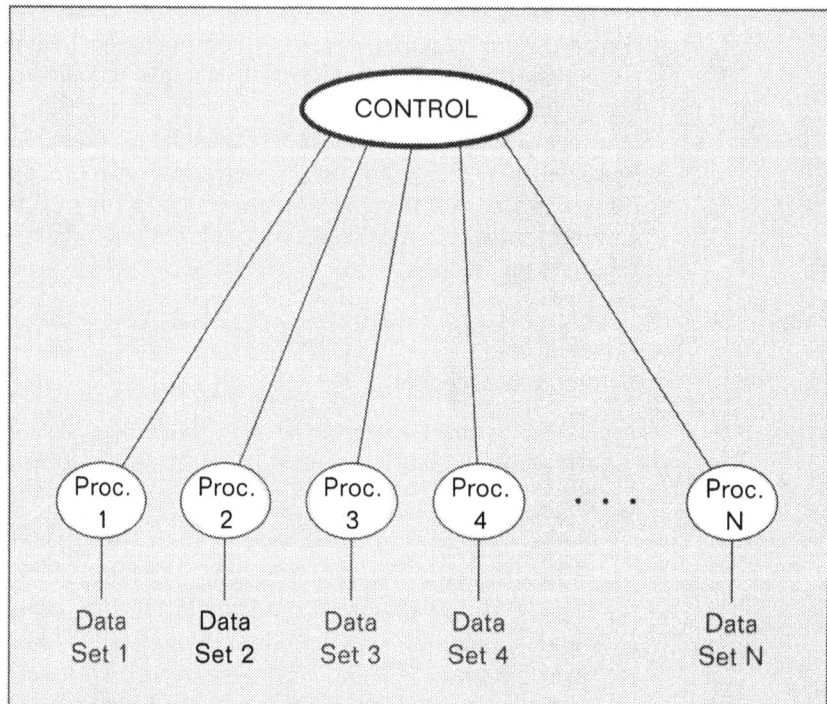

Figure 3.1 Processors in a Synchronous Computing Environment

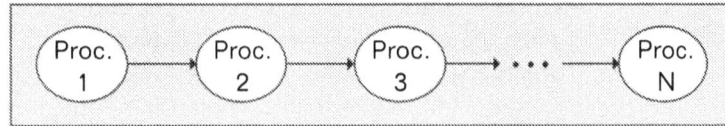

Figure 3.2 Processors in a Pipeline

circuits may decode, and a third set of circuits may be involved in the actual instruction execution.

With this organization applied to many data, the first worker or circuit does the first task. Then the second worker or circuit may start work on the first table or machine instruction, while the first worker starts on the next table or instruction. Eventually, every worker or circuit may simultaneously be working on a different phase of the job, each getting material or data from the previous stage of processing, and each, in turn, handing over his/her/its work to the next stage.

3. Processors may process data with different programs and different data. While this configuration allows processors to work independently much of the time, we have already observed that coordination sometimes is needed. This may be accomplished in several ways.

Processors may use *shared memory* to communicate. Each processor has its own local memory for much of its work, but each processor also can access some common or global memory as needed to obtain data or timing information from other processors. This approach can be visualized as shown in Figure 3.3.

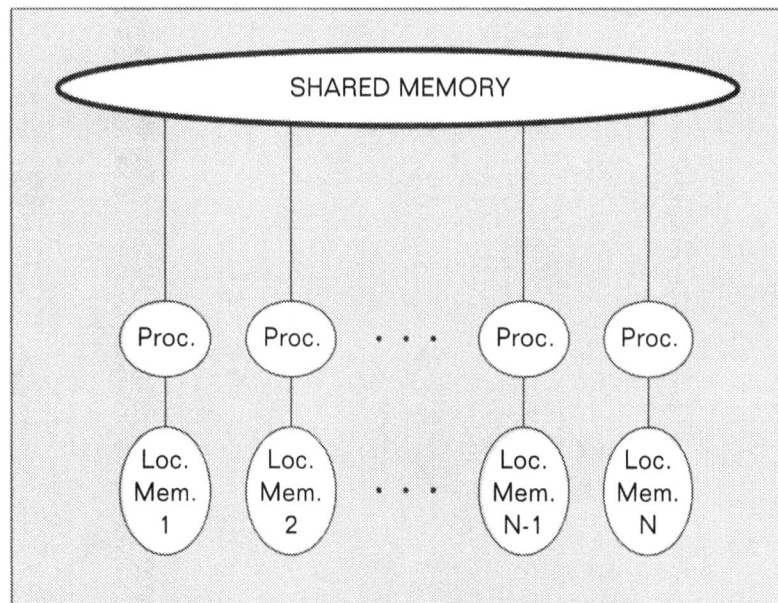

Figure 3.3 A Shared Memory Configuration of Processors

Processors may pass messages to coordinate their activities. In this context, when a processor requires specific information, it sends a request to another processor. When the second processor sends a response back, the first processor may continue with the computation.

While such message passing can work well, it is possible that the processing of messages may consume a significant amount of time. Processors may need to check whether messages from others are pending, and then responses may need to be formulated and returned. Such message processing may add considerable overhead to a computation. To help resolve this burden, processors usually are not attached directly to all others. Instead, processors may have relatively few connections, in order to minimize the need to check requests from many locations. In such configurations, however, messages from one place to another may need to go through several intermediaries, and this can slow down processor communication somewhat. Figure 3.4 illustrates this approach by showing the location of eight processors in a typical hypercube.

All of these hardware configurations allow interprocess communication and coordination, although each is designed for one type of computation. Synchronous processing is particularly effective when many values are needed following the same basic formula; pipelining works well when an algorithm has many distinct steps and those steps are applied to many data sets (to produce tables or to decode many instructions); independent processors may be effective when an algorithm has several distinct and independent parts, so that one processor may work on one task while another processor does another task.

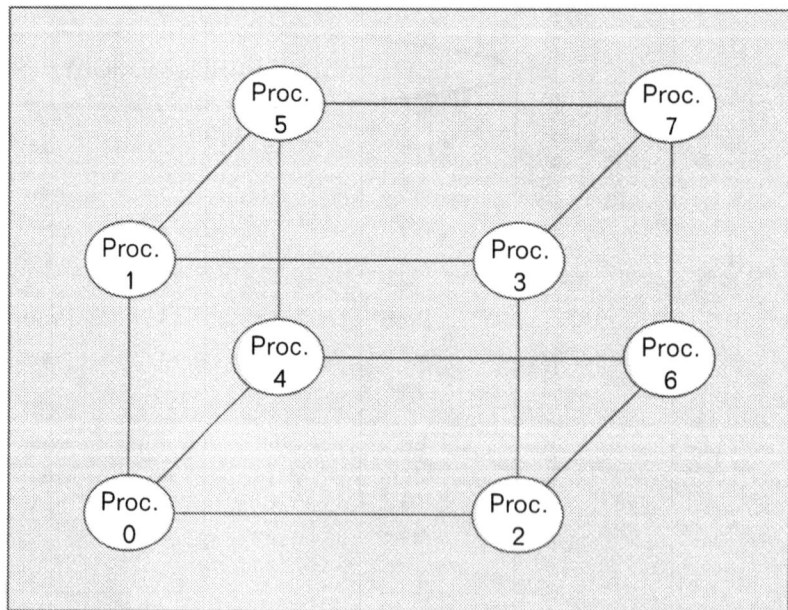

Figure 3.4 Processors in a (3-dimensional) Hypercube

Algorithm Approaches

A second approach to parallelism follows a problem-solving perspective, considering the nature of a specific problem and identifying opportunities for concurrent work. The following, particularly elegant, classification of such problem-solving approaches was described by Nicholas Carriero and David Gelernter in "How to Write Parallel Programs: A Guide to the Perplexed," *ACM Computing Surveys*, Vol. 21, No. 3, September 1989, pp. 323–357.

> *"From a problem-solving perspective, parallel algorithms may be classified into three general categories, result parallelism, specialist parallelism, and agenda parallelism."*

Result Parallelism   Consider the overall project of cooking a multi-course dinner, including an appetizer, soup, three entrees, wine, bread, a salad, dessert, and hot tea. With result parallelism, one organizes a separate team to prepare each course. Carrying this one step further, if each guest gets an individual plate for his or her appetizer, one might even organize a separate team to prepare each plate for each course. One constraint on the salad team might be that its final work, the serving of the guests, might depend upon the bread team finishing its work. Even in this case, however, the salad team can prepare its food while other activities are going on. Only one step, the serving, must wait for other tasks to occur.

This example illustrates several important characteristics of the *result-parallelism* approach to problem solving.

1. Problem solving begins by focusing on the desired results or final data.
2. Attention is paid to developing each component separately (as much as possible).
3. Each result has an associated process, whose goal is to process the individual component or data structure.
4. Each worker or group of workers is assigned to produce one part of the result. (In order to work, there must be at least as many workers as results, so this approach to parallelism may require a great many workers.)
5. Some workers may have to wait until other activities occur, but preliminary work still might be possible in parallel. If a worker does need to wait, that person simply remains idle until work can resume. The worker does not waste time moving from one task to another.
6. An individual works for one result, and when that result is complete, the person or process is not reassigned. Instead, the person is free to leave, take a nap, play a game of tennis, or relax in the sauna.

Specialist Parallelism   While result parallelism focuses upon data, the second type of parallelism, *specialist parallelism*, focuses upon the skills, tasks, or processes that are needed to perform the overall work.

One might consider the preparation of a dinner as involving the work of various types of culinary artists. For example, preparing a multi-course dinner requires people to wash food, slice or dice, measure ingredients, mix ingredients together, cook on the stove, arrange food on plates nicely, and so forth. With this form of parallelism, each person restricts his or her attention to a single activity, and the person may be extremely skilled in that specialized work. In the course of preparing a meal, all of these specialized skills are needed, and at various stages of the work, several specialists may be simultaneously working on different parts of the dinner.

Within this organization, it is also important to note that one specialist may work on parts of several courses. The chopping specialist, for example, may need to slice or dice ingredients for the appetizer, the soup, each entree, the salad, and the dessert. Similarly, a beverage specialist may work on both the wine and the hot tea.

This approach sometimes is observed in a pizza restaurant, where one person may make the dough, a second roll it into the correct size, a third add toppings, another cook, another serve the product, and yet another clean the dishes. In this setting, each person practices his or her trade in one part of the kitchen, and food is passed from one station to another. Furthermore, if the restaurant is large enough to fully implement specialist parallelism, the person preparing dough never does anything else. A similar statement applies to all of the other roles as well. Each person has become so proficient in one stage of the process that it is not cost-effective to allow that person to do anything else. (Even if the cook is idle for a few moments, one would not want him or her to be away from the ovens washing dishes in case other pizzas were ready to cook or had finished cooking.)

This example illustrates several important characteristics of specialist parallelism.

1. Specialists work on their tasks, when possible. At the start, many specialists may need to wait for preliminary work to be done, and there may be little opportunity for parallelism. As work progresses, however, many activities may proceed in parallel.

2. When several specialties are needed in succession, work may be pipelined.

3. This problem-solving approach focuses on the elements of an algorithm, and each element centers on a specialty, worker, process, or procedure.

4. When workers or processes need to coordinate their work, they may pass food or messages to and from each other. In specialist parallelism, data may be sent from process to process, as needed.

Agenda Parallelism   In the third type of parallelism, *agenda parallelism*, work is organized into a logical network or graph of tasks. From this structure, a list of activities is identified. When all parts of the list or agenda are complete, then the work is done. This work is completed by a group of generalists, who begin with the first few items on the agenda. Then, when an individual has completed an individual agenda item, he or she sets to work on the next task on the agenda.

In preparing a dinner, one must follow a sequence of activities for each course. A recipe indicates the sequence in which work must proceed. When putting a multi-course dinner together, one must coordinate all of these recipes. For example, if one is baking bread, one may need to start preparing the dough early so that it has adequate time to rise. Thus, if one is to make a single sequence of activities for preparing the entire dinner, one might list several tasks involving bread, several steps for the appetizer, and then some for one of the entrees. If a second entree can be prepared quickly, that might not be started until later. Any complete agenda or list of activities, however, must contain *all* stages needed for *each* course, listed in the correct order.

In agenda parallelism, the entire group of workers begins working on the first few items on this complete agenda. One may start making dough, a second may begin cleaning vegetables for the appetizer, another may put the wine in the refrigerator to cool. Then, as each worker finishes a small task, he or she looks at the agenda or master schedule to determine what task is next and begins work on this revised goal. Thus, after preparing the bread dough, for example, a person might start chopping ingredients for the third entree. Work continues until all tasks on the agenda are complete.

Agenda parallelism therefore is governed by an identified agenda or list of tasks that must be accomplished. Such work has the following characteristics:

1. At the start, all workers focus on the first agenda items.

2. Whenever an individual or group finishes one task, the generalist, worker, or process looks at the agenda to determine what task is next and goes to work. When done, each individual tackles the next remaining task.

3. In this work, activities and data may be distributed over the entire work area, and processes go from one activity or data structure to the next.

4. Agenda parallelism differs from result and specialist parallelism in that processes and data are not tightly coupled. In result parallelism, the concluding data are most important, and one or more processes are devoted to each result needed. In specialist parallelism, specialized algorithms or parts of algorithms are most important, and data are passed from one specialist to another. In agenda parallelism, processes and data exist independently of each other; data have an independent existence, and processes operate on some data and then on others as specified by the agenda.

Example: Determining Which Students Can Graduate

To illustrate how to develop parallel algorithms following the approaches just discussed, consider the problem of reviewing the transcripts of undergraduate students to determine which students have met all requirements for graduation. More precisely, suppose the Registrar's Office has a complete listing of all courses that each student has taken. We want to determine which students have actually met all requirements, in terms of both their majors and the college-wide requirements.

For computer science, we might think of the students and requirements as making up a grid, such as the one shown in Table 3.1. This sample table shows the various college-wide requirements as well as the specific requirements for a computer science major. Students majoring in other subjects would be expected to meet the same college-wide requirements, but would have different requirements for their respective majors. Student 1 in Table 3.1 seems to have met all requirements listed. Student 2 meets all requirements of the major, but needs two semesters of a foreign language and one semester of Western Studies. Student 3 needs one more computer science elective and one more semester of foreign language. The table also shows that more than one course sometimes may be used to satisfy a requirement.

Overall, our goal is to review all candidates for graduation, comparing the courses they have taken with the various college and major requirements. While this task is reasonably straightforward in principle, complications can arise in practice. For example, different courses sometimes may be used to meet specific requirements, the college may or may not allow one course to satisfy more than one requirement, or there may be specific GPA (grade point average) requirements.

If we were to use a result-parallel approach to solve this problem, we would focus upon the appropriate conclusion for each student. In this view, a process would logically be assigned to each student, and the process would check all requirements for that student. That is, for each student, this view of problem solving might center on the question, Can this student graduate? A separate process would be assigned to each student to find out. Alternatively, we would work at an even finer level of detail, assigning one process to each box in the table. Using

Table 3.1   Chart of Graduation Course Requirements and Students

	Student 1	Student 2	Student 3	. . .
College Requirements				
English Writing & Composition	English I	English I	Technical Writing	
Foreign Language (2 sem)	Spanish I, II		French I	
Western Studies (2 sem)	American Studies I, II	American History I	European History I, II	
World Studies	World Music	Asian Culture	South American Studies	
. . .				
Computer Science Major				
Discrete Mathematics	Math 1-2	Math 1-2	Math 3	
Introduction to CS I	CS I	AP Exam	Honors CS I	
Introduction to CS II	CS II	Honors CS II	CS II	
Machine Organization	Organization I	Electronics	Organization I	
Algorithms & Data Types	Algebra I, II	Algebra I, II	Algebra I, II	
. . .				
Electives (3 needed)	341, 335, 336	345, 410, 411	336, 345	

Using this approach, multiple processors would review different students concurrently, so columns of the table would be processed in parallel.

The specialist-parallel approach to this problem might focus upon the rows of the table. One process might check the English Writing and Composition requirement, a second might review foreign language courses, a third might focus upon courses in Western Studies, and so on. Alternatively, one process might specialize in college-wide requirements; a second, the major requirements for computer science majors; a third, the major requirements for English majors; and so on.

The agenda-parallel approach might begin with the observation that the overall review of students requires checking each square in the table or, at a higher level, each student's transcript. From the agenda perspective, these tasks would be organized into an overall list of work to be done. Then, the first of these tasks would be started by the available processors. As each processor finishes working on its task, it then takes the next item on the agenda and begins working on that. This continues until all work has been completed.

Throughout our discussion up to this point, our algorithm design has been motivated by an analysis of the work needed to evaluate Table 3.1. Each approach organized this work in a reasonable way, so that some activities could proceed concurrently with others. At a somewhat lower level of detail, note that the particular approach we choose may have implications for the data structure used to implement our algorithm. In any approach, we may want to store a list of courses taken by a student in a record, list, or tree structure. Similarly, we may need a Boolean flag within the data structure to indicate whether the student can graduate or not. This storage is required for any processing, because all algorithms must review which courses the student has taken.

When we organize processing by students (as in the first result-parallel approach), one process reviews all of the graduation requirements at once, and the process does not finish until it has determined whether all conditions have been met. Because the process is doing all of this work at one time, no additional storage is needed within the data structure for intermediate results. In contrast, if separate processes are handling individual requirements for a student, then each process may need to set a flag indicating whether or not a particular requirement has been met. (A final process then might examine all of these flags in order to reach a final conclusion.) In this case, the data structure for each student needs additional flags for each requirement, so separate processes can record their results. Furthermore, indicators may be needed within the data structure to indicate when various requirements have been checked. Overall conclusions are possible only when all requirements have been checked and when the results of each test indicate that a requirement has been satisfied.

So far, we have found several reasonable approaches to solving our problem taking advantage of parallel processing, and we may wonder, Is one approach clearly better than the others? or, How can we decide which of these approaches to follow? In practice, the answers to such questions can be rather difficult.

The creation of each process requires some processing overhead. Thus, we may want to avoid algorithms that require a very large number of processes, each doing very little. For example, we may want to avoid an algorithm that creates a separate process for each entry in the table, because the time needed to create a process may be significantly higher than the time required to check the table entry. While this observation may weigh against result-parallelism at its finest level of detail, we have already noted that we can combine such results by student. Using result parallelism, we could create a separate process for each column in our table, while specialist parallelism might create a separate process for each row (or group of rows). Agenda parallelism might consider all of the rows or all of the columns as its agenda, and processors work at one student or one requirement at a time, until all checks are made. Any of these approaches could work satisfactorily.

Some other factors influencing the choice of algorithm may depend upon the hardware that is available. For example, if we plan to use a machine designed for synchronous processing, then we could run the same checks on all students (or students within a designated major) at once. First, each processor could check a first requirement (for example, English Composition and Writing). Next, each processor could move to the second requirement (for instance, foreign language), and so on. In this setting, the hardware is designed to apply the same processing steps to many data sets, and this seems to be a natural setting for a result-parallel algorithm.

If our equipment supports pipelining, then we might wish to have each processor focus on a single requirement, following specialist-parallelism. The first processor could check the English Writing and Composition course for each student in turn. When finished with a student, this first processor might either conclude that the student has not met the requirement or pass the student's record on to the second processor to check the next requirement. The student's record is passed from one processor to the next until all requirements are met or until a condition is not satisfied. This pipelining would work quite well in checking requirements for all computer science majors. However, this flow of work would be less satisfactory in handling all majors at once, because a specialist for one major or major requirement could not provide meaningful information concerning students in another major. In such cases, a specialist could only pass the transcript to the next process, without making any helpful conclusions.

In a shared-memory environment, specialist processors could also check individual requirements, setting flags indicating whether or not specific requirements are met. This environment allows specialists to work on individual majors effectively. Because all processors can access the same information, each processor can focus upon the students within its major without interfering greatly with the checking of other students by other processors. A message-passing environment also can handle this type of specialist parallelism effectively, because student information for a specified major can be sent only to an all-college-requirement processor and to the processor specializing in a student's major.

This example illustrates that result-parallelism, specialist-parallelism, and agenda-parallelism all can provide helpful perspectives in developing parallel algorithms. Each approach allows us to identify what might be done concurrently and how important elements can fit together. With this as a start, we can refine algorithms to reduce administrative overhead. Also, the nature of the available hardware may affect our final choice of algorithm.

Example: The Flow of Pollutants in a Stream

As a further review of the three algorithmic approaches, suppose we are interested in determining the flow of pollutants in the air or in a body of water. For example, we might want to track the flow of chemicals seeping from a landfill site into a river system.

While the details of such a study may be quite complex and unfamiliar, the general approach need not be intimidating at all. Tables typically give water flow rates at different points within rivers and lakes. Many bodies of water are charted, so the direction and speed of water at each point are well known. (In tidal basins, flows and directions may change throughout the day, but even these effects are well tabulated.)

When a pollutant enters a river, stream, or lake, one may wish to know how much of the pollutant moves to which parts of the water body when. One way to answer these questions is to consider the water system as being divided into many points. We record the level of pollutants P[i,j,k,t] for each point (i,j,k) in the body of water at each time t. (We could also consider dividing the region into logical cubes or rectangular pieces with center (i,j,k).) The flow of one such river is shown in Figure 3.5.

At any time, we know the flow of water, and we know that any chemicals present at one point move to an adjacent point shortly thereafter. A pollutant at one position at one instant, moves to nearby points within a few time intervals, following the tabulated flow of the water.

Initially, we know the flow of water at each point, we may know how pollutants enter the body of water (runoff from nearby fields, for example), and we may know how much pollutant is entering from various sources. With these initial conditions, we can compute P[i,j,k,t], the pollution at point (i,j,k), and time t from nearby pollutant levels at time t−1.

Now consider how such computations might proceed, following each problem-solving approach to parallelism.

Result parallelism focuses on the desired outcomes P[i,j,k,t], associating a process with each point and time. (Technically, P[i,j,k,t] gives a matrix, and a process corresponds with each matrix entry.) The goal of each process is simply to compute one specific pollutant level at one point and one time. Initially, we may know the pollutant levels at the point where the chemical enters the water, and the levels elsewhere are 0. Thus, we may know initial values for P[i,j,k,0], the pollution at points (i,j,k) at time 0. Also, if a chemical continues to leak, we may know P[i,j,k,t] at those points next to the source of the pollution. At this point, processes for time 1 may perform their computations, but most or all of the other processes must wait. However, each process works eventually, once computations for all previous time intervals are completed. When any particular process finishes computing its value, it terminates; it does not move on to other computations, because the computation of other values has already been assigned to other processes.

The agenda approach would form a pool of tasks (sorry about the pun) to be done (point (0,0,0) at time 1, point (0,0,1) at time 1, ..., point (0,0,0) at time 2, and

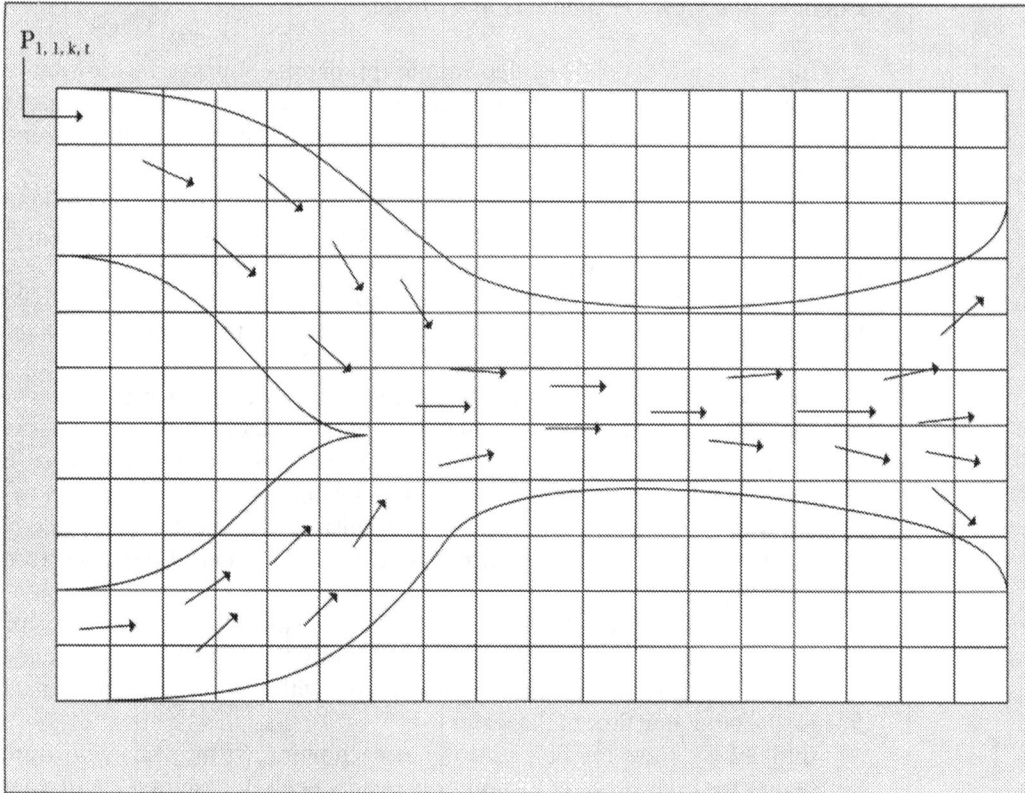

Figure 3.5 Flow of Water, as Forks of a River Merge and Separate

so on). This gives a complete, but lengthy, list of all computations that need to be done. When several processes are available to do this work, they initially are set to work on the first items on the agenda. Then, when one process becomes free, it selects the next item on the agenda and begins that computation. Eventually, all items on the agenda are completed, and the work is finished.

Specialist parallelism could create a series of processes, each specializing in one task. For example, each process might focus upon the pollution level at a specific point. In this work, when a process needs information about the pollution levels at other points, it sends messages requesting the data and receives messages back.

Speed Up and Cost

In solving problems, we may want to know how effective p processors may be in comparison to one processor. In this regard, we usually consider two distinct measures. Sometimes, we may simply want a job done as fast as possible. We may not care how many processors are utilized or how much total work is done by all processors; we simply want answers quickly. In such a setting, we might want a conclusion, such as "processing speed is increased by a factor of 2 or 3 or . . ." Of course, such results may depend upon how many data items are being processed. This gives rise to the following definition:

Let **T(n)** be the shortest time required to solve a problem involving n data items using a single processor (or process), and let **$T_p(n)$** be the time required to solve the same problem with p processors (or processes). Then the **speedup $S_p(n)$** achieved using the p processors (or processes) is

$$S_p(n) = \frac{T(n)}{T_p(n)}$$

Thus, if p processors can finish a job in half the time, then

$$T_p(n) = \frac{T(n)}{2}$$

and

$$S_p(n) = 2$$

Unfortunately, working with many processors (or processes) may require extra work. For example, messages may have to be formulated, sent, received, and processed. Ideally, we hope that p processes give a speedup by a factor of p, but this is rarely the case. Thus, another way of measuring the effectiveness of an algorithm with p processors is to compare the amount of processing with one processor to the total amount of processing required for all p processors.

As above, T(n) gives the time for a single processor. On the other hand, if p processors each require time $T_p(n)$, then the total amount of work done by all p processors must be $pT_p(n)$. This motivates the following definition:

The **efficiency $E_p(n)$** of a parallel algorithm is defined as

$$E_p(n) = \frac{T(n)}{pT_p(n)}$$

When efficiency is 1, then T(n) is the same as $pT_p(n)$, and virtually no additional work (overhead) is required to complete the task. Each processor does about 1/p of the task, and work is speeded up by a factor of p. On the other hand, if efficiency is low, then T(n) is much less than $pT_p(n)$ (or T(n)/p is much less than $T_p(n)$). In this case, each processor is doing much more than 1/p of the original work, and the overhead for the algorithm is considerable.

SUMMARY

A module is a construct that allows related parts of a program to be defined and compiled separately. The interface section of a module specifies what the module does; the implementation section of a module specifies how the module does it. Modules support information hiding by allowing the user of the module to see the interface section but keeping the implementation section hidden.

The documentation that appears in the interface section of the module should be the definition of the abstract data type. There should be no mention of any implementation details. The documentation that appears in the implementation section of the module should include all the implementation details necessary for a programmer to maintain the code.

Modules are ideal for implementing abstract data types. Along with the use of opaque types, private types, and implementation-defined structures, a module provides complete encapsulation for an abstract data type.

Modules incorporating an abstract data type can be made more general by requiring that the user of the module provide an auxiliary module that defines the type of the items in the abstract data type, the maximum number (if appropriate), and a comparison function that compares two items in the structure.

In solving problems and meeting specifications, we might expect that multiple processors (or processes) could do a task faster than one. This motivates the study of concurrent processing. However, one must be careful in considering such work, because coordination among processors may be necessary in order to avoid one processor interfering with the computation of another.

There are two basic approaches to parallelism. The first, a bottom-up approach, begins with a study of hardware. Processors may run the same programs on different data in lock-step (synchronous processing, data-parallel programming); processors may be arranged in a pipeline configuration, where one processor hands its data on to the next for further work; or processors may try to work independently. In the last case, coordination may be achieved by allowing the processors to access the same data (shared memory) or by providing ways for the processors to send data back and forth (message passing).

The second approach to parallelism, a top-down approach, focuses first on data or algorithms. Result parallelism looks first at the final data values that are desired and assigns a separate process to compute each such result. Specialist parallelism organizes work according to the special skills or computations that may be needed. Agenda parallelism constructs a list of tasks that must be done to obtain a solution and processes work on successive tasks.

In analyzing the effectiveness of parallel algorithms, speedup is a measure of how much faster p processors can be than one processor, while efficiency considers how much more work p processors must do.

EXERCISES

1. Run an experiment on a computer, with a language accessible to you, to determine if the compiler uses short-circuit evaluation. For example, for an array [1..Max] of Real, determine what happens when the following statement is executed:

   IF (I ≤ Max + 1) AND (A[I] < > 0.0)
       THEN Write ("Yes");

2. Do the generic data types, described in the text, allow a program to declare both a list of integers and a list of characters in the same program? If so, explain how this might be done. If not, explain why not.

3. Define a DataDefn Module for use with ListOfItem where the items represent test scores marked on a 0.0 ... 100.0 scale.

4. Define a SortedList Module where the values are stored in an array-based list and the comparison operator is supplied by the user.

5. Define the DataDefn Module to go with Exercise 4, where the items are personnel records. They should be ordered by name (last, first).

6. *Building a house:* Consider the overall project of building a house, including foundation, walls, heating and cooling vents, plumbing, wiring, and so forth. Suppose you are responsible for organizing this construction, and you have several (at least 10) assistants to help.

   a. Explain how you might organize the building construction if you follow a result-parallel approach.

   b. Explain how you might organize the building construction if you follow a specialist-parallel approach.

   c. Explain how you might organize the building construction if you follow an agenda-parallel approach.

   In your discussions, be sure to distinguish each approach from the others.

7. In many team sports, several people are active at the same time. For each of the following, decide whether the work of individuals on the team demonstrates result parallelism, specialist parallelism, or agenda parallelism. In each case, justify your answer.

   a. A basketball team consists of a center, two forwards, and two guards.

   b. A track team has five runners, all of whom compete in the 440-yard dash.

   c. A motor-racing team includes a driver, a mechanic, and a pit crew, where each member of the pit crew has a designated task when the car comes in for service during a race. (For example, one member of the pit crew is assigned to change each wheel, another member is responsible for filling the car with fuel, and yet another crew member cleans the windshield.)

   d. A golf team consists of several players. In a tournament, the individual with the best overall score wins the tournament.

   e. A junior high school baseball team places a priority on including all of its members in every game. At the start of each game, names are picked out of a hat to determine who plays which positions. After every three innings, these players are shuffled to different positions, again according to a random draw.

8. A newspaper staff wishes to use a computing network to help streamline its production of the paper. Machines are needed for reporters to type their stories, for advertising staff to produce ad layouts, for editorial staff to combine individual stories into pages, and for production staff to run the presses.

   a. Describe how these machines might be organized, so that data can be moved from one place to the next with minimal overhead.

b. If you were responsible for purchasing equipment for this newspaper, would each machine you purchase have the same computing power (for example, processing speed, memory size)? Please explain.

c. Which type of parallelism best represents your organization or equipment: result parallelism, specialist parallelism, or agenda parallelism?

9. *Determining the Mandelbrot Set:* A picture of a Mandelbrot set depends upon making a computation for each point in the plane. On the basis of that computation, a point is colored black or white. [*Note:* Technically, a point c in the plane is considered to be a complex number. Given c, one applies the function $f(c) = c^2 + c$ many times, considering the sequence c, f(c), f(f(c)), f(f(f(c))), and so on. If the numbers of this sequence approach zero, c is considered to be part of the Mandelbrot set, and colored white. On the other hand, if this sequence approaches infinity, c is not in the Mandelbrot set, and is colored black.] When displaying a Mandelbrot set on the screen of a workstation, one computation is required for each pixel or dot on the screen. Consider how processing might be organized to display a Mandelbrot set on a screen, following result parallelism, agenda parallelism, and specialist parallelism.

10. *The n-body Problem:* In physics, the n-body problem follows the movement of n objects in space, assuming that each of these objects affects the others (for example, through gravitational or electrical forces) and that these objects are not affected by anything else.

More specifically, suppose we are given the initial position and velocity of n objects in space. We want to compute the forces on these objects over successive time intervals and determine the positions and velocities of the bodies after successive intervals. Of course, after a short time interval, each body may have moved somewhat from its previous position, so all forces on each body may change over time.

To solve the problem, think of the solution as involving the computation of two matrices, P[i,j] and V[i,j], where P[i,j] gives the position of body i at time j, and V gives similar values for velocity. Physics provides specific formulae for computing each position and velocity at one time interval from the positions and velocities at earlier time intervals.

Consider how processing might be organized to solve the n-body problem, following result parallelism, agenda parallelism, and specialist parallelism.

11. The speedup of a problem using p processes can never exceed p. Analyze the definition of the term "speedup," and discuss why p must be a bound for speedup [*Hint:* If speedup did exceed p, show how one could improve upon the algorithm for one processor.]

12. Explain why the efficiency of a parallel algorithm can never exceed 1.

13. In the discussion within this chapter, a processor is considered to be a single specialized chip, while a process is a job or task running on a processor. For example, if several users are seated at terminals connected to the same central processor, then each user is running one or more processes on that processor.

In formulating a parallel algorithm, explain why several processes running on a single processor can never solve a problem more quickly than a single process running on that machine. Assume that no other users are running jobs on the machine. If other users are also using the same machine, what effects may you experience if you divide your algorithm into parallel parts? Does this use of parallelism by you have any impact on other users? Explain.

14. This chapter presents an example to show some of the difficulties that can arise when two people transfer money between accounts at the same time. Within a computer, similar contention is a regular part of normal operations. For example,

    Two programs may request memory at the same time.

    Two users may want to use the same disk file(s).

    Two users may ask that two files be printed at the same printer.

    For each of the above situations, discuss what problems might arise if both programs or users are granted their requests concurrently. If you have taken a course on operating systems, describe some mechanisms that can be used to resolve such contention.

Unstructured Data Types

4

From a functional point of view, an unstructured data type is a composite data type where items are put into a collection of items and retrieved from that collection of items. There is no relationship among the items in the composite structure other than the fact that they reside in the same structure. The set is the classic unstructured data type. Two other common data types in this category are the record and the keyed table (sometimes called the symbol table).

We begin this chapter by reviewing the notation for axiomatic specifications, the technique we use to specify all abstract data types.

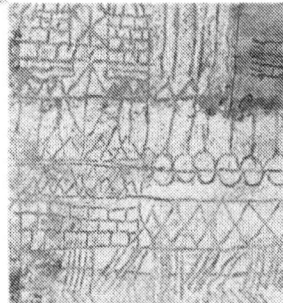

Review of Axiomatic Specifications

The abstract data type being defined is called the designated domain or the carrier domain. The other data types involved in the operations on the carrier domain are called auxiliary domains. There are four types of operations (functions) that can be defined on an abstract data type: primitive constructors, constructors, observers, and iterators.

Primitive constructors return an instance of the carrier domain without taking one as input; that is, a primitive constructor creates a new instance of the abstract data type. This new instance is either empty or has no defined values stored within it. For obvious reasons, these operations often are called Create. Create may be parameterless, or it may take a type (or types) or a constant (or constants) as a parameter that imposes certain bounds on instances of the data type being created.

Constructors take an instance of the carrier domain as an argument and return an object of the carrier domain. *Observers* are operations that take an instance of the carrier domain and return results of a different type; that is, they observe an instance of the carrier domain.

Iterators are operations that allow the user to view the items stored in an instance of the carrier domain. In some data types, separate iterators are not necessary; in other data types, iterators have no meaning; and in others, iterators must be explicitly defined using an additional auxiliary data type to hold the items to be viewed.

Basic constructors include primitive constructors and the constructors into which the structure expression can be reduced. In the Stack ADT, the basic constructors are Create and Push; in the UnsortedList ADT, they are Create and Make. All of the other operations are defined in terms of the basic constructors. These operations do not have axioms describing their behavior, unless the behavior is constrained in some way.

We need a way of expressing two situations that produce exceptions that come up in our specifications of data types. The first situation occurs when the application of an operation causes an error. Trying to Pop a stack when the stack is empty is such a situation.

The second situation occurs in cases where the Create operation takes a parameter that represents a constraint on the structure. Here, we could view the operation as creating the shell or template in which the allowable places are defined in advance. When a retrieval operation is applied to a place in a constrained structure type where no value has yet been stored, an error has occurred. Note that this is a different kind of error than trying to access a place outside the limits of a structure. For example, if you define an array Numbers to have 10 places indexed from 1 to 10, trying to access Numbers[0] or Numbers[11] is an error. However, accessing Numbers[2] before you have stored any values into it gives you logical garbage.

To handle these two situations, we introduce two universal constants, *Error* and *Undefined*. Error is returned when the application of the operation causes an error. Undefined is returned when access to the slot in a structure is allowable, but the contents of the slot have not been given a value. Every domain is augmented with Error and/or Undefined. Error and Undefined specify two different types of errors.

Set

The user of the abstract data type Set expects it to model the mathematical data type set. An empty set is created, and items of the component type are inserted into the set and deleted from the set. The only parameters needed for either operation are the set and the item.

Specification

The names that we choose for the operations are, for the most part, obvious. Store is the exception: we usually think of inserting an item into a set. We choose to use the verb Store here to be consistent with its use in later data types. (Insert is reserved for a second operator that adds an item to an abstract data type but has a side effect of altering the position of other items within the structure.)

```
structure  Set (of ItemType)
interface  Create                    → Set
           Store(Set, ItemType)      → Set
           IsEmpty(Set)              → Boolean
           Card(Set)                 → Integer
           IsIn(Set, ItemType)       → Boolean
           Delete(Set, ItemType)     → Set
    end

axioms     for i1, i2 in ItemType, S, T in Set, let
       Store(S, i1) =
              IF IsIn(S, i1)
                  THEN    S
              END IF

       IsEmpty(Create) = True
       IsEmpty(Store(S, i1)) = False

       Card(Create) = 0
       Card(Store(S, i1)) = 1 + Card(S)

       IsIn(Create, i1) = False
       IsIn(Store(S, i2), i1) =
              IF i1 = i2
                  THEN    True
                  ELSE    IsIn(S, i1)
              END IF

       Delete(Create, i1) = Create
       Delete(Store(S, i2), i1) =
              IF i1 = i2
                  THEN    S
                  ELSE    Store(Delete(S, i1), i2)
              END IF
    end
end Set
```

A set does not have duplicates. This is represented in the constraint on the Store operation. The Store does nothing if the item is already in the set. This property can be expressed in another way by putting no constraints on Store and letting Delete take care of removing all the extra duplicates. Card then has to be altered accordingly.

Delete(Create, i1) = Create
Delete(Store(S, i2), i1) =
    IF i1 = i2
        THEN   Delete(S, i1)
        ELSE   Store(Delete(S, i1), i2)
    END IF

Card(Create) = 0
Card(Store(S, i1)) = 1 + Card(Delete(S, i1))

Because there is no structure in a set that allows us to move from one element to another in order to view each element, we define an iterator that takes each of the items in the collection and puts them in an unsorted, nonindexed, linear list. Once items are in the list, we can view each item in turn. The operations on this type of list are defined in the Application section in Chapter 1. The constructor operation that takes a list and an item and returns a list is the Make operation.

We call the iterator operation Members. In order to define the interface for Members, we must add the ADT UnsortedList to the set of domains for Set.

Members(Set) → UnsortedList
Members(Create) = Create
Members(Store(S, i1)) = Make(Members(S), i1)

Notice that Create is used twice in the same axiom. There is no ambiguity, however, because the context determines which empty structure is being defined. The Members operation takes a parameter of type Set, so the Create on the left of the equal sign refers to an empty set. Members returns a parameter of type UnsortedList, so the Create on the right of the equal sign refers to the empty unsorted list.

If we use the second set of axioms where there is no constraint on Store (duplicates are inserted), the general axiom for Members must take care of not adding duplicates to the list.

Members(Store(S, i1)) = Make(Members(Delete(S,i1)), i1)

While we identified two different sets of axioms for the Set ADT, we consistently use the first approach here, where the removal of duplicates is included as part of the Store operation. This approach makes the Store operation a bit more complicated, but it greatly simplifies other operations (for instance, Delete, Card, Members), as shown above.

The ADT Set has four very commonly used binary operations associated with it: Difference, Union, Intersection, and IsSubset. Let us use the axioms to specify these four binary operations. The interfaces are as follows:

Difference(Set, Set)   → Set
Union(Set, Set)   → Set
Intersection(Set, Set) → Set
IsSubset(Set, Set)   → Boolean

The difference between two sets is defined as the set made up of all the items that are in the first set but not in the second set. There are two ways in which we can specify this. The first is to look at each of the items in the first set and ask if it is in the second set. If the item is not in the second set, then it is placed in the result. When does the process stop? When the first set is empty. This can be specified using the following two axioms:

Difference(Create, T) = Create
Difference(Store(S, i1), T) =
    IF IsIn (T, i1)
        THEN   Difference (S, T)
        ELSE   Store(Difference(S, T), i1)
    END IF

The second way to specify set difference is to look at each of the items in the second set and remove them from the first set. The base case then is when the second set is empty.

Difference(S, Create) = S
Difference(S, Store(T, i1)) = Difference(Delete(S, i1), T)

The base case is different in the two specifications. If the first set is being examined, the base case returns the empty set. If the second set is being examined, the base case returns the first set. Note also that the instance that is being examined (decomposed) in the general axiom is the instance that reaches Create in the base axiom. We are not saying that set difference is commutative; it is not. We are saying that there are two approaches to defining the result. One approach decomposes the first set, putting those items that are not in the second set into the result. The other decomposes the second set, removing each item from the first set. The results are the same in each case.

The Union operation returns a set made up of all those items that are in either or both sets. One of the sets is examined item by item; the base case returns the other set. It does not matter whether the first argument or the second is decomposed, but the base axiom must be consistent. That is, the Create must be in the position of the set being decomposed.

Union(Create, T) = T
Union(Store(S, i1), T) = Store(Union(S, T), i1)

As an aside, it is worthwhile to note that these axioms for Union apply whether the Store axioms check for duplicates or not. If they do, then Store prevents duplicates from arising. If they do not, then we have already commented that other operations must take possible redundant copies into account.

The Intersection operation returns a set made up of all the items that appear in both sets. Again, the items in one set are examined one at a time. If an item is in the other set, then it is put into the result. The base case returns the empty set, that is, Create.

```
Intersection(Create, T) = Create
Intersection(Store(S, i1), T) =
    IF IsIn(T, i1)
        THEN  Store(Intersection(S, T), i1)
        ELSE   Intersection(S, T)
    END IF
```

We have chosen to decompose the first set. This was an arbitrary choice; the second set would have done just as well.

The IsSubset operation returns True if all of the items in the first set are also in the second set. The items in the first set are examined one by one. If an item that is not in the second set is encountered, then False is returned; otherwise, the next item is examined.

```
IsSubset(Create, T) = True
IsSubset(Store(S, i1), T) =
    IF IsIn(T, i1)
        THEN  IsSubset(S, T)
        ELSE   False
    END IF
```

How would these axioms have to be changed in order to specify a proper subset rather than a simple subset? In a proper subset, the second set would have to contain at least one item that is not in the first in addition to all those that are in the first set. We leave this change as an exercise for you.

It is interesting to note that all of the operations for the Set ADT are fully specified; none returns Error or Undefined.

Implementation

There are two basic ways in which to implement sets. The first explicitly records the presence or absence of each item in the base type (ItemType) in the representation of a set variable. The second records only those items that are in a set variable at a particular time. If an item is not listed as being in the set, it is not in the set. That is, the presence of each item in the set is explicitly recorded; the absence of an item is implicit.

Explicit Representation

The explicit representation of each item in the component type in each set variable is called a **bit vector** representation. There is a one-to-one mapping from each item in the component type (ItemType) to a Boolean flag. If the item is in a set variable, the flag is True; if the item is not in the set variable, the flag is False. The languages that have a built-in set data type use this technique where the Boolean flag is represented by a bit—hence, the name bit vector.

> **Bit Vector** An implementation that maps each item in the component type to a Boolean flag.

We can use an array-based implementation for the bit vector because the cardinality of ItemType gives us the size of the array. For example, if we want to implement a set type, we use the following declarations:

Interface Section SetADT;

```
(* To access ItemType and MaxItems. *)
USES <data defining module>

TYPE
    ItemRange = 1..MaxItems;
    SetType = ARRAY [ItemRange] OF Boolean;

VAR
    Item       : ItemType;
    S1, S2, S3 : SetType;

FUNCTION Map(Item : ItemType) : ItemRange;
(* Item is mapped into a number between 1 and the cardinality   *)
(* of ItemType (MaxItems). This mapping is one-to-one.          *)
```

To be a bit more precise, an abstract set has the form

Store (Store (. . . (Store (Create, i_1)) . . .), i_{n-1}), i_n)

Furthermore, the Store axiom indicates that the set does not change if there is an attempt to store an item that is already in the set. Thus, any abstract set can be reduced to a set of the above form, where $i_1, i_2, \ldots, i_{n-1}, i_n$ are distinct. This provides a *reduced set expression* for a set. Additionally, it should be noted that Delete and the various observer functions do not distinguish various orders in which the elements are stored. For example, IsIn returns True if an element is anywhere in the set. (Of course, this indifference to the order of Store operations would change if we were to add an operation Head. But then, of course, we would have a new ADT with a Head operation, not a Set.)

With this framework, the reduced set expression

Store (Store (. . . (Store (Create, i_1)) . . .), i_{n-1}), i_n)

corresponds to the array

	Map(i_{n-1})			Map(i_1)			Map(i_n)		
...	True	False	...	False	True	False	...	False	True	False	...

This array has True in an entry j if a Store operation includes item j, and the array has False in an entry j if no Store operation includes item j. This relationship between the formal axioms and the array provides an appropriately precise correspondence between the set specified formally and our implementation.

But before we look at the algorithms themselves, we look at an illustration of a concrete example where ItemType is the subname of the characters 'A' . . . 'J'. The mapping into an index is the ordinal position of the letter in the subrange (first position is 1). That is, 'A' maps into 1; 'B' maps into 2; and so on. An instance of an empty set would look like this:

[1]	[2]	[3]	[4]	[5]	[6]	[7]	[8]	[9]	[10]
False	False	False	False	False	False	False	False	False	False

The set expression

(Store(Store(Store(Create, A), F), I)

is represented as follows:

[1]	[2]	[3]	[4]	[5]	[6]	[7]	[8]	[9]	[10]
True	False	False	False	False	True	False	False	True	False

The algorithms for the set operations become operations on Boolean values. As described in Chapter 3, we use a language-independent pseudocode to express all of our algorithms. In this example, we let the user declare the variables of SetType and pass such variables as parameters.

Create(VAR Set: SetType)

```
FOR Counter ← 1 TO MaxItems Do
    Set[Counter] ← False
END FOR
```

Store(VAR Set: SetType, Item: ItemType)

```
Set[Map(Item)] ← True
```

IsEmpty(Set: SetType) : Boolean

```
IsEmpty ← True
Counter ← 1
LOOP
    IF Set[Counter]
        THEN  IsEmpty ← False
    END IF
    IF NOT IsEmpty OR (Counter = MaxItems)
        THEN  EXIT
        ELSE  Counter ← Counter + 1
    END IF
END LOOP
RETURN IsEmpty
```

Card(Set: SetType) : ItemRange

There are two ways of determining the cardinality of a set. One is to have a counter that is set to zero by Create, incremented by Store, and decremented by Delete. If we choose to do this, we need to change our SetType to include a variable to record the cardinality. The other alternative is to count the number of Trues in the bit vector. These are the same alternatives that are available for keeping track of the length of a linked structure. Here, we choose to count the number of True values.

```
Number ← 0
FOR Counter := 1 TO MaxItems DO
    IF Set[Counter]
        THEN Number ← Number + 1
    END IF
END FOR
RETURN Number
```

IsIn(Set: SetType, Item: ItemType) : Boolean

```
RETURN Set[Map(Item)]
```

Delete(VAR Set: SetType, Item: ItemType)

```
Set[Map(Item)] ← False
```

Members(Set:SetType, VAR List: ListType)

We search for True in the bit vector, and when we find it, we insert the item in the list. However, we need to convert the index back into the item before we put it into the list. Therefore, we assume a reverse function MapBack, which takes a number between 1 and MaxItems and returns the corresponding item.

```
Create(List)
FOR Counter := 1 TO MaxItems DO
    IF Set[Counter]
        THEN  Insert(List, MapBack(Counter))
    END IF
END FOR
```

Difference(Set1, Set2: SetType, VAR Set3: SetType)

```
Create(Set3)
FOR Counter ← 1 TO MaxItems DO
    Set3[Counter] ← Set1[Counter] AND NOT Set2[Counter]
END FOR
```

Union(Set1, Set2: SetType, VAR Set3: SetType)

```
Create(Set3)
FOR Counter ← TO MaxItems DO
    Set3[Counter] ← Set1[Counter] OR Set2[Counter]
END FOR
```

Intersection(Set1, Set2: SetType, VAR Set3: SetType)

```
Create(Set3)
FOR Counter ← TO MaxItems DO
    Set3[Counter] ← Set1[Counter] AND Set2[Counter]
END FOR
```

IsSubset(Set1, Set2: SetType) : Boolean

```
IsSubset ← True
Counter ← 1
LOOP
    IF Set1[Counter] <> Set2[Counter]
        THEN  IsSubset ← Set2[Counter]
    END IF
    IF NOT IsSubset OR (Counter = MaxItems)
        THEN  EXIT
        ELSE  Counter ← Counter + 1
    END IF
END LOOP
RETURN IsSubset
```

Correctness As with any proposed implementation, we must check that the code produces actions that meet the specifications. In the interest of saving space, we check only representative operations here. You are asked to fill in the additional details in the Exercises at the end of the chapter.

Create In the axiomatic form, Create represents a set with no Store operations applied. The corresponding bit vector would be an array with no True entries. Thus, all such entries would be False. This is what the code performs.

Store The Store axiom states the following:

```
Store(S, i1) =
    IF IsIn(S, i1)
        THEN   S
    END IF
```

Now suppose we have the bit vector or array A that corresponds to S. If i1 is already in S, then A[Map(i1)] is already True. Thus, the implementation code, which sets this array element to True, does not change the array. Thus, the array for Store (S, i1) is the same as the array for S, as required.

If i1 is not already in S, then the correspondence between the new abstract set and our implementation indicates that the flag corresponding to Map(i1) should be set to True. Because the implementation code does precisely this work, we conclude that the code is correct.

IsEmpty Axiomatically, the empty set Create involves no Store operations, and the corresponding implementation array would have no True entries. The IsEmpty searches the array to find a true entry. If True is found, then IsEmpty is set False and returned. If no such True entry is found, then the array of all False entries corresponds to Create, and True is returned, as required.

The proofs of correctness for the remaining operations follow a similar pattern. In each case, the axiomatic view of a set as a sequence of Store operations is related to the corresponding bit pattern. Then, the required axiomatic relationships are translated to a statement concerning the array, and the code is examined to check that the processing of the array is done correctly.

Complexity In Chapter 2, we note that complexity of an algorithm is expressed in terms of a size factor. What is the size factor in this implementation? We have two choices: the number of items in a set and the number of items in the universe set (MaxItems). An examination of each of the algorithms shows that either the algorithm is a single statement or it contains a loop going from 1 to MaxItems. Because the algorithms do not vary with the number of items in the set (number of True values), the size factor must be MaxItems. But for any specific instance of the data type Set, the cardinality of the universe set is a constant! Therefore, the complexity of the operations on the bit vector representation are all bounded by the constant MaxItems and are therefore $O(1)$. Note, however, that the constant can be quite large.

On the other hand, if we are talking about the complexity of the implementation of the abstract data type Set, where the set of values varies, then the complexity is O(MaxItems). As the set of values changes, MaxItems changes, but for any execution of a specific instance of the Set data type, the complexity is O(1).

Programming languages that have the set as a built-in data type usually implement the set as a bit vector. Binary operations on variables of this type are very efficient because they make use of the underlying machine code. The union of two set variables is the machine code bitwise OR; intersection is bitwise AND; and difference is bitwise AND of the first set with the complement of the second.

Implicit Representation

Set variables implemented as bit vectors (**explicit set representation**) use the same amount of space regardless of how many items are in the set. The space is proportional to the cardinality of the universe set. (Actually, the space equals the size of the universe set.) This can limit the component types to comparatively small finite sets.

The second way of implementing sets is to keep a list of the items that are in the set. That is, given the abstract set expression

$$\text{Store (Store (\ldots (Store (Create, } i_1)) \ldots), i_{n-1}), i_n)$$

we explicitly store the elements, $i_1, \ldots, i_{n-1}, i_n$, in an appropriate implementation structure. This requires only space proportional to the number of items in a set at any one time. The limit here is the cardinality of the individual sets rather than the cardinality of the universe set. In this **implicit set representation** we infer a value is not in the set if its value is not on the list.

> **Explicit Set Representation** Space and time are proportional to the size of the universe set.
>
> **Implicit Set Representation** Space and time are proportional to the size of the instance of the set.

To implement these algorithms, we use one of the list primitives developed in Chapter 2. In good top-down fashion, we do not have to make a choice of which list primitives to use; we write the set algorithms using the list primitive interfaces without stating which list implementation we are referring to.

The parameters to the set operations are of types SetType and ItemType. The parameters to the list operations are of types ListType and ItemType. SetType and ListType must be aliased (that is, SetType = ListType) in the TYPE section of the module. In order to distinguish between set operations and list operations with the same names, we preface the operation name with the ADT name separated by a period.

Create(VAR Set: Set Type)

```
List.Create(Set)
```

Store(VAR Set: SetType, Item: ItemType)

```
IF NOT List.IsIn(Set, Item)
    THEN   List.Insert(Set, Item)
END IF
```

IsEmpty(Set: SetType) : Boolean

```
RETURN List.IsEmpty(Set)
```

Card(Set: SetType) : Integer

```
RETURN List.Length(Set)
```

IsIn(Set: SetType, Item: ItemType) : Boolean

```
RETURN List.IsIn(Set, Item)
```

Delete(VAR Set: SetType, Item: ItemType)

```
List.Delete(Set, Item)
```

Members(Set: SetType, VAR List: ListType)

Because of the implementation being used, the observer operation Members is a copy of the set itself.

```
List ← Copy(Set)
```

Difference(Set1, Set2: SetType, VAR Set3: SetType)

In order to implement any of the binary set operations, we need a mechanism to methodically cycle through the elements of a set. There are no set operations that allow us to do this, but the Members operation returns a list of the items in a set. We apply the Members operation to the two input sets returning two lists. Then we can use Head and Tail to cycle through the lists. The following algorithm implements the first difference axiom that we looked at:

```
Create(Set3)
Members(Set1, List1)
Members(Set2, List2)
WHILE NOT List.IsEmpty(List1) DO
    Item ← Head(List1)
    List1 ← Tail(List1)
    IF NOT List.IsIn(List2, Item)
        THEN  Set.Store(Set3, Item1)
    END IF
END WHILE
```

Union(Set1, Set2: SetType, VAR Set3: SetType)

```
Set3 ← Copy(Set2)
Members(Set1, List1)
WHILE NOT List.IsEmpty(List1) DO
    Item ← Head(List1)
    List1 ← Tail(List1)
    Set.Store(Set3, Item)
END WHILE
```

Intersection(Set1, Set2: SetType, VAR Set3: SetType)

```
Create(Set3)
Members(Set1, List1)
Members(Set2, List2)
WHILE NOT List.IsEmpty(List1) DO
    Item ← Head(List1)
    List1 ← Tail(List1)
    IF List.IsIn(List2, Item)
        THEN   Set.Store(Set3, Item1)
    END IF
END WHILE
```

IsSubset(Set1, Set2: SetType) : Boolean

```
Members(Set1, List1)
Members(Set2, List2)
IsSubset ← True
WHILE NOT List.IsEmpty(List1) AND IsSubset DO
    Item ← Head(List1)
    List1 ← Tail(List1)
    IsSubset ← List.IsIn(List2, Item)
    END IF
END WHILE
RETURN IsSubset
```

Correctness   The set is being implemented as a list. Because we have not specified which list implementation we are using, we must look at each list implementation in order to verify this code. Here, we look at the unordered linked-list implementation. We leave the verification for the other list primitives for you as exercises. The linked-list implementation of a set is particularly easy to verify because the abstract set

$$\text{Store (}\dots \text{(Store (Create, } i_1\text{)) }\dots\text{), } i_{n-1}\text{), } i_n\text{)}$$

corresponds to the linked list

$$\text{List.Insert (List.Insert (}\dots \text{ (List.Insert (Create, } i_1\text{)) }\dots\text{), } i_{n-1}\text{), } i_n\text{)}$$

where duplicates are omitted rather than inserted in the list. With this correspondence, the correctness of the Create, Store, IsEmpty, Card, IsIn, and Delete operations follows trivially. In this implementation, the Members operation simply returns a copy of the implementation structure, that is, a list. The WHILE loop in the Difference, Union, and Intersection code produces the items $i_n, i_{n-1}, \ldots, i_1$ in that order, which is the order that would be produced by the set axioms. The WHILE loop in IsSubset examines the items in the set in the same order as the axioms and stops if an item is found in the first set that is not in the second set or the items in the first have all been examined. This is exactly what the axioms for IsSubset do.

Complexity The complexity of Create, IsEmpty, Card, IsIn, and Delete are the same as the complexity of the corresponding list operations. The complexity of Store is the complexity of List.IsIn plus List.Insert. The complexity of Members is the length of the list being copied: List.Length. The complexity of the binary operations Difference, Union, Intersection, and IsSubset depend on the complexity of Members, List.IsIn, List.Insert, Head, and Tail. Head is constant time because it is accessing the last item put on the list. In the case of a linked implementation, the last item put on the list is the first item in the list. In the array-based implementation, the last item put on the list is in the Length position. Conceptually, Tail requires the copying of a list each time, but in practice this operation is commonly implemented by setting an internal index or pointer to the "new" first element in a list each time. Head then accesses the element associated with this index or pointer. Thus, abstractly, Tail might have O(Length), but normally the implementation has O(1) to set an index or pointer. Assuming an efficient implementation, Head and Tail are both O(1).

IsIn is O(Length) in the unsorted array implementation and the linked list representations. IsIn is $O(\log_2 \text{Length})$ in the sorted array implementation and the binary search tree implementation. List.Insert is O(Length) in both the array and linked list representations, and $O(\log_2 \text{Length})$ or O(Length) in the binary search tree implementation, depending on whether the tree is balanced. In each operation, IsIn and List.Insert are embedded in a loop that executes once for each item in the first set.

Converting Length to the generic N, it looks like the best we can do for each binary operation is $O(N\log_2 N)$, and three of our implementations are $O(N^2)$. This is true using the algorithms developed in the previous section. There is, however, an O(N) algorithm for each of these binary operations if the lists in the implementation are sorted! We can change our algorithms to take advantage of the order of the elements in the two lists. We can merge any two sorted lists in O(N) time. As an example, we redo the Difference operation using a merge as the basis.

We move down each list in parallel, comparing the current items. If the item from the first list is less, then it means that this item is not on the second list (in the second set). Therefore, we put it in the result and get the next item on the first list. If the two items are equal, the item does not go into the result, so we get the next item from each list. If the item from the second list is less, we cannot make a decision about the current item from the first list; we must see the next item on the second list. This process is expressed in the following algorithm using a case statement within a loop.

Difference(Set1, Set2: SetType, VAR Set3: SetType)

```
CreateL(Set3)
Members(Set3, List1)
Members(Set3, List2)
IF NOT List.IsEmpty(List1) AND NOT List.IsEmpty(List2)
    THEN
        Item1 ← Head(List1)
        List1 ← Tail(List1)
        Item1 ← Head(List2)
        List2 ← Tail(List2)
        LOOP
           CASE Compare(Item1, Item2) OF
              LessThan    :  Set.Store(Set3, Item1)
                             IF List.IsEmpty(List1)
                                 THEN  EXIT
                                 ELSE
                                     Item1 ← Head(List1)
                                     List1 ← Tail(List1)
                             END IF
              Equal       :  IF NOT List.IsEmpty(List1) AND
                                     NOT List.IsEmpty(List2)
                                 THEN
                                     Item1 ← Head(List1)
                                     List1 ← Tail(List1)
                                     Item2 ← Head(List2)
                                     List2 ← Tail(List2)
                                 ELSE EXIT
                             END IF
              GreaterThan:  IF List.IsEmpty(List2)
                                 THEN  EXIT
                                 ELSE
                                     Item2 ← Head(List2)
                                     List2 ← Tail(List2)
                             END IF
           END CASE
        END LOOP
END IF
WHILE NOT List.IsEmpty(List1) DO
    Item1 ← Head(List1)
    List1 ← Tail(List1)
    Set.Store (Set3, Item1)
END WHILE
```

We leave the O(N) versions of Intersection, Union, and IsSubset as an exercise.

Why did we bother to include the original $O(N^2)$ and $O(N\log_2 N)$ algorithms for binary set operations when O(N) algorithms exist? We want to make the point that the most efficient algorithm may not be the first algorithm that you develop. The $O(N^2)$ and $O(Nlog_2N)$ algorithms are correct, and correctness is the most important property of an algorithm. These algorithms that do not take advantage of the sorted property of the implementation mirror the specification. Such an algorithm should be your first approximation. If you are implementing an algorithm that is not going to be run very often and you are in a hurry, these slower algorithms may be fine. However, if you are implementing an algorithm that is to be used over and over again, it is worthwhile to look for a more efficient algorithm. One may or may not exist. Note that the efficiency gained by merging two sorted lists is dependent on the implementation structure and has no effect on the logical behavior of the operations.

Software tools exist that allow you to trace the execution of your program and determine which parts are being executed most frequently. For code that is to be run many times, you might use one of these tools and see if the frequently executed sections can be made more efficient.

As an example of fine-tuning an implementation in terms of both time and space, in the next section we examine several algorithms that have been studied by computer scientists over many years in an attempt to make them as efficient as possible.

Union/Find Algorithms

Before leaving the discussion of set implementations, we look at an implementation that is very efficient provided the operations are restricted to set union and an observer function that returns which set a particular item is in. The algorithms that work with this structure are known as the *union/find algorithms*. There is one additional constraint for this application: an item can be in only one set at a time. This means that the sets are mutually disjoint. The context for these algorithms guarantees a small enough cardinality of the base type to allow an explicit representation.

The applications that use the Union/Find algorithms all take the form of asking the question, Are two items in the same set? If they are, nothing is done. If they are not, the two sets are combined into one. Find(Item) must return which set Item is in. The general algorithm can be expressed as follows:

Process(Item1, Item2)

```
IF Find(Item1) <> Find(Item2)
    THEN  Union(Find(Item1), Find(Item2))
END IF
```

We need a way of naming sets; that is, what does the Find operation return? It does not matter which sets two items are in, only whether they are in the same or different sets. We arbitrarily choose one member of a set to be the "owner" of the set, and mark it. Find(Item) returns the owner of the set that includes Item. Because the sets are mutually disjoint, Item can only be in one set. We can visualize these sets as items with pointers to the owner.

For example, suppose that our items are integer numbers.

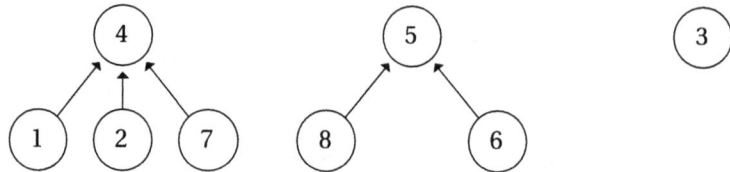

We have three sets: the set owned by 4, the set owned by 5, and the set owned by 3. Process(1, 7) would do nothing because both 1 and 7 are in the set owned by 4. Process(6, 3) would take the Union of 5 and 3 because 6 is in the set owned by 5, and 3 is in the set owned by itself. Taking the union of two disjoint sets involves making one the owner of the other. Suppose we make 3 the owner of 5. Now our set structure looks like this:

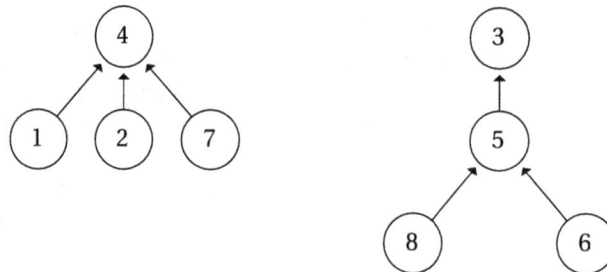

Because the sets are mutually disjoint, we can represent the collection of sets in an array (Sets). As in the bit vector representation, we have a function Map that takes an item and maps it into an integer number between 1 and MaxItems. The components of the array are integer numbers between 0 and MaxItems. If Sets[Map(Item)] is zero, Item is the owner of the set that contains Item. If Sets[Map(Item)] is nonzero, it is the index of another item in the same set. All the items are initialized into one-item sets where each item is the owner of its set. Find returns the index of the position that contains a zero. The Union of two disjoint sets just places the index returned from one Find operation into Sets indexed by the result of the other Find operation.

To clarify this, we summarize the algorithms and work an example or two. Note that Process is the only operation in the interface section; all of the other operations are hidden in the implementation section.

Interface Section Union/Find

(∗ To access ItemType, MaxItems (the cardinality of ItemType) and function   ∗)
(∗ Map which maps an item of ItemType into the range 1..MaxItems.   ∗)

USES <insert module name>

PROCEDURE Process(Item1, Item2: ItemType)

Implementation Section

TYPE
    ItemRange = 1..MaxItems;
    ItemRangePlusZero = 0..MaxItems;
    SetsArray = ARRAY [ItemRange] OF ItemRangePlusZero

Create

Because the implementation structure is hidden within the implementation section of the module, the Create operation is executed by the module as initialization.

```
FOR Counter ← 1 TO MaxItems DO
    Sets[Counter] ← 0
END FOR
```

Find(Item: ItemType) : ItemRange

```
Index ← Map(Item)
WHILE Sets[Index] <> 0 DO
    Index ← Sets[Index]
END WHILE
RETURN Index
```

Union(Owner1, Owner2: ItemRange)

```
Sets[Owner1] ← Owner2
```

Process(Item1, Item2: ItemType)

```
Index1 ← Find(Item1)
Index2 ← Find(Item2)
IF Index1 <> Index2
    THEN  Union(Index1, Index2)
END IF
```

In the following example, we successively apply our operations to sets. The union/find algorithms can be used to process equivalence pairs (pairs of items).

The process starts with each item in an equivalence class by itself. Pairs of items that are equivalent are read in. If they are in the same equivalence class already, no action is taken. If they are not in the same class, the two classes are merged.

We represent the classes as sets. For this example, we bypass the mapping function and deal only with cardinal numbers between 1 and 9. The collection of one-item classes (sets) is shown below in array Sets. At the start, each item is in its own set. (Thus, in this array, Set[Item] is 0, as each Item is the owner of the set that it is in.)

Sets	0	0	0	0	0	0	0	0	0
	[1]	[2]	[3]	[4]	[5]	[6]	[7]	[8]	[9]

Process(2, 4) is called: Find(2) returns 2 and Find(4) returns 4, so Union(2, 4) is executed.

Sets	0	4	0	0	0	0	0	0	0
	[1]	[2]	[3]	[4]	[5]	[6]	[7]	[8]	[9]

Here, 4 is made the owner of the set containing 2. That set now contains both 2 and 4. Next, Process(2, 6) is called: Find(2) returns 4 and Find(6) returns 6, so Union (4, 6) is executed.

Sets	0	4	0	6	0	0	0	0	0
	[1]	[2]	[3]	[4]	[5]	[6]	[7]	[8]	[9]

Here, 6 is made the owner of the set containing 4. Next, Process(4, 6) is created. Find(4) returns 6 and Find(6) returns 6, so no further processing is done.

Process(7, 9), Process(6, 7), and Process(5, 3) are executed. Find(7) returns 7 and Find(9) returns 9, so Union(7, 9) is executed. Find(6) returns 6 and Find(7) returns 9, so Union(6, 9) is executed. Find(5) returns 5 and Find(3) returns 3, so Union(5, 3) is executed. The resulting Sets follows:

Sets	0	4	0	6	3	9	9	0	0
	[1]	[2]	[3]	[4]	[5]	[6]	[7]	[8]	[9]

Sets now represents four disjoint sets (there are four zeros). They can be visualized as follows:

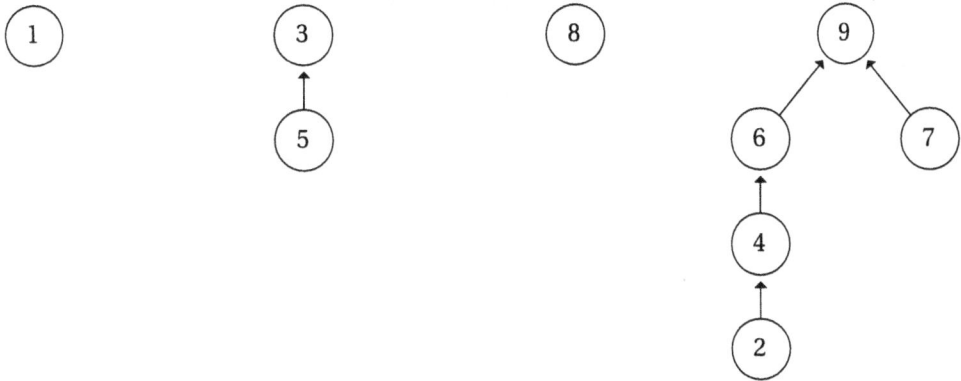

Complexity The Find operation involves following a chain from the initial item to a cell that contains a zero. For example, Find(2) in the diagram above goes through two intermediate places before Sets[9] results in a zero. If the order of the processing is

Union(9, Union(8, Union(7,. . .(2, 1)))))))))

the array Sets is as follows:

Sets	0	1	2	3	4	5	6	7	8
	[1]	[2]	[3]	[4]	[5]	[6]	[7]	[8]	[9]

and Find(9) goes through all the other items in the set to find the owner. Therefore, the complexity of Find is O(N), where N is the number of items in a set. Union involves only one statement, so it is O(1).

Computer scientists have been studying the union/find algorithms for years to find ways of making them more efficient. Two improvements are the applications of the weighting rule and the collapsing rule.

Weighting Rule When two sets are merged, the index of the second set (Index2) is stored in Sets[Index1], making the owner of the set containing the second item the owner of the combined set. This means that one link has been added to the chain for every item in the set containing the first item. We arbitrarily choose to let the owner of the second set be the owner of the combined set. If we let the owner of the set with the most items be the owner of the combined set, we extend the chain for the fewer number of items.

To continue our example, consider what happens if we execute Process(6, 3). Find(6) returns 9 and Find(3) returns 3, so Union(9, 3) is executed resulting in the tree in diagram (a) below. Contrast that with the tree in diagram (b), which would result from Union(3, 9). (In the diagram, we ignore the sets that do not involve 3 or 9.)

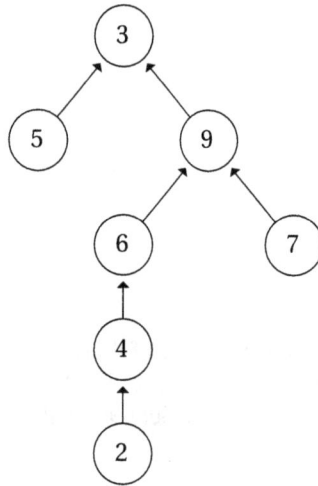

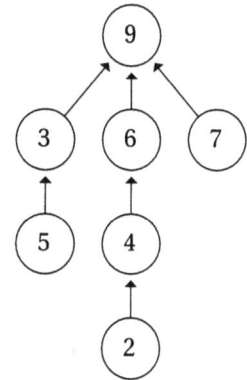

(a)   (b)

The *weighting rule* says to make the owner of the combined set the owner with the most items in its set. We have an operation—Card—that tells how many items are in a set. The algorithm for this change is given below.

Union(Owner1, Owner2: ItemRange)

```
IF Card(Owner1) > Card(Owner2)
    THEN   Sets[Owner2] ← Owner1
    ELSE   Sets[Owner1] ← Owner2
END IF
```

Because Card is O(N), this approach may not seem to be an improvement. We need to keep a length field so that we do not have to count each time. Within the context of trying to make these algorithms run as efficiently as possible in terms of both time and space, we can use a little tricky code to save space by keeping length as a negative value of ItemRange in place of the zero in the owner's slot. That is, a negative value indicates that the index is the owner of the set, and the absolute value of an initial negative value gives the number of items in the set. A positive value is just a pointer to the next item in the set.

Card(Owner: ItemRange): ItemRange

Card ← Abs(Sets[Owner])

We must also update the number of elements in the combined set. This leads to a revised algorithm for Union.

Union(Owner1, Owner2: ItemRange)

```
IF Card(Owner1) > Card(Owner2)
    THEN
        Sets[Owner1] ← Sets[Owner1] + Sets[Owner2]
        Sets[Owner2] ← Owner1
    ELSE
        Sets[Owner2] ← Sets[Owner1] + Sets[Owner2]
        Sets[Owner1] ← Owner2
END IF
```

Let us work through the example in the preceding section, using the weighting rule. The original array Sets is initialized to all negative ones.

Sets

−1	−1	−1	−1	−1	−1	−1	−1	−1
[1]	[2]	[3]	[4]	[5]	[6]	[7]	[8]	[9]

There are nine disjoint sets with one item in each set. We place the number −1 in each array element to indicate that that element is the owner of its set and that each set contains one element.

If Process(2, 4) is called, Find(2) returns 2 and Find(4) returns 4. Card(2) and Card(4) are both 1, and we make 4 the owner of the set containing 2. Sets[2] becomes 4, indicating this ownership. Sets[4] becomes −2, indicating that there are now two elements in the set owned by 4.

Sets

−1	4	−1	−2	−1	−1	−1	−1	−1
[1]	[2]	[3]	[4]	[5]	[6]	[7]	[8]	[9]

When Process(2, 6) is called, Find(2) returns 4 and Find(6) returns 6. Card(4) is 2 and Card(6) is 1, so 4 is made the owner: Sets[6] is 4 and Sets[4] is −3. (The − indicates that the value stored is the number of items now in the set owned by 4.)

Sets	−1	4	−1	−3	−1	4	−1	−1	−1
	[1]	[2]	[3]	[4]	[5]	[6]	[7]	[8]	[9]

Process(4, 6): Find(4) returns 4 and Find(6) returns 4, so no further processing occurs. Process(7, 9): Find(7) returns 7 and Find(9) returns 9. The cardinality of both is 1, so Sets[7] is 9 and Sets[9] is −2.

Sets	−1	4	−1	−3	−1	4	9	−1	−2
	[1]	[2]	[3]	[4]	[5]	[6]	[7]	[8]	[9]

Process(6, 7): Find(6) returns 4 and Find(7) returns 9. Because Card(4) is greater than Card(9), 4 is made the owner: Set[9] is 4 and Set[4] is −5.

Sets	−1	4	−1	−5	−1	4	9	−1	4
	[1]	[2]	[3]	[4]	[5]	[6]	[7]	[8]	[9]

Process(5, 3): Find(5) returns 5 and Find(3) returns 3. The cardinalities are the same, so Sets[5] is 3 and Sets[3] is −2.

Sets	−1	4	−2	−5	3	4	9	−1	4
	[1]	[2]	[3]	[4]	[5]	[6]	[7]	[8]	[9]

Sets now represents four disjoint sets (there are four negative numbers). This can be visualized as follows:

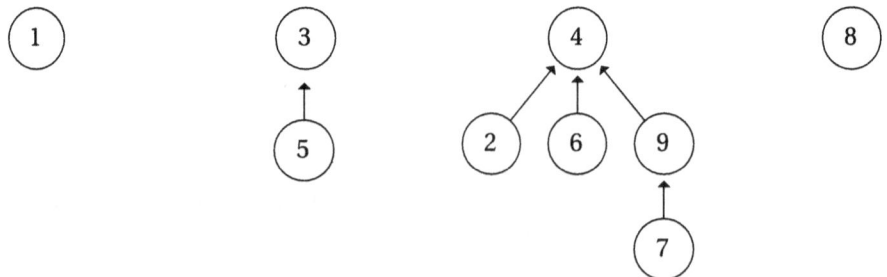

Look back at the sets we had when the weighting rule was not applied. The sets are the same, but the chains are different.

The constant associated with the Union complexity is increased somewhat because the count must be updated, but the complexity remains O(1). What, then, is the complexity of the Find using the weighting rule? The data structure that is being built is actually a tree structure with a pointer to parent. No node in a tree built using this algorithm has a level greater than $\log_2 N$, so the complexity of the Find operation when the weighting rule is used is $O(\log_2 N)$.

Collapsing Rule The collapsing rule is a rule that shortens any chain that is encountered if the chain is longer than one link. The rule may be applied in conjunction with the weighting rule or by itself. The collapsing rule says to go back through the chain after each Find and set the items in the path to point directly to the owner. For example, given the tree in part (a) of the diagram below and the command Find(2), the path is retraced from Sets[2] to Sets[9], setting Sets[2], Sets[4], and Sets[6] to 9. The resulting tree is shown in part (b) of the diagram.

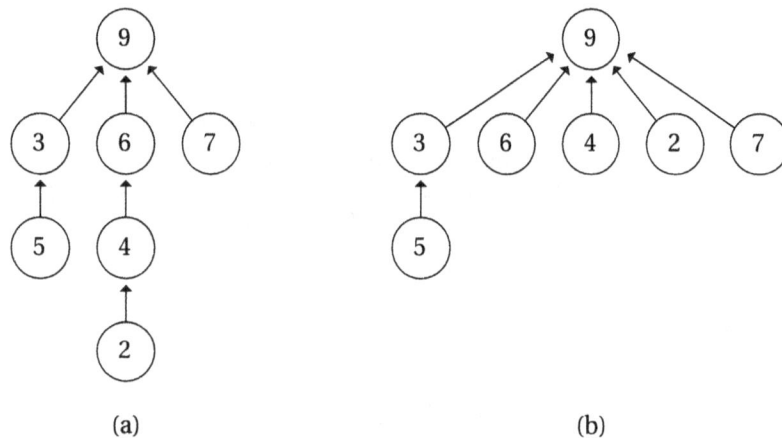

(a)   (b)

Find(Item: ItemType) : ItemRange

```
Index ← Map(Item)
WHILE Sets[Index] > 0 DO (* or <> 0 if the weighting rule is not used *)
    Index ← Sets[Index]
END WHILE
Owner ← Index
Index ← Map(Item)
WHILE Index <> Owner DO
    TempIndex ← Set[Index]
    Sets[Index] ← Owner
    Index ← TempIndex
END WHILE
RETURN Owner
```

Application

In the previous section, we mentioned that the union/find algorithms can be used to process equivalence pairs. The process starts with each item in an equivalence class by itself. Pairs of items that are equivalent are processed. If the two items are in the same equivalence class, no action is taken. If they are in different classes, the two classes are merged.

The union/find algorithms can also be used to detect cycles in a graph. Kruskal's algorithm for forming the minimum cost spanning tree in a graph uses the union/find algorithms to determine if the inclusion of an edge in the spanning tree causes a cycle. While you are not expected to know about graphs and spanning trees at this point, note that these union/find algorithms are mentioned again later in the text, when we look at Kruskal's algorithm.

Record

Because records are built into most modern programming languages, you have undoubtedly used them. In fact, we used the record when defining the array-based list primitives. A list is a record with two fields: an integer field that contains the number of items in the list and an array field that contains the items themselves.

Records have historically been considered structured data types because of the way they are implemented by the compiler. However from the user's perspective, the accessing mechanism does not depend on any structure; each component has its own name. Thus, a record is a nonstructured data type from the user's view.

Specification

The record data type is a nonhomogeneous data type where <field, information> pairs are stored. The Create operation takes a set of fields and returns the structure with the fields defined but the associated information undefined.

structure	Record (of <FieldType, InfoType>)	
interface	Create(FieldType)	$\rightarrow$ Record
	Store(Record, FieldType, InfoType)	$\rightarrow$ Record
	Find(Record, FieldType)	$\rightarrow$ InfoType

    end

axioms for fields in FieldType, f1, f2 in fields, i in InfoType, R in Record, let
      Find(Create(fields), f1) = Undefined
      Find(Store(R, f2, i), f1) =
         IF f1 = f2
            THEN i
            ELSE Find(R, f1)
        END IF
    end
    end Record

Because the constants in the fields are known in advance, there is no need to define an iterator. The same is true for a set if the component type is limited in size. However, because this is not the general case, we include an iterator for the ADT Set.

Implementation and Application

Records are built into most modern programming languages, so we do not discuss their implementation in detail. In Chapter 5, we discuss the base address plus offset technique in relation to the implementation of arrays. The same approach is typically used for implementing records.

If you are programming in a language that does not support records, you must use simple variables, one for each field. If you need an array of records, you normally use parallel arrays, one for each field in the record. The fields in a record are bound together through a common index into each of the arrays.

Because we have already used records to implement our list primitives, we do not look at another application.

Keyed Table

The ADT Keyed Table stores <key, information> pairs with no additional logical structure. The pairs are inserted into the collection and removed by specifying the key, and the collection is searched for the information associated with a key. There are no common binary operations applied to keyed tables.

Keyed tables are very useful structures. Anytime you want to store information that can be retrieved by some unique value, you are using a keyed table. The field that contains the value by which you want to retrieve the information is the Key field. In the early literature, keyed tables were called *symbol tables* because their early use was in assemblers, where the key (called the *symbol*) was the programmer's identifier and the information (called the *value*) was the location assigned by the assembler to that identifier. Some authors still refer to the keyed table as a collection of <key, value> pairs, but we prefer to use the more general term <key, information>. Value often implies a scalar, and the information associated with a key is not limited to a single value.

Specification

In one sense, the keyed table is like the record: the items contained in the collection are made up of pairs, the first element of which is used to identify and retrieve the second. The difference between a record and a keyed table is that the fields in a record come from a closed, predefined type. The Create operation in a record creates a structure where the fields are defined but do not yet have associated information. In a keyed table, the keys in a <key, information> pair may or may not be known in advance. The Create operation is not parameterized; it returns an empty collection.

structure KeyedTable (of <KeyType, InfoType>)
interface Create   → KeyedTable
          Store(KeyedTable, KeyType, InfoType)   → KeyedTable
          Delete(KeyedTable, KeyType)   → KeyedTable
          Find(KeyedTable, KeyType)   → InfoType
          IsIn(KeyedTable, KeyType)   → Boolean
          IsEmpty(KeyedTable)   → Boolean
end
axioms   **for k1, k2 in KeyType, i in InfoType, KT in KeyedTable let**

Store(KT, k1, i) =
   IF IsIn(KT, k1)
      THEN Error
   END IF

Delete(Create, k1) = Create
Delete(Store(KT, k2, i), k1) =
   IF k1 = k2
      THEN KT
      ELSE   Store(Delete(KT, k1), k2, i)
   END IF

Find(Create, k1) = Error
Find(Store(KT, k2, i), k1) =
   IF k1 = k2
      THEN i
      ELSE   Find(KT, k1)
   END IF

IsIn(Create, k1) = False
IsIn(Store(KT, k2, i), k1) =
   IF k1 = k2
      THEN True
      ELSE   IsIn(KT, k1)
   END IF

IsEmpty(Create) = True
IsEmpty(Store(KT, k1, I)) = False
   end
end KeyedTable

In the following iterator definition, we use the data type SortedList to hold the keys to impose an order on the way in which the keys are viewed. The ADT SortedList is defined in Chapter 6. The constructor operation that we need is Insert. Insert takes a list and an item and inserts the item into its sorted place in the list.

ListOfKeys(KeyedTable) → SortedList
ListOfKeys(Create) = Create
ListOfKeys(Store(KT, k1, I)) = Insert(ListOfKeys(KT), k1)

Unbounded vs. Bounded Abstract Data Types

In Chapter 1, we state that if we implement a stack in an array-based list, we need an operation to determine if the stack is full. However, we cannot just add an operation to the implementation. Our implementation must match the specifications exactly.

The abstract data types that we have specified so far have been **unbounded data types**; that is, there has been no limit imposed on the number of components in an instance of the data type by the specifications. The cardinality of ItemType imposes a limit on the size of a set, but this is a property of ItemType, not the Set ADT specification. If we are going to use an array-based implementation structure, the abstract data type must be a **bounded data type**. Because we wish to introduce an array-based structure as the implementation structure for the abstract data type KeyedTable, we now look at how to specify a bounded abstract data type.

> **Unbounded Data Type** A data type in which there are no limits on the number of items that can be stored in an instance of the data type.
>
> **Bounded Data Type** A data type in which there is a limit on the number of items that can be stored in an instance of the data type.

For a structure to be bounded, there must be a constant that defines the maximum number of items that can be stored in the structure. We introduce this constant as a parameter to the Create function.

Create(Max) $\rightarrow$ KeyedTable

In addition, our axioms must specify that we cannot store more than Max items in the data type. There are two ways in which to write the axioms. We can specify an IsFull function, but provide no axioms for it (just as we do for Store):

IsFull(KeyedTable) $\rightarrow$ Boolean
Store(KT, k1, i) =
    IF IsFull(KT)
        THEN Error
    END IF

or we can make it explicit, by defining a Size function:

Size(KeyedTable) $\rightarrow$ Integer
Size(Create(Max)) = 0
Size(Store(KT, k1, i)) = 1 + Size (KT)

Store(KT, k1, i) =
    IF Size(KT) = Max
        THEN Error
    END IF

In the first case, the specification of IsFull is omitted, although we could define it in terms of the Size operation. In the second case, the axioms for Size are given explicitly. In both cases, the details of Store are not defined, except that a certain condition is specified as an error. To complete the specification of the bounded ADT KeyedTable, Max must be added to the function Create in the base cases of the other axioms. Because Max is an integer value, Integer must be added to D, the set of domains. Here is the specification of the bounded ADT KeyedTable that we implement in the next section.

structure KeyedTable (of <KeyType, InfoType>)
interface Create(Max) $\rightarrow$ KeyedTable
IsFull((KeyedTable) $\rightarrow$ Boolean
Store(KeyedTable, KeyType, InfoType) $\rightarrow$ KeyedTable
Delete(KeyedTable, KeyType) $\rightarrow$ KeyedTable
Find(KeyedTable, KeyType) $\rightarrow$ InfoType
IsIn(KeyedTable, KeyType) $\rightarrow$ Boolean
IsEmpty(KeyedTable) $\rightarrow$ Boolean
end
axioms **for k1, k2 in KeyType, i in InfoType, KT in KeyedTable let**

Store(KT, k1, i) =
IF IsFull(KT)
THEN Error
ELSE
IF IsIn(KT, k1)
THEN Error
END IF

Delete(Create(Max), k1) = Create(Max)
Delete(Store(KT, k2, i), k1) =
IF k1 = k2
THEN KT
ELSE Store(Delete(KT, k1), k2, i)
END IF

Find(Create(Max), k1) = Error
Find(Store(KT, k2, i), k1) =
IF k1 = k2
THEN i
ELSE Find(KT, k1)
END IF

IsIn(Create(Max), k1) = False
IsIn(Store(KT, k2, i), k1) =
IF k1 = k2
THEN True
ELSE IsIn(KT, k1)
END IF

IsEmpty(Create(Max)) = True
IsEmpty(Store(KT, k1, i)) = False
   end
end KeyedTable

ListOfKeys(KeyedTable) → SortedList

ListOfKeys(Create(Max)) = Create
ListOfKeys(Store(KT, k1, i)) = Insert(ListOfKeys(KT), k1)

Implementation

We are going to examine two different techniques for implementing the Keyed-Table ADT. The first uses the list primitives from Chapter 3; the second uses a technique known as hashing.

Lists

Our list primitives are lists of items where the only assumption is that the items can be compared using the relational operators. We can expand our list primitives to include lists of <key, information> pairs. Now that we have defined the ADT Record, we can encapsulate these <key, information> pairs into a record that we refer to as an Item. Thus, the list primitives can be converted to lists of records. The only code that must be changed is the code that compares two items. This comparison has to be done between the fields of two records instead of between two simple variables. You may ask, Which field? The Key field, of course. But what if the Key field is a composite? To be general, we let the only person who knows what the data actually look like—the user—define a comparison function that takes two items of ItemType and compares their key fields, returning (LessThan, EqualTo, GreaterThan) as described in Chapter 3.

Our interface changes slightly because we are implementing a bounded data type. The interface section for the bounded ADT KeyedTable is shown below. The KeyedTable is declared within the implementation section of the module

Module DataDefn;

Interface Section DataDefn;

```
TYPE
    RelationType = (LessThan, EqualTo, GreaterThan);
    KeyType = (* any type *);
    InfoType = (* rest of information in the record *);
    ItemType = RECORD
        Key     : KeyType;
        Info    : InfoType
    END RECORD;
```

```
FUNCTION Compare(Item1, Item2 : ItemType) : RelationType;
    (* Pre:  None                                                    *)
    (* Post: Compare returns                                         *)
    (*            LessThan if Item1 is "less than" Item2             *)
    (*            EqualTo if Item1 is "equal to" Item2               *)
    (*            GreaterThan if Item1 is "greater than" Item2       *)
```

Implementation Section DataDefn

(* Implementation of Function Compare appropriate for KeyType   *)

END MODULE

Module KeyedTable;

Interface Section KeyedTable;

```
(* Access ItemType, MaxTables, KeyType, and InfoType.     *)
USES <data defining module>

PROCEDURE Create(MaxTable : integer)
(* Post:     KeyedTable has been created.                              *)

FUNCTION IsEmpty : Boolean
(* Post:     IsEmpty returns False if the Table contains at least one item;  *)
(*           True otherwise                                           *)

FUNCTION IsFull : Boolean
(* Post:     IsFull returns True if there are MaxTables items in the Table.  *)

PROCEDURE Store(Item : ItemType);
(* Pre:      NOT IsFull AND NOT IsIn(Item.Key)                        *)
(* Post:     Item is stored in the Table.                             *)

PROCEDURE Delete(Key : KeyType)
(* Pre:      IsIn(Item.Key)                                           *)
(* Post:     Item whose key value is Key is removed.                  *)

FUNCTION Find(Key : KeyType) : InfoType
(* Pre:      IsIn(Key)                                                *)
(* Post:     Returns Info field of the record whose key field is Key.  *)

FUNCTION IsIn(Key : KeyType) : Boolean
(* Post:     Returns True if a record exists whose key field is Key.   *)

PROCEDURE ListOfKeys(VAR List : KeyListType)
(* Post:     A sorted list of keys is returned in List.               *)
```

Writing the implementation section for Module KeyedTable is trivial, given the list primitives. The list operations Store, Delete, IsIn and IsEmpty can be used with the changes mentioned above. This leaves only the Find and ListOfKeys operations to be coded. We leave this as an exercise for you. Because you are writing the implementation, we also leave as an exercise the proof that your implementation satisfies the given axiomatic specifications.

Error Checking The specifications put constraints on the Store operation. The axioms state that there are two error conditions: trying to store information with the same key as an item already in the table and trying to store an item when the table is full. For this module, we choose to let the user check for error conditions. Therefore, the user of this module must not call Store without checking to be sure that no item with the same key exists in the table and that the table is not full. The specifications also state that trying to find a key that does not exist in the keyed table is an error, so the user must call IsIn before calling Find. Each of these assumptions is stated in the preconditions of the appropriate operation.

Complexity The complexity of the operations on a keyed table is the complexity of the underlying list operations. The change from a list of scalar items to a list of records does not change the complexity of the operations.

There are two new operations: Find and ListOfKeys. Find is essentially the same as IsIn; therefore, it is the same complexity, $O(N)$ or $O(\log_2 N)$. ListOfKeys requires a traversal of the structure making a list of the keys. If the implementation keeps the records in sorted form, the order of ListOfKeys is $O(N)$, the order of the traversal. If the implementation does not keep the records in sorted form, the order of ListOfKeys is the order of the traversal plus the time required to sort the list of keys. Because we can sort the list in $O(N\log_2 N)$ time, this would result in a complexity of $O(N) + O(N\log_2 N)$, which is $O(N\log_2 N)$. An alternate strategy would be to traverse the unordered list, inserting the keys into an ordered list as we go. The complexity here also ranges from $O(N\log_2 N)$ to $O(N^2)$, depending on the complexity of inserting the item into an ordered list.

Hashing

Hashing is a technique that is used for storing and retrieving information associated with a key and that makes use of the individual characters or digits in the key itself. Hashing is an excellent technique for implementing keyed tables. Before we write the algorithms for a second implementation of Module KeyedTable using hashing, we need a few definitions.

A **hash table** is an array-based structure used to store <key, information> pairs. To store an item in a hash table, a **hash function** is applied to the key of the item being stored, returning an index within the range of the hash table. The item is then stored in the table at that index position. Each index position in a hash table is called a **bucket**. To retrieve an item in a hash table, you follow the same scheme used to store the item.

> **Hash table** An array [0..MaxTable − 1] of buckets.
>
> **Hash function** A function that maps a key into the range 0..MaxTable − 1, the result of which is used as an index into a hash table.
>
> **Bucket** An index position in a hash table that stores a fixed number of items (usually one).

A problem arises, however, when the hash function returns the same value when applied to two different keys. When this happens, we say that a **collision** has occurred and the two keys are called **synonyms**. To handle the situation where two items need to be stored in the same index position, we can define the hash table so as to have room for two items at the same index position; that is, we can let each bucket contain two items. But what happens if a third key hashes to the same index value? When more keys hash to the same index position than there is room for in a bucket, an **overflow** occurs. There are two different kinds of hash tables, depending upon how overflows are handled: open hash tables and closed hash tables.

> **Collision** The result of two keys hashing into the same bucket (index position).
>
> **Synonyms** Keys that hash to the same bucket.
>
> **Overflow** The result of more keys hashing to the same index position than there is room for in the bucket. (Collision and overflow are synonymous when the bucket size is 1.)

An **open hash table** is one in which a bucket does not contain an item, but rather a pointer to a list or chain of items that are synonyms (hash to that index position). A **closed hash table** is one where the buckets contain items. When an overflow occurs in a closed hash table, the table is searched for a free position in which to store the synonym. (We look at the algorithms for overflow resolution in detail in the next section.) Unfortunately, there is little consistency in the literature concerning terminology for open and closed hashing. For example, other terms for open hashing include bucketed hash tables, hash chaining, method of chaining, and external linking. Other terms for closed hashing include unbucketed hash tables, hashing, double hashing, and scatter storage within a vector.

> **Open Hash Table** One in which buckets contain pointers to lists of synonyms.
>
> **Closed Hash Table** One in which buckets contain the items themselves, and in which overflow is resolved by looking (probing) for a free spot.

Choosing the size of the table (MaxTable) can be a tricky problem in both open and closed tables. You need a table large enough to hold all the records, but not so large that its space requirements interfere with other processing demands. For example, the possible number of keys (records) where the key is 10 uppercase letters is 26^{10}. That is a very large number! Clearly, you do not have that many very often. One guideline is to choose a prime number somewhat larger than your outside guess for a ClosedTable. (We say more about the size of tables shortly.)

Choosing an appropriate hash function is also tricky. The literature is full of hash functions, ranging from the simple to the exceedingly complex. What you want from a hash function is a flat or uniform distribution, where any random key has an equal chance of hashing into any of the buckets. Getting a uniform distribution from a set of arbitrary keys is very difficult.

It is comforting to know that some of the simpler hash functions are, on average, as good as the more complex ones. One simple function involves squaring the key and taking an appropriate number of bits from the middle of the result. Another involves breaking up the key into groups of characters and adding up the groups. A third involves dividing the key by the table size and taking the remainder (MOD function). If a key is alphanumeric rather than numeric, the sum of the Ord of the characters can be used in place of the letters themselves.[1]

Open Hashing   An open hash table is simply an array indexed by a function of the key where the component type of the array is a pointer to ListType, that is, an array of lists of items. The bucket size is 1. The following declarations define an open hash table. We use record notation to designate the Key field of ItemType. (See Figure 4.1.)

Interface Section OpenKeyedTable

(* To gain access to MaxTable, ItemType, KeyType, InfoType, and   *)
(* function Hash that converts the Key field of ItemType into IndexRange.   *)
USES <data defining module>

(* To gain access to ListType. *)
USES <an implementation of ListADT>
TYPE
    IndexRange = [0..MaxTable−1];
    PtrType = ↑ListType;
    OpenHashTable = ARRAY [IndexRange] OF PtrType;

Store, Delete, Find, and ListOfKeys involve finding which list to process and then applying the appropriate list operation. However, Create and IsEmpty are different. Both must traverse the array of lists. We show Create, IsEmpty, and Store here, leaving Delete, Find, and ListOfKeys as an exercise.

Create

```
FOR Counter ← 0 TO MaxTable−1 DO
    OpenTable[Counter] ← NIL
END FOR
```

---

[1] See "The Art of Computer Programming: Sorting and Searching," by D. Knuth, Addison-Wesley, Reading, Massachusetts, 1973, or "Hash Table Methods," by W. Mauer and T. Lewis, *ACM Computing Surveys*, vol. 7, no. 1, March 1975, for more information.

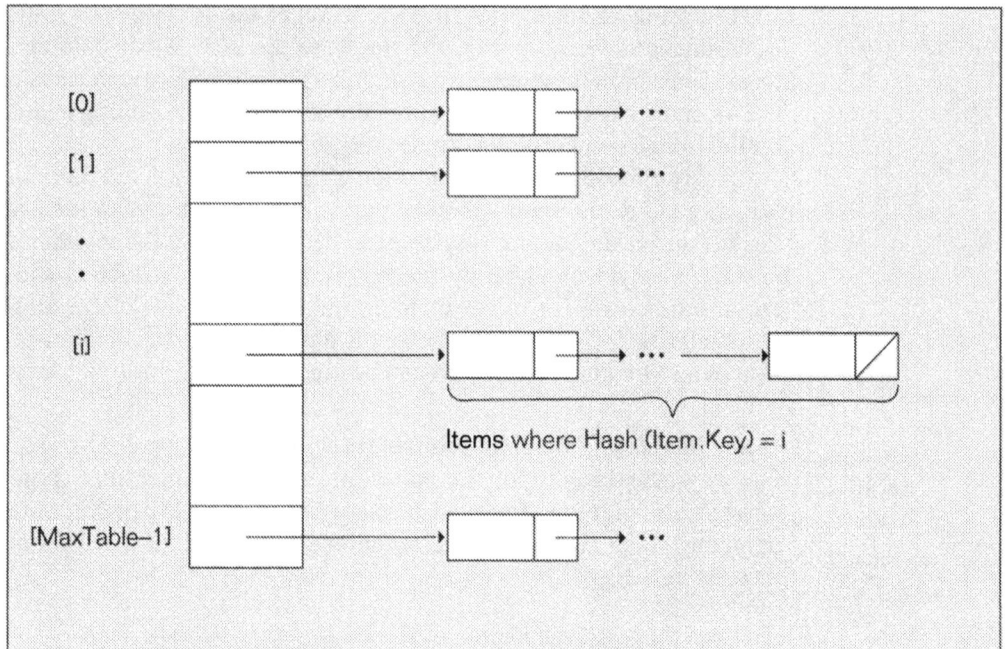

Figure 4.1 Open Hash Table

IsEmpty : Boolean

```
Empty ← OpenTable[0] = NIL
Counter ← 1
WHILE Empty AND Counter <= MaxTable−1 DO
    Empty ← OpenTable[Counter] = NIL;
    Counter ← Counter + 1
END WHILE
RETURN Empty
```

Store(Item: ItemType)

```
Index ← Hash(Item.Key)
List.Insert(OpenTable[Index], Item)
```

Complexity In the open-hash table implementation, there are two size factors: MaxTable, the size of the array of lists, and Length, the size of the lists themselves. Create and IsEmpty have complexity O(MaxTable); Store, Delete, Find, and ListOfKeys have complexity O(Length). But which Length are we talking about? There are MaxTable lists and MaxTable lengths. The ideal situation is one in which the total number of items in the table are evenly spread across the MaxTable lists. If we let N be the number of items in the table, the best-case complexity is O(N/MaxTable). What about the worst-case complexity? All of the N items can be in one list, giving O(N) for Store, Delete, and Find. ListOfKeys is the same order in this implementation as in the list implementation: it ranges from $O(Nlog_2N)$ to $O(N^2)$, depending on the complexity of inserting the item into an ordered list.

Closed Hashing The following declarations define a closed hash table. (See Figure 4.2.)

Interface Section ClosedKeyedTable

(* To gain access to MaxTable, ItemType, KeyType, InfoType, and   *)
(* function Hash that converts the Key field of ItemType into IndexRange.   *)
USES <data defining module>

TYPE
   IndexRange = [0..MaxTable−1];
   ClosedHashTable = ARRAY [IndexRange] OF ItemType;

The bucket size in Figure 4.2 is 1; NumberStored/MaxTable is the **loading density**. If Hash(Key1) = Hash(Key2), then Key1 and Key2 are synonyms and a collision has occurred. If the record with Key1 has already been stored in the table and a record with Key2, is inserted into the table, overflow occurs. A search is made for a bucket in which to store the record containing Key2, using one of several different strategies: linear probing, quadratic probing, or rehashing.

> **Loading density** The number of items stored in a closed table divided by the number of places in the table.

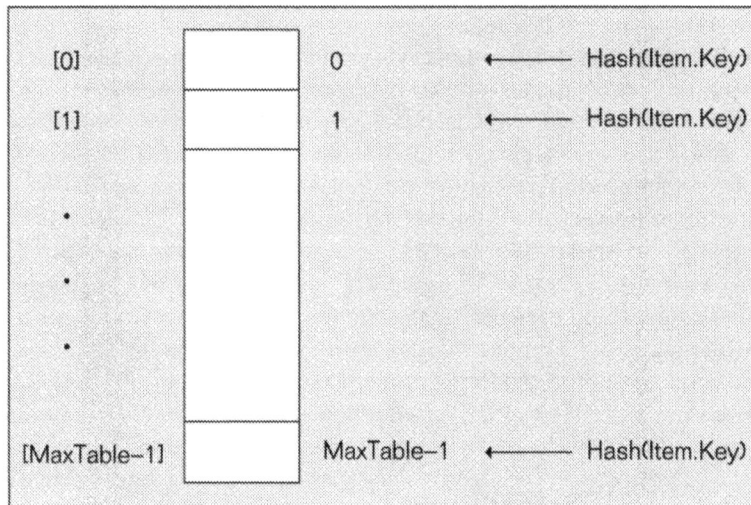

Figure 4.2 Closed Hash Table, No Overflows

Linear probing This search strategy looks for the next free spot until one is found or the original bucket is accessed again. For example, if Hash(Key1) returns 4 and ClosedTable[4] already has a record stored there, ClosedTable[5], ClosedTable[6], and so on are examined until a free bucket is found or ClosedTable[4] is accessed again and no free bucket has been found.

Quadratic probing Although linear probing is easy to implement, it tends to form clusters of synonyms, resulting in secondary clustering (merging of clusters). *Quadratic probing* slows down the growth of secondary clusters. In quadratic probing, the following formula is used to determine which place in the table to check next:

$$((Hash(Key1) \pm i^2) \; MOD \; MaxTable)$$

where i goes from 1 to (MaxTable−1)/2. If MaxTable is a prime number of the form (4∗integer + 3), quadratic probing covers all of the buckets in the table.

Rehashing This strategy makes use of a series of hash functions Hash1(Key1), Hash2(Key1), . . . until a free space is found or it is determined that the table is full.

Before writing the algorithms, we consider an example that looks for situations that might cause problems in the implementation. We use quadratic probing to resolve overflow. MaxTable is seven (7 = 4∗1+3), the keys are numeric values, and the hash function is the key MOD MaxTable.

In our example, the Create operation involves simply drawing an empty table. When implementing Create, we need some way of indicating that the table is empty.

[0]	
[1]	
[2]	
[3]	
[4]	
[5]	
[6]	

The first five keys are 22, 17, 32, 5, and 7. After they have been inserted, the table looks like this:

[0]	7
[1]	22
[2]	
[3]	17
[4]	32
[5]	5
[6]	

The next key to be inserted is 24, which hashes to the position already occupied by key 17. Applying the formula

$$((Hash(Key1) \pm i^2)) \text{ MOD MaxTable}$$

we get

$$((24 \text{ MOD } 7) + 1) \text{ MOD } 7 = [4] \text{ (occupied)}$$

$$((24 \text{ MOD } 7) - 1) \text{ MOD } 7 = [2] \text{ (free)}$$

Position [3 + 1] is occupied, but [3 − 1] is not, so key 24 goes into the position [2].

[0]	7
[1]	22
[2]	24
[3]	17
[4]	32
[5]	5
[6]	

The next key to be inserted is 8, which hashes to position [1]. This position is occupied, so we again apply the formula until we find an empty position.

1. $((8 \bmod 7) + 1) \bmod 7 = [2]$ (occupied)

2. $((8 \bmod 7) - 1) \bmod 7 = [0]$ (occupied)

3. $((8 \bmod 7) + 4) \bmod 7 = [5]$ (occupied)

4. $((8 \bmod 7) - 4) \bmod 7 = [4]$ (occupied)

5. $((8 \bmod 7) + 9) \bmod 7 = [3]$ (occupied)

6. $((8 \bmod 7) - 9) \bmod 7 = [6]$ (free)

Therefore, key 8 goes into position [6]. There are several things to notice about this example. The first is that we need the true MOD function, not the remainder operation that is called MOD in both Pascal and Modula-2. The MOD and remainder operations produce the same results when both values are the same sign, but different results when the signs are different. In the fourth and sixth cases, the first value is negative. Here we want to wrap around the table when moving either forward or backward. If A in the expression A MOD B is negative, use the following formula to get the true MOD:

$$B - (\text{Abs}(A) \bmod B)$$

Key 8 is stored in position [6]. Incidentally, Ada has both the remainder operator (called REM) and the MOD operator.

[0]	7
[1]	22
[2]	24
[3]	17
[4]	32
[5]	5
[6]	8

Now we write the implementation algorithms for the ADT ClosedKeyedTable. Although the user provides a hash function, we show one here as an example. The items are characters, and the hash function returns the sum of the ordinal codes of the characters' MOD MaxTable. As in our example, we use quadratic probing, which requires an auxiliary function NextProbe.

Hash(Key: KeyType) : IndexRange

```
Sum ← 0
FOR Counter ← 1 TO KeyLength DO
    Sum ← Sum + Ord(Key[Counter])
END FOR
RETURN Sum MOD MaxTable
```

NextProbe(HashedKey, TimesCalled: IndexRange) : IndexRange

To calculate the next position to examine, we need to know the value of i in the formula and whether we are to add i^2 or subtract it. A counter set to 0 at the first call and incremented each successive time NextProbe is called for the same key can be used to determine both the value of i and whether to add or subtract the value.

i = (TimesCalled DIV 2 ± 1)
   + when (TimesCalled MOD 2) is 0
   − when (TimesCalled MOD 2) is 1

  We can use the built-in MOD function for this formula, but remember to check the sign of the first value for the quadratic probing formula.

```
I ← TimesCalled DIV 2 + 1
I_Squared ← I * I
IF (TimesCalled MOD 2) = 0
    THEN    Quotient ← HashedKey + I_Squared
    ELSE    Quotient ← HashedKey − I_Squared
END IF
IF Quotient < 0
    THEN    NextProbe ← MaxTable − (Abs(Quotient) MOD MaxTable)
    ELSE    NextProbe ← Quotient MOD MaxTable
END IF
RETURN NextProbe
```

Create

The table is initialized in the executable section of the module. Because we are storing items in the table randomly, we need a way in which to determine if a bucket is in use. In our example, we could tell if the slot was empty because it was blank. In our program, we need to define a special constant called BlankKey of KeyType. The Key fields of all the buckets must be initialized to BlankKey.

```
FOR Counter ← 0 TO MaxTable−1 DO
    ClosedTable[Counter] ← BlankKey
END FOR
```

IsEmpty: Boolean

How do we determine if the table is empty? We have two choices: we can search the table or we can keep a count of the number of entries in the table. IsFull, the mirror image of IsEmpty, has the same two choices. Which is better? As is so often the case in design decisions, there is not a specific answer.

Keeping a counter requires that all insertions and deletions be recorded. This adds a small constant to each of these operations. On the other hand, searching the table is an O(MaxTable) operation. If IsEmpty and IsFull are going to be called frequently, then a counter should be kept. If they are not expected to be called often, then a counter is probably not worth it. In this case, we keep a counter (call it Length). We must remember to set Length to 0 when the table is initialized.

```
RETURN (Length = 0)
```

IsFull : Boolean

```
RETURN (Length = MaxTable)
```

Store(Item: ItemType)

```
HashKey ← Hash(Item.Key)
Attempts ← 0
Probe ← HashKey
LOOP
    IF ClosedTable[Probe].Key = BlankKey
        THEN
            ClosedTable[Probe] ← Item
            Length ← Length + 1
            EXIT
        ELSE
            Probe ← NextProbe(HashKey, Attempts)
            Attempts ← Attempts + 1
    END IF
END LOOP
```

IsIn (Key: KeyType)

To locate an item in the table, we must follow the same steps we use to store an item in the table. However, instead of checking for a bucket with a Key field of BlankKey, we look for a Key field equal to Key. In fact, if we find a Key field equal to BlankKey, we know that the item we are searching for is not in the table.

This brings up a very important point relating to another operation: How do we delete an item? We cannot simply set its Key field to BlankKey, for that would break the search chain. For example, assume that we are searching for the record whose key is 24 in the table we created previously.

[0]	7
[1]	22
[2]	24
[3]	17
[4]	32
[5]	5
[6]	8

Key 24 hashes to position [3], which contains the key 17. The quadratic probing formula is calculated with i equal to 1, and position [4] is examined. This position contains the key 32. The quadratic probing formula is again used, giving position [2]. The key is examined and determined to be 24, the key we are looking for. Now look what happens if we delete key 32 and try to find key 24. We follow the same procedure as before, but when we examine position [4], we see that it is empty (its key is BlankKey). The assumption is that this is where key 24 would be if it were in the table; hence, key 24 is not in the table. We have broken the search chain to key 24 by removing key 32.

Therefore, we must determine a way of marking an item as deleted, rather than actually deleting it. That is, its key must remain in the search chain. When we are searching the table for a particular Key and we reach a deleted item, we continue searching. When we are searching the table for a free space and we reach a deleted item, we can reuse that place.

We use the same technique we used to define an empty place and define a constant DeleteKey of KeyType. When IsIn encounters a key value of DeleteKey, the search continues; when IsIn encounters a key value of BlankKey, False is returned. When Store encounters either a key value of BlankKey or a key value of DeleteKey, the item is stored in that bucket.

There is one more problem to take care of: What if the table is full and the item is not in the table? How can we recognize this situation? We can count the number of times we look in the table and stop when we examine MaxTable keys or we can remember the place in the table where we started searching. Because the NextProbe function requires that we count the number of times it is called, the first approach is more efficient. Notice that we do not have to handle DeleteKey explicitly. If we do not find a match or BlankKey, we look at the next item in the chain.

```
HashKey ← Hash(Key)
Attempts ← 0
Probe ← HashKey
LOOP
    IF ClosedTable[Probe].Key = Key
        THEN
            IsIn ← TRUE
            EXIT
        ELSIF ClosedTable[Probe].Key = BlankKey
            THEN
                IsIn ← FALSE
                EXIT
            ELSIF Attempts = MaxTable
                THEN
                    IsIn ← FALSE
                    EXIT
                ELSE
                    Probe ← NextProbe(HashKey, Attempts)
                    Attempts ← Attempts + 1
    END IF
END LOOP
```

Delete (Key: KeyType)

```
HashKey ← Hash(Key)
Attempts ← 0
Probe ← HashKey
LOOP
    IF ClosedTable[Probe].Key = Key
        THEN
            ClosedTable[Probe].Key ← DeleteKey
            Length ← Length − 1
            EXIT
        ELSE
            Probe ← NextProbe(HashKey, Attempts)
            Attempts ← Attempts + 1
    END IF
END LOOP
```

Find(Key:KeyType) : ItemType

Find is a logical subset of IsIn. The algorithm for Find, however, is much simpler than the algorithm for IsIn, because the precondition for Find states that the item is in the table.

```
HashKey ← Hash(Key)
Attempts ← 0
Probe ← HashKey
LOOP
   IF ClosedTable[Probe].Key = Key
      THEN
            Item ← ClosedTable[Probe]
            EXIT
   END IF
   Probe ← NextProbe(HashKey, Attempts)
   Attempts ← Attempts + 1
END LOOP
RETURN Item
```

ListOfKeys(List: ListType)

```
FOR Counter ← 0 TO MaxTable−1 DO
   IF (ClosedTable[Counter].Key <> DeleteKey) AND
         (ClosedTable[Counter].Key <> BlankKey)
      THEN  List.Insert(List, ClosedTable[Counter].Key)
   END IF
END FOR
```

Complexity IsFull and IsEmpty have bounded time because we have kept a counter as we store and delete items. ListOfKeys is O(N) where N is MaxTable. The other operations all have an event-controlled loop that terminates when a free bucket or a key is found or not found. An analysis of these functions requires some care and depends upon some mathematics.

In this analysis, let N be the size of our table (that is, the number of buckets, MaxTable), and suppose a bucket can store s items (normally, s = 1). Thus, overall, the table can store s * N items (pairs). In addition, suppose there are p pairs actually stored. Then the loading density is $\alpha = p / (s * N)$. Thus, α is the fraction of the table that is full. If α is close to 0, then there are very few actual pairs stored relative to the space available. If α is close to 1, then p and (s*N) are about equal, and the number of items stored is close to the maximum capacity of the table.

In what follows, we assume s = 1 for simplicity. In the exercises, you are asked to redo the analysis for an arbitrary value of s. Thus, in what follows, we assume our table can store N pairs and the loading density is $\alpha = p/N$.

Informally, if the loading density is small (that is, if there are a lot of free buckets), the loops involved in searching successive buckets are seldom repeated, so the order is O(1). As the loading density approaches 1, the order approaches O(N). Therefore, we say that these operations have an average-case complexity of O(1) and a worst-case complexity of O(N), where N is the table size.

More precisely, if there are p items in the table and the table can hold N items, then the fraction of the table that is filled is p/N. If we are using a uniform hashing function, then that function is equally likely to choose any location in the table for the start of a search. Thus, during a search, the likelihood that an item is already present at the position designated by the hashing function is p/N.

If there is a collision in the first position considered, then any of the collision resolution algorithms look at a second position. Disregarding the initial position, there are p−1 remaining elements in the N−1 remaining buckets. Thus, assuming the first collision, the likelihood that a collision also occurs at the second position is (p−1)/(N−1). Putting these two pieces together, the likelihood of a collision at both the first and the second positions examined is

$$\frac{p\,(P-1)}{N\,(N-1)}$$

Similarly, the likelihood of at least i collisions is

$$\frac{p\,(p-1)\,(p-2)\ldots(p-i+1)}{N\,(N-1)\,(N-2)\ldots(N-i+1)}$$

From probability theory, the expected number of steps for inserting an element is

$$E = \sum_{i=1}^{N} i * \text{probability (stopping in i steps)}$$

$$= \sum_{j=1}^{N} j * \text{probability (stopping in at least j steps)}$$

$$= \text{probability (stopping in one step) + probability (stopping in two steps)}$$

$$+ \ldots + \text{probability (stopping in P steps).}$$

$$= 1 + \frac{p}{N} + \frac{p\,(p-1)}{N\,(N-1)} + \ldots + \frac{p\,(p-1)\ldots 2 * 1}{N\,(N-1)\ldots(N-p+1)}$$

After a great deal of algebra, this reduces to the following formula, which gives the expected number of steps that will be needed in a search in order to find a free space.

$$E = \frac{(N + 1)}{(N + 1 - p)}$$

This formula also gives the expected number of steps for any search.

Before going further, it is worthwhile to make two observations. First, E grows very slowly from 1 to N−1 as p increases up to its limit of N−1. Second, if N is large enough, then this number E is small. For example, if N is about twice p, then E is about 2— that is, we can expect to find any element within two steps.

Finally, we consider the average work involved in building a table with M elements. To insert M items, the total work is the sum of the work involved for the first item plus the work for the second, the third, and so on. This gives the following:

$$\text{Total work} = \sum_{p=0}^{M-1} \frac{(N + 1)}{(N + 1 - p)}$$

To get the average work per insertion, we should divide by the number of elements, M. Again, using algebra, this average is

$$\text{Average Work} = \left(\frac{N}{M}\right) \log_e \left(\frac{N}{N + 1 - M}\right)$$

$$= -\left(\frac{1}{\alpha}\right) \log_e (1 - \alpha)$$

where $\alpha = M / N$ is the loading factor.

A review of this formula gives the same general conclusions that we reached informally earlier. When the loading factor is small, then the average amount of work is quite small (because $1 - \alpha$ is close to 1, and $\log_e 1$ is close to 0, even with the initial $1/\alpha$ factor). When the loading factor is large, then $1 - \alpha$ is close to 0, so its log is large (actually a large negative). Because α is about 1, $1/\alpha$ is also about 1, and multiplying by this factor still gives a large number. Thus, a large loading factor yields a high average amount of work.

Application

Keyed tables are used in two different contexts. The first context is one in which the values of the keys are known in advance. The second context is one in which there is no prior knowledge as to what the key values are going to be. These situations are called *static* and *dynamic*, respectively. The best implementation for a keyed table often depends on whether the context is static or dynamic.

Static

A static keyed table has a constant set of keys. They are known in advance and change very little. Payroll, inventory, and most data processing applications fall into this category. If the number of items is small enough to keep in memory, a sorted list is an appropriate implementation structure. Because the list of keys is stable, the primary operation is Find. The complexity of the sorted array implementation of Find is $O(\log_2 N)$. The binary search tree implementation is also $O(\log_2 N)$ but uses more space. If sufficient memory is available, a hash table is an excellent choice for implementing a static keyed table, as the complexity of both store and delete are $O(1)$.

Another type of static context is one in which we search the table both for keys that are in the table and for keys that are not. An example of this type of table is the Reserved Word Table in a compiler. This table is searched once for every occurrence of an identifier in a program. If an identifier is not in the Reserved Word Table, then it is looked for in another table. To optimize a table knowing what keys are in the table and what the probable distribution is of those that are not in the table, we build an optimal binary search tree. The algorithm for this structure is in Chapter 8.

Dynamic

Dynamic keyed tables are those that are built on the fly. The keys have no history associated with their use. Because we know nothing about them, not even how many there are, a balanced binary search tree is a good choice. A hash table may be appropriate only if a bound is known for the number of items to be stored and if there are few delete operations. In Chapter 8, we examine ways of ensuring that the performance of the tree operations is kept at $O(\log_2 N)$. The identifiers in a particular program fall into this category.

Direct access files (also called random access files) can be modeled as dynamic keyed tables. In Chapter 9, we discuss multi-way search trees, which are often used to implement keyed tables where the items are on secondary storage—that is, they are in files.

Names and Routing on the Internet

Because the previous discussion of applications still may seem rather abstract, we close this chapter with a more concrete example: the use of names and routing tables on the Internet, a national computer network. While a full description of this topic would fill volumes, we focus here upon the basic approach used to communicate from one machine to another via the Internet. In fact, the detailed protocols vary somewhat according to the application being run. For example, communication for electronic mail may follow a different form than a file transfer application follows. Most Internet applications, however, have many communication characteristics in common, and we focus upon this commonality here.

Overall, locations on the Internet may be described at three levels, the *domain name*, the *internet protocol number (IP number)*, and the *Ethernet address*.

The domain name is a logical name for a computing system attached to the Internet. For example, cs.utexas.edu is the logical name associated with a central machine in the Computer Sciences Department at The University of Texas at Austin, while ac.grin.edu refers to a central academic computing machine at Grinnell College. In fact, the names form a tree structure. EDU indicates that each of these are educational institutions: grin.edu and utexas.edu are children of the EDU node, math.grin.edu and ac.grin.edu are two nodes under the Grinnell College node, used for the Mathematics/Computer Science department and for general academic computing. (Other initial names are COM for commercial, GOV for governmental agencies, MIL for the military, and ORG for organizations.) Logical names are assigned through a central authority.

The IP number is a 32-bit address, which often is written as a four part decimal number. For example, ac.grin.edu corresponds to the IP address 132.161.10.8, while cs.utexas.edu corresponds to 128.83.139.9. IP numbers also are arranged hierarchically. All of Grinnell's addresses begin 132.161 . . . , with the machines related to academic computing being 132.161.10 . . . , while the machines related to the Mathematics and Computer Science Department are divided into three subnetworks with IP numbers 132.161.31 . . . , 132.161.32 . . . , and 132.161.33 . . . . As with domain names, IP numbers are defined so that no two correspond to the same location or machine.

The Ethernet address is a 48-bit address that is built into each actual machine or Ethernet board. Manufacturers register these numbers with a central authority. When machines are repaired or when Ethernet cards are replaced, new circuitry has a new Ethernet address, even though the rest of the computer may be the same. (This motivates the distinction between IP names and Ethernet addresses. In a communication network, one wants to designate the same machine, even if the board attached to the Ethernet wire has changed.)

On a logical level, when a user wants to send a message, she or he normally designates a domain name. The machine then must translate this to the Internet IP number. IP numbers in turn must be translated to Ethernet addresses when machines send actual packets of information over a specific wire.

The translation between domain and IP numbers, or between IP numbers and Ethernet addresses, is a natural application of keyed tables, and it is instructive to see how these tables may be implemented. As we consider these tables, we must note that the Internet is now so large that it is not practical for any one machine to record all possible addresses. Instead, central machines are designated as authorities for various parts of the network, and a local machine may or may not record the few names it actually uses.

To see how this type of lookup is done, suppose the local machine (steen-rod.math.grin.edu) needs to determine the IP number for cs.utexas.edu. When the machine is first turned on, it has no information concerning other IP numbers, but its initial configuration includes information that a local domain name server (DNS) can be reached at ac.grin.edu—IP number 132.161.10.8. If this server is unavailable, it has the IP number for a secondary Network Information Server (NIS). The DNS and NIS machines maintain databases with domain names and IP numbers in a binary format. In fact, it is common for this information to be stored in two hash tables, one with the domain name as key and the other with IP number as key.

In searching for the IP number for cs.utexas.edu, the local machine first asks its local DNS, which is the authority for the local network, but which may or may not know about the rest of the world. In handling this request for information, this local DNS uses its hash table to attempt to locate the needed IP number. If this information is not in the table, the search fails and the local machine then asks its secondary NIS source, which is the authority for a wider area of the network. If this fails as well, eventually a request is generated for the DNS for all .edu addresses. This DNS then either returns the information requested or indicates that it is available from a more specialized DNS, which handles information down one branch of the domain name tree. (For example, the .edu DNS may indicate that information regarding cs.utexas.edu can be obtained from a DNS specializing in utexas.edu and give the IP number for that specialized DNS.) In short, in determining the IP number that corresponds to a given domain name, a local machine may consult several specialized DNS machines that look the desired domain name up in appropriate hash tables before finding one that returns the appropriate IP number.

Of course, it might be that all designated DNS machines are unavailable at a particular moment. Because of this possibility, some systems also maintain a table for some local machines that are commonly accessed. While this table is often in text format rather than binary format, it can serve as a backup. Once the IP number is obtained, the communication can proceed, and the local machine may store this IP number in the local table for future reference.

Once the local machine learns the IP number for the destination of a message, it then must send the message itself. However, as noted earlier, the IP number designates a logical machine, not the physical connection of an Ethernet controller to a wire. Thus, another translation process is needed, and another keyed table is used—this one often stored in main memory. Again, suppose we start when a system has just been turned on.

When a machine needs to determine the Ethernet address associated with an IP number, it consults an in-memory table. At the start, this table is empty. Thus, the machine broadcasts a message to all machines on its local network, asking, "Which of you has the following IP number: . . ?" If the message is being sent to another machine in the local network, then the desired machine replies, and the machine can send the message. If the machine is outside the local network, no response is returned. Instead, the machine packages the message in a packet to a default router, which in turn can follow a similar process until the packet is delivered to the correct location.

While the mechanics of Internet communication are somewhat intricate and beyond the scope of this text, this illustration demonstrates two common and important applications of keyed tables. Conceptually, Internet communication requires at least two types of lookups to receive IP numbers from domain names and to obtain Ethernet addresses from IP numbers. Because the Internet involves a vast number of machines, it is impractical to keep all of this information locally. Instead, a machine may keep a table of recently obtained information, but it consults other machines when data are unknown. The central authorities for domain names are domain name servers, which often use hash tables for fast retrieval of information. A local machine needs rather few Ethernet addresses, however, and these are often kept in a small, in-memory table where a linear search is simple and effective.

SUMMARY

The Set ADT models the mathematical object set. A set can be implemented in two ways: explicitly and implicitly. An explicit implementation associates each item in the base type (ItemType) with a specific place in memory (bit, byte, or word). Each item's presence or absence is explicitly recorded in the location assigned to it. In the implicit implementation, the items that are present in a set are recorded in a list. Those items that are not on the list are not in the set. That is, an item's absence is implicit.

The union/find algorithms are applied to sets where the sets are mutually disjoint. Processing two items in this context involves determining which sets the two items belong to and merging the sets if they are different. The union/find algorithms can be made more efficient by the application of the weighting rule and the collapsing rule. The algorithm uses an explicit set representation.

The ADT Record is a collection of <field, information> pairs where the only operations are Store and Find. The Find function returns the information associated with a field. Records are built into most modern programming languages where the fields are accessed by name.

The ADT Keyed Table is the most general unstructured data type. It is a collection of <key, information> pairs. Information is stored, deleted, and retrieved by the associated key. We examined two implementation structures for a keyed table: a list of <key, information> pairs and a hash table where a function of the key (called a hash function) is used to locate the <key, information>'s location in an array. When a hash function returns the same value for two different keys, a collision occurs causing overflow. We discussed two ways of handling overflow: probing and chaining.

Overall, unstructured types are those data types in which no relationship exists among the items in the data type. They are simply collections of components. Sets, records, and keyed tables are unstructured data types. Unstructured data types are differentiated by how components are stored into the collection and how they are accessed within the collection. The components in the set are stored and accessed by literal values of ItemType. The components in the record and the keyed table are stored and accessed by field name and key value, respectively. The set of fields used to access components in a record are part of the data type itself. The set of keys used to access components in a keyed table are part of the data stored in the table.

EXERCISES

1. Define the following terms.

universe set	proper subset
empty set	cardinality of a set
power set	component type of a set
subset	

2. Give the axioms for the following operations involving sets. In this definition, do not assume that the Store operation is defined to avoid duplicates.

structure	Set (of ItemType)	
interface	Create	→ Set
	Insert(Set, ItemType)	→ Set
	Delete(Set, ItemType)	→ Set
	IsIn(Set, ItemType)	→ Boolean
	Union(Set, Set)	→ Set
	Difference(Set, Set)	→ Set

   axioms   **for all S, T in Set, a, b in ItemType, let**

   (* fill in the axioms *)

3. a. What is the carrier or designated domain in exercise 2?

   b. What are the auxiliary domains in exercise 2?

4. Describe the implementation technique used for sets when the only operations are Find and Union in mutually disjoint sets.

5. Describe two ways in which the speed of the algorithms described in Exercise 4 can be improved.

6. Describe the bit vector implementation of sets.

7. Finish the proof, begun in this chapter, that the given bit vector implementation of sets is correct. (In other words, prove that the implementation satisfies the axioms.)

8. Describe a method for implementing sets where the component type is infinite but all the sets are assumed to be finite.

9. List the ways in which the scheme described in Exercise 8 can be implemented.

10. Give the order of the operations on sets for each of the ways listed in Exercise 8.

11. Compare and contrast the implementations in Exercises 4, 5, and 8.

12. Distinguish between set implementations that are proportional to the size of the set and implementations that are proportional to the cardinality of the universe set.

13. Write the algorithms for O(N) Union, Intersection, and IsSubset where space is proportional to the size of the set.

14. In Chapter 2, we defined five implementation approaches for a List ADT. We used one of these (the unsorted linked list) to implement the Set ADT in this chapter and verified this implementation. For the four remaining implementation approaches, describe how a reduced set expression

   $$Store(Store(\ldots (Store(Create, i_1) \ldots i_{n-1}), i_n)$$

   would correspond to the data structure created by each implementation approach. That is, give the mapping for Create and Store in each approach.

15. The results of processing a series of equivalence pairs using the Union/Find algorithms are shown below:

Sets	2	−2	4	−3	4	−1	8	−3	8
	[1]	[2]	[3]	[4]	[5]	[6]	[7]	[8]	[9]

   a. How many equivalence classes are there?

   b. What changes would the processing of the input pair (1,5) make?

   c. Was the weighting rule used?

   In words, describe a reasonable algorithm for each of the following operations, given the structure listed beside the operation. Give the order of your algorithm. Assume that there are N items in a set. For binary operations on sets, assume that both sets contain N items.

16. Set Union (bit vector implementation).

17. Set Union (both unordered linked lists).

18. Set Intersection (both ordered arrays).

19. Set Intersection (one an ordered array, the other an unordered linked list, the answer is in an ordered array).

20. IsSubset (one a binary search tree, the other an ordered linked list).

21. Insert (unordered array; precondition: item not in set).

22. Delete (unordered array; precondition: item is in set).

23. Insert (ordered linked list; precondition: item not in set).

24. Union (one an ordered linked list, and one a sorted array, answer left in ordered array that was input, no additional array or linked list can be used).

25. Delete (ordered array; precondition: item is in set).

26. Write the axioms for the operation ProperSubset.

27. a. Write the algorithm for the Find and ListOfKeys operations using the list primitives.

    b. Prove that your implementation satisfies the given axiomatic specifications for a keyed table.

28. Modify the axioms for the ADT Keyed Table to include the IsFull function.

29. A particular application for the ADT Keyed Table needs an operation that modifies the value of a <key, value> pair. The interface is

    Replace(KeyedTable, KeyType, ValueType) → KeyedTable.

    If the key is in the table, value replaces the original value. If the key is not in the table, the table is unchanged. Write the axiom for Replace.

30. Write an algorithm for a hash function that divides an eight-digit number into four groups of two digits and sums the groups. The result is MOD MaxTable.

31. The analysis of the complexity of the insertion operation for a hash table derived the formula $E = (N + 1) / (N + 1 - p)$, although several algebraic manipulations were not given explicitly. Fill in the details for this analysis.

32. Modify the analysis of the complexity of the insertion operation for a hash table to include the possibility that each bucket can store s items.

33. The discussion of Internet addressing indicated the need to translate from domain names to IP numbers and from IP numbers to Ethernet addresses.

    a. If you have access to the Internet, determine the domain name and IP number for your machine and for your server.

    b. Use the lookup facility available on your machine to confirm the IP number for ac.grin.edu and cs.utexas.edu stated in the text. (On a Unix system, you might try using a program called /usr/etc/nsloopup.)

    c. Determine what Ethernet addresses are stored on your machine. (On a Unix system, you might try using the program /usr/etc/arp, a program that handles the address resolution protocol.)

34. Implement Find, Delete, and ListOfKeys for the KeyedTable ADT using open hashing.

Semi-Structured Data Types

5

From the user's point of view, a semi-structured data type is a collection of items that has a special or designated item but no logical relationship among the rest of the items in the collection. The operation that views or deletes an item knows that this designated item is to be returned or deleted. The stack, the FIFO queue, and the priority queue fall into this category.

Stack

The stack usually is the second user-defined data type that students encounter (the list is the first). The stack is introduced with pictures showing stacks of pennies, stacks of shirts, or stacks of plates in a cafeteria line. All of these analogies exhibit the characteristic that defines the stack: you cannot access the second item without first accessing the one on the top.

Specification

In the stack, the designated item is the item that has been in the collection for the shortest time. In Chapter 1, we use the axioms for an *unbounded* stack in order to illustrate the axiomatic approach to specifying the behavior of an abstract data type. Here we give the specifications for the abstract data type *bounded* Stack.

```
structure  Stack (of ItemType)
interface  Create (Max)              → Stack
           IsFull (Stack)            → Boolean
           Push(Stack, ItemType)     → Stack
           Pop(Stack)                → Stack
           Top(Stack)                → ItemType
           IsEmpty(Stack)            → Boolean
    end
axioms     for all S in Stack, i in ItemType, let
           Push(S, i) =
             IF IsFull(S)
                 THEN  Error
             END IF

           Pop(Create(Max)) = Error
           Pop(Push(S, i)) = S

           Top(Create(Max)) = Error
           Top(Push(S, i)) = i

           IsEmpty(Create(Max)) = True
           IsEmpty(Push(S, i)) = False
    end
end Stack
```

Implementation

Chapter 1 presented a linked-list implementation of an unbounded stack and outlined a proof showing that the stated implementation was correct. The specification given here is for a bounded stack. The linked-list implementation with an additional IsFull operation works for the bounded stack as well. The Push must have a precondition that the stack is not full. The user can use the IsFull function to test for the full case. Because Max is a parameter of the Create operation, the IsFull is easy to implement. You can either keep a count of the number of items on the stack or you can count them whenever IsFull is called.

A bounded stack can be implemented using an array-based scheme as well. Because you have undoubtedly already implemented a stack in an array, and because we have already shown one stack implementation, we do not do so here.

Application: Paired Symbols

Two classic applications of a stack involve translating an arithmetic expression from one form to another and implementing recursion. Both of these applications are commonly used as examples in the second computer course so we only remind you of them here. If you have never seen the algorithms for expression conversion or studied how recursion is implemented, refer back to a Computer Science II textbook. Several are listed in the bibliography at the end of this book.

Another classic problem for which a stack is an appropriate data structure, and which we present here, is how to determine if a set of paired symbols is used appropriately. The specific problem is: given a set of different types of parentheses, determine if the open and close versions of each type are used correctly. The versions of parentheses include ( ), [], and {}.[1] Any number of other characters may appear in the input, but a closing symbol must match the last unmatched opening symbol, and all symbols must be matched when the input is empty. The input is from the keyboard.

We call the versions of parentheses special symbols. If the expression is correct, write a congratulatory message to the screen and halt. If an error is found, the program should print the current close symbol and the remaining unmatched open symbols and halt. Thus, the main program reads characters one at a time and does one of three tasks depending on whether the character is an open special symbol, a close special symbol, or not a special symbol.

This last case is the easiest. If the character is not a special symbol, it is discarded and another character is read. If the character is an open special symbol, it is saved. If the character is a close special symbol, it must be checked against the last open special symbol. If they match, the character and the last open special symbol are discarded and a new character is read. The Stack ADT is the appropriate data type in which to save the open special symbols because it is always the most recently saved symbol that we need to examine.

Now we are ready to write the algorithms, assuming an instance of a Stack ADT where ItemType is Character. The structure is declared within the module, so

---

[1] An overly zealous copy editor once changed one of the author's parenthesized expressions in Pascal from plain parentheses to alternating plain parentheses and square brackets. Fortunately, when all of the programs were tested, this change was caught.

the structure is not passed as a parameter. We also assume two instances of Set ADT (OpenSet and CloseSet) where ItemType is Character. They are declared within the user program.

Main Program

```
Initialize (OpenSet, CloseSet)
LOOP
    IF EOF
        THEN  EXIT
    END IF
    Read(A_Character)
    IF IsIn(OpenSet, A_Character)
        THEN
            Push(A_Character)
    ELSIF IsIn(CloseSet, A_Character)
        THEN  ProcessClose(A_Character, ErrorFlag)
        ELSE  (* Not a special symbol; do nothing.*)
    END IF
    IF ErrorFlag
        THEN  EXIT
    END IF
END LOOP
IF EOF AND NOT Stack.IsEmpty
    THEN  Write 'Premature end of data'
    ELSIF NOT ErrorFlag
        Write 'Congratulations!'
END IF
PrintStack
```

Initialize (VAR OpenSet, CloseSet: SetType)

```
Create(OpenSet)
Insert(OpenSet, '(')
Insert(OpenSet, '[')
Insert(OpenSet, '{')
Create(CloseSet)
Insert(CloseSet, ')')
Insert(CloseSet, ']')
Insert(CloseSet, '}')
```

ProcessClose(A_Character: Character, VAR ErrorFlag: Boolean)

```
IF Stack.IsEmpty
    THEN
        ErrorFlag ← True
        Write 'Extra close symbol', A_Character
```

```
        ELSE
            Pop(Item)
            CASE A_Character OF
            ')'   : ErrorFlag ← Item <> '('
            ']'   : ErrorFlag ← Item <> '['
            '}'   : ErrorFlag ← Item <> '{'
            END CASE
        IF ErrorFlag
            THEN  Write 'Symbols do not match', Item, A_Character
        END IF
    END IF
```

PrintStack

```
IF NOT Stack.IsEmpty
    THEN
        Write 'Unmatched open symbols'
        WHILE NOT Stack.IsEmpty DO
            Pop(A_Character)
            Write A_Character
        END WHILE
END IF
```

FIFO Queue

The First In First Out (FIFO) queue is the structure that models a waiting line. In fact, in some regions of the United States and in England, to queue means to line up. Hopefully, the first person in line is waited on first.

Specification

In the FIFO queue, the designated item is the item that has been in the collection for the longest time. The operation that puts an item into the FIFO queue is usually called Enque; the operation that removes an item is usually called Deque; and the operation that views the designated item is usually called First. We give the specifications for the unbounded queue here; you are asked to give the bounded version in the exercises at the end of this chapter.

```
structure  Queue (of ItemType)
interface  Create                    → Queue
           Enque(Queue, ItemType)    → Queue
           Deque(Queue)              → Queue
           First(Queue)              → ItemType
           IsEmpty(Queue)            → Boolean
     end
```

axioms   **for Q in Queue, i in ItemType, let**
    Deque(Create) = Error
    Deque(Enque(Q, i)) =
        IF IsEmpty(Q)
           THEN Create
           ELSE   Enque(Deque(Q), i)
        END IF

    First(Create) = Error
    First(Enque(Q, i)) =
        IF IsEmpty(Q)
           THEN i
           ELSE   First(Q)
        END IF

    IsEmpty(Create) = True
    IsEmpty(Enque(Q, i)) = False
  end
end Queue

Implementation

Although you have surely implemented a FIFO queue before, we examine several implementation alternatives. Initially, one might be tempted to translate the queue axioms directly to list primitives and then use list operations. One must be careful of this approach, however, because the queue operations have special characteristics that do not map directly to lists. After all, that is why the queue is a separate ADT. Much of what follows is modeled after our work with lists, but we must make some changes in the way in which we implement the list in order to be able to access the designated item directly.

Array-Based Implementation

As with stacks, any array-based implementation of queues can be used only to implement a bounded queue. The Enque operation cannot be applied in all cases. Conceptually, in the unsorted list primitive, the first item put in the list is in the first slot in the array; the second item put in the list is in the second slot in the array; and so on. If we remove an item, we close up the space, always keeping the items in the list contiguous beginning at the first slot in the array.

If we implement a queue using a list of items, the items are removed from the front of the list and added to the back of the list. The list (queue) items are contiguous, but the first item is not necessarily in the first slot of the array unless we move all the items down one slot every time we dequeue an item. The complexity of this Deque operation is O(N). With a little ingenuity, we can implement the queue as an array-based list and keep the complexity of both insertion (Enque) and deletion (Deque) at O(1).

The trick is to let the beginning of the list float throughout the array. This requires that we keep a logical pointer or index to both the first and last items in the list. For obvious reasons, we call these logical pointers First and Last. As a consequence of letting List.Data[First] float, we must allow List.Data[Last] to wrap around. That is, when Last is being incremented in order to store a new item in the list, it must be incremented MOD the array size. For example, look at the state of the list after we insert the letters 'a' through 'g'.

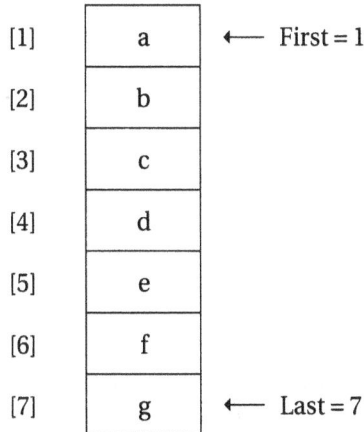

[1]	a	←—— First = 1
[2]	b	
[3]	c	
[4]	d	
[5]	e	
[6]	f	
[7]	g	←—— Last = 7

If the delete operation for the list removes the item at the beginning of the list, the list is represented as follows in the array after two calls to Deque.

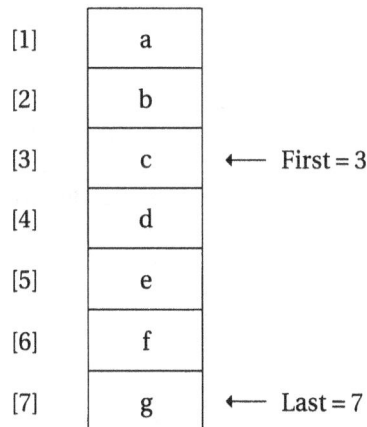

[1]	a	
[2]	b	
[3]	c	←—— First = 3
[4]	d	
[5]	e	
[6]	f	
[7]	g	←—— Last = 7

If we now insert 'h' into the list, where should it go? Last is at the end of the array, but the first two positions in the array are not in use, so we let Last wrap around and store 'h' in List.Data[1].

[1]	h	←— Last = 1
[2]	b	
[3]	c	←— First = 3
[4]	d	
[5]	e	
[6]	f	
[7]	g	

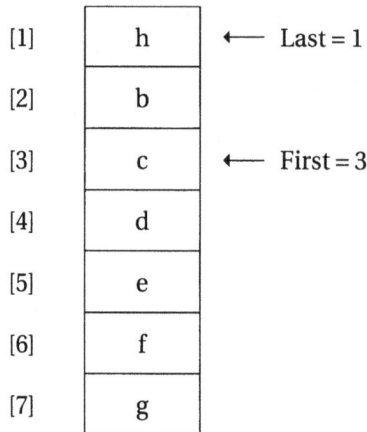

This wraparound structure can be visualized as a circle, as shown in Figure 5.1.

The list is List.Data[First]..List.Data[Last]: 'cdefgh'. Using this implementation of a list, we can implement our queue directly with List.Data[First] as the designated item. Before writing the code, however, we still need to handle one other issue: we cannot tell the difference between a full list and an empty list. For example, if the list contains only one item, First and Last are equal. If that item is removed, First is one slot ahead of Last. This same condition holds if the list is full.

The problem actually is somewhat subtle; it is not just a detail of our implementation. Here, we are using First and Last to identify positions in the array, and the number of empty elements in the array must be given by the relative positions of these variables. However, because these are numbers between 1 and MaxList, the number of items we can distinguish with these variables is limited to MaxList. On the other hand, our array may have 0 elements, 1 element, . . . , up to MaxList elements in it, and there are MaxList + 1 such possibilities. Mathematically, there is no way to record MaxList + 1 states when we can record only MaxList values. (Technically, this is called the Pigeon Hole Principle.)

The analysis also demonstrates two ways in which to solve this problem. One approach is to reserve an empty slot just before First and not allow an item to be stored there. This reduces the number of states we need to distinguish to MaxList, and we can do that with our current variables. Here, an empty list is one where First is one slot ahead of Last. A full list is one where First is two slots ahead of Last. This approach allows the following tests for IsFull and IsEmpty. We switch from MaxList to MaxQueue as we zero in on our queue implementation structure.

IsFull (Queue: QueueType): Boolean

```
RETURN ((Last MOD MaxQueue+ 1) MOD MaxQueue + 1) = First
```

IsEmpty (Queue: QueueType): Boolean

```
RETURN (Last MOD MaxQueue) + 1 = First
```

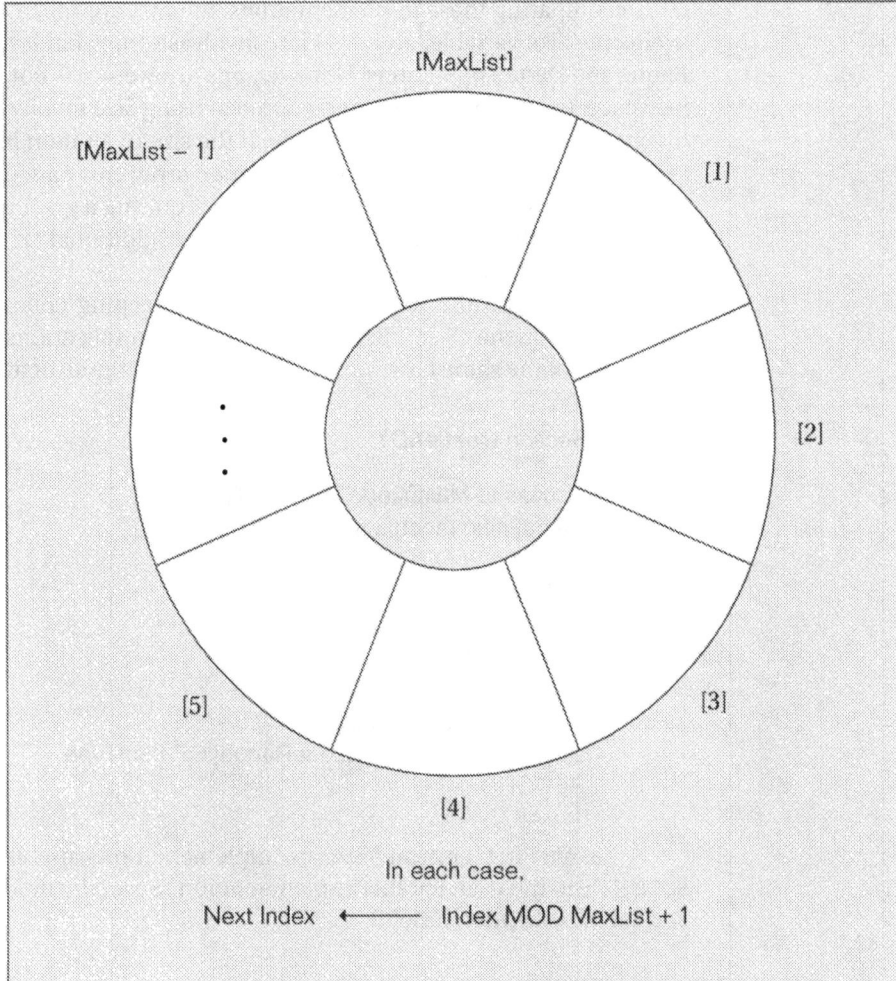

Figure 5.1 Circular Array-Based List

The second approach to resolve the full versus empty problem introduces another variable that is not limited to MaxList values. In particular, we can use a variable Size, which records the number of elements in the queue. With this approach, Size must be changed with each Enque and Dequeue operation, and IsFull and IsEmpty are implemented as follows:

IsFull (Queue: QueueType): Boolean

```
RETURN (Size = MaxQueue)
```

IsEmpty (Queue: QueueType) : Boolean

```
RETURN (Size = 0)
```

In comparing these implementations, the first approach using an empty slot avoids the Size variable, and therefore involves somewhat less processing for the Enque and Deque operations. However, one array entry is not used, thereby wasting space. In contrast, the second approach using Size involves less complex conditions at the cost of an extra variable. If the size of an item in the queue array is relatively small, then the size involved for an array entry and for the Size variable are about the same. If one is queuing items requiring a great deal of storage, then the Size variable represents less space than the additional array entry. Processing of the two approaches is roughly equivalent.

Now we write the remaining algorithms, keeping count of the number of items in the queue (Size). Because many queue applications require more than one queue of the same type, we let the user declare the structure.

Interface Section QueueADT;

```
(* To gain access to MaxQueue and ItemType.)
USES <data defining module name>
TYPE
    SizeRange = 0..MaxQueue;
    QueueRange = 1..MaxQueue;
    QueueType = RECORD
        Size        : SizeRange;
        First, Last  : QueueRange;
        Items       : ARRAY [QueueRange] OF ItemType
    END RECORD
```

Note that First, Last, and Size are implementation variables that should be inaccessible to the user. For this implementation, we let the module check for errors and set the exception ERROR.

Create(VAR Queue: QueueType)

```
Queue.First ← 1
Queue.Last ← MaxQueue
Queue.Size ← 0
```

Enqueue(VAR Queue: QueueType, Item: ItemType)

```
IF Queue.Size = MaxQueue
    THEN  ERROR
    ELSE
        Queue.Last ← Queue.Last MOD MaxQueue + 1
        Queue.Items[Queue.Last] ← Item
        Queue.Size ← Queue.Size + 1
END IF
```

Deque (VAR Queue: QueueType)

In the list data types, the delete operation took a parameter that indicated which item to delete. When removing an item from a semi-structured data type, it is the designated item that is removed. That is, the user does not know what the item is, but the data type does. Therefore, following our specifications, we do not return this item to the user here. The user can use the First function if this designated item is needed.

```
IF IsEmpty(Queue)
    THEN  ERROR
    ELSE
        Queue.First ← Queue.First MOD MaxQueue + 1
        Queue.Size ← Queue.Size − 1
END IF
```

First (Queue: QueueType, VAR Item: ItemType)

```
IF IsEmpty(Queue)
    THEN  ERROR
    ELSE   Item ← Queue.Items[Queue.First]
END IF
```

ExtendedDeque(VAR Queue: QueueType, VAR Item: ItemType)

Because our specifications give two functions—one to remove the designated item and one to view the designated item—we implement our operations in the same way. Note, however, that it is more common to combine these as one operation where the designated item is returned to the user. The following ExtendedDeque operation performs this combined task.

```
IF IsEmpty(Queue)
    THEN  ERROR
    ELSE
        Item ← Queue.Items[Queue.First]
        Queue.First ← Queue.First MOD MaxQueue + 1
        Queue.Size ← Queue.Size − 1
END IF
```

Correctness In verifying that this array implementation correctly meets our specifications, we begin by carefully describing the relationship between an axiomatic queue and the implemented version. Consider the following abstract queue expression.

$$\text{Store (Store (... (Store (Create, } i_1)) ...), i_{n-1}), i_n)$$

This corresponds to the array Items

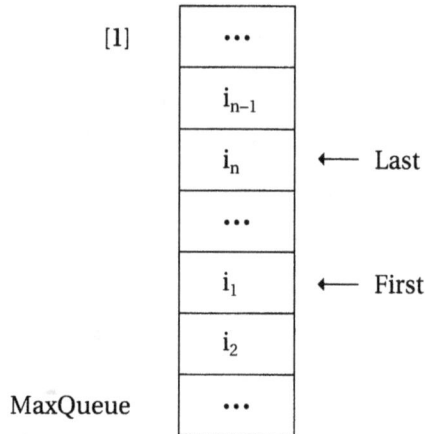

Noting that Queue.Size reflects the actual number of items in the queue, we begin our check to be sure our implementation satisfies the given axioms.

Create The empty list corresponds to the queue Create, with no Enque operations. The corresponding implementation should have no elements designated in the array; the size should be 0; and Size, First, and Last are in correct positions relative to each other. A simple check of the code for Create confirms that these conditions are met.

Enque An abstract queue expression Enque(Q, i) adds one additional item to the queue. The corresponding code adds the element to the array, and increments both Last (Mod MaxQueue) and Size. A verification of the other commands follows a similar form, given our careful description relating abstract queue expressions and the array-based queue structure.

As noted earlier, this implementation maps queue operations onto a list-like structure, although special care was needed to keep track of the location of the designated element. Remember that a queue is a semi-structured data type, not a list. Thus, even though we used an augmented list to implement the queue data type, we were careful in our discussions not to mix data types and data structures.

Linked-Structure Implementation

As an alternative to the array implementation, we could consider how to relate the queue directly to the unsorted linked-list primitives. Our first approach might be to translate Enque to store the item at the head of a list. The delete operation would need to find the designated item at the other end of the list, delete that item, and return it. With this traversal of the list, Deque would search the list each time it was applied. Thus, the complexity would be O(N): O(N) to find the end and O(1) to remove it.

As a second approach, we could add a new item at the end of the list and remove an item from the head of the list. In this approach, each queue entry points to another one that was enqueued after it. While this approach seems equally involved, we can save considerable work by keeping a pointer to the last item in the list as well as to the first item in the list. When enqueueing an item, we add it to the list's end and update a last pointer. When dequeueing an item, we remove it from the head of the list. This approach yields Enque and Deque operations that both have O(1) complexity. Also, instead of having two named pointers, the list could be circular with the external pointer pointing to the last item in the list. The designated item (first item), then, is List↑.Next↑.Item.

Application

The traditional application area for the ADT queue is in simulation. You have undoubtedly seen these applications. If not, refer back to any textbook designed to be used in a second-semester computer science course. We look at a different application here—*external sorting*.

What does external sorting have to do with queues? External sorting has to do with sequential files, and the behavior of a sequential file is exactly the same as that of a queue. The first item written on a sequential file is the first item read, and the last item written is the last item read. An item in the middle of a sequential file cannot be accessed until the items before it have been accessed. The fact that sequential files are on secondary storage and that a queue is an internal data type is an implementation issue, not a logical one. The only logical distinction between the two is that a file still exists after it has been accessed (read), while a queue does not. The read operation is not destructive for files, while Deque changes the queue. This can be solved by adding a CopyQueue operation. If every queue is copied before it is accessed, then the file can be completely modeled by the queue. In what follows, we do not replace the traditional input/output statements with Enque and Deque, but they are logically equivalent.

External Sorting

To a computer scientist, **sorting** is the process of arranging values in ascending or descending order. The values might be names or numbers—anything that can be compared.

This process of arranging values in order is probably one of the first algorithms a student learns (after finding the minimum and maximum). Increasingly complicated (and faster) algorithms are then introduced as the student progresses in her or his career as a student. However, many algorithms assume that the number of values to be sorted is small enough for the data to be stored in an array. Sorting data in an array is called **internal sorting** because all the values are in memory at one time.

Such examples work very nicely as illustrations, but they ignore many important applications. In this section, we look at how very large files are sorted—files that contain too many values to be held in memory at one time. First, we introduce some terminology.

Suppose R_1, R_2, . . . R_N are the records to be sorted. Each record has a field, called the *key*, to be used in determining the ordering. Clearly, a record may have several fields that may be used for ordering the records. For example, the records may contain both social security number and name. However, only one of these fields may be used at a time for sorting. The key field is the one that is to determine the order of that particular sort.

The problem, then, is how to sort these N records when they do not all fit into memory at one time. Sorting a file of records that is too large to fit into main memory is called **external sorting**.

> **Sorting** Arranging a collection of N records in ascending (or descending) order by the value of the key field in each record.
>
> **Internal Sorting** Sorting a collection of N records that can be in main memory all at one time.
>
> **External Sorting** Sorting a collection of N records that cannot fit into main memory all at one time.

To get an insight into how this might be done, let us look at what you might do if you were to do the task by hand. Suppose you had 1000 index cards that needed to be sorted by last name. Because you cannot hold 1000 index cards in your hand all at one time, you would probably take them in smaller stacks and sort these stacks. Let us suppose that you sort them in stacks of 50. Now you have 20 stacks of 50 sorted index cards.

You then can take two stacks of sorted cards and merge them, producing one stack of 100 sorted cards. The rest of the stacks then can be merged, two at a time. There are now 10 stacks of sorted cards, each with 100. These stacks of 100 can now be merged two at a time, giving 5 stacks, each containing 200 index cards. You could twice merge two stacks of 200. Now there are two stacks of 400 and one stack of 200. The two stacks of 400 can be merged, and the result finally merged with the remaining stack.

This is exactly the algorithm used to sort a large file of records. The process is divided into two phases: the sorting phase and the merging phase. The original file is sorted into stacks or piles of sorted records, and these sorted records are repeatedly merged into larger and larger piles of sorted records until they have all been merged into one file.

The number of records that can be reasonably sorted internally (called M) is determined on the basis of the amount of memory and the type of installation (that is, multiprogramming, batch, single-user, etc.). Each sorted sequence of M records is called a **run**. The first phase, then, is to sort the N records into runs of size M. This gives us $\lceil N/M \rceil$ runs to work with during the merge phase.

> **Run** A sorted sequence of M records.

In order to merge a pair of runs, we need to access them in parallel. If they are all in one file, we can read the first run into an array of size M and merge the array with the next run on the file. This works for merging the original runs, but does not work for merging the set of runs that are now 2*M in length. Why? Because M was chosen as the largest group of records we can hold in memory. We cannot read 2*M records into an array in order to merge them with the next run on the file. Therefore, we need more than one input file and one output file for the merge phase.

Two strategies can be used for the merge phase: a balanced merge and a polyphase merge. A balanced merge requires the same number of files for both input and output. A polyphase merge uses only one file for output but two or more files for input. We look first at the balanced merge.

Balanced Merge The minimum number of files for a balanced merge is four: two for reading and two for writing. The sorting phase should leave half of the runs on one output file and half on the other. The two files become input files and are read in parallel to merge the original runs. If we know the number of records in the file to be sorted, we can divide the number of records by M and determine the number of runs. Half of the runs can be placed on one file and half on the other. In practice, we often have no idea of the size of the file.

Fortunately, we can guarantee that the runs are evenly divided no matter what the size of the output file if the runs are placed alternately in each file. For example, if M is 10 and N is 132, the 14 runs are distributed across File1 and File2 as follows by the run generation phase.

File1	File2
Run 1: Records 1 . . . 10	Run 2: Records 11 . . . 20
Run 3: Records 21 . . . 30	Run 4: Records 31 . . . 40
Run 5: Records 41 . . . 50	Run 6: Records 51 . . . 60
Run 7: Records 61 . . . 70	Run 8: Records 71 . . . 80
Run 9: Records 81 . . . 90	Run 10: Records 91 . . . 100
Run 11: Records 101 . . . 110	Run 12: Records 111 . . . 120
Run 13: Records 121 . . . 130	Run 14: Records 131 . . . 132

File1 and File2 would be reset and used as input files to the merge phase. File3 and File4 would be used as output files.

The first run on File1 ($R_1 \ldots R_{10}$) is merged with the first run on File2 ($R_{11} \ldots R_{20}$). The result ($R_1 \ldots R_{20}$) is written on File3. The second run on File1 ($R_{21} \ldots R_{30}$) is merged with the second run on File2 ($R_{31} \ldots R_{40}$). The result ($R_{21} \ldots R_{40}$) is written on File4. The third runs on File1 and File2 are merged on File3. The fourth runs on File1 and File2 are merged on File4. This process continues until File1 and File2 are empty.

File3	File4
Run 1: Records 1 . . . 20	Run 2: Records 21 . . . 40
Run 3: Records 41 . . . 60	Run 4: Records 61 . . . 80
Run 5: Records 81 . . . 100	Run 6: Records 101 . . . 120
Run 7: Records 121 . . . 132	<eof>

File3 and File4 are reset and become the input files to the next merge pass. File1 and File2 become empty output files. The first run on File3 is merged with the first run on File4. The result is written on File1. The second runs on File3 and File4 are merged onto File2. The third runs are merged onto File1. This process continues until File3 and File4 are empty.

File1	File2
Run 1: Records 1 . . . 40	Run 2: Records 41 . . . 80
Run 3: Records 81 . . . 120	Run 4: Records 121 . . . 132

Then the two sets of files again change roles, with File3 and File4 becoming output files and File1 and File2 becoming input files. The process continues until all the records have been merged onto one file.

File3	File4
Run 1: Records 1 . . . 80	Run 2: Records 81 . . . 132

File1	File2
Run 1: Records 1 . . . 132	<eof>

The merging of a complete set of runs from one set of files to the other is called a *merge pass.* (This example took four merge passes.) At each merge pass, the key of each record is examined. Movement from external storage into main memory (read) and from main memory back to secondary storage (write) is very slow and therefore very costly. If the number of merge passes (the number of times each record is read and written) can be reduced, the algorithm is much more efficient.

The number of merge passes can be reduced by increasing the number of files we are using for input and output during each pass. That is, we can generalize the balanced merge from a 2-way merge (two files being used for input and two files being used for output) to a K-way merge (K files being used for input and K files being used for output).

Before we design the algorithm for a K-way balanced merge, we consider an example. Given a file of 2005 records, an original run size of 100, and four files for input and four files for output (that is, $K = 4$), we look at the status after the original sorting phase and each merge pass. After the sorting phase, the 21 runs (2005/100) are distributed across the input bank of four files as follows. (We use the initial run number to indicate which records are on which file; that is, Run 1 is Record 1 . . . 100, Run 2 is Record 101 . . . 200, and so on.)

File1	File2	File3	File4
Run1	Run2	Run3	Run4
Run5	Run6	Run7	Run8
Run9	Run10	Run11	Run12
Run13	Run14	Run15	Run16
Run17	Run18	Run19	Run20
Run21	<eof>	<eof>	<eof>

After the first merge pass, the results are as follows, where Runs 1 . . . 4 means the result of merging runs 1 through 4.

File5	File6	File7	File8
Runs 1 . . . 4	Runs 5 . . . 8	Runs 9 . . . 12	Runs 13 . . . 16
Runs 17 . . . 20	Run 21	<eof>	<eof>

After the second merge pass, the results are as follows.

File1	File2	File3	File4
Runs 1 . . . 16	Runs 17 . . . 21	<eof>	<eof>

On the final merge pass, the results are left on File5.

File5	File6	File7	File8
Runs 1 . . . 21	<eof>	<eof>	<eof>

Our example named the files File1 to File8. Clearly, this is not very general. Do we have to have a different implementation for each value of K? No, we can define a data type that is an array of files. Our data structure can be visualized as two banks of files, one on the left and one on the right, their roles changing with each merge pass. Therefore, we call the arrays of files RightBank and LeftBank.

To simplify the algorithms, we assume that we are sorting integers. The concept is exactly the same as sorting a file of records, but we do not bother with the complexity of reading and writing arbitrary records. An exercise at the end of the chapter asks you to generalize the algorithm to sort records where the user supplies the type of the records and a comparison function to compare keys.

```
TYPE
    FileRecord = RECORD
        FileName  : File;
        Value     : Integer
    END RECORD

    BankType = ARRAY [0..K-1] OF FileRecord;

VAR
    LeftBank, RightBank : BankType
```

This structure can be pictured as follows.

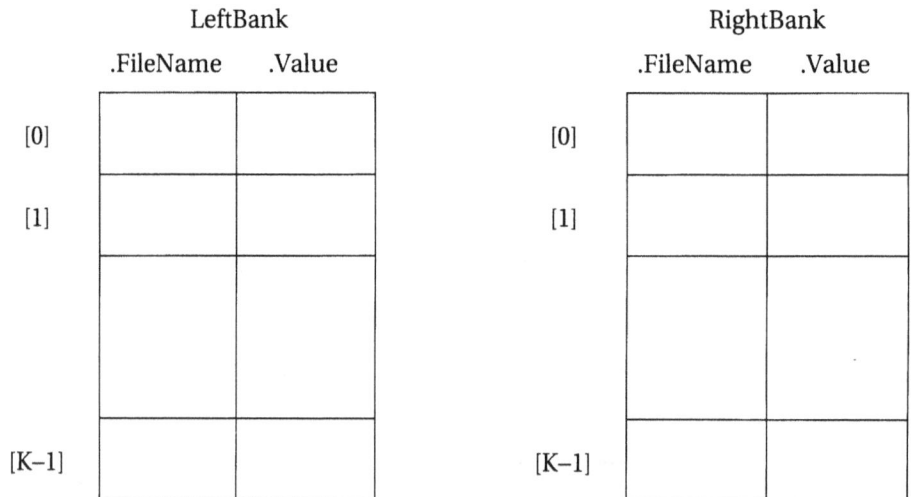

LeftBank and RightBank are arrays of records in which the first field is an *internal file variable* and the second field is a value from that file. Internal files are read and written within the program but do not exist after the sorting is complete. Therefore, they do not have to be text files; they can be internal representation files (sometimes called binary files). Reads and writes of these files involve no translation. What is stored in a place in memory is written to a binary file exactly as it is. What is read from a binary file is stored exactly as it is read. Because numeric values are not translated back and forth between their internal representation and their picture form (text format), binary files are particularly efficient.

The main module is easy enough. We first generate the initial runs, and then we merge them. We have pushed the details (as always) to the next level of the design.

Generate the Initial Runs

Most of our discussion has been spent on the merge process, because you should already be familiar with internal sorting algorithms. The choice of which internal sorting algorithm to use should be based on the characteristics of the data. Who knows those characteristics? The user, of course. For now, we just issue a call to a generic procedure Sort.

What are the control structures in this problem? We are to sort the input file in runs of size M. We do not know, however, that the file is an even multiple of M. Therefore, we have to guard against an end-of-file. We can use one loop with an EXIT on end-of-file.

We must also be careful to rotate the runs through the bank of files. That is, the first run should be on the first file, the second on the second file, and so on. In order to make the cycling through the bank of files easier, we have indexed them from 0 to K − 1. WhichFile (the index variabled) is initialized to 0 and incremented with the statement

WhichFile ← (WhichFile + 1) MOD K.

Thus, WhichFile cycles from 0 to K − 1. The algorithm for generating the sorted runs is shown below.

GenerateRuns (VAR LeftBank : BankType)

```
CreateBank(LeftBank)   (* Get LeftBank ready for writing. *)
WhichFile ← 0
Count ← 0                (* Records number of values read; cycles 0..M. *)
LOOP
    IF EOF
        THEN EXIT
    END IF
    Read Value
    Count ← Count + 1
    Data[Count] ← Value
```

```
        IF Count = M
            THEN
                Sort(Data, M)
                Write Data on LeftBank[WhichFile]
                WhichFile ← (WhichFile + 1) MOD K
                Count ← 0
        END IF
    END LOOP
    IF Count <> 0
        THEN
            Sort(Data, Count)
            Write Data on LeftBank[WhichFile]
    END IF
    ResetBank(LeftBank)
```

CreateBank and ResetBank are procedures that deal with preparing the files for writing and reading, respectively. These operations are of no relevance to the algorithms under discussion.

Merge the Runs

The original runs are now evenly distributed over LeftBank. The last operation in the sorting phase is to reset all the files. The postcondition for GenerateInitial-Runs should state where the file pointers are positioned when it finishes, and the preconditions for MergeRuns should state where it expects the file pointers to be positioned. (They had better be consistent!) RightBank can be made ready for writing by a call to CreateBanks.

So far in our discussion we have ignored several issues dealing with control of the process. For example, we have said that the first run on each file is merged, and then the second run on each file is merged. How do we recognize the end of a run? How do we recognize when the merge of a group of runs is complete? In fact, how do we expand our concept of merge from two files to K files? We consider these questions one at a time.

The simplest way to determine the end of a run is to use an end-of-run marker. As we will observe shortly, it is convenient for this end-of-run marker to be the largest value in the data type of the key. (If this value might actually be encountered in our data set from the file, then we have to use a different value.) If the key is an integer, the end-of-run marker could be the largest integer value (provided this value does not appear as a value within our data set). If the key is a character string, the end-of-run marker can be a string of all Z's (again assuming such a string is not found in the file data). This information should be provided by the user along with K and M (the original run size). In any case, the algorithm for the GenerateInitialRuns must include writing an end-of-run marker at the end of each run. In what follows, we assume that the end-of-run marker is the largest value in the data type. If this is not the case because that value also occurs in our file, then we may have to test specially for this marker in what follows.

Just exactly what are we doing when we merge two files? We are looking at two values, one from each file. The smallest is written out, and a new value is read from that file. When we merge K files, we look for the smallest value among the K files and write it out. The next value is read from the file from which the smallest value was read.

Now we can answer the question, When have we finished merging a set of runs? When the smallest key value is the end-of-run marker, the merge of that set of runs is complete. The end-of-run marker is the highest value possible for a key. If the end-of-run marker is the one returned as the smallest, then all the files are at the end-of-run marker and that merge is complete.

How can we tell when the last set of runs has been merged and the banks are ready to change roles? That is, how can we determine that a merge pass is complete? Here, there is both some good news and some bad news. On the positive side, we observe that a pass certainly is complete when all the input files in a bank are at <eof>. To simplify this further, it is sufficient to check only the first file in the bank. If there are any more runs to be merged, at least one of them must be in the first file.

On the negative side, different languages handle <eof> in different ways. Some, such as Pascal and Ada, use a Boolean function EOF(File) to look ahead to determine if the <eof> marker is the next item in the file. Others, such as Modula-2, require the user to read the next character and compare it to an EOF character. In the first case, an extra read causes an error when trying to read beyond the end of the file. In the second case, reading is required to determine that end of file has been obtained. While one can test for <eof> in either of these cases, the resulting code (or pseudocode) is somewhat different.

The only remaining control question is, When have we finished? We know that the final sorted file is in the first file of one of the banks. In fact, it is in the first file of the bank that is to be read from. We can recognize that we are finished by looking at the status of the second file in the input bank just before we start a new merge pass. If that file is at <eof>, then all the runs have been merged and the result is in the first file of that bank.

Merge (VAR RightBank : BankType)

```
CreateBank(RightBank)
LOOP
    Merge(LeftBank, RightBank, Finished)
    IF Finished
        THEN  EXIT
    END IF
    Merge(RightBank, LeftBank, Finished)
    IF Finished
        THEN  EXIT
    END IF
END LOOP
```

Merge(VAR InBank,OutBank: BankType,Finished: Boolean)

This MergeRuns procedure uses the following Merge procedure, which in turn uses two supplemental procedures. The pseudocode for these pieces that follow assumes that one must read an <eof> symbol and test for it to determine when the end of a file is encountered. In the exercises at the end of the chapter, you are asked to write code for the alternative setting, when a language supplies a lookahead Boolean function for testing the end of a file.

```
SetReadBank(InBank)          (* prepare to read from InBank *)
SetWriteBank(OutBank)        (* prepare to write to OutBank *)
GetFirstValues(InBank)
WhichFile ← 0
IF InBank[1].Value = EOF
    THEN
        Finished ← True
    ELSE
        LOOP
            Finished ← False
            FindSmallest(InBank, Value, FileNo)
            Write (OutBank[WhichFile], Value)
            IF Value = end-of-run marker
                THEN
                    WhichFile ← (WhichFile + 1) MOD K
                    GetFirstValues(InBank)
                    IF InBank[0] Value = EOF
                        THEN EXIT
                    END IF
                ELSE
            END IF  Read(InBank[FileNo].FileName, InBank[FileNo].Value)
        END LOOP
END IF
```

GetFirstValues(VAR InBank: BankType)

```
FOR Index ← 0 TO K −1 DO
    Read(InBank[Index].FileName, InBank[Index].Value)
END FOR
```

Find Smallest(InBank: BankType, VAR Value, VAR FileNo: Integer)

```
Value ← InBank[0].Value
FileNo ← 0
FOR Index ← 1 TO K−1 DO
    IF Value > InBank[Index].Value
        THEN
            Value ← InBank[Index].Value
            FileNo ← Index
    END IF
END FOR
```

Polyphase Merge   In balanced merging,

- the same number of files are used for both input and output, and
- the initial runs are evenly distributed across the bank of output files.

In polyphase merging,

- all but one of the files are used for input and only one file is used for output, and
- the initial runs are not evenly distributed across the banks of output files.

A polyphase merge uses K files for input and one file for output when merging. If one of the K input files becomes empty following the merging of a set of parallel runs, that file immediately becomes the new output file. The old output file is reset and becomes one of the input files.

The trick is to distribute the original runs across the K files in such a way that no two files become empty at the same time until the end and the last merge occurs when there is exactly one run left on each of the K input files. Before we look at the algorithm in detail, we consider an example that works correctly.

MergeRuns

Suppose that there are four files, one used for output and three for input. Suppose also that initially File1 has 13 runs, File2 has 11 runs, File3 has 7 runs, and File4 is empty (File4 is being used for output).

File1	File2	File3	File4
13runs	11runs	7runs	<eof>

After 7 parallel runs have been merged onto File4, File3 becomes empty. The four files now look like this:

File1	File2	File3	File4
6runs	4runs	<eof>	7runs

File3 becomes the new output file; File4 is reset, ready to merge the first 4 of its runs with 4 runs on File1 and 4 runs on File2. After 4 parallel runs have been merged, the 4 files look like this:

File1	File2	File3	File4
2runs	<eof>	4runs	3runs

File2 is now empty and becomes the new output file; File3 is reset, ready to merge the first 2 of its runs with those on File1 and File4. After 2 parallel runs have been merged, the files look as follows:

File1	File2	File3	File4
<eof>	2runs	2runs	1run

File1 becomes the new output file; File2 is reset, ready to merge one of its runs with those on File3 and File4. When File4 becomes empty, the files look as follows:

File1	File2	File3	File4
1run	1run	1run	<eof>

File1, File2, and File3 each have 1 run ready to be merged onto File4.

As promised, no two files become empty at the same time, and we end with an empty file and only one run left on each of the other files.

The merging part of the algorithm is much like that of the balanced merge. K files are being merged and can be thought of as a bank of K files. The output is actually simpler because we do not have to rotate among K output files. The only difficulty occurs when we change one file from an input file to an output file, and another file from an output file to an input file. In fact, this can be done with a simple swapping of the contents of two places. OutFile always contains the name of the file being used for output. When one of the input files (say, InBank[i]) is at <eof>, the variable pointers InBank[i] and OutFile are swapped.

The control points for a polyphase merge are a little different from those in a balanced merge. We need to test for an empty file each time a set of parallel runs has been merged. The end of the process is when there are data on only one file. In the case of the balanced merge, we know that the final result is on the first file. In the case of the polyphase merge, we do not know which file the final sorted version is on; we have to check each time a new output file is assigned to see if more than one of the files is at the end-of-file. We add a parameter to GetFirstValues that tells us that the merging process is over.

Assuming that the initial runs have been distributed properly, we can now write the algorithm for the polyphase merge. As with our merging of runs with the Balanced Merge Sort, the following code assumes that an end-of-file is determined by reading a value and then testing it against a special <eof> constant. Note that this code uses the FindSmallest procedure previously defined for the Balanced Merge Sort.

```
Create(OutFile)
SetReadBank(InBank)
GetFirstValues(InBank, OutFile, Finished)
WHILE Not Finished DO
    FindSmallest(InBank, Value, FileNo)
    Write(OutFile, Value)
    IF Value = end-of-run marker
        THEN   GetFirstValues(InBank, OutFile, Finished)
        ELSE   Read(InBank[FileNo].FileName, InBank[FileNo].Value)
    END IF
END WHILE
```

GetFirstValue(VAR InBank:BankType, VAR OutFile: File, VAR Finished: Boolean)

```
Count ← 0
ChangeOutFile ← False
REPEAT
    IF InBank[Count].Value = EOF
        THEN   (* Either switch output file or finished. *)
            IF NOT ChangeOutFile
                THEN   (* One <eof>, switch output file. *)
                    Reset(OutFile)
                    TempFile ← OutFile
                    OutFile ← InBank[Count]
                    InBank[Count] ← TempFile
                    Rewrite(OutFile)
                    ChangeOutFile ← True
                ELSE   (* Second <eof> encountered *)
                    Finished ← True
            END IF
        ELSE   (* Set up to merge next set of runs. *)
            Read(InBank[Count].FileName, InBank[Count].Value)
            Count ← Count + 1
    END IF
UNTIL (Count = K) OR Finished
```

Distribution of Initial Runs

A polyphase merge has the same complexity as the balanced merge has, but requires fewer files. However, the distribution of runs is more complicated. If we
had used a three-file example, the number of runs initially would have been a Fibonacci number. For a three-file system, the total number of runs must be equal

to a Fibonacci number, with the two input files containing runs the numbers of which are equal to the two previous Fibonacci numbers.

What about a four-file polyphase merge or a five-file polyphase merge? How must the runs be distributed? We can determine the distribution by working backwards. We know that we must end up with only one run on each of K files. From there, we can determine what must be on the files the last time the OutFile switched. We can continue working backwards until the total number of runs distributed across the K files is approximately equal to the original number of runs we expect to have. In our example, we consider a four-file system.

Given the following table, we need to fill in the shaded areas. Each row in the table represents a point where a file becomes empty (<eof>). With no loss of generality, we can allow the empty file to rotate.

	File1	File2	File3	File4	Total
(a)	1run	<eof>	<eof>	<eof>	1run
(b)	<eof>	1run	1run	1run	3runs
(c)		<eof>			
(d)			<eof>		
(e)				<eof>	
(f)	<eof>				

File2 is empty at (c) and has 1 run at (b). Therefore, 1 run must have been removed from File1, File3, and File4 in the transition from (c) to (b). Adding the 1 run to the state of File1, File3, and File4 in (b), we get the values for row (c).

	File1	File2	File3	File4	Total
(a)	1run	<eof>	<eof>	<eof>	1run
(b)	<eof>	1run	1run	1run	3runs
(c)	1run	<eof>	2runs	2runs	5runs
(d)			<eof>		
(e)				<eof>	
(f)	<eof>				

Applying the same logic, we see that the transition from (d) to (c) must have involved 2 runs. Adding 2 runs to the state of File1, File2, and File4 in (c), we get the values for row (d).

	File1	File2	File3	File4	Total
(a)	1run	<eof>	<eof>	<eof>	1run
(b)	<eof>	1run	1run	1run	3runs
(c)	1run	<eof>	2runs	2runs	5runs
(d)	3runs	2 runs	<eof>	4runs	9runs
(e)				<eof>	
(f)	<eof>				

We now work backwards again, adding the number of runs on File4 in (d) to the number of runs on the other files in (d) to generate the values in row (e). Why File4? Because File4 is the file that is empty in row (e). Notice also that File4 has the maximum number of runs in (d).

	File1	File2	File3	File4	Total
(a)	1run	<eof>	<eof>	<eof>	1run
(b)	<eof>	1run	1run	1run	3runs
(c)	1run	<eof>	2runs	2runs	5runs
(d)	3runs	2 runs	<eof>	4runs	9runs
(e)	7runs	6runs	4runs	<eof>	17runs
(f)	<eof>				

Because the maximum number of runs on (e) is 7 (the file that is empty in (f)), we add 7 to the number of runs for each file in (e) to get (f).

	File1	File2	File3	File4	Total
(a)	1run	<eof>	<eof>	<eof>	1run
(b)	<eof>	1run	1run	1run	3runs
(c)	1run	<eof>	2runs	2runs	5runs
(d)	3runs	2runs	<eof>	4runs	9runs
(e)	7runs	6runs	4runs	<eof>	17runs
(f)	<eof>	13runs	11runs	7runs	31runs

What we have constructed is a distribution for 31 runs such that the polyphase merge using four files works properly.

The algorithm can be summarized as follows:

Find the number of runs in row i that is positioned above the file marked <eof> in row succ(i). Add this value to each of the runs shown in (i) to generate the number of runs necessary on each file in row succ(i). Note that the number of runs added is the maximum in row i.

Tables showing the run distributions necessary for more files can be constructed in the same way. The distribution of the number of runs necessary is related to the generalized Fibonacci numbers.

We have already mentioned that there are times when we have no idea how many runs are to be generated. If this is the case, then a balanced merge is preferable. If, however, we can determine the run size such that the number of runs is close to the required number, dummy runs can be inserted to generate the necessary distribution for a polyphase merge.[2]

Priority Queue

A priority queue models the situation in which the item with the highest priority moves to the head of the line. In the television series MASH, when the wounded soldiers arrive at the field hospital the doctors quickly look at the patients and mark them in order of the severity of their wounds. The most severely wounded soldiers are operated on first. This ordering of the wounded creates a priority queue: the cases are ordered according to the severity of the wounds with the most critically wounded being the first one treated.

Specification

In the priority queue, the entries are made up of <item, priority> pairs. The designated entry is the item with the highest priority. The operation that deletes the designated entry is usually called Serve in a priority queue, and the operation that views the designated entry is usually called Next. In the following axioms, we use the relational operator greater than (>) to compare priorities. Note that highest priority may or may not mean greatest value.

First, we define a simple version of the serve axiom, which is analogous to the Pop and Delete operations for stacks and queues. We call this SServe (for Simple Serve).

---

[2] For more information, see Donald Knuth, *The Art of Computer Programming*, Vol. 3, Addison-Wesley Publishing Company, 1973.

structure PQueue (of <ItemType, PriorityType>)
interface Create $\rightarrow$ PQueue
Enque(PQueue, ItemType, PriorityType) $\rightarrow$ PQueue
SServe(PQueue) $\rightarrow$ PQueue
Next(PQueue) $\rightarrow$ ItemType
IsEmpty(PQueue) $\rightarrow$ Boolean
end
axioms **for PQ in PQueue, i1, i2 in ItemType, p1, p2 in Priority,Type let**

SServe(Create) = Error
SServe(Enque(Create, i1, p1)) = Create
SServe(Enque(Enque(PQ, i1, p1), i2, p2)) =
    IF p1 > p2
        THEN Enque(SServe(Enque(PQ, i1, p1)), i2, p2)
        ELSE   Enque(SServe(Enque(PQ, i2, p2)), i1, p1)
    END IF

Next(Create) = Error
Next(Enque(Create, i1, p1)) = i1
Next(Enque(Enque(PQ, i1, p1), i2, p2)) =
    IF p1 > p2
        THEN Next(Enque(PQ, i1, p1))
        ELSE   Next(Enque(PQ, i2, p2))
    END IF

IsEmpty(Create) = True
IsEmpty(Enque(PQ, i1, p1) = False

While these axioms parallel those we have seen previously for stacks and queues, it is somewhat traditional to combine the SServe and Next operations into a single operation Serve, which returns both the next item and the priority queue that results when this entry is removed. Serve has the following basic form:

Serve(PQueue) $\rightarrow$ PQueue $\times$ ItemType

Thus, Serve returns both a priority queue and an item, and a simple definition of Serve uses both SServe and Next as

Serve = (SServe $\times$ Next)

Alternatively, the definition of this combined axiom could be given directly, although here it is necessary to work with pairs or cross products (PQueue $\times$ Item-Type). To manipulate such pairs, we need to be able to extract either the first or the second part of the pair from the composite. This is done with projection operations π_1 and π_2, where

π_1 (PQ, i) = PQ

π_2 (PQ, i) = i

The complete axioms for Serve follow.

Serve(Create) = Error
Serve(Enque(Create, i1, p1)) = (Create, i1)
Serve(Enque(Enque(PQ, i1, p1), i2, p2)) =
    IF p1 > p2
        THEN (Enque(π_1(Serve(Enque(PQ, i1, p1))), i2, p2), π_2(Serve(Enque(PQ, i1, p1))))
        ELSE (Enque(π_1(Serve(Enque(PQ, i2, p2))), i1, p1), π_2(Serve(Enque(PQ, i2, p2))))
    END IF

While this definition may appear rather complex, note that the basic conditions for these definitions correspond to those for SServe and Next. Furthermore, the first component of Serve is the same as the axioms for SServe (except that π_1 is added, so Enque is applied to a priority queue rather than a pair). Similarly, the second component of Serve is analogous to the axioms for Next.

This combined axiom also suggests why it is customary to define SServe and Next (or Pop and Top, or Deque and First) as separate axioms, even though we may think of them in a combined setting. Separate axioms are often simpler to state and verify than combined ones. Furthermore, even when an axiom such as Serve does combine two simple operations, it may be easier to consider Serve as a pair (SServe × Next).

Implementation

In our implementations, we write code for Serve, although we assume that this operation has two simple components, SServe and Next, as noted above. Thus, as we consider different alternative implementation structures, we examine them using a Serve with two output parameters, bearing in mind that we are actually implementing both a Next and a SServe as specified.

Specifications are abstract, but implementations must be concrete. How are we going to represent this abstract data type in a computer program? The most obvious way is as a list of items, stored either in an array or in a linked structure. Let us consider how we might implement the priority queue using our list primitives from Chapter 2. Rather than having a list of simple items, we have a list of records. One of the fields in the record is the priority. As we look at these implementations, we review the complexity of each operation in the average case.

As List Implemented in an Array

Recall that a list kept in an array has two parts: the array and the length. We refer to the two parts as Items and Length. For variety, we call the array Items rather than Data here. The time required to insert and delete items in the list depends on the number of items in the list, Length.

Before we can analyze the order of the operations, we have another design decision: when we model the abstract priority queue

$$\text{Enque (Enque (\dots (Enque (Create, } i_1)) \dots), i_{n-1}), i_n)$$

we must decide if the list containing $i_1, \ldots, i_{n-1}, i_n$ is to be kept sorted or unsorted. In fact, we look at it both ways, unsorted first.

Create At the implementation level, Create simply means doing whatever initialization is necessary. In this case, the Length field is set to zero, which has constant time, $O(1)$.

Enque To find where an item belongs in an unsorted list is easy. If the list is unsorted, we can put it anywhere. The obvious place to put it is at the end of the list. This involves only incrementing Length and storing the item in Items[Length]. Both incrementing and storing have bounded time. Therefore, the complexity of inserting into an unsorted list kept in an array is $O(1)$.

Serve This operation has two parts: finding the item with the highest priority and removing it from the priority queue. To find an item with the highest priority in an unsorted list, we have to search the entire list. The time it takes to search the list is clearly dependent on the number of items in the list. Therefore, the order of finding the item to delete is $O(\text{Length})$.

Once we have found the item, we remove it by moving all those items in the rest of the list up one position in the array and decrementing Length. Moving items up one position in the array requires a loop going from the position of the item to the end of the list. How many items are there to be moved? We do not know precisely, but it could be Length $-$ 1. Therefore, the operation of removing the item is also $O(\text{Length})$. Alternatively, we could replace the item being removed by the item in the Length position. Putting these pieces together, the order of the deletion operation is $O(\text{Length})$.

IsEmpty To determine if a list is empty we compare the Length field to zero. This is a bounded (actually constant) time operation and so has $O(1)$.

If the list is kept sorted in order of priority, with Items[Length] as the highest priority, the complexity of Enque and Serve would change, but Create and IsEmpty would not.

Enque (sorted) This operation again breaks down into two operations: find the place and insert the item. Because the list is sorted, we can use a binary search to find the insertion point. Binary search is an $O(\log_2 N)$ operation. Inserting the item requires moving all the items in the array below the insertion point down one position. By the same argument used in the unsorted Serve operation, this operation is $O(\text{Length})$.

Serve (sorted) Because we know that Items[Length] has the highest priority, finding it and removing it have bounded time, $O(1)$.

As List Implemented in a Linked Structure

Because the size of the structure and the size of the list are identical, there is no need to keep a length field. Again, we analyze the structure as both unsorted and sorted beginning with the unsorted structure.

Create Initializing a linked list is just setting the external pointer to the list to NIL, which has O(1).

Enque The obvious place to put a new item into an unsorted list kept in a linked structure is at the beginning. The processing only requires getting a node, putting the item in the component field, and changing two pointers. Neither of these operations is dependent on how many items are in the list, so the operation is O(1).

Serve Finding the item to delete requires searching the list. Searching a linked structure is logically just like searching an array; the operation is dependent on the length of the list (O(Length)). Removing an item from a linked list is simpler than removing an item from an array-based list. All we have to do is change a pointer and dispose of the node. Again, putting these pieces together, the order of the Serve operation is O(Length).

IsEmpty To determine if a linked list is empty, we only have to compare the external pointer to the list to NIL, which is a constant time operation.

Enque (sorted) To find the insertion place in a sorted list, we must scan the linked list, which is O(Length). Inserting an item into a linked list at this point has O(1).

Serve (sorted) If the list is kept sorted with the highest-priority item first, serving is O(1).

Correctness In verifying either the array or the linked-list implementations of a priority queue, we follow the same steps outlined for previous structures. In the case of the unsorted array or linked structures, the implementation parallels the axioms very closely, so the verification is particularly straightforward. Both SServe and Next are defined by comparing a current priority with the next one. This is precisely the linear search used in the implementation.

For the sorted array or linked implementation, one must be careful to describe the correspondence between the abstract priority queue

$$\text{Enque (Enque (\dots (Enque (Create, } i_1)) \dots), i_{n-1}), i_n)$$

and the data, $i_1, \dots, i_{n-1}, i_n$, after it has been sorted. This correspondence can be simplified, however, by the observation that the only operations that use multiple Enque operations return the same results when the order in which the elements are enqueued is changed. Specifically,

$$\text{Next (Enque (Enque (PQ, a), b)) = Next (Enque (Enque (PQ, b), a))}$$

and

$$\text{SServe(Enque (Enque (PQ, a), b)) = SServe(Enque (Enque (PQ, b), a))}$$

Thus, in describing the correspondence between the abstract priority queue

$$\text{Enque (Enque (\dots (Enque (Create, } i_1)) \dots), i_{n-1}), i_n)$$

and a sorted array-based or linked list, we can assume $i_1, \ldots, i_{n-1}, i_n$ have been sorted. Then, by looking at one data item in the sorted version, one can make an inference concerning the results of the linear search described in the axioms. A careful proof of correctness must write out what one can infer from the implemented structure and translate such inferences to the axioms as written.

Other Implementation Structures

A priority queue can also be implemented in a binary search tree where the tree is ordered on priority.

Create Initializing a binary search tree involves only setting the external pointer to NIL, which is O(1).

Enque Inserting into a binary search tree is an $O(\log_2 N)$ operation, because each comparison to find the insertion point cuts the remaining tree in half.[3]

Serve Finding the item with the highest priority requires that we follow the path either as far right as possible or as far left as possible, depending on whether the highest priority is the highest or lowest value. Therefore, finding the item is O(log2N); removing it requires constant time, because it is a leaf.

IsEmpty Testing for empty is a simple comparison with NIL.

Comparison of Implementation Structures[4]

The average-case complexity of the operations on the priority queue are summarized in Table 5.1. Enque is the sum of Find Place and Insert Item, and Serve is the sum of Find Item and Delete Item. Because Create and IsEmpty are O(1) in every implementation, they are not included in the summary.

Application

In our opinion, the priority queue is one of the most (if not *the* most) versatile of all the abstract data types that we study in this book. Procedure FindSmallest in the merge algorithm used for external sorting is actually a priority queue. Finding the smallest value in a set of values is an application where "highest priority" becomes "smallest value." Likewise, finding the maximum value in a set of values is an application where "largest value" becomes "highest priority." The application we present here is a little more sophisticated; it uses the priority queue to improve the efficiency of the external sorting algorithms presented in the previous section.

---

[3] Of course, if we are not careful, the tree can degenerate into a linked list at the worst case, but we are looking at an average case here. In Chapter 8, we discuss techniques to guarantee that insertion into a balanced binary tree results in a tree that is still reasonably balanced.

[4] When the heap is defined in Chapter 7, we discuss its use as an implementation structure for a priority queue.

Table 5.1 Complexity Comparison for the Average Case for Alternative Implementation Structures for the ADT Priority Queue

	Enque Operation			Serve Operation		
	Find Place	Insert Item	Total	Find Item	Delete Item	Total
Array						
Sorted	$O(\log_2 N)$	$O(N)$	$O(N)$	$O(1)$	$O(1)$	$O(1)$
Unsorted	$O(1)$	$O(1)$	$O(1)$	$O(N)$	$O(N)$	$O(N)$
Linked						
Sorted	$O(N)$	$O(1)$	$O(N)$	$O(1)$	$O(1)$	$O(1)$
Unsorted	$O(1)$	$O(1)$	$O(1)$	$O(N)$	$O(1)$	$O(N)$
Binary Search Tree	$O(\log_2 N)$	$O(1)$	$O(\log_2 N)$	$O(\log_2 N)$	$O(1)$	$O(\log_2 N)$

Replacement Selection Run Generation for Balanced K-way Merge

The formula that gives the number of merge passes required for S runs is $\log_k S$. As k increases, $\log_k S$ decreases, and our sort is more efficient (although its order does not change). Are there other ways in which we can make our sorting algorithm more efficient? To begin, we look at the parameters.

Time is dominated by the input and output of records; that is, I/O is the bottleneck in any external sorting algorithm. We have decreased the number of merge passes by increasing the number of files that we are working with. If we could make each original run longer, we could decrease the number of merge passes further. However, M, the original run size, is chosen to be as big as possible. We seem to be at an impasse. In fact, improvement is impossible if we use the basic scheme of successively reading in M values and sorting them until we reach the end of the original file.

To make further headway, we need to consider a different approach for the generation of the original runs. Instead of thinking of the run as a basic unit, we consider each value in the run as the basic unit, and we construct the runs, one value at a time. We use the term value (standing for value of the key) rather than record in our discussion. In practice, we sort records, not values.

A bounded priority queue of size M is used to hold the values we have read in but have not yet written out. We begin the process by filling the priority queue with the first M values to be sorted, considering the lowest key value to have the highest priority.

LoadPriorityQueue

```
REPEAT
    Read Value
    Enque(PQ, Value)
UNTIL IsFull(PQ)
```

If we were to write out the entire contents of the priority queue, we would have the equivalent of the first run. However, we write out only the first value. We now have room in the priority queue for another value from the original input file. This next value is read and examined. If this value is greater than the value that was just written out, it can still go out on this run. If the value is less than the value just written out, it has to be saved to go out on the next run.

Where can we put this value to save it for the next run? Again, we are faced with the problem of having used all available space for the priority queue. We put this value on the queue as well, but mark it for the next run. That is, we have two runs coexisting in the priority queue at one time. (Alternatively, we could use two priority queues of size M/2; see Exercises.) The priority function, which compares the priority of two items, considers the values for the current run to be higher-priority than those being saved for the next run. When all the values that can go out on the current run are written out, an end-of-run marker is written on the file, and the values remaining in the queue are written on this new (current) run.

Let us look at an example before continuing with the algorithm. In our example, we indicate those marked for the next run by underlining them.

Data: 2 4 1 7 6 3 8 2 4 6 9 1 3 4 6 5

M: 5

The first five values are read into the priority queue. We picture the priority queue as an array of five sorted values. This is for illustration purposes only, because we have already shown that the priority queue may be implemented in any number of ways.

PQ: 1 2 4 6 7

Serve(PQ, Value) returns a 1, which is written out. The next value from the input file is a 3, which is larger than the last value written, so it is entered into the priority queue marked for this run.

PQ: 2 3 4 6 7   Current Run: 1

Serve(PQ, Value) returns a 2, which is written out, and an 8 is read and enqueued.

PQ: 3 4 6 7 8   Current Run: 1 2

Serve(PQ, Value) returns a 3, and a 2 is read. The 2 cannot go out on the current run so it is marked for the next run.

PQ: 4 6 7 8 2   Current Run: 1 2 3

Serve(PQ, Value) returns a 4, and a 4 is read. The 4 can still go out on this run.

PQ: 4 6 7 8 2   Current Run: 1 2 3 4

Serve(PQ, Value) returns a 4 , and a 6 is read.

    PQ: 6 6 7 8 2   Current Run: 1 2 3 4 4

Serve(PQ, Value) returns a 6, and a 9 is read.

    PQ: 6 7 8 9 2   Current Run: 1 2 3 4 4 6

Serve(PQ, Value) returns a 6, and a 1 is read.

    PQ: 7 8 9 1 2   Current Run: 1 2 3 4 4 6 6

After the next three values have been written and replaced, the situation is as follows:

    PQ: 1 2 3 4 6   Current Run: 1 2 3 4 4 6 6 7 8 9

Serve(PQ, Value) returns a 1. We recognize that this is the first value in the next run. We put an end-of-run marker on the output file. Now the items in the priority queue are all for the current run, and the process continues. The last value in the input file (a 5) is entered into the priority queue. The input file is now empty, and the situation is as follows:

    PQ: 2 3 4 5 6   Run 1: 1 2 3 4 4 6 6 7 8 9

                         Current Run: 1

The priority queue is now written out, giving the following two runs.

Run 1: 1 2 3 4 4 6 6 7 8 9

Run 2: 1 2 3 4 5 6

Notice that Run 1 contains 10 values, twice M! In fact, experimentation has shown that the use of a priority queue normally doubles the expected size of a run using this technique.[5] Thus, while one might not expect to obtain runs of exactly twice the queue size, this example does represent a typical result. Furthermore, we note that this example was not rigged; the numbers were chosen out of thin air.

Now we must translate our by-hand algorithm into one that we can code for the computer. One way to mark the value for the next run is to attach the run number to the value (that is, consider the run number to be part of the key). After each run is completed, the current run number is incremented, thus making those values in the priority queue marked for the current run. The function that compares the priority of two items for the priority queue has to examine both the run number and the value to determine which of the two items has higher priority.

We can now write the replacement selection algorithm for generating runs. This algorithm assumes a K-way merge and distributes the runs across the K files

----

[5] See Knuth, Vol. 3.

on LeftBank. Also, as with our code for the Balance Merge and the Polyphase Merge Sorts, our pseudocode assumes that one must read the <eof> indicator before checking it. (It does not use a look-ahead function.) In this code, remember that the Value and Run fields of each item are combined to form a priority.

Generate Runs

```
FillPQ (PQ)
CurrentRun ← 1
WhichFile ← 0
LOOP
    Serve(PQ, OutItem)
    IF OutItem.Run <> CurrentRun
        THEN
            CurrentRun ← CurrentRun + 1
            Write end-of-run marker on LeftBank[WhichFile]
            WhichFile ← (WhichFile + 1) MOD K
    END IF
    WriteWord(LeftBank[WhichFile], OutItem.Value)
    Read Item.Value
    IF Item.Value = EOF
        THEN   EXIT
    END IF
    IF Item.Value >= OutItem.Value
        THEN   Item.Run ← CurrentRun
        ELSE   Item.Run ← CurrentRun + 1
    END IF
    Enque(PQ, Item)
END LOOP
FlushPQ (PQ)
```

Fill PQ (VAR PQ : PQType)

```
Create(PQ)
Item.Run ← 1
Read (Item.Value)
WHILE (Item.Value <> EOF)
    AND NOT IsFull(PQ) DO
    Enque (PQ, Item)
    Read Item.Value
END WHILE
```

The replacement selection algorithm for generating initial runs is embedded in a LOOP that continues until an <eof> is encountered on the input file. This can happen at any time during the process. By the nature of the algorithm, there are $M - 1$ values left to be written out when the <eof> is encountered. That is, the <eof> is detected when the algorithm attempts to get the next value to put into the priority queue. These M − 1 values remaining in the priority queue must be written out. They can all be part of the current run, they can be part of both the current run and the next run, or they can all be destined for the next run. These three cases must be taken care of.

Flush PQ (VAR PQType)

```
WHILE Not IsEmpty(PQ) DO
    Serve(PQ, OutItem)
    IF OutItem.Run <> CurrentRun
        THEN
            Write end-of-run marker on LeftBank[WhichFile]
            WhichFile ← (WhichFile + 1) MOD K
            CurrentRun ← CurrentRun + 1
    END IF
    WriteWord(LeftBank[WhichFile], OutItem.Value)
END WHILE
```

Before we conclude this discussion, a word needs to be said about how to compare two items when there are two parts to the comparison. That is, how do we determine higher priority when we have both the value and the run number?

If the run numbers are not the same, then the run numbers alone determine which item has higher priority. If the run numbers are the same, then the values must be checked to determine higher priority. It is the same scheme that would be used to compare dates. If the years are different, then we can use the years to decide which comes first. If the years are the same, then we must compare the months. If the months are the same, then we must compare the days. The following algorithm is for a Boolean function, which returns True if Item1 and Item2 have equal priority, or if Item1 has higher priority than Item2.

Is Higher Or Equal (Item1, Item2): Boolean

```
IF Item1.Run < Item2.Run
    THEN  RETURN True
    ELSIF Item1.Run > Item2.Run
        THEN  RETURN False
        ELSE  RETURN (Item1.Value < Item2.Value)
END IF
```

As indicated earlier, experiments indicate that the expected length of each run is approximately 2*M. What happens in cases where the original file is actually sorted? If the original file is sorted in the same order as we are sorting it, then the original run is the entire file. The merging phase is eliminated completely. The closer the file is to being sorted, the longer the runs are. This is certainly a good feature of the algorithm.

What happens when the file is sorted in reverse order? Each run is exactly M in length. In fact, this is the worst case; we can do no worse than our original approach, which was to sort the file in runs of size M. Of course, our algorithm does take slightly more space for each record, because we must associate the run number with the key. The amount of extra space can actually be reduced to one bit per record by using a Boolean flag to distinguish between the current run and the next run. This alternative to the algorithm is left as an exercise.

SUMMARY

Semi-structured data types can be characterized by the fact that the operation that deletes an item takes no item as a parameter. The item to be removed (or viewed) is the designated item. It is the definition of the designated item that distinguishes these data types. Because the names of the operations are different across the data types in this category, they are summarized below.

	Stack	FIFO Queue	Priority Queue
Store an Item	Push	Enque	Enque
Delete Designated Item	Pop	Deque	SServe
Observe Designated Item	Top	First	Next

The stack is abstract data type to be used to save values if you need to examine the values in the reverse order in which they were entered. The queue is the one to use if you need to examine values in the same order in which they were entered. The priority queue is the one to use if each value has a priority associated with it and you need to examine values in terms of their priority.

We illustrated the use of the stack in a problem to determine if pairs of symbols were used properly. External sorting was used to illustrate an important use of both a FIFO queue and a priority queue.

It is interesting to note that the priority queue can be used to simulate both the stack and the FIFO queue. If a time stamp is attached to each item to use as the priority, the designated item in the stack is the one with the most recent time stamp, and the designated item in the FIFO queue is the one with the oldest time stamp.

EXERCISES

1. Fill in the blanks in the following axiomatic specification for the ADT Queue.

   structure Queue (of ItemType)
   interface Create $\rightarrow$ _____
              Enque(Queue, ItemType) $\rightarrow$ _____
              Deque(Queue) $\rightarrow$ _____
              First(Queue) $\rightarrow$ _____
              IsEmpty(Queue) $\rightarrow$ _____

   axioms   **for all Q in Queue, i in ItemType, let**
       IsEmpty(Create) = _____
       IsEmpty(_____) = _____
       Deque(Create) = _____
       Deque(_____) = _____
       First(_____) = _____
       First(_____) = _____

2. Construct the queue containing the letters a, b, d, q, r (r is in the rear) using the operations defined in the axioms.

3. Define Enque and Deque for the ADT Queue using the UnsortedList developed in Chapter 1 as the underlying model.

4. The text suggests two ways of implementing the Queue ADT using an array. The first uses an empty slot between the First and Last array elements. The second maintains a Size variable. Evaluate the efficiency of the IsFull, IsEmpty, Enque, and Deque procedures in each implementation using a micro analysis of each arithmetic operation, assignment, and comparison performed. (Ignore any overhead of procedure calls to IsFull, IsEmpty, or Size when analyzing Enque and Deque, as a compiler might reasonably replace these calls by a copy of the code.)

   Because the MOD operation (Index MOD MaxQueue) might be implemented as a shift machine instruction if MaxQueue is a power of 2, one might assume that the time for each arithmetic operation, assignment, and comparison is the same (1 unit of time). In this case, determine if one of these implementations is more efficient than the other. Explain your answer.

5. Suppose the following operation is added to the definition of the ADT queue.

   Guess(Queue, Queue) $\rightarrow$ Queue
   Guess(Create, Q) = Q
   Guess(Enque(P, i), Q) = Enque(Guess(P,Q), i)

   Show the Queue expression in reduced form after the following series of operations, and prove that your result is correct.

   P1 $\leftarrow$ Create
   P2 $\leftarrow$ Enque(P1, 1)
   P3 $\leftarrow$ Enque(P2, 2)
   P4 $\leftarrow$ Enque(P3, 0)
   Q1 $\leftarrow$ Create
   Q2 $\leftarrow$ Enque(Q1, 6)
   Q3 $\leftarrow$ Enque(Q2, 7)
   Q4 $\leftarrow$ Guess(P4, Q3)

6. What is the result of the following code segment where Q is the result of Guess(P, Q) in Exercise 5?

```
WHILE NOT IsEmpty(Q) DO
    Write(First(Q));
    Deque(Q)
END WHILE
```

7. Say in words what Guess (as defined in Exercise 5) does.

8. Given a file of 500 records, a run size of 10, and eight files, show how the merge process works for a balanced merge by showing where the original runs are during each merge pass.

9. Given three files, F1 with eight runs, F2 with five runs, and F3 as the beginning output file, what file contains the final sorted output after a polyphase merge?

10. The pseudocode for the Balanced Merge Sort assumed that one tested for the end of a file by reading a value and comparing it to a special <eof> value. Such an approach is followed in Modula-2. Ada and Pascal, on the other hand, contain a special end-of-file function that indicates when the next item to be read is the <eof> designator.

    a. Rewrite the pseudocode for languages that use a special Boolean end-of-file function.

    b. Because you should change as few procedures as possible, explain why each procedure you modified had to be changed.

11. Determine the distribution of runs for a polyphase merge of 34 runs. Three files are used for the merge.

12. Determine the distribution of runs for a polyphase merge of 17 runs. Four files are used for the merge.

13. Suppose you have 2*K files available for merging. Thus, in a Balanced Merge Sort, you would use K files for input and K files for output for each pass. In a Polyphase Merge, you would use 2*K − 1 files for input and 1 file for output. While a Polyphase Merge combines more items per run, the two have the same order of complexity. Why?

14. The complexity analysis for the implementation of a priority queue by an unsorted or sorted array noted that Create has constant time, but it stated that the unsorted Enque and the sorted Serve have bounded time. Describe an instance where the time for unsorted Enque and sorted Serve would not be constant, even though it must be bounded.

15. Table 5.1 gives the complexity of alternative implementations for the ADT priority queue in the average case. Present analogous tables for the best- and worst-case analyses.

16. Assuming no two elements have the same priority, prove the assertion in the text that the ADT priority queue axioms imply that

    Next (Enque (Enque (PQ, a), b)) = Next (Enque (Enque (PQ, b), a))

    and

    SServe(Enque (Enque (PQ, a), b)) = SServe(Enque (Enque (PQ, b), a))

    for any priority queue PQ and any items a and b.

17. Given a queue size of 5, generate the initial runs using the replacement selection algorithm with the following data:

    1 4 7 6 3 8 2 4 3 10 11 2

18. How many runs are generated using replacement selection in the following cases?

    a. Original file is already sorted.

    b. Original file is sorted in reverse order.

    c. File is in unknown order.

19. Revise the Replacement Selection algorithm by using a Boolean flag to distinguish the current run from the next run. Thus, a Boolean flag replaces the run field described in the text.

20. Write a program that implements the Balanced Merge Sort and the Polyphase Sort based on a total of six files. The program also should use a standard sorting algorithm (based on 100 data items) and the Replacement Selection Algorithm (using a priority queue holding 100 items) to generate different runs.

    Now run the program on a reasonably large file of data and manually time how long each sorting algorithm takes, using both the sorting algorithm and replacement selection. How many merge passes are required in each case? How do the times compare?

21. Write the specifications for a bounded FIFO queue and bounded priority queue.

22. Generalize the external sort using a balanced merge to sort records where the user provides the type of the records and a comparison function that compares keys.

23. In the queue implementation, we used the formula

    Last ← Last MOD MaxQueue + 1

    to cycle through the elements in the array. In the external file application, we used the formula

    WhichFile ← (WhichFile + 1) MOD K

    to cycle through the array of files. Compare and contrast these two formulae.

24. Rewrite the replacement algorithm using two priority queues of size M/2 rather than one of size M. One priority queue holds the values for the current run, and the other holds the values for the next run.

25. The sample algorithm using a stack matched paired symbols. Rewrite this algorithm so that the different versions of parentheses must be used in the following order: (, [, {. (. . . . If an out-of-order open symbol is found, write an error message, print the contents of the stack, and halt.

Structured Linear Data Types

6

Linear data types are homogeneous data types that the user views as being ordered from beginning to end. If the user accesses the items by position within the ordering, the linear data type is an *indexed linear list*. If the user accesses the items by moving from one to the next, the data type is a *nonindexed linear list*. Often the term linear list is used to refer to all linear data types, leading to confusion about operations such as "storing an item" and "inserting an item." We think that the distinctions between access modes lead to two distinct categories of data types.

Within the indexed category, we recognize two distinct data types: the *array*, where an index (or pair of indices) is permanently bound to an item, and the *sequence*, where an index is temporarily bound to an item. That is, the index in the sequence only reflects an item's current position in the list. The binding of an item to a position may change as other items are inserted and deleted. Within the nonindexed category, we again recognize two types: one where the values in the list are unsorted and one where the values in the list are sorted.

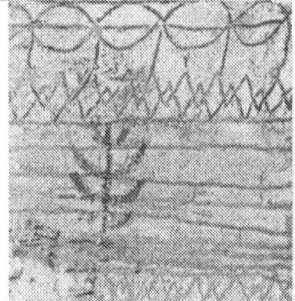

Arrays

Because arrays are built into most programming languages, we tend to take them for granted. They are a named collection of components, each of which we can access by its position within the collection. This definition suffices for the data structure array, but here we want to define the abstract data type array.

Specification

Arrays can be one-dimensional, two-dimensional, three-dimensional, and so on. We give the specifications for the one- and two-dimensional arrays, leaving the specification of higher-dimensional arrays as an exercise.

One-Dimensional Array

The one-dimensional array data type is a collection of <index, value> pairs where the bounds on the index set are known at the time an instance of an array data type is created. Like the record data type, a newly created instance of an array data type includes the specification of the available indices; the allowable indices are defined, but the value for each <index, value> pair is undefined.[1] An attempt to store an <index, value> pair when the index is not within the bounds of the array is an error condition and returns Error.

structure OneDArray (of <IndexType, ValueType>)
interface Create(IndexType, IndexType)   → Array
               LoBound(Array)   → IndexType
               HiBound(Array)   → IndexType
               Store(Array, IndexType, ValueType)   → Array
               Retrieve(Array, IndexType)   → ValueType
      end

axioms   **for all A in Array, i1, i2, i3, i4 in IndexType, and v in ValueType, let**
          LoBound(Create(i3, i4)) = i3
          LoBound(Store(A, i1, v)) = LoBound(A)

          HiBound(Create(i3, i4)) = i4
          HiBound(Store(A, i1, v)) = HiBound(A)

          Store(A, i1, v) =
              IF (i1 < LoBound(A)) OR (i1 > HiBound(A))
                  THEN Error
              END IF

          Retrieve(Create(i3, i4), i1) =
              IF (i1 < LoBound(A)) OR (i1 > HiBound(A))
                  THEN Error

---

[1] Because the terminology for arrays comes from mathematics, we use the term <index, value> pair rather than <index, information> pair. However, ValueType is not limited to being a scalar.

```
            ELSE   Undefined
        END IF

    Retrieve(Store(A, i2, v), i1) =
        IF (i1 < LoBound(A)) OR (i1 > HiBound(A))
            THEN   Error
            ELSE
                IF  (i1 = i2)
                    THEN v
                    ELSE   Retrieve(A, i1)
                END IF
        END IF
    end
end OneDArray
```

In reviewing these axioms, the parameters to Create specify the range of subscripts allowed for the array. The specifications for all other operations generate an error if one attempts to access the array outside of these limits.

Multi-Dimensional Array

Because the specifications for multi-dimensional arrays are direct extensions of the specifications for one-dimensional arrays, we give only the specifications for two-dimensional arrays here.

```
structure   Array (of <IndexType, IndexType, ValueType>)
interface   Create(IndexType, IndexType, IndexType, IndexType) → Array
            LoBound1(Array)                                  → IndexType
            HiBound1(Array)                                  → IndexType
            LoBound2(Array)                                  → IndexType
            HiBound2(Array)                                  → IndexType
            Store(Array, IndexType, IndexType, ValueType)   → Array
            Retrieve(Array, IndexType, IndexType)           → ValueType
    end
axioms      for all A in Array, i1, i2, i3, i4, i5, i6 in IndexType, and v in
ValueType, let
        LoBound1(Create(i3, i4, i5, i6)) = i3
        LoBound1(Store(A, i1, i2, v)) = LoBound1(A)

        HiBound1(Create(i3, i4, i5, i6)) = i4
        HiBound1(Store(A, i1, i2, v)) = HiBound1(A)

        LoBound2(Create(i3, i4, i5, i6)) = i5
        LoBound2(Store(A, i1, i2, v)) = LoBound2(A)

        HiBound2(Create(i3, i4, i5, i6)) = i6
        HiBound2(Store(A, i1, i2, v)) = HiBound2(A)
```

```
            Store(A, i1, i2, v) =
                IF (i1 < LoBound1(A)) OR (i1 > HiBound1(A))
                        OR (i2 < LoBound2(A)) OR (i2 > HiBound2(A))
                    THEN Error
                END IF

            Retrieve(Create(i3, i4, i5, i6), i1, i2) =
                IF (i1 < LoBound1(A)) OR (i1 > HiBound1(A))
                        OR (i2 < LoBound2(A)) OR (i2 > HiBound2(A))
                    THEN Error
                    ELSE  Undefined
                END IF

            Retrieve(Store(A, i1, i2, v), i3, i4) =
                IF (i3 < LoBound1(A)) OR (i3 > HiBound1(A))
                        OR (i4 < LoBound2(A)) OR (i4 > HiBound2(A))
                    THEN Error
                    ELSE IF (i1 = i3) AND (i2 = i4)
                        THEN v
                        ELSE  Retrieve(A, i3, i4)
                    END IF
                END IF
        end
    end Array
```

The axioms for arrays reflect the behavior that we associate with the array type built into most high-level programming languages. Retrieve returns the last value that was stored with a particular index or indices. If no value has been stored, then the value that is returned is undefined. In languages with strong type checking, an error is generated if the index or indices in an access (retrieve or store) are outside of the bounds of the array.

All array data types are bounded types. There is a constraint on the number of items that can be put into the structure. In the bounded ADT KeyedTable, the Create operation took a parameter that specified the maximum number of items that could be on the structure. In the array data type, the upper and lower bounds are specified for each dimension. In the ADT OneDArray, the bound on the number of items is HiBound − LoBound + 1. In the ADT TwoDArray, the bound is specified by two dimensions: (HiBound1 − LoBound1 + 1) ∗ (HiBound2 − LoBound2 + 1).

Implementation

The implementation of arrays in high-level programming languages is covered in the first year of most computer science curricula, so, rather than bore you with a detailed discussion, we just refresh your memory by presenting the major concepts.

Computer memory can be considered as one long list (no pun intended) of bits grouped together into bytes and/or words. We use the nonspecific term "cell" rather than word or byte to avoid machine-dependent details of how large specific structures might be. During the compilation phase of a program, the appropriate number of cells is determined for an array, and the code for accessing the individual components is generated. The mechanism for actually allocating space for the array depends upon the nature of the language.

In some cases, the location of the array can be determined at compile-time. For example, global variables in Pascal, C, Modula-2, and Ada are available throughout the running of a program, so these variables can be assigned memory locations before the program starts. FORTRAN sets up all variables in this way, with local variables associated with the subroutines in which they are defined. Thus, for FORTRAN, space for all variables can be allocated at compile-time.

However, when a language generates space for local variables as each procedure is called, as in Pascal, C, Modula-2, or Ada, such space normally is allocated in a part of the computer's memory called the run-time stack, and the location of that space depends upon when a procedure is called. In such circumstances, the compiler can generate code to allocate the correct amount of space, and the compiler can know where within a block of space to access a given data item.

Regardless of when the space is actually allocated, the location of the entire block of memory is referenced by the address of the first cell. This first address is called the *base address* of the array. When the compiler can allocate this space directly, an array variable and this address are entered directly into a keyed (symbol) table along with the parameters that are necessary to generate the accessing functions, LoBound, HiBound, and Size (the number of cells required to hold a value of type ValueType). Then any reference to this array variable is translated into the corresponding address. When a procedure is called and the actual allocation of space is done, the compiler stores this information in an appropriate symbolic form, and data for the accessing functions may be inserted into an array header at execution time.

In either approach, the compiler generates code to access each individual element using the following formula.

$$\text{Address}(I) = \text{BaseAddress} + (I - \text{LoBound}) * \text{Size}$$

The motivation for this formula is given in an example that follows. You are asked to supply details in the Exercises at the end of the chapter.

If the language has strong type checking like Pascal, Modula-2, and Ada do, then code also is generated to check the index I against HiBound and LoBound to ensure that the address generated is within the array. If the address is not within the bounds, a fatal error is generated. If the language does not have strong type checking, HiBound and sometimes LoBound are not used.

For example, suppose we are given the following declarations:

```
TYPE
    AType = ARRAY [1..5] OF Real;      (* Assumption: Real values take 2 cells *)


VAR
    A : AType;
```

If the base address of A is 100, the address of A[4] is calculated as

$$100 + (4 - 1) * 2 = 106$$

The following diagram may clarify this calculation.

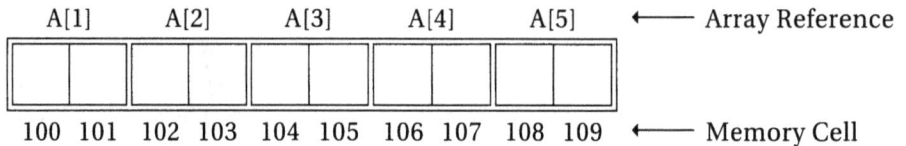

| A[1] | A[2] | A[3] | A[4] | A[5] | ⟵ Array Reference |

100 101   102 103   104 105   106 107   108 109   ⟵ Memory Cell

A[1] begins in cell 100 and takes two cells, A[2] begins in cell 102, and A[3] begins in cell 104. The position of A[4] can be found by beginning at the start of the array (cell 100) and moving three array elements beyond, to cell 106. Because each array element requires two cells, we move 3*2 cells beyond the base address 100.

In the case of a two-dimensional array, the formula becomes a little more complex, but the idea is the same: calculate the number of cells coming before the one you want and add it to the base address to give the address of the specified element.

Two-dimensional arrays can be stored in *row major order* or *column major order*. That is, elements in each row can be stored contiguously or elements in each column can be stored contiguously. The formula for calculating an address where the array is stored in row major order is

Address(I,J) = BaseAddress +
        (HiBound2 − LoBound2 + 1) * (I − LoBound1) * Size +
        (J − LoBound2) * Size

For example, consider the following declarations:

```
TYPE
    AType = ARRAY [1..2, 1..3] OF Real;      (* Assumption: Real values take 2 cells *)

VAR
    A : AType;
```

If the base address of A is 100, the formula calculates the address of A[2,3] as

$$100 + ((3 - 1 + 1) * (2 - 1) * 2 + (3 - 1)) * 2 = 110$$

Again, the motivation for this formula is illustrated by considering the following diagram of memory.

Memory Cell		Array Reference
100		
		A[1,1]
101		
102		
		A[1,2]
103		
104		
		A[1,3]
105		
106		
		A[2,1]
107		
108		
		A[2,2]
109		
110		
		A[2,3]
111		

A[2,3] begins at location 110 because all entries from row 1 come first, followed by two prior entries in row 2.

This approach to storing arrays is called the *base address plus offset* method. It can be logically extended to implement arrays with any number of dimensions. While this approach is efficient for many applications, other representations also are possible. We could store a one-dimensional array as a list of <index, value> pairs, using the ADT KeyedTable as an implementation structure where the index is the key and the value is the information. Similarly, a two-dimensional array may be stored as a list of <index, index, value> triples using the ADT KeyedTable with the <index, index> pair as a combined key. When we expect few elements in a two-dimensional array to be nonzero, we may store only the nonzero values. We discuss this last approach in more detail at the end of this chapter.

Complexity

The reason why most high-level languages use the base address plus offset method lies in the complexity of the accessing functions. The base address plus offset implementation gives bounded time, O(1) access.

In contrast, if an array is implemented through the use of a keyedtable, then the complexity of the Store or Find operations depends upon the implementation. Such times range from O(1) in a good hash implementation to O(N) in an unsorted list implementation, where N is the number of components in the array.

Application: Matrix Module

When you were first learning about arrays, your instructor may have made the analogy that a one-dimensional array is like a vector, and a two-dimensional array is like a matrix. They are alike in the way in which the individual items in the structures are accessed, but an array is an abstract data type built into a high-level language, and vectors and matrices are mathematical objects.

Vectors are mathematical objects upon which the binary operations addition, subtraction, and dot product are defined. Matrices are mathematical objects upon which the unary operation transpose and the binary operations addition, subtraction, and multiplication are defined. An array is an abstract data type where the only operations provided are store (array reference on the left of an assignment operator) and retrieve (array reference on the right of an assignment operator).

Because of the similarity of access, arrays are used frequently to implement vectors and matrices. In this application section, we use the built-in two-dimensional array data type to implement a library module of matrix operations including addition, subtraction, multiplication, and transpose. However, before talking about implementation issues, we review matrix multiplication. Matrix addition, subtraction, and transpose are very straightforward, but matrix multiplication is complex enough to warrant a review.

Review of Matrix Multiplication

If A and B are matrices (two-dimensional arrays) and if the number of columns of A is the same as the number of rows of B, then the matrices may be multiplied together. For example, suppose A and B are as follows:

$$A = \begin{pmatrix} 1 & 2 & 3 & 4 \\ 0 & 2 & 1 & 3 \\ 1 & 1 & 0 & 0 \end{pmatrix} \quad B = \begin{pmatrix} 1 & 1 \\ 0 & 1 \\ 2 & 3 \\ 4 & 2 \end{pmatrix}$$

Here, A is a 3 by 4 matrix, and B is 4 by 2, and

4 = number columns (A) = number rows (B)

In such a situation, we can form a new product matrix AB which has the same number of rows as A and the same number of columns as B. In the example, AB has 3 rows and 2 columns. An entry in this product is obtained by multiplying elements in a row of A with the corresponding elements in a column of B and adding the results, as shown on the following page.

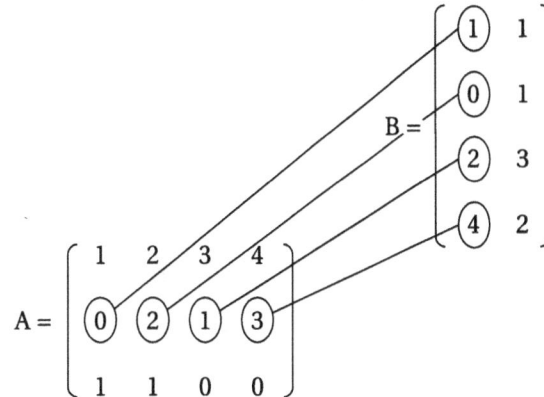

As illustrated in this diagram, the entry for the second row and first column of the product is obtained by multiplying the second row of A and the first column of B. The first entry (0) in the row is multiplied by the first entry (1) in the column, the second entries (2 and 0) are multiplied, and so forth with the third entries (1 and 2) and the fourth entries (3 and 4). Each of these products is then added to give the entry for the product matrix. Thus,

Product[2,1] = 0*1 + 2*0 + 1*2 + 3*4 = 14.

Similarly,

Product [3,2] = 1*1 + 1*1 + 0*3 + 0*2 = 2.

Continuing this approach for each of the other rows and columns, we obtain the following result.

$$\text{Product} = \begin{pmatrix} 23 & 20 \\ 14 & 11 \\ 1 & 2 \end{pmatrix}$$

More generally, suppose that A is an m by n matrix and B is an n by p matrix, as follows.

$$A = \begin{pmatrix} a_{11} & a_{12} & a_{13} & \cdots & a_{1n} \\ a_{21} & a_{22} & a_{23} & \cdots & a_{2n} \\ a_{31} & a_{32} & a_{33} & \cdots & a_{3n} \\ & \vdots & & \cdots & \vdots \\ a_{m1} & a_{m2} & a_{m3} & \cdots & a_{mn} \end{pmatrix} \quad B = \begin{pmatrix} b_{11} & b_{12} & b_{13} & \cdots & b_{1p} \\ b_{2b} & b_{22} & b_{23} & \cdots & b_{2p} \\ b_{31} & b_{32} & b_{33} & \cdots & b_{3p} \\ & \vdots & & \cdots & \vdots \\ b_{n1} & b_{n2} & b_{n3} & \cdots & b_{np} \end{pmatrix}$$

Then the product AB is an m by p matrix, where the entry in the ith row and jth column is

Product [i,j] = $a_{i1}*b_{1j} + a_{i2}*b_{2j} + a_{i3}*b_{3j} + \ldots + a_{in}*b_{nj}$

Implementation of Matrix Module

We must be careful in defining MatrixType, because the preconditions on our matrix operations ensure *matrix* compatibility, but they do not guarantee *array* compatibility. Specifically, Pascal and Modula-2 do not allow two arrays with different dimensions to be defined by the same data type. However, Ada has a construct called an unconstrained array, which is a mechanism designed to solve this type of compatibility problem—but only for one-dimensional arrays.

Here we are letting the user declare the maximum dimensions and define an array type of the appropriate size. The instances of an array of MatrixType are declared in the user program, and the matrix dimensions are set when a matrix is initialized.

Interface Section MatrixOperations

```
(* To access MaxRows, MaxColumns, and ValueType. *)
USES <name of data defining module>
TYPE
    RowRange = 1..MaxColumns;
    ColRange = 1..MaxRows;

    MatrixType = RECORD
        NumberRows,
        NumberColumns : Integer;
        Values : ARRAY [1..MaxRows, 1..MaxColumns] OF ValueType
    END RECORD;

PROCEDURE MatrixCreate (Rows, Columns : Integer; VAR Result : MatrixType);
(* Pre:      Rows ≤ MaxRows AND                              *)
(*           Columns ≤ MaxColumns                            *)
(* Post:     Result.NumberRows ← Rows;                       *)
(*           Result.NumberColumns ← Columns                  *)

PROCEDURE StoreValue (VAR One : MatrixType; Value : ValueType;
                          Row, Column : Integer);
(* Pre:      Row ≤ One.NumberRows AND                        *)
(*           Column ≤ NumberColumns                          *)
(* Post:     One.Values[Row, Column] ← Value                 *)

PROCEDURE MatrixAdd (One, Two : MatrixType; VAR Result : MatrixType);
(* Pre:      One.NumberRows = Two.NumberRows                 *)
(*           One.NumberColumns = Two.NumberColumns           *)
(* Post:     Result ← One + Two                              *)

PROCEDURE MatrixSub (One, Two : MatrixType; VAR Result : MatrixType);
(* Pre:      One.NumberRows = Two.NumberRows                 *)
(*           One.NumberColumns = Two.NumberColumns           *)
(* Post:     Result ← One − Two                              *)
```

PROCEDURE MatrixMult (One, Two : MatrixType; VAR Result : MatrixType);
(* Pre: One.NumberColumns = Two.NumberRows   *)
(* Post: Result ← One * Two   *)

PROCEDURE Transpose (One : MatrixType; VAR Result : MatrixType);
(* Pre: One has been created.   *)
(* Post: Result[i,j]← One[j,i]   *)

Because the definitions for matrix operations are commonly covered in courses in discrete mathematics or linear algebra, we give the algorithms here without further comment.

MatrixCreate (Rows, Columns: Integer) VAR Result: MatrixType

```
Result.NumberRows ← Rows
Result.NumberColumns ← Columns
```

StoreValue (VAR One: MatrixType, Value: ValueType, Row, Column: Integer)

```
One.Values[Row, Column] ← Value
```

MatrixAdd (One, Two: MatrixType , VAR Result: MatrixType)

```
MatrixCreate(Result, One.NumberRows, One.NumberColumns)
FOR Row ← 1 TO One.NumberRows DO
    FOR Col ← 1 TO One.NumberColumns DO
        Result.Values[Row,Col] ← One.Values[Row,Col] +
                                    Two.Values[Row,Col]
    END FOR
END FOR
```

MatrixSub (One, Two: MatrixType, VAR Result: MatrixType)

```
MatrixCreate(Result, One.NumberRows, One.NumberColumns)
FOR Row ← 1 TO One.NumberRows DO
    FOR Col ← 1 TO One.NumberColumns DO
        Result.Values[Row,Col] ← One.Values[Row,Col] −
                                    Two.Values[Row,Col]
    END FOR
END FOR
```

MatrixMult(One, Two: MatrixType, VAR Result: MatrixType)

```
MatrixCreate(One.NumberRows, Two.NumberColumns, Result)
FOR Row ← 1 TO One.NumberRows DO
    FOR Col ← 1 TO Two.NumberColumns DO
        DotProduct ← 0
        FOR K ← 1 TO One.NumberColumns DO
            DotProduct ← DotProduct + One.Values[Row,K] *
                            Two.Values[K,Col]
            END FOR (* summing *)
```

```
        Result[Row,Col] ← DotProduct
    END FOR
END FOR
```

Transpose (One: MatrixType, VAR Result: MatrixType)

```
MatrixCreate(One.NumberColumns, One.NumberRows, Result)
FOR Row ← 1 TO One.NumberRows DO
    FOR Col ← 1 TO One.NumberColumns DO
        Result.Values[Col, Row] ← One.Values[Row, Col]
    END FOR
END FOR
```

Complexity

Previously in this chapter, we discussed the complexity of both the base plus off-set method of implementing arrays and the use of the ADT KeyedTable. Here, we look at the complexity of the matrix operations.

MatrixCreate has bounded time because the time required to store Rows and Columns is independent of the values being stored. StoreValue also has bounded time, provided the array is implemented using the base plus offset approach. MatrixAdd and MatrixSub are O(NumberRows * NumberColumns); hence, $O(N^2)$ for a square matrix, where N is the number of rows and columns.

The classic matrix multiplication algorithm used in MatrixMult has three loops: the outer loop is from 1..One.NumberRows, the next loop is from 1..Two.NumberColumns, and the third loop is from 1..One.NumberColumns, making it an $O(N^3)$ algorithm for N × N matrices.

Matrix multiplication is an example of an interesting problem in complexity. If we consider all operations to be of equal time, then we cannot do any better than N^3. On real machines, however, multiplications and divisions take consider-ably longer than additions and subtractions, and this becomes important when working with very large matrices. So researchers look for faster matrix multiplica-tion algorithms using the number of multiplications as the measure of complexi-ty. That is, a better matrix multiplication algorithm is one that decreases the number of multiplications.[2]

Reducing the number of multiplications for a single multiplication A * B is tricky and requires a very careful analysis, beyond the scope of this text. However, a surprising savings can be gained when computing the product of several matri-ces if we carefully choose the order in which to multiply them. We look at this problem in the next section.

Factoring Algorithm for Multiplying a Series of Matrices   If a series of ma-trices must be multiplied together, savings in the total number of multiplications is possible by a simple rearrangement of the order in which they are multiplied.

---

[2] Winograd and Strassen each have matrix multiplication algorithms that use less than N^3 multi-plications. See references in the Bibliography.

We can compute the product of $M_1 * M_2 * M_3 * \ldots * M_n$ in many different ways because matrix multiplication is associative.

Consider the number of multiplications required to multiply four matrices (n = 4 above), and suppose the matrices have the following dimensions (the first value is the number of rows; the second value is the number of columns):

$M_1(10,2)$ $M_2(2,30)$ $M_3(30,10)$ $M_4(10,15)$

If we compute $(((M_1 * M_2) * M_3) * M_4)$, the number of multiplications is as follows:

Result1(10,30) ← M_1*M_2 requires 600 multiplications.

Result2(10,10) ← Result1*M_3 requires 3000 multiplications.

Result3(10,15) ← Result2*M_4 requires 1500 multiplications.

Thus, multiplying these four matrices together in left-to-right order requires 5100 multiplications. Because matrix multiplication is associative, can we do better by multiplying them in a different order? Suppose we try $(M_1 *(M_2 *(M_3 * M_4)))$.

Result1(30,15) ← M_3*M_4 requires 4500 multiplications.

Result2(2,15) ← M_2*Result1 requires 900 multiplications.

Result3(10,15) ← M_1*Result2 requires 300 multiplications.

Thus, multiplying in right-to-left order requires 5700 multiplications. What about M_1*M_2 multiplied by M_3*M_4?

Result1(10,30) ← M_1*M_2 requires 600 multiplications.

Result2(30,15) ← M_3*M_4 requires 4500 multiplications.

Result3(10,15) ← Result1*Result2 requires 4500 multiplications.

This is much worse; it requires 9600 multiplications! Next, we try M_1 times the result of $(M_2*M_3)*M_4$.

Result1(2,10) ← M_2*M_3 requires 600 multiplications.

Result2(2,15) ← Result1*M_4 requires 300 multiplications.

Result3(10,15) ← M_1*Result2 requires 300 multiplications.

This is much better; it requires only 1200 multiplications!

Clearly, the number of multiplications required for a series of matrix multiplications can be reduced by determining ahead of time the best order in which the multiplications should occur. Now the question is, How do we determine the best order? We could, of course, do what we have just done, that is, try all possible combinations. This process, however, is very inefficient. There are a lot of redundant calculations as you can see from the example. There should be a better way—and, of course, there is.

We begin with some notation for the product $M_1 * M_2 * M_3 * \ldots * M_n$. In this product, suppose matrix M_i has dimensions d_{i-1} by d_i, that is M_i has d_{i-1} rows and d_i columns. In our example, for four matrices, there are five dimensions to remember (d_0 to d_4), because the inner ones must be the same. Following the definition of matrix multiplication, therefore, the number of multiplications for the product $M_i * M_{i+1}$ is $d_{i-1} * d_i * d_{i+1}$. Now, suppose we want to find the best order in which to multiply the matrices $M_i * \ldots * M_j$.

As we proceed, the last work we do involves a final multiplication, as follows:

$$(M_i * \ldots * M_k) * (M_{k+1} * \ldots * M_j).$$

Here, we assume we already have multiplied matrices $M_i, \ldots, M_k$ and $M_{k+1}, \ldots, M_j$. Then, the matrix on the left has dimensions d_{i-1} by d_k, the one on the right has dimension d_{k+1} by d_j, and the number of multiplications in this last product is $d_{i-1} * d_k * d_j$.

Now, suppose that by great insight, intuition, previous work, or sheer luck, we already know the best order in which to multiply each of these smaller series of matrices. Let Min[i,k] be the minimum number of multiplications for the first of these series, and Min[k+1,j] be the minimum number for the second series. Then, the number of multiplications for the overall product is the number for the left and right subsequences plus the amount of this last product:

$$\text{Min}[i,k] + \text{Min}[k + 1,j] + d_{i-1}*d_k*d_j$$

If we were to know all Min[i,k] and Min[k + 1,j] for all subseries, then we could find the best overall way to do this order by considering all possible k's. That is,

$$\text{Min}[i,j] = \text{Minimum} \ (\text{Min}[i,k] + \text{Min}[k + 1,j] + d_{i-1}*d_k*d_j)$$
$$i \leq k \leq j - 1$$

In short, this formula is saying that the minimum number of multiplications required to multiply matrix i through matrix j, can be calculated by finding the best place to break this span into two pieces. Min[i,k] is the minimum required up through matrix k, Min[k + 1,j] is the minimum required from matrix k + 1 through j, and $d_{i-1}*d_k*d_j$ is the number of multiplications required to multiply these two halves together.

To actually perform these computations, we store these values in a two-dimensional array we call Min, and we carefully order the way in which we calculate the Min values. At the end of the calculation, the best order is in Min[1,N].

To motivate the algorithm, we consider an example first. Remember, we cannot write an algorithm for something until we completely understand the process, and formulas such as this sometimes can seem confusing in the abstract. We begin with four observations:

1. Min[i,i] = 0 for $1 \leq i \leq N$ as no multiplications are needed here.

2. Min[i,i+1] = $d_{i-1} * d_i * d_{i+1}$ as this is the number of multiplications determined above for the product $M_i * M_{i+1}$.

3. We are only interested in Min[i,j] for $1 \leq i < j \leq N$, so we do not have to calculate values for each cell in the array, only those in the upper triangular part.

4. In considering the best order of products, we need to record the k for which the minimum occurs. If we store this at each stage, we know what products to perform when we have finished our processing. That is, we know how to interpret the results in Min.

With these observations, we consider Min as an array of records that contains the minimum number of multiplications and k. We also need an array containing the dimensions of the matrices, indexed from 0 to N.

We now apply the algorithm to the previous example.

$$M_1(10,2) * M_2(2,30) * M_3(30,10) * M_4(10,15)$$

The array Dimensions has the dimensions of the matrices to be multiplied in the left-to-right order with the middle dimension repeated only once. Remember, we cannot rearrange the matrices; we can only vary the way in which we group (associate) them.

Dim			(* Dimensions *)	
10	2	30	10	15
[0]	[1]	[2]	[3]	[4]

The array Min is shown below with the diagonals initialized, following observation 1 above. Min[i,j].m is the minimum number of multiplications needed to multiply matrix i through matrix j, and Min[i,j].k shows where to break that span into two pieces. Because the diagonal represents the case where i and j are equal, no multiplications are done, so m and k are both zero.

Min	[1]	[2]	[3]	[4]
[1]	m: 0 k: 0			
[2]		m: 0 k: 0		
[3]			m: 0 k: 0	
[4]				m: 0 k: 0

The function we are minimizing is repeated below using our array of records notation, where d refers to the array Dimensions.

$$\text{Min}[i,j].m = \text{Minimum } (\text{Min}[i,k].m + \text{Min}[k+1,j].m + d_{i-1}*d_k*d_j)$$

$$i \leq k \leq j - 1$$

Following our earlier discussion of this formula, we note that Min[i,j] can be computed if we know all the Min[i,k] and Min[k+1,j] for the various subseries with $i \leq k \leq j-1$. In order for this to be true, we work in the table along the diagonals from left to right. That is, next we calculate the minimum (m) for Min[1,2], Min[2,3], and Min[3,4]. Notice that because j = i+1 on this diagonal, only one value of k is used in each of these calculations. (If there is only one value, it is the minimum.)

Min[1,2].m = Minimum

k=1: Min[1,1].m + Min[2,2].m + Dim[0]*Dim[1]*Dim[2] = 600

Min[2,3].m = Minimum

k=2: Min[2,2].m + Min[3,3].m + Dim[1]*Dim[2]*Dim[3] = 600

Min[3,4].m = Minimum

k=3: Min[3,3].m + Min[4,4].m + Dim[2]*Dim[3]*Dim[4] = 4500

Min with the values recorded is shown below.

Min	[1]	[2]	[3]	[4]
[1]	m: 0 k: 0	m: 600 k: 1		
[2]		m: 0 k: 0	m: 600 k: 2	
[3]			m: 0 k: 0	m: 4500 k: 3
[4]				m: 0 k: 0

Now we fill in the next diagonal, where we are calculating the best way to multiply three matrices together. Here, k can have two values.

Min[1,3].m = Minimum

k=1: Min[1,1].m + Min[2,3].m + Dim[0]*Dim[1]*Dim[3] = 800 ← minimum

k=2: Min[1,2].m + Min[3,3].m + Dim[0]*Dim[2]*Dim[3] = 3600

Min[2,4].m = Minimum

> k=2: Min[2,2].m + Min[3,4].m + Dim[1]*Dim[2]*Dim[4] = 5400
>
> k=3: Min[2,3].m + Min[4,4].m + Dim[1]*Dim[3]*Dim[4] = 900 ← minimum

There is only one cell left to calculate: Min[1,4].

Min[1,4].m = Minimum

> k=1: Min[1,1].m + Min[2,4].m + Dim[0]*Dim[1]*Dim[4] = 1200 ← minimum
>
> k=2: Min[1,2].m + Min[3,4].m + Dim[0]*Dim[2]*Dim[4] = 9600
>
> k=3: Min[1,3].m + Min[4,4].m + Dim[0]*Dim[3]*Dim[4] = 2300

The completed table is shown below.

Min	[1]	[2]	[3]	[4]
[1]	m: 0 k: 0	m: 600 k: 1	m: 800 k: 1	m: 1200 k: 1
[2]		m: 0 k: 0	m: 600 k: 2	m: 900 k: 3
[3]			m: 0 k: 0	m: 4500 k: 3
[4]				m: 0 k: 0

Min[1,4] contains 1200, the minimum value that we calculated earlier, which is comforting! Now, the question is, How do we interpret the k values in order to reconstruct the appropriate sequence?

Associating the Matrices   The k value tells us how to break up each subsequence. In the table, the k value for Min[1,4] is 1. Plugging these values (k = 1, i = 1, j = 4) back into the formula, we have

$$Min[1,4] = Min[1,k] + Min[k + 1,4] = Min[1,1] + Min[2,4]$$

which means that the best factoring of $M_1..M_4$ is the best factoring of $M_1..M_1$ times the best factoring of $M_2..M_4$. Because $M_1..M_1$ represents a single matrix, the best factoring is the matrix itself. What is the best factoring of $M_2..M_4$? We can look in the Min[2,4] cell to find out: Min[2,4].m is the minimum number of multiplications, and Min[2,4].k is the k in the best factoring.

The k value in Min[2,4] is 3, and plugging k, i, and j back into the formula, we have

$$Min[2,4] = Min[2,k] + Min[k + 1,4] = Min[2,3] + Min[4,4]$$

which means that the best factoring of $M_2..M_4$ is the best factoring of $M_2..M_3$ times the best factoring of $M_4..M_4$ (which is just M_4). We look up Min[2,3] to see how best to factor this sequence. The k value is 2, so

$$Min[2,3] = Min[2,k] + Min[k + 1,3] = Min[2,2] + Min[3,3]$$

Because each factor now represents a single matrix, the factorization is now complete. If we put parentheses in at each break, we have our order.

$$M_1*(M_2..M_4) = M_1*((M_2..M_3)*M_4) = M_1*((M_2*M_3)*M_4)$$

Now we are ready to write the algorithm that calculates the Min table. Notice the pattern in the subscripts, that is, the relationship among i and j and the number of values on each diagonal.

First diagonal (main) : j = i		$(1 \leq i \leq N)$
Second diagonal:	j = i + 1	$(1 \leq i \leq N - 1)$
Third diagonal:	j = i + 2	$(1 \leq i \leq N - 2)$
Fourth diagonal:	j = i + 3	$(1 \leq i \leq N - 3)$

After the m and k fields of the main diagonal are zeroed out, there must be a loop that calculates the minimum (m) and k for each diagonal. In the algorithm, we let the outer loop go from 2 to N so that the loop counter corresponds to the appropriate diagonal. The inner loop records the row position for each entry on that diagonal. This gives us the following algorithm, which calculates the values in Min and prints the final ordering of multiplications as its output. The arrays Min and Dim are global variables.

OptimumSequence

```
(* Main diagonal — diagonal 1 — contains only zeros *)
FOR Counter ← 1 TO N DO
    Min[Counter,Counter].m ← 0
    Min[Counter,Counter].k ← 0
END FOR
(* Fill in remaining diagonals in upper triangular matrix *)
```

```
FOR Diagonal ← 2 TO N DO
    FOR Row ← 1 TO N − Diagonal + 1 DO
        Minimum(Row, Row + Diagonal − 1, Dimension)
    END FOR
END FOR
Print 'minimum number of multiplications is' Min[1,N]
Print Factored Matrices
```

Minimum(i, j : Integer, Dim: AType)

```
m ← Min[i + 1,j].m + Dim[i − 1]*Dim[i]*Dim[j]
BestK ← i
FOR k ← (i + 1) TO (j − 1) DO
    Temp ← Min[i,k].m + Min[k + 1,j].m + Dim[i − 1]*Dim[k]*Dim[j]
    IF Temp < m
        THEN
            m ← Temp
            BestK ← k
    END IF
END FOR
Min[i,j].m ← m
Min[i,j].k ← BestK
```

We leave the algorithm for Print Factored Matrices as an exercise.

Complexity of Factoring Algorithm

Overall, the OptimumSequence algorithm has the following structure:

```
FOR Diagonal ← 2 TO N DO
    FOR Row ← 1 TO N − Diagonal + 1 DO
        Initialize m, BestK
        FOR k ← Row + 1 TO Row + Diagonal − 1 DO
            Update m, BestK
        END FOR
    END FOR
END FOR
```

In reviewing this code, the main work involves initializing/updating m and BestK a total of Diagonal times for each value of Row and Diagonal. The middle loop repeats this process (N − Diagonal) + 1 times, so for each value of Diagonal, the main computations are repeated Diagonal(N − Diagonal + 1) times. This, in turn, is repeated for Diagonal being 2, 3, 4, ..., N. Thus, the total amount of work is

$$2(N − 1) + 3(N − 2) + 4(N − 3) + \ldots + N(1)$$

After some algebra, the total amount of work can be shown to be

$$\frac{N^3}{6} + \frac{N^2}{2} - \frac{2N}{3}$$

and this algorithm has complexity $O(N^3)$. Informally, one can think that on average the middle and inner loops are repeated about $N/2$ times for each value of Diagonal. Putting these together, the innermost material is repeated about $N^2/4$ times for each value of Diagonal. Because the outer loop is repeated N times, the overall algorithm requires roughly $N^3/4$ operations. (While this informal estimate gives the wrong constant for the N^3 term, the order of the result is still correct.)

In summary, we have used the built-in array type to implement a module of matrix operations. In addition, we have examined an algorithm for determining the best factoring for a series of matrix multiplications. Notice that we also used two array data types in this algorithm: a one-dimensional array for the dimensions and a two-dimensional array (of records) for recording the minimum number of multiplications and the ordering information.

Application: Searching and Sorting

From previous courses, you know that searching and sorting are very common array applications. Specifically, suppose A[1..m] and B[1..n] are two arrays containing m and n elements, respectively, and consider the following problems:

1. Determine whether a specific value V is in array A:
   a. assuming A is not ordered.
   b. assuming A is ordered.
2. Assuming A is ordered, find the rank of V in A, where the rank is either the position of V in the array or the position in which one would insert V to maintain an ordered array.
3. Assuming A and B are ordered, merge A and B to obtain array C.
4. Sort array A.

While you probably learned to solve these problems in the past with algorithms for a single processor, here we consider each problem assuming multiple processors are available. Our approach illustrates some issues and approaches that are common for parallel algorithms. For example, we see ways in which to apply the perspectives of result parallelism, specialist parallelism, and agenda parallelism, as described in Chapter 3. However, for simplicity, we choose relatively straightforward algorithms that represent ideas, rather than more complex algorithms that may be somewhat more efficient. Refinements of these more complex algorithms may be found in more advanced books.

Parallel Searching

Just as in the traditional, uniprocessor environment, the problem of searching for an element within an array using many processors may be divided into two cases: one where the array is unsorted and one where the array is sorted.

Searching in an Unsorted Array To begin, we consider the problem of finding whether a specific value V is in array A. A first attempt at a solution uses pure result parallelism. We assign a separate process to each array element, and each process reports that V is 'Found' or 'Not Found'. Here, searching can proceed with separate processes searching separate array elements in parallel. However, we must consider how we as users get our final answer.

If each process reports directly to the user, then the user's process must handle all m messages:

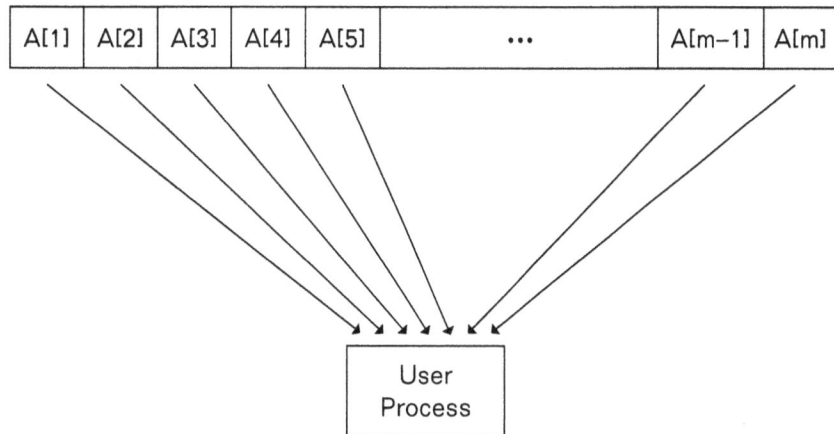

Here, searching takes one step, but reporting is $O(m)$ because the user must process each of the m messages. Thus, this approach does not effectively speed up the solution.

To avoid handling all of these messages, another approach might require the individual searching processes to report only if they find the desired item. While this reduces messages to the user, this approach also has a disadvantage: the user may not know how long to wait if no messages are received. When is it safe for the user to conclude that a value is not found?

As an alternative approach, we could begin by looking at each item in the array and then organizing the responses in a hierarchy, as shown in Figure 6.1. In this approach, results are determined at middle or upper levels of the hierarchy by returning 'Found' if V is present anywhere below. Otherwise, a location in the hierarchy returns 'Not Found'. This approach focuses upon the final results desired, with a separate process for each position in the hierarchy. Again, this solution is motivated by the result-parallel approach to problem solving, with a separate process for each result in the hierarchy.

In analyzing the efficiency of this approach, we note that each level of processes doubles the number of elements that can be processed. Thus, i levels can collect responses from 2^i array elements. To process m elements, there must be enough levels so that $2^i \leq m$ or $i \leq \log_2 m$. This discussion shows that you can search any array in approximately $\log_2 m$ steps if you have enough processors.

As a practical matter, the hierarchical algorithm in Figure 6.1 has a drawback: each process may require some processing overhead. To reduce the number of processes, we can modify the approach to agenda parallelism. In this setting, we list the tasks to be done, starting at the bottom and working towards the top. At first, the available processes work on the array elements themselves. When this work is done, processes move on to the next levels, from the array towards the user.

While our focus here has been on finding whether or not a value V is present in an array, it is worthwhile to note that a similar approach can be used to consider how many times V occurs in the array or where V is located. For any of these problems, the appropriate algorithm takes only O(log$_2$m) steps, without assuming that the array is sorted.

Searching in a Sorted Array If we are searching a sorted array, we can ask what additional efficiencies might be possible. We proceed by extending the binary search. Recall that the binary search is efficient for sorted arrays because, at each step, a midpoint is computed and then a comparison either finds the desired value or allows half of the array to be discarded from further consideration.

From another perspective, we could say that a binary search proceeds with the algorithm that focuses or specializes on a middle element that divides the array into

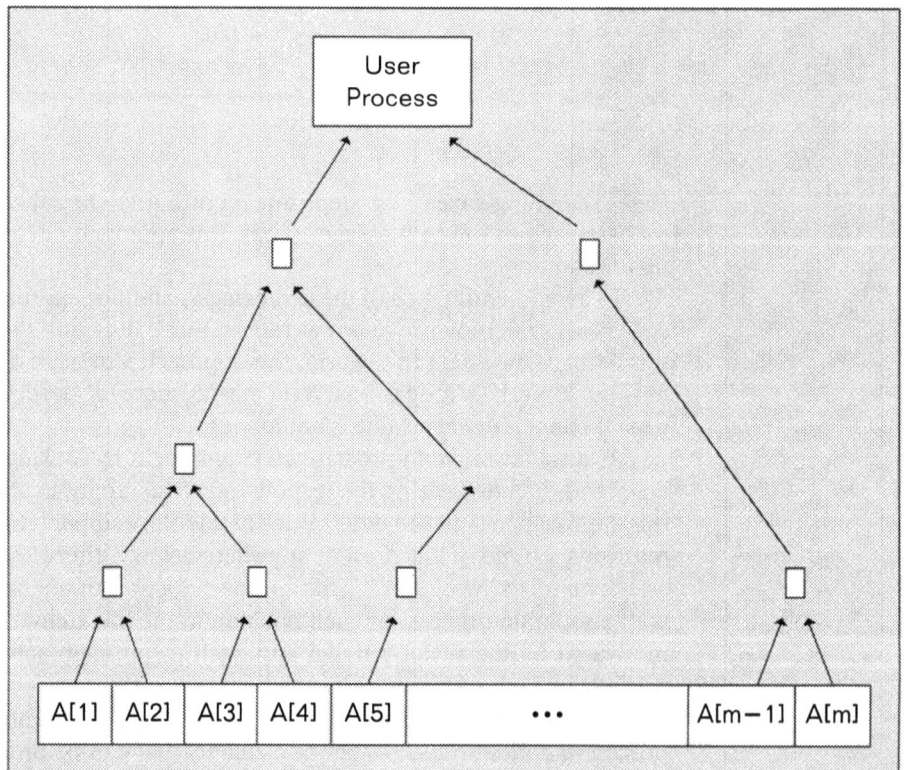

Figure 6.1 Processors Arranged in a Hierarchical Structure

two pieces (one piece before the middle element, one piece after the middle element). With s processes, we could divide the interval into s + 1 pieces, all approximately equal in length. This approach, called an *s-ary search*, follows specialist parallelism—that is, each processor specializes in one array element a fraction of the way through the segment of the array under consideration. In this processing, each process compares its designated array element with the desired one and either finds the value or concludes that part of the array can be discarded from further consideration. As with the search of unsorted arrays, however, we must be careful to limit the amount of interprocess communication required, to avoid bottlenecks.

Before looking at some details and complications, we consider the following example, which finds 11 in the following sorted array, using three processes.

A:	2	4	5	7	9	10	11	14	16	17	19	22	23	25	27
Index:	[1]	[2]	[3]	[4]	[5]	[6]	[7]	[8]	[9]	[10]	[11]	[12]	[13]	[14]	[15]

Throughout a search, each process focuses upon an array element:

> Process 1 focuses upon the array element about 1/4 of the way from the left of the array segment being searched toward the right edge.

> Process 2 focuses upon the array element about in the middle of the array (just as in a binary search).

> Process 3 focuses upon the array element about 3/4 of the way through the array, from the left edge toward the right.

Thus, each process specializes in one array element at a specific position within the part of the array being searched.

The searching process comprises several steps:

Step 1: Divide the array into four pieces by choosing three values: A[4], A[8], and A[12].

Step 2:

> Process 1 considers A[4] = 7 and determines the desired value 11 is bigger.

> Process 2 considers A[8] = 14 and determines 11 is smaller.

> Process 3 considers A[12] = 22 and determines 11 is smaller.

Step 3: The search can be narrowed to A[5]..A[7].
[Note that Process 2 can reach the conclusion in Step 3, because A[8] is the lowest array element considered so far where the desired value 11 is smaller.]

Step 4: Divide the array segment A[5]..A[7] into pieces by choosing three values: A[5], A[6], and A[7].

Step 5:

Process 1 considers A[5] = 9 and determines the desired value 11 is bigger.

Process 2 considers A[6] = 10 and determines 11 is bigger.

Process 3 considers A[7] = 11 and determines 11 has been found.

Step 6: Process 3 can report its finding.

Having studied this example, we are now ready to look at the s-ary search algorithm in somewhat more detail. As with the binary search, we use variables L and R to indicate that the search currently is limited to A[L]..A[R]. Processes then looks at selected elements in this array segment:

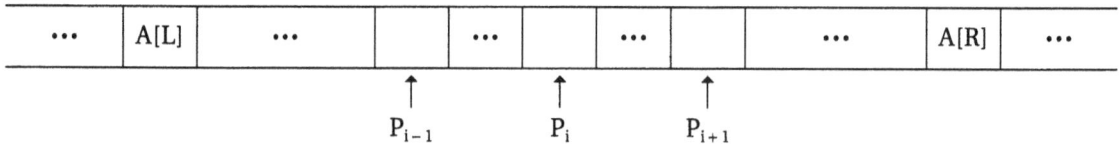

...	A[L]	...		...		...		...	A[R]	...

$$\uparrow \qquad \uparrow \qquad \uparrow$$
$$P_{i-1} \qquad P_i \qquad P_{i+1}$$

Each process P_i must look at an array element. If P_i determines that the desired element V equals the array element being examined, then it tells the user that V has been found, and it notifies the other processes that the search can stop. If the process P_i does not find V in its array element, it uses Boolean variable b_i to report the result of its comparison. If the array element is greater than V, then V must be found earlier in the array and b_i is set true. If the array element is smaller than V, then the searching for V must continue later in the array, and b_i is set false. After process P_i sets its b_i, it communicates this value to the next process P_{i+1} and receives the value of b_{i-1} from process P_{i-1}.

b_i = true means V comes earlier in the array

After communicating the b_i values, each process P_i examines its b_i value and the b_{i-1} value it received from the previous process. If b_{i-1} is true and b_i is false, then P_i can conclude that V must be searched for in the array segment between where P_{i-1} and P_i looked. In this circumstances, P_i reports its finding to the other processes and the search continues. Note that this circumstance can occur for only one P_i. (Why?)

This suggests the following initial algorithm outline for each P_i:

Continue for each P_i until 'Found' or 'Not Found' is reported.
 L and R are determined for P_i
 P_i determines where in the array segment A[L]..A[R] it should look.
 P_i examines its array element:
  If V equals the array element, P_i sends 'Found' to the user and
   other processes, and processing stops.
  P_i sets b_i true if the array element is greater than V;
   false, otherwise.

P_i sends P_{i+1} the value of b_i and receives b_{i-1} from P_{i-1}.
If b_i = true and b_{i-1} = false, then P_i calculates new values for L and R.
If more space in the array remains to be searched,
    then P_i sends revised values of L and R to other processes
        for the next iteration of processing.
    Otherwise, P_i reports 'Not Found' and processing stops.

The communication described here is manageable in many machine configurations. With shared memory, L, R, and each b_i are available to all processors. With message passing, one may be able to organize processes, so that each can broadcast values to others and so that adjacent processes can communicate efficiently. This organization of processes is shown in the following diagram.

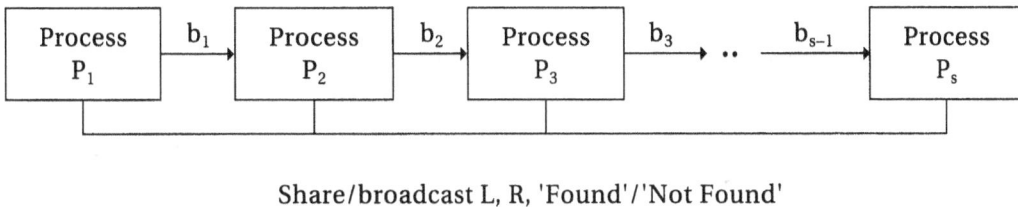

Share/broadcast L, R, 'Found'/'Not Found'

While this algorithm outline describes the idea of the s-ary search reasonably well, a few additional details remain. First, the user process must be considered, and initial values for L and R must be set. These details may be handled by a separate process, which we might label P_0. Second, we need to pay some attention to endpoints. In particular, there is no process to the left of P_1, so P_1 cannot receive any messages. Similarly, we must consider what to do if V is located at the right end of the array. If P_s examines an element to the left of V, then no process is available to determine that V comes later.

In practice, these situations can be handled in either of two ways. First, special code may be written for P_1 and P_s so that they handle these endpoint conditions appropriately. Alternatively, we can let P_0 handle the left endpoint—always sending false to P_1—and we could create another process, P_{s+1}, to receive the result from P_s, thereby handling the right endpoint. This latter approach can allow the same code to be used for each process, but it requires two additional processes to handle the two endpoints.

The remaining details of the algorithm involve determining where process P_i searches within A[L]..A[R]. Because this location depends somewhat on how endpoints are handled, we assume we have created extra processes P_0 and P_{s+1} for these endpoints, so that s processes are available to examine the middle of the array segment. With s processes, we can divide the array into s+1 segments, starting with index L. With some algebra, one can check that process P_i should examine array element

$$A[L + (i * (R - L + 1) \text{ DIV } (s + 1))]$$

To determine the efficiency of this s-ary search, note that each step divides the size of the array being considered from q elements into about $q/(s + 1)$ elements. Thus, if we start with an ordered array of m elements, then

After 1 step, work is narrowed to $m/(s + 1)$ elements.

After 2 steps, work is narrowed to $m/(s + 1)^2$ elements.

After 3 steps, work is narrowed to $m/(s + 1)^3$ elements.

.
.
.

After i steps, work is narrowed to $m/(s + 1)^i$ elements.

Work should continue until there are no elements left to consider in the array. Thus, work ends when $m/(s + 1)^i < 1$ or $m < (s + 1)^i$ or i is about $\log_{s+1}(m)$.

With one process (s=1), this algorithm is the traditional binary search, and this analysis of efficiency gives the familiar conclusion that the binary search takes about $\log_2(m)$ steps. With a limited number of processes, the result is still a logarithmic search, but the base of the logarithm is larger (and the number of steps is reduced by a constant factor). With an unlimited number of processes available, we could choose $s + 1 = m$, in which case, only 1 step would be required for the search. Each process can look at just one element in the array, and searching an ordered array would then be an $O(1)$ operation. (This may be the ultimate in specialist parallelism.)

Parallel Sorting

Our development of a parallel sorting algorithm for an array begins with a common approach for many parallel algorithms. First, we start with a traditional (nonparallel) algorithm. Next, we determine places where several processes can work in parallel to obtain some speedup. Then we modify some parts of the algorithm to give a further speedup. As we shall see, our final algorithm uses the specialist parallelism just described for the s-ary search within a larger context based upon result parallelism.

Our approach is motivated by the traditional Merge Sort. First, here is a quick review.

Part A: Merging two ordered lists We start with ordered lists $a_1, a_2, a_3, a_4, \ldots$ and $b_1, b_2, b_3, b_4, \ldots$. Then we compare a_1 and b_1 to find the smaller of the two, and we move this smaller item to the new list. Next, we compare the smallest remaining items on the two lists and move the smaller item to the new list. (If $a_1 < b_1$ in the first step, then a_1 is the first element of the new list, and we next compare a_2 with b_1.) We continue this process of comparing next elements and moving the smaller one to the new list as long as data remain on both lists. Finally, we copy any data remaining in one list (after the other list has been exhausted).

Part B: Using merging to obtain the Merge Sort We start by considering an array A of m elements to be m lists of one item each. As any list of one item is ordered, each sublist of A of size 1 is ordered. Next, we merge lists 1 and 2, 3 and 4, 5 and 6, and so on. Because each initial list is one item long, each new list contains two elements. Next, we merge adjacent lists again; the new lists now have four elements each. The next steps continue to merge adjacent lists, until all array elements are on one list. This sorts the array.

This merging process is illustrated in the following diagram:

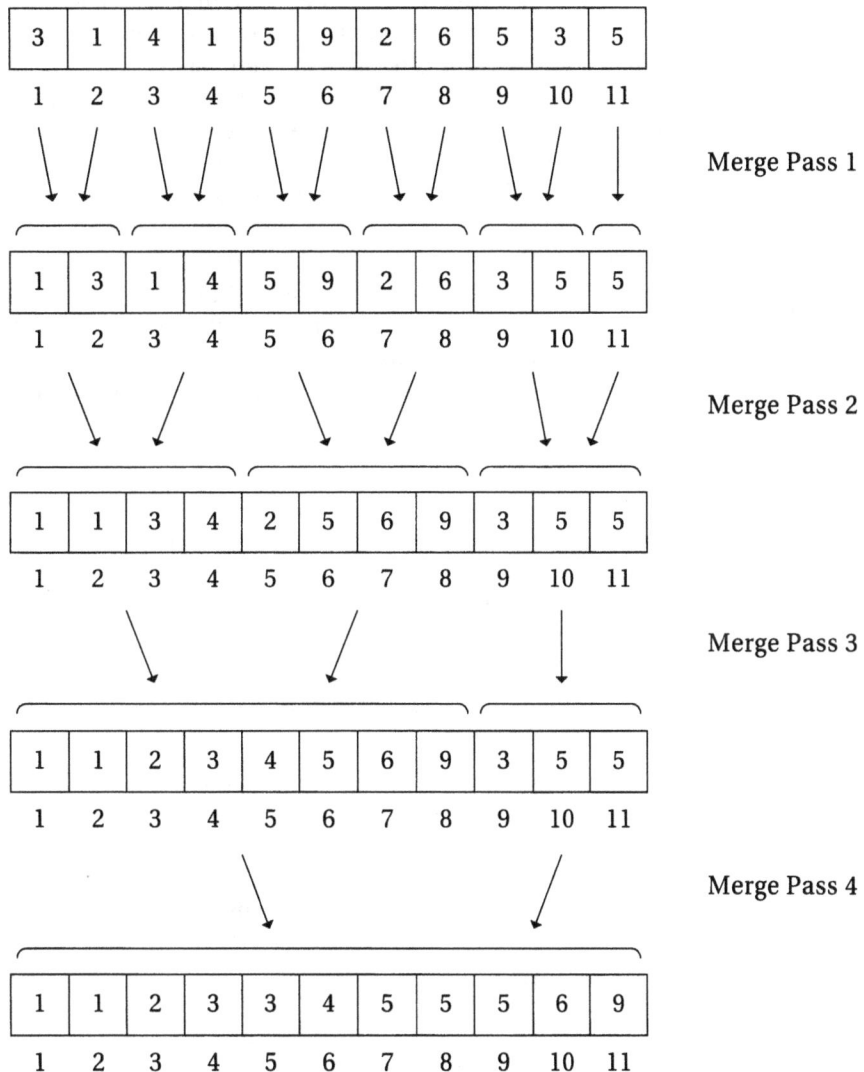

3	1	4	1	5	9	2	6	5	3	5
1	2	3	4	5	6	7	8	9	10	11

Merge Pass 1

1	3	1	4	5	9	2	6	3	5	5
1	2	3	4	5	6	7	8	9	10	11

Merge Pass 2

1	1	3	4	2	5	6	9	3	5	5
1	2	3	4	5	6	7	8	9	10	11

Merge Pass 3

1	1	2	3	4	5	6	9	3	5	5
1	2	3	4	5	6	7	8	9	10	11

Merge Pass 4

1	1	2	3	3	4	5	5	5	6	9
1	2	3	4	5	6	7	8	9	10	11

With each merge step, the length of the ordered sublists doubles, so that after i passes, the length of the ordered sublists is 2^i. Work then continues until $2^i > m$, where m is the array size. Thus, the number of passes is about $\log_2 m$.

For one pass, all m pieces of data are examined and moved, and this takes time proportional to m. With $\log_2 m$ passes and cm operations per pass (where c is a constant), the Merge Sort has $O(m \log_2 m)$.

We now review this algorithm to determine what opportunities we might have for parallelism. Following agenda parallelism, the different parts of a merge pass can be done by different processes. For merge pass i, one process can merge lists 1 and 2, a second process can merge lists 3 and 4, and so forth. At the early stages of the Merge Sort, this allows considerable parallelism. At the later stages, however, only a few lists are left in the merging process. Thus, while this parallelism may shorten some pass steps, the amount of speedup is limited.

Overall, the Merge Sort requires $\log_2 m$ passes, and the traditional merging requires m main steps per pass. While the use of multiple processors to handle different parts of the pass reduces the number of main steps for some passes, a more systematic reduction in the work required for each pass might improve performance significantly. For example, if we could use multiple processes to require $\log_2 m$ steps (per process) per main step, sorting would go from $O(m \log_2 m)$ to $O((\log_2 m)^2)$. If we could do each merging step in a bounded amount of time, then the revised Merge Sort could run as quickly as $O(\log_2 m)$.

Thus, we have reduced efficiency questions for a Merge Sort to the following problem: Given two ordered arrays A[1..m] and B[1..n] containing m and n elements, respectively, merge A and B to obtain an ordered array C. We attack this problem using result parallelism, and we consider where element A[i] should be placed in array C. First, for simplicity, assume all elements of A and B are distinct from each other. Focusing on A[i] in C, we have the following picture:

Array C

Elements A[1] . . . A[i−1] and Elements of B < A[i]	A[i]	. . .	C[m+n]

From this picture, we observe that elements A[1]..A[i − 1] are to the left of A[i] in C. Also, those elements of B less than A[i] are to the left of A[i]. This motivates the following definitions.

Let v be a number and let B be an ordered array of n elements. Then the *rank of v in B*, written *rank (v, b)*, is the number of elements of B that are less than or equal to v. Also, the *truncated rank of v in B*, written *trank (v, B)*, is the number of elements of B that are less than v.

For example, suppose B is the following array.

1	1	2	3	3	5	6	6	6	7	9
[1]	[2]	[3]	[4]	[5]	[6]	[7]	[8]	[9]	[10]	[11]

Then, rank $(4, B) = $ trank$(4, B) = 5$, rank $(6, B) = 9$, and trank $(6, B) = 6$. This example illustrates that if v is distinct from all of the elements of B, then rank$(v, B) = $ trank(v, B).

Continuing our assumption that the elements of A are distinct from the elements of B, an examination of the C array allows us to conclude that the position of A[i] is $(i - 1) + $ rank$(A[i], B)$: that is, the elements $A[1]..A[i - 1]$ come before A[i] in C and there are rank $(A[i], B)$ elements of B that come first. Under the same assumption, the position of B[j] in C is $(j - 1) + $ rank $(B[j], A)$.

If the elements of A and B are not distinct, then the picture of C may be slightly different. The elements less than A[i] or B[j] surely come before these elements. The elements $A[1]..A[i - 1]$ come before A[i], and the elements $B[1]..B[j - 1]$ come before B[j]. What remains is to determine an ordering for equal elements. Arbitrarily, we decide to put A's elements before B's. This yields the following picture for the elements B[j] in the C array.

Array C

Elements B[1] ... B[j–1] and Elements of A ≤ B[j]	B[j]	$\cdots$	C[m+n]

In allowing duplicates, the position of A[i] and B[j] must reflect possible duplications. Thus, the position of A[i] in C is $(i - 1) + $ trank $(A[i], B)$, and the position of B[j] in C is $(j - 1) + $ rank $(B[j], A)$.

These observations allow us to complete the merging process using the approach of result parallelism. We assign a separate process to each element of A and to each element of B. We want each process to place its value of A or B into the appropriate position in array C. Our discussion indicates that each process can proceed independently if we can compute all values trank $(A[i], B)$ and rank $(B[j], A)$. If we have enough processes (and we are not hampered by communication problems), then all elements of A and B can be moved concurrently.

Both trank $(A[i], B)$ and rank $(B[j], A)$ can be computed using the s-ary search described earlier in $O(\log_{s+1} n)$ and $O(\log_{s+1} m)$, respectively. With enough processes, we can compute ranks and truncated ranks for all elements in A and B very quickly. Once (truncated) ranks are known, merges can be completed very quickly by having each data element in A and B moved to C concurrently by separate processes.

Ignoring the possible overhead costs of having many processes, merging can be done in $O(1)$, so the Merge Sort can run in $O(\log_2 m)$. In practice, each process may have non-negligible overhead. The communication between processes, and the simultaneous access of shared memory, create additional constraints on algorithms running on real systems. Therefore, in actual programs, the task of sorting may be broken into sections, with each process performing a series of steps. Thus, in practice, the result parallelism described here is reorganized into tasks, giving rise to agenda parallelism.

Sequences

In all of the applications of the ADT Array, the indices were permanently bound to the values in the array. Now we look at the ADT Sequence, where the index only reflects an item's current position in the sequence.

Specification

The items in a sequence are also <index, value> pairs. However, the index represents the value's current position in the sequence and may change as other items are inserted into or deleted from the sequence. The Create operation has no parameters; it returns an empty sequence. There are two operations that add items to the collection of items: the Store operation, which places an item into a specified location in the sequence, and the Insert operation, which inserts an item into a specified position, shifting all those items in that position and subsequent positions down one place. The Store has no side effects on items in other places. Storing an item in the sixth place means that the item is placed in the sixth place, but inserting an item in the sixth place means that what was in the sixth place is now in the seventh place, what was in the seventh place is now in the eighth place, and so on.

In addition we need an operation that changes the sequence but does not change its length; that is, we need a replace. The characteristics of these operations are explicitly defined in the following set of axioms. An error condition occurs if an attempt is made to store or insert an item into a position in the list that does not already exist or that is greater than the length of the list plus 1. Therefore, we need an operation that returns the length of the sequence.

structure Sequence (of <IndexType, ValueType>)
interface Create $\qquad\qquad\qquad\qquad\qquad\qquad\quad \rightarrow$ Sequence
$\qquad\qquad$ Store(Sequence, IndexType, ValueType) $\qquad \rightarrow$ Sequence
$\qquad\qquad$ Length(Sequence) $\qquad\qquad\qquad\qquad\quad\ \rightarrow$ Integer
$\qquad\qquad$ Insert(Sequence, IndexType, ValueType) $\quad\ \rightarrow$ Sequence
$\qquad\qquad$ Delete(Sequence, IndexType) $\qquad\qquad\ \ \rightarrow$ Sequence
$\qquad\qquad$ Retrieve(Sequence, IndexType) $\qquad\qquad \rightarrow$ ValueType
$\qquad\qquad$ Find(Sequence, ValueType) $\qquad\qquad\quad\ \rightarrow$ IndexType
$\qquad\qquad$ Replace(Sequence, IndexType, ValueType) $\ \rightarrow$ Sequence
$\quad$ **end**

axioms for all S in Sequence, i1, i2 in IndexType, and v1, v2 in ValueType, let
$\qquad$ Length(Create) = 0
$\qquad$ Length(Store(S, i1, v1)) = 1 + Length(S)

$\qquad$ Store(S, i1, v1) =
$\qquad\qquad$ IF i1 > Length(S) + 1
$\qquad\qquad\qquad$ THEN Error
$\qquad\qquad\qquad$ ELSE   IF i1 < Length(S)
$\qquad\qquad\qquad\qquad$ THEN Replace(S, i1, v1)
$\qquad\qquad\qquad$ END IF
$\qquad\qquad$ END IF

Insert(Create, i2, v2) = Store(Create, i2, v2)
Insert(Store(S, Length(S) + 1, v1), i2, v2) =
    IF i2 > 2 + Length(S)
        THEN Error
        ELSE IF i2 = 2 + Length(S)
            THEN Store(Store(S, Length(S) + 1, v1), i2, v2)
            ELSE IF i2 = Length(S) + 1
                THEN Store(Store(S, i2, v2), i2 + 1, v1)
                ELSE Store(Insert(S, i2, v2), Length(S) + 2,v1)
            END IF
        END IF
    END IF

Retrieve(Create, i2) = Error
Retrieve(Store(S, i1, v1), i2) =
    IF IsIn(S, i2)
        THEN Retrieve(S, i2)
        ELSE IF i2 = i1
            THEN v1
            ELSE Error
    END IF
END IF

Delete(Store(S, Length(S) + 1, v1), i2) =
    IF i2 > Length(S) + 1
        THEN Error
        ELSE IF i2 = Length(S) + 1
            THEN S
            ELSE Store(Delete(S, i2), Length(S), v1)
        END IF
    END IF

Replace(Create, i2, v2) = Error
Replace(Store(S, Length(S) + 1, v1), i2, v2) =
    IF i2 = Length(S) + 1
        THEN Store(S, Length(S) + 1, v2)
        ELSE Store(Replace(S, i2, v2), Length(S) + 1, v1)
    END IF

Find(Create, v2) = Error
Find(Store(S, i1, v1), v2) =
    IF IsIn (S, v2)
        THEN Find (S, v2)
        ELSE IF v1 = v2
            THEN i1
            ELSE Error
    END IF
END IF

IsIn(Create, v2) = False
IsIn(Store(S, i1, v1), v2) =
    IF v1 = v2
        THEN   True
        ELSE   IsIn(S, v2)
    END IF
    end
  endSequence

Implementation

There are two things to notice about the ADT Sequence before we start to design an implementation. The first is that the sequence has no predetermined length: linked structures are best for unbounded data types. The second is that all the accesses are in terms of an index: arrays give O(1) access to an indexed position.

Thus, we have three choices. First, we can add an axiom that specifies an upper bound on the length of a sequence and implement the sequence using an array. Second, we can implement the sequence in an unbounded fashion and have the index be implied rather than explicit; that is, in the linked implementation, the index position has to be calculated each time. Third, we can use the linked implementation, storing both the index position and the data for that position in each node. While all three of these alternatives are feasible, we focus on only the first two here and compare the results. You are asked to implement the third approach in the exercises at the end of the chapter.

In the array implementation, the sequence

$$\text{Store}(\text{Store}(\ldots \text{Store}(\text{Create}, 1, v_1), \ldots), n-1, v_{n-1}), n, v_n)$$

corresponds to the array

1	2		n−1	n		Max
v_1	v_2	$\bullet\,\bullet\,\bullet$	v_{n-1}	v_n	$\bullet\,\bullet\,\bullet$	

Each index in the array up to n corresponds to the position number in a Store operation, and the contents of the array element correspond to the value stored. Because the Store axiom replaces what is there (if anything), duplicate items cannot be stored in a single position, and there is no ambiguity concerning which values should go into the array.

For this implementation, we let the user declare the instances of type BoundedSequenceType and handle errors through the exception ERROR.

(* Gain access to ValueType and Max. *)
USES <data defining module>

```
TYPE
    BoundedSequenceType = RECORD (* Bounded Representation *)
        Length     : Integer;
        Items      : ARRAY [1..Max] OF ValueType
    END RECORD
```

Create(VAR S : BoundedSequence)

```
Sequence.Length ← 0
```

Length(Sequence: BoundedSequenceType): Integer

```
RETURN Sequence.Length
```

**Store (VAR Sequence: BoundedSequenceType, Index: IndexType,
Value: ValueType)**

```
IF Index <= Sequence.Length + 1
    THEN
        Sequence.Items[Index] ← Value
        IF Index = Sequence.Length + 1
            THEN  Sequence.Length ← Sequence.Length + 1
        END IF
    ELSE   ERROR
END IF
```

**Insert (VAR Sequence: BoundedSequenceType, Index: IndexType,
Value: ValueType)**

```
IF Index <= 1 + Sequence.Length
    THEN
        Sequence.Length ← Sequence.Length + 1
        Counter ← Sequence.Length
        WHILE (Index < Counter) DO
            Sequence.Items[Counter] ← Sequence.Items[Counter − 1]
            Counter ← Counter − 1
        END WHILE
        Sequence.Items[Index] ← Value
    ELSE   ERROR
END IF
```

**Retrieve (Sequence: BoundedSequenceType, Index: IndexType, VAR Value:
ValueType)**

```
IF Index <= Sequence.Length
    THEN  Value ← Sequence.Items[Index]
    ELSE  ERROR
END IF
```

Delete (VAR Sequence: BoundedSequenceType, Index: IndexType)

```
IF Index <= Sequence.Length
    THEN
        Sequence.Length ← Sequence.Length − 1
        FOR Counter ← Index TO Sequence.Length DO
            Sequence.Items[Counter] ← Sequence.Items[Counter + 1]
        END FOR
    ELSE  ERROR
END IF
```

Replace (VAR Sequence: BoundedSequenceType, Index: IndexType, Value: ValueType)

```
IF Sequence.Length >= Index
    THEN  Sequence.Items[Index] ← Value
    ELSE  ERROR
END IF
```

Find (Sequence: BoundedSequenceType, Value: ValueType) : IndexType

```
Index ← 1
WHILE (Index <= Sequence.Length )
AND (Sequence.Items[Index] <> Value) DO
    Index ← Index + 1
END WHILE
IF Index <= Sequence.Length
    THEN   RETURN Index
    ELSE   ERROR
END IF
```

With the natural correspondence between the Store operations and the array elements, it is straightforward to check that this implementation satisfies the various Sequence ADT axioms. Details are left to the exercises.

Before we go on to the unbounded implementation, we determine the order of the operations in the bounded implementation. Create, Length, Store, Retrieve, and Replace are all O(1). Insert and Delete have loops from the index to the end of the sequence. Find has a loop from the beginning of the sequence up to the point where a certain value is found or all values have been checked. Therefore, Insert, Delete, and Find are O(Length(Sequence)), that is, O(N).

Turning to the linked-list implementation, we have chosen to keep an explicit length field, because so many of the operations check the length to determine if an error situation exists. The declarations and algorithms follow.

```
(* Unbounded implementation *)
TYPE
    PointerType = ↑ValueNode;
    ValueNode =  RECORD
```

```
        Value    : ValueType;
        Next     : PointerType
END RECORD

UnBoundSequenceType = RECORD
        Length   : Integer;
        Items    : PointerType
END RECORD
```

Create(VAR Sequence: UnBoundSequenceType)

```
Sequence.Length ← 0
Sequence.Items ← NIL
```

Length (Sequence:UnBoundSequenceType):Integer

```
Length ← Sequence.Length
```

Replace (VAR Sequence: UnBoundSequenceType, Index: IndexType, Value: ValueType)

```
IF Index <= Sequence.Length
    THEN
        FindIndexPosition(Sequence.Items, Index, Ptr)
        Ptr↑.Value ← Value
    ELSE   ERROR
END IF
```

FindIndexPosition (SequenceUnBoundSequenceType, Index: IndexType, VAR Ptr: PointerType)

FindIndexPosition is a hidden operation; that is, the user of the Sequence ADT does not have access to this operation. It is used only in implementing the other operations.

```
Counter ← 1
Ptr ← Sequence.Items
WHILE Counter < Index DO
    Counter ← Counter + 1
    Ptr ← Ptr↑.Next
END WHILE
```

Store (VAR Sequence: UnBoundSequenceType, Index: IndexType, Value: ValueType)

```
IF Index <= Sequence.Length + 1
    THEN
        IF Index = Sequence.Length + 1
            THEN  Insert(Sequence, Index, Value)
```

```
                        ELSE   Replace(Sequence, Index, Value)
                END IF
        ELSE   ERROR
    END IF
```

Insert(VAR Sequence: UnBoundSequenceType, Index: IndexType, Value: ValueType)

Insert can use FindIndexPosition, but the position we need here is the position before Index. Therefore, we pass Index − 1 as a parameter; that is, we need to change the pointer field of the item before the insertion point. We also need to check to see if we are inserting at the first position, in which case we must change the external pointer to the sequence Sequence.Items.

```
IF Index <= Sequence.Length + 1
    THEN
        New(NewNode)
        NewNode↑.Value ← Value
        Sequence.Length ← Sequence.Length + 1
        IF Index = 1
            THEN
                NewNode↑.Next ← Sequence.Items
                Sequence.Items ← NewNode
            ELSE
                FindIndexPosition (Sequence, Index − 1, Ptr)
                NewNode↑.Next ← Ptr↑.Next
                Ptr↑.Next ← NewNode
        END IF
    ELSE   ERROR
END IF
```

Retrieve(Sequence: UnBoundSequenceType, Index: IndexType, VAR Value: ValueType)

```
If Index <= Sequence.Length
    THEN
        FindIndexPosition(Sequence, Index, Ptr)
        Value ← Ptr↑.Value
    ELSE   ERROR
END IF
```

Delete (VAR Sequence: UnBoundSequenceType, Index: IndexType)

Again, we need the position before the deletion point, so the call to FindIndex Position must ask for the Index − 1 position. We also need to see if we are deleting the first item, so that the external pointer can be properly set. In the following code, we assume that unreferenced nodes are identified and deallocated by the system. Code must be added if we want to deallocate the space for nodes ourselves.

```
IF Index <= Sequence.Length
    THEN
        IF Index = 1
            Sequence.Length ← Sequence.Length − 1
            THEN  Sequence.Items ← Sequence.Items↑.Next
            ELSE
                FindIndexPosition(Sequence, Index − 1, Ptr)
                Ptr↑.Next ← Ptr↑.Next↑.Next
            END IF
    ELSE  ERROR
END IF
```

Find(Sequence: UnBoundSequenceType, Value: ValueType): IndexType

```
Ptr ← Sequence.Items
Index ← 1
WHILE (Index ≤ Sequence.Length) AND (Ptr↑.Value <> Value) DO
    Index ← Index + 1
    Ptr ← Ptr↑.Next
END WHILE
IF Index > Sequence.Length
    THEN   ERROR
    ELSE   RETURN Index
```

As with arrays, the correspondence between a sequence of Store operations and the implementation is straightforward, as is the verification that this implementation satisfies the Sequence ADT axioms. The proof of correctness is left as an exercise.

Create and Length are O(1). All other operations have O(Sequence.Length) because they must search for either the proper position or a specific value. The complexity of the two implementations is summarized in Table 6.1, where N is Sequence.Length.

Application: Strings

We have not included the string as a separate abstract data type. Instead, we believe that the string is a special case of the sequence where the ValueType is Character. The other operations normally associated with strings, such as concatenate, substring, and pattern match, can be specified using the sequence axioms.

We now use strings as the application for sequences. We specify additional string operations, consider the implications of these operations on the implementation structure, and then look at a well-known algorithm for string matching.

The interface and axioms for the additional operations are given below. Concat(S1, S2) forms a string with S2 placed at the end of S1; SubStr (S, i1, i2) forms the string of i2 characters, beginning at position i1 in string S; IsSubSequence (S1,

Table 6.1   Comparison of Bounded and Unbounded Implementation of the ADT Sequence

Operation	Bounded	Unbounded
Create	O(1)	O(1)
Length	O(1)	O(1)
Store	O(1)	O(N)
Insert	O(N)	O(N)
Replace	O(1)	O(N)
Delete	O(N)	O(N)
Retrieve	O(1)	O(N)
Find	O(N)	O(N)

S2) determines if the characters of S2 appear contiguously in the same order within S1. We also define an additional constructor that appends characters (values) onto the end of the string (sequence).

> **structure** Sequence (of <IndexType, ValueType>)
> **interface** Append(Sequence, ValueType)   → Sequence
> Concat(Sequence, Sequence)   → Sequence
> SubStr(Sequence, IndexType, IndexType)   → Sequence
> IsSubSequence(Sequence, Sequence)   → Boolean
> **end**
> **axioms**   **for all S1, S2 in Sequence, i1, i2 in Index, and v1, v2 in Value, let**
> Append(S1, v1) = Store(S1, Length(S1) + 1, v1)
>
> Concat(S1, Create) = S1
> Concat(S1, Append(S2, v1)) = Append((Concat(S1, S2), v1)
>
> SubStr(Create, i1, i2) = Create
> SubStr(Append(S1, v1), i1, i2) =
>   IF (i2 = 0) OR (i1 + i2 − 1) > Length(Append(S1,v1))
>   THEN Create
>   ELSE IF (i1 + i2 − 1) = Length(Append(S, v1))
>   THEN Append(SubStr(S1, i1, i2 − 1), v1)
>   ELSE   SubStr(S1, i1, i2)
>   END IF
>
> IsSubSequence(S1, Create) = True
> IsSubSequence(Create, S2) = False
> IsSubSequence(Store(S1, v1, i1, Store(S2, v2, i2)) =
>   IF (v1 = v2) AND Restmatch(S1, S2)
>   THEN True
>   ELSE   IsSubSequence(S1, Store(S2, V2, i2)
>   END IF

Restmatch(S1, Create) = True
Restmatch(Create, S2) = False
Restmatch(Store(S1, v1, i1), Store(S2, v2, i2) =
    IF (v1 = v2)
        THEN Restmatch(S1, S2)
        ELSE   Restmatch = False
    END IF
    end
endSequence

The axioms for Concat specify that the second string is concatenated onto the end of the first string. The axioms for SubStr specify that characters are collected from the right of the string, beginning with the last one. In contrast, the axioms for IsSubSequences specify that the match is from left to right. An exercise asks you to specify these axioms in a different way. Notice that we had to use an auxiliary function Restmatch in defining IsSubSequence in order to guarantee that the match returns true only if the pattern string (S2) is found in continuous positions within S1.

The axioms for the additional functions are actually recursive algorithms using the ADT Sequence. While they can be coded exactly as stated, this implementation is not very efficient. Instead, we consider nonrecursive algorithms for these string functions. Because we are using the Sequence ADT as the base for strings, we consider the two sequence implementations described previously. We discuss these algorithms and analyze which implementation is more efficient, but we leave the writing of the algorithms as an end-of-chapter exercise.

The Concat function takes two input strings, S1 and S2, and returns the string made of the second (S2) concatenated onto the back of the first (S1). This operation can be viewed as creating a completely new string or as altering the first string. If returning a new string in the array implementation, the first string is copied into the result string and the second string is copied into the result string following the first. Therefore, the complexity would be O(S1.Length + S2.Length). In the second case, where the result is returned in the first string, only the second string is copied, giving a complexity of O(S2.Length). The danger in the bounded implementation is that the strings tend to become large. The maximum on the string size would have to be set quite high.

In the unbounded implementation, if a new string is returned, both strings would have to be traversed and copied, giving O(S1.Length + S2.Length). If the first string is altered, the next field of the last item in S1 is set to point to the first item in S2. A traversal of the first string is required in order the find the last item. If the Concat operation is used frequently with this interpretation, a pointer to the last item in the string should be included in the record, and the algorithms adjusted accordingly. Without the additional pointer, the order is O(S1.Length); with the change, the order is O(1).

The SubStr operation takes a string and two integer values (i1, i2) and returns a string of length i2, beginning at the i1 position in the input string. This would be quite easy using the array implementation. Because there is direct access to where the new string begins, the order would be O(i2). In the unbounded version, the order would be O(i1 + i2), because S1 would have to be traversed from the beginning up to the last character in the substring.

The IsSubSequence function returns True if the second string (S2) is found in the first string (S1), and False otherwise. Both of the strings have to be traversed. Does it really matter which implementation we use? Yes, in this case it is critical, as we shall see by considering a simple, straightforward algorithm and analyzing its order for each implementation.

Rather than call these strings S1 and S2, we call the string being searched S and the pattern being searched for P. We begin by looking in S for the first occurrence of the first character in P. If we do not find a match, IsSubSequence returns False. If we do find a match (say at S_i), we continue to match successive characters until the match fails or the last character in P is matched successfully. If a failure occurs, we begin searching at S_{i+1} for the first character in P.

IsSubSequence

```
IF Length(S) >= Length(P)
    THEN
        Found ← False
        Sindex ← 0
        WHILE ((SIndex + Length(P)) < Length(S)) AND NOT Found DO
            SIndex ← SIndex + 1
            IF Retrieve(P, 1) = Retrieve(S, SIndex)
                THEN
                    PIndex ← 2
                    WHILE (PIndex < Length(P)) AND DO (Retrieve(P, PIndex)
                            = Retrieve (S, SIndex + PIndex − 1))
                        PIndex ← PIndex + 1
                    END WHILE
                    Found ← (PIndex = Length(P)) AND
                        (Retrieve(P, PIndex) = Retrieve(S, SIndex + PIndex − 1))
            END IF
        END WHILE
    ELSE    ERROR
END IF
RETURN Found
```

In the worst case, the outer loop executes approximately Length(S) times and the inner loop executes approximately Length(P) times. The ADT Sequence operations used are Length and Retrieve. In general terms, therefore, the work involved with this code may be described as follows:

```
WHILE (1..Length(S))
    Use Retrieve on P and S and compare results
    WHILE (1..Length(P))
        Use Retrieve on P and S and compare results
    Use Retrieve on P and S and compare results
```

Focusing upon the inner loop in the worse case, we find Retrieve is used about Length(S) * Length(P) times. Length is O(1) in both implementations. Retrieve is O(1) in the bounded, array-based version, and O(N) in the linked-list version, although Retrieve(P,1) is O(1) in both. (Why?)

In the array implementation, therefore, an O(1) operation is done Length(S) * Length(P) times, and the result has O(Length(S) * Length(P)). In the linked-list implementation, on average, Retrieve has to search down half of P and half of S for each comparison. Thus, the amount of work is proportional to the sizes of P and S, (that is, to Length(P) + Length(S). Because this work is done Length(S) * Length(P) times, the result has O(Length(S) * Length(P) * (Length(S) + Length(P))).

The complexity of the IsSubSequence function is one order greater in the unbounded implementation. Does this mean that the unbounded implementation should never be used if pattern matching is a required operation? No, the varying size of the strings may require that the unbounded implementation be used. The moral is that the total collection of operations must be examined before a decision is made.

Knuth-Morris-Pratt Pattern-Matching Algorithm

Pattern matching has intrigued computer scientists for years. In the straightforward algorithm, the search is always resumed by trying to match the first character in the pattern with the character in S that immediately follows the one that matched the first character in P on the previous failure. For example, look at the following string and pattern.

P: A B A B D

S: C A C A B A B A B D

Think of sliding the pattern to the right over the string until the first character in the pattern matches a character in S. The first match occurs at the second character in S.

P: A B A B D

S: C A C A B A B A BD

The match on the second character of the pattern fails, so the pattern is slid one character to the right until another match is found—in this case, the fourth character in the sequence matches the first character in the pattern.

P: A B A B D

S: C A C A B A B A B D

The match continues successfully until the last character in the pattern is reached, where the pattern has a D and the string has an A. Our algorithm continues trying to match the first character in the pattern with the fifth character in the string. But if we continue trying to match the third character in the pattern with the eighth character in the string, we find our complete match without having to go back to the beginning of the pattern.

P: A B A B D

S: C A C A B A B A B D

This observation leads to an algorithm for pattern matching known as the Knuth-Morris-Pratt algorithm. This algorithm examines the pattern and determines for each character in the pattern where to resume matching when a failure occurs. We call these positions *failure links* for each character in the pattern. The failure links for P in our example are given below.

P: A B A B D

Fail: 0 1 1 2 3

The failure links are actually indexes into the pattern. When a failure occurs, the index into the pattern (PIndex) is reset to the failure link associated with PIndex. Matching continues with the current position in the string (SIndex) and the pattern indexed by the new PIndex. The 0 for the first position of the failure links means that SIndex must be incremented, and the matching process begins again, looking for a match with the first character of the pattern. The consequence of this algorithm is that the character at SIndex may be examined more than once, but you never have to back up to examine a previous character in the string.

IsSubSequence(S, P: BoundedSequenceType; Fail: FailLinksType) : Boolean

(∗ KMP algorithm∗)

```
Found ← False
PIndex ← 1
SIndex ← 1
WHILE((SIndex+Length(P)−PIndex) <= Length(S)) AND NOT Found DO
    IF (Retrieve(P, PIndex) = Retrieve(S, SIndex))
        THEN
            IF PIndex = Length(P)
                THEN   Found ← True
                ELSE
                    SIndex ← SIndex + 1
                    PIndex ← PIndex + 1
            END IF
        ELSE IF Fail[PIndex] <> 0
                THEN PIndex ← Fail[PIndex]
                ELSE
                    SIndex ← SIndex + 1
                    PIndex ← 1
        END IF
END WHILE
RETURN Found
```

The effect of resetting PIndex is to slide the pattern to the right over the string. SIndex is always being incremented. This means that the same algorithm could be used with a pattern and a file where you read a new character instead of incrementing SIndex.

Now all we have to do is determine the failure links. If we have a failure at PIndex, we need to find a prior substring that ends in the character at position PIndex $-$ 1. That is, the failure link for PIndex should be the character position following an initial substring of P that matches a substring ending at PIndex $-$ 1. The second part of the Knuth-Morris-Pratt algorithm finds these substrings and stores the failure links in an array.

SetFailureLinks(VAR Fail: FailLinksType, P: String)

```
Fail[1] ← 0
FOR PIndex ← 2 TO Length(P) DO
    I ← Fail[PIndex − 1]
    WHILE (I > 0) AND (Retrieve(P,PIndex − 1) <> Retrieve(P,I)) DO
        I ← Fail[I]
    END WHILE
    Fail[Pindex] ← I + 1
END FOR
```

As an example, we apply the algorithm to the pattern ABABD.

Fail[1] ← 0
PIndex ← 2
I ← Fail[1] = 0
0 = 0: loop condition fails
Fail[2] ← 1

PIndex ← 3
I ← Fail[2] = 1
1 > 0 AND B <> A: loop condition succeeds
I ← Fail[1] = 0
0 = 0: loop condition fails
Fail[3] ← 1

PIndex ← 4
I ← Fail[3] = 1
1 > 0 AND A = A: loop condition fails
Fail[4] ← 2

PIndex ← 5
I ← Fail[4] = 2
2 > 0 AND B = B: loop condition fails
Fail[5] ← 3

Unsorted

The unsorted, nonindexed, linear structured data type is what most users mean when they say "linear list." The property of position that is used in the indexed linear structured data type is implicitly here, but is immaterial to the user. The operations do not use position as a parameter.

Specification

We worked through the specification of the UnsortedList ADT as an example in Chapter 1. We repeat it here without further comment.

structure UnsortedList (of ItemType)
interface Create   → UnsortedList
           Make(UnsortedList, ItemType)   → UnsortedList
           Delete(UnsortedList, ItemType)   → UnsortedList
           Head(UnsortedList)   → ItemType
           Tail(UnsortedList)   → UnsortedList
           IsEmpty(UnsortedList)   → Boolean
           IsIn(UnsortedList, ItemType)   → Boolean
           Length(UnsortedList)   → Integer
   end

axioms   **for i1, i2 in ItemType, L in UnsortedList, let**
Head(Create) = Error
Head(Make(L, i1)) = i1

Tail(Create) = Error
Tail(Make(L, i1)) = L

Delete(Create, i1) = Create
Delete(Make(L, i2), i1) =
    IF i1 = i2
       THEN L
       ELSE   Make(Delete(L, i1), i2)
    END IF

IsEmpty(Create) = True
IsEmpty(Make(L, i1)) = False

IsIn(Create, i1) = False
IsIn(Make(L, i2), i1) =
    IF i1 = i2
       THEN True
       ELSE   IsIn(L, i1)
    END IF

$$Length(Create) = 0$$
$$Length(Make(L, i1)) = 1 + Length(L)$$

    end
end UnsortedList

Implementation

In Chapter 2, we looked at the complexity of the operations of the UnsortedList ADT using both an array-based implementation and a linked implementation. The implementation of the ADT UnsortedList became the basis for two of our list primitives. In Chapter 3, we used the UnsortedList ADT to demonstrate our module pseudocode. Thus, enough has already been said about implementing unsorted lists.

Sorted

The sorted, nonindexed data type differs from the unsorted version in the same way that the array and sequence differ: the sorted type has three basic constructors and the unsorted has only two. The extra constructor imposes an ordering on the items within the data type. The Insert in the Sequence ADT uses the ordering of the indexes associated with an item to determine where the item goes within the sequence. The Insert in the SortedList ADT uses the inherent ordering of the items themselves to determine the position of the item.

Specification

Because the SortedList axioms for Delete, Head, Tail, IsEmpty, IsIn, and Length are the same as those for the UnsortedList, they are not repeated. The Insert operation is the only new operation to be considered here; Insert adds an element to a sorted list in a way that guarantees that the new list also is sorted.

    structure   SortedList (of ItemType)
    interface   Create $\rightarrow$ SortedList
                   Make(SortedList, ItemType) $\rightarrow$ SortedList
                   Insert(SortedList, ItemType) $\rightarrow$ SortedList
                   Delete(SortedList, ItemType) $\rightarrow$ SortedList
                   Head(SortedList) $\rightarrow$ ItemType
                   Tail(SortedList) $\rightarrow$ SortedList
                   IsEmpty(SortedList) $\rightarrow$ Boolean
                   IsIn(SortedList) $\rightarrow$ Boolean
                   Length(SortedList) $\rightarrow$ Integer
    end

axioms　　for i1, i2 in ItemType, L in SortedList, let
　　　　　Insert(Create, i1) = Make(Create, i1)
　　　　　Insert((Make(L, i2), i1) =
　　　　　　　IF i1 < i2
　　　　　　　　　THEN　Make(Insert(L, i1), i2)
　　　　　　　　　ELSE　Make(Make(L, i2), i1)
　　　　　　　END IF
　　end
end SortedList

Implementation

In Chapter 2, we examined the implementation of a sorted list when we defined the list primitives. We informally have used the SortedList ADT when discussing the implementation of both unstructured and semi-structured abstract data types. In fact, being able to implement a sorted list was a prerequisite for this course. Look carefully at the axioms for Insert; they specify exactly what you have been doing.

No iterator is defined for ADTs UnsortedList or SortedList because Head and Tail can be used to iterate through either list. However, the list is destroyed if we implement Tail literally. An alternate implementation for Head, Tail, and IsEmpty is to leave the list intact but have an associated pointer that initially points to the first item in the list. The Head operation returns the item pointed to by the pointer; Tail moves this pointer to point to the next item; and IsEmpty returns true if the pointer points beyond the last item. In the array version, IsEmpty is true if the pointer is Length + 1; in the linked version, IsEmpty is true if the pointer is NIL.

Application: Sparse Matrices

We have already shown a variety of applications for unsorted and sorted lists in the previous chapters. Here, we use variations of the SortedList ADT to show other implementations of the matrix module when we expect our matrix has relatively few nonzero elements. Such matrices are called **sparse matrices**. In certain circumstances, these implementations can save both space and time over our previous implementation.

> **Sparse Matrix** A matrix with relatively few nonzero elements.

For example, consider the following matrix with four rows and five columns:

Matrix A:

$$\begin{pmatrix} 0 & 10 & 0 & 0 & 0 \\ 15 & 0 & 8 & 0 & 6 \\ 0 & 20 & 0 & 0 & 0 \\ -20 & 0 & 0 & 16 & 0 \end{pmatrix}$$

Thirteen of the 20 places in the matrix are zero. With such a matrix, we store only the <row, column, value> triples shown below, rather than all matrix entries. The overall size of the matrix is stored separately.

Row	Column	Value
1	2	10
2	1	15
2	3	8
2	5	6
3	2	20
4	1	−20
4	4	16

There are several choices for the storage of these triples. One simple structure for this storage is the SortedList ADT. In this approach, we expand our definition of ItemType for the SortedList to be a record in which the key is the combined <row, column>. The extra information associated with the key is the value in that position. How is this different from representing the matrix as a keyedtable? The items are the same, but the operations on the structures are different. The keyedtable is unordered; the sortedlist is ordered. All accesses into the keyedtable are by key; all accesses into the sortedlist are by Head or Tail.

Of course, with any implementation, we still must have the same matrix operations, including MatrixCreate, StoreValue, MatrixAdd, MatrixSub, MatrixMult, and Transpose. For many of these operations, processing may be speeded up considerably if the <row, column, value> triples are kept in a sorted list, as we shall see. Specifically, suppose we order the keys first by row and then by column within the same row. In our example, this list would have the following form:

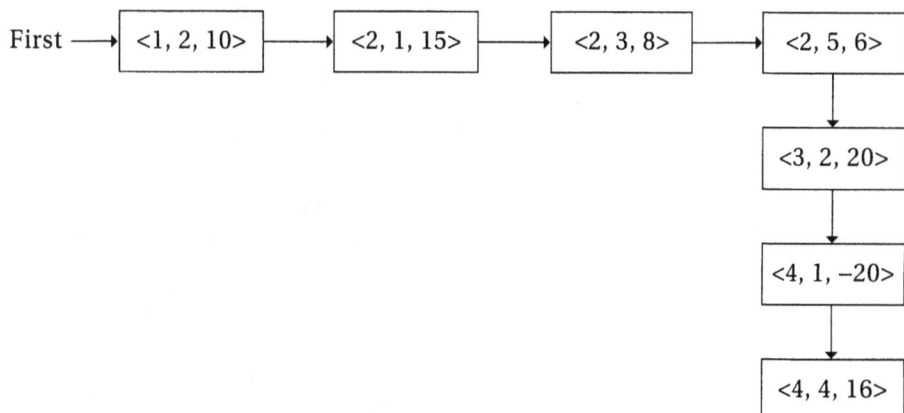

Our interface would look like this:

Interface Section MatrixOperations

```
(* To access ItemsType and Compare. *)
(* ItemType is a Row, Column, Value > *)
USES <name of data defining module>, SortedList

TYPE
    MatrixType = RECORD
        NumberRows,
        NumberColumns      : Integer;
        Values             : SortedList
    END RECORD;
```

MatrixCreate(Rows, Columns, A) simply records the dimensions of the array and sets Values to NIL. StoreValue(A, Value, Row, Col) adds or changes a corresponding entry on the list. For MatrixAdd(A, B, C) or MatrixSub(A, B, C), the resulting entry in C is zero unless the corresponding entry in either A or B is nonzero. To perform addition or subtraction, we could go through lists A and B following much the same approach as in Set Difference. If an entry on A comes before the next one on B, then the matrix value in B corresponding to that A entry must be zero, and the sum for that entry in C is just the A entry. Similarly, if an entry on B comes before the next one on A, then the B entry can be copied to C for the sum. If an entry on A has a corresponding entry on B, then these values can be added to get the C entry.

More precisely, suppose the subprogram Compare takes two entries of ItemType and compares them to see if the first entry comes before the second (in a scan by row), if they are the same row and column, or if the first comes after the second. Suppose also that GetNextEntry gets the next matrix entry and sets a Boolean flag if the last one has been processed, and CompleteList copies the unprocessed items in one of the matrices (if any exist). Then the algorithm for MatrixAdd is as follows:

MatrixAdd (A, B: MatrixType, VAR C: MatrixType)

```
Matrix Create(A.NumberRows, B.NumberColumns, C)
GetNextEntry (A.Values, Entry A, Continue)
GetNextEntry (B.Values, Entry B, Continue)
WHILE Continue DO
    CASE Compare(EntryA, EntryB) OF
        Before :  Insert(C.Values, EntryA)
                  GetNextEntry(A.Values, EntryA, Continue)
        Equal  :  EntryA.Value ← EntryA.Value + EntryB.Value
                  Insert(C.Values, EntryB)
                  GetNextEntry(A.Values, EntryA, Continue)
                  GetNextEntry(B.Values, EntryB, Continue)
        After  :  Insert(C.Values, EntryB)
                  GetNextEntry(B.Values, EntryB, Continue)
    END CASE
```

```
END WHILE
IF NOT IsEmpty(A.Values)
      THEN  CompleteList(C, A.Values, EntryA)
END IF
IF NOT IsEmtpy(B.Values)
      THEN  CompleteList(C, B.Values, EntryB)
END IF
```

The code for MatrixSub is similar.

The transpose operation involves interchanging rows and columns, so the triple <i, j, value> should give rise to the entry <j, i, value> in the transpose. GetNextEntry can be used to iterate through the input matrix. The row and column of each entry is interchanged and the entry is inserted into the result.

In matrix multiplication, each row of A must be accessed in parallel with a column of B. In the original listing, both A and B are ordered by row and then by column within the row. However, in computing the product, we need to access B by column and then by row within column. While this requires some care, the processing becomes simpler if we first consider Transpose (B), as the rows of Transpose (B) correspond to the columns of B itself.

In much of this work, processing is more efficient if we can access rows individually rather than having to traverse one linked list for every entry. Such access may be provided in several ways. An elementary approach uses the same SortedList ADT structure already discussed, but just adds another set of pointers to mark the start of each row. The corresponding diagram for our example is shown below.

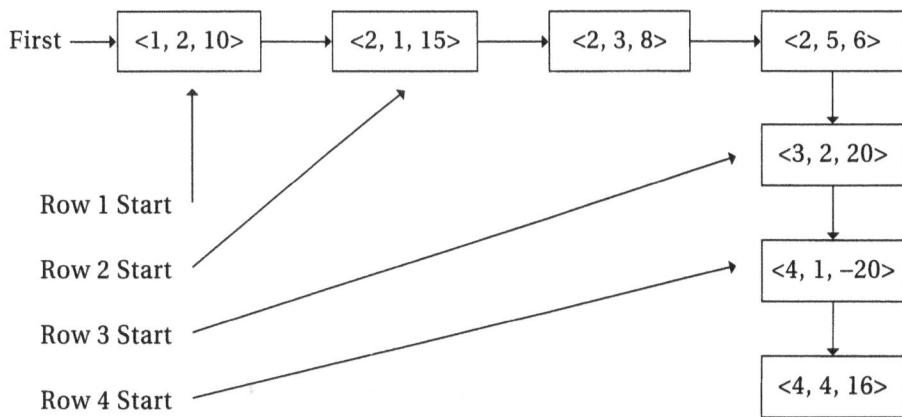

A variation of this approach reduces storage demands by removing the row number from the SortedList ADT entries. Only <column, value> pairs are stored, and row numbers are inferred by comparison with the row pointers. This approach yields the following structure for our example:

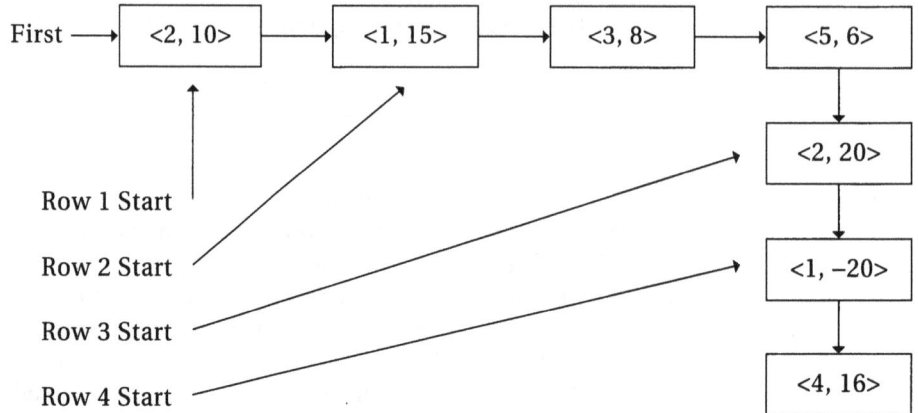

First → | <2, 10> | → | <1, 15> | → | <3, 8> | → | <5, 6> |

| <2, 20> |

| <1, −20> |

| <4, 16> |

Row 1 Start
Row 2 Start
Row 3 Start
Row 4 Start

In a variation of these approaches, the entries for each row could be kept in completely separate lists. For our example, these lists have the following form:

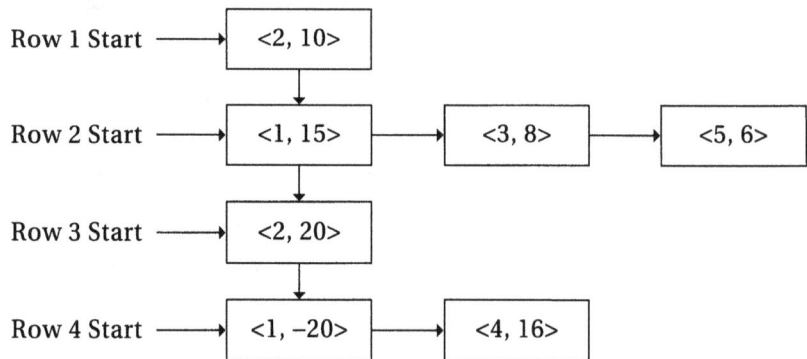

Row 1 Start → | <2, 10> |

Row 2 Start → | <1, 15> | → | <3, 8> | → | <5, 6> |

Row 3 Start → | <2, 20> |

Row 4 Start → | <1, −20> | → | <4, 16> |

Still another approach is motivated by the need in matrix multiplication to have access to columns as well as rows. In this approach, pointers are kept for each row as well as for each column. Applying this structure to our example yields the following:

Column
First Pointers

Row   [1]   [2]   [3]   [4]   [5]

[1] ——————————————→ <1,2,10>

[2] ——→ <2,1,15> ——————→ <2,3,8> ——————→ <2,5,6>

[3] ——————→ <3,2,20>

[4] ——→ <4,1,−20> ——————————————→ <4,4,16>

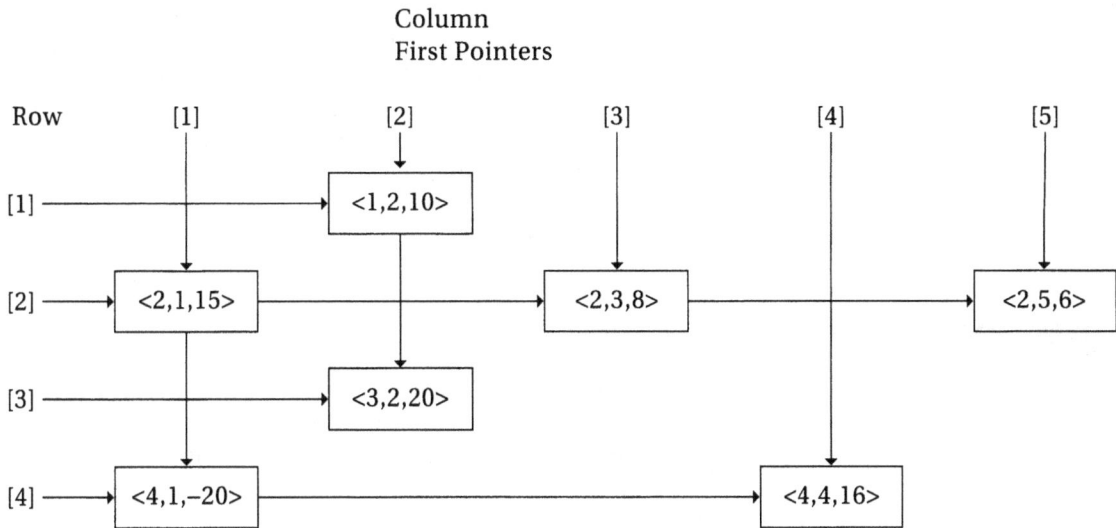

To clarify this structure, we could follow either row or column pointers in this figure for array A[1..4, 1..5] to conclude that A[1,2] = 10 and A[2,5] = 6. An array entry not shown in a list (for instance, A[1, 1]) has the default value (0 for A[1, 1]).

As a final variation, we might replace the initial array of first-row and first-column pointers by linked lists or trees. In these formats, we follow a linked list or a (binary search) tree to find the first nonzero entry in a row or column. Thereafter, we follow next pointers to find successive nonzero entries in the row or column.

Complexity

Just to review, in our discussion of sparse matrices, we considered the following implementations:

1. Single, sorted list of triples.
2. Single, sorted list of triples, with additional row pointers.
3. Single, sorted list of pairs, with additional row pointers.
4. Separate, sorted lists of pairs or triples, with a separate list for each row.
5. Pairs of triples stored in lists both by row and by column, with first pointers stored in arrays.
6. Pairs of triples stored in lists both by row and by column, with first pointers stored in linked lists.
7. Pairs of triples stored in lists both by row and by column, with first pointers stored in another structure (for example, in a binary search tree or hash table).

Each of these approaches can lead to code that correctly implements the operations described for matrix operations. Of course, the efficiency for these approaches varies. For example, approaches 1, 6, and 7 require only a simple initialization for the MatrixCreate command, while approaches 2, 3, 4, and 5 require that arrays of pointers be initialized to 0 or nil. Thus, approaches 1, 6, and 7 have O(1) for MatrixCreate, while the others have O(N), where N is the number of rows or columns. The efficiency of the other operations is left for you to determine in the exercises at the end of the chapter.

SUMMARY

Structured linear data types are sequential lists of items. If the items are accessed by their positions within the list, they are indexed linear lists; if the items are accessed sequentially by moving from one to the next, they are nonindexed linear lists. Arrays and sequences are indexed; sorted and unsorted lists are nonindexed.

Arrays are used so often to represent sequences in a program that the two are frequently confused. There are, however, two distinctions between arrays and sequences. Arrays are fixed in size (bounded); the Create operation returns the structure with the index part of the <index, value> pairs already defined. Also, for arrays, once a value is stored with an index, the value stays bound to the index until another value is stored with that same index.

In contrast, the sequence is usually thought of as an unbounded data type, and the binding of the index and the value is only temporary. This binding represents the current position of the value within the sequence. An array is *always* and *only* a bounded data type, but we could specify a bounded version of a sequence by having the maximum number of items as a parameter to the Create function and by specifying that the length of the sequence could not exceed that maximum. If the bounded version of the sequence is specified, then either an array-based or a linked implementation can be used.

Both arrays and records have their structures defined by the Create operation. The array, however, is linear because the index type is ordered, and the record is unstructured because the set of fields is not ordered.

Sorted and unsorted lists are those that are accessed sequentially from beginning to end. The items are not accessed by position. The only difference in the sorted and unsorted specifications is the additional operator Insert in the sorted version. The Insert uses the value of an Item to determine where in the list the item goes. In sorted lists, the items are ordered linearly in terms of the structure in which they reside and logically in terms of the values of the items. In unsorted lists, there does not need to be a relationship between the value of one item and the item next to it in the list.

EXERCISES

1. The chapter gives formulas for the effective address of an array element, given its base address and subscript(s), and the motivation for these formulas is shown through an example.

a. Prove that the formula for a one-dimensional array, as given in the text, is correct.

b. Prove that the formula for a two-dimensional array, as given in the text, is correct.

c. Derive a formula for an n-dimensional array, and justify your answer.

2. The matrix implementation given in this chapter uses the type declaration

```
TYPE
    MatrixType = RECORD
        NumberRows,
        NumberColumns  :Integer;
        Values          : ARRAY [1..MaxRows, 1..MaxColumns] OF ValueType
    END RECORD
```

While this leads to a natural implementation, the size of the matrix is limited to the dimensions specified by MaxRows and MaxColumns. Furthermore, a careful reading of the axioms for the Array ADT does not limit these dimensions.

How might the axioms for the Array ADT be modified to include a limit on the size of possible arrays?

3. The analysis of complexity for the Optimum Sequence Algorithm determined that the main work of computing and updating the variables m and BestK was repeated in the structure

```
FOR Diagonal ← 2 TO N DO
    FOR Row ← 1 TO N − Diagonal + 1 DO
        Compute m, BestK
        FOR k ← Row + 1 TO Row + Diagonal − 1 DO
            Update m, BestK
        END FOR
    END FOR
END FOR
```

This led to the total work being approximated by the sum

$$\text{TotalWork} = \sum_{D=2}^{N} D\,(N − D + 1)$$

where D stands for the variable Diagonal. The text then claimed that, using algebra, one could reduce this to the formula

$$2(N − 1) + 3(N − 2) + 4(N − 3) + \ldots + N(1)$$

This gave rise to the expression

$$\frac{N^3}{6} + \frac{N^2}{2} − \frac{2N}{3}$$

Fill in the algebraic details to prove that this result is correct. (*Hint*: You need formulas for the sums $\sum D$ and $\sum D^2$, which you can find in standard mathematics textbooks.)

4. a. Implement an unbounded sequence using a linked-list structure that stores both the index and the data for that position in a node.

b. Compare the efficiency of this approach with the two described in detail in the chapter.

5. a. Modify the Sequence ADT axioms in the text to specify a maximum size for a sequence.

   b. With this modification, show that the array implementation given in the book satisfies the Sequence ADT axioms.

6. Show that the linked-list implementation for the Sequence ADT given in the book satisfies the axioms as originally stated.

   a. State clearly the correspondence between the sequence of abstract Store operations

   $$\text{Store}(\text{Store}(\ldots \text{Store}(\text{Create}, i_1, v_1), \ldots), i_{n-1}, v_{n-1}), i_n, i_n)$$

   and the data stored within the associated linked list.

   b. Prove that this correspondence is maintained by the various Sequence ADT operations.

7. Consider the array $A[1], \ldots, A[63]$ of 63 elements. Suppose the s-ary parallel search algorithm is used with three processes (not including any processes used to handle endpoints). Suppose further that the item we are searching for is located in $A[37]$.

   Trace the s-ary search algorithm for this example by showing which array elements are examined by which processes at each step.

8. Consider the arrays $A = (2, 3, 4, 5, 7, 9, 10, 13, 14, 16, 17)$ and $B = (3, 6, 9)$. For each element in B, compute both rank (b_i, A) and trank (b_i, A).

9. Consider the arrays $A[1], \ldots, A[n]$ and $B[1], \ldots, B[2n]$, suppose all values in A and B are ordered and distinct, suppose rank $(A[i], B) = 2i - 1$ for each $i = 1, \ldots, n$, and suppose rank $(B[j], A) = j$ div 2 for $j = 1, \ldots, 2n$. When arrays A and B are merged to yield an array $C[1], \ldots, C[3n]$, show the relative positions of the elements of $A[i]$ and $B[j]$ in C. (In other words, what sequence of A's and B's yield C: $A[1], B[1], A[2]$, or $B[1], A[1], B[2]$, or $B[1], B[2], A[1]$, or something else?

10. Evaluate each of the following structures after the given operations.

    L1 ← Create
    L2 ← Store(L1, 1, a)
    L3 ← Store(L2, 2, x)
    L4 ← Store(L3, 3, b)
    R ← Retrieve(L3, 3)
    L5 ← Insert(L4, 2, q)

11. The ADT UnsortedList was defined using Head and Tail. If Last(S) is defined as i_n and Leader(S) is defined as $<i_1, i_2, \ldots i_{n-1}>$, then the ADT UnsortedList can also be defined in terms of Last and Leader. Fill in the blanks of the formal specification of the ADT UnsortedList using Last and Leader.

structure	UnsortedList (of ItemType)	
interface	Create	→ UnsortedList
	Make(UnsortedList, ItemType)	→ _____
	Last(UnsortedList)	→ _____
	Leader(UnsortedList)	→ _____
	Concat(UnsortedList, UnsortedList)	→ _____
	IsEmpty(UnsortedList)	→ _____
	Length(UnsortedList)	→ _____

Axioms for all L1, L2 in UnsortedList, i in ItemType, let

IsEmpty(_____)	=	_____
IsEmpty(_____)	=	_____
Last(Create)	=	_____
Last(Make(L1, i))	=	_____
Leader(Create)	=	_____
Leader(Make(L1, i))	=	_____
Length(Create)	=	_____
Length(Make(L1, i))	=	_____
Concat(L1, Create)	=	_____
Concat(_____)	=	_____

12. Write a procedure that takes the Min table that calculates the optimum way to multiply a series of matrices as input and prints out the matrices showing the order of multiplication using parenthesized notation.

13. Calculate the best way to factor the following series of matrix multiplications.

$$A(5,6)*B(6,8)*C(8,10)*D(10,3)*E(3,5)*F(5,5)$$

14. Rewrite the axioms for the String ADT operations so that

Concat decomposes the first argument,
SubStr works from the left of the string to the right, and
IsSubSequence looks for a match beginning at the end of the strings.

15. In some implementations of arrays, sequences, and lists, elements on these structures are copied to create new structures. In other implementations, external pointers are changed, but the internal structure is not actually changed. For example, consider the following operations for a sequence.

L1 ← Store(Store(Store(Create, 1, a), 2, b), 3, c)
L2 ← Delete (L1, 1)
L3 ← Insert(L2, 2, d)

Here, we would expect L2 to be

Store(Store(Create, 1, b), 2, c)

and L3 to be

Store(Store(Store(Create, 1, b), 2, d), 3, c)

However, if L2 were implemented by just returning a pointer to the old L1 structure and this was changed for L3, then L2 could be rather different (both L2 and L3, for example, have the same head). Explain when a copying mechanism could be added to these implementations to avoid this type of situation.

16. The chapter identified the following approaches to implementing sparse matrices.

a. Single, sorted list of triples.

b. Single, sorted list of triples, with additional row pointers.

c. Single, sorted list of pairs, with additional row pointers.

  d. Separate, sorted lists of pairs or triples, with a separate list for each row.

  e. Pairs or triples stored in lists both by row and by column, with first pointers stored in arrays.

  f. Pairs or triples stored in lists both by row and by column, with first pointers stored in linked lists.

  g. Pairs or triples stored in lists both by row and by column, with first pointers stored in another structure (for example, in a binary search tree or hash table).

  Show how the following matrix would be represented in each of these implementations.

$$\begin{pmatrix} 1 & 0 & 1 & 3 \\ 0 & 2 & 0 & 4 \\ 6 & 0 & 0 & 0 \\ 0 & 0 & 0 & 0 \\ 2 & 1 & 0 & 0 \end{pmatrix}$$

17. Consider each of the sparse-matrix implementations described in the previous exercise.

  a. Describe an algorithm for StoreValue, MatrixAdd, and MatrixMult for implementations a, d, e, and f.

  b. Determine the efficiency of each algorithm from part (a), assuming that approximately one-third of each row and column is nonzero.

  c. Determine the efficiency of each algorithm from part (a), assuming that each row and column has no more than 10 nonzero entries.

  Record your answers to (b) and (c) in the following table.

	Rows & columns 1/3 full			Maximum 10 nonzero entries per row or column		
Impl	Store	Add	Mult	Store	Add	Mult
a						
b						
c						
d						

18. The sparse-matrix implementation, described briefly in the text, is often coded by using an array for first pointers for the rows and another array of first pointers for columns.

  a. Code this sparse-matrix implementation.

  b. Determine the complexity of each operation in your implementation,

    i. assuming about half of each row and each column is zero

    ii. assuming there are no more than 10 nonzero entries in each row and column.

19. The sparse-matrix implementation coded in Exercise 18 still has the limitation that the number of rows and columns is limited by the size of the corresponding arrays of first pointers.

a. Remove this restriction by replacing the array of first pointers by a linked list of first pointers.

b. Determine the complexity of each operation in this new operation, assuming each of the circumstances given in the previous exercise.

20. Augment the String ADT specification with an operation Copy.

21. Implement Copy in both the bounded and unbounded implementations.

22. Write the algorithm for the bounded String ADT operation Concat.

    a. Assume that the Concat operation takes two parameters and alters the first.

    b. Assume that the Concat operation takes three parameters, where the third is the result.

23. Write the algorithm for the unbounded String ADT operation Concat.

    a. Assume that the Concat operation takes two parameters and alters the first.

    b. Assume that the Concat operation takes three parameters, where the third is the result.

24. Write the Append and SubStr operations on the unbounded String ADT.

25. Write the Append and SubStr operations on the bounded String ADT.

26. In defining IsSubSequence, we used an auxiliary function RestMatch. Below is another set of axioms for IsSubSequence. Explain the difference between this axiom and the one given in the text.

    IsSubSequence(S1, Create) = True
    IsSubSequence(Create, S2) = False
    IsSubSequence(Insert(S1, v1, i1), Insert(S2, v2, i2)) =
        IF (v1 = v2) AND IsSubSequence(S1, S2)
            THEN IsSubSequence(S1, S2)
            ELSE   IsSubSequence(S1, Insert(S2, v2, i2))
        END IF

27. Give the reduced expression for the following String ADT.

    Insert(Insert(Insert(Append(Store(Create, 1, a), b), 1, c), 2, d), 2, e)

28. Apply SubString(S, 1, 2) to the following String ADT expression.

    Append(Store(Store(Store(Create, 1, a), 2, b), 3, c), d)

29. Apply IsSubSequence(S1, S2) where S1 and S2 are the String ADT expressions shown below.

    S1: Append(Append(Append(Store(Create, 1, a), b), c), d)

    S2: Insert(Store(Create, 1, b), 1, a)

Binary Trees

In the first part of this book, we encountered a "chicken and egg" problem—that is, we needed a way in which to implement lists of items before we actually got around to defining a list as an abstract data type. Also, we implemented the ADT List in five ways. Four of the primitive implementations were linear; the fifth was a binary search tree implementation. We have not, however, relied upon your understanding of binary search trees thus far.

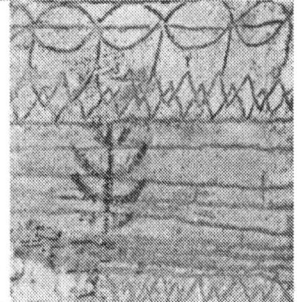

This chapter begins by defining the notion of general trees and introducing some terminology. Attention then focuses upon a particular type of tree, called a binary tree. The formal specifications for the ADT BinTree organize data in a hierarchical structure, but there need not be any special ordering relationship among the data. Implementations for binary trees include traditional approaches with pointers or arrays as well as threaded trees. Decision trees, an application of general binary trees, provide a useful way of viewing program execution and are a powerful tool for determining the best possible efficiency for solving some types of problems. The chapter closes by considering heaps as a special type of binary tree, giving formal specifications, describing a particularly efficient array implementation, and outlining the use of heaps to implement priority queues.

General Trees

The ADT Binary Tree is an abstract data type that models the mathematical object *tree* or *rooted tree*. A tree is defined recursively, as follows:

1. A set of zero objects is a tree, called the *empty tree* or the *null tree*.

2. If $T_1, T_2, \ldots, T_n$ are n trees for $n \geq 0$ and R is an object, called a *node*, then the set T containing R and the trees $T_1, T_2, \ldots, T_n$ is a tree. Within T, R is called the *root* of T and $T_1, T_2, \ldots, T_n$ are called *subtrees*.

When we visualize a tree, we use a box to represent the external name of the tree and circles, boxes, or text to represent the nodes. Lines are drawn from a root to the roots of each of its subtrees. The representation of a tree is shown in Figure 7.1. For reference, we also have labeled each node in these trees.

The tree in Figure 7.1 (a) is the empty tree; there are no nodes. The tree in (b) has only one node, the root. The tree in (c) has 16 nodes. The root node has four subtrees. The roots of these subtrees are called the *children* of the root. Because our definition is recursive, each of the roots of these subtrees has subtrees. There are 16 nodes in the tree, so there are 15 nonempty subtrees. The nodes with no subtrees are called *terminal nodes* or, more commonly, *leaves*. There are 10 leaves

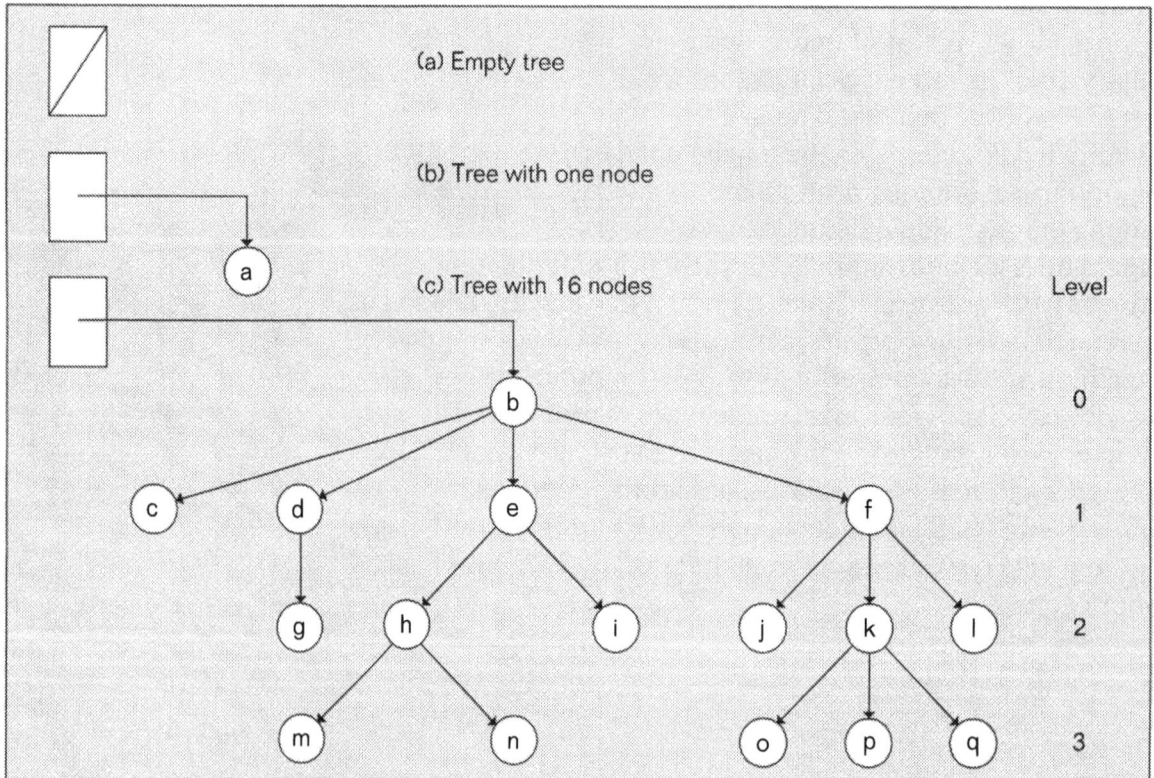

Figure 7.1 Trees with Nodes Labeled with Letters

in the tree in (c). The *degree of a node* is the number of subtrees that it has. Thus, the degrees of the nodes in Figure 7.1 range from zero to four. By definition, the degree of each leaf node is zero. The *degree of a tree* is the maximum degree of a node in the tree. As the tree in (a) has no nodes, there is no maximum degree of a node, and the degree of the tree is not defined. The tree in (b) has degree 0, and the tree in (c) has degree four.

Because family relationships can be modeled as trees, we often call the root of a tree (or subtree) the *parent*, and the roots of the subtrees the *children*. Consequently, the children of a node are called *siblings*.

A great deal of processing takes advantage of the relationship between a parent and its children, and we commonly say a *directed edge* (or, simply, an **edge**) extends from a parent to its children. Thus, edges connect a root with the roots of each subtree. For example, in Figure 7.1 (c), an edge extends from the root b to each of the nodes c, d, e, and f. Similarly, edges extend from e to i and from k to q. An *undirected edge* extends in both directions between a parent and a child. Thus, undirected edges also would extend from i to e and from q to k.

A *directed path* (or, simply, *path*) is a sequence of directed edges $e_1, e_2, \ldots, e_n$ where the node at the end of one edge serves as the beginning of the next edge. An *undirected path* is a similar sequence of undirected edges.

For example, in Figure 7.1 (c) one path containing three edges begins at the root and extends through nodes f, k, and q. Similarly, the path beginning with node h and containing nodes e, b, and d is an undirected path. In this chapter and the next two chapters, when we say *edge* we mean a *directed* edge from a parent to its child. (In Chapter 10, we again introduce the concept of an undirected edge.) Following the analogy of family hierarchies, if a path exists from one node to another, it is common to state that the first node is an *ancestor* of the second, and the second is a *descendant* of the first.

The *length* of a path is the number of edges it contains (which is one less than the number of nodes on the path). The *depth* or *level* of a node is the length of the directed path from the root to that node. The *height* of a tree is the length of the path from the root to a node on the lowest level. Thus, the level of the root of a tree is zero, and the level of each child of the root is one. Equivalently, the height of a tree is the largest level number of any node in the tree.[1]

There are three common ways to systematically order (or list) the nodes in a tree: *preorder*, *inorder*, and *postorder*. For each of these orderings, the empty tree gives rise to the empty list, and the tree with one node yields the list with one node. For trees with more than one node, the following statements are true.

- The preorder list contains the root, followed by the preorder list of the nodes of the subtrees of the root from left to right.

- The inorder list contains the inorder list of the left-most subtree, the root, and the inorder list of each of the other subtrees from left to right.

---

[1] Some texts designate the level of the root to be one. This changes the relation of the level number in various definitions but does not change the definitions themselves.

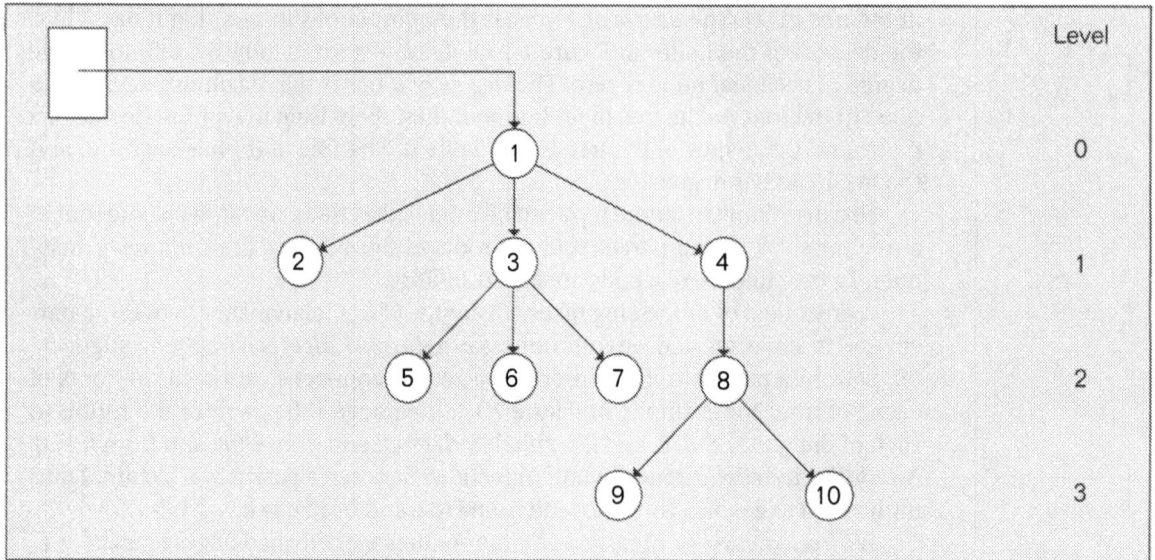

Figure 7.2 Tree with Nodes Labeled with Numbers

- The postorder list contains the postorder list of the subtrees of the root from left to right, followed by the root.

Figure 7.2 shows a tree whose nodes are labeled with numbers rather than letters. Following is a list of terms for review, using a concrete example from the tree in Figure 7.2.

Subtrees The nodes labeled 2, 3, and 4 are the roots of the subtrees (children) of the node labeled 1. The nodes labeled 5, 6, and 7 are the roots of the subtrees (children) of the node labeled 3; the node labeled 8 is the root of the subtree (child) of the node labeled 4. The nodes labeled 9 and 10 are the roots of the subtrees (children) of the node labeled 8.

Leaves The nodes labeled 2, 5, 6, 7, 9, and 10 are terminal nodes or leaf nodes.

Degree The nodes labeled 1 and 3 have degree 3. The node labeled 8 has degree 2. The node labeled 4 has degree 1. All the leaf nodes have degree 0. The degree of the tree is 3, because the maximum degree of any node is 3.

Levels The level numbers appear on the right of the tree. The level of the root is 0, the level of the nodes labeled 2, 3, and 4 is 1, the level of the nodes labeled 5, 6, 7, and 8 is 2, and the level of the nodes labeled 9 and 10 is 3.

Family relationships The node labeled 1 is the parent of the nodes labeled 2, 3, and 4. The node labeled 3 is the parent of the nodes labeled 5, 6, and 7. The node labeled 4 is the parent of the node labeled 8, which, in turn, is the parent of the nodes labeled 9 and 10. The nodes labeled 2, 3, and 4 are siblings. The nodes labeled 5, 6, and 7 are siblings. The nodes labeled 9 and 10 are siblings. Note that the node labeled 8 is not the sibling of the nodes labeled 5, 6, and 7.

Paths and path lengths Paths exist from all parents to children. A unique path exists from the root to each leaf node; these are shown below. The length of each path is also shown. Because any subpath is a path, all of the paths are represented.

$1 \rightarrow 2$	Length: 1
$1 \rightarrow 3 \rightarrow 5$	Length: 2
$1 \rightarrow 3 \rightarrow 6$	Length: 2
$1 \rightarrow 3 \rightarrow 7$	Length: 2
$1 \rightarrow 4 \rightarrow 8 \rightarrow 9$	Length: 3
$1 \rightarrow 4 \rightarrow 8 \rightarrow 10$	Length: 3

Height and depth The height of the tree is 3, the maximum level. The depth of the nodes labeled 2, 3, and 4 is 1. The depth of the nodes labeled 5, 6, 7, and 8 is 2. The depth of the nodes labeled 9 and 10 is 3, the same as the height of the tree. The depth of the nodes on the lowest level is always the same as the height of the tree.

Orderings The preorder, inorder, and postorder orderings of the nodes are given below.

$1 \rightarrow 2 \rightarrow 3 \rightarrow 5 \rightarrow 6 \rightarrow 7 \rightarrow 4 \rightarrow 8 \rightarrow 9 \rightarrow 10$ (preorder)

$2 \rightarrow 1 \rightarrow 5 \rightarrow 3 \rightarrow 6 \rightarrow 7 \rightarrow 9 \rightarrow 8 \rightarrow 10 \rightarrow 4$ (inorder)

$2 \rightarrow 5 \rightarrow 6 \rightarrow 7 \rightarrow 3 \rightarrow 9 \rightarrow 10 \rightarrow 8 \rightarrow 4 \rightarrow 1$ (postorder)

Binary trees are trees where the maximum degree of any node is two. Any general tree can be represented as a binary tree using the following algorithm.

1. Insert an arrow from each node to its right sibling (if one exists).
2. Remove arrows from each node to all but the left-most child.

We can apply this algorithm to the trees in Figure 7.1. The tree in (a) is empty, so there are no nodes, no siblings, no children, and, therefore, nothing to do: the binary representation of an empty general tree is an empty tree. The tree in (b) has one node, but no siblings and no children, so there is nothing to do. The binary representation of a one-node general tree is a one-node binary tree. The tree in (c) with these changes is shown on the next page in Figure 7.3.

While this, in fact, is a binary tree, it may not look like a usual tree structure. Think of the nodes in the figure as being connected by string and pick up the tree by the root. The result is Figure 7.4, which may look more familiar.

In comparing the trees in figures 7.1 and 7.4, both have 16 nodes—so far so good. Leaf nodes in the binary representation (Figure 7.4) should be those leaf nodes in the original tree that had no siblings to the right. Of the 10 leaf nodes in the original, 5 had no right siblings; there are 5 leaf nodes in the binary representation. Each left node in the binary representation was a left-most child; there

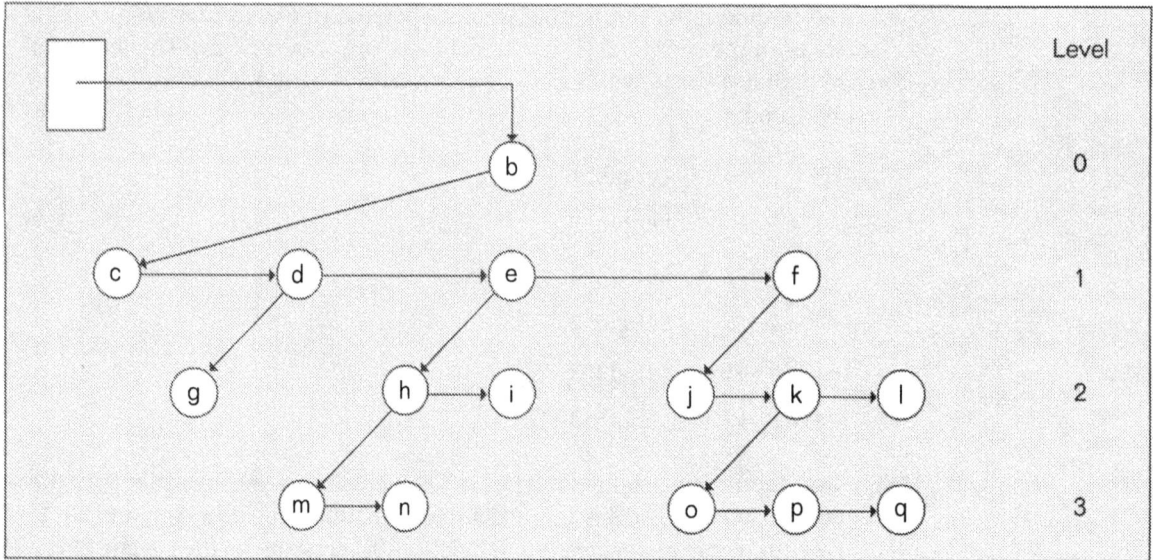

Figure 7.3 General Tree to Binary Tree

were 6 left-most children in the original and there are 6 left nodes in the binary representation. As a second example, we apply the algorithm to the labeled tree in Figure 7.2, resulting in Figure 7.5.

Notice that the transformation from Figure 7.2 to Figure 7.5 is reversible. That is, given a binary representation of a general tree, we can re-create the general tree. A left node is the left-most child of its parent. A right node is a sibling of its parent.

Binary trees have certain interesting properties. Because the maximum degree of any node is 2, we can determine the maximum number of nodes at any level: 2^k where k is the level number. A *full binary tree* is a binary tree where all of the leaves are on the same level and that level has the maximum number of leaves. A full binary tree has $2^{k+1} - 1$ nodes. A count of nodes in a binary tree is illustrated in Figure 7.6.

A *complete binary tree* is either a full tree or a tree that is full through the maximum level minus one, and the nodes on the last level are as far to the left as possible. The tree in Figure 7.6 is full through the third level, and is complete.

Binary Trees

As in the case of arrays and sequences and unsorted and sorted lists, there are two types of binary trees: one where there is only a store operation and one where there is also an insert operation. Here, we consider binary trees with only the Store operation. Discussions later in this chapter and in Chapter 8 cover binary trees with an Insert operation (heaps and binary search trees).

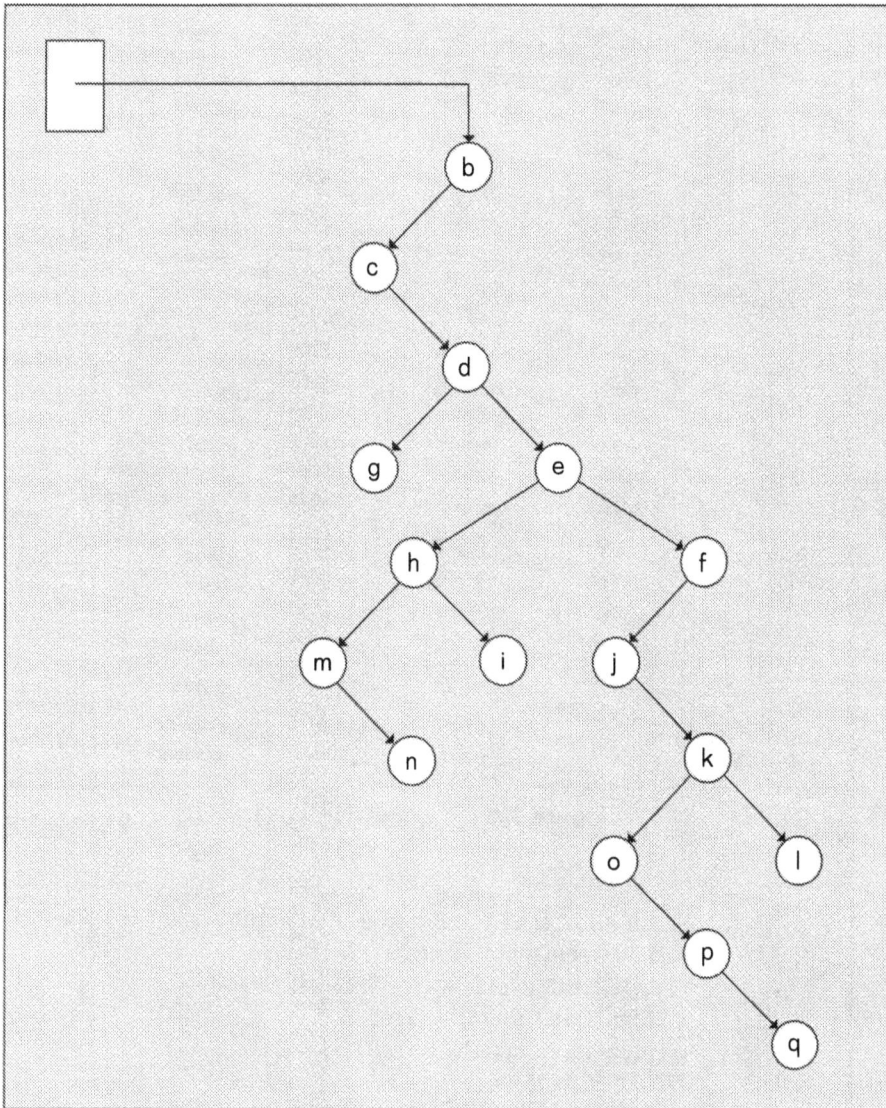

Figure 7.4 The Binary Tree of Figure 7.3 in a More Familiar Format

Specification

structure	BinTree (of ItemType)	
interface	Create	→ BinTree
	Make(BinTree, ItemType, BinTree)	→ BinTree
	LeftTree(BinTree)	→ BinTree
	RightTree(BinTree)	→ BinTree
	Item(BinTree)	→ ItemType
	IsEmpty(BinTree)	→ Boolean
end		

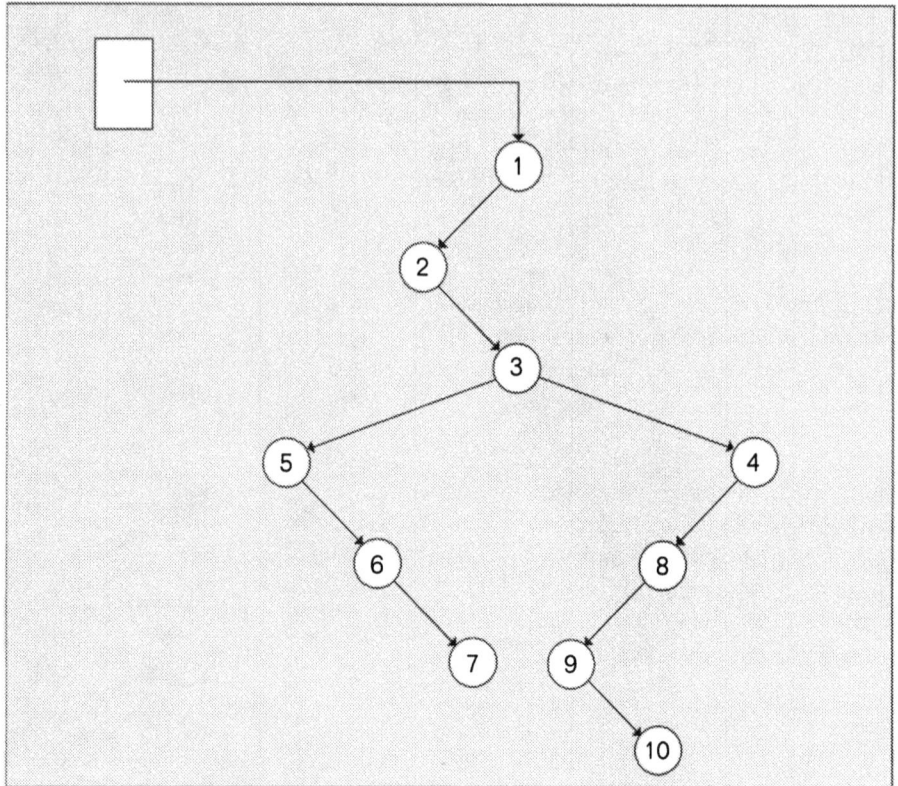

Figure 7.5 Tree from Figure 7.2 as a Binary Tree

axioms for all BT1, BT2 in BinTree, i1 in ItemType, let
       LeftTree(Create) = Error
       LeftTree(Make(BT1, i1, BT2)) = BT1
       RightTree(Create) = Error
       RightTree(Make(BT1, i1, BT2)) = BT2
       Item(Create) = Error
       Item(Make(BT1, i1, BT2)) = i1
       IsEmpty(Create) = True
       IsEmpty(Make(BT1, i1, BT2)) = False
   end
end BinTree

In later discussions, we need to identify the elements within a tree in a standard way. Assuming the values in the nodes have an intrinsic ordering of some type, this can be done by placing the tree elements in a nonindexed, sorted list, as specified in Chapter 6. (For example, if our tree contains strings, then the strings can be inserted into a sorted list in alphabetical order. Similarly, a natural ordering is available if the nodes contain numbers.) This gives rise to the following defi-

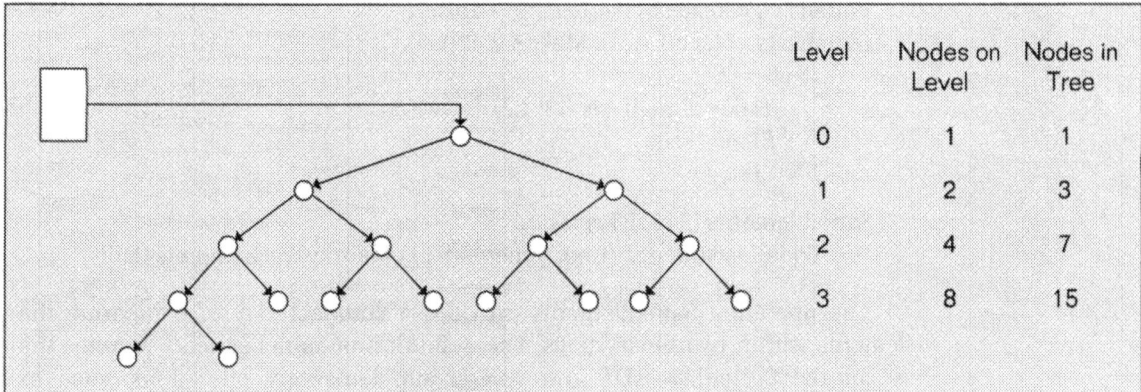

Figure 7.6 Node Count in a Binary Tree

nitions, which use the Create and Insert operations of the SortedList ADT. We also need the definition of the operation Merge, which combines two sorted lists to give a new sorted list.

> Merge (SortedList, SortedList)   → SortedList
> IdentifyTreeElements (BinTree)   → SortedList
>
> Merge (Create, L2) = L2
> Merge (Make (L1, i1), L2) = Merge (L1, Insert(L2, i1))
>
> IdentifyTreeElements (Create) = Create
> IdentifyTreeElements (Make(BT1, i1, BT2))
>   = Insert(Merge(IdentifyTreeElements(BT1),
>   IdentifyTreeElements (BT2)), i1)

This last axiom states that we can obtain the sorted list of tree elements for the tree Make (BT1, i1, BT2) by merging the lists obtained from the subtrees and then inserting element i1. (Recall that the Insert operation on sorted lists adds an element to a list in an appropriate location to maintain the ordering of the new list.)

Given two binary trees, the IdentifyTreeElements operation provides a relatively simple way to determine if the elements in the two trees are the same (although the organization of the elements within the trees may be quite different). We simply compare the elements in the two sorted lists. This gives rise to the operation SameElements. As an auxiliary function, we define the operation Equal-Lists, which determines if two sorted lists are the same.

> EqualLists (SortedList, SortedList)   → Boolean
> SameElements (BinTree, BinTree)   → Boolean
>
> EqualLists (Create, Create) = True
> EqualLists (Make(L1, i1), Create) = False

EqualLists (Create, Make(L2, i2)) = False
EqualLists, (Make(L1, i1), Make(L2, i2)) =
    IF i1 = i2
        THEN EqualLists (L1, L2)
        ELSE False
    END IF

SameElements (BT1, BT2) =
    EqualLists(IdentifyTreeElements(BT1),IdentifyTreeElements (BT1))

The operation SameElements provides a compact way of comparing the elements within two binary trees. The definition of SameElements requires the use of the SortedList ADT and several supplementary operations, such as IdentifyTreeElements and EqualLists. These definitions seem somewhat complex, so you may wonder why we did not define SameElements directly in terms of binary tree operations, avoiding the use of sorted lists completely. While such an approach is possible, it is even more complicated than the approach shown here. For example, binary trees can have any shape, and the axioms do not dictate where elements might be. Also, duplicate data values may be present. The exercises at the end of this chapter pursue this direct definition of SameElements further.

If we want to list all of the elements in the tree systematically, then we need to define an iterator operation. In the following, we give the axiomatic specifications for a preorder traversal utilizing the Queue ADT (of ItemType) augmented with the operation Concat, which concatenates two Queues. The end of chapter exercises ask you to write the specifications for the inorder and postorder traversals.

Concat(Queue,Queue)   → Queue
PreOrder(BinTree)   → Queue

Concat (Q, Create) = Q
Concat (Q, Enque(P, i1)) = Enque (Concat (Q, P), i1)

PreOrder(Create) = Create
PreOrder(Make(BT1, i1, BT2)) =
    Concat(Concat(Enque(Create, i1), PreOrder(BT1)), PreOrder(BT2))

Note carefully the difference between the list returned from IdentifyTreeElements and the queue returned from PreOrder. The list from IdentifyTreeElements is a listing of the values in the nodes in the tree ordered by the intrinsic ordering of the values themselves; the queue from PreOrder lists the values in the nodes in the order in which the nodes are visited in a preorder traversal. (For a binary search tree, which we discuss in Chapter 8, the list from IdentifyTreeElements and the queue returned from an inorder traversal are the same.)

Implementation

The interface section of the ADT Binary Tree module is shown below. The data structure is hidden within the implementation section of the module. The operations are all implemented as functions. BinTree can either be an opaque type, or the definition of BinTree can be filled in at a later time.

Interface Section ADTBinaryTree;

(* To access ItemType. *)
USES < data defining module >

TYPE
　　BinTree;　　(* Opaque type or filled in later. *)

FUNCTION Create : BinTree
(* Post:　　Returns a Tree.　　　　　　　　　　　　　　　　　　　　*)

FUNCTION Make(Left : BinTree; Item : ItemType; Right : BinTree) : BinTree
(* Pre:　　Left and Right have been initialized.　　　　　　　　　*)
(* Post:　　Returns a Tree with Left as Left(Make), Right as Right(Make)　*)
(*　　　　and Item as Item(Make).　　　　　　　　　　　　　　　*)

FUNCTION LeftTree(Tree : BinTree) : BinTree
(* Pre:　　NOT IsEmpty(Tree).　　　　　　　　　　　　　　　　*)
(* Post:　　Returns Left subtree of Tree.　　　　　　　　　　　　*)

FUNCTION RightTree(Tree : BinTree) : BinTree
(* Pre:　　NOT IsEmpty(Tree).　　　　　　　　　　　　　　　　*)
(* Post:　　Returns Right subtree of Tree.　　　　　　　　　　　*)

FUNCTION Item(Tree : BinTree) : ItemType
(* Pre:　　NOT IsEmpty(Tree).　　　　　　　　　　　　　　　　*)
(* Post:　　Returns Item field of Tree.　　　　　　　　　　　　　*)

FUNCTION IsEmpty(Tree : BinTree) : Boolean
(* Pre:　　Tree has been initialized.　　　　　　　　　　　　　*)
(* Post:　　Returns True if Tree is empty; False otherwise.　　　　*)

Because most modern programming languages have pointer variables, it may seem natural to discuss immediately the implementation of a binary tree as a dynamic structure using referenced variables. However, at this stage we resist this approach, because such details are always machine- or language-dependent. A more universal approach uses node operations instead, at an intermediate level of abstraction. Our node of type TreeNodeType contains three fields: Left, Item, and Right.

| Left | Item | Right |

The following node manipulation functions are available. We define the algorithms later.

FUNCTION GetNode: TreeNodeType
(* Post: Returns a Node.   *)

FUNCTION GetLeft(Node : TreeNodeType) : TreeNodeType
(* Post: Returns the Left field of Node.   *)

FUNCTION GetRight(Node : TreeNodeType) : TreeNodeType
(* Post: Returns the Right field of Node.   *)

FUNCTION GetItem(Node : TreeNodeType) : ItemType
(* Post: Returns the Item field of Node.   *)

PROCEDURE SetLeft(VAR Node1 : TreeNodeType; Node2 : TreeNodeType)
(* Post: Left(Node1) ← Node2.   *)

PROCEDURE SetRight(VAR Node1 : TreeNodeType; Node2 : TreeNodeType)
(* Post: Right(Node1) ← Node2.   *)

PROCEDURE SetItem(VAR Node : TreeNodeType; Item : ItemType)
(* Post: Item(Node) ← Item.   *)

FUNCTION NULL(Node : TreeNodeType) : Boolean
(* Post: Returns True if Node is empty; False otherwise.   *)

PROCEDURE FreeNode(Node : TreeNodeType)
(* Post: Returns an unneeded Node.   *)

We use these operations to write the algorithms for the binary tree operations.

Create: BinTree

```
RETURN NULL
```

Make(Left : TreeNodeType, Item : ItemType, Right: TreeNodeType) : BinTree;

```
TempNode ← GetNode
SetLeft(TempNode, Left)
SetRight(TempNode, Right)
SetItem(TempNode, Item)
RETURN TempNode
```

LeftTree, RightTree, Item, and IsEmpty are directly coded as the node primitives GetLeft, GetRight, GetItem, and NULL.

If we use pointer variables, GetNode is implemented as

```
New(Ptr)
RETURN Ptr
```

and NULL implemented as

```
RETURN (Node = NIL)
```

However, we may also implement the tree structure using an array of records rather than pointer variables. In this approach, a node is stored as an entry within a large, predefined array, and an array subscript designates individual nodes. This approach parallels the work done by the operating system in allocating space dynamically for objects designated by pointer variables. Here, GetNode identifies a new location not currently designated within the array, while FreeNode designates that an array entry is no longer needed. The pool of nodes used in building the tree is described by the following declarations.

```
CONST
    NULL = 0;

TYPE
    TreeNode= 0..MaxNodes;
    BinTree = TreeNode;

    TreeNodeType = RECORD
        Left, Right   : BinTree;
        Item          : ItemType
    END;

    NodesType = ARRAY [1..MaxNodes] OF TreeNodeType;

VAR
    Nodes   : NodesType;
    Avail   : BinTree;
```

Nodes is a pool of record variables of type TreeNode, and we can think of an array index as the address of a node within the array that represents storage. For example, Nodes[Ptr].Left and Nodes[Ptr].Right are logically equivalent to Ptr↑.Left and Ptr↑.Right in a pointer implementation.

In working with this pool, we must keep track of which entries within the array contain actual data and which are available for use. This is done by storing the index of a free entry in variable Avail or FirstAvail, and by having each free entry designate a next entry (making the collection of free array entries into a linked list). As a node is needed, the index to one of the record variables is given to the user and this record is deleted from the free list. When a node is no longer needed, it is returned to the free list. This work is done by GetNode, which is logically equivalent to New, and FreeNode, which is logically equivalent to Dispose. In practice, either the Left field or the Right field can be used to link the nodes. The storage pool might be initialized as shown below.

Avail

| 1 |

Nodes

	.Left	.Item	.Right
[1]			2
[2]			3
[3]			4
[4]			5
[5]			6
.			
.			
.			
[MaxNodes]			0

In this approach, the index 0 is used to designate the end of the available list, just as a NIL value might be used for pointer variables.

The first time GetNode is executed, 1 is returned and Avail is updated to point to the record indexed in the Right field of the node returned, the next free node. The next time GetNode is executed, 2 is returned and Avail becomes 3, and so on.

To deallocate space, the FreeNode operation places the item designated at the beginning of the Avail list. For example, if the first two items are allocated as discussed previously, and then FreeNode(1) is executed (Nodes[1] is being freed), the current value of Avail is then stored in the Right field of Nodes[1] and Avail is set to 1. The structure looks like that shown below if Avail is 3 when FreeNode(1) is executed. (Note that the Avail list is acting like a stack.)

Avail

| 1 |

Nodes

	.Left	.Item	.Right
[1]			3
[2]				← Handed out by GetNode, not part of the pool of available space.
[3]			4
[4]			5
[5]			6
.			
.			
.			
[MaxNodes]			0

Given this structure, we define our node operations as follows:

Get Node: TreeNode

```
Temp ← Avail
Avail ← Nodes[Avail].Right
RETURN Temp
```

Get Left(Node: TreeNode): TreeNode

```
RETURN Nodes[Node].Left
```

Get Right(Node: TreeNode) : TreeNode

```
RETURN Nodes[Node].Right
```

Get Item (Node: TreeNode): ItemType

```
RETURN Nodes[Node].Item
```

Set Left (VAR Node1 : TreeNode; Node2 : TreeNode)

```
Nodes[Node1].Left ← Node2
```

Set Right(VAR Node1 : TreeNode Node2 : TreeNode)

```
Nodes[Node1].Right ← Node2
```

Set Item (VAR Node : TreeNode Item : ItemType)

```
Nodes[Node].Item ← Item
```

NULL (Node : TreeNode) : Boolean

```
RETURN (Node = 0)
```

Free Node (Node : TreeNode);

```
Nodes[Node].Right ← Avail
Avail ← Node
```

The axiomatic specifications for the PreOrder traversal use a queue with an additional binary operation Concat. Concat places the second queue behind the first queue. The PreOrder axioms specify that PreOrder(Create) returns the empty queue, and PreOrder applied to any other tree returns the item in the node (root) followed by the PreOrder traversal of the left subtree and the PreOrder traversal of the right subtree. The axioms are our algorithm! This can be coded almost verbatim from the axioms except that we must pass a Queue as a parameter. Recall that all structures that are being passed as a parameter have been created.

PreOrder (Tree: TreeNode, VAR Queue: QueueType);

```
IF NOT NULL(Tree)
    THEN
        Enque(Queue, GetItem(Tree));
        PreOrder(GetLeft(Tree), Queue);
        PreOrder(GetRight(Tree), Queue)
END IF
```

Complexity

What is the size factor when working with a binary tree? Each of the operations that build or look at parts of a binary tree have bounded time. The iterator PreOrder, however, visits every node in the tree. Therefore, the size factor is the number of nodes in the tree. This is true for all trees. When we add an Insert operation to the BinaryTree ADT and have a binary search tree, then Insert might have order N, depending upon the specific form of the tree. This parallels the array and the sequence and the unsorted and sorted lists. Array store has bounded time; sequence Insert has the order of the number of items in the sequence. Unsorted list store has bounded time; sorted list Insert has the order of the number of items in the list.

Threaded Trees

How many NIL pointers (or NULL pointers in an array-based implementation) are there in a tree with N nodes? *There are N+1!* (The proof of this fact is left as an exercise.) These NIL pointers can represent a considerable waste of space, thus giving us an incentive to use this space to improve processing efficiency. One such application is the use of these NIL pointers to make traversals faster. In a left NIL pointer, we store a pointer to the node's inorder predecessor; in a right NIL pointer, we store a pointer to the node's inorder successor. This allows us to traverse the tree both left-to-right and right-to-left without using recursion. These pointers are called *threads*. How do we tell a tree node from a thread? For the moment, we assume that we have a function IsThread that returns True if the pointer is a thread, and False if it is a pointer in the tree.

Be careful about terminology—both threads and tree pointers are pointers to nodes in the tree. The difference is that threads are not structural pointers in the tree. They can be removed and the tree does not change. Tree pointers are the pointers that hold the tree together.

We look at several examples, develop the traversal algorithms, and examine how the threads can be set. But first, we define a header node that makes processing easier. The IsThread(Right(Header)) is always False, and Right(Header) is Header. IsThread(Left(Header)) is True if the tree is empty. We draw the threads as dashed lines and the nonthreads (the structural pointers) as solid lines.

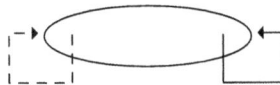

The binary tree in Figure 7.7 has the threads drawn in, and the nodes are numbered so that we can discuss them. The numbers are not necessarily values in the tree.

In good top-down fashion, we first write the algorithm for an inorder traversal, assuming that we have a function Successor(T) that returns the successor to node T. If we start with T being the header node, then we know that we have finished when we arrive back at T.

TraverseInorder (HeaderT: TreeNode)

```
Next ← Successor(HeaderT)
WHILE Next <> HeaderT DO
    Visit Item(Next)
    Next ← Successor(Next)
END WHILE
```

The inorder successor of node T is the left-most node in T's right subtree. We call the root of T's right subtree RightT. So now there are three possibilities: RightT

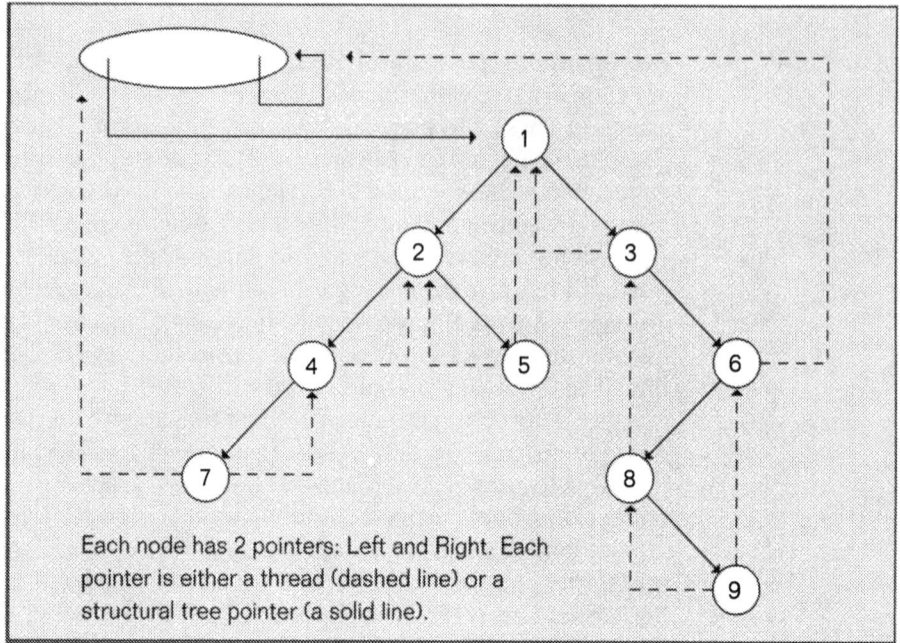

Figure 7.7 A Threaded Binary Tree

can have no left subtree, in which case RightT is the successor of node T; RightT can have a left subtree, in which case we must traverse to the left as far as possible; or RightT can be a thread, in which case RightT is the successor. The three possible cases are shown below in Figure 7.8.

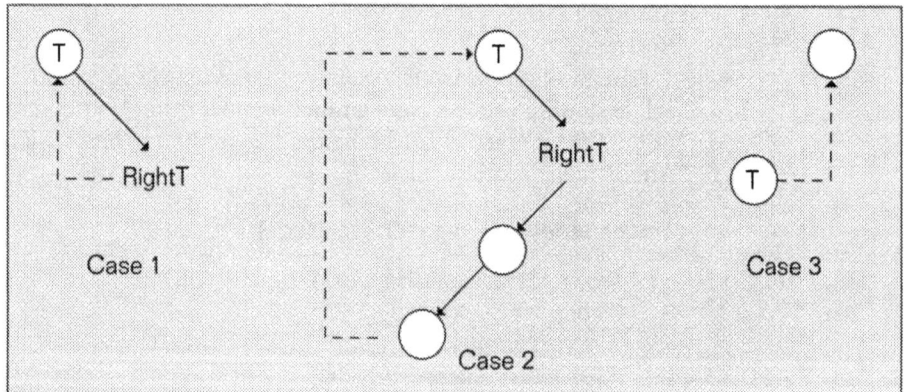

Figure 7.8 The Successor Node T

Note that in the first two cases the left child of the successor node is a thread pointing back to T. In the third case, the right child is a thread pointing to the successor. Now we can write the algorithm.

Successor (T: TreeNode): TreeNode

```
Temp ← Right(T)
IF NOT IsThread(Right(T))
    THEN
        WHILE NOT IsThread(Left(Temp)) DO
            Temp ← Left(Temp)
        END WHILE
END IF
Successor ← Temp
```

An exercise at the end of the chapter asks you to write the algorithm to find the predecessor of a node T. Before we move on to show how to insert the threads, we write out a code walk through of Traverse Inorder and Successor to be sure that they work on the tree from Figure 7.7. In the following discussion, we change the shape of a node from a circle to an oval when we visit it. The process begins with TraverseInorder(HeaderT).

```
Next ← Successor(HeaderT)
    Temp ← Right(HeaderT)
    IsThread(Right(HeaderT)) is False
    IsThread(Left(HeaderT)) is False
        Temp ← Left(Right(HeaderT)) (* that is, HeaderT*)
    IsThread(Left(Temp)) is False
        Temp ← Left(Temp)                    (* Temp is 1 *)
    IsThread(Left(Temp)) is False
        Temp ← Left(Temp)                    (* Temp is 2 *)
    IsThread(Left(Temp)) is False
        Temp ← Left(Temp)                    (* Temp is 4 *)
    IsThread(Left(Temp)) is False
        Temp ← Left(Temp)                    (* Temp is 7 *)
    IsThread(Left(Temp)) is True
    Successor ← Temp
Next ← Successor                             (* Next is 7 *)
Next <> HeaderT
Visit Next                                   (* Mark 7 *)
```

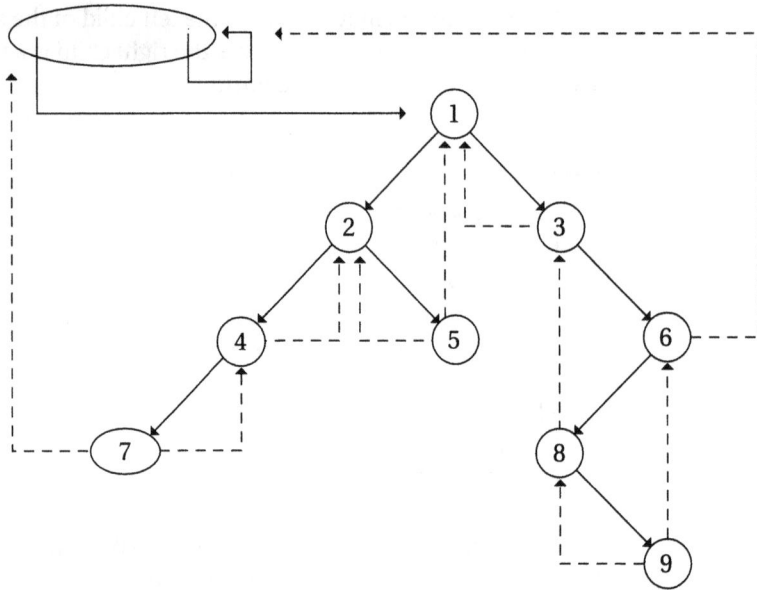

Next ← Successor(Next)
    Temp ← Right(Next)
    IsThread(Right(Next)) is True
    Successor ← Temp
Next ← Successor   (∗ Next is 4 ∗)
Next <> HeaderT
Visit Next   (∗ Mark 4 ∗)

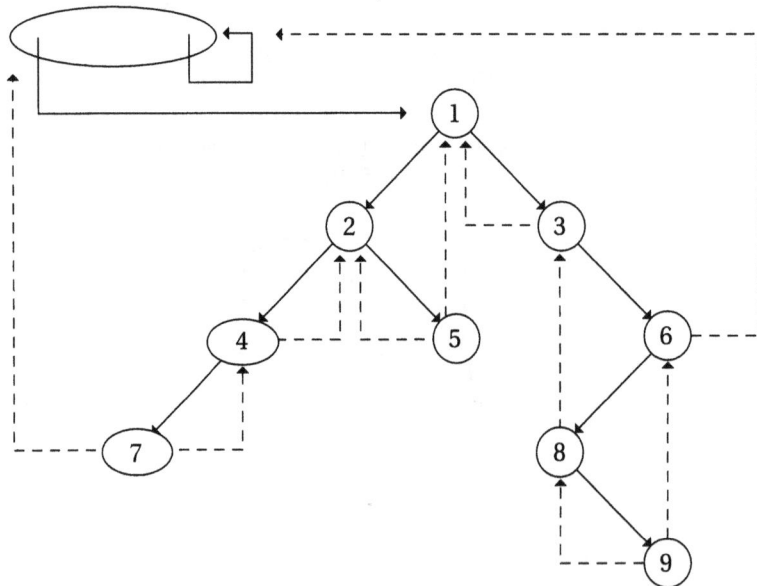

```
Next ← Successor(Next)
    Temp ← Right(Next)
    IsThread(Right(Next)) is True
    Successor ← Temp
Next ← Successor                          (* Next is 2 *)
Next <> HeaderT
Visit Next                                (* Mark 2 *)
```

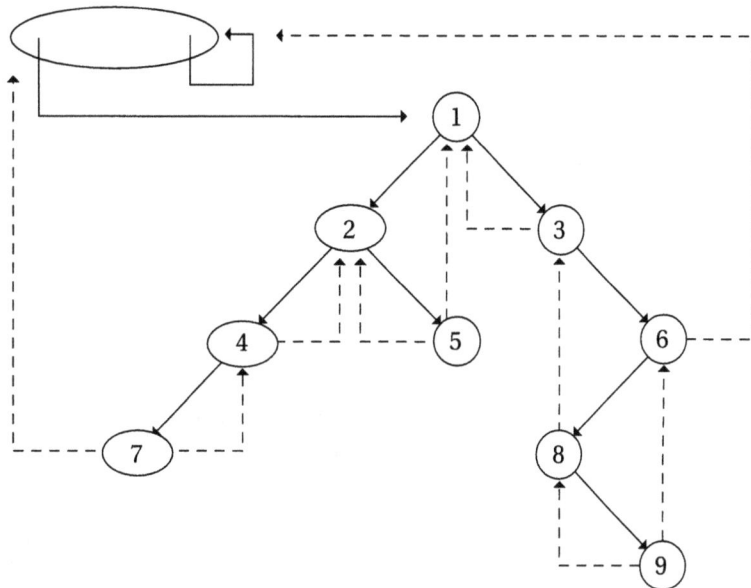

```
Next ← Successor(Next)
    Temp ← Right(Next)                     (* Temp is 5 *)
    IsThread(Right(Next)) is False
    IsThread(Left(Temp)) is True
    Successor ← Temp
Next ← Successor
Next <> HeaderT
Visit Next                                (* Mark 5 *)
```

Next ← Successor(Next)
    Temp ← Right(Next)
    IsThread(Right(Next)) is True
    Successor ← Temp   (* Temp is 1 *)
Next ← Successor
Next <> HeaderT
Visit Next   (* Mark 1 *)

As you can see, the nodes were marked in the order prescribed by an inorder traversal. To check that the algorithm ends properly, consider what happens when node 6 has been marked. At that point, Temp is 6.

```
Next ← Successor(Next)
     Temp ← Right(Next)              (* Temp is HeaderT *)
     IsThread(Right(Next)) is True
     Successor ← Temp
Next ← Successor                     (* Next is HeaderT *)
Next <> HeaderT is False
```

Complexity The complexity of any tree traversal is O(N), where N is the number of nodes in the tree. Of course, this is the best possible order for processing N items, and this order is the same as the recursive solution. Here, however, we are saving the space required for the run-time stack. We also may save *time* whenever the traversal moves us upward in the tree. Furthermore, this iterative solution eliminates any overhead of procedure calls that normally are required in a recursive solution.

If we implement IsThread as the testing of a binary bit, then we have added only two bits to each node. There is another advantage to threaded traversals: a traversal can begin anywhere in a tree. That is, you can traverse the rest of the tree beginning with any arbitrary node. What about the time required for threading the tree or updating the threads when a tree is altered? Yes, these do take time. Before you decide to use a threaded tree, you must consider how volatile the tree is (that is, how many changes are likely) and how often it must be traversed.

Threading a Binary Tree If we are given a binary tree, it is natural to ask how threads might be added to it so that it becomes threaded. Threading a binary tree is an interesting problem, because a particularly obvious approach is wrong. A first idea might be to find each NIL (or NULL) pointer and insert the proper thread. However, when you reach a NIL pointer, you have no way of determining what the proper thread is. The proper algorithm is based on taking any nonleaf node and setting the threads that should point to it. The algorithm for finding a node's predecessor and successor are well defined: the successor of any node A is the left-most node in A's right subtree, and the predecessor is the right-most node in A's left subtree. The algorithm must traverse the tree level by level, setting all the threads that should point to each node as it processes the node. Therefore, each thread is set before the node containing the thread is processed. In fact, if the node is a leaf node, it need not be processed at all.

The code itself uses the following two auxiliary procedures:

```
PROCEDURE SetRightThread(T, SuccT: TreeNode)
(* Post:    Right(T) is set to SuccT AND IsThread(Right(T) is True.     *)

PROCEDURE SetLeftThread(T, PredT: TreeNode);
(* Post:    Left(T) is set to PredT AND IsThread(Left(T) is True.     *)
```

We use a queue to traverse the tree by level. After the threads to the node being processed are inserted, its children go on the queue (if they exist). During preprocessing, the thread to the header must be inserted in the tree's left-most node as the left thread, and the thread to the header must be inserted in the tree's right-most node as the right thread. We now can write out the algorithm for threading a binary tree with header node.

```
Create(Q)
Enque(Q, Tree)
SetLeftThread(Node(MinElement), Header)
SetRightThread(Node(MaxElement), Header)
WHILE NOT IsEmpty(Q) DO
      Deque(Q, T)
      SetRightThread(Pred(T), T)
      SetLeftThread(Succ(T), T)
      IF NOT IsThread(GetLeftT)
          THEN  Enque(Q, GetLeftT)
      END IF
      IF NOT IsThread(GetRightT)
          THEN  Enque(Q, GetRightT)
      END IF
END WHILE
```

Inserting into a Threaded Tree   A variation of the threading problem arises if we want to insert a new node into a tree that already has been threaded. What are the possible cases? While we might want to contemplate the insertion of a node into the middle of a tree, in the context of threaded trees, it would seem to make more sense to insert the new node as a leaf. This new node could be inserted on the left side or the right side of a given node. An outline of the code for insertion on the left is shown below. Insertion on the right utilizes analogous code.

(* Case 1: Insert on left of existing node *)

```
SetLeftThread(Node, Left(T))
Set Left(T) to Node
Set RightThread(Node, T)
```

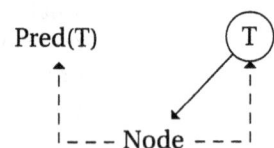

Pred(T)   (T)

Further details are left as exercises at the end of the chapter.

Application: Decision Trees

While many applications use trees to store data for rapid retrieval, such applications often impose some additional structure on a tree. For example, data in a left or right subtree may have a particular relationship (for instance, greater than or smaller than) with the data in a node. Such trees and their applications are discussed later in this chapter and in later chapters.

Here we consider the use of trees to organize the results that may arise from making various decisions. Consider, for example, the execution of a program. When the program begins, the machine does some work to load the code and some constants. Furthermore, the beginning part of the program code may initialize some variables, print some information to the user, and read some input data. The program always follows these steps whenever it is run. However, most programs involve more than simple input and output, they contain some conditional statements (for example, IF or CASE statements) or conditional loops (WHILE and REPEAT loops). In these situations, the work that is done depends upon the results of testing variables and expressions. For example, after testing a Boolean expression in an IF statement, the program may execute a THEN clause or an ELSE clause. Similarly, after examining an exit condition, the program may repeat code within a WHILE loop, or the program may continue with the code following the loop.

One way of visualizing the different ways in which a program may execute is to arrange the code in a tree structure, called a *decision tree*. The root of the decision tree consists of the code that always is run at the start of the program, up to the first conditional statement. At the first conditional statement, however, the program executes one code segment or another, depending upon the value of the condition. Such a circumstance is shown in the decision tree by drawing a child of the root for each code option that the program might follow. For an IF statement, there are two children of the root: one if the Boolean expression is True and the THEN clause is executed, and another in case the expression is False. For a CASE statement, a different child is drawn for each different case identified by the code, because different code is followed for each of these situations. These situations are shown in Figure 7.9.

For a WHILE loop, the body of the loop might be executed 0, 1, 2, 3, or more times, after which program execution continues with the code that follows the WHILE statement. Viewed in another way, the machine first tests the exit condition and then either exits the loop or starts the loop body for the first time. If the loop is executed the first time, then eventually the machine reaches the exit condition a second time and either exits the loop or continues with the loop a third time. Work within the loop continues until the machine tests the exit condition and determines that the loop should not continue. This sequence of potential tests is also shown in Figure 7.9.

In tracing program execution, we incorporate each individual decision into another branch within an overall decision tree. If each option is based on the test of a Boolean expression, the result is a binary tree, such as the one shown in Figure 7.10.

Searching an n-Element Ordered List, Implemented in an Array

To be somewhat more concrete, consider code that determines where a value V is located within a sorted, nonindexed list, that has been implemented as the sorted array A. For simplicity in the code that follows, we assume that V is located somewhere within A.

```
First ← 1
Last ← n
REPEAT
    Middle ← (First + Last) DIV 2
    IF V < A[Middle]
        THEN   Last ← Middle − 1
        ELSE   First ← Middle + 1
    END IF
UNTIL V = A[Middle]
```

At the start of this code, we assume that the machine has already determined n values for the array A, and we assume that we have decided upon the value V. The first part of the decision tree for this code is shown in Figure 7.11.

At the start of the given code, we initialize First, Last, and Middle. This work occurs every time the program is executed, and it never varies from one run of the program to the next. All of this activity is represented within the root node of the decision tree; no decisions have been made up to this point.

The next line of the binary search, however, checks to determine if V comes

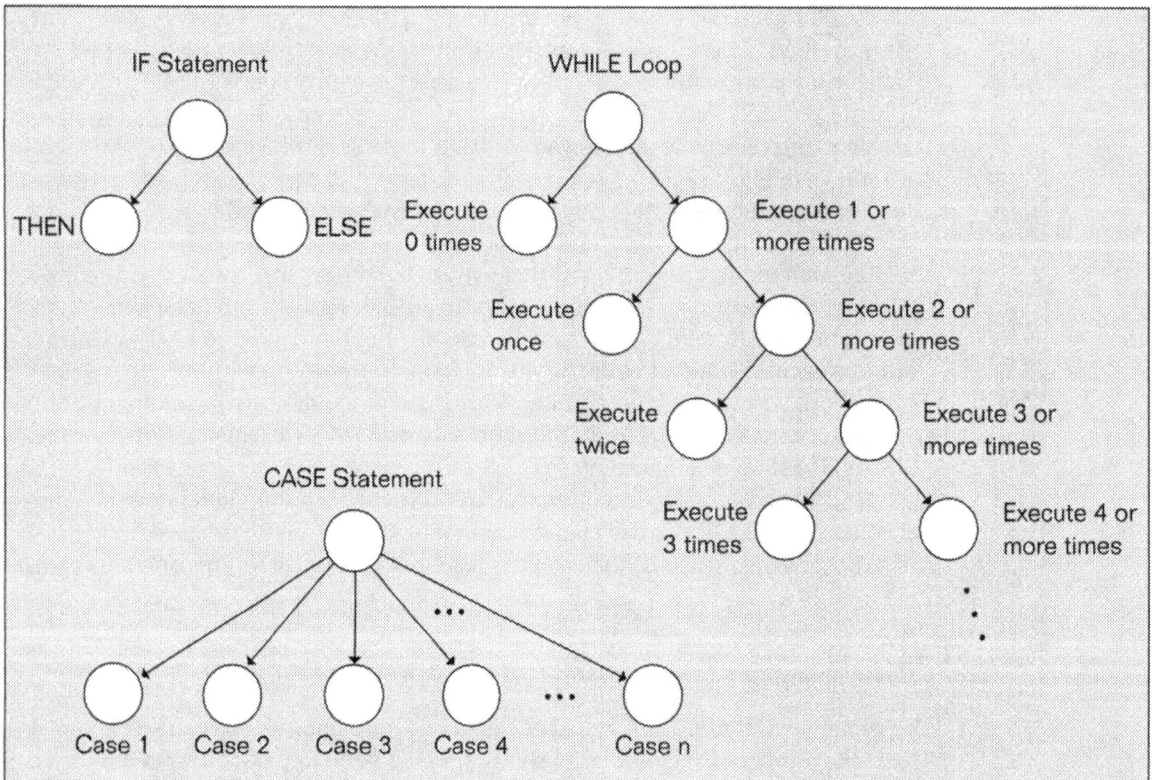

Figure 7.9 Branching Structure in a Decision Tree for Various Programming Statements

before the middle array element, and the machine executes the THEN or ELSE clause appropriately. In the decision tree in Figure 7.11, these alternatives are shown as two branches to the children of the root. In one case, Last is updated, and in the other case, First is revised.

These two assignment statements begin their respective nodes as children of the root. Then, in either case, the machine next tests the exit condition of the RE-PEAT loop. Each of these children of the root then have branches indicating whether the result of the test of this exit condition is True or False. If the test produces a True value, the execution of the code segment is complete, and we have moved to a leaf of the tree. If a False condition is found, program execution continues at the top of the loop again, with a recomputation of Middle and another test to determine if V comes before this new middle value.

Again, the result of the test $(V < A[Middle])$ may be True or False, and this is reflected by the THEN and ELSE branches to the respective children. The testing

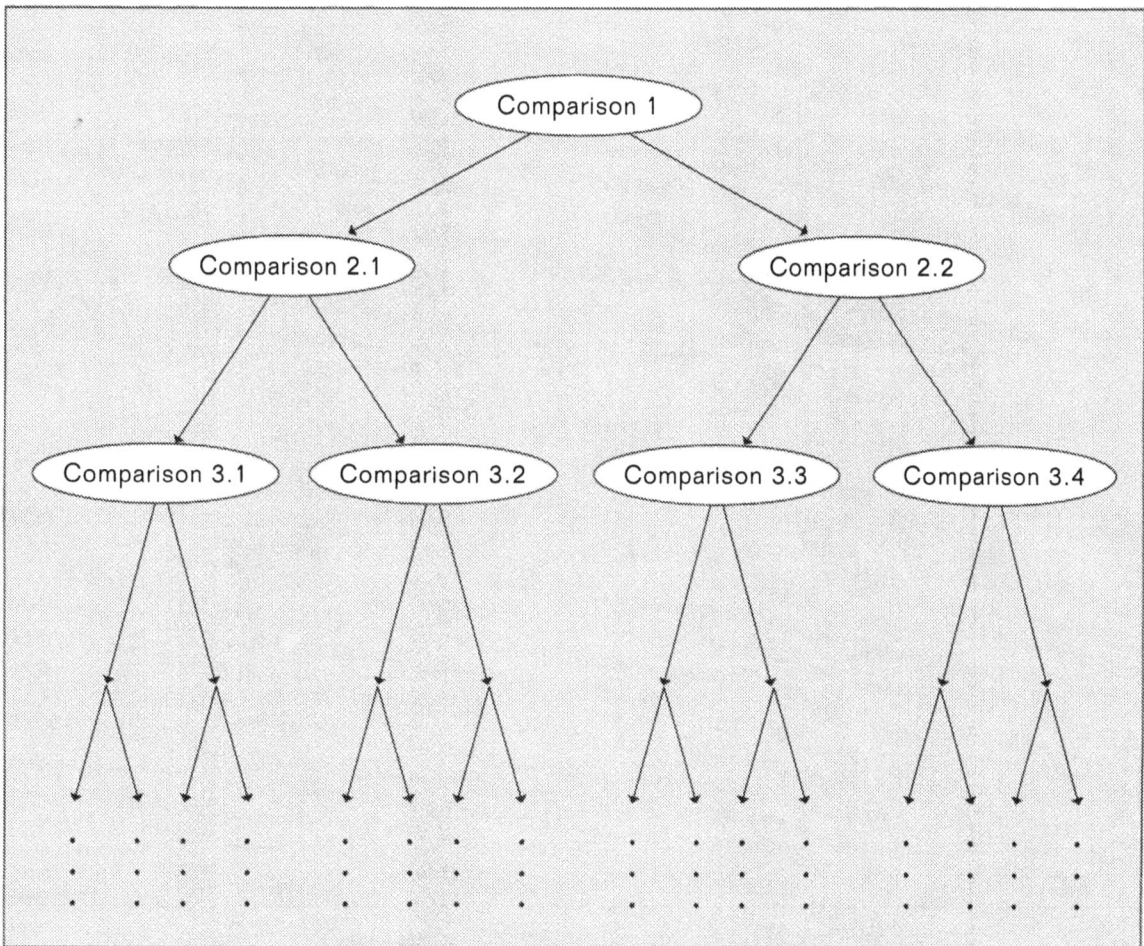

Figure 7.10 A Decision Tree Based on Evaluations of Boolean Expressions

of the exit condition the second time through the loop produces the next branching in the tree. Eventually, the binary search finishes when V is found, and Middle contains the index of V within the array A. This result arises in the leaves of the tree.

This discussion suggests that decision trees can provide a way of visualizing all possible execution paths that might be followed within a program or code segment. (To test your understanding of this tree, examine the various branches and conditions and explain why the machine cannot actually get to the "Done" node at the extreme left side of this decision tree at level 2—two levels below the root.)

Decision trees not only provide a mechanism for visualizing code execution, they also provide a framework for us to analyze how general algorithms might work. For example, suppose we want to study all algorithms that determine where an element V might be located within an ordered list A. While we have already commented upon the nature of the decision tree for a binary search, our discussion can be applied to the decision tree of any searching algorithm. For any algorithm, we can expect that there are various comparisons that must be made, and there are branches at various nodes.

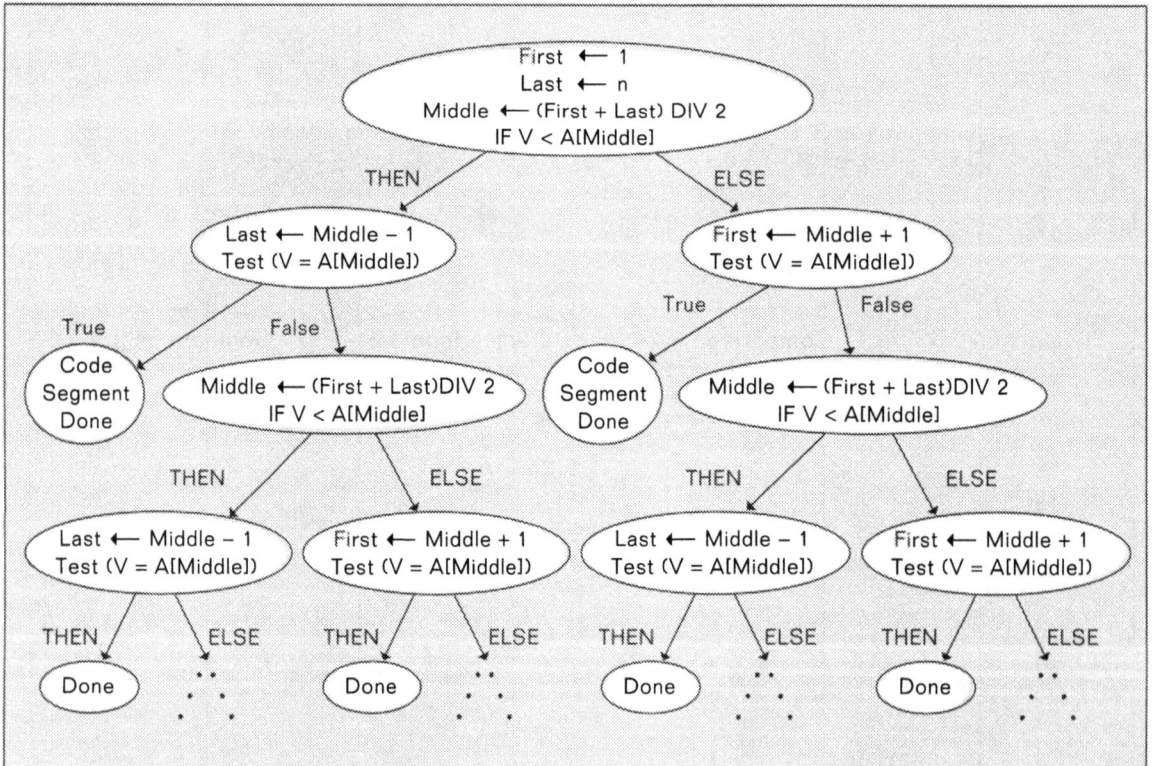

Figure 7.11 Decision Tree for a Binary Search

By the end of any such search, an algorithm must have set a variable (for example, Middle) to the location of V within A, based upon where V is found after a comparison of V with some elements of A.

With this in mind, what can we say about the nature of the decision tree? There are n possible places where V might be located within A, and each position gives rise to a different result for any search algorithm. Because any search algorithm must produce the correct result for any of these n possible outcomes, we conclude that the decision tree must have at least n leaves. (Because the location variable [for example, Middle] can have any of n different values, and because each path to a leaf gives rise to a specific ending value for that variable, n different outcomes must give rise to at least n different leaves.)

How big, then, must a tree be in order to contain n leaves? In order to have as many leaves as possible at a given level, we want a tree to be quite full. Furthermore, we have already noted that, at level h in a full tree, we can have 2^h nodes. Thus, in order to have as short a tree as possible with n leaves, we want a rather full tree of height h, where n (the number of leaves) is 2^h. With $n = 2^h$, we conclude $h = \log_2 n$. In other words, the decision tree for any searching algorithm must have a height of at least $h = \log_2 n$.

How does this information about decision trees relate to algorithms? We have already noted that each node in a decision tree corresponds to some work within an algorithm. Furthermore, as an algorithm runs, work starts at the root of the decision tree and moves progressively downward through the tree from level to level until program execution comes to a leaf. When the code in the leaf terminates, the algorithm is complete. With this outline of processing, we conclude that the number of main steps (or comparisons) in an algorithm corresponds to the number of nodes executed within the decision tree. The maximum number of steps for an algorithm, therefore, corresponds to the height of the tree! Within a node, we may be doing several assignments or other activities, so the decision tree does not directly give us the exact amount of work required for an algorithm. However, ignoring the details of each step, the height of the decision tree does provide us with information concerning the number of major steps in an algorithm. In Chapter 2, we used this type of macroanalysis of an algorithm to determine the order of an algorithm. *The order of an algorithm corresponds to the height of the algorithm's decision tree.*

More precisely, the preceding discussion has shown that any searching algorithm must contain at least $\log_2 n$ steps. This gives rise to the following important result.

> **Theorem:** Any algorithm that searches a sorted, nonindexed list of n elements to find the location of a specified value must be at least $O(\log_2 n)$.

The binary search has this order. Therefore, we can conclude that there are no algorithms for this task of a faster order than the binary search. Of course, this macroanalysis does not count individual machine statements, so it is possible that the binary search may be refined or that other algorithms may run somewhat faster (for instance, 10% or 30% faster). However, this analysis does demonstrate that we need not look for another searching algorithm of better order, at least in the single-processor context where our decision-tree analysis applies.

Sorting an Array-Based List

The same type of analysis just used for searching within a sorted, array-based list can be extremely useful for studying other problems as well. For example, suppose we want to sort the values within a list, placing them in ascending order. Again, we assume that an algorithm makes comparisons and moves data from place to place on the basis of the relative values of the list elements. (Such an assumption certainly applies to most common sorting algorithms, such as the bubble sort, selection sort, insertion sort, heap sort, quicksort, and merge sort. It does not apply to the radix sort, however.)

With an algorithm based on comparisons and data movements, the decision tree has a root, representing any possible input list. At the leaves, different comparisons and data movements have been made, depending upon how the initial data were ordered. As each leaf corresponds to one such initial ordering, the number of leaves in a decision tree must be at least the number of such orderings.

If the list has n elements, these elements can be arranged in n! ways. (Any of the n elements could be placed first in the list; any of the remaining n − 1 could be second, any of the remaining n − 2 could be third; and so on.) We conclude that the decision tree for a sorting algorithm must contain at least n! leaves.

As noted above, if the decision tree has height h, then the tree has no more than 2^h leaves. Thus, to have n! leaves, we must have $2^h \geq$ n!. Taking the log of both sides, we have h $\geq \log_2$ (n!) or h $\geq \log_2$ n $+ \log_2$ (n − 1) $+ \log_2$ (n − 2) $+ \ldots + \log_2$ 2 $+ \log_2$ 1. Unfortunately, solving this expression precisely for h is quite complex.

Informally, we may think of $\log_2$(n!) as being something like n $\log_2$ n, as follows. Replace each term in the sum $\log_2$ n $+ \log_2$ (n−1) $+ \log_2$ (n−2) $+ \ldots + \log_2$ 2 $+ \log_2$ 1 by $\log_2$n. While this approximation is clearly higher than desired, it does allow us to approximate the sum as the sum of n terms, each of which is $\log_2$n. Thus, the sum is roughly n $\log_2$ n.

More formally, Sterling's formula (for large n) states that n! is approximately $(2n\Pi)^{1/2}(n/e)^n$. Applying this result to the height of our decision tree, we conclude that the tree must have a height of h, where $2^h \geq (2n\Pi)^{1/2}(n/e)^n$. Solving this for h shows that h is approximately log $(2\Pi$ n)/2 $+$ n $(\log_2$ n $- \log_2$ e). Ignoring constants and lower-degree terms, we conclude that h has order n $\log_2$ n.

Because this conclusion concerning the height of an algorithm's decision tree provides an approximation of the efficiency of the algorithm, we are led to the following theorem.

> **Theorem:** Any sorting algorithm based on comparisons of data and data movements must have at least O(n $\log_2$ n).

Of course, if you know more about the data, if you use a different basis for your algorithm, or if you have multiple processors available, then the assumptions of this analysis may not apply, and other conclusions might be possible. However, in many contexts, we can conclude that we cannot do better than O(n $\log_2$ n) sorts. Because such algorithms as the heap or merge sorts fall into this category, we conclude that we cannot find algorithms that are dramatically better. Some approaches or refinements may increase efficiency somewhat, but we cannot expect new algorithms that are fundamentally better.

Heaps

A **heap** is a binary tree with two properties. The first property concerns the shape of the binary tree. The second property relates the values in the nodes to one another. The **shape property** specifies that the tree is complete; that is, the tree is either full or the tree is full at each level except the last one and, at the last level, all nodes are on the left as much as possible. Recall that the tree in Figure 7.6 is a complete tree.

The relationship among the values in the nodes of a heap (the **value property**) is stated in terms of priority. The value in any node has higher or equal value than any node in either its left or its right subtree. The definition of the ADT Heap states that both the shape property and the value property hold.

> **Shape property** An organization of nodes within a binary tree in which the tree is either (1) full or (2) full to the next-to-the-lowest level and with all leaves on the lowest level as far as possible to the left.
>
> **Value property** A property of binary trees in which the value of any node in the tree has equal or higher value than any node in either its left subtree or its right subtree.
>
> **Heap** A binary tree with both the shape and value properties.

While the value property is stated in relation to node values, the relationship among the values may be regarded as any ordering that determines a priority. High-priority items should be at the top of a heap, while lower-priority items should be farther down. From this perspective, the ordering could be specified as alphabetical or reverse-alphabetical order of strings, ascending or descending order of numbers, or seniority of people, among other things. In our discussion, we use the relational operators, but they should be interpreted in terms of priority. For example, "less than" is interpreted as "lower priority."

Specification

While the specifications for the ADT Heap must ensure both the shape property and the value property, such specifications can be written in at least two rather different styles. The first of these approaches formally defines what we mean by the shape and value properties, states that heaps have these properties, and specifies that the Insert and Delete operations must maintain these properties. This approach does not indicate where to insert or delete elements; after an insertion or deletion, any organization of data is allowed, provided the heap properties are maintained.

The second approach maintains the shape and value properties by limiting how insertion and deletion can occur. In this approach, properties hold because, after an insertion or deletion, data must be organized in a specific way.

As we shall see, the first of these approaches is more general. The second approach, however, is quite common and may seem more familiar. We compare the two approaches after presenting both to the specification of a heap.

A General Heap Specification

The first approach for specifying the Heap ADT focuses only upon the heap properties: a binary tree satisfying the shape and value properties. Already, we have written specifications for SameElements, which indicate when two trees have the same values. Next, we write specifications for the shape and value properties. Of these operations, the axioms to test the value property are simpler, because we only need to check that the value at each node is greater than or equal to the value at each child (if any). (We do not have to check the values at every node of every subtree. Why?) In the following definitions, we look at four separate cases: the case of an empty tree, the case of a node with no children, the case of only one child, and the case of two children for a node.

HasValueProperty (BinTree)   →Boolean

HasValueProperty (Create) = True
HasValueProperty (Make (Create, i1, Create)) = True
HasValueProperty (Make(Make (BT1, i2, BT2), i1, Create)) =
    (i1 ≥ i2) AND HasValueProperty (Make (BT1, i2, BT2))
HasValueProperty (Make(Create, i1, Make (BT3, i3, BT4))) =
    (i1 ≥ i3) AND HasValueProperty (Make (BT3, i3, BT4))
HasValueProperty (Make(BT1, i2, BT2), i1, Make (BT3, i3, BT4)) =
    (i1 ≥ i2) AND HasValueProperty (Make (BT1, i2, BT2))
    AND (i1 ≥ i3) AND HasValueProperty (Make (BT3, i3, BT4))

In developing the specification of the shape property, we need to consider the various ways in which a tree might meet this property. One possibility is that a tree can be full, in which case, for every node, the height of its left subtree is the same as the height of its right subtree. The following definitions specify axioms for the height of a tree and for a full tree.

Height(BinTree)   →Integer
Full(BinTree)   →Boolean

Height(Create) = 0
Height(Make(H1, i1, H2)) = 1 + Max(Height(H1), Height(H2))

Full(Create) = True
Full(Make(H1, i1, H2)) =
    IF Height(H1) <> Height(H2)
        THEN   False
        ELSE   Full(H1) AND Full(H2)
    END IF

A tree could satisfy the shape property even if it were not full, but the last row would have some leaves on the left but none on the right. A few such cases are illustrated below.

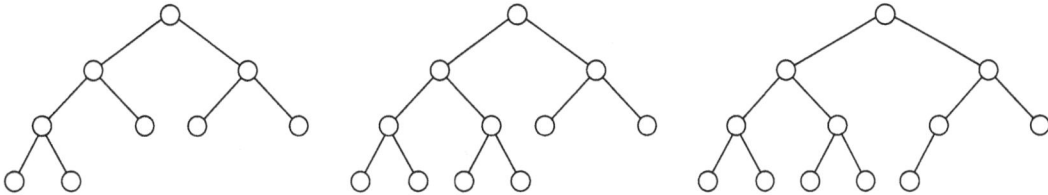

The tree on the left illustrates that the right subtree of the root may be full, while the left subtree may be complete, but not full. The middle example illustrates that both the left and right subtrees may be full, but the left one may have one additional level of nodes. The right tree illustrates that the left subtree may be full, while the right one may be complete, but not full. In each case, the heights of the various subtrees must agree, or they can differ by one only in certain ways. The axioms for the HasShapeProperty make these observations more precise.

HasShapeProperty(BinTree) $\rightarrow$ Boolean

HasShapeProperty(Create) = True
HasShapeProperty(Make(H1, i1, H2)) =
    Full (Make(H1, i1, H2))
    OR (Full (H1) AND Full (H2) AND (Height(H1) = 1 + Height(H2)))
    OR (HasShapeProperty(H1) AND Full (H2) AND (Height(H1) = 1 + Height(H2)))
    OR (Full(H1) AND HasShapeProperty (H2) AND (Height(H1) = Height(H2)))

With these operations defined, we can determine whether a binary tree is a heap simply by checking both properties.

    IsHeap(BinTree) $\rightarrow$ Boolean
    IsHeap(BT1) = HasShapeProperty (BT1) AND HasValueProperty (BT1)

We now state the axioms for the Heap ADT. The first several operations provide the basic operations to construct trees, to move from a heap to a subtree, to extract data from a node, and to determine if the heap is empty. The operations Insert and Delete maintain the heap structure itself. Insert adds a data item to the heap, while Delete removes the root and allows a reorganization of the remaining nodes to maintain the shape and value properties.

structure Heap (Of ItemType)
interface Create → Heap
Make(Heap, ItemType, Heap) → Heap
Left(Heap) → Heap
Right(Heap) → Heap
Data(Heap) → ItemType
IsEmpty(Heap) → Boolean
Insert(Heap, ItemType) → Heap
Delete(Heap) → Heap
end
axioms **for all H1, H2 in Heap, i1 in ItemType, let**
Left(Create) = Error
Left(Make(H1, i1, H2)) = H1

Right(Create) = Error
Right(Make(H1, i1, H2)) = H2

Data(Create) = Error
Data(Make(H1, i1, H2)) = i1

IsEmpty(Create) = True
IsEmpty(Make(H1, i1, H2)) = False
end
end Heap

In defining the Insert and Delete operations, we only want to specify that the resulting structures are heaps and contain the correct elements. In this general approach to specification, the axioms say nothing about the resulting structure of the heap. As in the semi-structured data types in Chapter 5, the Delete operation knows which item to delete: the one with the highest priority that is in the root node.

Insert (H1, i1) = any H2 where
  IsHeap(H2)
    AND EqualLists (Insert (IdentifyTreeElements(H1), i1),
      IdentifyTreeElements(H2))

Delete(H1) = any H2 where
  IsHeap(H2)
    AND EqualLists (IdentifyTreeElements(H1),
      Insert (IdentifyTreeElements(H2), Data(H1)))

To clarify these axioms further, we reemphasize that the Insert and Delete operations allow us to rearrange elements in a heap in any way we wish, provided the required properties still hold. For example, consider the heaps shown in Figure 7.12.

Each of the two options shown in Figure 7.12 are heaps with the data desired after inserting the value 3 into the original heap. In option 1, the new value 3 is simply placed at the end of the third row, while the other data values remain in their original positions. In option 2, all values (except the root value) have been moved around within the structure, and the new value 3 is tucked into the middle. Our axioms allow each of these results (and many others as well), because each structure is a heap with the correct data.

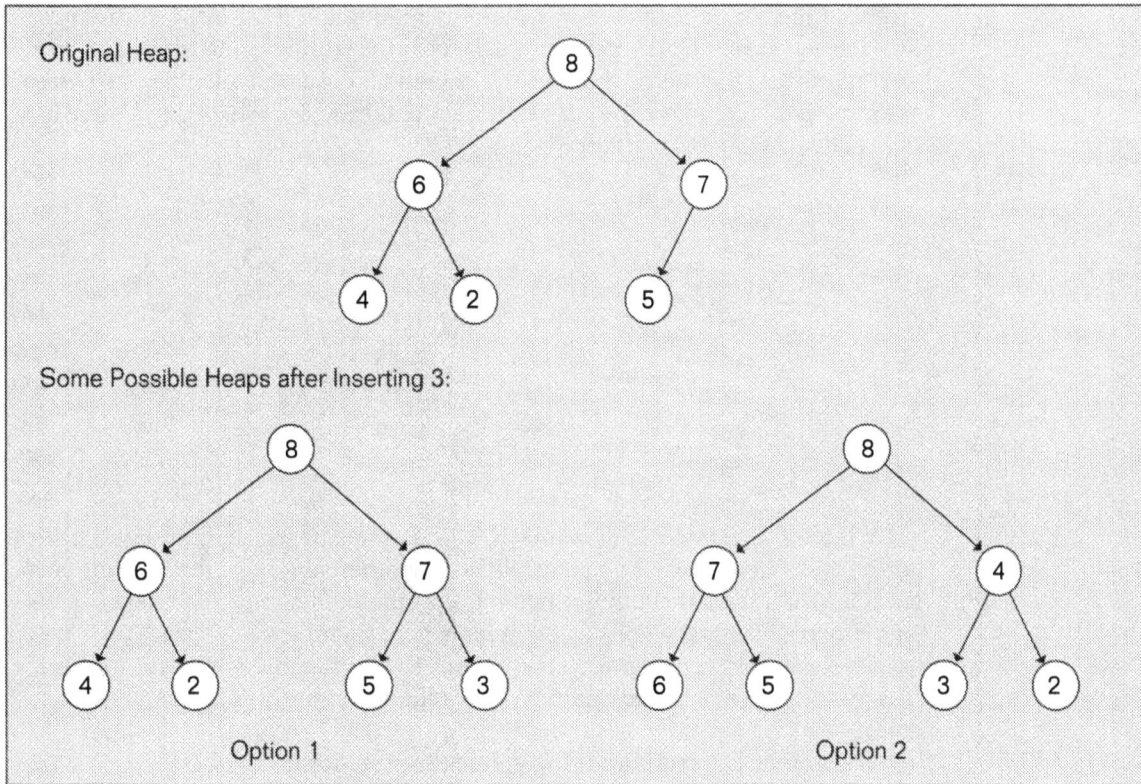

Figure 7.12 Two Possible Results for Inserting into a Heap

A More Constrained Heap Specification

The second approach to the specification of the Heap ADT is more definite about where a new item is inserted within a heap. The specification of the more elementary operations—Create, Make, Left and Right, Data, and IsEmpty—remain the same in this second approach. Only the Insert and Delete axioms are more constrained, because we rely upon these operations to ensure both the shape property and the value property. First, we discuss the Insert operation in some detail. Then we present the Delete specifications with much less discussion.

In considering the Insert operation, we first focus on the shape property. What are the cases? An empty tree, a full tree, and a tree that is complete, but not full. Inserting into an empty tree just returns a one-node tree. This is the base case.

Insert(Create, i1) = Make(Create, i1, Create)

Inserting into a full tree means that the level is increased by one and that the node is the left subtree of the left-most node. Given the left-most node, the axiom becomes

Insert(Make(Create, i2, Create), i1) = Make(Make(Create, i1, Create), i2, Create)

Inserting into a complete tree requires finding the right-most node on the lowest level. This is a little more complex! As in the writing of the general axioms, we must look at the shape when the tree is complete, but not full. Here, two cases seem relevant: one where the last leaf is a left child and one where the last leaf is a right child. These are illustrated below.

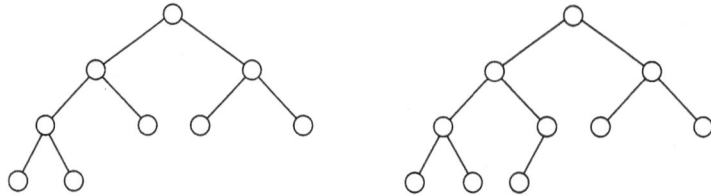

What are the circumstances in each case that tell us which direction to move down the tree to the insertion point? Keep moving left as long as the left subtree is not full. When the left subtree is full, move to the right subtree and begin again. This process eventually ends at the node where the new value goes. If the new node is to be a right child, the left child is full, so you go right. If the new node is to be a left child, the left child and the right child are empty, falling into the second base case.

The axioms for creating a complete tree are as follows:

Insert(Create, i1) = Make(Create, i1, Create)

Insert(Make(Create, i2, Create), i1) = Make(Make(Create, i1, Create), i2, Create)

Insert(Make(H1, i2, H2), i1) =
    IF Full(H1)
        THEN   Make(H1, i2, Insert(H2, i1))
        ELSE   Make(Insert(H1, i1), i2, H2)
    END IF

With this analysis, we try these specifications with a few trees to check that we have not missed a case. The nodes are labeled, so we can talk about them.

Insert(H, G)

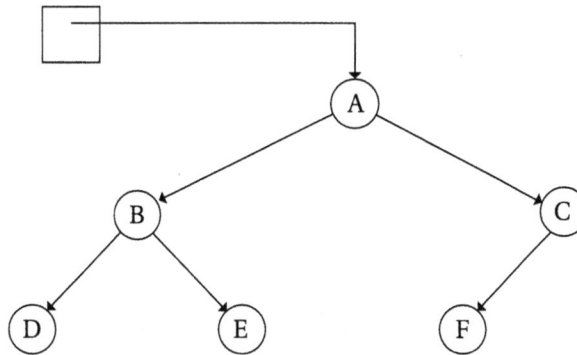

A's left tree is full, so we go right, giving us the following tree.

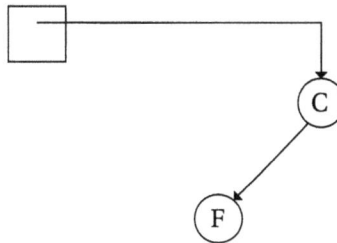

C's left tree is full, so we go right (giving us an empty tree where we use the base case) and insert G.

Insert(H, X)

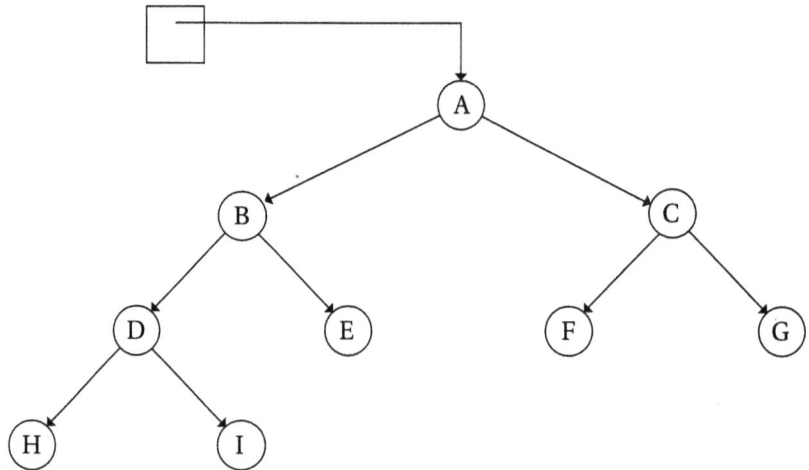

A's left child is not full, so we go left. B's left child is full, so we go right. We are at the second base case, so X is inserted as the left subtree of E.

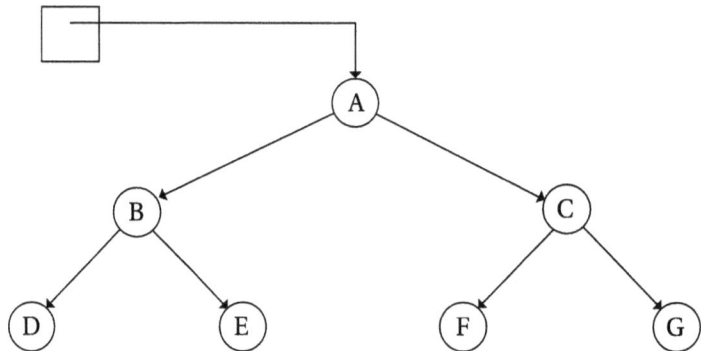

So far, our axioms for Insert seem to work as we wish. We also can check that the case of an empty tree works correctly. What about a full tree—the other special case?

Insert(H, Z)

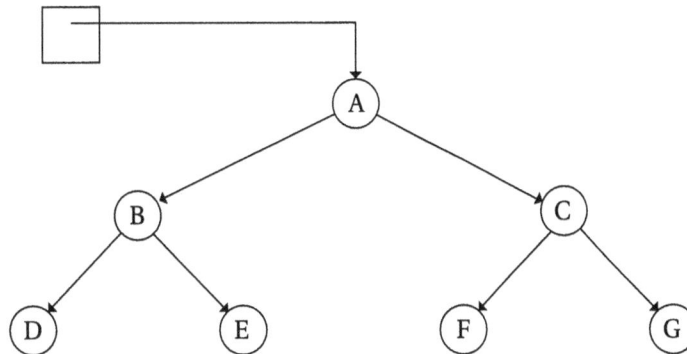

A's left child is full, so we go right—*no, we want to go left!* What is wrong? We did not take care of the case where both subtrees are full. If the tree itself is full, we want to go left. This only happens when a tree is full to begin with. We add this constraint to our axiom, remembering that any subtree of a full tree is full.

```
Insert(Make(H1, i2, H2), i1) =
    IF Full(H1) AND NOT Full(Make(H1, i2, H2))
        THEN   Make(H1, i2, Insert(H2, i1))
        ELSE   Make(Insert(H1,i1), i2, H2))
    END IF
```

Before you go on to read the complete set of axioms for the Insert operation for a Heap ADT, try taking the axioms that we just constructed for inserting into a complete tree and adding the relationship constraint to it. Remember, the "less than" relational operator stands for "lower priority."

The complete axioms for Insert follow.

```
Insert(Create, i1) = Make(Create, i1, Create)
Insert(Make(Create, i2, Create), i1) =
    IF i1 < i2
        THEN   Make(Make(Create, i1, Create), i2, Create)
        ELSE   Make(Make(Create, i2, Create), i1, Create)
    END IF
Insert(Make(H1, i2, H2), i1) =
    IF Full(H1) AND NOT Full(Make(H1, i2, H2))
        THEN
            IF i1 < i2
                THEN   Make(H1, i2, Insert(H2, i1))
                ELSE   Make(H1, i1, Insert(H2, i2))
            END IF
```

```
        ELSE
            IF i1 < i2
                THEN    Make(Insert(H1, i1), i2, H2)
                ELSE    Make(Insert(H1, i2), i1, H2)
            END IF
        END IF
```

Turning to the axioms for the Delete operation, we recognize that the item to be deleted is in the root of the tree. We want to remove this item. To do so, the shape property specifies that we need to remove a node in the bottom row of the tree, as far to the right as possible. This item then must be placed back in the tree in a way that ensures that the value property is maintained.

To accomplish this task, we need several auxiliary functions. Operation Last returns the value in the right-most node on the lowest level; DelLast deletes this right-most node on the lowest level; and ReHeap takes a tree that is almost a heap and restores the heap property. The definition of these auxiliary operations follows.

```
Last(Heap)                      → ItemType
DelLast(Heap)                   → Heap
ReHeap(Heap)                    → Heap

Last(Create, i1, Create) = i1
Last(Make(H1, i1, H2)) =
    IF Full(Make(H1, i1, H2)) OR NOT Full(H2)
        THEN    Last(H2)
        ELSE    Last(H1)
    END IF

DelLast(Create, i1, Create) = Create
DelLast(Make(H1, i1, H2)) =
    IF Full(Make(H1, i1, H2)) OR NOT Full(H2)
        THEN    Make(H1, i1, DelLast(H2))
        ELSE    Make(DelLast(H1), i1, H2)
    END IF

ReHeap(Make(Create, i1, Create)) = Make(Create, i1, Create)
ReHeap(Make(H1, i1, Create)) =
    IF i1 < Data(H1)
        THEN    Make(Make(Create,i1,Create), Data(H1), Create)
        ELSE    Make(H1, i1, Create)
    END IF
ReHeap(Make(H1, i1, H2)) =
    IF (i1 > Data(H1)) AND (i1 > Data(H2))
        THEN    Make(H1, i1, H2)
        ELSIF   Data(H1) > Data(H2)
            THEN    Make(ReHeap(Make(Left(H1), i1, Right(H1))), Data(H1), H2)
            ELSE    Make(H1, Data(H2), ReHeap(Make(Left(H2), i1, Right(H2))))
    END IF
```

With these auxiliary functions, the Delete operation is obtained by replacing the root of the tree with the right-most node at the lowest level and reorganizing the node values to guarantee that the value property holds. The Delete axioms follow.

Delete(Create) = Error
Delete(Make(Create, i1, Create)) = Create
Delete(Make(H1, i1, H2)) =
    ReHeap(DelLast(Make(H1, Last(Make(H1, i1, H2)), H2)))

We leave it to the reader to check that these axioms for Delete maintain the desired properties of a heap.

As already noted, the axioms for Create, Make, Left, Right, Data, and IsEmpty are unchanged in this more constrained approach to specification. Only the axioms for the Insert and Delete operations are different. As we have already seen, the Insert operation also uses the Full operation, defined previously in this chapter. The Delete operation uses several auxiliary operations.

Comparison of Specification Approaches

The more general approach to the specification of the Heap ADT (Approach 1) defines a heap as a binary tree with the shape and value properties. This gives a programmer complete freedom in implementing a heap. In many situations, such freedom is precisely what is desired in writing specifications: we do not want specifications to constrain an implementor unnecessarily. Instead, a programmer writes code in any way he or she desires, perhaps taking advantage of special opportunities for efficiency. However, this general approach also does not allow us to make any conclusions about the relationship of one heap to a new heap with one data item added. This approach allows a reshuffling of items after every Insert operation. Thus, while we have allowed a programmer to make the implementation code efficient, we have not mandated any type of efficiency.

In the more constrained approach to specification (Approach 2), we indicate exactly how items should be placed during the Insert operation. While this constrains a programmer considerably, it also allows us to make some conclusions concerning efficiency. For example, we have O(1) access to the node with the highest priority: it is the root. We also know that insertion is going to be $O(\log_2 N)$ because the shape property guarantees that the tree is balanced. Similarly, the Delete operation has $O(\log_2 N)$, because each of the auxiliary operations—Last, DelLast, and ReHeap—moves from the root of the heap to a leaf, and such processing has $O(\log_2 N)$ by the shape property.

In reviewing the two approaches, note that Approach 2 specifies a particular heap that is the result of the insertion or deletion of an item. It is straightforward to check that the resulting heap of Approach 2 satisfies both the shape and value properties specified by Approach 1. Thus, an ADT satisfying Approach 2 also satisfies Approach 1. The converse, however, is not true, because Approach 1 allows many different heaps as the result of insertion or deletion, while Approach 2 mandates a specific result. Thus, Approach 1 really is more general than Approach 2.

Implementation

The shape property of a heap makes it possible to implement a heap using an array rather than pointer variables. If we move a heap into an array level by level, we know exactly where the children of each node are: given a node in location i, the left child is in location 2*i, and the right child is in location 2*i + 1. (See Figure 7.13.) This relationship between a node and its children also suggests that for any node in location j, its parent is in position j DIV 2.

You can think of the heap as being implemented as a list of nodes where the relationship that exists among the nodes is represented in their relative position within the list.

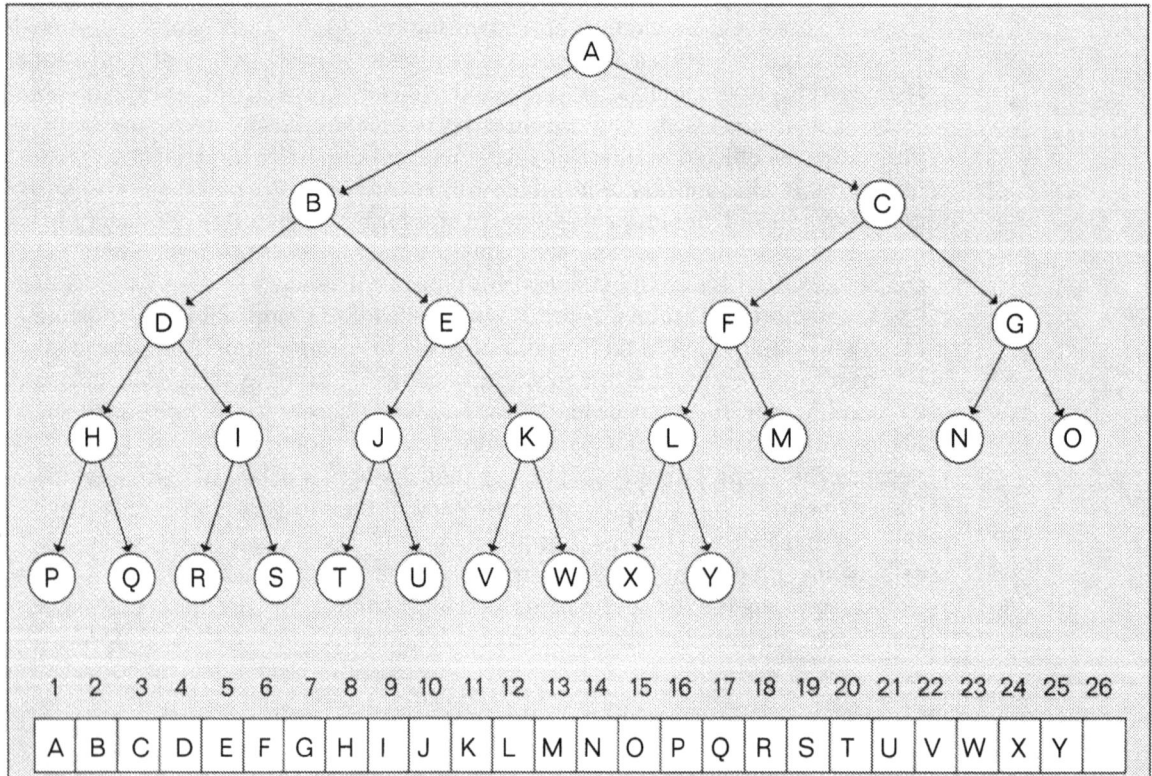

Figure 7.13 Heap and Implementation

```
(* To Access MaxHeap and ItemType. *)
USES < data defining module >

TYPE
    Nodes Type = 1..MaxHeap;
    HeapType = RECORD
        Heap      : ARRAY[NodesType] OF ItemType;
        Length    : 0..MaxHeap
    END;


VAR
    AHeap: HeapType
```

Using this implementation, the item with the highest priority is in AHeap.Heap[1]. The bottom, right-most item in the heap is in AHeap.Heap[AHeap.Length]. With these observations, we write the algorithms for the ADT Heap.

The heap is declared within the Heap ADT. The only operations in the interface are Create, Insert, Delete, IsEmpty, and IsFull. As discussed in Chapter 5, any array implementation limits the correctness of our code to those cases in which the array does not become full. We combine the Data and the Delete into a single procedure Delete, which returns a copy of the deleted item just as we did with the semi-structured data types in Chapter 5. For this module, we let the user be responsible for error checking.

```
PROCEDURE Create
(* Post:    Heap has been initialized.                       *)

PROCEDURE Insert(Item: ItemType)
(* Pre:     NOT IsFull                                        *)
(* Post:    Item is in Heap; Heap is a heap.                  *)

PROCEDURE Delete(VAR TopHeap: ItemType)
(* Pre:     NOT IsEmpty                                       *)
(* Post:    The item with the highest priority is returned    *)
(*          in TopHeap and is removed from the heap.          *)
(*          Heap is still a heap.                             *)

FUNCTION IsEmpty: Boolean;
(* Pre:     Heap has been initialized.                        *)
(* Post:    IsEmpty is True if there are no items in Heap;    *)
(*          False otherwise.                                  *)

FUNCTION IsFull: Boolean;
(* Pre:     Heap has been initialized.                        *)
(* Post:    IsFull is True if there is no more room in Heap;  *)
(*          False otherwise.                                  *)
```

We make our algorithms more specific than usual, because we know what our implementation is going to be. The following are the operations Create, IsEmpty, and IsFull. These are reasonably straightforward, so we give them without explanation.

Create

Our basic approach for working with the nodes of a tree utilizes the Length field to keep track of the last array element utilized for data within the array. Because the initial tree is empty, no array elements are utilized, and this Length is 0.

```
AHeap.Length ← 0
```

Is Full: Boolean

```
RETURN (AHeap.Length = MaxHeap)
```

Is Empty: Boolean

```
RETURN (AHeap.Length = 0)
```

Insert (Item: ItemType);

Turning to the Insert operation using this array implementation, we note that the bottom, right-most element in the tree is at position AHeap.Length. When a new element is added to the heap, the shape property dictates that the new element must go into the next position on the current level or into the first position in the next level if the tree is full. In the mapping from the tree into the array, the next position in the tree corresponds to the next free array slot; that is, AHeap.Length must be incremented by 1 and the new element must be put into AHeap[AHeap.Length].

In order to maintain the value property, we have to examine the relative values of various tree elements. We cannot simply add a new element at the end of the tree and expect the result to be a heap. This examination of tree elements can occur in several ways. For example, we could start at the root of the heap and move downward, inserting or updating elements until we reach the bottom position. Alternatively, we could start at the last array position of the tree and work our way upward. Because each of these ideas leads to a reasonable algorithm, we present both algorithms here. A third approach, which follows the specifications for Approach 2 very closely, is outlined in the exercises at the end of the chapter.

A Bottom-Up Approach to Insertion

The bottom-up approach to insertion places the inserted value at the end of the array and then moves data as necessary. More specifically, the algorithm begins with the statements:

AHeap.Length ← AHeap.Length + 1
AHeap.Heap[AHeap.Length] ← Item

This produces a new, larger tree that includes the new item, and this tree satisfies the shape property, as already explained. Furthermore, with the exception of the new item at the right-most bottom of the tree, the new tree satisfies the value property. As an example, consider the heap of Figure 7.14.

Now suppose we wish to insert the value 8. Our first step increments the Length field and places the value 8 at the end of the array.

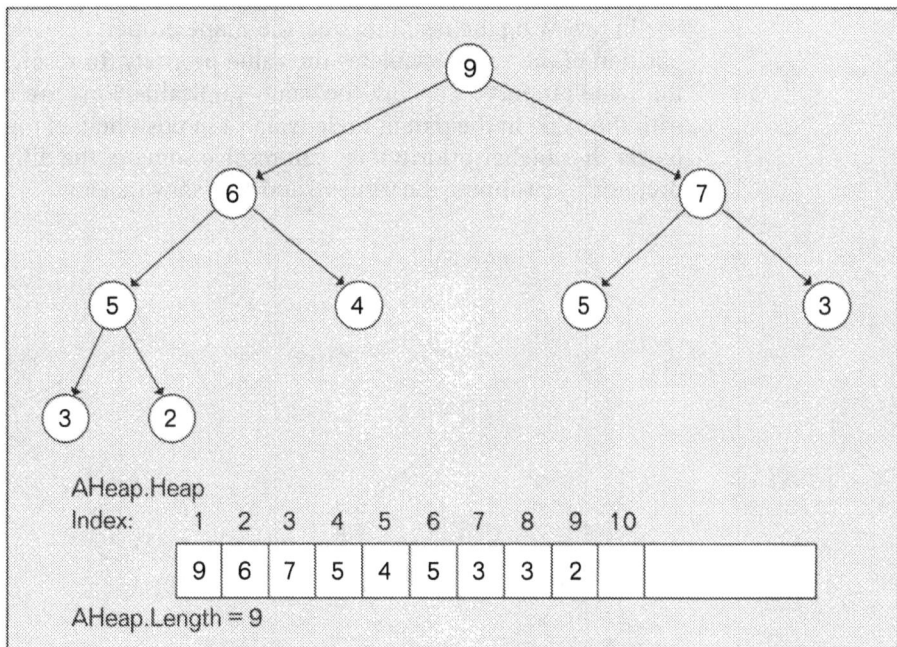

Figure 7.14 A Heap Implemented with an Array

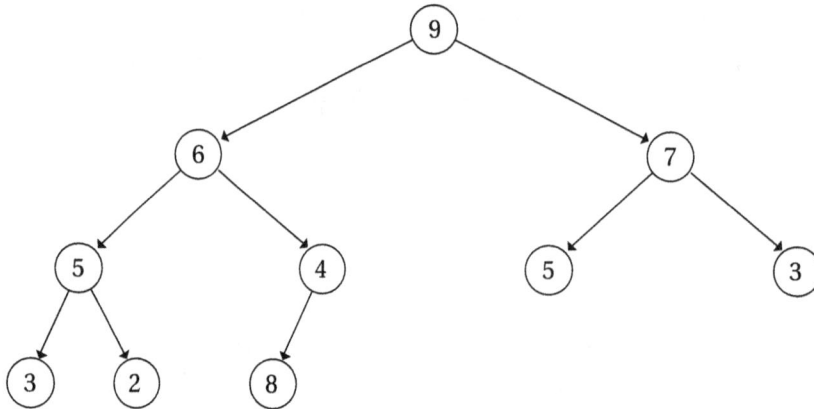

AHeap.Heap
Index: 1 2 3 4 5 6 7 8 9 10

9	6	7	5	4	5	3	3	2	8	

AHeap.Length = 10

In reviewing the resulting tree, the shape property clearly holds, and only the position of the value 8 violates the value property. To resolve this difficulty with the value property, we work the value 8 upwards. First, we compare the value 8 with the value in the parent node (value 4 in position 5 of the array). Because 8 is bigger (has higher priority), we can resolve some of the difficulty with the value property by swapping the values 8 and 4, as shown below.

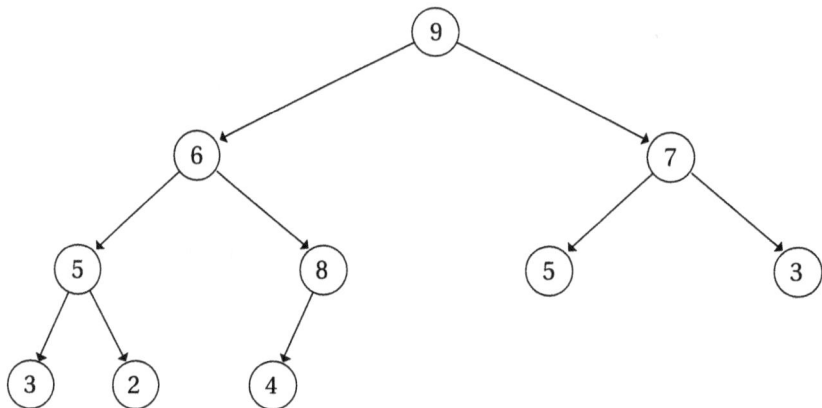

AHeap.Heap
Index: 1 2 3 4 5 6 7 8 9 10

9	6	7	5	8	5	3	3	2	4	

AHeap.Length = 10

Now, at least the bottom two rows satisfy the shape property. However, the 8 is still larger than the value 6 in its parent node. To resolve this difficulty, we swap the 8 and the 6 to get the following tree.

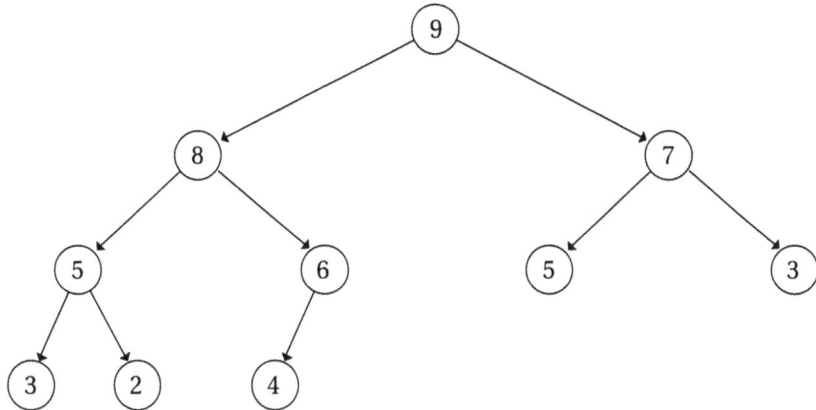

AHeap.Heap
Index:

1	2	3	4	5	6	7	8	9	10		
9	8	7	5	6	5	3	3	2	4		

AHeap.Length = 10

In swapping the 8 and the 6, note that the 6 was already bigger than all values in its left subtree, and 8 is bigger than 6. Thus, placing 8 in the higher node still maintains the value property for the left part of the heap. The nodes below the 6 in the resulting tree were also below the 6 in the original heap. Thus, the value property also is maintained in this subtree, and the value property now has been checked for the bottom three rows of the new tree.

Comparing the 8 with the next node up, we find that 8 is smaller than 9, so the value property must hold throughout this new tree.

The general algorithm follows this example. We place a new element at the end of the array, as the bottom, right-most element in the tree. This guarantees that the new tree satisfies the shape property. Next, we compare the new element with the value in its parent node and swap if necessary. By continuing to work upward, comparing each element with the element above and swapping as needed, we can reorganize elements in the tree to meet the value property. The movement of the new element upward continues until the value in the parent node is larger (has higher priority) than the new one or until we have reached the root of the tree. During this process, we note that we can work upward in a tree easily in this array implementation: if a node has location j in the array, its parent has location j DIV 2. Having made this observation, we can write the algorithm.

```
AHeap.Length ← AHeap.Length + 1
AHeap.Heap[AHeap.Length] ← Item
Child ← AHeap.Length
Parent ← Child DIV 2
WHILE (Child > 1) AND (AHeap.Heap[Parent] < AHeap.Heap[Child]) DO
    Swap (AHeap.Heap[Parent], AHeap.Heap[Child])
    Child ← Parent
    Parent ← Child DIV 2
END WHILE
```

Because the resulting tree satisfies both the shape and the value properties and contains the desired elements, this new tree meets the Approach 1 specifications for the Insert operation of the Heap ADT. (In the exercises at the end of the chapter, you are asked to determine if this new tree also meets the Approach 2 specifications for Insert.)

A Top-Down Approach to Insertion

While the implementation just discussed inserts the new element at the bottom of the tree and works upward, a second approach works from the top downward. Before describing the details of the algorithm, let us consider an example. Suppose we wish to insert a new value, 5, into the heap of Figure 7.14. As already noted, to maintain the shape property, a new node must go into position 10 in the array. In this approach, however, instead of working from this leaf node upward, we work from the root down. More specifically, our processing follows the path from the root of the tree downward to the position of this new node. This path is shown in the following figure.

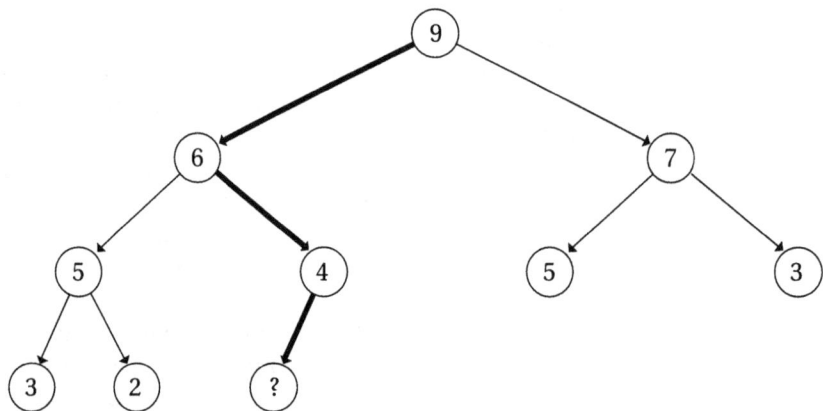

AHeap.Heap

Index:	1	2	3	4	5	6	7	8	9	10			
	9	6	7	5	4	5	3	3	2	?			

AHeap.Length = 10

To insert the value 5, we start at the root. As the value in the root (9) is larger than 5, we cannot place the 5 in the root if we wish to satisfy the value property. Thus, we move downward along the designated path, to the node containing the value 6 (the node at array position 2). Again, the value in the node (6) is bigger than the item to be inserted, so the value property does not allow us to insert the 5 here. Again, we move downward along the path, to the node with the value 4 (in position 5). Here, the value to be inserted (5) is larger than the value at the node (4). Thus, we replace the 4 with the 5 and seek to insert the 4 lower in the tree. Because the node at the next level downward is the new node, we place the 4 there. This gives the following tree.

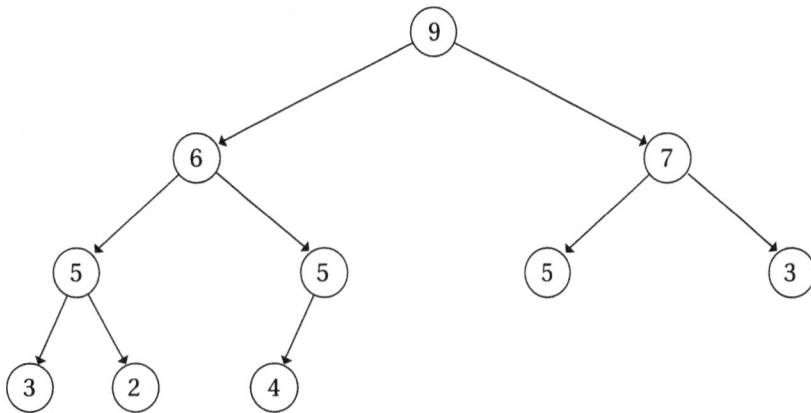

AHeap.Heap

Index:	1	2	3	4	5	6	7	8	9	10			
	9	6	7	5	5	5	3	3	2	4			

AHeap.Length = 10

The resulting structure satisfies the shape property, because the new node is added as the right-most node at the bottom level of the tree. Also, the value property is satisfied because, at each stage, we either maintain the same structure found previously or we replace the value at a node by a larger value.

To clarify this approach even further, suppose we wish to insert the value 8 into this new heap. Again, an insertion requires the addition of a new node at the end of the array, and we can identify the path from the root to this new node as shown below.

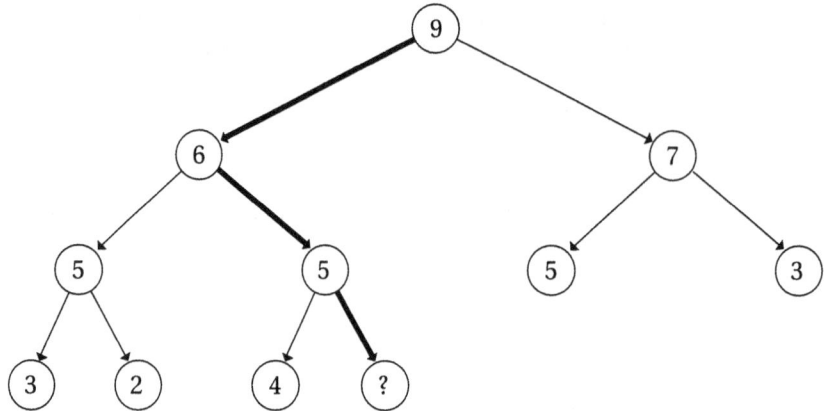

AHeap.Heap
Index: 1 2 3 4 5 6 7 8 9 10 11

| 9 | 6 | 7 | 5 | 5 | 5 | 3 | 3 | 2 | 4 | ? | | |

AHeap.Length = 11

To insert the new value 8, we again start at the root. The value at the root, again, is larger than the new value, so we do not replace the root's value, but rather move to the next node in the path to the new node; that is, we move to the node containing the value 6. This time, the new value 8 is larger than the value at the node we are examining. Thus, we replace the value at the node by the 8 and insert the 6 farther down in the tree. The current state of the tree is as follows.

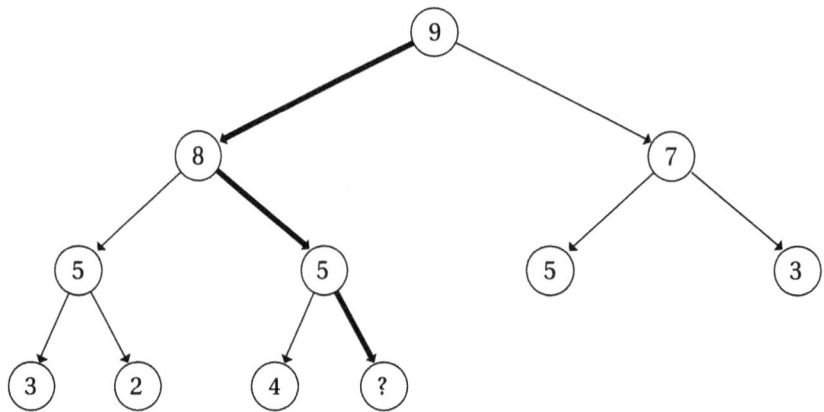

AHeap.Heap
Index: 1 2 3 4 5 6 7 8 9 10 11

| 9 | 8 | 7 | 5 | 5 | 5 | 3 | 3 | 2 | 4 | ? | | |

AHeap.Length = 11

Because we replaced the 6 by a larger value, 8, and because we already checked that the 8 was smaller than the parent node (9 in the root), our replacement maintains the value property throughout this structure.

To continue the algorithm, we still need to insert the value 6 farther down in the tree. As we resume our path downward, we compare the 6 with the value (5) at the next node in the path. Because 6 is larger, we replace the 5 with the 6 and note that we have to insert the value 5 farther down in the tree. As before, the resulting tree still has the value property. This tree is shown below.

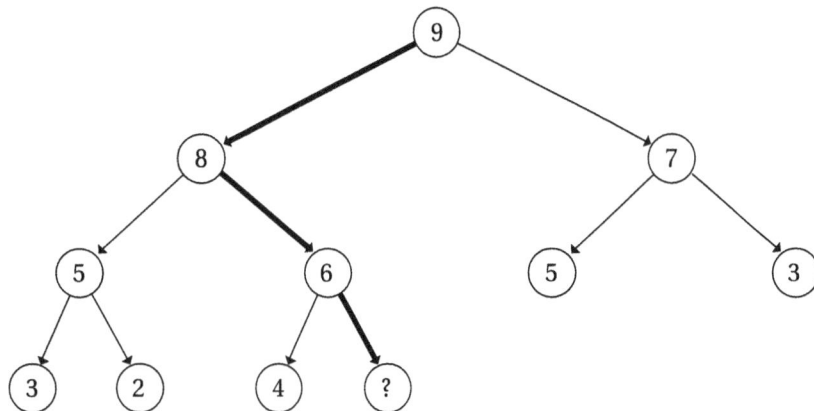

AHeap.Heap

Index:	1	2	3	4	5	6	7	8	9	10	11	
	9	8	7	5	6	5	3	3	2	4	?	

AHeap.Length = 11

At this point, we have reached the new node to be added to the tree, and we can insert the 5 without further checking. We have already determined that the item to be inserted (5) is smaller than what has come before. Thus, the resulting tree still satisfies the value property. The resulting tree is shown on the next page.

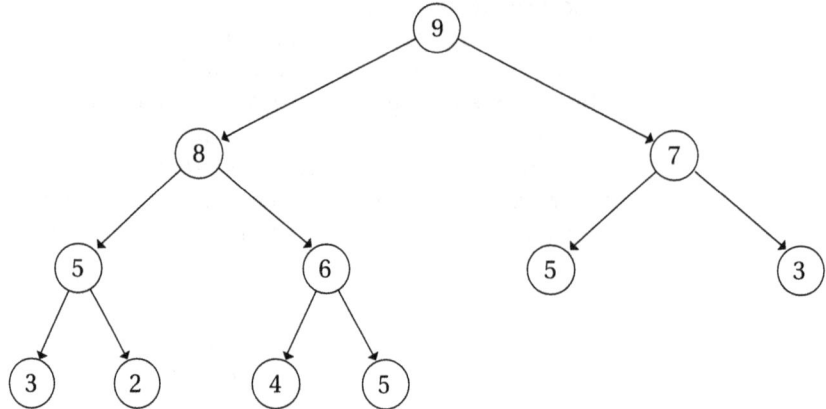

AHeap.Heap
Index:

1	2	3	4	5	6	7	8	9	10	11	
9	8	7	5	6	5	3	3	2	4	5	

AHeap.Length = 11

These examples illustrate the main ideas of the top-down approach. We start at the root of the tree and work along the path to the new node at the bottom. At each stage, we compare the value to be inserted with the value at a node. If the node value is bigger, we simply continue down the tree. If the value to be inserted is bigger, we replace the node value with the value to be inserted and continue downward. In the later steps, this replaced value becomes the value to be inserted farther down in the tree.

While this outline is reasonably straightforward, one vital detail remains. How can we determine the appropriate path from the root to the new node in the tree? This question can be answered in at least two different ways. One way to determine this path follows directly from the Approach 2 specifications of the Heap ADT: we can use Full, which in turn uses Height. While we could use the axioms directly, Height and Full would do a lot of redundant processing. This prompts us to ask if there is an easier way. We know that the maximum number of nodes in a tree with i levels is $2^i - 1$. If AHeap.Length equals the maximum number of nodes, the tree is full. What about a subtree? Each time we move to a subtree, we cut the maximum number of nodes in half. This leads to the following hypothesis: *If AHeap.Length is greater than the index of the root plus the maximum number of nodes in the subtree, the subtree is full.* You are asked to complete this approach to determining the path in the exercises at the end of the chapter.

A second way to determine the appropriate path from the root to the new node in the tree takes advantage of the special numbering of nodes in the array. Before stating the general approach, we look at an example. Suppose we want to insert a new element into the heap of Figure 7.13. The heap in that figure already has 25 nodes, so the new node goes in array position 26. Also, the path from the root (array position 1) to this new node involves nodes at array positions 1, 3, 6, 13, and 26. Below, we write out these array positions using their binary representation.

1	1
3	11
6	110
13	1101
26	11010

In reviewing these binary numbers, we see that each binary number has one binary digit more than its predecessor. Furthermore, each binary number is obtained from its predecessor by adding a 0 or a 1 at the right—the leading digits in the numbers are the same in each case.

This pattern is not accidental. We already know that in this array implementation, we can get from a node at position i to its left child by looking at array position 2*i. The right child is at position 2*i + 1. In the binary system, multiplication by 2 corresponds to a shifting of all digits to the left and adding the digit 0 (much like multiplication by 10 in the decimal system). Thus, the position of the left child can be obtained by adding the digit 0 at the right of the binary representation of the parent, while the right child can be obtained by adding the digit 1.

These observations have several interesting consequences. First, we can use the digits of the binary representation of the position of a node to identify the path from the root to that node. The initial 1 corresponds to the root. For subsequent digits, a 0 indicates that we should go left in the path, while a 1 indicates that the path goes right. This is illustrated below for the path to node number 26 mentioned above.

26 =	1	1	0	1	0
	↑	↑	↑	↑	↑
	root	right	left	right	left

Second, given the binary representation of the position of a new node, we can use subsequent digits to determine the positions of all nodes on the path from the root. For position 26 = (binary 11010), the root is at position (binary 1), the leading binary digit of 26; the next node in the path is at position (binary 11), the leading two binary digits of 26; the third node in the path is at position (binary 110), the leading three binary digits of 26; and so forth.

Thus, given the binary representation of the position of a new node in the tree, we can compute all nodes in the path to it from the root by taking progressively more binary digits from the left of the binary number. In practice, the mechanism to extract these digits from a number may depend upon the capabilities of the language and of the machine at hand. For example, a shift operation can make such computations extremely efficient. Another simple approach uses a bit mask to hide the right bits of a number. This is illustrated in the table on the next page.

Index (of New Node)		Bit Mask		Index DIV BitMask	
(Decimal)	*(Binary)*	*(Decimal)*	*(Binary)*	*(Decimal)*	*(Binary)*
26	11010	16	10000	1	1
26	11010	8	1000	3	11
26	11010	4	100	6	110
26	11010	2	10	13	1101
26	11010	1	1	26	11010

This table illustrates that if we divide the index of where the new node must go by the appropriate power of 2, we obtain the appropriate index for successive positions along the path to that node. At the start, the required power of two is the largest power of 2 less than or equal to the node's index. Subsequent powers of 2 are obtained by dividing the Bit Mask successively by 2. This discussion motivates the following code.

```
AHeap.Length← AHeap.Length + 1;
(*Compute the initial BitMask *)
BitMask← 1
WHILE BitMask * 2 < AHeap.Length DO
    BitMask← BitMask * 2
END WHILE
(* Work downward from the root *)
TreePosition← AHeap.Length DIV BitMask
WHILE TreePosition < AHeap.Length DO
    IF Item > AHeap.Heap[TreePosition]
        THEN Swap (Item, AHeap.Heap[TreePosition])
    END IF
    BitMask← BitMask DIV 2
    TreePosition← AHeap.Length DIV BitMask
END WHILE
AHeap.Heap[AHeap.Length]← Item
```

As previously noted, the tree maintains its value property after each iteration down the insertion path. At the end of this insertion process, all desired values are present in the tree, with a new node in the correct location to maintain the shape property.

Delete (VAR TopHeap: ItemType)

We use the specifications for Delete following the more constrained approach to motivate our implementation. Because we know just where nodes are located in our array, some simplifications are possible. The top of the heap is just the item in AHeap.Heap[1]. Last finds the right-most node, which is in AHeap.Heap[AHeap.Length]. DelLast just removes the right-most node; decrementing AHeap.Length does this. What, then, does Delete actually do? It creates a heap where the value in the right-most node is put into the first position, and the right-most node is then removed from the tree.

ReHeap takes this new heap and restores the heap value property by determining if the value in the root has higher priority than the value in the root of either subtree. If this is true, the heap property is intact. If not, the value in the root is exchanged with the value in the root of either the left or right subtree, depending on which has higher priority. The subtree where the change occurs then has its heap property restored in the same way. The process is guaranteed to end because a leaf node is a heap. How do we recognize a leaf node? Twice its index is greater than the length of the heap. There is one additional difficulty: we need to avoid moving beyond the end of the tree in cases where a node near the bottom of the tree has a left child but not a right one.

```
WITH AHeap
    TopHeap ← Heap[1]
    Heap[1]← Heap[Length]
    Length ← Length − 1
    IsAHeap ← False
    HeapIndex ← 1
    WHILE NOT IsAHeap DO
        IsAHeap ← (HeapIndex*2 > Length) OR
                    (Heap[HeapIndex] > Heap[HeapIndex*2] AND
                    (HeapIndex*2 = Length OR
                    Heap[HeapIndex] > Heap[HeapIndex*2 + 1]))
        IF NOT IsAHeap
            THEN
                IF HeapIndex*2 = Length OR
                        Heap[HeapIndex*2] > Heap[HeapIndex*2 + 1]
                    THEN    Max ← HeapIndex*2
                    ELSE    Max ← HeapIndex*2 + 1
                END IF
                Swap(Heap[HeapIndex], Heap[Max])
                HeapIndex ← Max
        END IF
    END WHILE
```

Complexity

The shape property ensures that the insertion into and deletion from a heap is $O(\log_2 N)$, where N is AHeap.Length. In its worst case, the bottom-up insertion algorithm continues until the root is encountered, but the shape property guarantees that this can involve no more than $O(\log_2 N)$ steps. The top-down algorithm first computes BitMask and then travels the full height of the tree. In both cases, however, the shape property again guarantees that neither of these steps requires more than $O(\log_2 N)$ steps, although this top-down approach requires two loops of this length instead of just one. Similarly, the deletion algorithm has worst case $O(\log_2 N)$, because it follows a path downward from the root. If the heap property is reestablished before a leaf is found, the algorithm stops.

Would we ever want to implement a heap using pointer variables? Probably not, for two reasons. The first is that pointers require extra space and are unnecessary because of the shape property. The second is that the algorithms would have to mirror the axioms, including many unnecessary calls to recursive functions. Of course, the array implementation has the same limitations of all array-based structures: we have to know a maximum number of items to begin with.

Application: Implementation of Priority Queues

Because of the shape and value properties of a heap, it makes an ideal implementation structure for a priority queue. The operations and axioms for a priority queue may be considered as a selected subset of those for the Heap ADT. In particular, the Priority Queue ADT of Chapter 5 allows us to Create a priority queue, Enque an item with a given priority, retrieve the data for the top priority item (Next), remove this top priority item (SServe), and determine if there are any items on the priority queue (IsEmpty). These operations of the Priority Queue ADT correspond exactly to the operations Create, Insert, Data, Delete, and IsEmpty of the Heap ADT, except that the priority is given explicitly for Enque and only implicitly in our definition of Insert for heaps.

With this observation, we can use our efficient implementation of the Heap ADT to give an efficient implementation of priority queues. In fact, this is the best implementation of a priority queue. Insertion and Deletion are worst case $O(\log_2 N)$.

SUMMARY

A tree is a finite set of zero or more nodes such that, if the set is not empty, there is a designated node called the root, and the remaining nodes are partitioned into zero or more disjoint sets of nodes where each set is a tree. A binary tree is a tree where the maximum number of subtrees for each node is two. Any tree can be represented as a binary tree. A binary tree is full if it contains the maximum number of nodes for a binary tree with that number of levels. A binary tree is complete if it is full or if it is full through the next to the last level and if all the nodes on the last level are as far left as possible.

Threading a tree is an implementation technique in which the NIL pointers in a tree are replaced with pointers to a node's predecessor and successor. Threading allows the tree to be traversed without having to use a stack or recursion.

A heap is a complete tree that has the property that the value in a node has a priority greater than or equal to the priority of any value in any node of its sub-trees. Heaps may be specified using two rather different approaches. The first approach gives an implementor complete flexibility in determining how to insert or delete items from a heap, provided the shape and value properties of a heap are maintained. The second approach specifies how data are to be moved within a heap during the insert and delete operations. This second approach, while giving a programmer much less flexibility than the first approach, allows us to conclude that the insertion and deletion operations have $O(\log_2 N)$. Such results motivated our use of the heap to represent a priority queue.

EXERCISES

1. Define the following terms.

leaf	sibling	descendant	full tree
degree	ancestor	level	complete tree

2. a. If the root is considered to be at level 0, how many nodes are there in a full binary tree with N levels?

   b. How many nodes are there on level i in a full binary tree?

3. The text states that a tree with N nodes must have $N+1$ NIL pointers. This fact can be proved in several ways.

   a. Prove this result with a direct (not inductive) argument.

   b. Prove this result using mathematical induction.

4. Fill in the following blanks.

   ```
   structure  BinTree (of Item)
   interface  Create                                    → BinTree
              Make(BinTree, ItemType, BinTree)          → _____
              LeftChild(BinTree, ItemType, BinTree)     → BinTree
              RightChild(BinTree, ItemType, BinTree)    → _____
              Root(BinTree)                             → _____
              Insert(BinTree, ItemType)                 → _____
              Find(BinTree, ItemType)                   → _____
       end
   axioms     for all l, r in BinTree, i, i1, i2 in ItemType, let

              (* fill in the axioms *)
   ```

5. Suppose the following operation has been added to the ADT Queue.

   Append(Queue, Queue) → Queue
   Append(Q, Create) = Q
   Append(Q, Enque(P, d)) = Enque(Append(Q, P), d)

Assuming the ADT Queue (with the Append operation) has been added to the domain of the ADT BinTree, give the axioms for the following operations that traverse the BinTree, leaving the result in a queue.

PostOrder(BinTree) → queue
InOrder(BinTree) → queue

6. Suppose a stack was used instead of a queue to store the elements from preorder and postorder traversals. How would the items retrieved from the stacks following these traversals relate to the items retrieved from queues created by similar traversals? Justify your result.

7. Write pseudocode to add a node as the leaf of a threaded binary tree, updating the threads appropriately.

8. In defining the specifications for operation HasValueProperty, we stated, "We do not have to check the values at every node of every subtree." Prove that this statement is true. That is, prove that if the value at each node is greater than or equal to the value at each child, then the value at each node is also greater than or equal to the value at every node of every subtree. (*Hint:* Use induction.)

9. The operation SameElements returns True or False, depending upon whether two binary trees contain the same elements. In this chapter, this operation was defined using the ADT SortedList as an auxiliary data type.

   a. If you know that each tree contains no duplicate data, then one can determine if two trees contain the same elements by testing to see if each node in one tree is found within the other tree.

   Write specifications for an operation IsIn that returns True if a given data value is found within a binary tree, and False otherwise.

   Use the operation IsIn to define SameElements, assuming any given tree contains no duplicate data.

   b. Find an example of two trees, each containing some duplicate data, where each tree contains the same number of nodes, each data value in one tree is also in the other, but the two trees do not contain exactly the same data. (In other words, the duplicate values in one tree may not be repeated the same number of times in the other tree.) This example shows that the solution in part (a) does not solve the general problem of determining when two trees have the same elements.

   c. Define an operation CountOccurences that counts the number of times a specific element appears within a binary tree.

   Either use CountOccurences to define the operation SameElements or explain why such an operation is inadequate to define SameElements (without using still other tree operations beyond Create and Make).

   d. Define an operation Delete that removes one occurrence of an element from a binary tree, leaving another binary tree containing all other elements of the original tree (in some position).

   Define the operation SameElements using a combination of IsIn and Delete, as described above.

10. A threaded binary tree optimizes the tree for traversals. Describe in a paragraph or two how this technique works.

11. Give the algorithm for inserting a node into a threaded tree as a right child.

12. Give the algorithm for finding the predecessor of a node in a threaded binary tree.

13. Give the algorithm for threading a binary tree.

14. Draw the threads in the following binary tree.

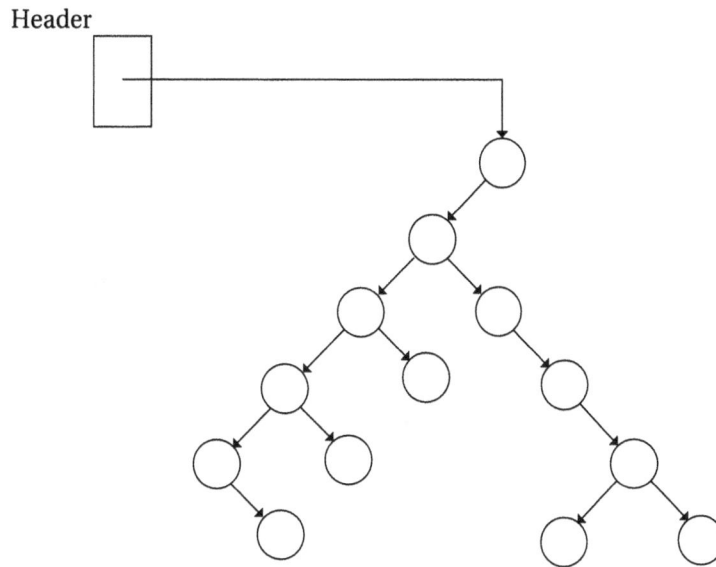

15. Any tree can be represented as a binary tree. Give the algorithm for transforming an n-ary tree into a binary tree.

16. Discuss why we might want to be able to represent an n-ary tree as a binary tree.

17. Convert the following tree to a binary tree.

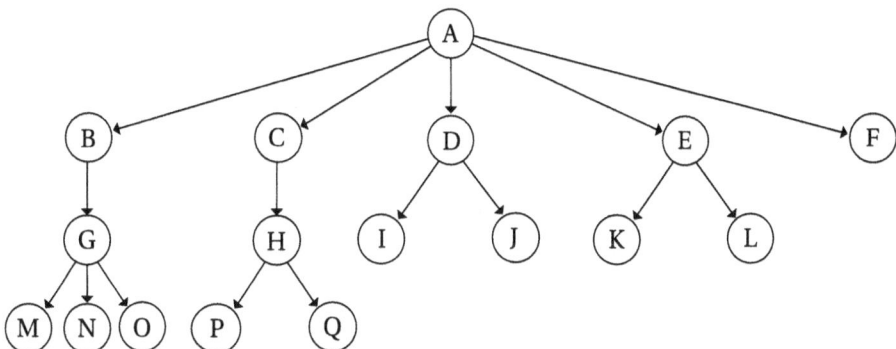

18. The following tree is the binary representation of an n-ary tree. Draw the original tree.

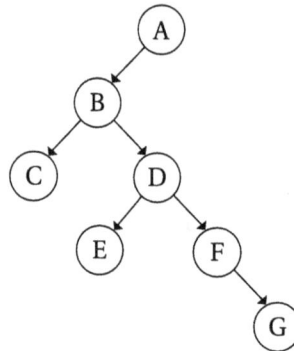

19. The right child in a binary representation of an n-ary tree was what in the original tree?

20. The left child in a binary representation of an n-ary tree was what in the original tree?

21. Why does the root not have a right child in the binary representation of an n-ary tree?

22. The following operation is added to the definition of the ADT Stack.

    Guess(Stack, Stack) → Stack

    Guess(S1, Create) = S1
    Guess(S1, Push(S2, i)) = Push(Guess(S1, S2), i)

    a. Say in words what Guess does.

    b. The ADT Stack (with the Guess operation) has been added to the domain of the ADT BinTree. Give the axioms for the following operations, which traverse the BinTree, leaving the result in a Stack so that proper ordering of the tree elements is obtained when the stack is Popped.

    PostOrder(BinTree) → Stack
    PreOrder(BinTree) → Stack
    InOrder(BinTree) → Stack

23. Implement the node primitives using pointer variables.

24. The ADT Binary Tree does not have a Delete operation.

    a. Define a Delete operation without overspecifying the shape of the resulting tree.

    b. Write an appropriate algorithm to implement your Delete operation.

25. Consider the decision tree in Figure 7.11, which is based upon a binary search of an ordered, nonindexed list, implemented as an array. Examine the various branches and conditions and explain why the machine cannot actually get to the "Done" node at the extreme left side of this decision tree at level 2—two levels below the root.

26. Consider the following segment, which finds the smallest of three numbers.

```
Read (A, B, C)
IF A < B
    THEN IF A < C
              THEN Smallest ← A
              ELSE Smallest ← C
         END IF
    ELSIF B < C
         THEN   Smallest ← B
         ELSE   Smallest ← C
END IF
```

Draw the decision tree that corresponds to this code.

27. Show that the heap that results from the more constrained heap specifications for Insert must satisfy the shape and value properties. And thus, show that any Insert operation that satisfies the more constrained axioms also satisfies the more general axioms.

28. This chapter presents code to implement the Insert operation in either of two ways: a bottom-up algorithm and a top-down algorithm.

    a. For each of these algorithms, write a paragraph explaining why the algorithm produces a binary tree that satisfies the general Heap ADT specifications for Insert (Approach 1).

    b. Examine each of these implementations to determine if they satisfy the more constrained Heap ADT specifications for Insert (Approach 2). For each implementation, either prove that the axioms are met or give a counterexample that illustrates how they can fail.

29. This chapter suggests that one can write an Insert operation for the Heap ADT in a top-down fashion, directly from the axioms, using Full and Height to determine when to move left and right from node to node. In the array implementation of a heap, the chapter also suggests that the value of Full can be inferred directly from a current position in the tree, the current level of the tree, and the location of the end of the array (where the new node is inserted).

    Write an implementation following this top-down approach to the Insert operation.

30. Figure 7.12 shows two possible heaps that might result from the insertion of the value 3 into an original heap of six nodes.

    a. Draw two additional heap structures that could result from this insertion.

    b. How may different heap structures could result from this insertion (including the two shown in Figure 7.12 and the two more you drew in part (a) of this exercise).

31. a. Write code to determine if a particular value is stored within a binary tree, implemented as an array of records. (In this exercise, you should not anticipate later

chapters by assuming that the tree has any special properties. For example, do not assume that the tree is a search tree. Also, do not assume that the tree is a heap.)

b. If the tree has n nodes, determine the order of your algorithm.

c. Could you make your code more efficient if the tree were a heap? If so, how, and what would be the order of your revised code? If not, explain why.

32. The axiom for the Merge function used the Insert operation to insert the items from L1 into L2. Rewrite this axiom without using the Insert operation.

Binary Search Trees

The binary search tree is a binary tree with the property that the value in a node is greater than any value in the node's left subtree and less than or equal to any value in the node's right subtree. This value property guarantees fast search time provided the tree is relatively balanced. In this chapter, we define the properties of the binary search tree and examine two types of binary search trees: static trees, where the set of values in the nodes is known in advance and never changes, and dynamic trees, where the values in a tree may change over time. We examine ways of building trees of each type in order to guarantee that the trees remain balanced.

Shape and Searching

Nodes within binary trees are organized into a hierarchical structure, starting at a root node and continuing through several levels of children. This chapter considers several ways of adding additional properties to this hierarchical structure in order to improve the efficiency of some common processing tasks. In particular, suppose the data within the nodes can be ordered in some way. (For example, we might order strings alphabetically or numbers by size.) With this assumed ordering, a **binary search tree** is a binary tree with the property that, for every node R, all children in R's left subtree contain values less than the value in R, and all children in R's right subtree contain values greater than or equal to the value in R. For example, Figure 8.1 shows two binary search trees that use the alphabetical order of strings as their underlying ordering.

> **Binary Search Tree** A binary tree with the following property: The values in a node's left subtree are less than the value in the node, and the values in a node's right subtree are greater than or equal to the value in the node.

In Figure 8.1 (a), Harry is the root, and all strings in the left subtree come before Harry in alphabetical order. Similarly, all strings in the right subtree come after Harry. Likewise, the left subtree of the node labeled "Bill" contains data that always comes before Bill in alphabetical order, and Bill's right subtree contains data coming after Bill. This same ordering property applies to all nodes in both parts of Figure 8.1.

Figure 8.1 also demonstrates that binary search trees may have rather different shapes. The tree in part (a) is rather full; all nodes are within 3 levels of the root. This tree is not full (Why?), but it is quite compact. In contrast, the same data are stored in part (b) of the figure, but here Ellen is 10 levels away from the root. In fact, the tree in part (b) looks very much like a linear list!

In order to find an element within a binary search tree, we start at the root and compare the desired value with the data found in this node. If we are lucky, the desired item is in this root node. However, if we are unlucky, we determine if the desired item comes before or after the data at the present node. If the item comes before, we continue our search in the left subtree. Otherwise, we look in the right subtree. Thus, to find MacKay in the tree of Figure 8.1 (a), we compare MacKay with Harry. Because Harry comes first alphabetically, we continue our search with the right subtree; in other words, we search for MacKay within the subtree with Steven as root. Because MacKay comes before Steven, we move to the left subtree of Steven. The next comparison of data identifies the location of MacKay within the tree.

Figure 8.1 (a) suggests that full trees can allow a reasonably fast search of a structure in order to find a desired item. (We found MacKay in the third round of comparisons, for example.) In fact, our example suggests that the maximum amount of work required for searching a binary search tree is related to the number of levels within the tree. We make this observation more precise shortly.

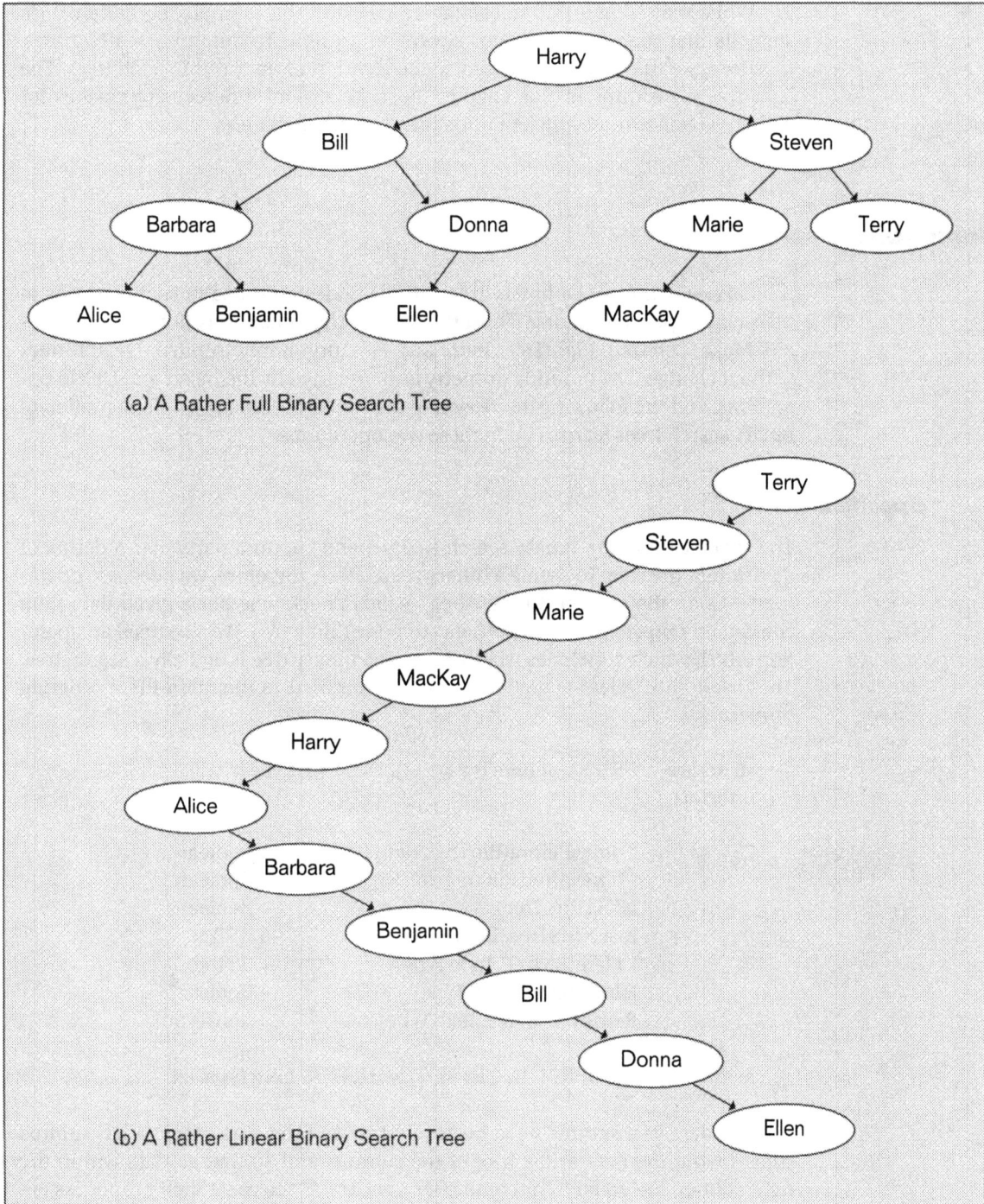

(a) A Rather Full Binary Search Tree

(b) A Rather Linear Binary Search Tree

Figure 8.1 Two Binary Search Trees

While searching in full trees may be efficient, the example in Figure 8.1 (b) suggests that such trees may not always be present. To minimize search times, therefore, we may want to reorganize the location of data within such trees. The later tree algorithms in this chapter illustrate several different approaches for making searches more efficient under varying circumstances.

Elementary Search Trees

A binary search tree is a binary tree with its nodes arranged in such a way as to maintain a special ordering. Thus, the general tree operations (for instance, Create, Make, LeftTree, RightTree, Item, and IsEmpty) apply to binary search trees without change. The ordering property is maintained by the Insert and Delete operations, and the following discussion of the specification and implementation of binary search trees focuses upon these two operations.

Specification

The specification of a binary search tree depends upon a particular ordering of data within the tree. To define a binary search tree, therefore, we need two operations—ComesBefore and ComesAfter—which check whether a given data item consistently precedes or follows data stored within a tree. We also need an operation IsBST, which concludes whether or not a binary tree is actually a search tree. The Insert and Delete operations then are specified to maintain these ordering properties.

structure	BSTree (of ItemType)
interface	.

.
.

ComesBefore(BinTree, ItemType)	$\rightarrow$ Boolean
ComesAfter(BinTree, ItemType)	$\rightarrow$ Boolean
IsBST(BinTree)	$\rightarrow$ Boolean
Insert(BSTree, ItemType)	$\rightarrow$ BSTree
Delete(BSTree, ItemType)	$\rightarrow$ BSTree
IsIn(BinTree, ItemType)	$\rightarrow$ Boolean
Retrieve(TSTree, ItemType)	$\rightarrow$ ItemType

end
axioms   **for all BT1, BT2 in BinTree, i1, i2, i3 ItemType, let**

The data in a subtree must be ordered so that the data within a left subtree come before the data at the root of the subtree, and so that all data within the right subtree are equal to or come after the data at the root. Such properties are stated precisely as follows.

ComesBefore(Create, i1) = True
ComesBefore(Make(BT1, i2, BT2), i1) = (i2 < i1)
   AND ComesBefore(BT1, i1) AND ComesBefore (BT2,i1)
ComesAfter(Create, Item) = True
ComesAfter(Make(BT1, i2, BT2), i1) = (i2 ≥ i1)
   AND ComesAfter(BT1, i1) AND ComesAfter(BT2, i1)

A binary search tree is a binary tree satisfying the ordering properties for all nodes.

IsBST(Create) = True
IsBST(Make(BT1, i1, BT2) =
   ComesBefore(BT1, i1) AND ComesAfter (BT2, i1)
     AND IsBST(BT1) AND IsBST(BT2)

The Insert and Delete operations create new trees with the desired elements and with the following order properties.

Insert(BT1, i1) = any BT2 where
   IsBST(BT2) AND EqualLists(Insert(IdentifyTreeElements(BT1), i1),
                 IdentifyTreeElements(BT2))
Delete(Create, i2) = Error
Delete(BT1, i2) = any BT2 where
   IsBST(BT2) AND EqualLists(IdentifyTreeElements(BT1),
              Insert(IdentifyTreeElements(BT2), i1))

As with the specification of the Insert and Delete operations for the Heap ADT in the previous chapter, these operations for binary search trees allow an implementor complete flexibility in determining the shape of trees and in placing data within nodes, provided the resulting structures have the desired properties. Thus, these specifications allow either tree in Figure 8.1, following a sequence of Insert commands, to place the given names in a binary search tree. This flexibility in the definition of Insert and Delete is particularly important later in this chapter, where we try to optimize search times under varying assumptions.

Given that the order properties hold, the Retrieve and IsIn functions are straightforward.

IsIn(Create, i1) = False
IsIn(Make(BT1, i2, BT2), i1) =
   IF i1 = i2
     THEN   True

```
            ELSE
                IF i1 < i2
                    THEN    IsIn(BT1, i1)
                    ELSE    IsIn(BT2, i1)
                END IF
        END IF

    Retrieve(Create, i1) = Error
    Retrieve(Make(BT1, i2, BT2), i1) =
        IF i1 = i2
            THEN   i2
            ELSE
                IF i1 < i2
                    THEN    Retrieve(BT1, i1)
                    ELSE    Retrieve(BT2, i1)
                END IF
        END IF
```

The Retrieve operation looks strange; in fact, it looks like it does nothing. If an item is not in the tree, an error is returned. If an item is in the tree, a copy of the item is returned. If ItemType is a scalar type or a string, Retrieve does, in fact, do nothing. However, in practice, ItemType is usually a record with a key field, and the relational operators are replaced with a user-defined comparison function. Therefore, Retrieve returns a copy of a record where the key field in the argument is the same as the key field in the record.

Implementation

There are various techniques for implementing binary search trees, and we study several of them. We begin with the simple scheme that uses a record with three fields. This time we use pointer variables.

```
(* To access ItemType and Compare. *)
USES < module that defines ItemType >

TYPE
    TreePointer = ↑TreeNode;
    TreeNode = RECORD
        Item    : ItemType;
        Right,
        Left    : TreePointer
    END RECORD ;
```

Create (VAR Root: TreePointer)

```
Root ← NIL
```

Other binary tree operations, such as LeftLeft, GetRight, GetItem, SetLeft, SetRight, and SetItem, all translate directly from the array implementation in Chapter 7 to pointers. The Insert and Delete operations require some discussion, however, as these must maintain the proper ordering of data within nodes. The IsIn and Retrieve operations follow the same search path as the Insert and Delete.

A simple implementation of the insert operation places new data in nodes that become leaves of an existing tree. The main consideration is the placement of the new node in an appropriate position. The precise location for this new node is motivated by the required ordering of data. To insert into a null tree, clearly the new node becomes a new root. For a non-null tree, the ordering property specifies whether the new node should be added to the left or the right subtree. From the standpoint of the root of the tree, the ordering property is maintained as long as the new node is inserted somewhere in the correct subtree. This discussion motivates the following recursive procedure.

Insert (VAR Root: TreePointer, Item: ItemType); (∗ Recursive Version ∗)

```
IF Root = NIL
    THEN
        New(Root)
        Root↑.Item ← Item
        Root↑.Left ← NIL
        Root↑.Right ← NIL
    ELSE
        CASE Compare(Item, Root↑.Item) OF
            Less   :    Insert(Root↑.Left)
            Equal,
            Greater:    Insert(Root↑.Right)
        END CASE
END IF
```

When this recursive procedure comes to a NIL pointer at the bottom of the tree, the new data item is inserted. Thus, the new tree contains the new item together with all previous data values, as required by the specifications. Furthermore, at each stage, the recursion to the left or right within the tree guarantees that the new tree has the required ordering property for each node and subtree. Thus, this Insert procedure satisfies the required conditions for a binary search tree.

An iterative solution to this problem unwinds the recursion, moving a pointer variable down the tree, level by level, until a NIL pointer is found for the insertion of a new leaf. Details of this iterative procedure are left as an exercise at the end of the chapter.

With this Insert procedure, we can build a binary search tree from a file as follows.

BuildSearchTreeFromFile (VAR Root: TreePointer)

```
Root ← NIL
Open file for reading node data
WHILE NOT EOF DO
    ReadFromFile (Item)
    Insert (Root, Item)
END WHILE
```

The implementation of the Delete operation is somewhat more complex, because the node being deleted could occur anywhere within the tree. We begin by searching down a tree to find the node to be deleted. Subsequent processing, however, may be divided into three main cases: a left subtree is empty, a right subtree is empty, or neither a left nor a right subtree is empty. (If both the left and the right subtrees are empty, we may follow either of the first two cases.)

In order to gain insight into the construction of a simple algorithm for deletion, we look at each of these cases in turn. First, we consider the case where the left subtree below the node to be deleted is empty.

Example: Delete(T, 5)

Before Deletion   After Deletion

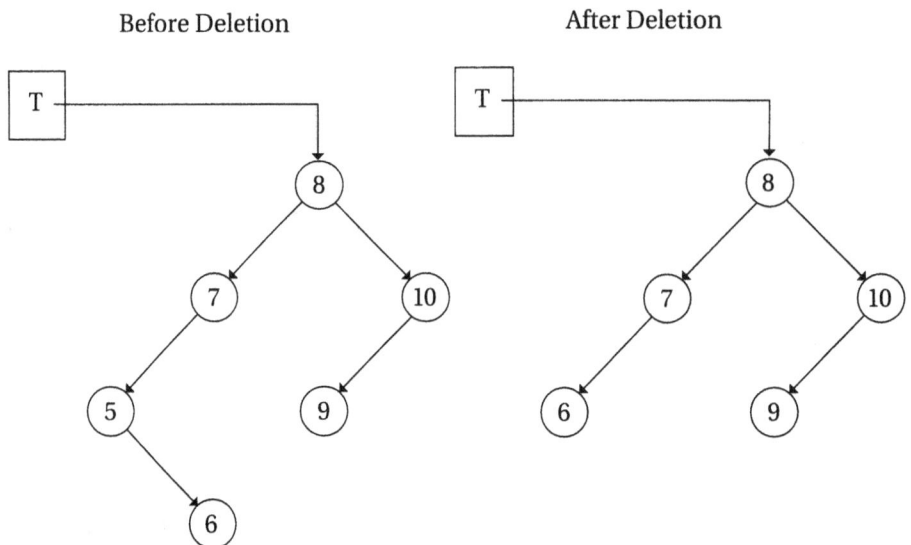

In this example, removing the node containing 5 divides the tree into two pieces: the upper tree with values 7, 8, 9, and 10, and the lower tree with value 6. In the final tree, these pieces must be connected, and we can accomplish this by inserting the lower tree in place of the node being deleted. Furthermore, we observe that the new structure must be a search tree because the lower subtree contained data smaller than the root. Thus, attaching this subtree to the left of the root maintains the order property.

Now we consider the case where the left subtree is not empty, but the right subtree is.

Example: Delete(T, 7)

Before Deletion

After Deletion

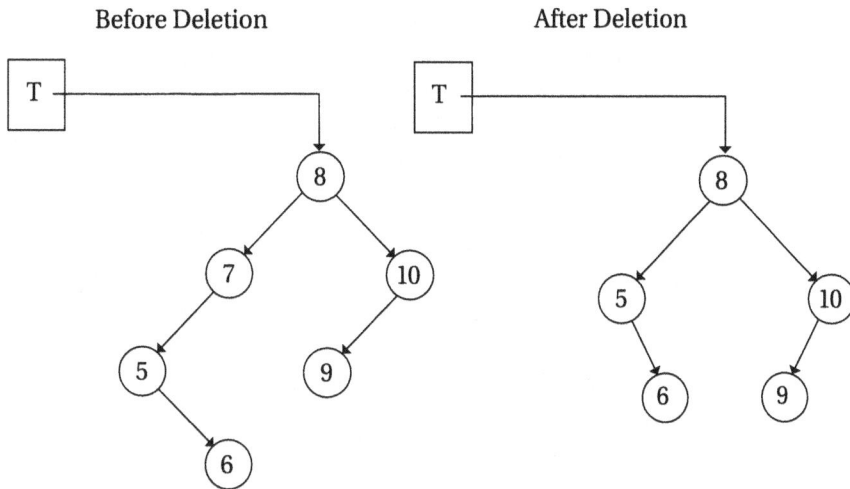

As before, the removal of the node containing 7 splits the tree into two pieces, and these pieces must be combined to obtain a new search tree. Here again, the lower tree can be inserted into the upper structure in place of the node being deleted, and the result is still a search tree. As before, this replacement maintains the proper ordering of data values.

The third case is where neither subtree is empty.

Example: Delete(T, 8)

Before Deletion

After Deletion

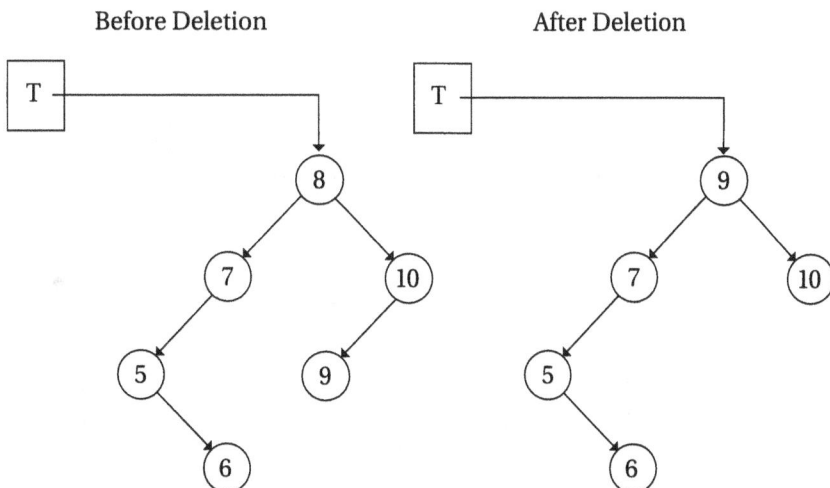

Here, the removal of the node containing 8 splits the tree into two parts, but it is not as clear exactly how to put the pieces together. The ordering property requires that all nodes in the left subtree be to the left of all nodes in the right subtree. With this in mind, consider the minimal element in the right subtree. This element (9) is smaller than or equal to any other element in the right tree and greater than the elements in the left subtree. Thus, this is a natural candidate to be the root of the new tree. Once we identify this smallest element in the right subtree, we can move it to the root of the old tree and delete it from the right subtree.

How do we find this smallest element in the right subtree? We just start at the root of that right subtree and continually move left (to smaller values) until we come to a node that has no left child.

With these examples, we can write the code for the Delete operation. In the following recursive version, the first task is to find the desired item. Once found, we follow the cases described in our examples. As with the specifications, this code assumes that the given item is found in the tree.

Delete (VAR Root: TreePointer, Item: ItemType);

```
CASE Compare(Item, Root↑.Item)
    Less     :   Delete (Root↑.Left, Item)        (* Delete in left subtree *)
    Greater  :   Delete (Root↑.Right, Item)       (* Delete in right subtree *)
    Equal    :   IF Root↑.Left = NIL              (* Node found *)
                    THEN   Root← Root↑.Right
                    ELSIF  Root↑.Right = NIL
                        THEN   Root← Root↑.Left
                    ELSE
                        MinRight ← Root↑.Right
                        WHILE MinRight↑.Left <> NIL DO
                            MinRight ← MinRight↑.Left
                        END WHILE
                        Root↑.Item ← MinRight↑.Item
                        Delete (Root↑.Right, MinRight↑.Item)
                    END IF
END CASE
```

The iterative version of this algorithm replaces the above recursion using pointers to work down through the tree level by level. Details are left as an end-of-chapter exercise.

Complexity of Elementary Insertion

What is the complexity of the Insert algorithm? The recursive algorithm requires a step for each level that is processed. For a full binary tree of N nodes, this maximum level is $\log_2 N$, in which case inserting into a binary search tree is $O(\log_2 N)$. However, if the tree contains $O(N)$ levels, then insertion might degenerate to $O(N)$.

Figures 8.2, 8.3, and 8.4 show that the number of levels in a tree may vary considerably according to the order in which nodes are inserted. In each of these figures, the values in the data sets are the same; only the order of the items in the input file is different in each case.

Even a cursory examination of the binary search trees in Figures 8.2, 8.3, and 8.4 indicates that search performance of the tree in Figure 8.2 is probably worse than in the other two. Closer examination indicates that the search performance of the tree in Figure 8.3 is probably better than that in Figure 8.4. Unfortunately, though, for many purposes, "clearly" and "probably" are not good enough. We need to find a quantitative measure of performance in a binary search tree. One such measure is the average number of comparisons it takes to find an item in the tree.

To be more precise, suppose all data elements in the tree are equally likely to arise during our search for values. In this setting, we can compute the total number of comparisons in a search by taking each item in the tree and counting the number of comparisons it takes to locate the item. The average number of comparisons is this total divided by the number of nodes. This formula follows the normal method for finding an average: find the total number of comparisons and divide by the number of items.

Applying this measure to the trees in Figures 8.2, 8.3, and 8.4, we get the following averages.

Figure 8.2: $1 + 2 + 3 + 4 + 5 + 6 + 7 + 8 + 9 + 10 + 11 + 12 = 78/12 = 6.5$

Figure 8.3: $1 + 2 + 2 + 3 + 3 + 3 + 3 + 4 + 4 + 4 + 4 + 4 \quad = 37/12 = 3.08$

Figure 8.4: $1 + 2 + 2 + 3 + 3 + 3 + 3 + 4 + 4 + 4 + 5 + 5 \quad = 39/12 = 3.25$

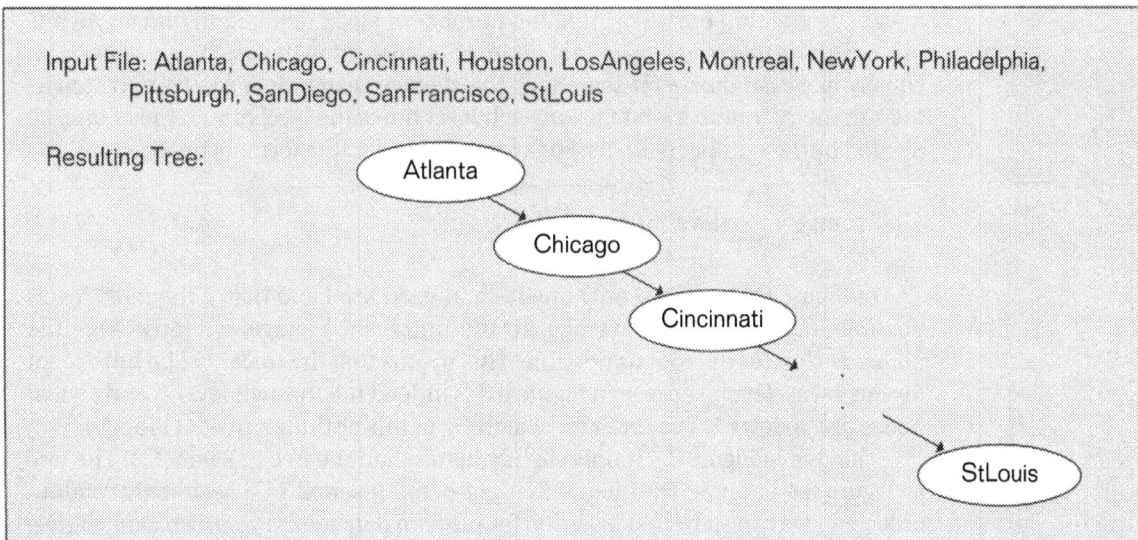

Input File: Atlanta, Chicago, Cincinnati, Houston, LosAngeles, Montreal, NewYork, Philadelphia, Pittsburgh, SanDiego, SanFrancisco, StLouis

Resulting Tree:

Atlanta

Chicago

Cincinnati

StLouis

Figure 8.2   A Binary Search Tree Generated from a File Using Simple Tree Insertion

Input File: Montreal, Cincinnati, Pittsburgh, Atlanta, Houston, Philadelphia, SanFrancisco, Chicago, LosAngeles, NewYork, SanDiego, StLouis

Resulting Tree:

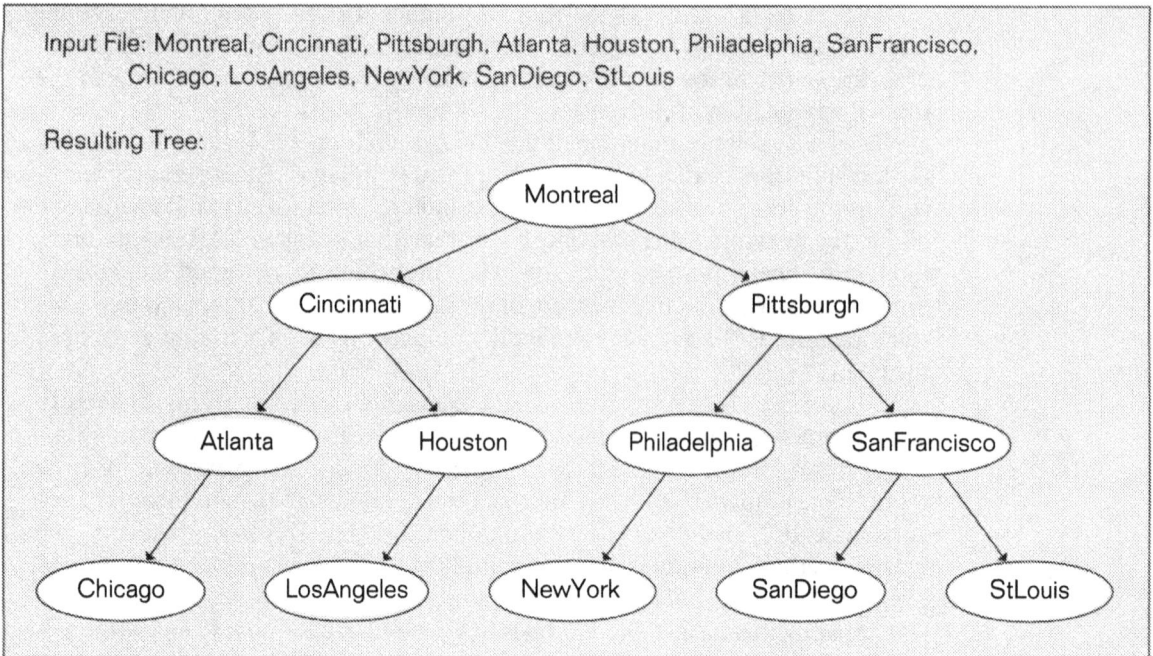

Figure 8.3 A Binary Search Tree Generated from a Different File Using Simple Tree Insertion

Now we can state quantitatively that based on average search time, the performance of the tree in Figure 8.3 is the best, and the performance of the tree in Figure 8.2 is the worst. In fact, a few moments reflection proves that no tree can be worse than the tree in Figure 8.2 or any better than the tree in Figure 8.3.

Because the root has level 0 and because movement from level to level requires a main step within our algorithm, the number of steps required to find an item is just one more than the level of that node. Thus, assuming that each data value is an equally likely candidate for searching, the average search time can be rewritten as the sum of the number of items on each level times the level number plus one, all divided by the number of items. For a tree of N nodes, the formula becomes

$$\text{Average} = \sum_{i=1}^{N} (\text{level}(\text{node}_i) + 1) / N$$

In Figure 8.2, we have only one item at each level and hence the most levels possible, maximizing the average. To minimize the average, we must have the nodes as close to the root as possible. This means that the tree must be full except for the lowest level. The tree in Figure 8.3 is indeed full through level 2, and all leaf nodes are on level 3. The order for searching in this optimum tree is $O(\log_2 N)$.

The tree in Figure 8.3 is only slightly better than the tree in Figure 8.4. The tree in Figure 8.4 is a tree with items that are being inserted in a seemingly random order, and we can show that insertion for random data tends to give a balanced tree. If all permutations of the N items are equally probable, the average search time in the tree created by the items being entered randomly is close to the optimum. The tree in Figure 8.4 is actually the order of final team batting averages at the end of the

Input File: NewYork, Cincinnati, Montreal, Chicago, Pittsburgh, StLouis, Philadelphia,
    SanFrancisco, SanDiego, Atlanta, Houston, LosAngeles

Resulting Tree:

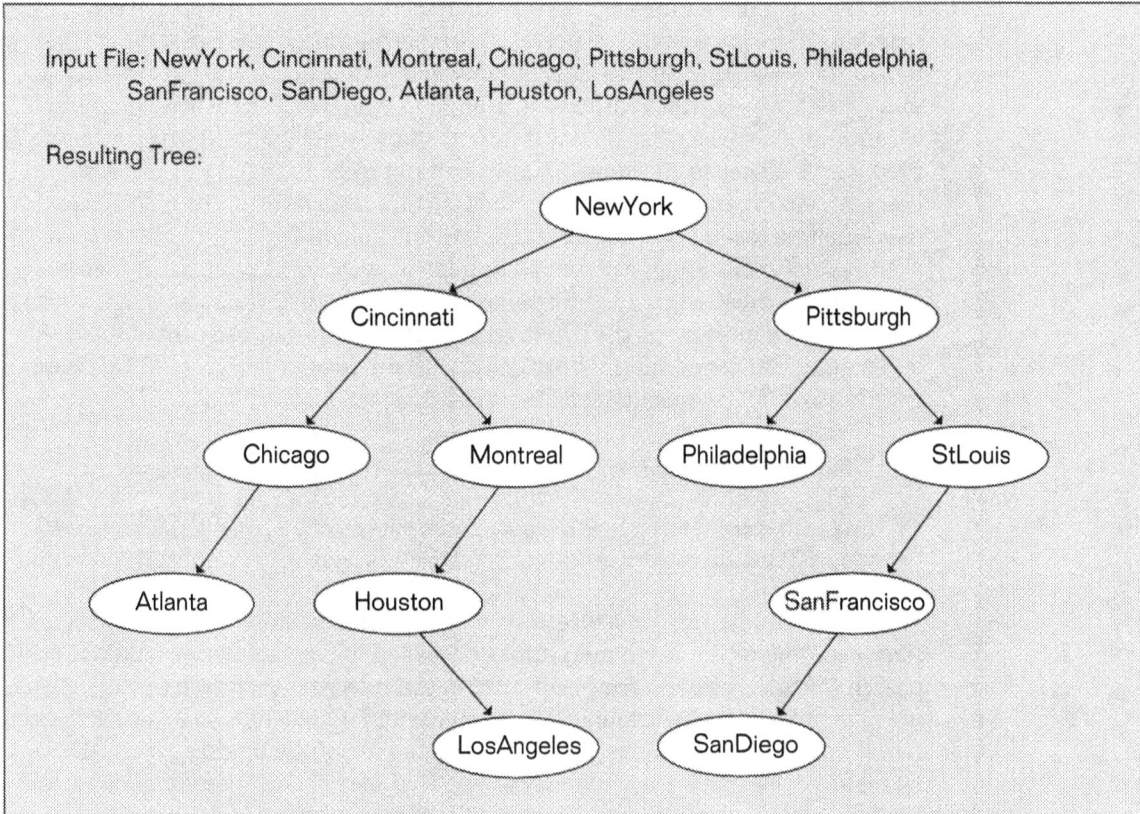

Figure 8.4 A Binary Search Tree Generated from a Different File Using Simple Tree Insertion

1987 National League Season. If we assume that each team has an equal chance of ending up in any spot, this order seems reasonably random. In this case, the tree is not badly out of balance, and the average search time approaches $\log_2 N$.

Static Binary Trees

Any analysis of the efficiency of an algorithm depends upon the context in which that algorithm is used. For example, our analysis of searching a binary search tree in the previous section assumed that the tree contained the item in question and that there was an equal probability of each item being the target of the search. If we know little about the nature of the items in the tree except that they cover all possibilities, then these assumptions may be reasonable. In some cases, however, we may know significantly more about the items under consideration.

For example, consider a spelling checker that stores a dictionary of correctly spelled words. Words not in the dictionary are considered misspelled. We know that some words, such as *the* and *is*, are likely to arise much more often than more specialized words like *algorithm* and *implementation*. Three types of words are searched for in this dictionary: a correctly spelled, commonly used word; a correctly spelled, seldom used word; and an incorrectly spelled word. To optimize searching in the dictionary, we need to optimize for these three cases. We can perform a statistical analysis of a large number of books, articles, and papers to determine which words typically are used often and which are much less common. If we arrange the correctly spelled words in a binary search tree with the commonly used words closer to the root, then we can optimize searching in the first two cases. An incorrectly spelled word is not in the tree, however, and our search ends only when we reach a NIL pointer at the bottom of the tree.

In order to talk about a search ending unsuccessfully at a particular place, we add square boxes to our tree diagrams wherever a NIL pointer appears. These square boxes represent places where an unsuccessful search "falls out of the tree," and so they are called **failure boxes** or **external nodes**. A tree drawn with these extra boxes is called an **extended binary search tree**.

Failure Boxes (External Nodes) Boxes drawn to replace NIL pointers in a tree.

Extended Binary Search Tree A binary search tree where NIL pointers are replaced by nodes that are external to the tree, called failure boxes.

For example, names in a directory of cities might be stored in a binary search tree according to the city names. Cities not listed in the directory would not appear in the tree. A small example of such an extended binary search tree is shown in Figure 8.5. This is an extended binary tree with four *internal nodes* and five *external nodes*. Internal nodes are those that are part of the original tree. External nodes are those that are added to show where failures occur. For example, the failure box to the left of the node containing Atlanta represents the place where a search ends when the value being searched for is lexically less than Atlanta. The

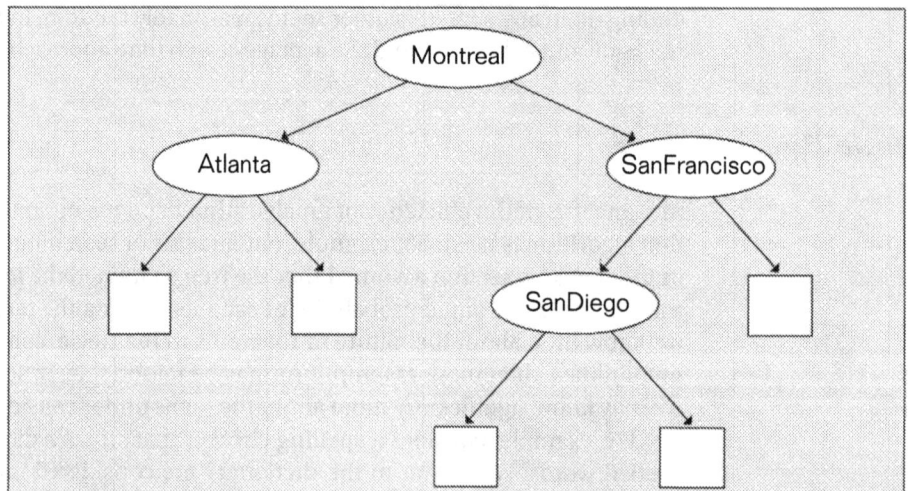

Figure 8.5 A Binary Search Tree with Failure Boxes

box to the right of Atlanta represents the place where a search ends when the value being searched for is lexically greater than Atlanta but less than Montreal.

Once we know the frequency with which various internal or external nodes are likely to be accessed within a tree, we can try to create trees based on this known information. Because the information about the tree data is known before we start and does not change during processing, such trees are called *static binary search trees*. In such circumstances, we can try to create trees that give a minimal average search time. In order to make this notion of minimal average search time more precise, it is helpful to consider how average search time might be computed when we know how often we are likely to want to locate the various nodes.

In general, we compute an average by adding the relevant quantities for each element under consideration and then dividing by the total number of elements. For example, in Figure 8.5, suppose we count the number of times we search for each of the four cities over a period of time. Our count might be as follows, assuming that we only count those searches involving the cities actually cited in the tree.

Atlanta	4
Montreal	2
SanFrancisco	3
SanDiego	1

In this example, we performed 10 searches: Atlanta was needed the most (four times), while SanDiego was needed only once. Previously, we noted that the amount of work required to find an item in a binary search tree depends upon the level of the node for that item. We need one basic step to find the root (Montreal), two steps to find Atlanta or SanFrancisco (nodes at level 1), and three steps to find SanDiego (at level 2). Thus, the total work for these searches is

Atlanta	**Montreal**		**SanFrancisco**		**SanDiego**	
$2 + 2 + 2 + 2 +$	$1 + 1$	$+$	$2 + 2 + 2$	$+$	3	$= 19$

In this sum, it takes two basic processing steps to find Atlanta, and our statistics indicate that we needed to find Atlanta four times. Thus, 2 occurs four times at the start of this sum. The average search time is 19 divided by the total number of searches $(1 + 2 + 3 + 4)$, and we have

$$\text{Average search time} = \frac{19}{10} = 1.9$$

More generally, suppose we consider N nodes in a tree—$node_1$, $node_2$, . . . , $node_N$—and suppose an analysis shows that these nodes are requested with frequency $p_1, p_2, \ldots, p_N$, respectively.

The number of basic processing steps for $node_i$ is $(\text{level}(node_i) + 1)$. In computing the total work required to process these nodes, we add the amount of work $(\text{level}(node_i) + 1)$ for each node and for each time the node is wanted. Thus, the amount of work for each node is $p_i(\text{level}(\text{node}_i) + 1)$. Adding these amounts together, we determine that the total work for a search is

$$\text{Total work} = \sum_{i=1}^{N} p_i(\text{level}(\text{node}_i) + 1)$$

Because the total number of items searched is $p_1 + p_2 + \ldots + p_N$, the average amount of work for a search is

$$\text{Average work} = \frac{\displaystyle\sum_{i=1}^{N} p_i(\text{level}(\text{node}_i) + 1)}{\displaystyle\sum_{i=1}^{N} p_i}$$

To simplify this expression, observe that the fraction $p_i / \sum p_i$ is simply the fraction of the time that we searched for node_i. If we consider the p_i as fractions or probabilities rather than actual frequencies, then the sum in the denominator simplifies to 1. In any case, whether we consider p_i as frequencies or probabilities, the sum $\sum p_i$ is a constant, based upon the total number of items searched.

The point of this discussion is that the main component of the expression for the average work in searching a tree is the sum

$$\sum_{i=1}^{N} p_i(\text{level}(\text{node}_i) + 1)$$

The larger this number, the higher the average time for searching a tree. This sum is called the *weighted internal cost* or the *weighted internal path length* of a binary search tree. In keeping with this terminology, sometimes the frequencies are called *weights*.

A similar analysis applies to searching a tree when frequencies are known for both the internal and the external nodes. In considering external nodes, however, there are two common interpretations of how much work is done when a search ends in failure. For example, in Figure 8.5, the external node to the left of Atlanta is located one level lower than Atlanta itself, so this failure node has level 2. But how much work must we perform to locate this external node? Because Atlanta has level 1 and the left NIL pointer for the failure node typically is stored in the Atlanta node, some people argue that we locate the failure node in two main steps. Others argue that the square boxes representing a failure node involve an extra amount of work and that searching requires three main steps in order to find the failure node to the left of Atlanta. Computer scientists tend to take the first of these two views as the information concerning NIL pointers is already contained in a parent node (such as Atlanta). We adopt this position in this text.

To be precise, we define the level of an external node as one more than the level of its parent node, but we define the number of main steps for finding that external node as the node's level, not the level plus one.

With this understanding of the amount of work required to determine that a search ends at a specific failure node, we consider the total amount of work involved in searching trees where the search may end in failure, as in the case of a spelling checker.

Already, we have let p_i be the frequency that a search ends at (internal) node i. Next, we number the N + 1 failure nodes with indices from 0 to N, and we let q_i be the frequency that a search ends at failure node i for i = 0, . . . , N. Following the motivation of our earlier discussion, we define the *weighted external cost* or the *weighted external path length* of a binary search tree to be

$$\text{Weighted external cost} = \sum_{i=0}^{N} q_i \, \text{level(failure node}_i)$$

The *weighted cost* or *cost* of a binary search tree combines the weighted internal and external costs, as follows:

$$\text{Weighted cost} = \sum_{i=1}^{N} p_i \, (\text{level(node}_i) + 1) + \sum_{i=0}^{N} q_i \, (\text{level(failure node}_i))$$

Also, when counting failure as a possible outcome of a search, the weight or total frequency of all searches is

$$\text{Weight} = \sum_{i=1}^{N} p_i + \sum_{i=0}^{N} q_i$$

To summarize, the total cost represents the total amount of work (or the number of steps) required to search for all types of data, and the total frequency indicates the amount of data for which we are searching. Thus, the average amount of work for our searches is found by taking the total cost (or weighted cost) and dividing by the total frequency (or weight). In other words,

$$\text{average work over all types of data} = \frac{\text{weighted cost}}{\text{weight}}$$

Similarly, the weighted internal cost represents the total amount of work needed to find the data stored in the tree, and the average amount of work for finding data in the tree is found by dividing this weighted internal cost by the total frequency of the data in the internal nodes. Also, the weighted external cost represents the total amount of work needed to determine that data are not in the tree.

As an example, Table 8.1 shows various computations for the extended tree in Figure 8.6, with the given weights or frequencies for each internal and external node.

While the term *internal weighted cost* is a synonym for *internal weighted path length*, the choice of terminology often depends upon the nature of the application. For example, in trying to minimize the amount of work or time for an

Table 8.1

	Figure 8.6 (a)	Figure 8.6(b)
Weight or Total Frequency	$2+4+3+5+6+5+3+9+1+5+3 = 46$	$2+4+3+5+6+5+3+9+1+5+3 = 46$
Weighted Internal Cost	$4*2+2*1+3*2+5*3+6*4 = 55$	$4*2+2*1+3*3+5*2+6*3 = 47$
Weighted External Cost	$2*5+2*3+2*9+3*1+4*5+4*3 = 69$	$2*5+2*3+3*9+3*1+3*5+3*3 = 70$
Weighted Cost	$55 + 69 = 124$	$47 + 70 = 117$
Average Search Time	$\dfrac{124}{46} = 2.70$	$\dfrac{117}{46} = 2.54$

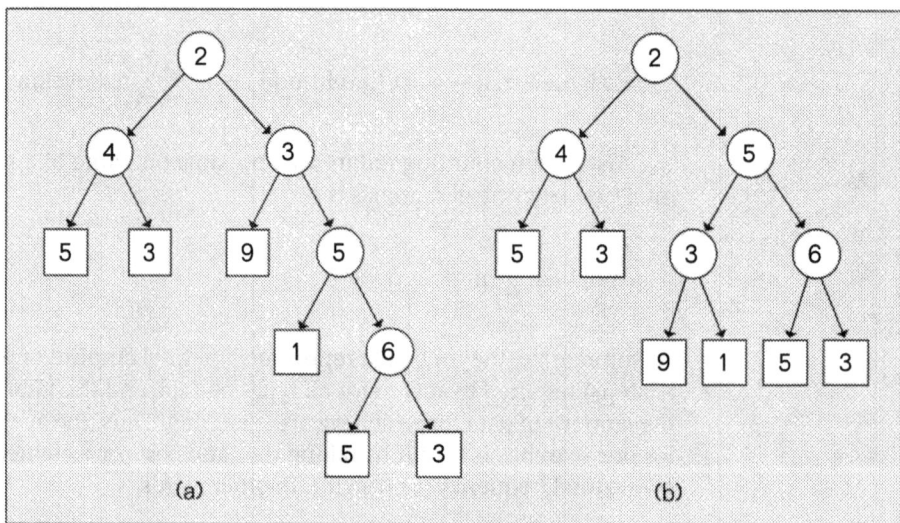

Figure 8.6 Extended Tree with Weights

operation, we often use the term *internal weighted cost.* If we want to focus upon the length of search paths, then it is more common to use the term *internal weighted path length.* Similar comments apply to the synonyms *external weighted cost* and *external weighted path length,* which we use interchangeably in the rest of the chapter.

Optimal Binary Search Trees

Now that we know how to compute the average search times for trees with known frequencies, we turn our attention to constructing a binary search tree with the minimum average search time. As we consider the problem, we must try to organize internal nodes and failure nodes within a tree for efficiency. However, any such binary search tree contains the same internal and external nodes in the same inorder traversal order. Only the relative positions of these nodes may change. Thus, the total frequency or weight is the same for any such tree, and we can minimize average search times by minimizing the weighted cost.

Our goal then is to construct a binary search tree with minimum weighted cost, in which we have information on the occurrence of the items in the tree as well as information on the probability of reaching the failure nodes. Such a tree is called an *optimal binary search tree.*

In order to discuss the construction of such trees, we need some notation. We assume that we are given n items in a tree and their associated weights

$\{a_1, a_2, \ldots a_n\}$ (* items in tree *)

$\{p_1, p_2, \ldots p_n\}$ (* weights associated with items *)

where $a_1 < a_2 < \ldots < a_n$. Similarly, we assume that we have the failure boxes and their associated weights

$\{e_0, e_1, \ldots e_n\}$ (* failure boxes *)

$\{q_0, q_1, \ldots q_n\}$ (* associated weights *)

where the failure nodes are listed from left to right within the tree.

The relationship of these items and failure boxes is illustrated by the nodes in Figure 8.7.

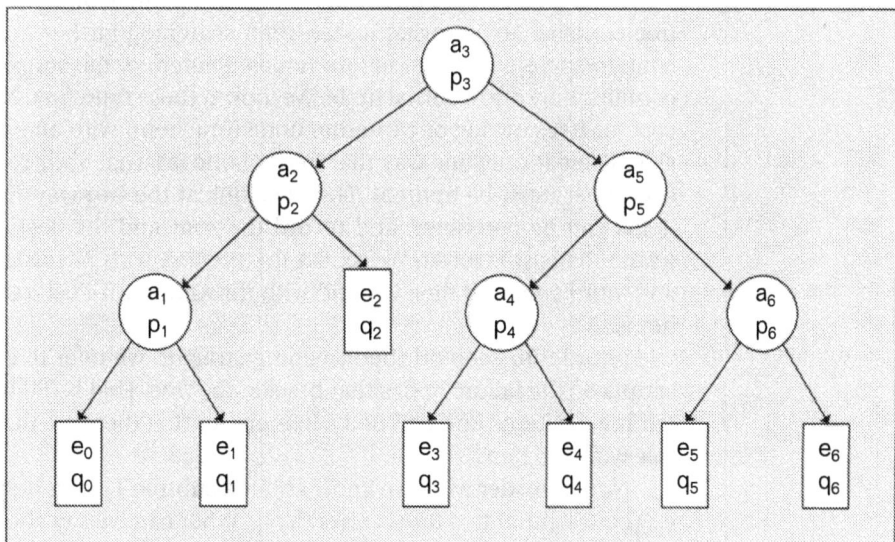

Figure 8.7   Extended Tree Showing Items, Boxes, and Weights

Notice that the subscript on each item in the binary search tree corresponds to the item's place in the inorder traversal. The relationship of the e_i to the a_i is as follows:

$$e_0 < a_1 < e_1 < a_2 \ldots < a_n < e_n$$

This means that e_i represents the end of an unsuccessful search, where the item being searched for is between a_i and a_{i+1}. In our earlier notation, e_i has weight q_i. As we look at the algorithm to calculate the optimum tree, we also consider a specific example where the items are names.

$$\{ \text{Ann, Betty, Judy, Sarah, Susy} \}$$
$$P_i \ \{ \quad 9, \quad 3, \quad 4, \quad 8, \quad 1 \quad \}$$
$$Q_i \ \{1, \quad 2, \quad 4, \quad 5, \quad 2, \quad 2 \}$$

The weight associated with the name Ann is 9. The weight associated with the name Betty is 3. The weight associated with the name Judy is 4. The weight associated with a name lexically less than Ann is 1. The weight associated with a name lexically between Ann and Betty is 2. The weight associated with a name lexically greater than Susy is 2. The task then is to build a binary search tree that optimizes both successful and unsuccessful searches.

The motivation for our approach is based upon the observation that every subtree of an optimal search tree must be optimal. If a subtree were not optimal, then we could optimize it and thereby reduce the cost of the tree to which it is a subtree. But this is a contradiction because the tree is already given to be optimal.

With this observation in mind, we begin by constructing some very small, optimal trees. From these small trees, we can build bigger trees that are optimal.

What nodes might be in a subtree of an optimal binary search tree? If the subtree contains any internal nodes, then searching farther down in the tree must contain some additional failure nodes. Therefore, the simplest tree for our data contains only one external node. We look at these trees first. Next, we compute the cost for trees having one internal node (one item) with an external node on each side. There is only one way that trees of one internal node can be constructed, so such trees must be optimal. Then we look at the two ways in which trees of two items can be combined and record the root and the cost of the configuration where the cost is lower. We repeat the process with possible trees of three items and four items, and then we end with the minimum-cost tree of (in this case) five items.

In order to keep our bookkeeping straight, we refer to each tree by the subscripts on the failure nodes that bracket the tree. That is, T_{02} refers to the tree containing the items Ann and Betty. Remember that there are three failure boxes for a tree with two items.

Now consider what we know about a subtree T_{ii} with only one external node, e_i. The weight of this tree is given by q_i. What can we say about its weighted cost? Here, the external node is the root, so it has level 0. Because the weighted cost for an external node is $q_i * \text{Level}(e_i)$, the weighted cost for any T_{ii} is $q_i * 0$, or 0.

While this computation involving only trees with one external node is rather modest, at least we have made a start. Next, we consider how we can compute the weighted cost of more complex trees. Three more observations are helpful.

1. The sum of the weights is fixed for any T_{ij}.

2. For any tree T, let T_L be the left subtree of the root and let T_R be the right subtree of the root. Then the level of a node in T is one more than the level of the node in T_L or T_R, because the level of a node in T counts the root, while the level of a node in either subtree of the root does not count this root. If $Level_T(a_i)$ denotes the level of node a_i in tree T, then this observation states the following:

$$Level_T(a_i) = Level_{TL}(a_i) + 1 \quad \text{for those nodes } a_i \text{ in the left subtree } T_L \text{ of T}$$

$$Level_T(a_i) = Level_{TR}(a_i) + 1 \quad \text{for those nodes } a_i \text{ in the right subtree } T_R \text{ of T.}$$

3. Let $WC(T)$, $WC(T_L)$, and $WC(T_R)$ be the weighted costs of T, T_L, and T_R, respectively. Then we have the following computational formula:

$$WC(T) = Weight(T) + WC(T_L) + WC(T_R)$$

This formula holds by expanding the definition of $WC(T)$ and grouping the resulting terms into the nodes in the left and right subtrees, as shown below.

First, $WC(T)$ is the sum of weights $\times$ levels, with the sum taken over all internal and external nodes.

$$WC(T) = \sum_{a_i \text{ in T}} p_i (Level_T (a_i) + 1) + \sum_{e_i \text{ in T}} q_i(Level_T(e_i))$$

Next, we group the terms of the sum into the root, plus the nodes in the left subtree of the root, plus the nodes in the right subtree.

$$WC(T) = p_{root} * 1$$
$$+ \sum_{a_i \text{ in } T_L} p_i (Level_T (a_i) + 1) + \sum_{e_i \text{ in } T_L} q_i (Level_T(e_i))$$
$$+ \sum_{a_i \text{ in } T_R} p_i (Level_T (a_i) + 1) + \sum_{e_i \text{ in } T_R} q_i (Level_T(e_i))$$

Now, we rewrite the levels of the nodes as levels in the subtrees, following our second observation.

$$WC(T) = p_{root} * 1$$
$$+ \sum_{a_i \text{ in } T_L} p_i (Level_{TL} (a_i) + 1 + 1) + \sum_{e_i \text{ in } T_L} q_i(Level_{TL}(e_i) + 1)$$
$$+ \sum_{a_i \text{ in } T_R} p_i (Level_T R(a_i) + 1 + 1) + \sum_{e_i \text{ in } T_R} q_i(Level_{TR}(e_i) + 1)$$

Each term in this sum has a frequency times 1 as one of its terms. If we collect these terms at the start of the sum, we get the following expression:

$$WC(T) = p_{root} * 1 + \sum_{a_i \text{ in } T_L} p_i + \sum_{e_i \text{ in } T_L} q_i + \sum_{a_i \text{ in } T_R} p_i + \sum_{e_i \text{ in } T_R} q_i$$

$$+ \sum_{a_i \text{ in } T_L} p_i (Level_{TL}(a_i) + 1) + \sum_{e_i \text{ in } T_L} q_i(Level_{TL}(e_i))$$

$$+ \sum_{a_i \text{ in } T_R} p_i (Level_T R(a_i) + 1) + \sum_{e_i \text{ in } T_R} q_i(Level_{TR}(e_i))$$

While this expression may look messy, the first line is just the sum of all of the weights of the nodes in T. Thus, the first line is just the weight of T. Also, the second line is just the definition of the weighted cost $WC(T_L)$ of the left subtree T_L, while the third line is just the definition of the weighted cost $WC(T_R)$ of the right subtree T_R. Writing this out as a formula, we get the above result, namely,

$$WC(T) = Weight(T) + WC(T_L) + WC(T_R)$$

This third observation states that we can compute the weighted cost of a tree directly from the weight of the tree and the weighted costs of its subtrees. Furthermore, this formula suggests that we can obtain the best weighted cost for a tree if we can organize nodes so that the sum of the weighted costs of the left and right subtrees is a minimum. As we organize our work into an algorithm, we also find it useful to keep track of the root of each subtree.

We are now ready to look at more complex trees. As we proceed, we record three values at each stage of the algorithm:

w_{ij} the sum of the weights in T_{ij}

c_{ij} the minimum cost for a configuration of T_{ij}

r_{ij} the root of the minimum cost configuration

In order to organize our computations, we store these values in a table format, where the i and the j are indexes, but we only use the upper half of the table. That is, the main diagonal represents the failure boxes. The next diagonal represents all trees with one internal node. From then on, each diagonal represents the minimum for larger and larger trees.

From our discussion of the trivial trees T_{ii}, we can fill in the weight of each tree as q_i and the cost as 0. The root does not involve an internal node in this case, so we let r_{ii} be 0. Using our example involving nodes containing names, this first stage in our algorithm gives the following entries in a table.

	[0]	[1]	[2]	[3]	[4]	[5]
[0]	w: 1 c: 0 r: 0					
[1]		w: 2 c: 0 r: 0				
[2]			w: 4 c: 0 r: 0			
[3]				w: 5 c: 0 r: 0		
[4]					w: 2 c: 0 r: 0	
[5]						w: 2 c: 0 r: 0

T_{ij} is the tree between e_i and e_j. By observation 1, the weight of this tree is the sum of the weights of all of its internal and external nodes. Turning to the weighted cost of each tree with one internal node and two external nodes, we have $WC(T_{ij})$ = weight $T(_{ij})$ + $WC(T_{ii})$ + $WC(T_{jj})$. We have already computed the weighted cost of each external node to be 0, so the cost and the weight are the same for these trees with one internal node.

	Ann 9	Betty 3	Judy 4	Sarah 8	Susy 1
	1 2	2 4	4 5	5 2	2 2
	T_{01}	T_{12}	T_{23}	T_{34}	T_{45}

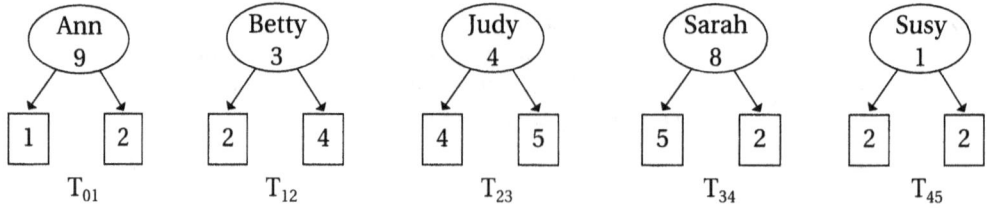

We now move these values into the table. Remember that the information for T_{01} goes in to entry [0,1] of the table and so on.

	[0]	[1]	[2]	[3]	[4]	[5]
[0]	w: 1 c: 0 r: 0	w: 12 c: 12 r: 1				
[1]		w: 2 c: 0 r: 0	w: 9 c: 9 r: 2			
[2]			w: 4 c: 0 r: 0	w: 13 c: 13 r: 3		
[3]				w: 5 c: 0 r: 0	w: 15 c: 15 r: 4	
[4]					w: 2 c: 0 r: 0	w: 5 c: 5 r: 5
[5]						w: 2 c: 0 r: 0

Now we must calculate minimum-cost trees for all possible combinations of two internal nodes. We can combine Ann and Betty to get T_{02} in two ways: with

Ann as the root and with Betty as the root. We can combine Betty and Judy in two ways (T_{13}): with Betty as the root and with Judy as the root. The same is true with Judy and Sarah (T_{24}) and Sarah and Susy (T_{35}). Because we are building an optimal binary *search* tree, there is no other possible combination of two internal nodes.

To clarify our process, Figure 8.8 shows the possible subtrees for T_{02}, the tree that contains Ann and Betty as internal nodes. Adding the weights for these two nodes, we determine that the weight for either tree is 19. We compute the weighted cost using the formula $WC(T_{02}) = $ weight $(T_{02}) + WC(T_L) + WC(T_R)$.

In this case, if Ann is the root, then T_{00} is the left subtree and T_{12} is the right subtree. Similarly, if Betty is the root, then T_{01} is the left subtree, and T_{22} is the right subtree. Examining the two computations, we conclude that the optimal T_{02} occurs if Ann (node 1) is the root. We record this information in entry [0, 2] of our table.

The table is repeated below with the next diagonal filled in. For convenience, the p's and the q's are also repeated.

p's		9	3	4	8	1
q's	1	2	4	5	2	2
	[0]	[1]	[2]	[3]	[4]	[5]

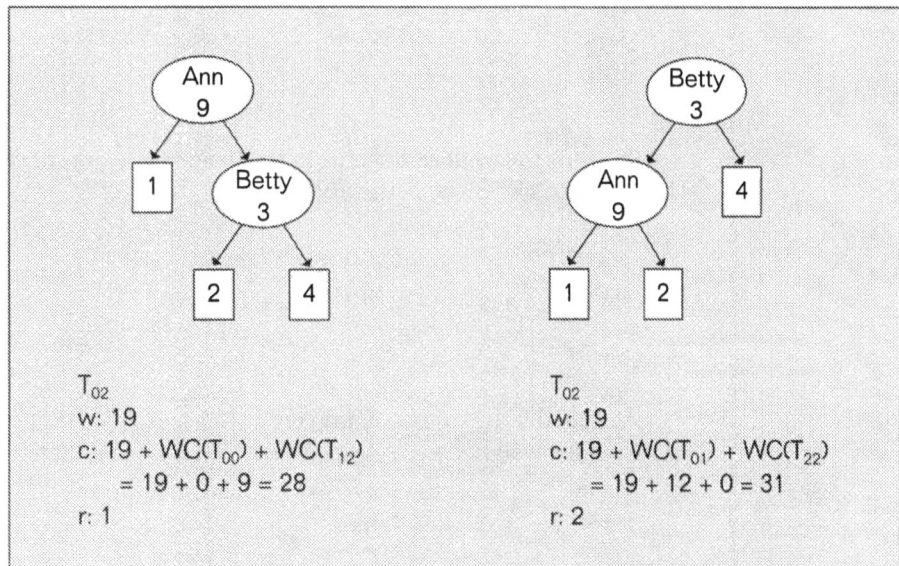

Figure 8.8 Alternate Calculations for T_{02}

	[0]	[1]	[2]	[3]	[4]	[5]
[0]	w: 1 c: 0 r: 0	w: 12 c: 12 r: 1	w: 19 c: 28 r: 1			
[1]		w: 2 c: 0 r: 0	w: 9 c: 9 r: 2	w: 18 c: 27 r: 3		
[2]			w: 4 c: 0 r: 0	w: 13 c: 13 r: 3	w: 23 c: 36 r: 4	
[3]				w: 5 c: 0 r: 0	w: 15 c: 15 r: 4	w: 18 c: 23 r: 4
[4]					w: 2 c: 0 r: 0	w: 5 c: 5 r: 5
[5]						w: 2 c: 0 r: 0

Turning to the next diagonal in the table, the weight of each tree is the sum of the p's and q's involved in the tree.

$$w_{03} : 1 + 2 + 4 + 5 + 9 + 3 + 4 = 28$$

$$w_{14} : 2 + 4 + 5 + 2 + 3 + 4 + 8 = 28$$

$$w_{25} : 4 + 5 + 2 + 2 + 4 + 8 + 1 = 26$$

In general, the weight of any tree T_{ij} is $q_i + q_{i+1} + .. + q_j + p_{i+1} + .. + p_j$. Alternatively, the weight can be determined from the table itself.

$$w_{ij} \leftarrow w_{ij-1} + w_{i+1j} - w_{i+1j-1}$$

To determine the cost of a tree, we calculate the cost of each combination of two subtrees that can combine to create the tree. T_{03} can be configured as

$T_{00} + T_{13}$ or as $T_{01} + T_{23}$ or as $T_{02} + T_{33}$. The cost of each configuration is calculated using our weighted cost formula with the weighted costs of the subtrees as stored in the table. Once we calculate the cost for each possible root in T_{ij}, we choose the minimum and record the result in the table.

The calculations for the trees with three nodes are shown below. In each case, the weighted cost of the tree is the cost of the minimum configuration.

c_{03}: (weight: 28)

$T_{00} + T_{13} + \text{weight} = 0 + 27 + 28 = 55$

$T_{01} + T_{23} + \text{weight} = 12 + 13 + 28 = 53 \ (* \text{ minimum } *)$

$T_{02} + T_{33} + \text{weight} = 28 + 0 + 28 = 56$

c_{14}: (weight: 28)

$T_{11} + T_{24} + \text{weight} = 0 + 36 + 28 = 64$

$T_{12} + T_{34} + \text{weight} = 9 + 15 + 28 = 52 \ (* \text{ minimum } *)$

$T_{13} + T_{44} + \text{weight} = 27 + 0 + 28 = 55$

c_{25}: (weight: 26)

$T_{22} + T_{35} + \text{weight} = 0 + 23 + 26 = 49$

$T_{23} + T_{45} + \text{weight} = 13 + 5 + 26 = 44 \ (* \text{ minimum } *)$

$T_{24} + T_{55} + \text{weight} = 36 + 0 + 26 = 62$

Similarly, we can calculate the possible costs for trees with four internal nodes.

c_{04}: (weight: 38)

$T_{00} + T_{14} + \text{weight} = 0 + 52 + 38 = 90$

$T_{01} + T_{24} + \text{weight} = 12 + 36 + 38 = 86$

$T_{02} + T_{34} + \text{weight} = 28 + 15 + 38 = 81 \ (* \text{ minimum } *)$

$T_{03} + T_{44} + \text{weight} = 53 + 0 + 38 = 91$

c_{15}: (weight: 31)

$T_{11} + T_{25} + \text{weight} = 0 + 44 + 31 = 75$

$T_{12} + T_{35} + \text{weight} = 9 + 23 + 31 = 63 \ (* \text{ minimum } *)$

$T_{13} + T_{45} + \text{weight} = 27 + 5 + 31 = 63 \ (* \text{ minimum } *)$

$T_{14} + T_{55} + \text{weight} = 52 + 0 + 31 = 83$

We leave the calculations for trees with five internal nodes to you. The completed table is shown here.

	[0]	[1]	[2]	[3]	[4]	[5]
[0]	w: 1 c: 0 r: 0	w: 12 c: 12 r: 1	w: 19 c: 28 r: 1	w: 28 c: 53 r: 2	w: 38 c: 81 r: 3	w: 41 c: 92 r: 3
[1]		w: 2 c: 0 r: 0	w: 9 c: 9 r: 2	w: 18 c: 27 r: 3	w: 28 c: 52 r: 3	w: 31 c: 63 r: 3
[2]			w: 4 c: 0 r: 0	w: 13 c: 13 r: 3	w: 23 c: 36 r: 4	w: 26 c: 44 r: 4
[3]				w: 5 c: 0 r: 0	w: 15 c: 15 r: 4	w: 18 c: 23 r: 4
[4]					w: 2 c: 0 r: 0	w: 5 c: 5 r: 5
[5]						w: 2 c: 0 r: 0

Each successive diagonal of the table represents optimal trees being built with one more internal node. The last diagonal of the table (the upper right-hand corner) gives the optimal tree spanning all of the internal nodes. The binary search tree generated in this way is optimal but may not be unique. At the stage where four internal nodes are combined, the cost calculation for T_{15} shows that there are two configurations that give the same minimum cost: $T_{12} + T_{35}$ and $T_{13} + T_{45}$. This indicates that there are two minimal cost solutions for T_{15}: one where the root is the identifier associated with p_3 and one where the root is the identifier associated with p_4.

Now that we have the table, we must be able to generate the tree. The roots of the optimal subtrees allow us to do this. The root of 3 in the upper right corner of the table means that the optimal subtrees of T_{05} are T_{02} and T_{35}. The root of T_{02} is 1, which means that the optimal subtrees of T_{02} are T_{00} and T_{12}. The root of T_{35} is 4, which means the optimal subtrees of T_{35} are T_{33} and T_{45}. The process continues expanding subtrees until all are expanded.

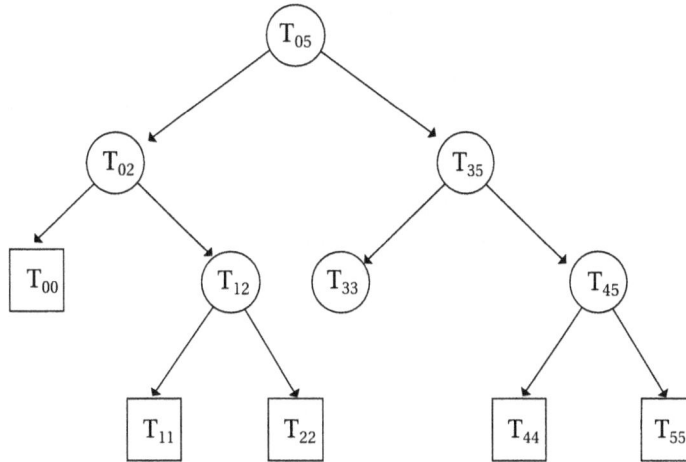

The subtrees whose subscripts are the same are the external nodes and are ignored. Other subtrees are replaced by the identifier associated with the root. That is, the roots refer to the subscript on the p's. Each p is associated with an identifier. Therefore, the optimum binary search tree is as follows.

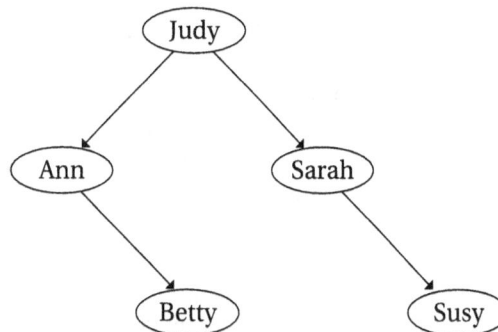

In summary, we can compute an optimal binary search tree by looking at optimal subtrees. At first, we have little choice concerning the configuration of the subtrees with a single external node or with one internal node attached to two external nodes. In considering larger subtrees, we assume that we have computed the optimal binary search trees of smaller size. Then, for a large tree, we consider all possible roots. For each root, we use our previous work to determine the best possible left and right subtrees, and we compute the weighted cost for that root. Comparing the weighted costs for each root, we locate a minimum, and this identifies the shape of the optimal binary search tree of this larger size.

While the details of this algorithm are new, note that our approach here is similar to the one we used to determine the best order in which to multiply a series of matrices. Turn back to Chapter 6 and review that algorithm. What do matrices and optimal binary search trees have in common? Their solutions look at simple cases first and then combine them two at a time to evaluate larger cases. We leave the coding of this algorithm as an end-of-chapter exercise.

Application: Symbol Tables

While compilers and assemblers scan a program, each identifier must be examined to determine if it is a key word. This information concerning the key words in a programming language is stored in a symbol table as defined in Chapter 4. Such tables provide an excellent example of an appropriate use of an optimal binary search tree. This symbol table is clearly static; that is, the names in the table (reserved words in the language) do not change. The weights associated with the internal nodes are based on the probability of the occurrence of a particular key word. Statistics on which these weights are based can be gathered from a representative set of programs written in the language.

For example, if we were to build a static symbol table for the reserved words in Modula-2, we would collect the frequency of occurrence of the reserved word from a representative collection of Modula-2 programs. We would expect that the reserved word END would occur the most frequently. If this proved true, we would want END to be recognized quickly, that is, to be located at a level close to the root.

What do the failure nodes represent in this application? The failure nodes have the weights associated with falling out of the tree between a pair of reserved words. For example, there are 40 reserved words in Modula-2. The first two are AND and ARRAY. The failure box e_0 represents searching the optimal binary search tree for a character string that is lexically less than AND. The failure box e_1 represents searching for a character string that is lexically greater than AND but less than ARRAY.

The weight q_0 would be based on the frequency of searching the table for a character string that is lexically less than AND. The statistics associated with such character strings could also be collected over a set of Modula-2 programs. Note that these character strings represent user-defined identifiers. The Modula-2 predefined identifiers could be included within the table of reserved words, kept with the user-defined identifiers, or kept in a table by themselves.

Huffman Algorithm

The construction of an optimal binary search tree applies to the situation where we know the frequencies of both internal and external nodes and where we want to organize these nodes into a binary search tree in such a way as to minimize the search time. We now look at the following related, but different, problem:

> Given a set of external nodes (failure boxes), $\{e_0, e_1, \ldots e_n\}$, and a set of associated weights, $\{q_0, q_1, \ldots q_n\}$, construct the binary tree with the minimum weighted external path length. (Recall that external path length is just another name for external weighted cost.)

This problem differs from the problem that motivated the optimal binary search tree in two ways. First, we do not concern ourselves with any internal nodes—we may consider the weights of all internal nodes to be 0. Second, we no longer require that the resulting tree be a search tree.

The Huffman algorithm builds such a tree from the bottom up, always making sure that the nodes are put together so that the nodes with the smallest weights are combined first. This guarantees that the nodes with larger weights are added to the tree closer to the root and therefore have a shorter path length from the root.

To start with, each failure box is considered a tree and the set of failure boxes is a forest (a collection of trees). A new binary tree is created at each iteration by taking the two trees available with the minimum weights and combining them. The weight of the newly formed tree is the sum of the weights of its subtrees. If there are N failure boxes, it takes $N - 1$ iterations to form them into one binary tree. This tree is the tree with the minimum weighted external path length.

Before we design the algorithm, we work through a concrete example. Ten failure boxes are listed below with their associated weights.

Box	Weight
e_0	18
e_1	54
e_2	30
e_3	18
e_4	14
e_5	8
e_6	2
e_7	5
e_8	0
e_9	6

We begin by considering each failure box to be a tree. The two trees (failure boxes) with the minimum weights are combined into a tree whose weight is the sum of the two trees used to form it.

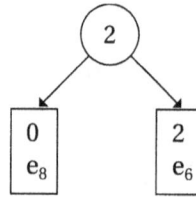

The process repeats again with the two trees with the minimum weight: the tree with the weight of five and the newly formed tree with the weight of two.

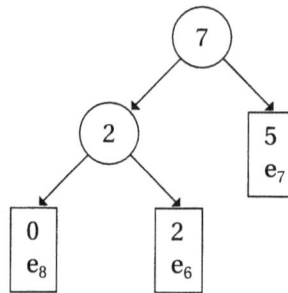

At the next iteration, the newly formed tree is joined with the tree whose weight is six, and the result is then joined with the tree whose weight is eight at the following iteration.

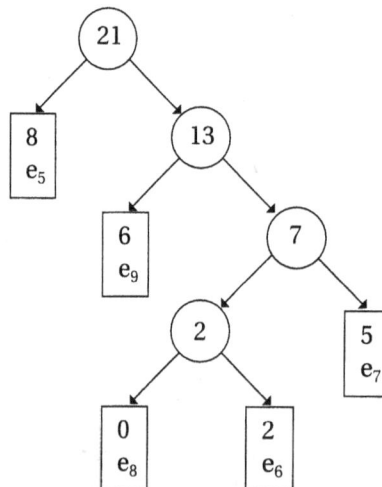

At this point, there is a tie: there are two weights of 18 and one of 14. The fact that there is a tie means that there is no unique solution. There are alternate configurations for the tree with minimum weighted external path length. In this example, we choose the 18 associated with the failure box 0. At the next iteration, the remaining tree with a weight of 18 is joined with the tree whose weight is 21.

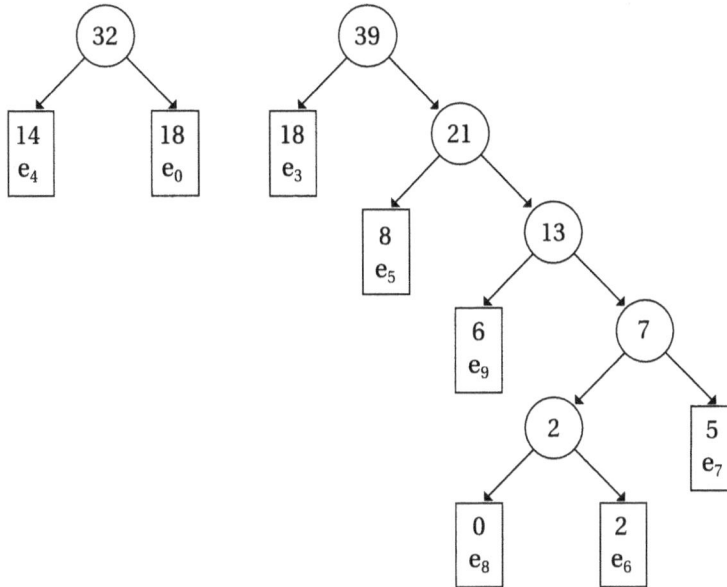

In the next two iterations, the trees whose weights are 32 and 30 are combined, and the trees whose weights are 39 and 54 are combined. The resulting tree is shown in Figure 8.9. The weighted external path length of this tree is 424. Because we had a choice between two trees with a weight of 18 to combine with the tree with a weight of 14, there is an alternate solution. However, its weight is also 424.

Notice that the tree we have constructed is an extended tree. The external nodes contain two values: an item and a weight associated with the item. The tree that was constructed is a tree that optimizes reaching failure boxes. In fact, *it is not a binary search tree at all.* It is a binary tree optimized to reach the failure nodes as quickly as possible. If it is not a binary search tree, what is in the nodes? How do you determine whether to take the left branch or the right branch? These questions are answered in our application section, which begins on page 347. For the moment, we write the algorithm to construct the Huffman tree. Have faith!

The by-hand algorithm can be coded with the use of a priority queue. The elements on the priority queue are trees. The priority is the weight of the tree. The highest priority is the lowest weight. The priority queue is initialized to trees having the original frequencies. For a tree with N failure nodes, it takes $N - 1$ iterations to build the tree with minimum weighted external path length. However, a

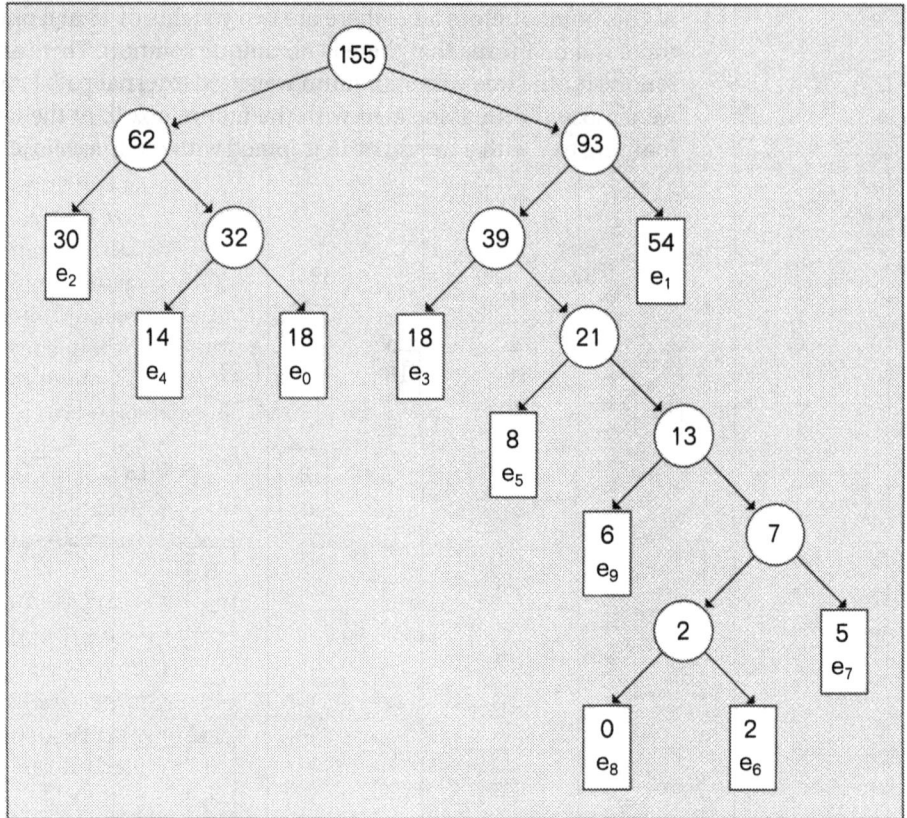

Figure 8.9 An Optimal, Extended Binary Tree (Not a Search Tree)

simpler control structure is to check the priority queue. When there is only one tree on the priority queue, the algorithm is finished.

We use the array of records implementation for the ADT binary tree given in Chapter 7. ItemType must have a character field and a weight field. External nodes need both fields, whereas internal nodes only use the weight field. As we pointed out, a Huffman tree is not a binary search tree.

```
TYPE
    BinTree = 0..MaxNodes;

    ItemType = RECORD
        Weight      : Integer;
        Digit       : Integer
    END RECORD;

    TreeNodeType = RECORD
        Left, Right  : Integer;
        Item         : ItemType
    END RECORD ;
```

```
NodesType      = ARRAY[1..MaxNodes] OF TreeNodeType;
TreeNode       = BinTree;
```

Huffman (VAR Root: BinTree)

```
Initialize Forest
LOOP
    Serve(PQ, LeftSubTree)
    IF Empty(PQ)
        THEN EXIT (* LeftSubTree is the root *)
    END IF
    Serve(PQ, RightSubTree)
    Item.Weight ← GetItem(RightSubTree).Weight +
                    GetItem(LeftSubTree).Weight
    HuffTree ← Make(LeftSubTree, Item, RightSubTree)
    Enque(PQ, HuffTree)
END LOOP
Root ← LeftSubTree
```

InitializeForest

```
Create(PQ)
WHILE More External Nodes DO
    (* NextItem is a local variable of ItemType. *)
    Read NextItem.Weight
    Read NextItem.Digit
    TempTree ← Make(Null, NextItem, Null)
    Enque(PQ, TempTree)
END WHILE
```

Application: Variable-Length Codes

In the example that we worked out by hand, we had 10 failure boxes with associated weights. Suppose we associate each failure box with a decimal digit (e_0 with the digit 0, e_1 with digit 1, and so on) and interpret the associated weights to mean the frequency of occurrence of that digit within a passage of text. In fact, the "weights" in the example were actually the frequency of occurrence of the digits 0 . . . 9 in a passage of text containing 23,040 characters. We can use the frequency statistics to devise a scheme for representing the digits in an efficient manner.

When storing digits in text form, each digit takes one byte of storage. The minimum external path length tree can be used to assign unique codes of various lengths to each item represented in a failure box. If items that appear frequently are encoded with fewer bits, then storage is minimized.

To assign a unique code to each failure box, start at the top of the tree and assign a 0 to each left link and a 1 to each right link. The series of 0's and 1's from the root to a failure box is the code for the item in the failure box. The tree from our example of digits is shown below with the codes for each item listed below the external node.

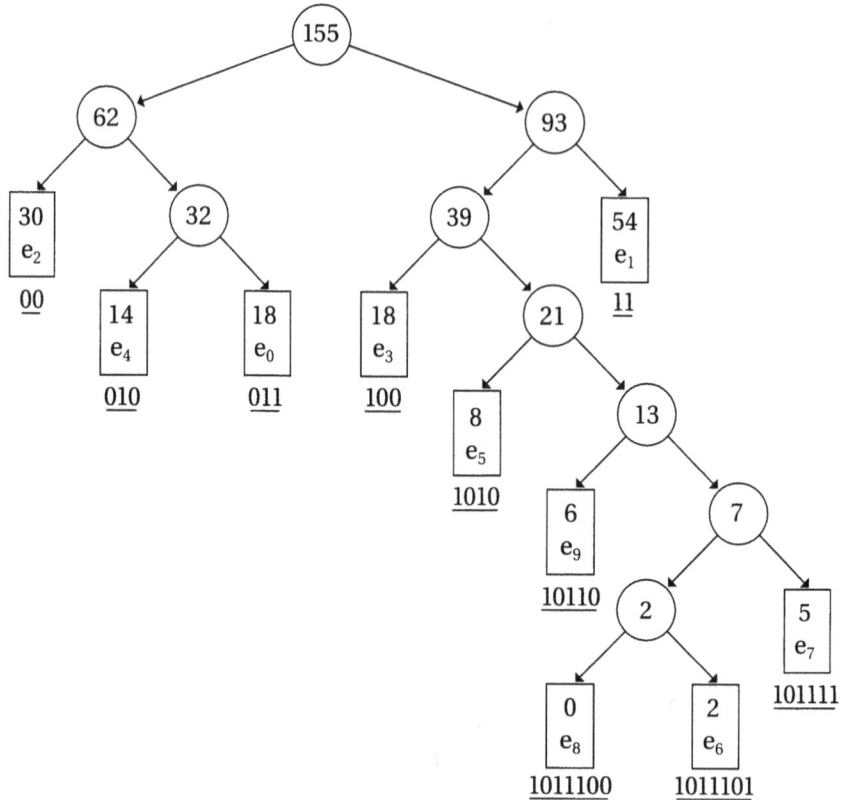

As usual, it is easy to follow a by-hand algorithm like, "Begin at the top of the tree, assigning a 0 to each left link and a 1 to each right link." But how do we write the computer algorithm to do this task? Well, "Begin at the top . . ." is a traversal of the tree recognizing when we reach an external node. Our traversal needs a parameter in which we build up the bit pattern for each external node as we traverse the tree. When we reach an external node (leaf node), we need to save the character, the parameter that holds the bit pattern, and the number of bits in the pattern. We can define an array [0..9] and store the bit pattern in the array indexed by the digit for which it is the pattern. This array also needs to be a parameter of the traversal.

We need to add the following declarations.

```
TYPE
    BinaryType = (Zero, One);

    CodeType = RECORD
        Length    : 0..16;
        Code      : PACKED ARRAY[1..16] OF BinaryType
    END RECORD ;
    CodesType = ARRAY [0..9] OF CodeType;
```

DeterminePatterns (HuffTree: BinTree, ACode: CodeType,
VAR Codes: CodesType)

```
ACode.Length ← 0
Traverse (HuffTree, ACode, Codes)
```

Traverse (HuffTree: BinTree, ACode: CodeType, VAR Codes:
CodesType)

```
IF NOT NULL(GetLeft(HuffTree))
    THEN (* HuffTree is an internal node. *)
        ACode.Length ← ACode.Length + 1
        Code.Code[Length] ← Zero
        Traverse(GetLeft(HuffTree), ACode, Codes)
        ACode.Code[Length] ← One
        Traverse(GetRight(HuffTree), ACode, Codes)
    ELSE (* Tree is an external node. *)
        Codes[GetItem(HuffTree).Digit] ← ACode
END IF
```

The codes generated from a Huffman tree have the *prefix property*, which means that none of the shorter codes duplicate the beginning of the longer codes. The digits 1 and 2 can be uniquely encoded using only two bits each, as 11 and 00, respectively. When decoding a stream of binary bits and 11 is encountered at the beginning of a digit, it is a 1; when 00 is encountered, it is a 2. The codes are summarized below.

Codes	.Code	.Length
[0]	011	3
[1]	11	2
[2]	00	2
[3]	100	3
[4]	010	3
[5]	1010	4
[6]	1011101	7
[7]	101111	6
[8]	1011100	7
[9]	10110	5

Based on the frequency statistics generated from the sample text, the minimum number of bits necessary to represent a digit is two, and the maximum is seven. The greater the frequency of occurrence of a digit in the sample, the shorter the code for the digit. Therefore, when decoding a number encoded using these codes, the more frequently occurring digits can be decoded faster.

The number 921 would be encoded by taking the code for the digit 9 (10110), followed by the code for the digit 2 (00), followed by the code for the digit 1 (11).

921: 101100011

To go the other way, we follow the path in the tree, going right or left depending on the binary digit, until we reach an external node. The binary string 0101110110011 would be decoded as follows.

010   ends in the external box containing the digit 4.

11   ends in the external box containing the digit 1.

10110   ends in the external box containing the digit 9.

011   ends in the external box containing the digit 0.

Therefore, 0101110110011 is the encoded version of 4190.

Because the codes generated have the prefix property, no digit delimiter is necessary. Morse code does not have this property; a pause is necessary between letters. Although we have applied this algorithm to digits, it can, of course, be applied to all characters, giving us a way in which to encode any information in text form.

There are two main areas where Huffman codes are used: in data compression and in message transmission. In data compression, we wish to store a large file on auxiliary storage using as little space as possible. A set of codes can be tailor-made for a particular file by using the frequencies for each character in the file itself to form the Huffman tree. Once the Huffman tree has been constructed, the codes for each character can be defined. The file is read in text format. Each character is encoded and written out as a sequence of zeros and ones. When the encoded file is read, the Huffman tree is used to decode the characters as they are read. This implies that the Huffman tree must be saved along with the compressed file or that the frequencies must be saved and the Huffman tree reconstructed.

In message transmission, the goal is to send as few bits as necessary over the medium of transmission. The codes can be tailored to the area of discourse, thus making each message as short as possible. Because of the prefix property of the codes, no end-of-character symbol is needed. Note that in both data compression and message transmission, blanks and punctuation marks are just characters that are included in the coding. In fact, the blank occurs so often that it probably has a very short code.

It was not an accident that we used the array-of-records representation of the ADT Tree to form the Huffman tree. Both of the applications require that the Huffman tree be present when messages or files are decoded. A tree built using pointer variables cannot be saved between runs. Therefore, we either have to encode and decode the tree somehow, save the frequencies and reconstruct the tree, or use the array-of-records representation. We chose the last of the three options.

Dynamic Binary Trees

Our discussion of static binary trees began with the assumption that we knew how often we might search for various nodes. In such circumstances, we minimize weighted costs in order to minimize average search times. When node frequencies are not known before processing begins, we have what is called a *dynamic tree*, and we must try a different approach in order to keep search times low. Dynamic trees are used to implement dynamic symbol tables (of course). The algorithms developed in the previous section are not applicable to dynamic trees.

Typically, we assume that all internal and external nodes are equally likely to occur. Searches within a tree, then, involve moving from level to level to find each node. To review, the amount of work necessary to search a tree, therefore, is

$$\text{Work within tree} = \sum_{i=1}^{N} (\text{level}(\text{node}_i) + 1)$$

$$= \left(\sum_{i=1}^{N} \text{level}(\text{node}_i) \right) + N$$

The N simply reflects the number of nodes in the tree, so we cannot affect this part of the formula by rearranging the tree. Rather, to analyze the efficiency of searching a tree, we consider the first part of this sum. This is called the *internal path length I*, the sum of the lengths of the paths from the root to each internal node. Similarly, the *external path length E* is the sum of the lengths of the paths from the root to each external or failure node. The formula for the external and internal path lengths can be more formally expressed in terms of level numbers of the internal and external nodes.

$$I = \sum_{i=1}^{N} \text{level}(\text{node}_i) \qquad E = \sum_{e=0}^{N} \text{level}(\text{failure node}_e)$$

As an example, consider the binary tree in Figure 8.5. The internal path length of the extended tree is 4. The external path length of the same tree is 12. Similarly, if we ignore the weights in Figure 8.6 (a), the internal path length of the tree is 7 and the external path length is 17. The internal and external path lengths in Figure 8.7(b) are 6 and 16, respectively.

If we compare these results with the number of internal nodes in the tree, a pattern emerges. In each case, the external path length is the internal path length plus 2*N, where N is the number of internal nodes. That is,

$$E = I + 2N$$

where E is the external path length and I is the internal path length. This is always true. The proof is left as an end-of-chapter exercise. (*Hint*: Use induction over the number of nodes.) The implication from this relationship is that optimizing either E or I optimizes the other. Because each of these sums involves the levels of various nodes, we expect that we can keep both E and I relatively low if we can place most nodes in levels with fairly low numbers. This suggests that we want to construct trees that are reasonably full.

AVL Trees[1]

Our best strategy for trying to minimize search times in dynamic trees is to let nature take its course (insert the values in the order in which they come), *but* monitor the shape of the tree and intervene if the shape deviates too much from the optimal shape. The operational words are *monitor* and *intervene.* Binary search trees that grow naturally until they get out of balance and are rebalanced are called *balanced trees.* Different definitions of monitor and intervene define different kinds of balanced trees. AVL trees represent one perspective on balancing a binary search tree, and we discuss this approach here. Another perspective considers balanced binary trees as a special case of more general, multi-way search trees. Red/Black trees illustrate this approach, and we outline these trees in Chapter 9. See the Bibliography at the back of the book for other examples.

A tree is called *height-balanced at node S* if the heights of the left and right subtrees of S differ by no more than 1. An *AVL tree* is a binary search tree in which every subtree is height-balanced. (Figure 8.10 shows a tree with the heights of each node specified.) Each subtree of an AVL tree is itself an AVL tree.

Figure 8.11 shows the shape of seven binary trees. The trees that are starred (*) are AVL trees. The others are not AVL trees because the heights of the subtrees of one of the nodes differ by more than 1.

Insertion in AVL Trees

Because AVL trees are binary search trees, the construction of AVL trees must guarantee that data and nodes obey the order property of search trees. Typically,

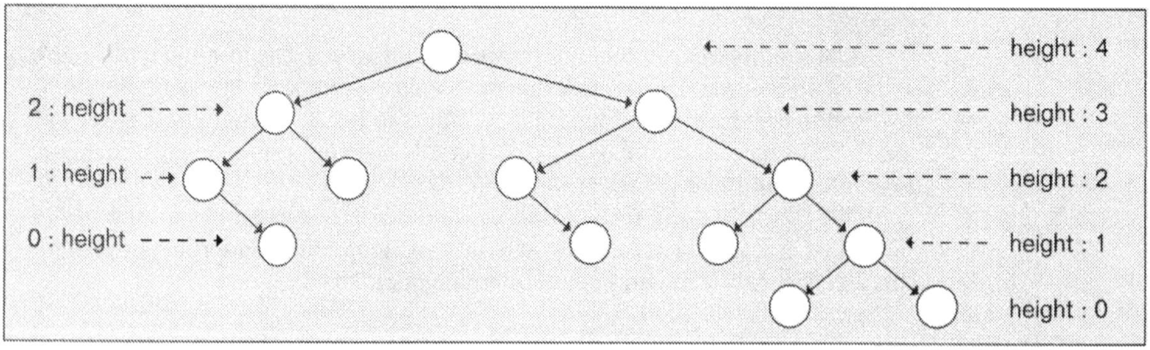

Figure 8.10 Height of Subtrees in an AVL Tree (Height of a tree is height of its tallest subtree)

[1] AVL trees are named for the Russian scientists who first investigated them: Adel'son-Vel'skii and Landis.

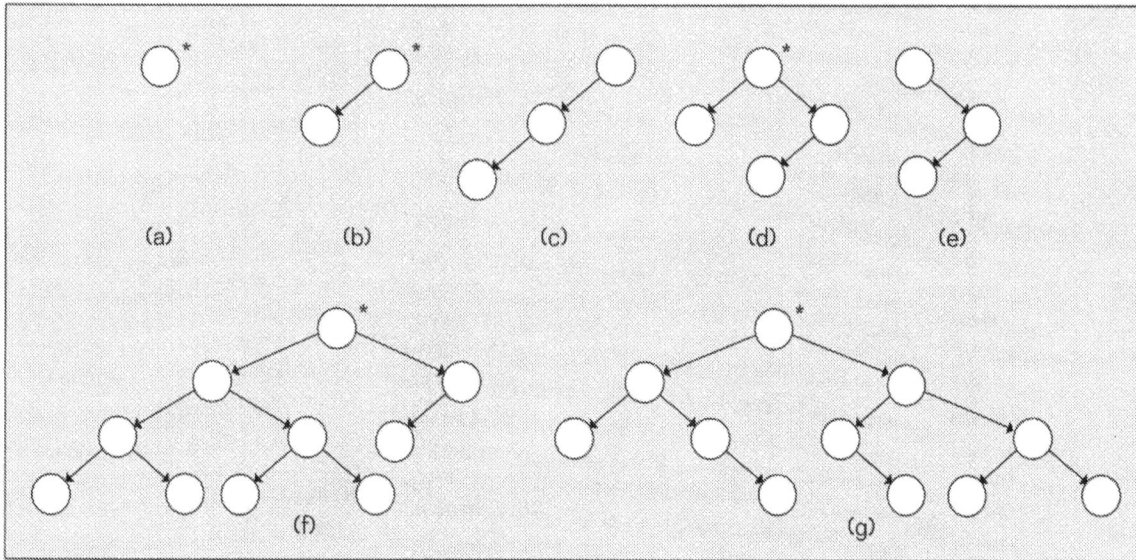

Figure 8.11   Shapes of Binary Search Trees (*Trees are AVL trees)

this is accomplished by organizing both the insertion and the deletion operations in two stages. First, we follow the insertion algorithm for simple insertion into a binary search tree. This guarantees that the tree we are building contains the correct values and obeys the order property of search trees. Next, during this simple insertion we watch the heights of each subtree. The heights of the subtrees of any node are allowed to get out of balance by only one level. If the heights of the subtrees of any node differ by 2, we intervene and rebalance the tree, still maintaining the order property of search trees.

In order to monitor the shape of the tree, we must have some way of determining that the heights of the subtrees of each node are within the allowed range. One way would be to keep track of the height of each subtree in the tree by recording the height in the root of the subtree. To determine the relative heights of the subtrees of each node we could compare the heights in the roots of the subtrees.

Another, more descriptive, way is to keep track of the shape of the tree for which each node is the root. That is, the shape of each tree (subtree) is either balanced, leaning left, or leaning right. We could use the following symbols to represent these states: = (balanced), / or ↙ (leaning left), and \ or ↘ (leaning right). Figure 8.12 shows the trees in Figure 8.11 with the shape symbols inside each node.

Although the shapes in Figure 8.12 demonstrate the use of the shape symbols, an examination of the pattern of the symbols in the AVL trees and the non-AVL trees does not give us any information on how to monitor the shape of the tree. That is, looking at the pattern of shape symbols in a non-AVL tree gives us no clue as to how it went out of balance. The key to monitoring the shape of the tree is to determine when it is going to go out of balance and intervene at that point. This determination is based on the shape of the tree into which a node is being inserted and the insertion point itself.

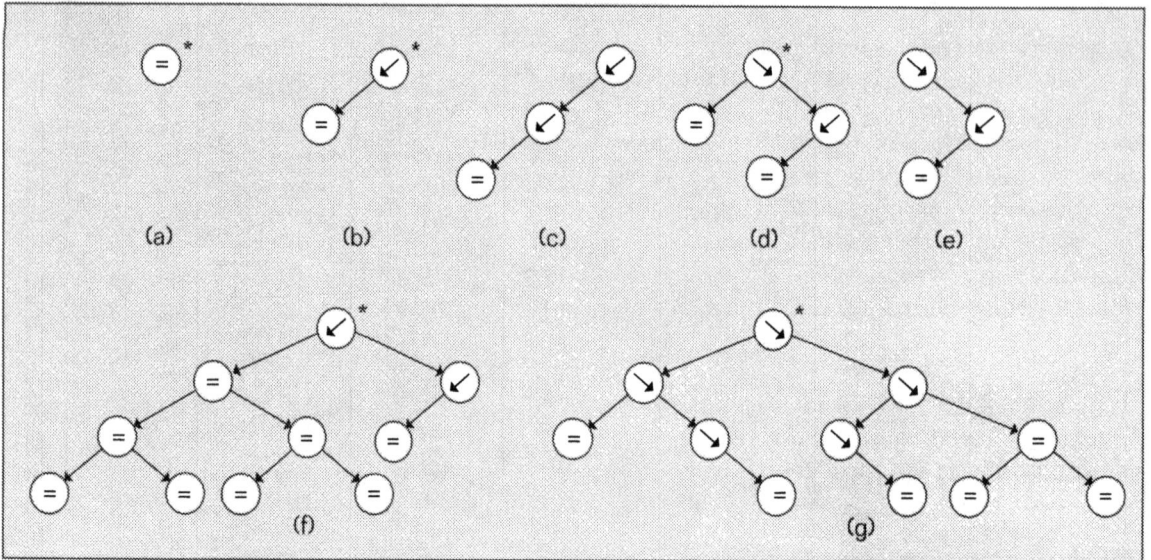

Figure 8.12 Shapes of Binary Search Trees (* Trees are AVL trees)

Examples There are several cases where an insertion causes the tree to become unbalanced. We now look at four such cases and determine the combination of events that predict when trouble is looming.

Example 1

Insert Austin into the following tree

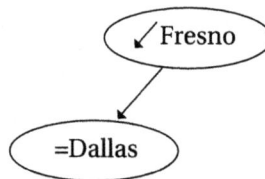

We can see immediately that there is going to be trouble. If we insert Houston, the balance factor (or shape symbol) of Fresno changes, but the tree is still balanced. On the other hand, inserting Austin causes the height of the left subtree of the node containing Fresno to be 2 more than the right subtree of the node containing Fresno. The tree must be reorganized so that the shape is balanced and the tree is still a binary search tree. That is, the reorganization must maintain the search property. In this case, a simple rotation to the right suffices.

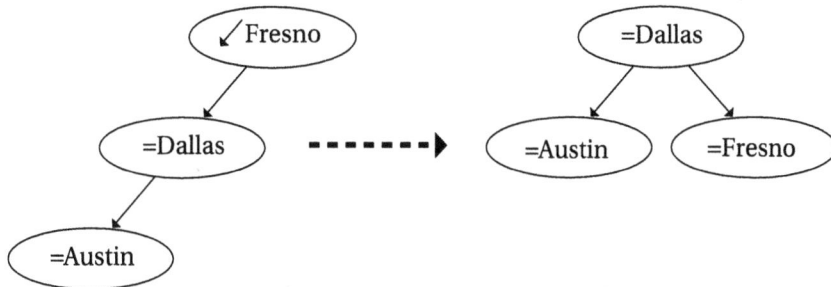

The node containing Dallas becomes the root node; the node containing Fresno becomes the right child of the root; and the node containing Austin remains the left child of Dallas. The new node always has an = shape symbol, but the symbols on the other nodes must be updated. The rotation algorithm has to be responsible for updating the shape symbols of the nodes involved in the rotation.

Example 2

Insert Houston into the following tree

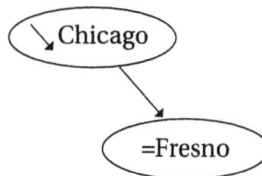

Again, we can see immediately that the insertion causes problems. In fact, this looks like the mirror image of the previous example; we are working with the right subtree rather than the left subtree. Indeed, it *is* a mirror image, and the solution is a mirror image also. Rotate the tree to the left.

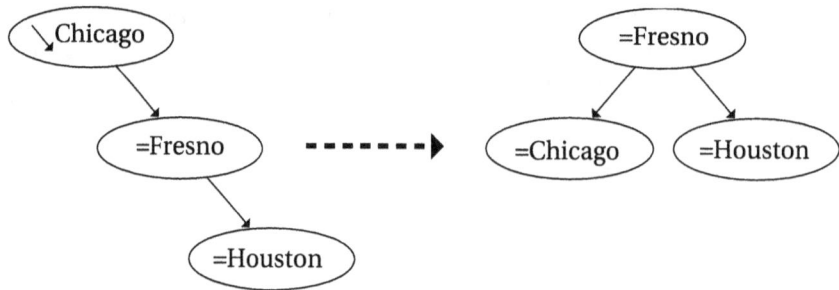

Example 3

Insert Greensboro into the following tree

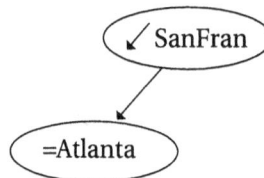

At first, this looks much like the two previous examples, but look at the result of inserting Greensboro.

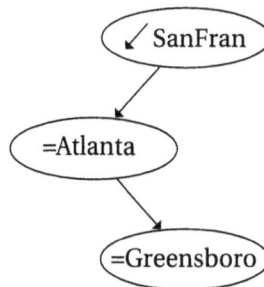

What happens if we try a simple rotation here? In the two previous examples, we rotated the middle element up to be the root. If we do that here, we have a tree that is not a binary search tree. There is no way that Atlanta can be in the root node and the tree can be an AVL tree. Clearly, for three nodes to be an AVL tree, the middle value must be in the root node.

A simple rotation worked in the two previous examples because the node containing the middle value was on the middle level. While we could simply rearrange the nodes in this example to make Greensboro the root, we need a more general approach (other than trial and error) for more complex trees. One reasonably straightforward approach uses the following two rotations. The first rotates the middle value (Greensboro) into the middle level by rotating the subtree with root containing Atlanta to the left. The second rotation restores the balance by rotating the subtree whose root contains SanFran to the right. The first rotation retains the binary search property but does not restore the shape property. The second rotation restores the shape property while also maintaining the binary search property.

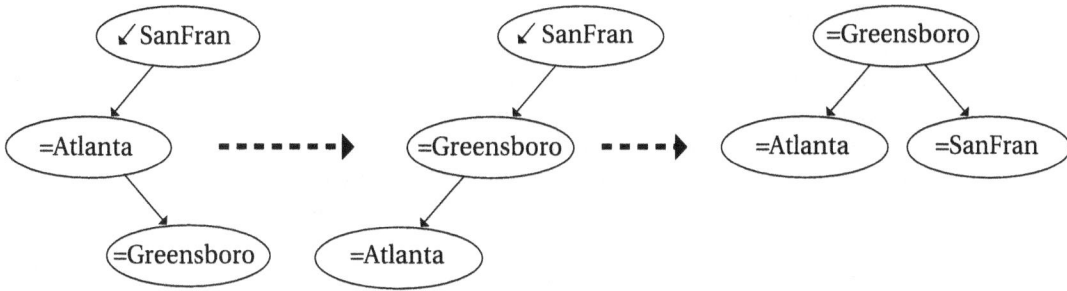

Example 4

Insert SanDiego in the following tree

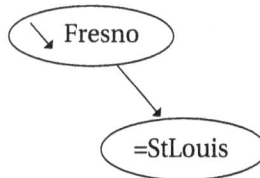

SanDiego is greater than Fresno and less than StLouis, so this looks like the mirror image of the previous example. A double rotation can be followed: the subtree whose root contains StLouis is rotated to the right and the whole tree is rotated to the left.

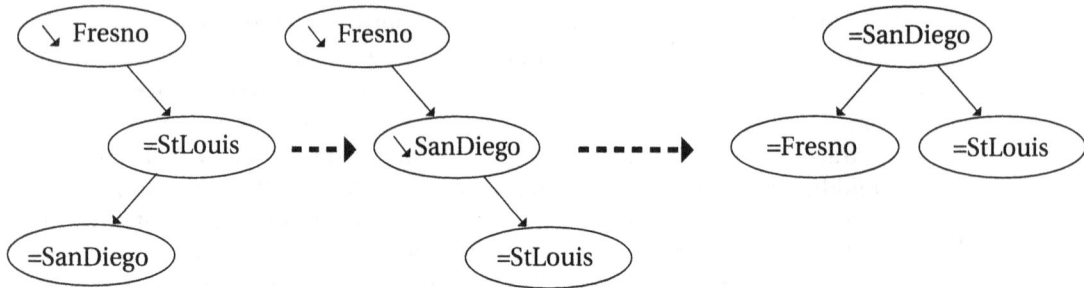

What do these four examples have in common? The shape of the tree is already leaning *and* the node is being inserted into the heavy side.

Note that this trouble cannot arise if the shape is equal. When a tree already balances, the insertion of one node cannot change the height of a subtree by 2 (enough to throw the tree out of balance). Such an insertion, however, would cause us to update the shape symbol of the parent. The problem of balancing is even simpler if the tree is unbalanced to one side and we add the node on the other side. Here, the addition may cause the new tree to become balanced. For example, if the tree is leaning to the right and the insertion is in the left subtree, then the shape of the tree becomes balanced.

This informal review of cases suggests that insertion violates the height-balanced property only when the insertion of the node increases the height of a subtree in the direction that the subtree is already leaning. While such informal reasoning is extremely useful in guiding our development of an algorithm, we need to be somewhat more formal if we want our algorithm to be completely correct. For example, we must be sure that the above examples cover all of the relevant cases. Furthermore, for each case already considered, we need to consider what happens if our trees contain more than just a few nodes.

Pivot Node on the Insertion Search Path In addressing these issues, we need some additional terminology. In the simple insertion process, we begin at the root and proceed downward to a leaf, moving left or right at subsequent nodes according to whether the new data item comes before or after the existing data. This process gives a path from the root through the tree to the position where the new node is placed. We call this path the **insertion search path**. For example, if we add Rochester to the tree in Figure 8.3 (page 324), the insertion search path would be Montreal, Pittsburgh, SanFrancisco, SanDiego, Rochester. (See Figure 8.13.)

When we are inserting into an AVL tree, it is important to understand how the insertion can change the balance of the tree. The addition of the new node has no effect on the balance of any subtrees that do not contain the insertion search path. For example, in Figure 8.13, the left subtree, which has Cincinnati as root, is completely unaffected by the addition of the new node. Because that part of the tree was height-balanced before the addition, it still must be that way after the addition.

As noted earlier, it is possible that all nodes along this insertion search path were balanced initially. If this is not the case, it is convenient to give a name to the

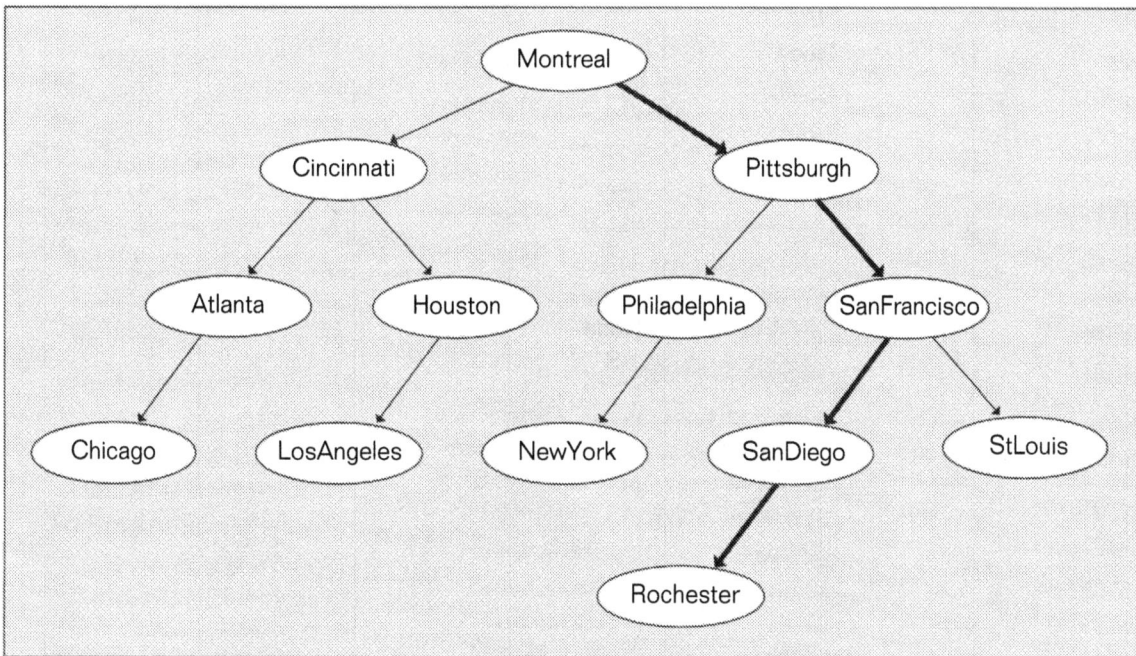

Figure 8.13 Insertion Path for Adding Rochester to the Tree in Figure 8.3

node whose shape symbol determines whether the insertion causes problems or not. In each example, this node was the root. In the general case, this node is the unbalanced node closest to the insertion point along the insertion search path. This node is called the **pivot node**.

Following the insertion search path may uncover many nodes whose shape symbol is not =. However, it is the last such node visited before the insertion point is reached that is the pivot node. If there are no unbalanced nodes on the path from the root to the insertion point, we do not identify a pivot node.

> **Insertion Search Path** The path from the root to a newly inserted node, following the simple binary-search-tree insertion algorithm.
>
> **Pivot Node** The last unbalanced node passed before reaching the insertion point. If all nodes visited are balanced, we do not designate a pivot node.

With this terminology, we now consider the various cases that can arise during insertion. These cases are illustrated in Figure 8.14.

Case 1: All nodes along the insertion search path are balanced initially.
Case 2: The new node is added on the short side of the pivot (in P's left subtree in Figure 8.14).
Case 3: The new data item does not come between the pivot and the following node on the long side, but rather is added on the long side away from the pivot (in R's right subtree in Figure 8.14).

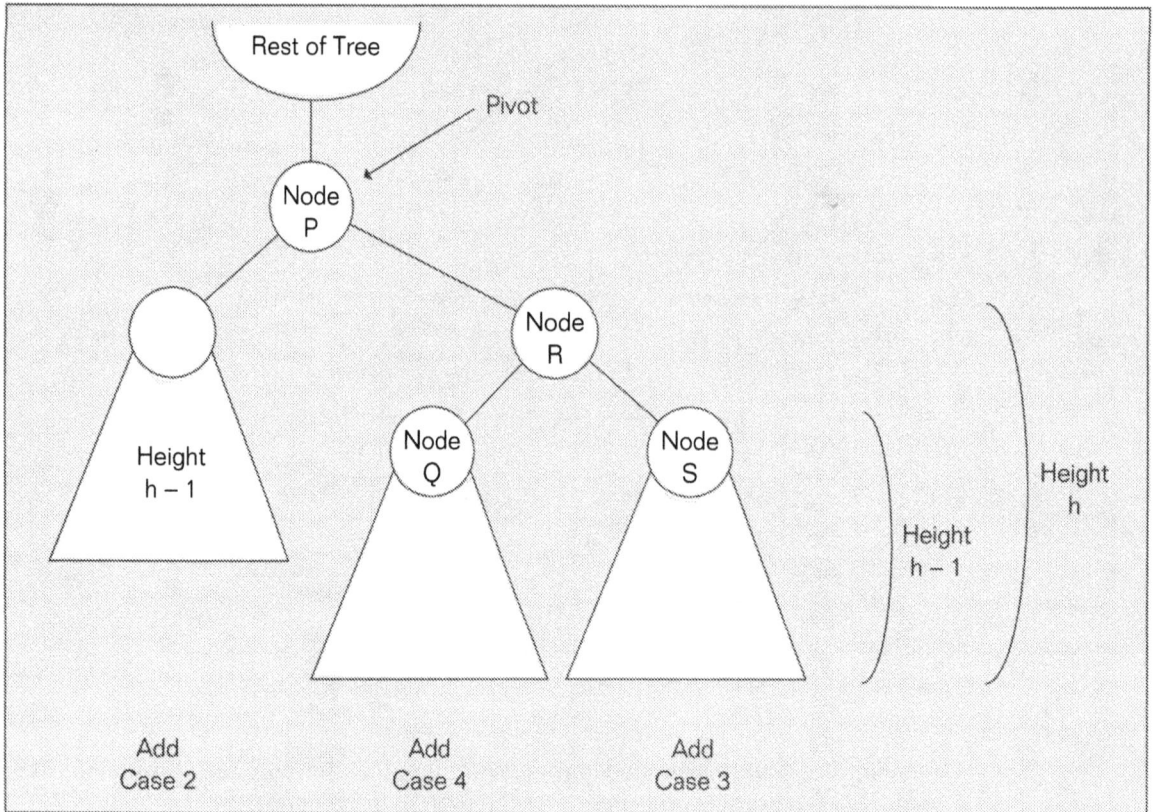

Figure 8.14 Cases for Adding a New Node to an Unbalanced Tree

Case 4: The new data item comes between the pivot and the following node on the long side (in R's left subtree in Figure 8.14).

An examination of Figure 8.14 shows that these are the only possible cases, because additions to all parts of the tree are covered in this listing. Fortunately, our previous examples already have provided some insight into Cases 2, 3, and 4 .

With this identification of cases, we now can use our examples to guide us in describing what action is needed in each circumstance.

For Case 1, all nodes are balanced initially. The addition of a new node adds length 1 to each subtree along the insertion search path. The resulting tree is still height-balanced, but the shape symbol must be changed from = to ∨ or ∨, depending upon whether the insertion is on the left or on the right of a given node.

For Case 2, we are adding on the short side of the pivot. Because the pivot node is the nearest unbalanced node to the new one, the paths on this short side must be balanced. When this happens, the addition of a new node increases the height of this short subtree, and the pivot node becomes balanced. In Figure 8.14, adding in Case 2 gives another level at the bottom of the short tree, which balances the trees below the pivot. Therefore, the balance symbol at the pivot becomes =. Within that short tree below the pivot, however, each node along the insertion search path becomes unbalanced, and the shape symbols of the nodes along that path must be adjusted, as in Case 1.

For Case 3, we are adding below node S in Figure 8.14. Informally, we can balance the tree by rotating R up to be a new pivot and moving the pivot down the other side. Where do Node Q and its subtree go? These nodes can be reattached to the old pivot. This rotation process is sometimes called a *type 1 rotation* and is shown in Figure 8.15.

In reviewing Figure 8.15, note that all parts of the tree still have the order property required for a binary search tree. The short size stays on the same side of the old pivot P, as does the subtree containing node Q. Similarly, the trees containing nodes Q and S remain on the same sides of the new pivot, node R. Furthermore, in analyzing the heights of the various subtrees, we conclude that both sides of node R now have the same height. Thus, node R is now balanced as claimed earlier.

Case 4 is somewhat trickier, although the appropriate positions of various subtrees can be found, as shown in Figure 8.16. Moving these subtrees into position in this case is sometimes called a *type 2 rotation*.

While this type 2 rotation may seem somewhat complex, our examples have illustrated that we may decompose this processing into two parts. First we perform a type 1 rotation at node R, in the direction away from the pivot. Then we perform a second type 1 rotation in the opposite direction at the pivot. (In the end-of-chapter exercises, you are asked to check that these two type 1 rotations move the various nodes and subtrees to the correct positions.)

As with the type 1 rotation, the result of a type 2 rotation still has the appropriate ordering of data to maintain a binary search tree structure, and the result is still height-balanced.

Now that we have identified all cases for maintaining an AVL tree structure during the insertion process, we turn to writing the steps in pseudocode.

Insertion Algorithm   We first write code for the type 1 and type 2 rotations. In both cases, two versions are needed, because the long side of the tree can be either to the left or to the right of the pivot. For the type 1 rotations, if the long side is to the right, we want to rotate the nodes counterclockwise. If the long side is to the left, a clockwise rotation is needed. These procedures also must set the shape symbols appropriately for the old and new pivots. The code for the counterclockwise rotation follows. Because the pivot changes after this rotation, the procedure requires a pointer parameter from the pivot's parent.

Type1RotationCounter (VAR Root: TreePointer, Item: ItemType);

```
OldPivot ← Root
Temp ← Left(Right (Root))
Root ← Right (Root)
Left(Root) ← OldPivot
Right(OldPivot) ← Temp
ShapeSymbol (Root) ← =
ShapeSymbol (OldPivot) ← =
```

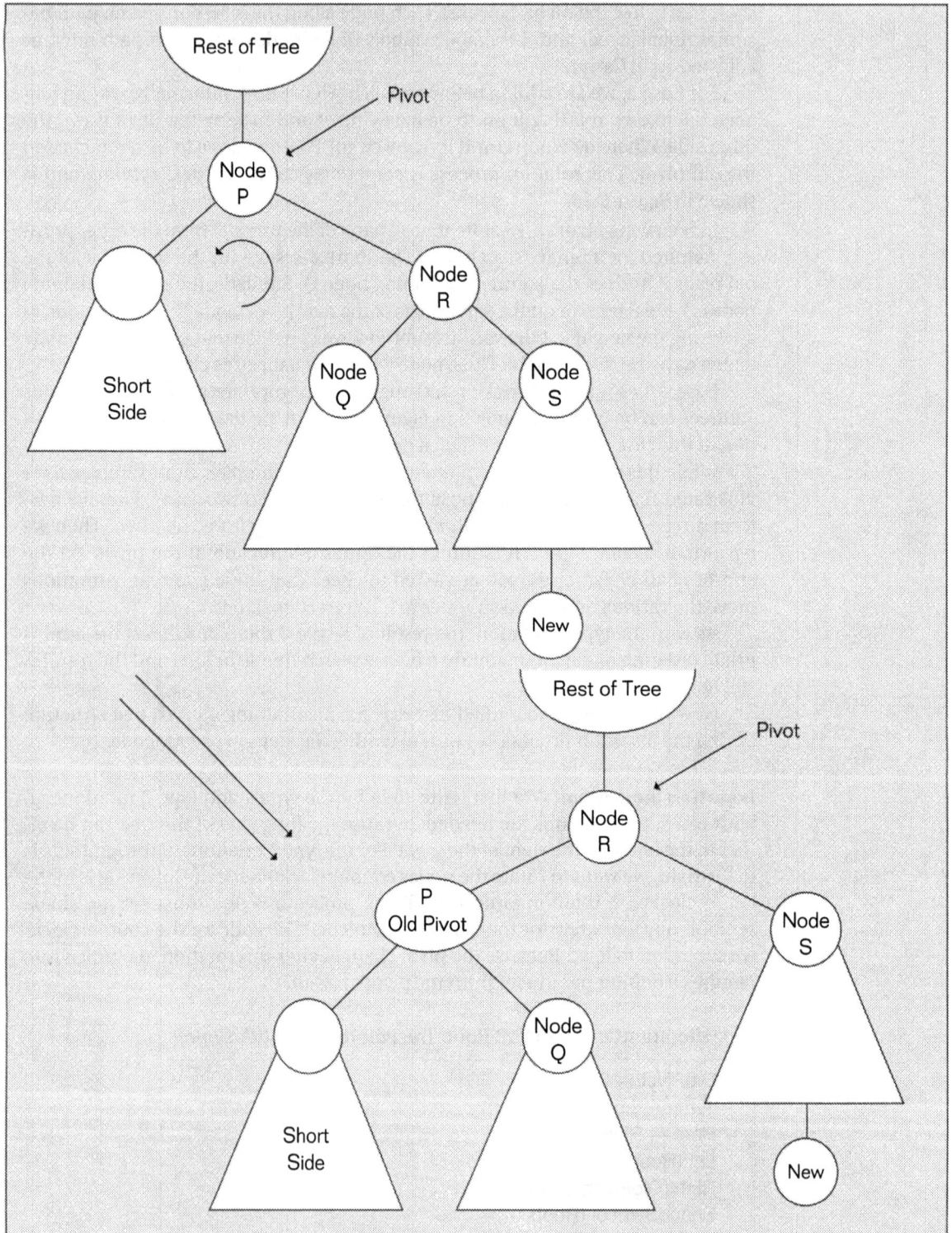

Figure 8.15   A Type 1 Rotation

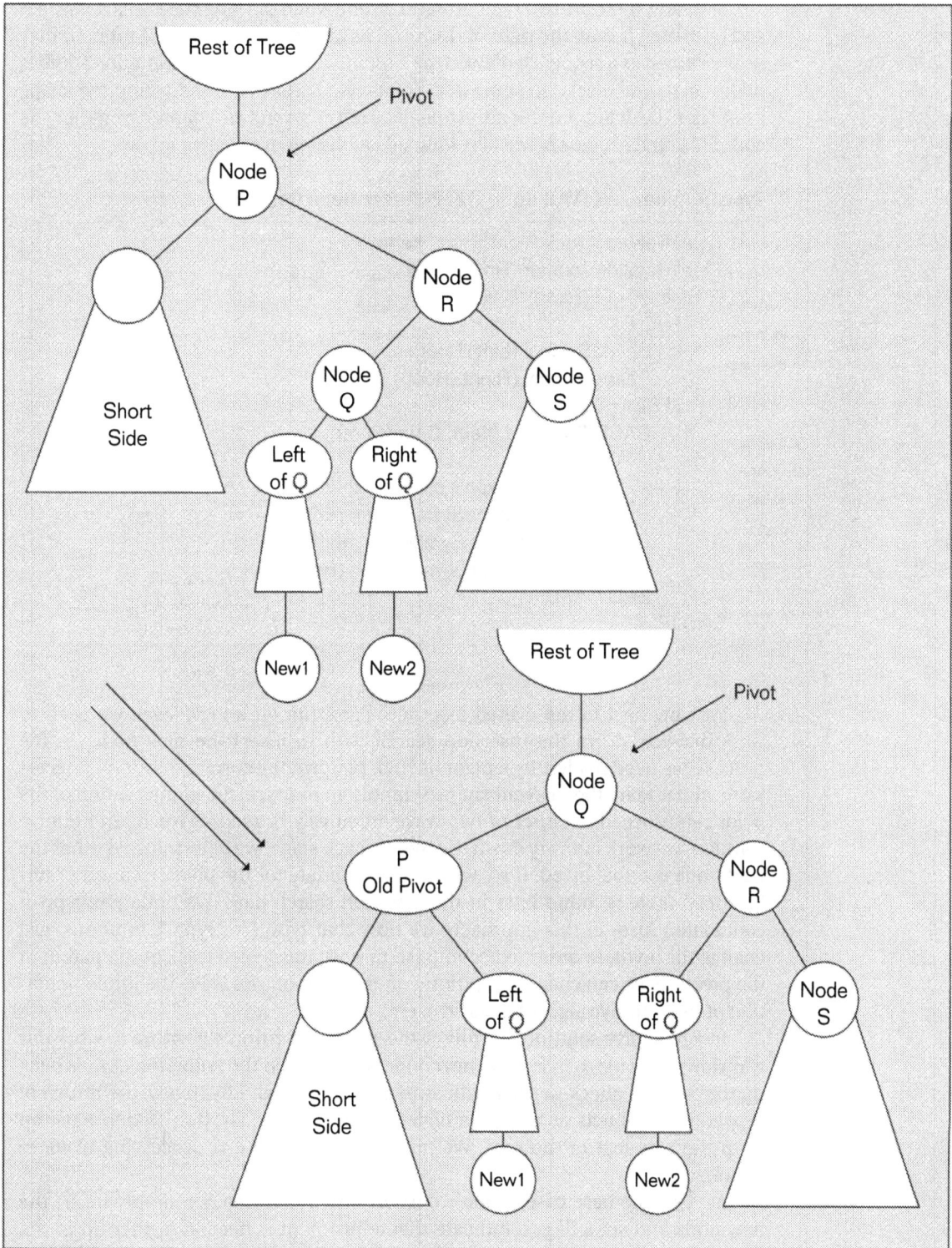

Figure 8.16 A Type 2 Rotation

Similarly, there are two type 2 rotations: one when the long subtree is on the left and one when it is on the right of the pivot. As already noted, a type 2 rotation may be performed as a sequence of two type 1 rotations. Also, the type 2 rotation shuffles nodes at several levels, so some additional care is needed in adjusting the shape symbols. (The details for this adjustment are left as an end-of-chapter exercise.) The code for a type 2 rotation, with the long side to the left of the pivot follows.

Type2RotationLeft (VAR Root: TreePointer), Item: ItemType

```
Type1RotationClock Right (Root, Item)
Type1RotationCounter (Root, Item)
IF Right (Right (Root)) = NIL
    THEN
        ShapeSymbol (Left (Root)) ← =
        ShapeSymbol (Right (Root))
    ELSE
        CASE Compare (Item, Data (Root))
            Greater,
            Equal  :  ShapeSymbol (Right (Root)) ← /
                      ShapeSymbol (Left (Root)) ← =
            Less   :  ShapeSymbol (Right (Root)) ← =
                      ShapeSymbol (Left (Root)) ← \
        END CASE
END IF
```

We now turn to the overall insertion algorithm. At a high level, we need to work our way down the insertion search path to insert the new node. In the process, we need to identify a pivot (if any), perform the correct rotation (if necessary), and update the relevant shape symbols. In practice, the identification of the pivot can proceed in either of two ways: iteratively or recursively. In an iterative solution, we work our way down the tree. At each stage, we determine whether the next node is unbalanced. If so, we have a candidate for the pivot. (If another unbalanced node is found later in the insertion search path, we update our pivot candidate.) Also, in this approach, we note that type 1 or type 2 rotations also change the pivot. In order to accomplish this, we must keep track of the parent of the pivot, so we can change its pointer after a rotation. We leave the implementation of this iterative algorithm as an exercise.

In a recursive solution, we follow the simple insertion algorithm to work our way down the tree to insert the new node. Then, when the recursion comes back up the tree, we check to see if adjustments are needed. Effectively, the return of procedure calls acts as a mechanism for tracing the insertion search path up from the new leaf to the root. We now look at this return processing in more detail.

As a simple base case, when we insert into a null tree, we simply insert the new node and set a flag to indicate that adjustment is needed farther up in the tree.

In the general case, once we have inserted farther down in the tree, we check to see if adjustment is still needed. (If we are processing at the pivot or below, we need to review the tree for balance and make adjustments as needed. If we are processing a node above the pivot, no adjustments are needed.)

In the case where a node below the pivot is balanced, both subtrees of the node were balanced previously, so the addition of the new node causes one subtree to become taller than it was previously. This requires an adjustment of the node's shape symbol. Also, because we have not reached the pivot yet in our processing back up the tree, adjustment is still needed farther up the tree.

We identify the pivot node because it is unbalanced and because processing farther down the tree indicates that adjustments in the tree are still needed. Here, we must distinguish between Cases 2, 3, and 4, and we must take appropriate action. Once the tree has been rebalanced and shape symbols have been adjusted, no further adjustments are needed farther up in the tree.

The various cases just described are shown in the following algorithm. On the way down the insertion search path, we need information concerning the tree's root and the item to be inserted. During the return process, we need to know if adjustments have already been completed farther down in the tree. Overall, these requirements can be met if the procedure has three parameters, as shown.

Insert (VAR Root: TreePointer, Item: ItemType, VAR AdjustmentNeeded: Boolean)

```
IF Root = NIL
   THEN
      MakeNode (Root, Item)
      AdjustmentNeeded← True
   ELSE
      CASE Compare(Item, Data(Root)) OF
         Less   :   Insert (Left(Root) Item, AdjustmentNeeded);
                    IF AdjustmentNeeded
                       THEN   (* Recompute node balances *)
                       CASE ShapeSymbol OF
                          =  :   ShapeSymbol ← /
                          \  :   (* Added on short side *)
                                 ShapeSymbol ← =
                                 AdjustmentNeeded ← False
                          /  :   (* Added on long side *)
                                 CASE Compare(Item, Data(Left(Root)) OF
                                    Less    :   Type1RotationClock (Root, Item)
                                    Greater,
                                    Equal   :   Type2RotationLeft (Root, Item)
                                 END CASE
                                 AdjustmentNeeded ← False
                       END CASE
                    (* ELSE AdjustmentNeeded is False, no balancing needed *)
                 END IF
```

```
                Greater,
                Equal   :   Insert (Right(Root) Item, AdjustmentNeeded);
                            IF AdjustmentNeeded
                                THEN   (* Recompute node balance *)
                                    CASE ShapeSymbol (Root) OF
                                          =   :   ShapeSymbol (Root) ← \
                                          /   :   (* Added on short side *)
                                                  ShapeSymbol (Root) ← =
                                                  AdjustmentNeeded ← False
                                          \   :   (* Added on long side *)
                                                  CASE Compare(Item, Data (Right (Root))) OF
                                                      Greater,
                                                      Equal   :   Type1RotationCounter(Root, Item)
                                                      Less    :   Type2RotationRight (Root, Item)
                                                  END CASE
                                                  AdjustmentNeeded ← False
                                    END CASE
                                (* ELSE AdjustmentNeeded is False; no balancing needed *)
                            END IF
        END CASE
END IF
```

Make Node (VAR Root: TreePointer; Item: ItemType;)

```
New (Root);
Data (Root) ← Item
ShapeSymbol (Root) ← =
Left(Root) ← NIL
Right(Root) ← NIL
```

While this code is somewhat lengthy, it is not as complex as it may seem at first. The base case to insert a new leaf follows the simple insertion algorithm, except for setting an additional flag. The general case then splits into two parts, depending upon whether the new node should be added on the left or the right of the current node on the insertion search path. The two cases are symmetrical, with only the directions reversed. In each situation, we first insert farther down in the tree. When this has been completed, we determine if adjustments are needed in the current node. If so, the appropriate situations are identified and corrections are made. If not, the procedure returns to nodes higher in the tree.

Deletion Algorithm

In many ways, the deletion algorithm is a mirror image of the insertion algorithm. However, there is one main difference: any changes in the tree caused by an insertion are isolated between the Pivot node and the insertion point. In deleting from an AVL tree, it is more difficult to predict where the changes occur. It is easier to work backwards from the deletion point to where we can see that the height of the subtree has not been changed. Because "work backwards" sounds recursive, we also develop a recursive deletion algorithm.

As is the case with any deletion from a binary search tree, we reduce the case to deleting a node with, at most, one child. If the node to be deleted is an interior node, we replace it with its predecessor (or successor) and delete the predecessor (or successor). This process has already been discussed as part of simple deletion, earlier in this chapter.

Before we begin to develop the algorithm, we consider several examples of deletions in order to gain insight into what is happening. In the case of insertion, the issue is what to do when a subtree is made taller. In the case of deletion, the issue is what to do when a subtree becomes smaller.

Examples

Example 1

Delete Roger from the following tree (We became tired of cities.)

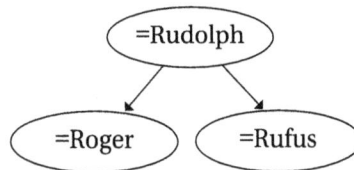

Deleting Roger leaves its parent leaning to the right, but does not reduce the height. No rearrangement of nodes is required.

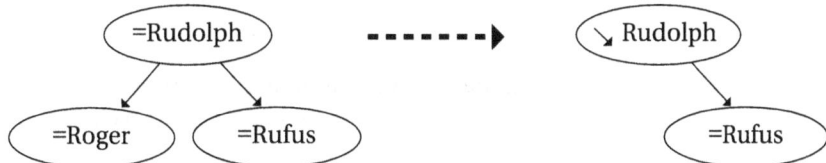

The implication is that deleting a node whose parent has = as its shape symbol only requires changing the shape symbol of the parent.

Example 2

Delete Betty from the following tree

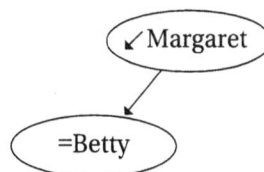

Deleting Betty simply changes Margaret's shape symbol to =. The subtree whose root is Margaret has been shortened.

Example 3

Delete Mary from the following tree

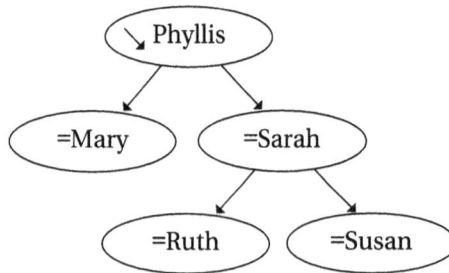

Deleting Mary leaves the tree unbalanced, but a simple rotation to the left should fix it. The height of the tree has not been changed.

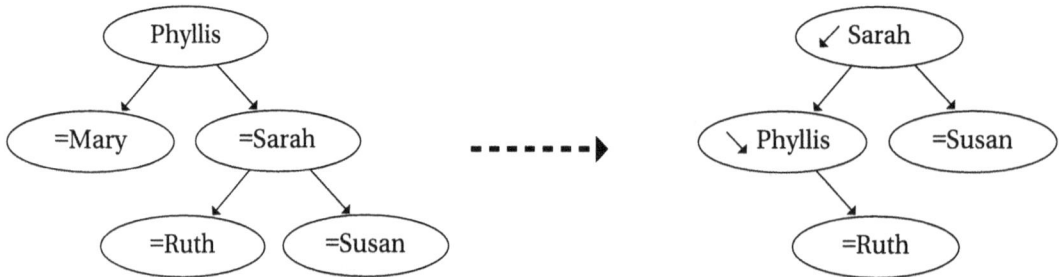

Example 4
Delete Ann from the following tree

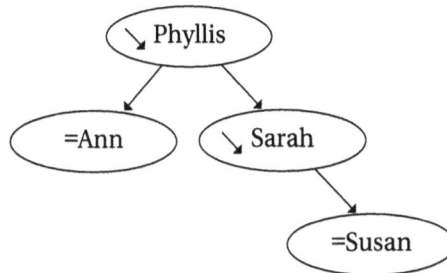

A single rotation to the left takes care of the problem because the middle level contains the middle value. The height of the tree has been shortened.

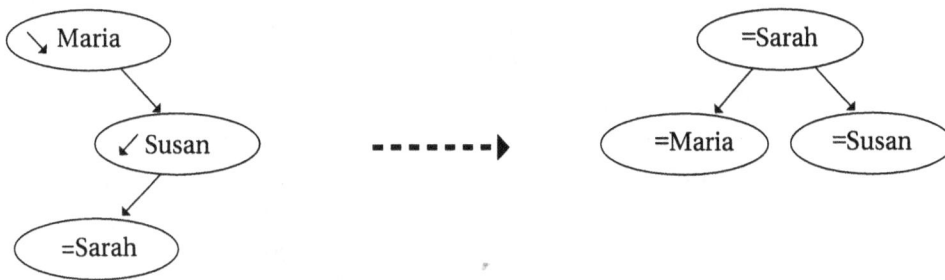

Example 5
Delete Judy from the following tree

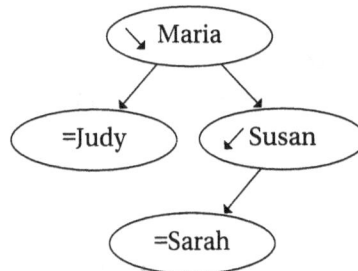

Deleting Judy leaves the tree out of balance. This looks suspiciously like the cases of insertion where a double rotation was necessary. The value in the middle level is not the middle value. Rotating Sarah right and Maria left should solve the problem. The height of the tree is shortened.

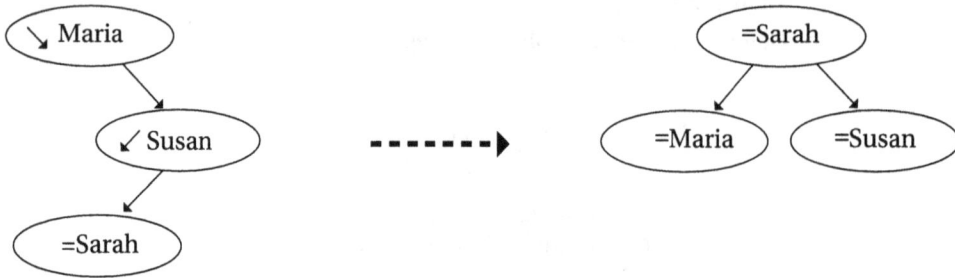

These examples show all the patterns that can occur when we delete from the left subtree. The mirror image patterns are there when we delete from the right subtree. Changes propagate back up the tree when the height of the subtree is shortened. We now examine the patterns and determine which deletions cause the height of the tree to change and which do not.

1. Deleting from a parent whose shape symbol points in the direction of the deletion changes the shape symbol of the parent to =. The parent is now balanced, but the height of the tree is shorter. (See deleting Betty.)

2. Deleting from a parent whose shape symbol is = requires neither a rotation nor a change in the height of the tree. (See deleting Roger.)

3. Deleting from a parent whose shape symbol is leaning in the opposite direction of the deletion seems to give conflicting results. (See deleting Mary, Ann, Judy.)

   a. If the sibling of the deleted node has a shape symbol of =, a single rotation is required but the height does not change. (See deleting Mary.)

   b. If the sibling of the deleted node has a shape symbol that is the same as that of the parent, a single rotation is required and the height is one level shorter.

   c. If the sibling of the deleted node has a shape symbol that is opposite from that of the parent, a double rotation is required and the height is one level shorter. (See deleting Judy.)

Deletion Algorithm The details of the delete algorithm follow from the examples and our observations. In deleting an item, we first locate the node containing it. If this node is not a leaf, we replace it by its successor, and recursively replace the successor. Following the deletion, we then rebalance the tree if necessary and update the various balance symbols. As with our recursive insertion algorithm, a flag parameter to the deletion algorithm indicates if a change has occurred to the height of the tree at the previous level. We call that flag Changed.

Delete (VAR Tree: TreeNodeType, Value: ItemType, VAR Changed: Boolean)

```
CASE Compare (Item, Value(Root)
    Equal:   IF Right(Root) <> Nil
                THEN   (* replace node by successor and delete successor *)
                Temp := Right (Root)
```

```
                              WHILE Left (Temp) <> Nil
                                    DO Temp  := Left (Temp)
                              END WHILE
                              Value (Root)       := Value (Temp)
                              Delete (Right(Root), Value (Temp), Changed)
                              IF Changed
                                    THEN AdjustFromRight (Root, Changed)
                              END IF
                           ELSE (* node has no successor * )
                              IF Left (Root)  = Nil
                                    THEN (* deleting leaf node *)
                                          Root   := Nil
                                          Changed   := True
                                    ELSE (* left node is leaf if right Nil in AVL
                                          tree *)
                                          Root   := Left (Root)
                                          Changed   := True
                              END IF
                           END IF
                     Less: Delete (Left (Root), Item, Changed)
                              IF Changed
                                    THEN AdjustFromLeft (Root, Changed)
                              END IF
                     Greater: Delete (Right(Root), Item, Changed)
                              IF Changed
                                    THEN AdjustFromRight (Root, Changed)
                              END IF
         END CASE
```

AdjustFromLeft (Node: TreeNodeType, Value: ItemType, VAR Changed: Boolean)

```
CASE ShapeSymbol(Node) OF
    =  :  ShapeSymbol(Node) ← \
          Changed ← False
    /  :  ShapeSymbol(Node) ← =
          Changed ← True
    \  :  CASE ShapeSymbol(Right(Node)) OF
             =  :  RotateLeft(Node)
                   ShapeSymbol(Node) ← /
                   ShapeSymbol(Left(Node)) ← \
                   Changed ← False
             \  :  RotateLeft(Node)
                   ShapeSymbol(Node) ← =
                   ShapeSymbol(Left(Node)) ← =
                   Changed ← True
```

```
        /   :   SaveShape ← ShapeSymbol(Left(Right(Node)))
                RotateRight(Right(Node))
                RotateLeft(Node)
                Changed ← True
                ShapeSymbol(Node) ← =
                CASE SaveShape OF
                    \   :   ShapeSymbol(Right(Node)) ← =
                            ShapeSymbol(Left(Node)) ← /
                    /   :   ShapeSymbol(Right(Node)) ← \
                            ShapeSymbol(Left(Node)) ← =
                    =   :   ShapeSymbol(Right(Node)) ← =
                            ShapeSymbol(Left(Node)) ← =
                END CASE
        END CASE
END CASE
```

The Adjust From Right algorithm is left as an end-of-chapter exercise. The Delete algorithm takes the node to be deleted. If this is an interior node, the value from the predecessor is inserted into the node and the predecessor is deleted. On return from Delete, Tree is the parent of that node.

SUMMARY

Binary search trees are binary trees in which the value in a node is greater than the values in its left subtree and less than or equal to the values in its right subtree. The shape of a tree determines the average search time for the values in the tree.

In inserting or deleting items from binary search trees, several algorithms may be followed. The simplest algorithms maintain data in a proper order for searching, but the trees may become quite unbalanced, because many insertions or deletions are performed. More sophisticated algorithms adjust the shape of the tree to improve average search times.

Static binary search trees are those in which the values in the nodes are known in advance. An optimal binary search tree can be constructed based on the statistics associated with the known values. When search frequencies are known in advance, nodes can be placed in a search tree to minimize average search times. Optimal binary search trees may be of particular value in writing compilers or in storing dictionaries or directories.

The Huffman algorithm produces a different type of static tree, which minimizes processing if all information is stored in failure nodes and if the application does not require the binary tree to be a search tree. Such trees have important application to problems requiring data compaction and transmission.

Dynamic binary search trees are those in which there is no prior information about the values. Balancing techniques can be used to ensure that the shape of the tree stays within certain bounds. The AVL algorithm is one of these techniques.

EXERCISES

1. Define the search property of a binary search tree.

2. Figure 8.1 shows two binary search trees.

   a. Suppose that these trees were constructed using the simple insertion algorithm. Find an ordering of input data that would result in these trees.

   b. In Figure 8.1 (a), Harry is located in the root, while in Figure 8.1 (b), Harry is shown about halfway down the tree. Find an ordering of data that also produces a list-like tree structure, where Harry is located at the far end of the list.

   c. Using your experience in parts (a) and (b), consider any set of n pieces of data, d_1, d_2, ..., d_n, and suppose $d_1 < d_2 < ... < d_n$. Describe how you could order the input data, so that the resulting tree would be a linear-looking structure with d_i at the end.

   This exercise demonstrates that simple insertion can produce a list-like structure for any data set for at least one ordering of the input data.

3. Suppose a binary search tree is created using the elementary Insert operation with the following 12 states in the order shown: Alabama, California, Colorado, Georgia, Iowa, Louisiana, NewYork, NoCarolina, NoDakota, SoCarolina, SoDakota, Texas.

   a. Draw a picture of the resulting tree.

   b. What is the average number of comparisons required to find an item in this binary search tree, assuming all names are equally likely?

4. Suppose a binary search tree is created using the elementary Insert operation with the following 12 states in the order shown: Louisiana, Colorado, NoDakota, Alabama, Georgia, NoCarolina, SoDakota, California, Iowa, NewYork, SoCarolina, Texas.

   a. Draw a picture of the resulting tree.

   b. What is the average number of comparisons required to find an item in this binary search tree, assuming all names are equally likely?

5. Suppose a binary search tree is created using the elementary Insert operation with the following 12 states in the order shown: NewYork, Colorado, Louisiana, California, NoDakota, Texas, NoCarolina, SoDakota, SoCarolina, Alabama, Georgia, Iowa.

   a. Draw a picture of the resulting tree.

   b. What is the average number of comparisons required to find an item in this binary search tree, assuming all names are equally likely?

6. Draw the extended tree for the trees shown in Exercises 4 and 5.

7. Give the internal and external path lengths for the extended binary trees in Exercise 6.

8. This chapter gives recursive algorithms for both the simple insertion and the simple deletion of an item into a binary search tree.

   a. Write the iterative algorithm for simple insertion. The algorithm should unwind the recursion, moving a pointer variable down the tree, level by level, until a NIL pointer is found for the insertion of a new leaf node.

   b. Write an iterative algorithm for simple deletion.

9. The third case for the simple deletion algorithm occurs when both the left and right subtrees of the node to be deleted are nonempty. In the text, this case is handled by re-

placing the data to be deleted by the smallest value in the right subtree and deleting this smallest value farther down in the tree. Another possible approach might be to promote the largest value in the left subtree instead, because such an approach might seem symmetrical to the argument given in the text.

Give an example to show that this work with the largest value in the left subtree may fail if the trees contain duplicate data.

10. Differentiate between a static binary search tree and a dynamic binary search tree.

11. If the binary search tree in Exercise 5 is a static tree with the following weights

    $p = \{1, 3, 2, 5, 7, 2, 3, 1, 7, 4, 2, 3\}$

    what is the average cost of a successful search? Note that the weights are given in order.

12. If the binary search tree in Exercise 11 is extended and the failure boxes have the following weights

    $q = \{1, 3, 4, 2, 3, 5, 1, 2, 3, 4, 5, 6, 7\}$

    what is the weighted external path length? Use the following p's and q's for Exercises 13 and 14.

    $p = \{3, 2, 4, 6, 1\}$ (* Boxer, Doberman, Lab, Spaniel, Visla *)
    $q = \{5, 9, 2, 3, 7, 1\}$

13. Fill in the following table, which calculates the optimal binary search tree.

	[0]	[1]	[2]	[3]	[4]	[5]
[0]	w: c: r: 0	w: c: r:	w: c: r:	w: c: r:	w: c: r:	w: c: r:
[1]		w: c: r: 0	w: c: r:	w: c: r:	w: c: r:	w: c: r:
[2]			w: c: r:	w: c: r:	w: c: r:	w: c: r:
[3]				w: c: r:	w: c: r:	w: c: r:
[4]					w: c: r:	w: c: r:
[5]						w: c: r:

14. Draw the optimal binary search tree calculated in Exercise 13.

15. Write the algorithm to construct the table that determines the optimal binary search tree.

16. Write the algorithm to generate the tree from the table that is the output from the algorithm constructed in Exercise 15.

17. Normally, we may think of an optimal binary search tree as being as full as possible.

    a. Construct an example of a tree with four internal nodes and with associated weights for both internal and external nodes so that the optimal binary search tree is linear, such as appears in Figure 8.1 (b) (reduced to just four internal nodes).

    b. Expand your example in part (a) to include a fifth node, where the new optimal binary search tree is still optimal.

    c. Based upon your experience in parts (a) and (b), do you believe that Figure 8.1 (b) could represent an optimal binary search tree for some collection of weights? Justify your answer.

18. Define an AVL tree.

19. Draw the AVL tree created by inserting the following numbers in the order shown. Apply the appropriate rotations if required.

    200, 220, 240, 180, 160, 190, 185, 195, 187

20. Assuming that the subtree in question is extended, fill in the following table showing which rotation is necessary in each case.

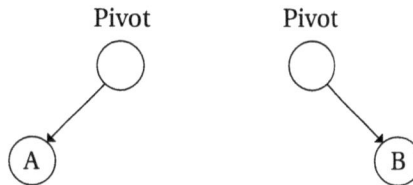

Insertion	Single		Double	
	Right	Left	Right/Left	Left/Right
Right(A)	_____	_____	_____	_____
Left(A)	_____	_____	_____	_____
Right(B)	_____	_____	_____	_____
Left(B)	_____	_____	_____	_____

21. The text asserts that for any tree, the external path length E equals the internal path length I plus twice the number N of nodes in the tree. That is, $E = I + 2N$.

    Prove this assertion. (*Hint*: Use induction over the number of nodes.)

22. Write out the details to show that a type 2 rotation can be obtained as the composite of two type 1 rotations.

23. The code given in the text for a type 2 rotation involves some careful analysis in order to set the shape symbols correctly. Draw a multi-level tree that illustrates why this code is needed.

24. The text gives a recursive algorithm for inserting an item into an AVL tree, and it also gives a brief outline for an iterative version of the algorithm. Write out the details for this iterative algorithm.

25. The text gives the code for the procedure AdjustFromLeft, which is used in deleting a node from an AVL tree. Write the corresponding procedure AdjustFromRight.

26. Prove that the deletion algorithm for AVL trees is correct. Your work can proceed in two steps.

    a. The discussion of deletion from an AVL tree identifies several cases that the deletion algorithm must handle. Explain why these are the only cases that can arise.

    b. Give a careful argument to prove that the algorithm handles each of these cases correctly. Specifically, for each case, explain why the algorithm preserves both the shape property of AVL trees and the order property of any binary search tree.

27. Consider the following binary search tree.

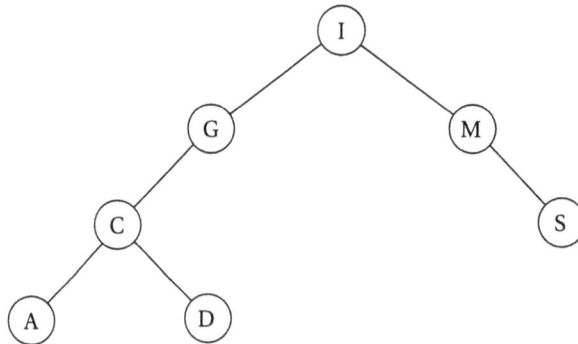

    a. This binary search tree is not currently an AVL tree. What is the unique letter that can be inserted to make it an AVL tree?

    b. Assume that that letter has been inserted. Now draw the tree that would be obtained if the letter F were inserted.

28. Give the algorithm for constructing a Huffman tree from a set of frequencies.

29. Construct a Huffman tree from the following set of frequencies. (Always put the smaller subtree to the left. If there is a tie, put the leaf to the left.)

    Letters: {a, e, i, o, u, s, t, b}
    Frequencies: {1, 3, 5, 2, 4, 6, 7, 8}

30. Determine the codes for each of the letters, based upon the Huffman tree in Exercise 27.

31. Encode the following message, based upon the Huffman tree in Exercise 27:

    betitisasitis

32. Decode the following message, based upon the Huffman tree in Exercise 27:

    011010001111000011111000011111111111

33. Define what is meant by the *prefix property*.

Multi-Way Search Trees

While Chapters 7 and 8 covered a wide variety of tree structures, all of the trees had the common property that only one piece of data was stored in a node. The node might have held a number, a name, or even a whole record of information, but all data in a node were considered part of a single, logical package. In this chapter, we consider the possibility of storing several logically unconnected data objects within each node. In this chapter, each data object is unique unless specified otherwise.

Tree structures with more than one value in a node are called multi-way trees. Like binary trees, multi-way trees can have the search property. In this chapter, we examine multi-way search trees and techniques for building them that guarantee balanced trees. Such trees are used extensively to index large data files.

Multi-Way Trees

Figure 9.1 shows a tree in which each node contains the names of 1 or more of the first 15 presidents of the United States. Informally, such a tree might be called a *multi-way tree*.

In Figure 9.1, the root contains the names of two presidents, Jefferson and Tyler. At level 1, the node on the left and the node on the right each contain two names, while the node in the middle contains just one name, Madison. At level 2, the left-most node contains three names, while the three nodes on the right contain just one name each. One node at level 2 also contains two names.

As with the general trees in Chapter 7, we identify the *degree of a node* as the number of subtrees that have the node as a parent. In Figure 9.1, the root node and the Polk/Fillmore node each have degree 3, while the node containing Madison has degree 2. The other nodes in Figure 9.1 all have degree 0, and such nodes are called *leaves*.

In their pure form, multi-way trees provide a hierarchical structure for storing data. Such trees may have a wide variety of shapes and properties. For example, the structure chart for a volunteer organization might have the names of people on a Board of Directors as the root. Under this root, we might find a node for each of the major committees, such as Finance, Membership, Community Service, Publicity, and so forth. Within each of these nodes, the names of the members of the committees might be tabulated. Subcommittees of these committees might make up the next level of nodes, again with each node containing the names of the people on a particular subcommittee. Such structure charts can be useful mechanisms for visualizing the various working groups within an organization.

While general multi-way trees may have a variety of applications, they are most helpful if we can organize data in ways that allow efficient searching. This need to be able to find particular data elements quickly motivates the concept of a multi-way search tree.

Because the formal definition of multi-way search trees involves stating a number of details, we look at an example first. Figure 9.2 shows a multi-way search tree with names of animals as the data.

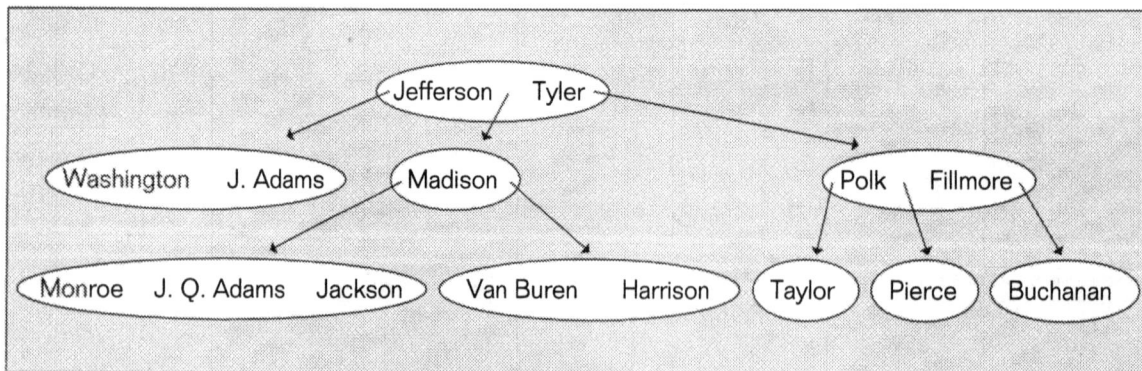

Figure 9.1 A Multi-Way Tree

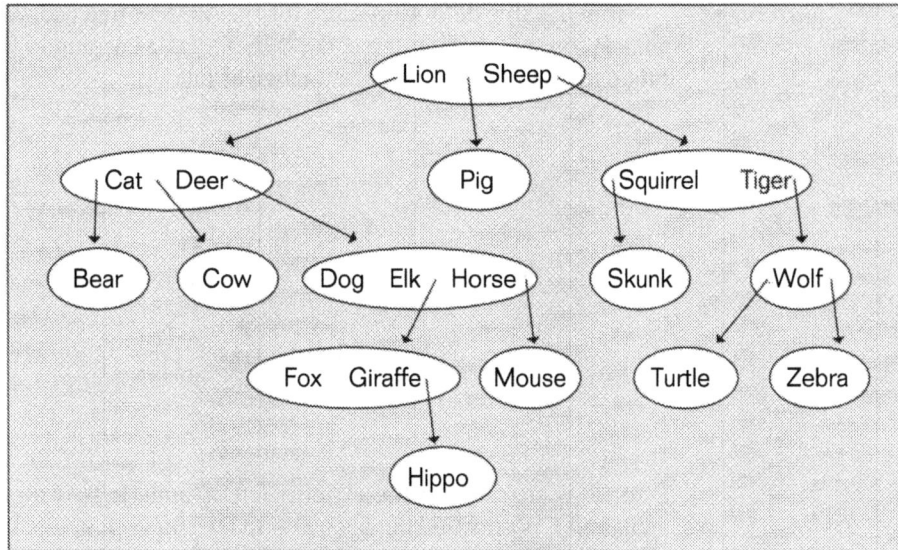

Figure 9.2 A Multi-Way Search Tree

In Figure 9.2, some nodes contain only one data item. When nodes contain several pieces of data, these data are listed in ascending order from left to right. Thus, in the root, Lion comes before Sheep in alphabetical order, so Lion is located to the left of Sheep within the node. Similarly, Cat is to the left of Deer; Dog is to the left of Elk, which is to the left of Horse; Fox is to the left of Giraffe; and Squirrel is to the left of Tiger. Beyond this ordering of data within nodes, the subtrees have a particular relationship to their parent nodes. For example, each data item in the left subtree of the root comes before Lion alphabetically. Similarly, the data in the middle subtree of the root (Pig) come between Lion and Sheep, and each data item in the right subtree comes after Sheep.

This same pattern may be observed at every node within the tree. Every data item within a left subtree always comes before the smallest data item in its parent, and every data item in a right subtree comes after every element in its parent. Furthermore, if a subtree is attached between two items in a node, then all data items in the subtree come between the two items in the parent. For example, Fox, Giraffe, and Hippo all come between Elk and Horse, so the Fox/Giraffe/Hippo subtree is attached between Elk and Horse in the Dog/Elk/Horse node. Similarly, the subtree containing Cow is attached to the Cat/Deer node between Cat and Deer.

We may think of a multi-way search tree as a logical extension of a binary search tree, where several keys may be provided within each node. In a binary search tree, each node contains one data item, the left subtree contains data smaller than this item, and the right subtree contains data that are greater than or equal to the data in the root node. In a multi-way search tree, several data are stored, and the ordering of data constrains which subtree can contain which data items.

To make this definition more formal, we first need some notation. Suppose a node P contains k data items, $D_1, D_2, \ldots, D_k$, as arranged from left to right, and suppose P has k + 1 subtrees, attached as follows:

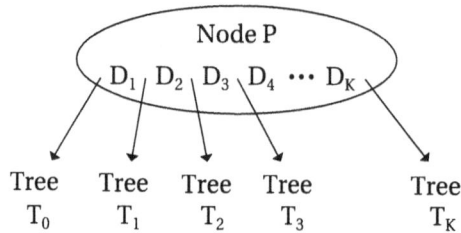

Thus, T_0 is attached to the extreme left of node P, T_k is attached at the extreme right, and T_i is attached between D_i and D_{i+1} for i = 1, 2, . . . , k − 1.

With this notation, we say that a *multi-way tree satisfies the order property at node P* if the following conditions are satisfied.

1. $D_1 \le D_2, \le \ldots \le D_k$.

2. All data, if any, in T_0 are less than D_1.

   All data, if any, in T_k are greater than or equal to D_k.

   All data, if any, in T_i are greater than or equal to D_i and less than D_{i+1} for i = 1, 2, . . ., k − 1.

A multi-way tree is a multi-way *search* tree if it satisfies the order property at all of its nodes. This definition of a multi-way search tree allows any or all subtrees of a node to be empty. However, if a subtree of a node is not empty, then all data in that subtree must have the appropriate ordering with respect to the data within the parent node.

As with binary search trees, the ordering of data within a multi-way search tree allows searching to be quite efficient. For example, suppose we want to find Hippo within the tree in Figure 9.2. Starting at the root, Hippo comes before Lion, so we must look within the left subtree of the root. Next, we determine that Hippo comes after Deer, so we move to the Dog/Elk/Horse node. At this stage, Hippo comes between Elk and Horse, so we look at the subtree between these two values. This leads to the Fox/Giraffe node. Finally, Hippo comes after Giraffe, so we go to the right subtree to find the desired data item.

Because multi-way search trees may contain many branches at each node, these trees have the potential to allow searching with very few steps. In Chapter 7, for example, we noted that searching in a full binary tree with N nodes could find any item in $\log_2 N$ steps. Similarly, in a reasonably full tree with k branches per node, searches must end within $\log_k N$ steps. With four branches per node, therefore, searches generally are done in half the number of steps as in a binary search tree. (Proof of these details are left as exercises at the end of the chapter.) Of course, searching within a multi-way search tree may require more processing per node, but fewer nodes must be processed if the tree is reasonably full.

Without further constraints, however, multi-way search trees may suffer from the same shape problems that were encountered with general binary search trees. Insertion into multi-way trees and deletion from these trees may leave the trees quite unbalanced unless we develop algorithms that guarantee some amount of balance.

As we did in our discussion of binary search trees, we begin with some specifications, followed by a description of a simple insertion and deletion algorithm for maintaining such structures. We then look at more sophisticated multi-way search trees, where we can guarantee that the trees maintain some amount of balance. Balanced, multi-way search trees have important applications, particularly in areas involving files.

Specification

The definition of a multi-way search tree states that data within nodes and sub-trees must be ordered in an appropriate way. The axiomatic specifications for the Insert and Delete operations parallel these properties within the context of the constructor operations Create and Make. We also include the IsEmpty operation in our axioms. For simplicity, we define only a three-way search tree. A similar approach may be followed for more general, multi-way search trees.

In a three-way search tree, an individual node may have up to three subtrees. Thus, nodes can have the following structure.

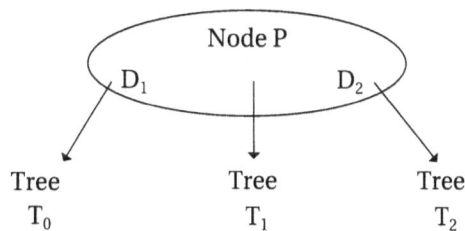

If both D_1 and D_2 are in this structure, then $D_1 \leq D_2$, all data in subtree T_0 are less than D_1, all data in subtree T_1 are less than D_2 and greater than or equal to D_1, and all data in subtree T_2 are greater than or equal to D_2. It is also possible, however, that a node might contain only one data item. By convention, we place that item in D_1 in such circumstances, and D_2 is undefined. With only one data item in a node, subtrees T_0 and T_1 still exist, following the normal ordering of binary search trees. However, without data item D_2, there cannot be a subtree T_2 attached to the far right of the node. One way to say this is that T_2 must be undefined if D_2 is undefined. However, for any three-way search tree, D_1, T_0, and T_1 must always be defined (although the subtrees could be empty).

With this possibility that a data field in a node could be undefined or that a right subtree could be undefined, the specification of the various operations must allow the appropriate fields to be undefined. In particular, it must be possible to apply operations to structures in certain cases where some parameters have undefined values.

The simplest way to accomplish this is to include the value *Undefined* in each domain and to include axioms in which fields are allowed to be undefined under certain circumstances. In what follows, therefore, we assume that types ItemType and TWTree are extended to include *Undefined*. Beyond the operations Create, Make, Insert, Delete, and IsEmpty, we also need axioms that allow us to check that a tree has the appropriate order properties. As with our specifications of binary search trees, we call these operations ComesBefore and ComesAfter. In addition, insertion and deletion require that we have a mechanism for comparing elements in different trees. This motivates the observer function TreeToList, which generates a sorted list from the elements of a three-way search tree.

> **structure** TWTree (of ItemType)
> **interface**
> | | |
> |---|---|
> | Create | $\rightarrow$ TWTree |
> | Make(TWTree, ItemType, TWTree, ItemType, TWTree) | $\rightarrow$ TWTree |
> | IsEmpty(TWTree) | $\rightarrow$ Boolean |
> | ComesBefore(TWTree, ItemType) | $\rightarrow$ Boolean |
> | ComesAfter(TWTree, ItemType) | $\rightarrow$ Boolean |
> | IsTWST(TWTree) | $\rightarrow$ Boolean |
> | TreeToList(TWTree) | $\rightarrow$ SortedList |
> | Insert(TWTree, ItemType) | $\rightarrow$ TWTree |
> | Delete(TWTree, ItemType) | $\rightarrow$ TWTree |
> | IsIn(TWTree, ItemType) | $\rightarrow$ Boolean |
> | Retrieve(TWTree, ItemType) | $\rightarrow$ ItemType |
> **end**

The axioms for Make guarantee that undefined values occur only in specified places.

> **axioms**   **for all TWT1, TWT2, TWT3 in TWTree and i1, i2, i3 in ItemType, let**
>
> Make(TWT1, i1, TWT2, i2, TWT3) =
>   IF NOT ((TWT1 <> Undefined) AND (i1 <> Undefined)
>   AND (TWT2 <> Undefined)
>   AND (((i2 = Undefined) AND (TWT3 = Undefined))
>   OR ((i2 <> Undefined) AND (TWT3 <> Undefined))))
>   THEN Error
>   END IF

With this axiom, any use of Make requires that a node have at least one data item. This motivates the following axioms for IsEmpty.

IsEmpty(Create) = True
IsEmpty(Make(TWT1, i1, TWT2, i2, TWT3)) = False

The definition of a search tree requires that data in subtrees contain values that come before or after various items in a root node. This ordering property is made precise with the ComesBefore and ComesAfter operations. In specifying each of these operations, we must consider nodes that contain either one or two values.

ComesBefore(Create, i1) = True
ComesBefore(Make(TWT1, i1, TWT2, i2, TWT3), i3) =
  ComesBefore(TWT1, i3) AND (i1 < i3) AND ComesBefore(TWT2, i3)
   AND ((i2 = Undefined)
     OR ((i2 < i3) AND ComesBefore(TWT3, i3)))

ComesAfter (Create, i1) = True
ComesAfter(Make(TWT1, i1, TWT2, i2, TWT3), i3) =
  ComesAfter(TWT1, i3) AND (i1 $\geq$ i3) AND ComesAfter(TWT2, i3)
   AND ((i2 = Undefined)
     OR ((i2 $\geq$ i3) AND ComesAfter(TWT3, i3)))

A three-way search tree is a tree in which the data within each node are ordered and the subtrees have the appropriate relationship with data in a parent node. This is specified formally as follows:

IsTWST(Create) = True
IsTWST(Make(TWT1, i1, TWT2, i2, TWT3)) =
  ComesBefore(TWT1, i1) AND ComesAfter(TWT2, i1)
   AND IsTWST(TWT1) AND IsTWST(TWT2)
   AND ((i2 = undefined)
    OR ((i1 $\leq$ i2)
     AND ComesBefore(TWT2, i2)
     AND ComesAfter(TWT3, i2) AND IsTWST(TWT3))

The construction of a SortedList with elements from a three-way search tree involves inserting all elements in a node into the list generated from the subtrees. This process uses the Merge operation to combine sorted lists, as defined and used in Chapter 7.

TreeToList(Create) = Create
TreeToList(Make(TWT1, i1, TWT2, i2, TWT3)) =
  IF (i2 = Undefined)
   THEN Insert(Merge (TreeToList(TWT1), TreeToList(TWT2)), i1)

ELSE   Insert(Insert(Merge
(Merge(TreeToList(TWT1), TreeToList(TWT2)),
TreeToList(TWT3)), i2), i1)
END IF

Finally, the Insert and Delete operations create new trees with the desired elements and with the order properties for three-way search trees. The specifications for these operations use the EqualLists operation, which compares two sorted lists, as defined in the specifications of Chapter 8.

Insert(TWT1, i1) = any TWT2 where
    IsTWST(TWT2) AND EqualLists (Insert(TreeToList(TWT1), i1),
        TreeToList(TWT2))

Delete(Create, i1) = Error
Delete(TWT1, i1) = any TWT2 where
    IsTWST(TWT2) AND EqualLists (TreeToList(TWT1),
        Insert(TreeToList(TWT2), i1))

Each of these operations follows a pattern that is similar to the corresponding operations for binary search trees, specified in Chapter 8. Also as noted in Chapter 8, these Insert and Delete axioms allow the implementor considerable flexibility in creating new trees. After an insertion or a deletion, the resulting structure must have the appropriate elements and a proper ordering of data. The specific shape of the trees or the placement of data items within the tree is not restricted, provided the resulting tree is still a three-way search tree.

As in the case of IsIn and Retrieve in a binary search tree, the algorithms are straightforward given that the search properties hold. We leave them as an end-of-chapter exercise.

Implementation

As with the processing of binary search trees, there are several variations of insertion and deletion for multi-way search trees. The simplest insertion algorithms place a new element in a new tree but do not attempt to balance the resulting tree. More advanced algorithms maintain a more balanced structure.

Simple Insertion and Deletion

Because a node in a three-way search tree may contain two data elements and pointers to up to three subtrees, a simple implementation for these trees would use a record structure for each node with appropriate fields for the data and pointers. In working with a node, we must have a mechanism for determining if the second data field within a node is defined or not. One approach involves defining a Boolean function HasSecondValue, which is applied to a node to determine if the second data field contains actual information. A second approach might add a Boolean flag to a record to indicate whether the second value is defined. A third approach is to have the data definition module define a special constant *NoValue*. In this third approach, the second data field contains NoValue if that field is undefined. Otherwise, the information is considered actual data. In what follows, we use this third approach with a NoValue constant, and we connect nodes in a tree using pointer variables. We also assume that the items in the tree can be compared with the relational operators and are distinct.

```
(* To access NoValue and ItemType. *)
USES < module defining data dependent identifiers >


TYPE
    NodePointer = ↑NodeType;
    NodeType = RECORD
        Value1, Value2      :   ItemType;
        Left, Middle, Right :   NodePointer
    END RECORD;
```

Simple insertion into a three-way search tree is similar to simple insertion into a binary search tree. We compare the item to be inserted with data in successive nodes until we find a place to add the new data. With three-way search trees, however, new data can be added in either of two ways. First, after searching a tree, we could place a new item in a new node and attach this node where a NIL pointer had been previously. This is the same approach that always is followed in a binary search tree. Alternatively, if a node only contains one data field, then a new item could be added within an existing node. Of course, data within a node must be ordered, so care must be taken to put the new item in the appropriate place.

A recursive insertion algorithm for three-way search trees, expanding and refining simple insertion for binary search trees, follows.

Insert (VAR Root: NodePointer, Item: ItemType);

```
IF Root = NIL
    THEN   (* Insert Item as new node in a previously null tree *)
        New (Root)
        Root↑.Value1 ← Item
        Root↑.Value2 ← NoValue
        Root↑.Left ← NIL
        Root↑.Middle ← NIL
    ELSIF Root↑.Value2 = NoValue
        THEN   (* Node contains only one value. *)
            IF Root↑.Value1 < Item
                THEN
                    IF Root↑.Middle = NIL
                        THEN   (* Insert Item as data field on right *)
                            Root↑.Value2 ← Item
                            Root↑.Right ← NIL
                        ELSE    Insert(Root↑.Middle, Item)
                    END IF
```

```
            ELSIF Root↑.Left = NIL
                THEN   (* Value1 becomes Value2, Insert Item as Value1 *)
                    Root↑.Value2 ← Root↑.Value1
                    Root↑.Value1 ← Item
                    Root↑.Right ← Root↑.Middle
                    Root↑.Middle ← Root↑.Left
                    Root↑.Left ← NIL
                ELSE   Insert(Root↑.Left, Item)
            END IF
        ELSE        (* Node contains 2 value; Insert lower in tree. *)
            IF Item < Root↑.Value1
                THEN   Insert (Root↑.Left, Item)
                ELSIF  Item < Root↑.Value2
                    THEN   Insert (Root↑.Middle, Item)
                    ELSE   Insert (Root↑.Right, Item)
            END IF
    END IF
END IF
```

To illustrate how this code works, we insert the values

5 7 10 4 3 6 2 1 0

in order into a tree that is initially empty. In our example, we use a slash (/) to indicate that a value is undefined. Because the simple insertion for three-way search trees is quite similar to the corresponding algorithm for binary search trees, we show the results of each insertion without additional comment.

Insert 5:

Insert 7:

Insert 10:

Insert 4:

Insert 3:

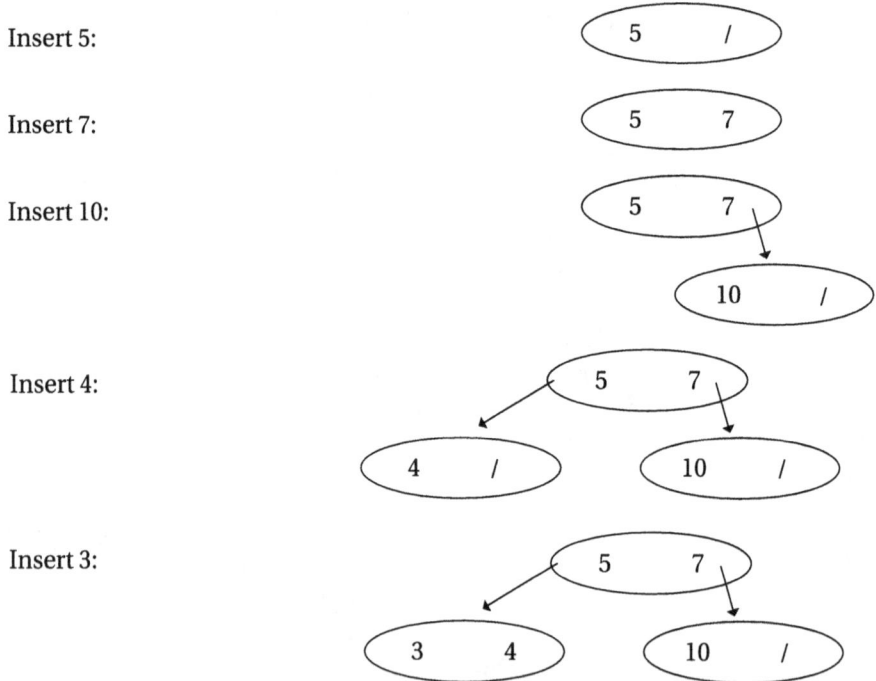

Insert 6:

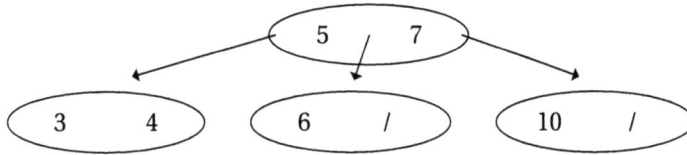

Insert 2:

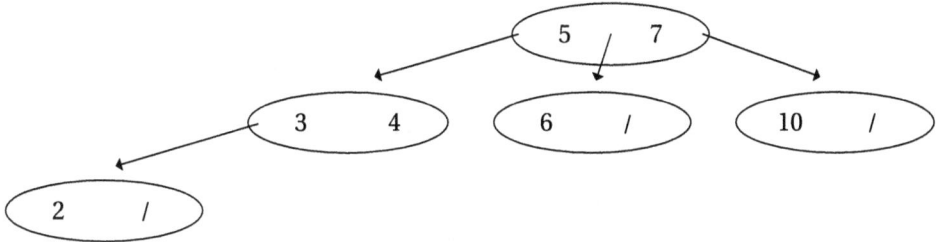

Insert 1:

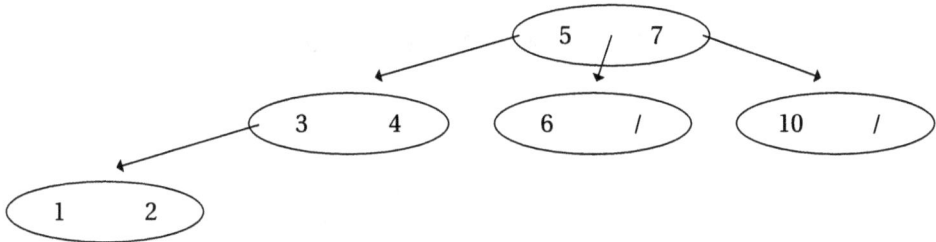

Insert 0:

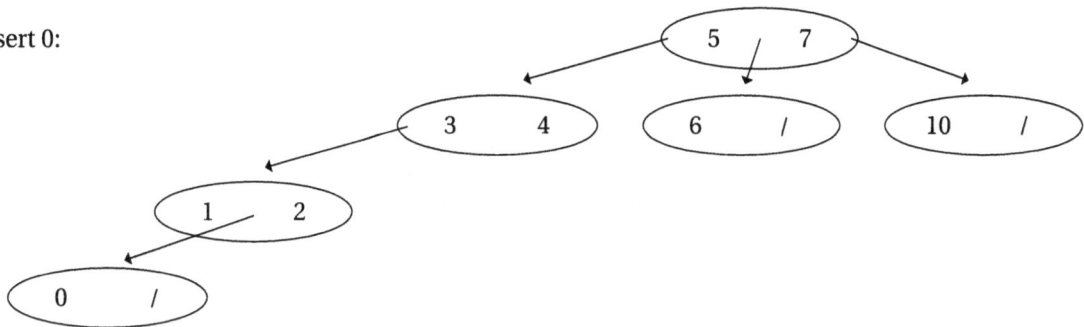

Like binary search trees, this simple insertion algorithm for three-way search trees can create an unbalanced tree. In the example, the left side of the tree extends below the other parts of the tree by several levels. Simple insertion is fairly easy to code but does not guarantee that the resulting tree is balanced.

Just as the simple insertion algorithm was a natural extension of the corresponding algorithm for binary search trees, the simple deletion algorithm extends the binary search tree algorithm. First, the tree is searched to find the item designated for deletion. Then, if either the right or left subtree below the item is empty, an element can be deleted without difficulty. If both subtrees are nonempty, however, then the deletion of an element requires the reattachment of two subtrees to a single node. As with the simple deletion algorithm for binary search trees, this can be accomplished by finding the smallest element in a right subtree, placing it into the node, and deleting it from the subtree. Through this process, some care is needed in case a node contains only one data value.

The deletion algorithm requires the identification of the minimum value in a three-way search tree; we write a function to accomplish this task first. We then present a recursive version of the simple deletion algorithm.

MinElement (Root: NodePointer): ItemType;

```
TempPtr ← Root
WHILE TempPtr↑.Left <> NIL DO
    TempPtr ← TempPtr↑.Left
END WHILE
RETURN TempPtr↑.Value1
```

Delete (VAR Root: NodePointer, Item: ItemType);

```
IF Root↑.Value1 = Item
    THEN   (* Remove Value1 from node *)
        IF Root↑.Left = NIL
            THEN   IF Root↑.Value2 = NoValue
                THEN   Root ← Root↑.Middle
                ELSE   (* Middle and right subtrees moved left *)
                    Root↑Left ← Root↑.Middle
                    Root↑Middle ← Root↑.Right
                    Root↑.Value2 ← NoValue
                END IF
            ELSIF Root↑.Middle = NIL
                THEN IF Root↑.Value2 = NoValue
                    THEN Root ← Root↑.Left
                    ELSE    (*Right Subtree moved left *)
                        Root↑Middle ← Root↑.Right
                        Root↑.Value2 ← NoValue
                    END IF
                ELSE
                    (* Replace Value1 by min. item in middle subtree *)
                    RightMin ← MinElement (Root↑.Middle)
                    Root↑.Value1 ← RightMin
                    Delete (Root↑.Middle, RightMin)
            END IF
    ELSIF Root↑.Value2 = Item
        THEN   (* Remove Value2 from node *)
            IF Root↑.Middle = NIL
                THEN   (* Right subtree moved to middle *)
                    Root↑.Middle ← Root↑.Right
                    Root↑.Value2 ← NoValue
                ELSIF Root↑.Right = NIL
```

```
            THEN
                (* Right subtree is empty and can be ignored *)
                Root↑.Value2 ← NoValue
            ELSE
                (* Replace Value2 by minimum item in right subtree *)
                RightMin ← MinElement (Root↑.Right)
                Root↑.Value2 ← RightMin
                Delete (Root↑.Right, RightMin)
        END IF
    ELSE    (* Look farther down in tree *)
        IF (Item < Root↑.Value1)
            THEN   Delete (Root↑.Left, Item)
            ELSIF (Root↑.Value2 = NoValue) OR (Item < Root↑.Value2)
                THEN   Delete (Root↑.Middle, Item)
                ELSE   Delete (Root↑.Right, Item)
        END IF
END IF
```

As with the simple insertion algorithm, simple deletion maintains the ordering of data required for three-way search trees, but no attempt is made to keep the trees balanced. IsIn and Retrieve follow the same search path used in the insertion algorithm.

2-3 Trees

While the simple insertion and deletion algorithms can create unbalanced trees, the implementation that we look at now guarantees a balanced tree. Just as an AVL tree is an implementation that builds a binary search tree that is height-balanced, so the following algorithm builds a three-way search tree that is guaranteed to be balanced. Throughout this discussion, we assume that all data values to be stored within the tree are distinct; duplicate data values are not allowed.

A *2-3 tree* is a three-way search tree, where all leaves are required to be on the same level and where there are no null pointers on either side of a data value except at the leaves. Because 2-3 trees are three-way search trees, each node can contain one or two elements. If a nonleaf node contains one element, it has two children. If a nonleaf node contains two elements, there are three children. Each node looks like the following.

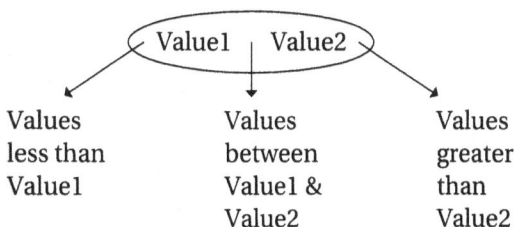

Values	Values	Values
less than	between	greater
Value1	Value1 &	than
	Value2	Value2

Some 2-3 trees are shown in Figure 9.3.

Unlike binary search trees, which grow *from the top down*, 2-3 trees grow *from the bottom up*. We work through an example showing how to build a 2-3 tree and then describe the appropriate operations and properties more precisely.

Suppose the words canary, dromedary, cat, elephant, fox, and dog are inserted in that order into an empty tree. The tree is initialized with the word canary in the first node. There is room in the same node for the word dromedary, so it is stored in the same node.

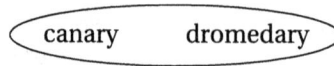

The next word to be inserted is cat. Cat is greater than canary, but less than dromedary. The pointer between them is nil, so cat belongs in this node. However, there is no room in the node because it is full. This node must be split and the

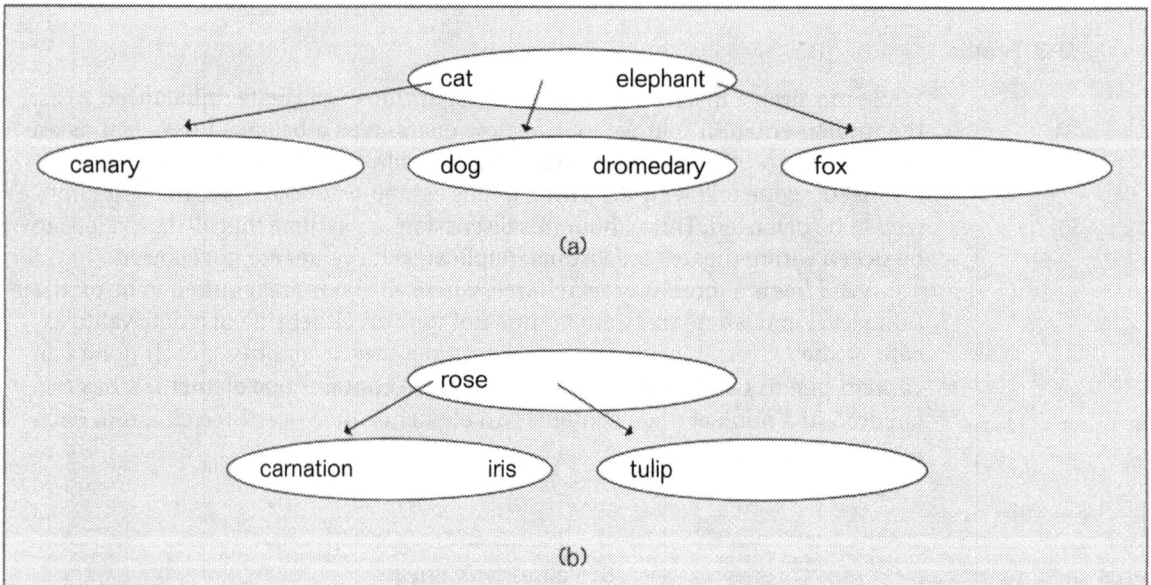

Figure 9.3   Examples of 2-3 Trees

middle value moved up to a node above to form a separator. (Remember that a 2-3 tree is a search tree.)

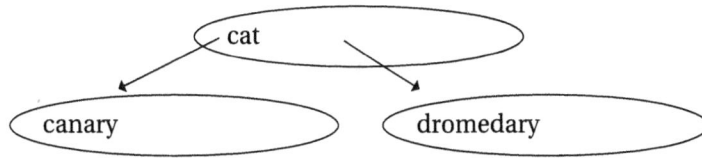

The next word to be entered is elephant. The tree is searched until the place where elephant should go is found. Elephant is greater than cat, so the right branch is taken. Elephant is greater than dromedary, but the next branch is nil, which means that this is a leaf node. The node with dromedary has only one value in it, so elephant can be put there.

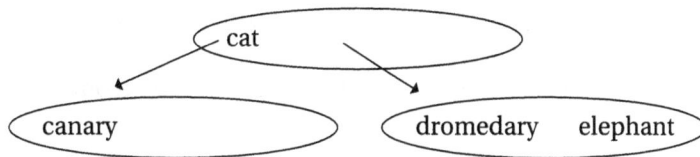

The next word to be inserted is fox. Fox is greater than dromedary and greater than elephant. The right pointer is nil, so fox belongs in this node. It cannot go here, however, because the node already has two values. The node must be split and the middle value moved up to the node above it to be used as a separator between the newly split nodes.

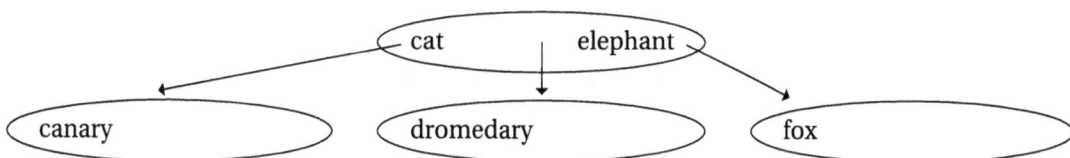

The next word is dog. Its place is found and there is room for it.

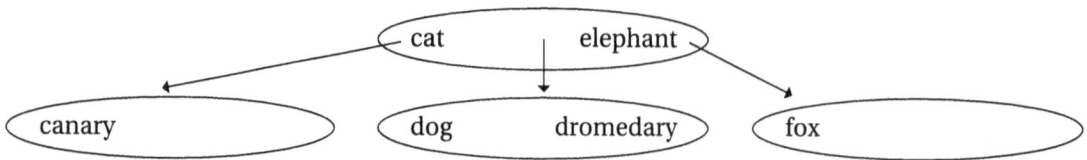

Next, we consider what happens when we add a few more words: ant, horse, and fly. Ant can go with canary, where it belongs, and horse can go with fox, where it belongs.

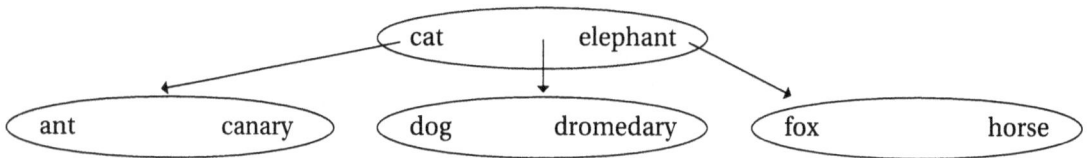

What do we do with fly? It belongs in the node with fox and horse, but there is no room. The node has to split and the middle value move up as a separator. But there is no room in the node above to accommodate fox, the middle value. That node just has to split.

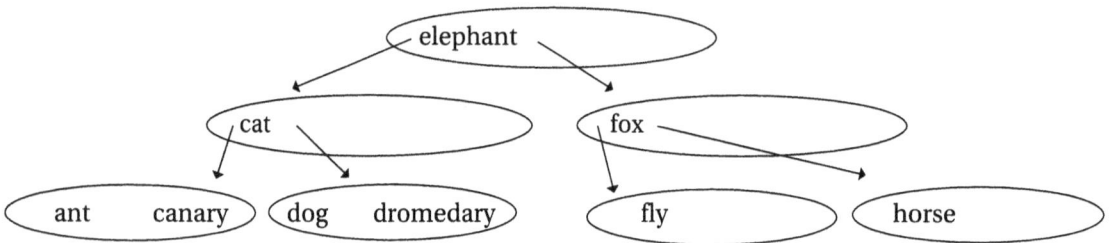

The properties of a 2-3 tree are summarized as follows:

1. All leaf nodes are at the same level.
2. There must be at least one value in each node.
3. All values are inserted into leaf nodes.
4. Except at the leaves, every node has one more non-nil child than it has keys.

In order to maintain these properties, the insertion algorithm must split a leaf node if there is no room for the item being inserted. That is, the algorithm must find the proper node. If it is full, the node must be split and the middle value moved up to the parent node to act as a separator between the newly formed nodes. If the parent node is full, moving the middle value up may cause the parent node to split, sending its middle value up to its parent, and so on.

If the node that must be split is the root node, the tree grows a level. A new node must be created, and the separator becomes the only value. This node then becomes the new root. Properties 1 and 4 guarantee that the tree is completely balanced, thus minimizing search time.

The one drawback is that there may be wasted space in the nodes themselves. A full node has two values and three non-nil pointers. The algorithm that creates the 2-3 tree does not guarantee that the nodes are full. A legal 2-3 tree can have only one value and two non-nil pointers in each node.

The insertion algorithm can be summarized as follows.

Insert

```
Find where value belongs
IF the node contains only one value
    THEN Insert value in node
    ELSE
        Split node
        Insert middle value into parent
END IF
```

The deletion algorithm must also maintain the 2-3 properties. If we are deleting from a binary search tree, we have three cases:

a. The value being deleted is in a leaf node.

b. A pointer on one side of the value is nil, while the pointer on the other side of the value designates a nonempty subtree.

c. The pointers on both sides of the value are non-nil.

Because a 2-3 tree is always balanced, only the first and third cases apply. We now look at several examples before we state the algorithm.

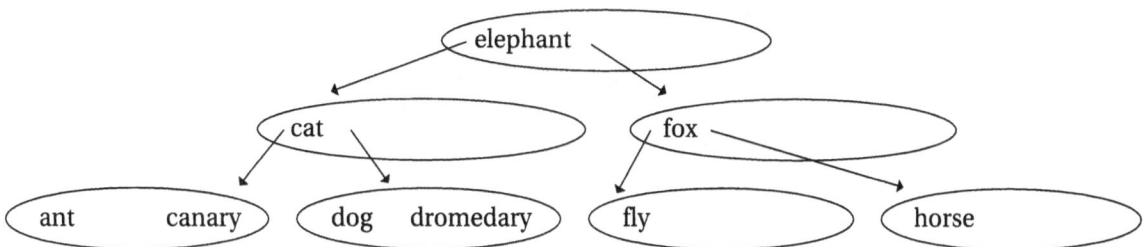

If we want to delete ant or canary, there is no problem. There is still a value left in the node, so Property 2 holds. We delete canary.

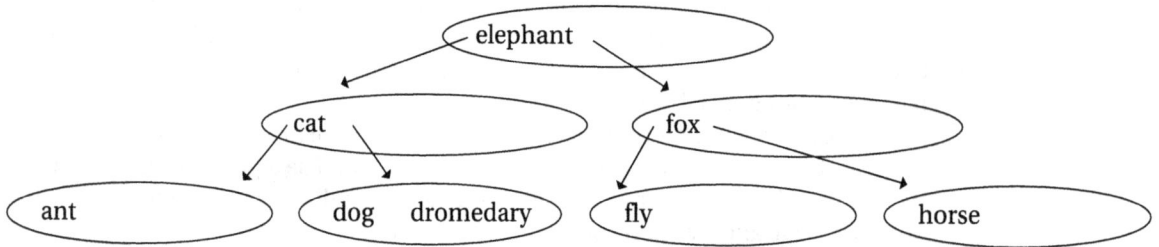

A problem occurs if we try to delete ant. Removing ant leaves a node with no values in it, breaking property 2. There are two steps that we can take to patch things up. The first is to try to borrow one value from the sibling of the empty node. If the sibling of the empty node has two values, we can borrow one of the values. If the empty node is a left child, the lowest value in its sibling can be moved up to the parent and the separator can be moved from the parent into the empty node. This is what happens in this case.

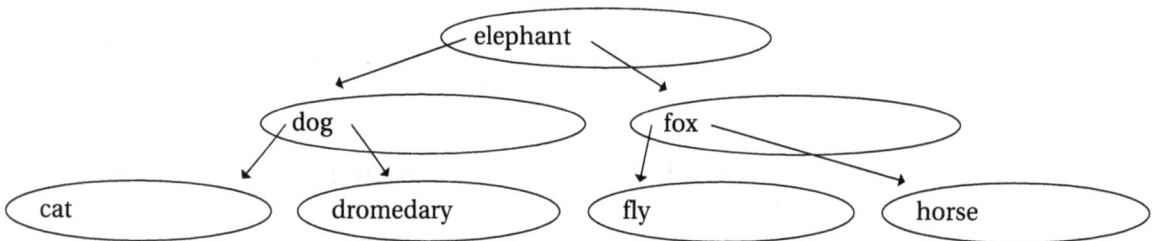

If the empty node is a right child, the highest value of its sibling can be moved to the parent node and the separator moved to the empty node. Figure 9.4 shows these two rotations.

What happens if a sibling of the empty node does not have two values? In that case, the separator is moved from the parent into the sibling of the empty node. The empty node just goes away. Because there are not two nodes for the separator to distinguish between, the sibling and the separator can reside in the same node. This, of course, may or may not cause problems farther up the tree.

For example, if we delete fly in the previous example, there is no value to borrow, so the separator from the parent node must be brought down. This, in turn,

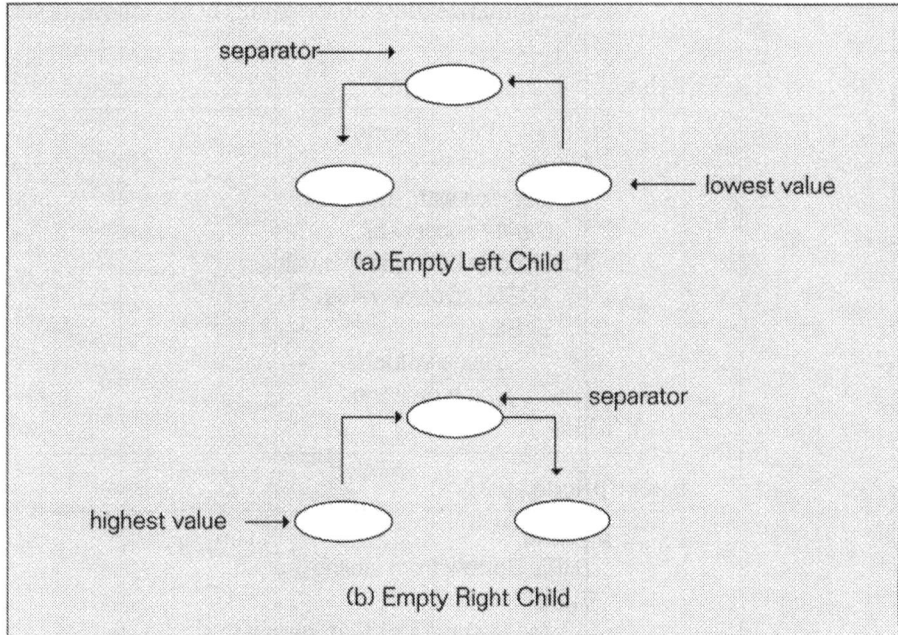

Figure 9.4 Borrowing Rotations[1]

leaves the parent node without a value. Its sibling has no values to spare, so the separator from its parent must be moved down. This leaves the parent node empty. However, in this case, the parent is the root and the tree simply collapses a level.

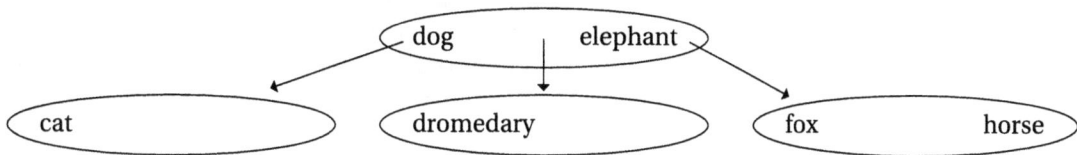

---

[1] While "borrow" is the term commonly used, it may be somewhat misleading. Clearly, the values "borrowed" are not returned.

We can summarize these observations in the following very general algorithm.

Delete

```
IF value is not in leaf node
    THEN
        Replace with successor
        Delete successor
    ELSIF node contains two values
        THEN   Delete value
        ELSE
            Delete value
            Patch up node
END IF
```

PatchUpNode

```
IF possible
    THEN Borrow from sibling
    ELSE
        Move separator from parent to sibling
        IF parent does not contain two values
            THEN Patch up node
        END IF
END IF
```

Detailed Examination of Insertion Algorithm

The insertion algorithm is reasonably easy to visualize. We can draw lines to boxes and easily determine what should be in the boxes that represent nodes, as well as which lines should go to which boxes. Unfortunately, we cannot write a program with lines and boxes. We have to use variables and pointers.

We now go over in great detail how this by-hand, picture algorithm can be converted into an algorithm appropriate for a computer. While the resulting algorithm is reasonably interesting, our primary motivation here is to demonstrate a way of translating from pictures to a program.

Once again, we write out the algorithm developed earlier.

Insert

```
Find where value belongs
IF the node contains only one value
    THEN   Insert value in node
    ELSE
        Split Node
        Insert middle value in parent
END IF
```

The first part of the algorithm seems easy enough. It involves no manipulation of nodes or pointers (boxes or lines). The ELSE branch is more complex. We need to get a new node and move one value to it and insert the middle value in the parent node to act as a separator between the two halves of the node we split.

If we are inserting a value into an internal node to act as a separator between two lower nodes, we must have pointers to these lower nodes. We now look carefully at a split, determine what the separator value is, and locate where the pointers to the lower nodes are. We insert the value 2 into the following 2-3 tree.

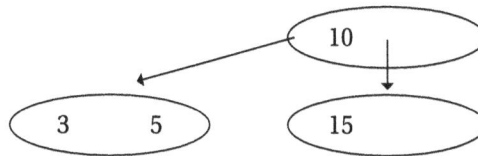

```
                                    10

              3      5           15
```

The value 2 is less than 10, so the left branch is taken. We are now at a leaf node, so this must be where the value belongs. How do we recognize that this is a leaf node? The left branch is NIL. We get a new node and move the largest value (5 in this case) into it. The smallest value (2 in this case) remains in the original node. The middle value (3 in this case) has to move up to be a separator between the original node and the new node. The separator and a pointer to the new node must be passed back to the parent node. Notice that the new node contains the value(s) that immediately succeed the separator value. The parent node must now be adjusted.

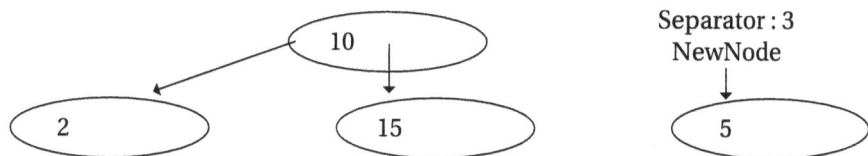

```
                         10              Separator : 3
                                         NewNode

        2             15                    5
```

(* NewNode and Separator must be inserted in node with value 10 *)

At this point, it is clear that we must have a way to work back up the tree. If a lower node splits, the parent must be adjusted. The split may propagate up the tree and eventually cause the root node to split. This suggests a recursive process. The search tree is traversed recursively until we reach a leaf node. The value is inserted in the leaf node, perhaps causing the leaf to split. On returning from each recursive call, we determine if a split has occurred at the lower level. If a split has occurred, the separator is inserted into what is the parent of the lower node. This insertion may or may not cause a splitting of the current node.

As we have seen, splitting the leaf node is straightforward. It is what happens at the next level that must now be examined. In our example, there is room for the separator in the parent node. Because we are returning from splitting the left child, we know that the separator must now become the first value in the parent of the node that was split. Therefore, the current first value and the pointer to its right subtree must be moved to the right. Because no split occurs at this level, the algorithm is complete.

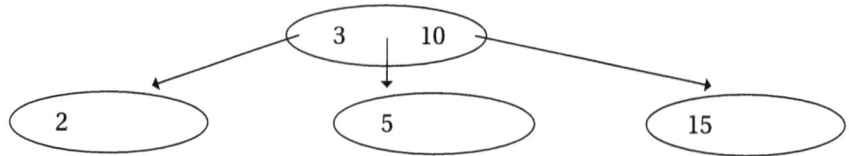

The next case we examine is the one in which the parent node is full, causing the parent node to split. Suppose we insert 2 into the following tree.

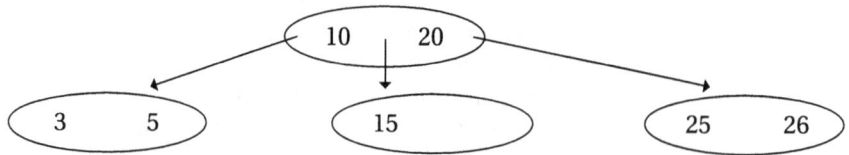

The place to insert the value 2 is found, and the node is split, giving the following situation on the return from the recursive call.

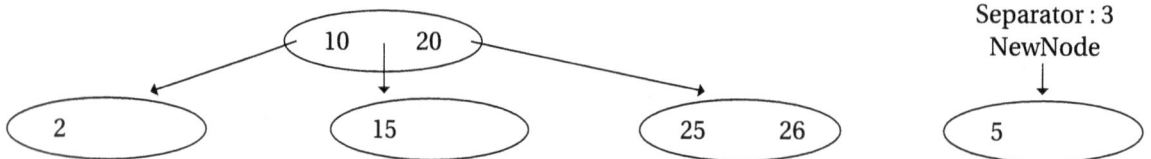

The node into which the separator and the new node must be inserted already has two values. Therefore, this node (call it the current node) must be split. A new node must be created, and the values and the children pointers must be adjusted between the current node and the new node. The middle value must be sent up to the next level as a separator between the current node and the new node. The result is as follows.

Separator : 10
NewNode

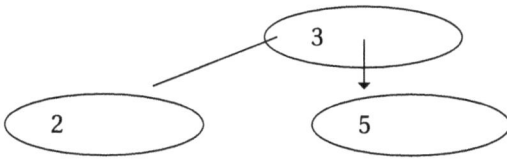

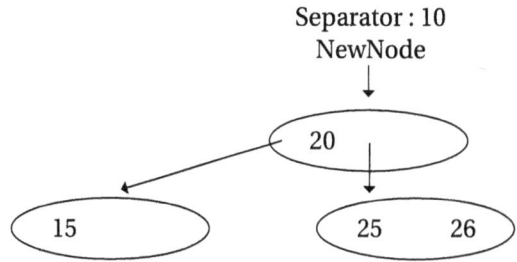

The operations that achieved these results are as follows: the middle child, Value2, and right child of the current node move into the left child, Value1, and middle child fields of the new node. The separator and the new node from the lower level are moved into the Value1 and middle child fields of the current node. What was the Value1 field of the current node is returned, along with the new node created at this level, to the next level up in the tree.

At this point, the algorithm has returned from the first call to the recursive routine. A split has occurred, so we must create a new root node. The original tree is the left child, the separator becomes Value1 in the new root node, and the new node returned from the lower level is the middle child.

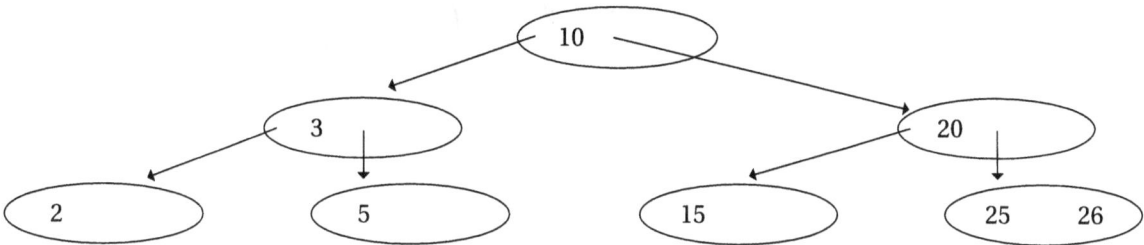

The shifting of values from the current node to the new node (if there is a split) and the replacement of the separator and new node depend upon which child is split at the lower level. The movements that have been illustrated so far have dealt with splitting a left child. We now examine splitting a node reached from a middle child. We insert 19 into the following 2-3 tree.

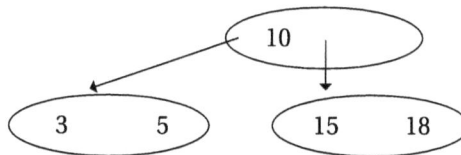

The leaf node where 19 belongs is located and the node is split, giving the following situation on return from the last recursive call.

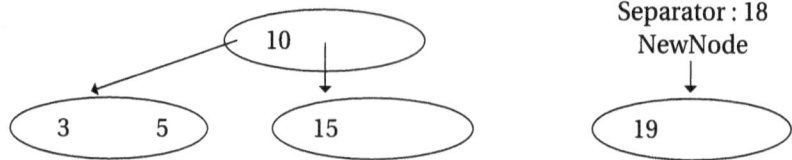

In this case, there is room in the parent node. The separator becomes Value2, and the new node is the right child, as shown below.

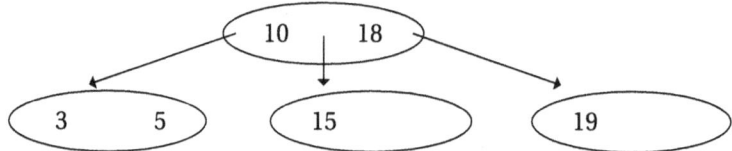

Now we insert 19 into a tree where the parent node is already full.

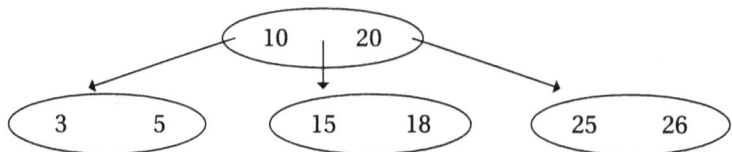

After inserting the value 19 and splitting the node, the situation is as follows on return from the recursive call.

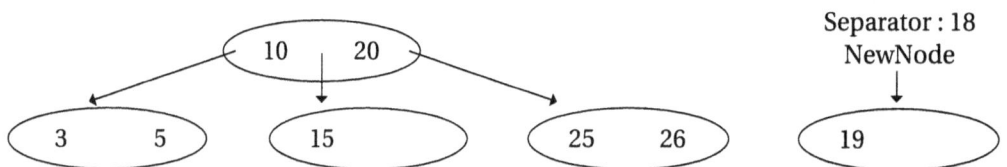

The node into which the separator is to be inserted is full. Therefore, it must be split to look like the following.

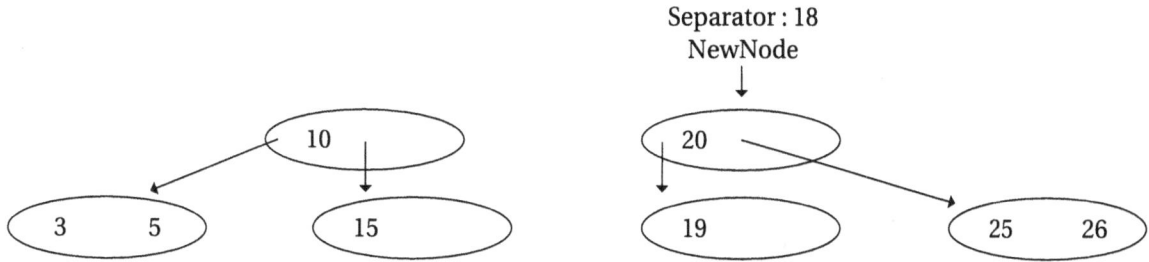

Separator : 18
NewNode

The first three fields of the current node remain the same. Because the split occurred in a middle child, the separator continues to be the separator at the next level. The new node from the previous split becomes the left child in the new node at this level. Value2 and the right child of the current node move into the Value1 and middle child fields, respectively, of the new node created at this level. The pointer to this new node is then returned, along with the separator to the next level.

If there were more levels in the tree, the process we have described would simply continue. In this case, the root node splits and the 2-3 tree is returned as follows.

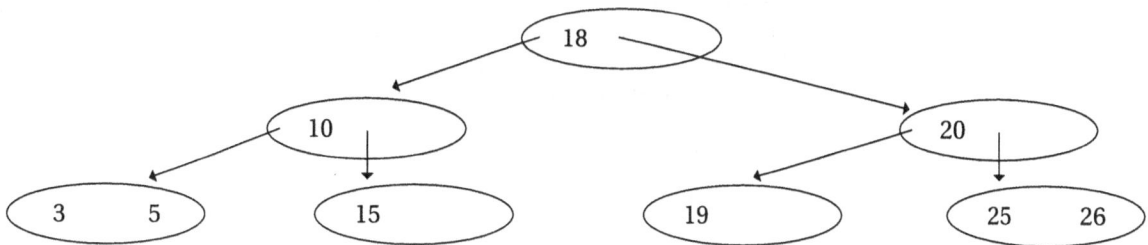

One more case needs to be examined: the case where the right child splits. When this happens, we know that there is no room in the parent for the separator. There cannot be a right child unless there are two values in the node. We insert 24 into the following 2-3 tree.

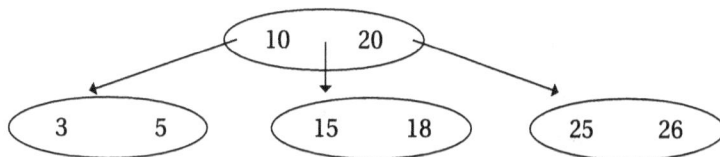

After the insertion of 24, the situation looks as follows returning from the recursive call.

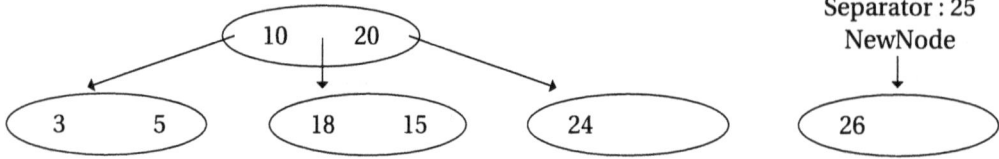

The node into which 25 is to be inserted is full, causing a split that looks as follows.

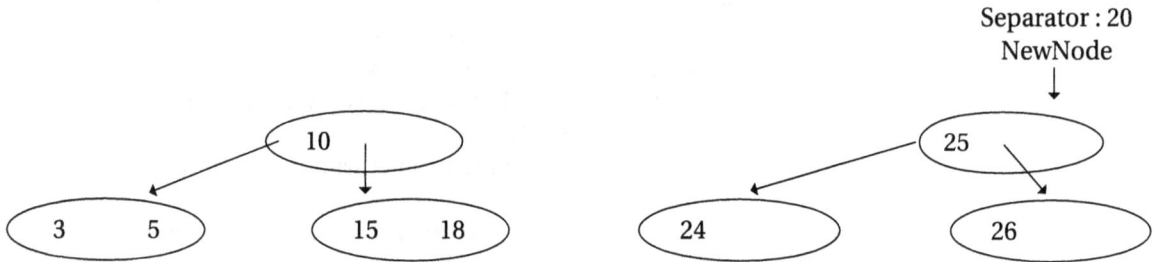

As in the case where the middle child splits, the first three fields of the current node remain the same. The right pointer in the current node becomes the left pointer in the new node. The separator becomes the first value in the new node. The new node from the lower level becomes the middle child in the new node at this level. What was Value2 in the current node becomes the separator at the next level. Because our examples have had only two levels, the root again splits and the final tree looks like the following.

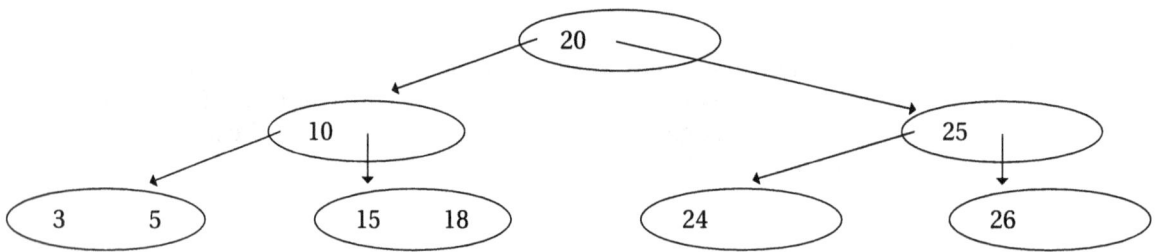

We are almost ready to write the algorithm, but first there are a few more things to consider. Our diagrams show blank value fields wherever a value has been moved into another node. How do we represent a blank value? As discussed previously, for general three-way search trees, we use the constant NoValue. In our diagrams, we have left the NIL pointer fields blank. We must be sure to set them to NIL in our algorithm.

One control question still needs to be answered: how do we determine if a split has occurred? We can return NewNode as a NIL pointer if there has not been a split, or we can have an explicit parameter, Split. An explicit parameter makes the code clearer and is, therefore, better style.

We have discussed the recursive part of the algorithm in great detail and have mentioned that there is a nonrecursive part where the root node has split. This is handled on return from the original call to the recursive algorithm. The special case where the 2-3 tree is empty should be handled before the recursive algorithm is called.

Now we can write the detailed algorithm. The following pseudocode uses the same record structure that we described for general three-way search trees.

Insert (VAR Tree: NodePointer, Value: ItemType)

```
(* Check for empty Tree *)
IF Tree = NIL
    THEN   InitializeNewNode(Tree, Value)
    ELSE
        Insert2(Tree, Value, Separator, NewNode, Split)
        IF Split
            THEN
                InitializeNewNode(TempTree, Separator)
                TempTree↑.Left ← Tree
                TempTree↑.Middle ← NewNode
                Tree ← TempTree
        END IF
END IF
```

InitializeNewNode (VAR Node: NodePointer, Value: ItemType)

```
New (Node)
Node↑.Left ← NIL
Node↑.Middle ← NIL
Node↑.Right ← NIL
Node↑.Value1 ← Value
Node↑.Value2 ← NoValue
```

Insert2(VAR Tree: NodePointer, Value: ItemType, VAR Separator: ItemType, VAR NewNode: NodePointer, VAR Split: Boolean)

```
IF Tree↑.Left = NIL
    THEN   (* a leaf node *)
        InsertNode (Separator, NewNode, Split)
    ELSIF Value < Tree↑.Value1
        THEN   (* follow left branch *)
            Insert2(Tree↑.Left, Value, Separator, NewTree, Split)
            IF Split
                THEN   AdjustLeftSplit(Tree, Separator, NewTree, Split)
            END IF
```

```
                ELSIF (Tree↑.Right = NIL) OR (Value < Tree↑.Value2)
                    THEN   (* follow middle branch *)
                        Insert2(Tree↑.Middle, Value, Separator, NewTree, Split)
                        IF Split
                            THEN   AdjustMiddleSplit (Tree, Separator,
                                                            NewTree, Split)
                        END IF
                    ELSE   (* follow right branch *)
                        Insert2(Tree↑.Right, Value, Separator, NewTree, Split)
                        IF Split
                            THEN   AdjustRightSplit(Tree, Separator,
                                                            NewTree, Split)
                        END IF
        END IF
```

**InsertNode (VAR Tree: NodePointer, Value: ItemType, VAR Separator: ItemType,
VAR NewNode: NodePointer, VAR Split: Boolean)**

```
IF Tree↑.Value2 = NoValue
    THEN   (* there is room *)
        Split ← False
        IF Value < Tree↑.Value1
            THEN
                Tree↑.Value2 ← Tree↑.Value1
                Tree↑.Value1 ← Value
            ELSE Tree↑.Value2 ← Value
        END IF
    ELSE   (* the node must split *)
        Split ← True
        InitializeNewNode(NewNode, Tree↑.Value2)
        IF (Value < Tree↑.Value1)
            THEN
                Separator ← Tree↑.Value1
                Tree↑.Value1 ← Value
                InitializeNewNode(NewNode, Tree↑.Value2)
            ELSIF Value < Tree↑.Value2
                THEN
                    Separator ← Value
                    NewNode↑.Value1 ← Tree↑.Value2
                ELSE
                    Separator ← Tree↑.Value2
                    InitializeNewNode(NewNode, Value)
        END IF
        Tree↑.Value2 ← NoValue
END IF
```

AdjustRightSplit (VAR Tree: NodePointer, VAR Separator: ItemType,
 VAR NewTree: NodePointer, VAR Split: Boolean)

```
Initialize(NewNode, Separator)
NewNode↑.Left ← Tree↑.Right
Separator ← Tree↑.Value2
NewNode↑.Middle ← NewTree
Tree↑.Right ← NIL
TreeValue2 ← NoValue
Split ← True
NewTree ← NewNode
```

AdjustLeftSplit (VAR Tree: NodePointer, VAR Separator: ItemType,
 VAR NewTree: NodePointer, VAR Split: Boolean)

```
IF Tree↑.Right = NIL
    THEN    (* room in node *)
        Tree↑.Right ← Tree↑.Middle
        Tree↑.Value2 ← Tree↑.Value1
        Tree↑.Value1 ← Separator
        Tree↑.Middle ← NewTree
        Split ← False
    ELSE
        InitializeNewNode(NewNode, Tree↑.Value2 )
        NewNode↑.Left ← Tree↑.Middle
        NewNode↑.Middle ← Tree↑.Right
        Tree↑.Middle ← NewTree
        Tree↑.Right ← NIL
        Split ← True
        Swap(Separator, Tree↑.Value1)
        Tree↑.Value2 ← NoValue
        NewTree ← NewNode
END IF
```

AdjustMiddleSplit (VAR Tree: NodePointer, VAR Separator: ItemType,
 VAR NewTree: NodePointer, VAR Split: Boolean)

```
IF Tree↑.Right = NIL
    THEN    (* room in tree *)
        Tree↑.Value2 ← Separator
        Tree↑.Right ← NewTree
        Split ← False
    ELSE
```

```
            InitializeNewNode(NewNode, Tree↑.Value2)
            NewNode↑.Left ← NewTree
            NewNode↑.Middle ← Tree↑.Right
            Tree↑.Right ← NIL
            Split ← True
            Tree↑.Value2 ← NoValue
            NewTree ← NewNode
    END IF
```

Detailed Examination of Deletion Algorithm

Again, we must map our boxes and arrows into variables and pointers. The algorithm defined for boxes and arrows is repeated below.

Delete

```
IF value is not in leaf node
    THEN
            Replace with successor
            Delete successor
    ELSIF node contains two values
            THEN   Delete value
            ELSE
                Delete value
                Patch up node
    END IF
```

PatchUpNode

```
IF possible
    THEN   Borrow from sibling
    ELSE
            Move separator from parent to sibling
            IF parent does not contain two values
                THEN   Patch up node
            END IF
    END IF
```

As we can see, there are several recursive features about this first approximation. If we find the value we are deleting in a nonleaf node, we replace it with its successor and delete the successor. If we must collapse a node, this might propagate up the tree, eventually causing the root node to collapse.

Our experience with the insertion algorithm gives some insights into a second approximation of the delete algorithm—namely, that the deletion algorithm must indeed be recursive and that several cases must be examined. "Patch up node" can be incorporated in the algorithm immediately following the recursive calls. That is, on return from each recursive call, we can test to see if the node has no values and needs to be adjusted.

Our original algorithm was written to replace the value with its successor if the value to be deleted is not a leaf node and to begin the algorithm again, deleting the successor. These two actions can be combined in one call to the delete procedure. If the value to be deleted is not in a leaf node, we remember the node that contains the value and continue searching. When we reach a leaf node, we are where the value would be if it were in a leaf node. That is, we are at the node that contains the predecessor (or successor) of the value for which we are searching.

If we follow the branch to the left of the value we are looking for, and if we find it in an interior node, we eventually reach the node containing its predecessor. If we follow the branch to the right of the value, we reach the node with its successor.

For example, if we are deleting pony from the following 2-3 tree, the predecessor of pony is horse and the successor of pony is shark.

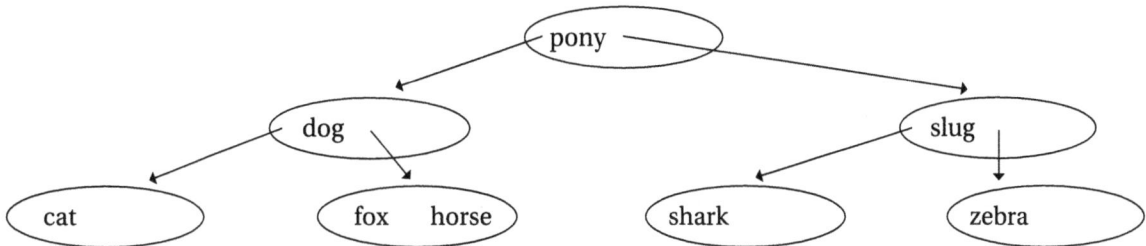

This implies that the deletion algorithm must have a parameter that is the nonleaf node where the value is found if it is found in an interior node. When a leaf node is finally encountered, this parameter can be tested. If this parameter is not NIL, the predecessor (or successor) is placed in that node and the deletion algorithm then deletes the predecessor (or successor) value.

Now we examine the possible cases that can occur when deleting from a leaf node. If the leaf node contains two values, the value can be deleted with no further action necessary.

If the leaf node is a left leaf, there are two possibilities: it can borrow from its right neighbor or it can collapse and combine the empty node with its neighbor. If it collapses with its neighbor, the separator is no longer needed, so it moves down into the neighbor. For example, suppose we delete the value 3 from the following 2-3 tree.

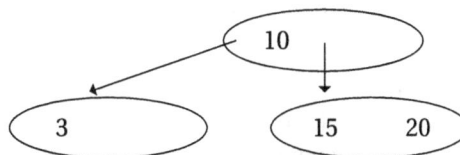

In this case, the neighbor has two values, so the separator can be moved to the empty leaf and the lowest value from the neighbor can be moved to the separator. Value2 would have to be moved into the Value1 field, giving the following result.

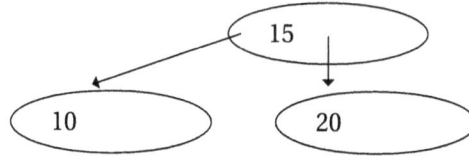

If the neighbor does not have two values, the two nodes must be combined (or *coalesced*, as it is sometimes called). This situation is shown on the left below. The result would be as shown on the right. 10 and 15 are combined in the node that originally contained 3; the nodes that contained 10 and 15 are now empty and can be disposed of. We leave the empty nodes and pointers in the diagrams, however.

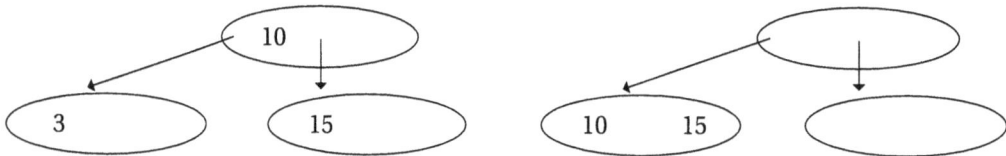

The parent node has only one child and no values. This node would have to be patched up at the next level. If there had been two values in the parent node when the separator was brought down, the parent could have been adjusted and no further patching up would have been necessary. This is demonstrated in the next diagram, where 3 is deleted from the first tree. Note the empty node would be returned and the pointer to it set to NIL.

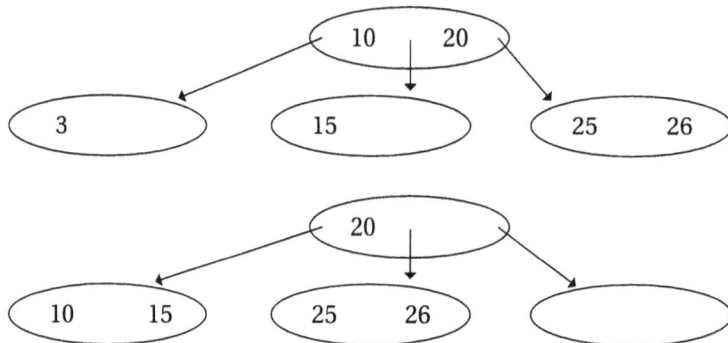

If the deletion is made from a middle child, the same situations apply. The cases are shown in Figure 9.5. Figure 9.6 demonstrates the cases where a value is being deleted from a right child.

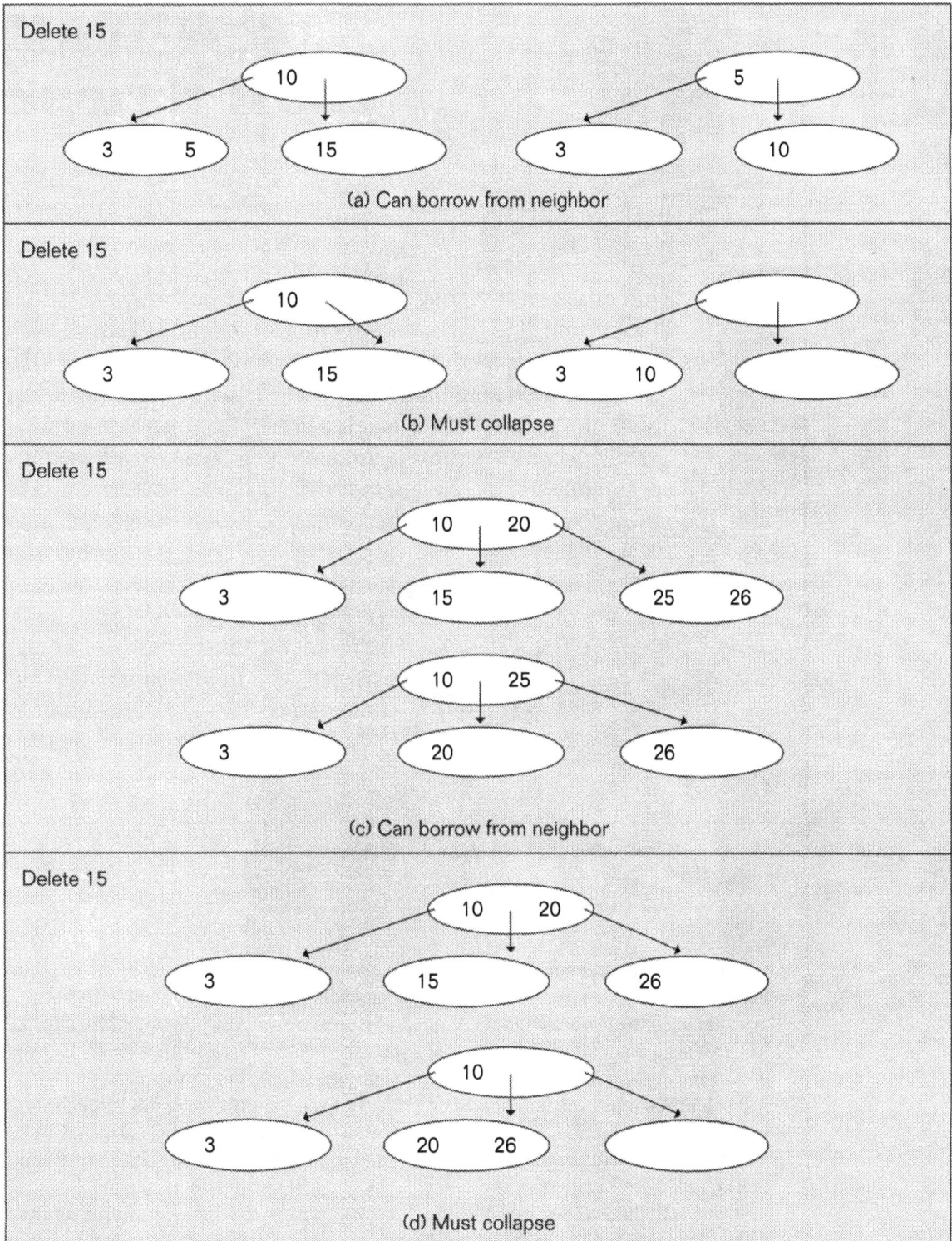

Figure 9.5 Deleting from a Middle Child

Delete 25

(a) Can borrow from neighbor

Delete 25

(b) Must collapse

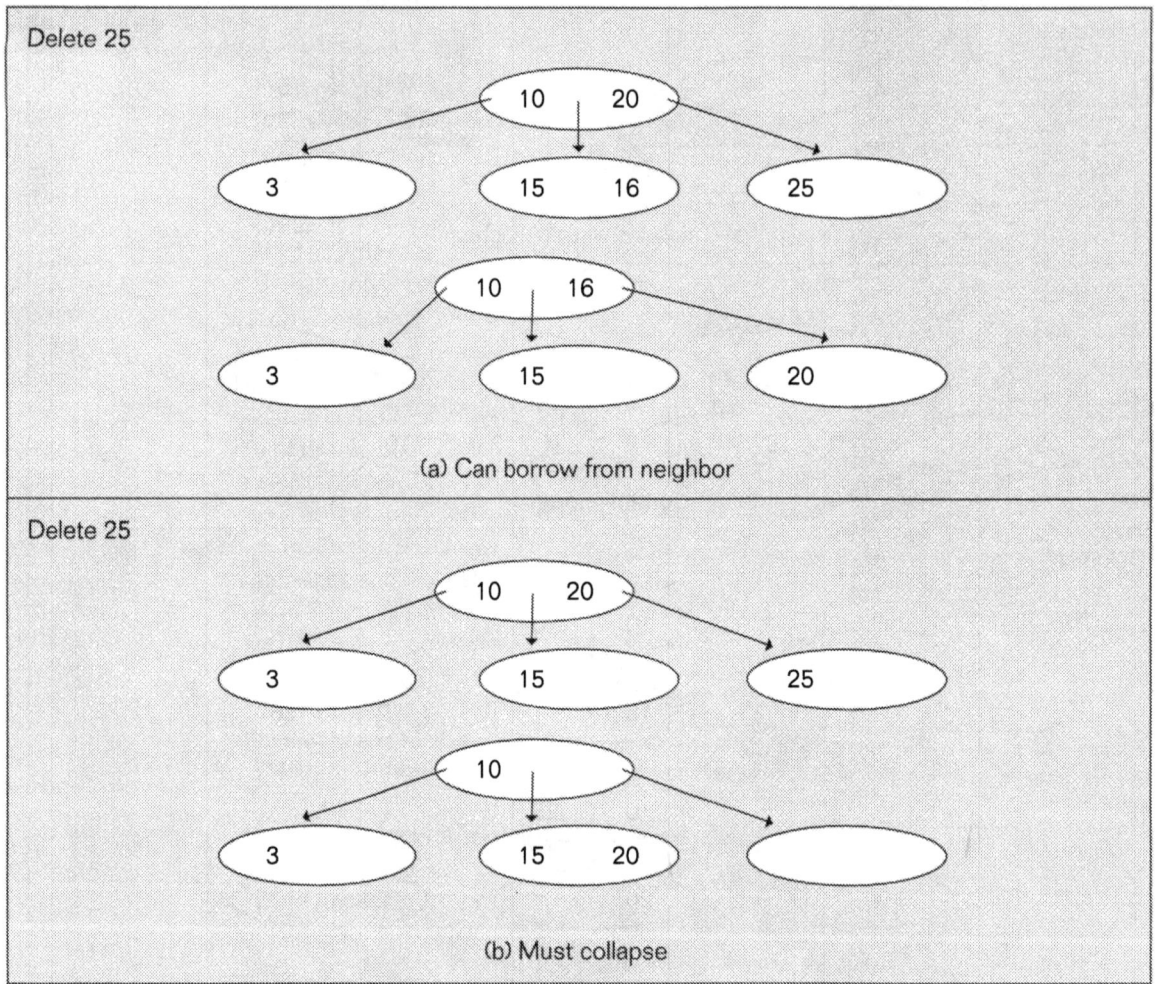

Figure 9.6 Deleting from a Right Child

Each of our trees has only two levels. We should look at the case where the deletion propagates up the tree to make sure that there is no problem with pointers that we have not seen yet. Figure 9.7(a) is the original tree. Figure 9.7(b) shows the tree with 15 deleted. Figure 9.7(c) shows the result of collapsing a node. Figure 9.7(d) shows the result of applying a left rotation to solve the problem.

Clearly, something is wrong. The node that was empty now has a value, but it still has only one child. The node from which we borrowed a value now has one value and three children. An analysis of what the values in the left child represent tells us what we must do.

The left child of the node from which we borrowed a value contains all the values greater than the separator but less than Value1. We have moved the separator to the node on the left and moved Value1 into the separator slot. To maintain the relationship among these values, we must move the left-most child of the

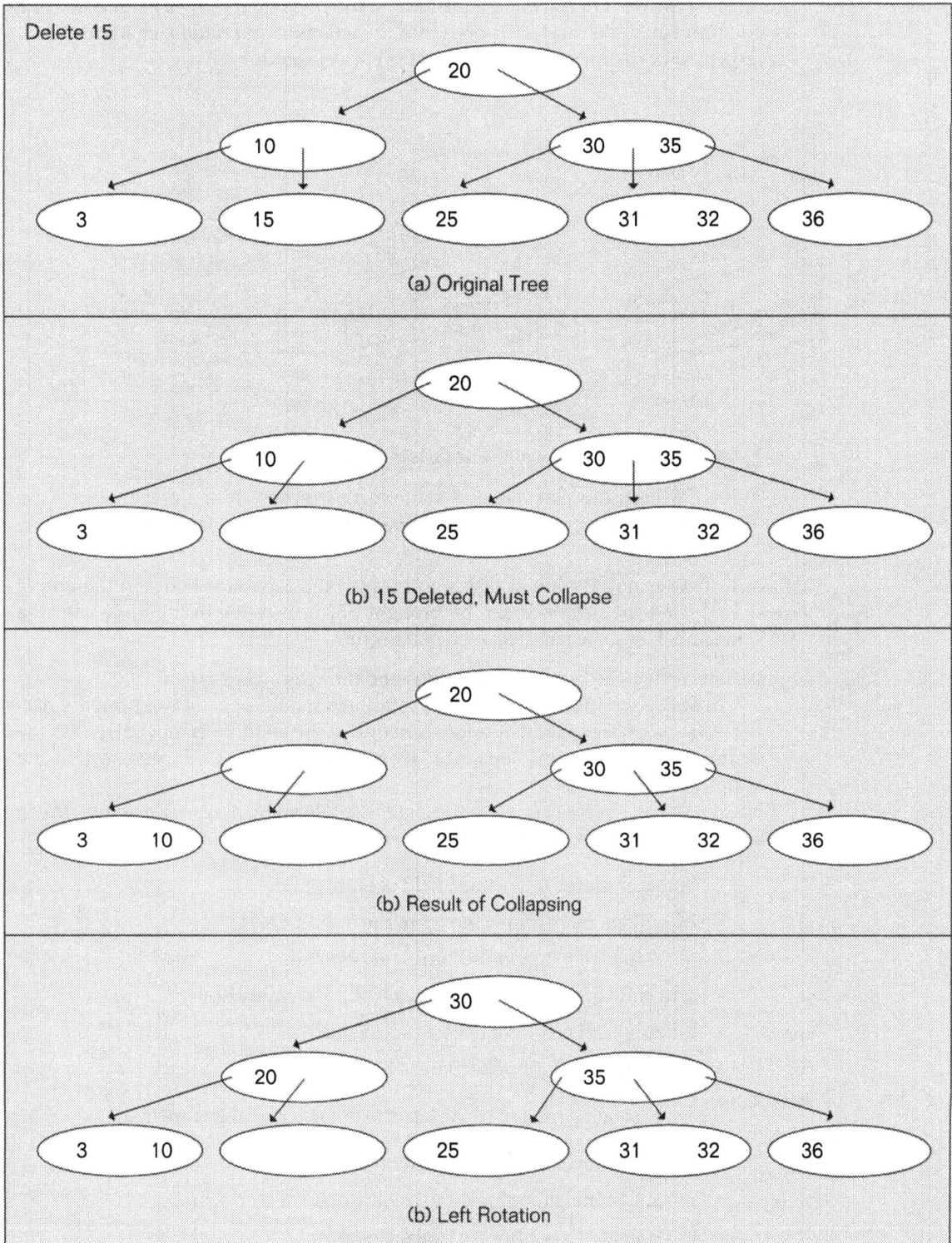

Figure 9.7 Deletion Propagates to Internal Node

node on the right to the middle position of the node on the left. The middle child and the right child must be moved into the left child and middle child positions, respectively. The following tree shows the correct rotation.

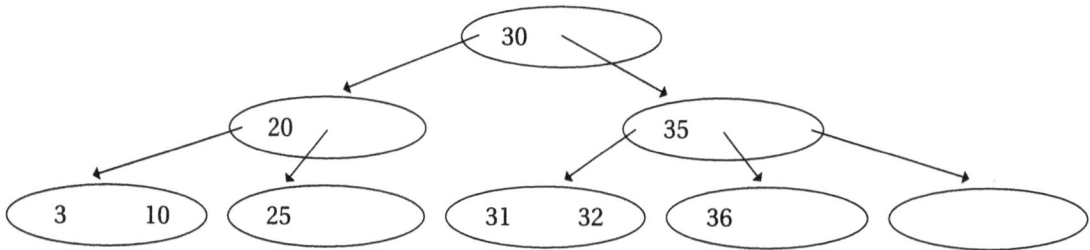

Two things can happen when a node is empty.

1. If a neighbor has two values, a value can be moved from a neighbor into the parent node, and the separator can be moved from the parent into the empty node.

2. If there is not a value available to borrow, the separator between the empty node and the neighbor can be brought down to reside in the node with the neighbor, and the parent can be patched up.

We now review the borrowing rotations and then the collapsing.

In both a left rotation and a right rotation a separator is moved from the parent into one of its children. A node from one of the children is moved up into the parent node to be a new separator. The children must be adjusted so that the search property holds.

If a value is being rotated to the right, the following changes are made. *(Note: Empty node refers to the node without a value.)*

- Separator moves into Value1 field of empty node.
- Left child of empty node moves to the middle child.
- Value2 field of neighbor becomes the separator.
- Right child of neighbor becomes left child of empty node.
- Value2 field of neighbor becomes NoValue.
- Right child of neighbor becomes NIL.

If a value is being rotated to the left, the following changes are made..

- Separator moves into Value1 field of empty node.
- Left child of neighbor moves to middle child of empty node.
- Value1 field of neighbor becomes separator.
- Middle child of neighbor moves to left child of neighbor.

- Value2 field of neighbor moves to Value1 field.

- Right child of neighbor moves to middle child of neighbor.

- Value2 field of neighbor becomes NoValue.

- Right child of neighbor becomes NIL.

Now we summarize the steps that occur when two nodes collapse. The exact pattern of value and pointer shifting depends on which node is empty. We first summarize what happens if the left node is empty.

- Separator moves into Value1 field of empty node.

- Value1 field of neighbor moves into Value2 field of empty node.

- Left child of neighbor moves into middle child of empty node.

- Middle child of neighbor moves into right child of empty node.

- Shift parent node.

    Value2 of parent moves to Value1 field.

    Value2 of parent becomes NoValue.

    Right child of parent moves to Middle child.

- Right child of parent becomes NIL.

If the middle child becomes empty and cannot borrow, the following steps are taken to collapse the node with its neighbor.

- Separator moves into Value2 position of left neighbor.

- Left child of empty node moves to right child of left neighbor.

- Shift parent node (same as above).

The only case left to examine is the one where the empty node is a right child—the simplest case of all.

- Separator moves to Value2 position of neighbor.

- Left child of empty node moves to right child of neighbor.

- Separator becomes NoValue.

- Right child of parent becomes NIL.

In the insertion algorithm, we needed several parameters in which to pass information back from the lower levels. This is not the case with the deletion algorithm. We know we have to adjust a node if there is no value in it; that is, if NoValue is in the Value1 position. We do, however, need access to both a node and its parent at every level because the siblings of a node can only be accessed through the parent. Therefore, the recursive delete algorithm must have both a node and its parent as parameters.

We are now ready to rewrite the deletion algorithm. As in the case of the insertion algorithm, the original call is to a nonrecursive procedure that checks for the case where the tree contains only one node and calls the recursive delete. As in the case of the insertion, if the root is changed, the nonrecursive shell takes care of it.

Delete (VAR Tree: NodePointer, Value: ItemType)

```
IF Tree↑.Left = NIL
    THEN
        IF Value = Tree↑.Value1
            THEN
                Tree↑.Value1 ← Tree↑.Value2
                Tree↑.Value2 ← NoValue
            ELSE   Tree↑.Value2 ← NoValue
        END IF
    ELSE
        IF (Value = Tree↑.Value1) OR (Value = Tree↑.Value2)
            THEN   ValueNode ← Tree
        END IF
        IF Value <= Tree↑.Value1
            THEN    Delete2(Tree, Tree↑.Left, Value, ValueNode)
            ELSIF (Tree↑.Right = NIL) OR (Value <= Tree↑.Value2)
                THEN   Delete2(Tree, Tree↑.Middle, Value, ValueNode)
                ELSE   Delete2(Tree, Tree↑.Right, Value, ValueNode)
        END IF
        IF Tree↑.Value1 = NoValue
            THEN   Tree ← Tree↑.Left
        END IF
END IF
```

Delete2(VAR Parent, Node: NodePointer, Value: ItemType,
VAR ValueNode: NodePointer)

```
IF Node↑.Left <> NIL
    THEN
        IF (Value = Node↑.Value1) OR (Value = Node↑.Value2)
            THEN   ValueNode ← Node
        END IF
        IF Value < Node↑.Value1
            THEN   Delete2(Node, Node↑.Left, Value, ValueNode)
            ELSIF (Node↑.Right = NIL) OR (Value <= Node↑.Value2)
                THEN   Delete2(Node, Node↑.Middle, Value, ValueNode)
                ELSE   Delete2(Node, Node↑.Right, Value, ValueNode)
        END IF
```

```
    ELSE   DeleteValue(Node, Value, ValueNode)
END IF
IF Node↑.Value1 = NoValue
    THEN   PatchUp(Parent, Node)
END IF
```

**Delete Value(VAR Node: NodePointer, Value: ItemType,
    VAR ValueNode: NodePointer)**

```
IF ValueNode <> NIL
    THEN
        IF Node↑.Value2 <> NoValue
            THEN
                Replace(Value, Node↑.Value1, ValueNode)
                Node↑.Value2 ← NoValue
            ELSE
                Replace(Value, Node↑.Value1, ValueNode)
                Node↑.Value1 ← NoValue
        END IF
    ELSIF Node↑.Value2 = NoValue
        THEN   (* 1 value in node, must be Value *)
            Node↑.Value1 ← NoValue
        ELSE   (* 2 values in node, remove Value *)
            IF Value = Node↑.Value1
                THEN
                    Node↑.Value1 ← Node↑.Value2
                    Node↑.Value2 ← NoValue
                ELSE   Node↑.Value2 ← NoValue
            END IF
END IF
```

Replace(Value, Successor: ItemType, VAR ValueNode: NodePointer)

```
IF Value = ValueNode↑.Value1
    THEN   ValueNode↑.Value1 ← Successor
    ELSE   ValueNode↑.Value2 ← Successor
END IF
```

PatchUp(VAR Parent, Node: NodePointer)

```
IF Node = Parent↑.Left
    THEN   (* Left child is empty *)
        Neighbor ← Parent↑.Middle
        IF Neighbor↑.Value2 <> NoValue
            THEN   RotateLeft(Neighbor, Parent↑.Value1, Node)
            ELSE   (* must collapse *)
                Node↑.Value1 ← Parent↑.Value1
                Node↑.Value2 ← Neighbor↑.Value1
```

```
                        Node↑.Middle ← Neighbor↑.Left
                        Node↑.Right ← Neighbor↑.Middle
                        ShiftParentNode(Parent)
                END IF
        ELSIF Node = Parent↑.Middle
            THEN   (* Middle child is empty *)
                Neighbor ← Parent↑.Left
                IF Neighbor↑.Value2 <> NoValue
                    THEN   RotateRight(Neighbor, Parent↑.Value1, Node)
                    ELSIF Parent↑.Right <> NIL
                        THEN
                            Neighbor ← Parent↑.Right
                            IF Neighbor↑.Value2 <> NoValue
                                THEN   RotateLeft(Neighbor, Parent↑.Value2,
                                       Node)
                                ELSE   (* must collapse *)
                                    Parent↑.Left↑.Value2 ← Parent↑.Value1
                                    Parent↑.Left↑.Right ← Node↑.Left
                                    ShiftParentNode(Parent)
                            END IF
                        ELSE   (* Parent↑.Right <> NIL *)
                            Neighbor↑.Value2 ← Parent↑.Value1
                            Parent↑.Value1 ← NoValue
                    END IF
            ELSE   (* Right child is empty *)
                Neighbor ← Parent↑.Middle
                IF Neighbor↑.Value2 <> NoValue
                    THEN   RotateRight(Neighbor, Parent↑.Value2, Node)
                    ELSE   (* must collapse *)
                        Neighbor↑.Value2 ← Parent↑.Value2
                        Neighbor↑.Right ← Node↑.Left
                        Parent↑.Value2 ← NoValue
                        Parent↑.Right ← NIL
                END IF
        END IF
    END IF
```

**RotateLeft(VAR Neighbor: NodePointer, VAR Separator: ItemType,
    VAR Node: NodePointer)**

```
Node↑.Value1 ← Separator
Node↑.Middle ← Neighbor↑.Left
Separator ← Neighbor↑.Value1
Neighbor↑.Value1 ← Neighbor↑.Value2
Neighbor↑.Value2 ← NoValue
Neighbor↑.Left ← Neighbor↑.Middle
Neighbor↑.Middle ← Neighbor↑.Right
Neighbor↑.Right ← NIL
```

RotateRight(VAR Neighbor: NodePointer, VAR Separator: ItemType,
VAR Node: NodePointer)

```
Node↑.Value1 ← Separator
Node↑.Middle ← Node↑.Left
Node↑.Left ← Neighbor↑.Right
Separator ← Neighbor↑.Value2
Neighbor↑.Value2 ← NoValue
Neighbor↑.Right ← NIL
```

ShiftParentNode (Parent: NodePointer)

```
Parent↑.Value1 ← Parent↑.Value2
Parent↑.Middle ← Parent↑.Right
Parent↑.Value2 ← NoValue
Parent↑.Right ← NIL
```

The number of pages devoted to 2-3 trees far exceeds the structure's importance. However, we have used the development of the 2-3 tree algorithms to show how to go from a problem statement, to pictures with boxes and arrows, to a general algorithm, to a detailed algorithm. Each step in this process requires careful attention to detail, and no step can be skipped. The more complex the algorithms become, the more important it is to use a careful, organized approach to program development.

B-Trees

If 2-3 trees generalize the idea of binary search trees, can the search tree concept be extended even further to nodes with more values and children? The answer is, Yes, it can. The 2-3 tree is a member of a larger class of trees known as *B-trees*. A B-tree is an M-way search tree with the following properties.

1. All leaves are on the same level.
2. Insertions are made in the leaf nodes.
3. All nodes have, at most, M children.
4. All nodes (except the root) have at least $\lceil M/2 \rceil$ nonempty children.
5. The number of keys is one less than the number of children.

A node in a B-tree has the following form.

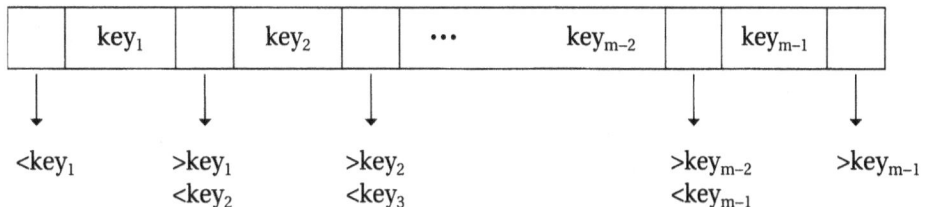

	key_1		key_2		...	key_{m-2}		key_{m-1}	

$<key_1$ $>key_1$ $>key_2$ $>key_{m-2}$ $>key_{m-1}$
          $<key_2$ $<key_3$ $<key_{m-1}$

If there are M children, there are M − 1 key values. The left-most child points to a subtree with keys that are less than key$_1$. The second child points to a subtree with keys that are greater than key$_1$ and less than key$_2$. The right-most child points to a subtree with keys that are greater than key$_{m-1}$.

Because B-trees are often used to index large collections of data, the literature talks about inserting and deleting keys rather than items. We are actually inserting records identified by a key. The information associated with the key may be general information or a pointer to where the general information can be found. For the following discussion, we assume that the keys are unique. If they are not, the associated information may point to a list of the items with the same key. We are interested in the properties of the structure, not in how an individual program might use the structure. We also simplify the discussion by talking about comparing keys with the relational operators. In practice, the user provides a comparison function that compares the keys of two records as we did in Chapter 8.

We work through an example of a B-tree where M is 5. The following constraints apply: $3 \leq$ children ≤ 5 and $2 \leq$ keys ≤ 4.

Insert a, b, g, f: We get a node and initialize it with all children set to NIL. a goes into the first key position; b goes into the second key position; and g goes into the third key position. When f is inserted, g must be moved into the fourth key position so that f can be stored in the third key position. The keys must remain in alphabetical order.

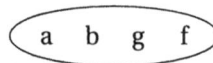

Insert k: Our one-node tree does not have room enough to insert k. We must split this node into two nodes and insert a node between them. The middle of the five key values goes into the first position of a new node, which becomes the root of the resulting tree. The two keys that are lower than the middle key remain as the first two keys in the original node. The two keys that are greater than the middle key go into the first two positions in a new node. The new root has the left-most child pointing to the original node, and the second child pointing to the new node.

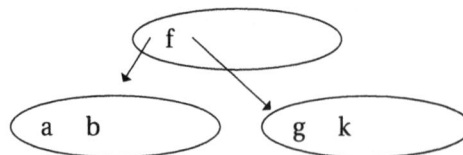

Insert d, h, and m: d is less than f, so the left-most child is followed to the node with a and b. There is room for d in this node. Both h and m are greater than f, so the second child pointer is followed to the leaf node with g and k. There is room, so they are inserted.

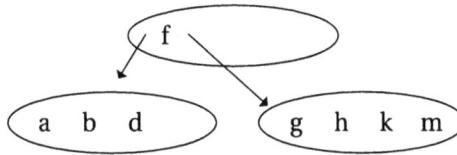

Insert l: l is greater than f, so the second child is followed to the leaf node with g, h, k, and m. This leaf is full, so the node splits with the middle key going up to be a separator in the parent node.

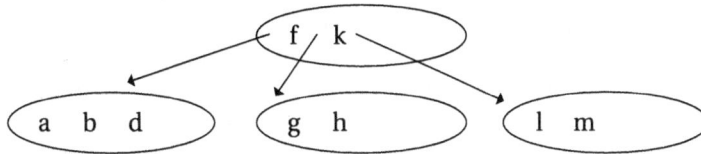

Insert s, i, and r: There is room for each of these values in the proper leaf nodes.

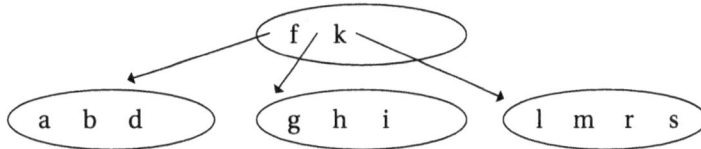

Insert x: x is greater than f and greater than k, so the third child pointer is followed to the proper leaf node. It is full, so the node splits with the middle key, r, going up to be a separator between the splitting node and the new node.

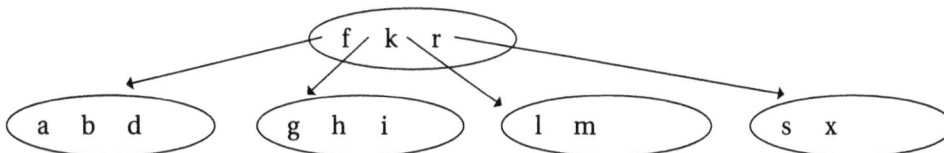

Insert c, e, n, o and p: When we insert c and e, the left-most node splits, sending c to the parent as a separator. When we insert n, o, and p, that node splits, sending n to the parent. There is no room for n in the parent, so the root node splits. The middle key is k, so k moves up to be the separator in the new root node.

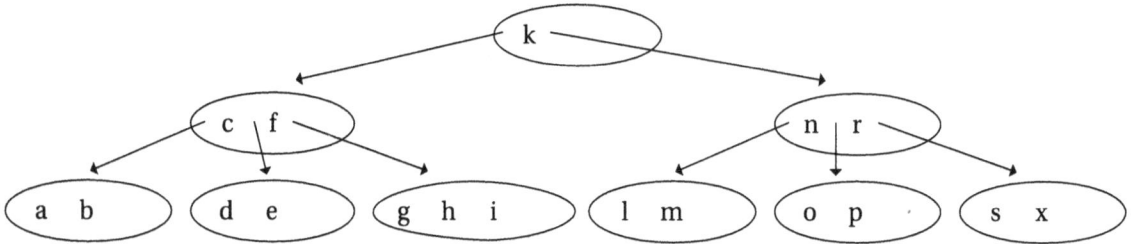

As you can see, the process of working with B-trees is a logical extension of working with 2-3 trees. One more word before we write the insertion algorithm. If the minimum number of keys is even, the middle key is distinct when you add one more key to it; if the minimum number of keys is odd, you have a choice. We write the algorithms assuming the minimum number of keys is even, because it is easier. Bear this in mind when you are implementing these algorithms.

We need two parameters while we are looking for the insertion point: the Tree to search and the Key value. We need three parameters if there is a split so that we can take care of it as we recurse: a Boolean value Split, the MiddleKey, and the NewNode.

Insertion (VAR Tree: NodePointer, Key: KeyType)

```
Insert(Tree, Key, Split, MiddleKey, NewNode)
IF Split
    THEN
        Get NewTree
        LeftMostchild(NewTree) ← Tree
        Next child (NewTree) ← NewNode
        First Key (NewTree) ← MiddleKey
END IF
```

**Insert (VAR Tree: NodePointer, Key: ItemType, VAR Split: Boolean,
VAR MiddleKey: ItemType, VAR NewNode: NodePointer)**

```
IF Tree is a leaf
    THEN
        IF Number of keys < M−1 (* less than maximum *)
            THEN
                Insert Key
                Split ← False
            ELSE
                Get NewNode
                Leave (M − 1)/2 keys in Tree
```

```
                    Move (M − 1)/2 keys to NewNode
                    MiddleKey ← MiddleValue
                    Split ← True
            END IF
        ELSE
            Find Path(NextTree)
            Insert(NextTree, Key, Split, MiddleKey, NewNode)
            IF Split
                THEN
                    IF Number of keys in Tree < M − 1
                        THEN
                            Insert Key w/pointer
                            Split ← False
                        ELSE
                            Get NewNode
                            Leave (M − 1)/2 keys in Tree
                            Move (M − 1)/2 keys and pointers to NewNode
                            MiddleKey ← Middle Value
                            Split ← True
                    END IF
            END IF
    END IF
```

Now we try deleting a few values from the following tree.

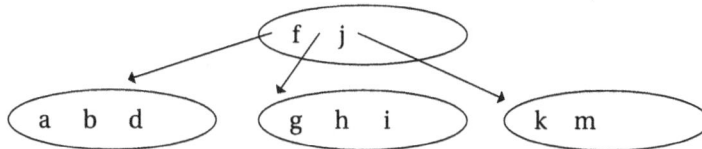

Delete d and b: Deleting d leaves the leaf node with two values. Deleting b causes
a problem because this leaves only one key in the node and there must be
two.

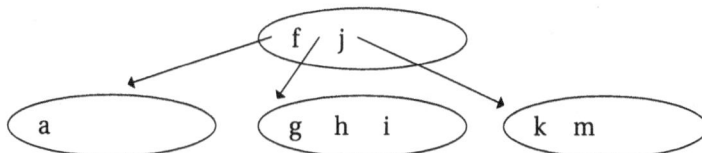

The sibling of the node has three keys. We can borrow g by moving f into the
node that needs a key and by moving g into the parent node to replace f as the
separator.

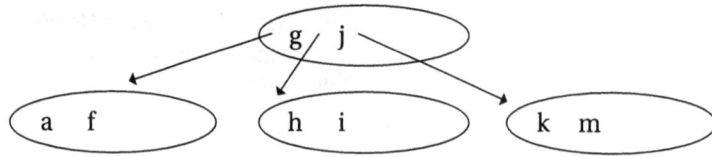

Notice that this is exactly what we did in the 2-3 tree when we rotated keys from one sibling to parent to other sibling.

Delete i: We are in trouble again because deleting i leaves that node with only one key. Neither sibling has an extra key. We can combine (coalesce) the node with either of its siblings. Note that if we cannot borrow from a sibling, we can always coalesce with it.

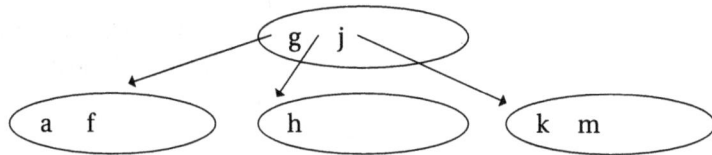

We move h to the node on the left and remove the pointer to the node that used to contain h. The separator, g, is no longer needed and is moved into the node on the left as well.

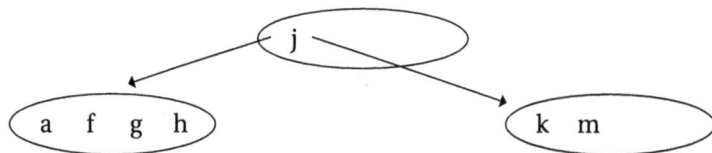

What about the case where the key to be deleted is not in a leaf node? We can do exactly what we did with binary search trees: replace the key to be deleted with its successor and delete the successor. The general algorithm for deletion is given below.

DeleteKey(VAR Tree: NodePointer, Key: KeyType)

```
Delete(NIL, Tree, Key)
IF Tree has only a Left Pointer
    Tree ← Left Pointer
END IF
```

Delete (VAR Parent, Tree: NodePointer, Key: KeyType)

```
IF Key in current node (* i.e., Tree *)
    THEN
        IF Tree is NOT a leaf
            THEN
                FindSuccessor(Tree, Key, NewKey)
                Replace Key with NewKey
                Delete(Parent, Tree, NewKey)
                IF Tree contains < M/2 −1 keys
                    THEN   PatchUp(Parent, Tree)
                END IF
            ELSE
                Remove key
                IF Tree contains < M/2 −1 keys
                    THEN   PatchUp(Parent, Tree)
                END IF
        END IF
    ELSE
        Find Path(NextTree)
        Delete(Tree, NextTree, Key)
        IF Tree contains < M/2 −1 keys
            THEN   PatchUp(Parent, Tree)
        END IF
END IF
```

PatchUp (VAR Parent, Node: NodePointer)

If we can both borrow and coalesce, does it matter which we do? If we borrow, the changes are localized and do not propagate back up the tree. If we coalesce, the changes may propagate all the way back up the tree, reducing the number of levels by one. It is really a toss-up. We decide to borrow first.

```
IF Right Sibling exists AND has > ⌈M/2⌉ −1 keys
    THEN   BorrowFromRight(Parent, Node, Right)
    ELSIF Left Sibling exists AND has > ⌈M/2⌉ −1 keys
        THEN   BorrowFromLeft(Parent, Node, Left)
        ELSIF Right Sibling exists
            THEN   Coalesce(Parent, Node, Right)
            ELSE   Coalesce(Parent, Left, Node)
END IF
```

Coalesce (VAR Parent, Node1, Node2: NodePointer)

```
Move Separator and Keys from Node2 into Node1
Remove Separator and Node1 pointer from Parent
```

BorrowFromRight (VAR Parent, Node, Right: NodePointer)

> Move Separator to Node
> Move LeftMostKey of Right to Parent as separator

BorrowFromLeft (VAR Parent, Node, Left: NodePointer)

> Move Separator to Node
> Move RightMostKey of Left to Parent as separator

Because we went into so much detail about converting the 2-3 tree pictures and the general algorithm to a detailed algorithm, we leave this conversion to you.

B⁺-Trees

B-trees are internal data structures. That is, the nodes contain whatever information is associated with the key as well as the key values. A variant of the B-trees is often used as an *index tree*. In an index tree, the pointers in the internal nodes point to other index nodes; and the pointers in the leaf nodes are not NIL, but rather point to where the information associated with each key is stored on disk. This means that each key must appear in a leaf node. B-trees whose keys are only in the internal nodes of the tree and whose pointers in the leaf nodes point to where the related information is stored externally are called *B⁺-trees*.

This seemingly minor change has some major effects on the algorithms. For example, the leaf nodes and the internal nodes are treated differently when they split. When a leaf node splits, a *copy* of the middle key is moved up to be a separator at the next level. When an internal (index node) splits, the key itself is moved up to act as a separator. For example, inserting a, b, g, f, and k produces the following B⁺-tree. The arrows from the leaf nodes point to where the information associated with the key can be found.

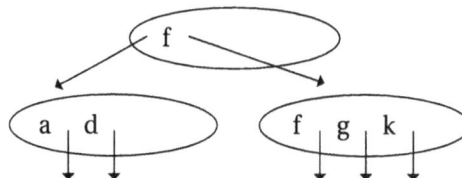

Another change is that keys are deleted only from the leaf nodes. If a key to be deleted is also part of the indexing structure (that is, appears in an internal node), it can remain in the index. For example, deleting f and j from the following tree

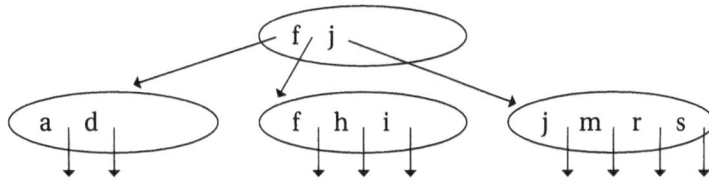

gives the B$^+$-tree shown below. The index says that all keys less than f are in the left subtree and those greater than or equal to f are in the right subtree. Likewise, all keys less than j are in the left subtree and those greater than or equal to g are in the right subtree. This is still true.

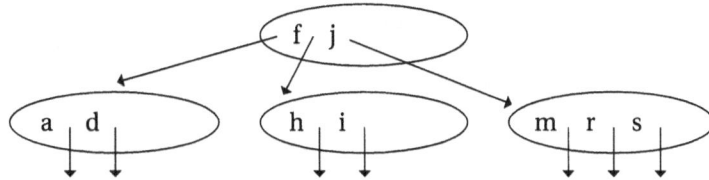

   Borrowing and coalescing are also slightly different because the old separator key can be discarded. For example, deleting g from the following B$^+$-tree leaves the left-most node one key short.

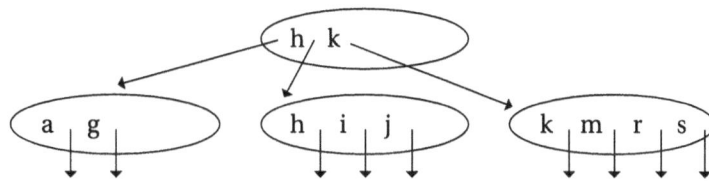

Here is the result of borrowing h.

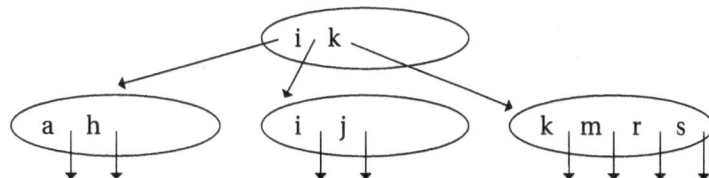

Notice the difference: in the B-tree, we rotated keys from one sibling to parent to other sibling. Here, the borrowed key goes directly into the sibling node and a copy of the new left-most node becomes the separator in the parent. If we borrow from the left, however, a copy of the borrowed key becomes the separator.

If we coalesce, h, i, and j go into the left-most node.

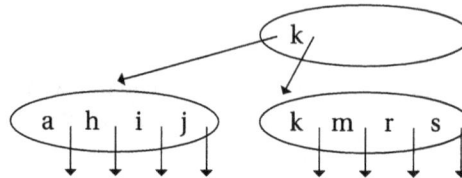

Because the pointers in the leaf nodes are not NIL, we must have another way in which to recognize a leaf node. One way is to have a field in each node to mark the node as either an internal node or a leaf node. Another way is to continue using the left-most child pointer as the flag, because we only need $M - 1$ pointers to point to the storage locations for $M - 1$ keys. By convention, we could let the pointer to the right of a key point to the data, and we could let the left-most pointer be NIL in a leaf node. This scheme handles pointers consistently on insertion because the new pointer in the recursive call is stored to the right of the separator key being inserted.

If we do not use the left-most pointer to determine if we are at a leaf node, we can use it to link all the leaf nodes together. Having the leaf nodes linked together allows us to process the items in the file in order as well as access the items randomly via the index.

We leave the rewriting of the algorithms for B^+-trees as an end-of-chapter exercise.

Other Tree Structures

Because multi-way search trees provide such a versatile way to store data for reasonably fast retrieval, it is hardly surprising that they are a popular data type. With this popularity, it also should not be surprising that many people have developed special algorithms and alternative structures to make these search trees even more effective. We have seen several variations already, including simple multi-way search trees, 2-3 trees, B-trees of order m, and B^+-trees.

In this section, we outline two additional search tree structures that illustrate some further extensions and refinements. As in the structures discussed earlier, we assume that all data values are distinct; duplicate values are not allowed. In each case, we leave various details as exercises to be done at the end of the chapter.

2-3-4 Trees

Multi-way search trees, where each node has 0, 2, 3, or 4 children, and where all leaves and null pointers are at the same level, are called *2-3-4 trees*. Stated another way, 2-3-4 trees are trees with 1, 2, or 3 data items in each node, where there are subtrees to the left and right of each data item, and where all leaves are at the same level. Such a 2-3-4 tree is shown in Figure 9.8.

Figure 9.8 illustrates that a 2-3-4 tree may be viewed as a general four-way search tree, with the additional properties that all leaves are at the same level and the pointer on each side of a data item is never null, except at the last level.

In order to preserve the leaf level and null properties of a 2-3-4 tree, insertion of a new value is always done at a leaf. In Figure 9.8, for example, we could add the values 17, 18, 64, 68, or 80 without difficulty. In each case, there is plenty of space in a leaf node for these values, and insertion can proceed easily. This type of insertion into a leaf was equally straightforward in each of our earlier multi-way search trees.

So what can go wrong with insertion? Clearly, we have trouble inserting into a leaf only if there is insufficient space for the extra value. In the algorithms for 2-3 trees or B-trees of order m, we solved this problem by splitting up the leaf node and inserting a value in a parent node. If the parent was also full, we split it and inserted another value farther up the tree. In short, when a leaf was full, we moved back up the tree, perhaps as far as the root, splitting nodes as necessary until we found appropriate space for the required values.

Insertion into a 2-3-4 tree anticipates this potential problem as part of the downward search process. In moving down the tree, whenever a node with three values is encountered, it is split, with a new value inserted into the parent. (If the upper level is full, it would have been split earlier in the process.) This basic algorithm is outlined below.

Insert (VAR Root: NodePointer, Value: ItemType)

```
IF Root has three data values
      THEN   split the root into a new root and two children
END IF
Ptr ← Root
WHILE Ptr not at leaf node DO
      Determine location of appropriate node at next level
      IF Node at next level contains three data values
```

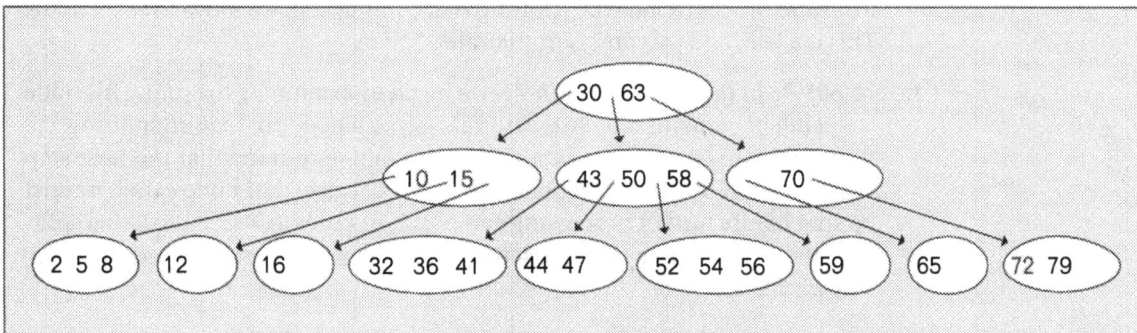

Figure 9.8 A 2-3-4 Tree

```
        THEN
            Split the node at the next level
            Insert middle value into the node given by Ptr
        END IF
        Move Ptr to appropriate node at next level
    END WHILE
    Insert Value into node given by Ptr
```

We illustrate this insertion with three examples, all based upon the tree in Figure 9.8.

Insert (7) Our insertion algorithm begins at the root. The root contains only two elements, so it need not be split. Now we compare 7 with the values in the root and determine that we should move left. Next, we examine the (10/15) node. It is not full either, so no splitting is needed. We compare 7 with these data values and discover that we must go left. This time, however, we find that the next node contains three values (2/5/8). Thus, before proceeding further, we split this node, promoting the 5 into the (10/15) node. This gives the following tree.

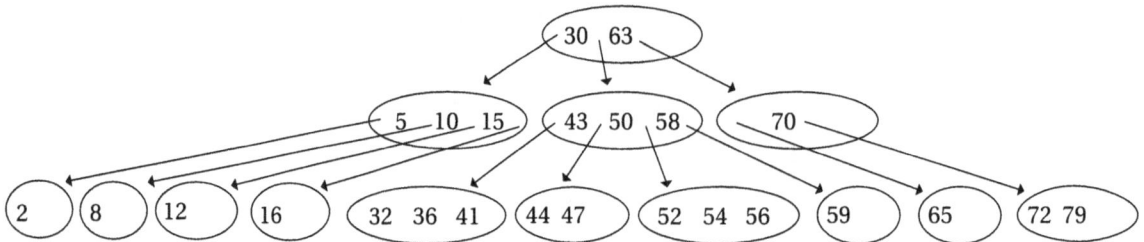

Thus, while still processing the (10/15) node, we anticipate that the following node is full, and we split the (2/5/8) node before moving to that point in our insertion process. Once the splitting is accomplished, we move to the 8 node. This is a leaf, and we can insert the value 7 here.

Insert (60) As in the previous example, we begin by examining the root. This node is not full (it contains only two data values), so it does not require splitting. We then compare 60 with the data in the root and determine that the next step moves toward the 43/50/58 node. However, because that node is full, it must be split before further processing can occur. In order to accomplish this splitting, the middle value (50) is inserted into the higher level. This produces the following tree.

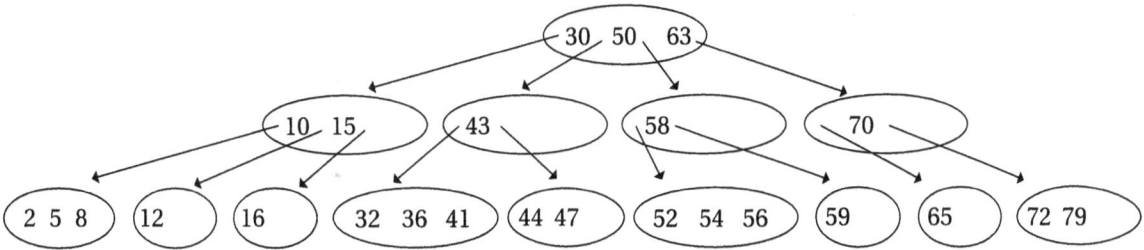

Following this splitting, we move to the 58 node. Next, we look ahead to the next node in the search path. This node (with 59) has only one data value, and we can move to it directly. Now we find that we are at a leaf, and the value 60 can be inserted, as required.

In this example, note that the 43/50/58 node was split as soon as it was encountered in the insertion/search process. In this case, we had room in the leaf for the new data value 60, but the algorithm does not take chances. Whenever a node with three data values is encountered, it is split immediately, before further searching or insertion is attempted.

Insert (53) The first steps necessary to insert 53 into the tree from Figure 9.8 mimic those for inserting 60. First, we examine the root, and it does not require splitting. Next, we look ahead at the 43/50/58 node and split it as before, getting the same result. The next step for inserting 53 leads to the 52/54/56 node, which again requires splitting immediately. This can be done by inserting the 54 into the 58 node. The result is shown below.

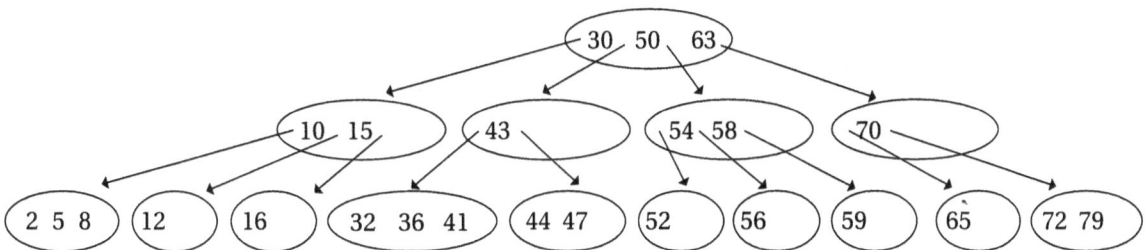

With this splitting, we now move to the next level, discover we are at a leaf, and store the 60 in the 59 node.

In this example, note that the early splitting of the 43/50/58 node created nodes with room for more values at that level. Then, when we needed to split the 52/54/56 node, we had room for the value 50 in the previous level.

This anticipation of possible future space needs allows the insertion algorithm for 2-3-4 trees to complete its work with a single pass down the tree, without needing to patch up the tree on a return pass toward the root. 2-3-4 trees maintain a balanced tree and split full nodes as insertion processing proceeds.

As we move from this general description of the algorithm to actual code, we need a more precise picture of a node. One convenient form numbers the data fields and pointer fields within a node.

Data[1]		Data[2]		Data[3]	
Next[0]	Next[1]	Next[2]		Next[3]	

In this diagram, the pointers for the subtrees on each side of Data[i] are numbered i − 1 and i.

This diagram gives rise to the following declarations.

```
TYPE NodePtr = ↑NodeType;
     NodeType = RECORD
         Data:   ARRAY [1..3] OF ItemType;
         Ptr:    ARRAY [0..3] OF NodePtr
     END RECORD;
```

The Insertion algorithm uses two procedures: one to create a new node and one to clean up an existing node.

CleanNode (VAR NPtr: NodePtr)

```
(* Set last two data fields to NoValue and last two pointer fields to NIL *)
NPtr↑.Data[2] ← NoValue;
NPtr↑.Data[3] ← NoValue;
NPtr↑.Ptr[2] ← NIL;
NPtr↑.Ptr[3] ← NIL;
```

CreateNode (VAR NPtr: NodePtr, Left, Right: NodePtr, Item: ItemType)

```
(* Create new node for NPtr, with designated Left and Right subtrees for *)
(* Item. Data values 2 and 3 within the node have NoValue *)
New(NPtr);
NPtr↑.Data[1] ← Item;
NPtr↑.Ptr[0] ← Left;
NPtr↑.Ptr[1] ← Right;
CleanNode(NPtr);
```

Insert (VAR Root: NodePtr, Item: ItemType);

The remaining details of the Insert algorithm follow the preceding discussion rather closely.

```
IF Root = NIL
    THEN  CreateNode (Root, NIL, NIL, Item)
    ELSE   (* Tree not empty *)
        NPtr ← Root; (* NPtr establishes current search position in tree *)
        IF Root↑.Data[3] <> NoValue
            THEN (* Split Root *)
                CreateNode (Right, Root↑.Ptr[2], Root↑.Ptr[3], Root↑.Data[3]);
                CreateNode (NewRoot, Root, Right, Root↑.Data[2])
                CleanNode(Root);
                Root ← NewRoot;
                IF Item < Root↑.Data[1]
                    THEN NPtr← Root↑.Ptr[0]
                    ELSE NPtr← Root↑.Ptr[1]
                END IF
        END IF (* Root split, if necessary *)
    (* Move down tree to leaf *)
    WHILE (NPtr↑.Ptr[0] <> NIL) DO   (* While not leaf find node at next level *)
    Index ← 0;
        WHILE (Item >= NPtr↑.Data[Index+1]) DO
            AND (NPtr↑.Data[Index+1]<>NoValue) DO
            Index ← Index + 1
        END WHILE
    (* Next level at NPtr↑.Ptr[Index] *)
    (* Split next level, if node currently is full *)
    NextNode ← NPtr↑.Ptr[Index]
    IF NextNode↑.Data[3]) = NoValue
        THEN   NPtr ← NextNode
        ELSE (* Split next node *)
            FOR J ← 2 Downto Index + 1 DO
                NPtr↑.Data[J+1] ← NPtr↑.Data[J] ;
                NPtr↑.Ptr[J+1] ← NPtr↑.Ptr[J]
            END FOR
            NPtr↑.Data[Index+1] ← NextNode↑.Data[2];
            CreateNode (NPtr↑.Data[Index+1] ,   NextNode↑.Ptr[2],
                        NextNode↑.Ptr[3], NextNode↑.Data[3]);
            CleanNode (NextNode);
            IF Item < NPtr↑.Data[Index+1]
                THEN   NPtr ← NPtr↑.Ptr[Index]
                ELSE   NPtr ← NPtr↑.Ptr[Index+1]
            END IF
    END IF
    END IF
END WHILE
```

```
      (* At Leaf *)
      IF Item < NPtr↑.Data[1]
          THEN   (* Insert item at left position in node *)
                NPtr↑.Data[3] ← NPtr↑.Data[2];
                NPtr↑.Data[2] ← NPtr↑.Data[1];
                NPtr↑.Data[1] ← Item
          ELSIF (Item < NPtr↑.Data[2]) OR (NPtr↑.Data[2] = NoValue)
                THEN   (* Insert item in middle position of node *)
                    NPtr↑.Data[3] ← NPtr↑.Data[2];
                    NPtr↑.Data[2] ← Item
                ELSE   (* Insert item in right position of node *)
                    NPtr↑.Data[3] ← Item
          END IF
      END IF (* check of Root *)
```

While this algorithm is very effective for handling data involving distinct values, this approach can fail when duplicate data values are allowed. The exercises at the end of the chapter ask you to find examples that 2-3-4 trees cannot handle correctly when data values are duplicated.

Red/Black Trees

While 2-3-4 trees are always balanced and require only a downward pass for insertion, they require that nodes be reasonably large. In particular, nodes must allow room for three data values, even though only one or two values might actually be present. *Red/Black Trees* resolve this problem by using a binary tree structure to represent the nodes of a 2-3-4 tree. Specifically, nodes with one, two, or three data values can be represented as binary structures, as shown in Figure 9.9.

With this representation, any 2-3-4 tree can be translated directly to a binary search tree. Note, however, that two representations of the node with two data items are possible, so there is a choice in the binary tree representation. At times in our processing, we must be able to tell which binary tree node corresponds to the root of a 2-3-4 tree node. In order to do this, we add a color to each node (or to each pointer to the node). By convention, the root of the binary 2-3-4 node is considered to be Black, and the children are considered Red. For example, in the representation of the node with values A, B, and C, we consider the B node in the binary tree to be Black, while both A and C are Red.

As an illustration, we translate the 2-3-4 tree of Figure 9.8 into a Red/Black tree. The result is shown in Figure 9.10, with black nodes designated by an asterisk (*).

With this representation, the insertion algorithms for 2-3-4 trees can be translated directly into the framework of Red/Black trees. Red and Black colors denote the different types of nodes within the tree structure, and code details must check which type of node is being processed at a particular time. Otherwise, algorithms for Red/Black trees can parallel those for 2-3-4 trees rather closely.

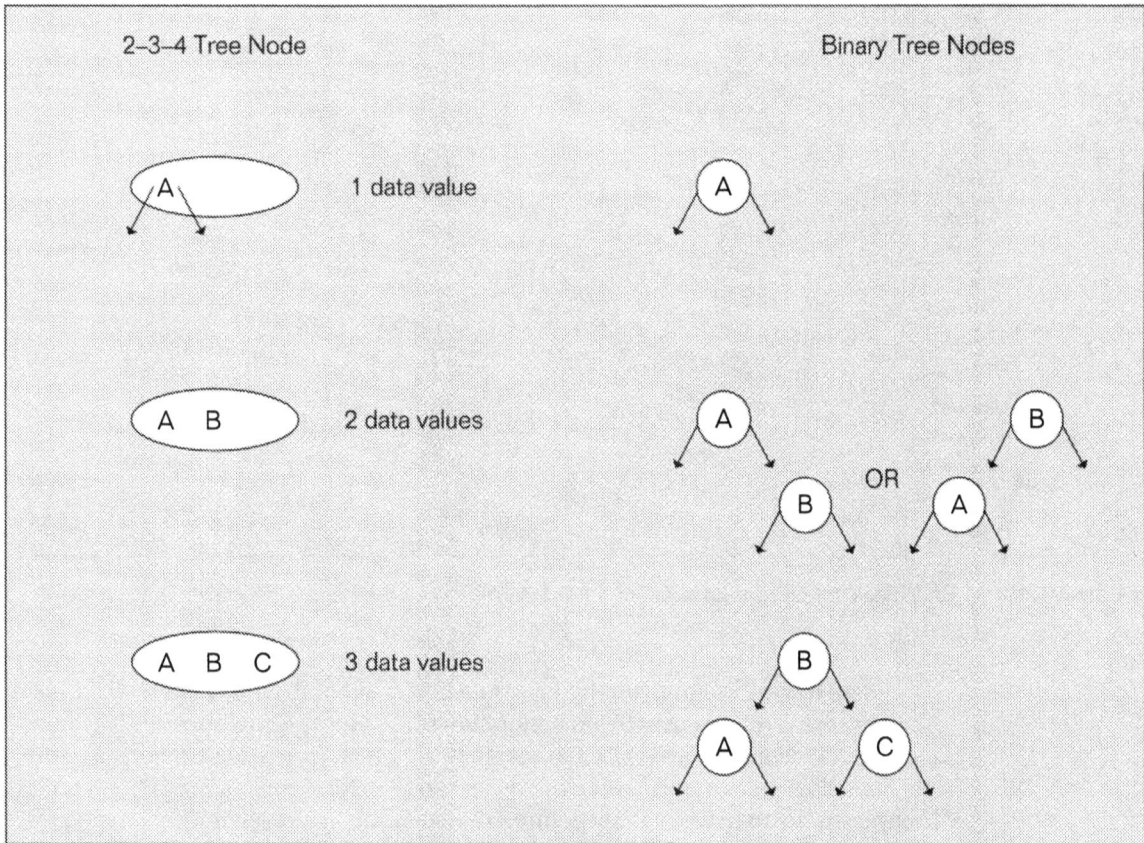

Figure 9.9   Red/Black Tree Representation of 2-3-4 Tree Nodes (Root nodes in binary tree are considered Black; Children in binary tree are considered Red)

In this representation, each node in a 2-3-4 tree is replaced by a binary tree node at no more than two levels. While the resulting Red/Black tree need not be balanced, it follows that the levels of various subtrees can never differ by more than a factor of 2. While this balancing is not as effective as AVL trees or general B-trees, Red/Black trees do guarantee some degree of balance.

Complexity

We have described a rather wide variety of multi-way search trees in this chapter; all but the simplest are balanced. Furthermore, if each node contains $K - 1$ keys, then insertion search paths to any key can be no longer than $\log_K N$ in searching a tree with N data items.

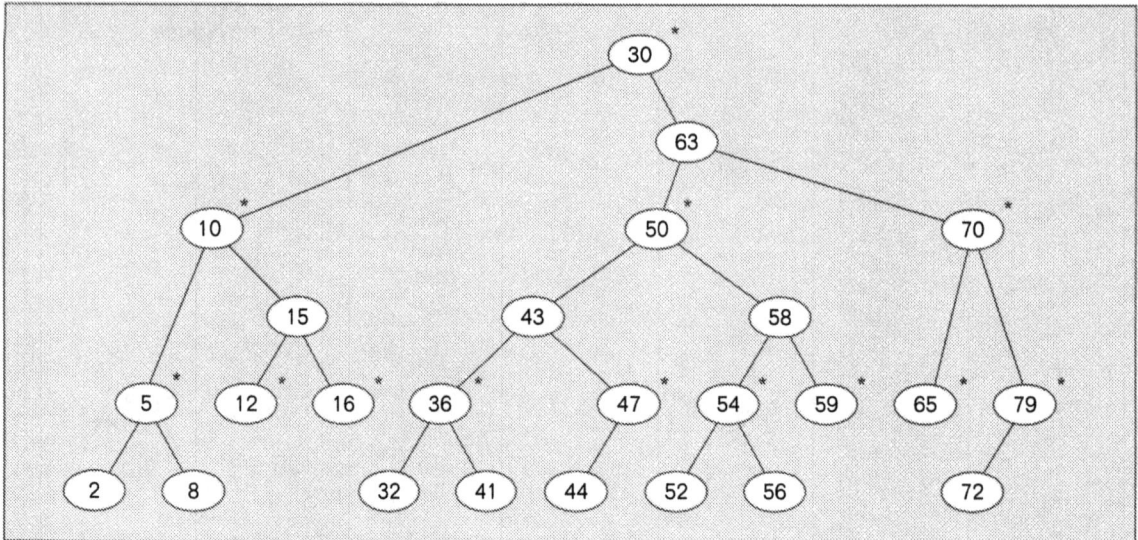

Figure 9.10 A Red/Black Tree Representation of the 2-3-4 Tree from Figure 9.8 (* denotes a Black node)

Red/Black trees may not be balanced, but they model 2-3-4 trees, which *are* balanced. 2-3-4 trees may be no better than some binary search trees, but even in such circumstances, we know that search times must have $O(\log_2 N)$. Search paths in Red/Black trees may be twice as long as those in 2-3-4 trees, as each 2-3-4 node may translate to a two-level structure in a Red/Black. However, in the worst possible case, this would only double the search times in a Red/Black tree, and the result would still be $O(\log_2 N)$.

Insertion and deletion in 2-3 trees or B-trees may require traversing from the root down to a leaf and then propagating back up the tree to the root, but the order is still $\log_K N$ for a multi-way search tree with k keys in each node.

Application: Files

Multi-way search trees have two important properties that make them particularly useful. Such trees are balanced (or reasonably so), ensuring that search times are logarithmic. In addition, the nodes for such trees can contain many values.

The balanced property makes multi-way trees useful for any application requiring searching, although we may prefer binary search trees for many applications because they are relatively simple to code.

However, when applications require searching for data within files, B-trees and B^+-trees can be particularly helpful. In accessing file data, most time is spent finding a data item and reading it into a buffer. Once the first item is obtained, successive items can be read fairly quickly until the buffer is full.

Now suppose we store a tree as a random-access file of records, with an index giving the location of the next record within the file. Due to the time required to read a buffer, searching in this context can be most efficient if we minimize the number of buffers of material that we must read. Processing a buffer can be done quickly, for once the buffer is read, work can be done entirely within main memory.

To minimize disk accesses to a tree structure, we store several pieces of data within each node so that each node is the size of the buffer. If we can store 5, 10, or 20 data items within a node, then we can process all of those data with a single disk access. For searching, this suggests storing data in a B-tree of order m, where m is the largest size possible to allow the entire node to fit inside a buffer. With a large size m, many data items can be stored in relatively few levels of the tree. Access for each item requires only a search from the root, and few tree levels ensure few disk accesses to find each item.

Similarly, B^+-trees are frequently used for indexing large files. The size of the node is often chosen to be the buffer size for the input/output system. Each disk access brings in one node. This may not seem efficient, but think how many records can be accessed with three disk accesses if the node contains 99 keys and the first node is in memory.

The first disk access brings in a node that can access one of 100 indexes. The second disk access gets the appropriate second-level index. The third disk access gets the record.

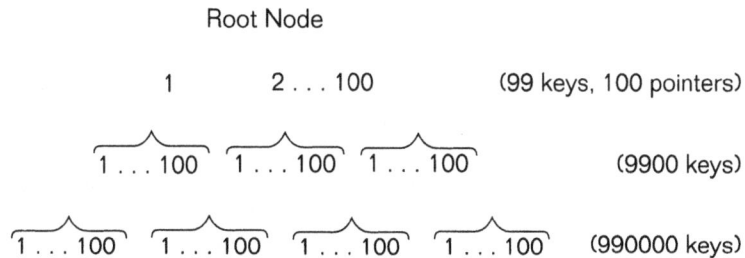

Root Node

| 1 | 2 . . . 100 | (99 keys, 100 pointers) |

| 1 . . . 100   1 . . . 100   1 . . . 100 | (9900 keys) |

| 1 . . . 100   1 . . . 100   1 . . . 100   1 . . . 100 | (990000 keys) |

Using this scheme, we can access one of 999,999 records with three disk accesses. The values within each node are ordered, so we can use a binary search on each index node to enhance efficiency. You do not have to draw pictures and count; the formula that gives the number of nodes in an m-way search tree of height h is

$$\sum_{i=0}^{h-1} m^i = \frac{(m^h - 1)}{(m-1)}$$

Because there is a maximum of m−1 keys in each node, the number of keys in an m-way search tree of height h is

$$\left\lceil \frac{(m^h - 1)}{(m-1)} \right\rceil * (m-1) = m^h - 1$$

The disadvantage, of course, is that the nodes may not be full. For example, if each of the nodes contains the minimum number of keys, the index references only 5201 records.

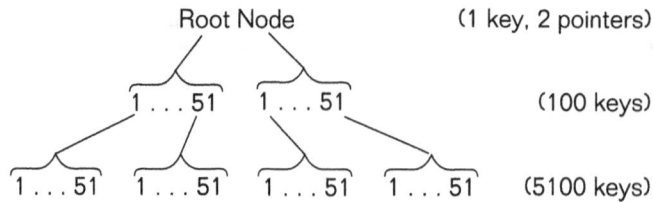

SUMMARY

Multi-way trees are trees in which several data items may be stored within each node. Such trees organize data in a hierarchical structure, generalizing the concept of binary trees.

Multi-way search trees are multi-way trees in which data are ordered so as to allow efficient searching. The values within a node are ordered. The left-most subtree contains all the values in the tree that are less than the first value. The next subtree contains all the values in the tree that are greater than the first value but less than the second value. This property holds for all the values in a node, with the right-most subtree containing all the values greater than the right-most value.

Simple insertion and deletion allow easy maintenance of multi-way search trees, but such trees can become very unbalanced. More sophisticated algorithms and structures ensure that balance is maintained.

2-3 trees are search trees that allow one or two data items to be stored in each node, and each node has 0, 2, or 3 children. All leaves are maintained at the same level.

More generally, B-trees are multi-way search trees that are constructed in such a way that all leaf nodes are on the same level and each node (except the root) contains at least $\lceil M/2 \rceil$ subtrees. 2-3 trees represent a special case—B-trees of order 3. B^+-trees are B-trees in which the internal nodes contain search keys and the leaf nodes contain pointers to the places where the records associated with each key can be found.

2-3-4 trees are search trees with one, two, or three data values in each node and with all leaves at the same level. Insertion into such trees may be done with a single pass downward from the root. In contrast, B-trees may require an initial downward pass, followed by an upward pass. Red/Black trees provide a binary search tree representation of 2-3-4 trees.

Balanced, multi-way search trees are used because searching in balanced trees can be done efficiently and because their nodes may hold many data items. This second property is particularly helpful in organizing file data.

EXERCISES

1. List the properties of a 2-3 tree.

2. List the properties of a B-tree.

3. Distinguish between a multi-way tree and a B-tree.

4. Distinguish between a B-tree and a B^+-tree.

5. Prove that in a reasonably full, multi-way search tree of N nodes with k branches per node, searches must end within $\log_k N$ steps.

6. The text claims that searches in a multi-branch search tree with four branches per node generally are done in half the number of steps as in a binary search tree. Prove this statement, using the result from the previous step and utilizing appropriate properties of logarithms.

7. Consider the definition of a multi-way search tree, and suppose that a node contains two data items that are equal. What, if anything, can you say about the middle subtree of this node? Explain your answer.

8. Consider the simple insertion algorithm for three-way search trees as described in the text. Is it possible to insert a sequence of elements starting with a null tree and following this algorithm, so that some node can contain two data elements while its parent contains only one data element? If so, give an example of such an insertion sequence. If not, explain why.

9. The text presents a simple recursive algorithm for inserting into a three-way search tree. Write an iterative algorithm to perform the same task.

10. Consider the simple deletion algorithm for three-way search trees as described in the text. Is it possible to delete a sequence of elements starting with a completely full and balanced tree and following this algorithm, so that some node can contain two data elements while its parent contains only one data element?

11. Write the axioms for IsIn and Retrieve for a three-way search tree.

12. The text presents a simple recursive algorithm for deleting from a three-way search tree. Write an iterative algorithm to perform the same task.

13. Write the algorithms for IsIn and Retrieve for a three-way search tree.

14. a. Write a procedure that performs an inorder traversal of a three-way search tree.

    b. Write the data from Figure 9.1 in the order corresponding to an inorder traversal.

    c. (For students with some history background) What can you say about the ordering of presidents given in part (b)?

15. a. Build a 2-3 tree by inserting the following letters

    a z s r n b c l p m

    b. Show the 2-3 tree after the deletion of z, n, and l.

16. a. Draw the 2-3 tree that would result from the following insertions.

    10, 20, 30, 15, 25, 35

    b. Draw the 2-3 tree that would result from deleting 25 and then 20.

17. The discussion of the deletion algorithm for 2-3 trees mentions that successor or predecessor values may be considered under certain circumstances.

    a. Suppose all data values in the tree are distinct. Could the deletion algorithm use either the successor or predecessor values in its processing? Explain.

    b. Suppose some data values in a 2-3 tree are not distinct. Could the deletion algorithm use either the successor or predecessor values in its processing? Explain.

18. The detailed discussion of insertion and deletion for 2-3 trees noted that the algorithm development could provide some more general insights into approaches for clarifying algorithms and writing code. Write a paper one to two pages in length describing the problem-solving principles that are illustrated by this development of these algorithms.

19. The discussion of 2-3 trees begins by stating the assumption that all data to be stored in the tree will be distinct.

    a. Consider a tree with the values 'a' and 'a' in the root node and no other nodes, and suppose the value 'd' is to be inserted. Explain why these data cannot be placed within a 2-3 tree.

    b. Consider the 2-3 tree with 'd' in the root, 'a' and 'a' in the left subtree, and 'e' in the right subtree. Which value(s) can be removed from this tree so that the result will still be a search tree? Justify your answer.

20. a. Build a B-tree of degree 5 with the following keys inserted in the order in which they are listed.

    10 20 30 40 50 25 42 44 41 32 38 56 34 58 60 52 54 46

    b. Show the tree after each of the following operations:

    Delete 32
    Insert 62, 65, 66
    Delete 54
    Delete 40

21. Complete the Insertion and Deletion algorithms for B^+-trees.

22. Chapter 7 gave the specifications for an in order traversal of a binary tree. Give the specifications for the traversal of an arbitrary three-way tree.

23. Suppose the numbers 7, 60, 17, 18, and 29 are inserted into the tree in Figure 9.8, following the insertion algorithm for 2-3-4 trees. Show the tree that results.

24. a. Repeat Exercise 23, using a Red/Black representation of the 2-3-4 tree.

    b. Using your experience from part (a) as a guide, write code to implement the algorithm to insert data into Red/Black trees.

25. The text states that difficulties can arise with 2-3-4 trees when duplicate data are allowed.

    a. Consider a 2-3-4 tree T with one node containing three copies of a single data item D. Following the algorithm described in the text, draw a picture of the tree that results when a fourth copy of D is inserted into T.

    b. Does your answer to (a) represent a 2-3-4 tree? Explain.

    c. Is it possible to place four identical data items into a 2-3-4 tree? Explain.

    d. Suppose a single node contains two duplicate values, and suppose the insertion algorithm is used to split that node. Is the resulting tree a 2-3-4 tree in all cases, in some cases, or in no cases? Explain your answer.

Directed Graphs or Digraphs

10

Graphs are mathematical objects. Paralleling the presentation used in Chapter 7, we spend the first part of this chapter looking at the mathematical object and divide graphs naturally into two categories: directed and undirected. After an informal discussion of the general idea of a graph, this chapter focuses on the specification, implementation, and application of *directed* graphs. Chapter 11 continues with a discussion of *undirected* graphs.

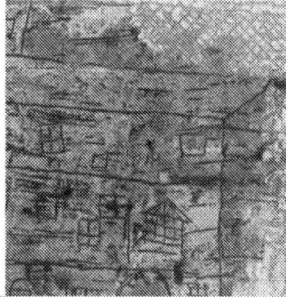

Definitions

Mathematically, a **graph** is a nonempty set of vertices and a set of <vertex, vertex> pairs, called **edges**. We specify a graph as G(V, E), where V is the set of vertices and E is the set of edges. When a discussion involves only one graph, we may refer to sets V and E directly. When several graphs are under consideration, then we write V(G1) or E(G1) to refer to the vertices and edges for the specific graph G1.

> **Graph** A nonempty set of vertices and a set of edges.
>
> **Edge** A designated pair of graph vertices.

This formal notion of a graph may be clarified by three examples.

Example 1: Courses and Prerequisites

We consider computer science and mathematics courses as making up the vertices of a graph and draw an edge from course A to course B if A is a prerequisite for B. Such a graph, based upon some courses at a hypothetical college, is shown in Figure 10.1.

This graph shows that students must take Computer Science I and Calculus I first, as these two courses have no prerequisites themselves but are prerequisites for other courses. Computer Organization must be taken after Computer Science II, but it must precede Operating Systems and Algorithms & Data Types.

Notice that we use directed lines (with arrows) connecting pairs of vertices to represent the edges in this graph. In a tree, there is a designated node—the root—and we commonly draw the root at the top of the paper and indicate the children as lines radiating out below it. In a graph, there is no designated item, so there is no standard way of arranging the vertices of a graph. For example, the graph in Figure 10.1 could just as easily be drawn as shown in Figure 10.2.

While we may find the organization of one of these figures easier to read than the other, both represent the same graph because both have exactly the same vertices and edges.

Example 2: Students in the Same Classes

Now we create a second graph by considering a set of students as the vertices. In this case, we connect two students by an edge if they have at least two classes together. Such a graph (for a very small student body) is shown in Figure 10.3. Because the relationship of being in a class together is symmetric, we can draw the graph with arrows going both ways (part (a) of the figure) or with no arrows at all (part (b)).

In this graph, V is the set {Sarah, Susy, Chris, Judy, June, Phil, Bobby, Maricarmen} and E is the set of edges {(Susy, Chris), (Judy, Phil), (Bobby, Maricarmen)}. Also, from this diagram, we can conclude that Bobby and Maricarmen have at least two classes together, while June sees different students in every one of her classes or is the only one in each of her classes.

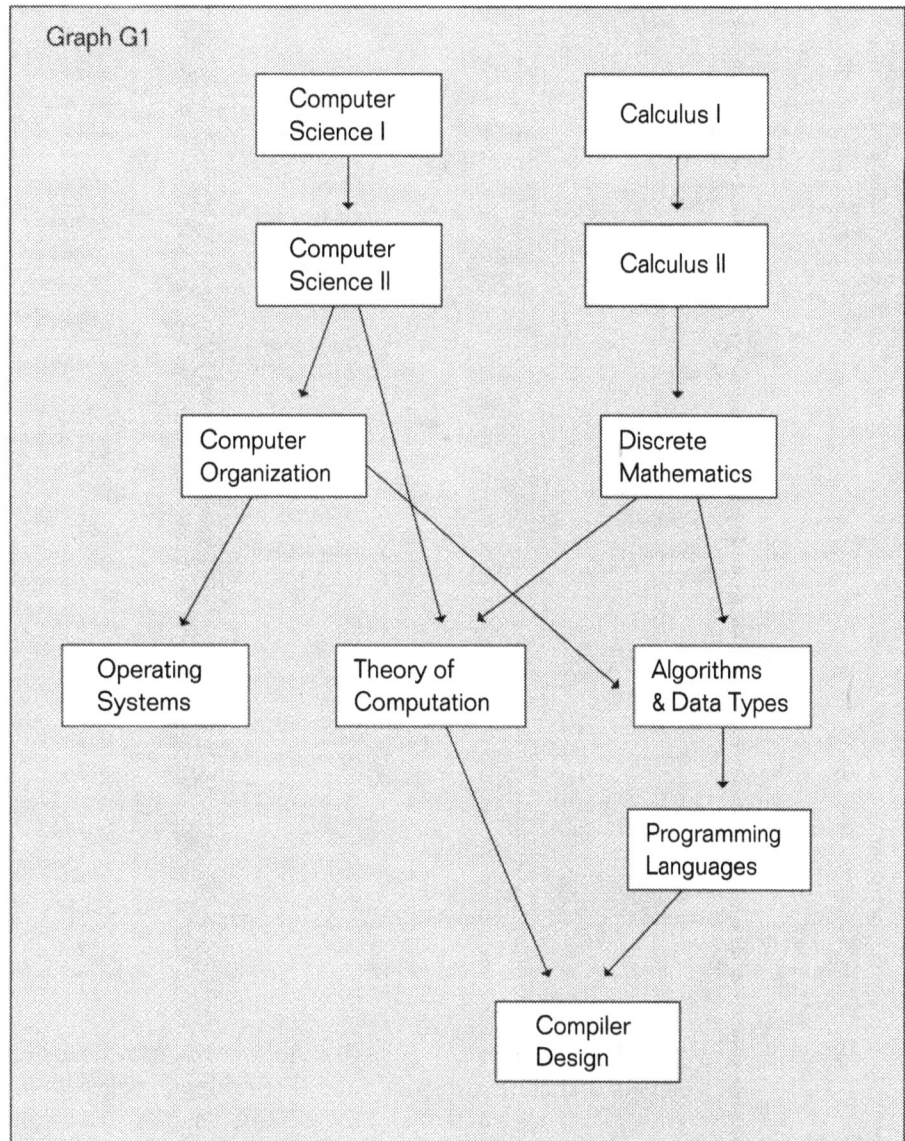

Figure 10.1 Some Courses and Prerequisites

Example 3: Maps

As a third example, we might consider geographical locations as the vertices of a graph. Roads connecting these locations are then interpreted as graph edges. With this interpretation, many road maps may be considered graphs.

The road-map example becomes more complex, however, when we allow the possibility that some streets may be one-way and some may be two-way. Such a

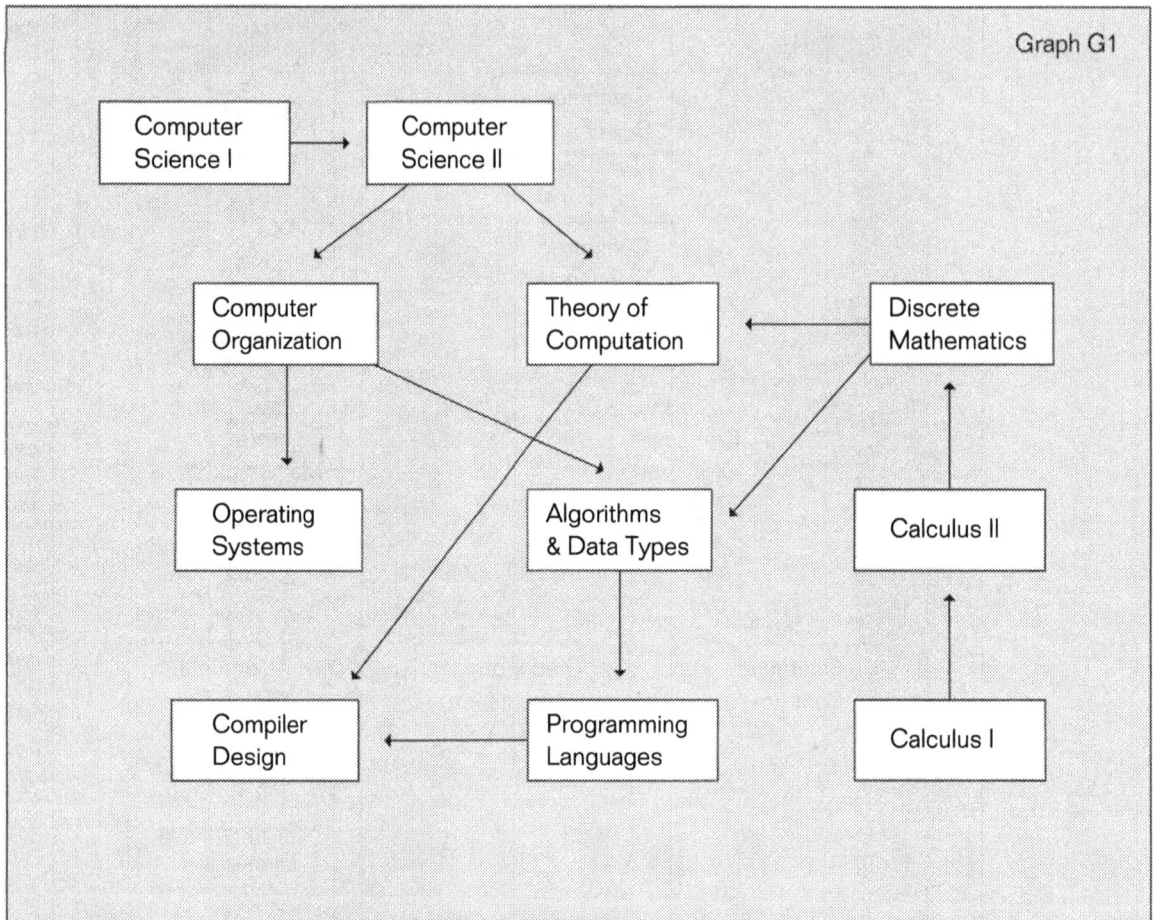

Figure 10.2 Same Courses and Prerequisites as in Figure 10.1, Same Graph, Different Layout

situation is shown in Figure 10.4. Edges with arrowheads on both ends indicate streets that allow two-way travel. For example, edges go in both directions between the Supermarket and the Library. The town also contains some one-way streets. Following one-way streets, we could go from the Police Station to the Donut Shop to the Drug Store to the Post Office to the Clothing Store and back to the Donut Shop, but no part of this route allows travel in the other direction.

When direction matters only sometimes, we need a way to specify which edges go in both directions and which go in only one direction. Figure 10.4 shows one way to illustrate this situation graphically, using double-ended and single-ended arrows. A second approach is shown in Figure 10.5, where the same small town is considered. In Figure 10.5, each edge has a single direction, and we show two edges (one in each direction) in those cases where one can travel along a road in either direction.

This example illustrates the need to distinguish between two types of graphs: undirected and directed.

Graph G2

a) Drawn with arrows in both directions

b) Drawn without arrows

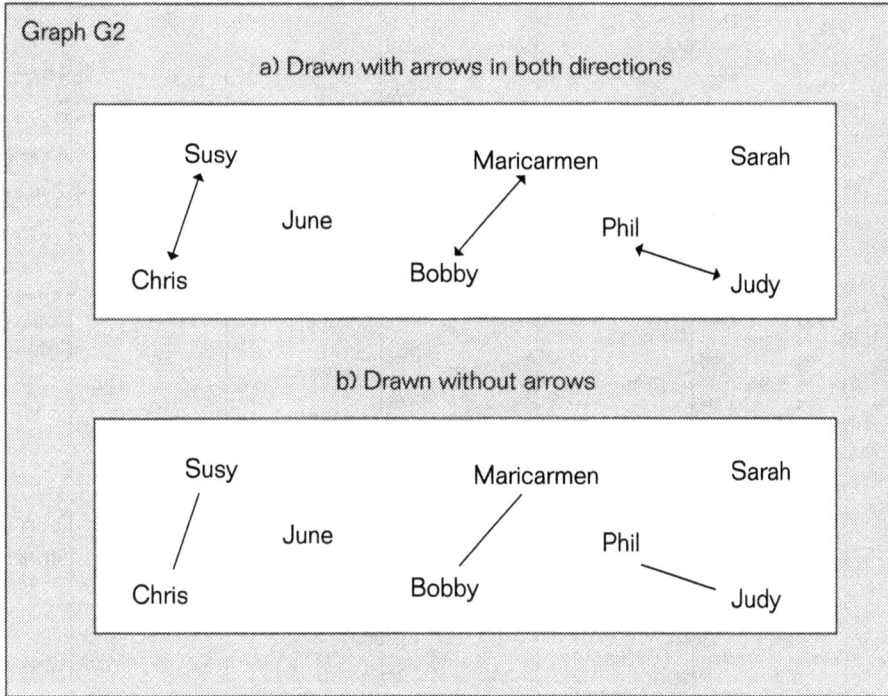

Figure 10.3   Students Sharing Two or More Classes

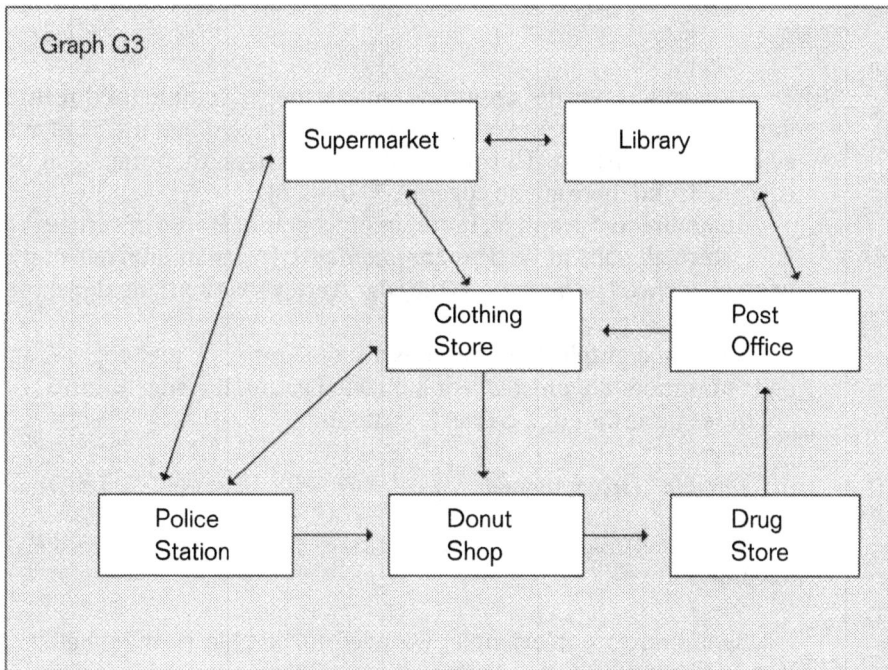

Graph G3

Figure 10.4   Layout of a Small Town

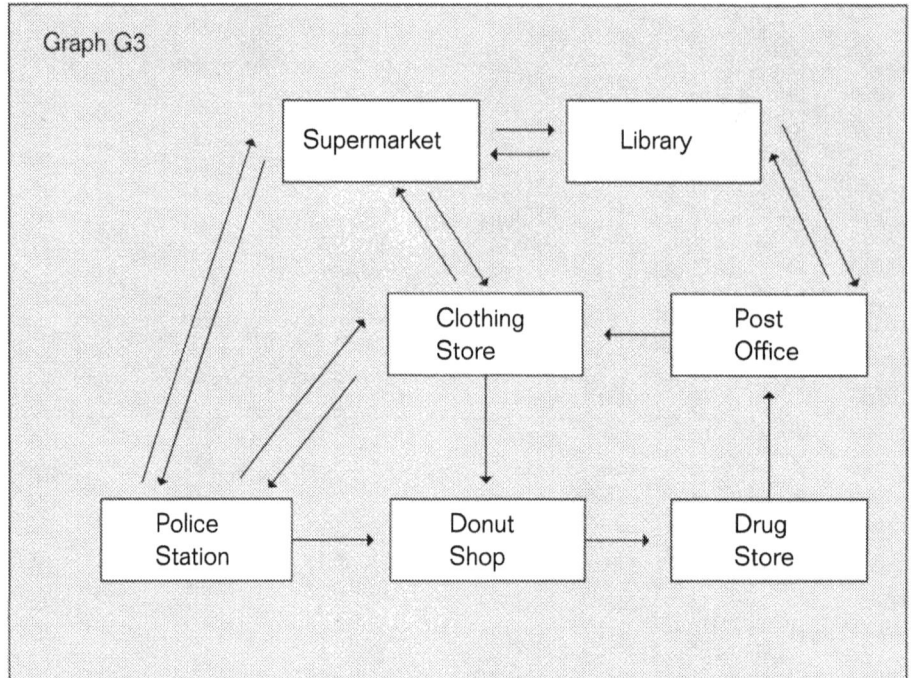

Figure 10.5 Layout of a Small Town Using Unidirectional Edges

Throughout our discussion, we follow the commonly used restrictions that duplicate edges between vertices are not allowed and that the head and tail of an edge must be distinct. Thus if A and B are vertices, then there can only be one edge (A, B) and there are no edges (A, A) or (B, B).

An **undirected graph** or, more simply, a **graph**, is a set of vertices V and edges E, in which all pairs of vertices are *unordered*. For an undirected graph, the edge (vertex1, vertex2) is the same as the edge (vertex2, vertex1); no direction is implied in the edge.

A **directed graph**, or **digraph**, is a set of vertices V and edges E, in which all pairs of vertices are *ordered*. For a directed graph, the edge <vertex1, vertex2> is not the same as the edge <vertex2, vertex1>.

> **Directed Graph** or **Digraph** A graph where edges have a specified direction.
>
> **Undirected Graph** or **Graph** A graph where all edges go in both directions between vertices.

Returning to our example, we need to be able to tell whether the graph that is being specified in written form is directed or not. If there is an edge <Supermarket, Library>, then we must know if the edge <Library, Supermarket> is automatically present or only present only if it is specified explicitly. To clarify such situations, we use the convention that directed edges are shown in angle brackets, while undirected edges are shown in parentheses. When drawing graphs, we use arrows for directed graphs and no arrows for nondirected graphs (see Figure 10.3(b)). Thus, for our directed graphs in Figures 10.4 and 10.5, we have the following specification.[1]

V(G3) = {Supermarket, Library, Clothing Store, Post Office, Police Station, Donut Shop, Drug Store}

E(G3) = {<Supermarket, Library>, <Library, Supermarket>,
      <Library, Post Office>, <Post Office, Library>,
      <Clothing Store, Supermarket>, <Supermarket, Clothing Store>,
      <Supermarket, Police Station>, <Police Station, Supermarket>,
      <Police Station, Clothing Store>, <Clothing Store, Police Station>,
      <Police Station, Donut Shop>, <Donut Shop, Drug Store>,
      <Drug Store, Post Office>, <Clothing Store, Donut Shop>,
      <Post Office, Clothing Store>}

These examples illustrate that directed and undirected graphs arise in a wide variety of applications. In the following discussion concerning the specification, implementation, and application of graphs, we find some additional terminology useful. Most of the following definitions apply to both directed and undirected graphs.

A *complete* graph is a graph that contains the maximum number of edges; that is, every vertex is connected to every other vertex by an edge. In an undirected graph, there are $N(N - 1)/2$ edges in a complete graph, where N is the number of vertices; that is, the number of unordered, distinct pairs of N objects is $N(N - 1)/2$. The number of edges in a complete, directed graph of N vertices is $N(N - 1)$.

The following definitions apply to any type of graph with vertices V and edges E, and we use graph G2 and the following graph G4 to clarify the various terms introduced.

V(G4) = {Sarah, Susy, Chris, Judy, June, Phil, Bobby, Maricarmen}
E(G4) = {<Judy, June>, <June, Bobby>, <Bobby, Susy>, <Susy, Sarah>}

In graph G4, the vertices correspond to various people we know, and an edge is drawn from one person to another if we know that the first is (just a little) older than the second. (Because we do not know the ages of all of our friends, there are no edges connecting some people.) A picture of this simple graph is shown in Figure 10.6.

If (vertex1, vertex2) is in E(G), we say that vertex1, vertex2 are *adjacent* and that the edge (vertex1, vertex2) is *incident on* vertices vertex1 and vertex2. If <vertex1, vertex2> is in E(G), vertex1 is *adjacent to* vertex2 and vertex2 is *adjacent from* vertex1 and the edge <vertex1, vertex2> is *incident on* vertex1 and vertex2.

---

[1] None of our examples has had an edge from a vertex to itself, because this is normally not the case. If such an edge is appropriate, we explicitly say so.

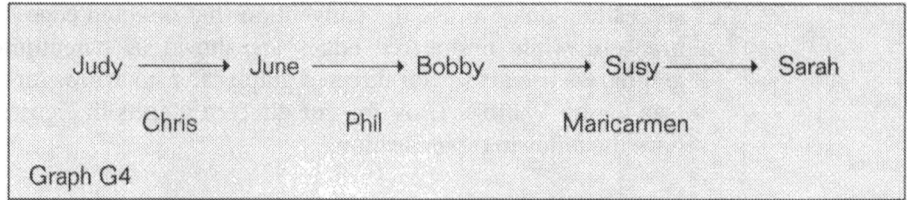

Figure 10.6 People and Decreasing Seniority (when known)

Susy and Chris are adjacent in the graph G2, and <Susy, Sarah> is incident on Susy and Sarah. Judy is adjacent to June in G4, Sarah is adjacent from Susy in G4, and <Susy, Sarah> is incident on Susy and Sarah in G4.

Given the edge <vertex1, vertex2>, vertex1 is the **tail** of the edge and vertex2 is the *head* of the edge. The *degree* of a vertex is the number of edges incident upon it. In a directed graph, the **in-degree** of a vertex is the number of edges in which the vertex is a head, and the **out-degree** is the number of edges in which the vertex is a tail.

> **In-degree** The number of vertices adjacent *to* a vertex.
>
> **Out-degree** The number of vertices adjacent *from* a vertex.

Judy is the tail of the edge <Judy, June>, and June is the head of the edge <Judy, June>. Even if the graph is not directed, for convenience we sometimes call Susy the tail and Chris the head in the edge (Susy, Chris). However, because the undirected edge (Susy, Chris) is the same as (Chris, Susy), we also could call Chris the tail and Susy the head if we wanted to think of the edge as going from Chris to Susy.

A **path** from vertex1 to vertex2 is a sequence of edges, where the head of one edge is the tail of the next edge in the sequence. A *simple path* is a path where all the vertices are different except possibly the first and the last. A *cycle* is a path of at least two distinct edges starting and ending at the same vertex. Because a cycle has at least two distinct edges, a cycle in an undirected graph must have at least three vertices, but a cycle in a directed graph needs only two vertices. A graph that contains no cycles is called *acyclic*. The **path length** is the number of edges in the path.

> **Path** A sequence of edges, where the head of one edge is the tail of the next.
>
> **Path length** The number of edges in the path.

In our example, a simple path exists from Judy to Sarah in G4:

Judy → June → Bobby → Susy→ Sarah

The graph G5 specified on the next page and shown in Figure 10.7 demonstrates a simple path whose first and last vertices are the same.

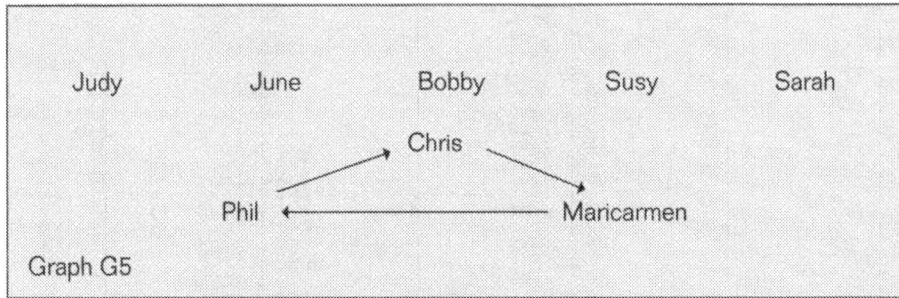

Figure 10.7 Graph with a Simple Path

V(G5) = {Sarah, Susy, Chris, Judy, June, Phil, Bobby, Maricarmen}
E(G5) = {<Phil, Chris>, <Maricarmen, Phil>, <Chris, Maricarmen>)

A path exists from Phil to Chris to Maricarmen, and back to Phil. An interpretation of the edges in G5 might be, "has lent money to." Here, each of three people may have made loans to each other at various times. (If these loans were for the same amount, then all loans may be resolved if the three simply agree to forgive each other's loans. Alternatively, if any borrower repaid the loan, that money might be used to repay other loans, and the money would find its way back to its initial owner.)

A *strongly connected* graph is a directed graph in which a path exists between each pair of vertices. A *connected* graph is an undirected graph in which a path exists between each pair of vertices.

A *traversal* of a graph is a systematic visit to all of the vertices in a graph.

A *subgraph* of G is a graph G′ in which the vertices in G′ are also in G and the edges in G′ are also in G; that is, V(G′) ⊆ V(G) and E(G′) ⊆ E(G). Subgraphs are *disjoint* if they have no vertices in common.

We review all of these definitions by considering the following graphs, which are drawn in Figure 10.8.

```
G6(V,E):
   V(G6) = {A, B, C, D, E, F, G}
   E(G6) = {(A,B),(A,D),(A,G),(B,C),(C,A),(F,D),(G,E)}
G7(V(G6),E)
   E(G7) = {<A,B>,<A,C>,<B,D>,<B,E>,<C,F>,<F,G>}
G8(V(G6),E)
   E(G8) = {<A,B>,<B,C>,<C,A>,<D,E>,<E,D>,<D,F>,<F,D>,<F,E>,<E,F>}
```

G6 is an undirected graph. It is connected because any of the vertices can be reached from any other vertex. The degree of vertex A is 4; the degree of G, D, C, and B is 2; and the degree of E and F is 1. The edge(A,C) is incident on A and C; edges (D,F) and (G,E) are incident on D and F, and G and E, respectively; vertices A and C, D and F are adjacent, as are G and E. There is a cycle from A to B to C to A.

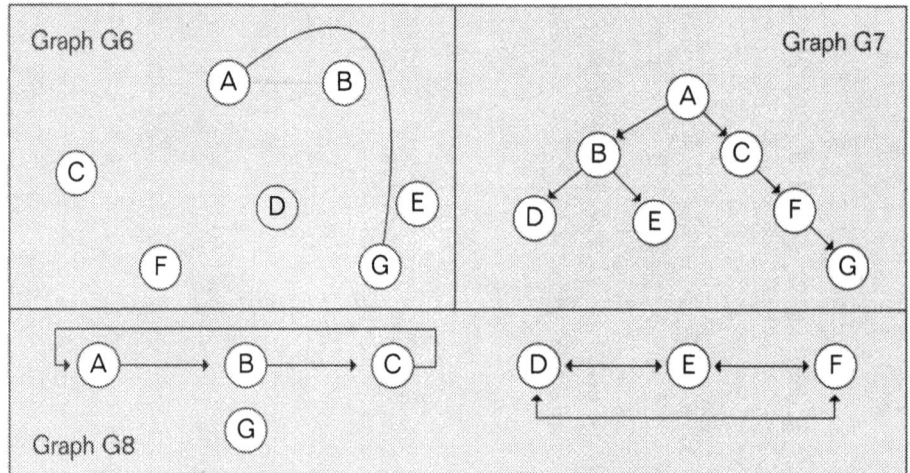

Figure 10.8 Some Directed and Undirected Graphs

G7 is a directed, acyclic graph. The in-degree of A is 0; the in-degree of each of the other nodes is 1. G7 looks like a binary tree. In fact, a binary tree is an acyclic, directed graph where the in-degree of one vertex is 0, the in-degree of all other vertices is 1, and the out-degree is 0, 1, or 2.

G8 is a directed graph made up of three disjoint subgraphs. The subgraph made up of vertices A, B, and C contains a cycle. The in-degree and out-degree of each vertex in this subgraph is 1. Vertex A is adjacent to B, B is adjacent to C, and B is adjacent to A. B is adjacent from A, C is adjacent from B, and A is adjacent from C.

The subgraph of G8, made up of the vertices D, E, and F, is complete; that is, there are N*(N − 1) = (3*2) edges. This subgraph is also strongly connected. Any complete directed graph is also strongly connected. The in-degree and out-degree of each vertex in this subgraph is 2. D is adjacent to and from E, E is adjacent to and from D, E is adjacent to and from F, F is adjacent to and from E, F is adjacent to and from D, and D is adjacent to and from F. The third subgraph of G8 is made up of the single element G. A graph is a nonempty set of vertices and a set of edges. The single vertex G is a graph in which the set of edges is empty.

Before we look at the abstract data type that models the mathematical object, we should mention one more point about graphs. There are times when an application requires information to be attached to either the vertices or the edges. If either the vertices or the edges have information associated with them, the graph is called a **labeled graph**. If the information is numeric, the graph is called a **weighted graph**. G9, shown in Figure 10.9, is a labeled graph in which the vertices are cities, and the labels on the graph represent the mileage between the cities.

> G9(V,E)
>   V(G9) = {Austin, Houston, SanAntonio, Waco, Dallas}
>   E(G9) = {(Austin, Houston, 163), (Austin, SanAntonio, 78),
>   (Austin, Waco, 100), (Austin, Dallas, 200)}

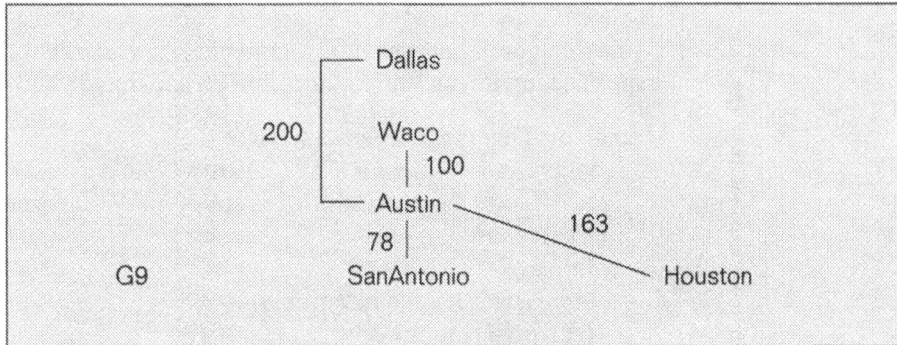

Figure 10.9 A Weighted Graph with Cities and Distances

> **Labeled graph** A directed or undirected graph, where *information* is attached to either the vertices or the edges.
>
> **Weighted graph** A directed or undirected graph where *numbers* are associated with each edge.

For the remainder of this chapter, we restrict our attention to directed graphs. We return to undirected graphs in Chapter 11. Directed graphs are often called digraphs, and throughout the rest of this book, we use the two terms interchangeably.

Specification

Mathematically, a directed graph is a nonempty set of vertices and a set of edges. All the examples in the previous section began with a graph as a given. If we want to talk about a graph where the edges are different, we just create a new digraph with a different set of edges. In defining an abstract data type, however, it can be more useful to specify a growing, changing structure. When we want to view the same structure with a few changes, we do not simply begin again. Instead, we must specify how to make changes and what the changes mean.

In the axiomatic specification, we must specify both the set of vertices and the set of edges. While many of the directed graph ADT operations simply store or retrieve vertex or edge information, a few do more and deserve some comment. First, we think of the Create operation as providing the appropriate framework for future processing of a digraph. Thus, Create provides a structure with no vertices and no edges, just as the Create operations we have defined for previous ADTs do. This specification, therefore, allows the ADT digraph to have an empty set of vertices, while the mathematical notion normally requires the set of vertices to be nonempty. Second, our definition for the axiom for deleting a vertex from the digraph also deletes all the edges for which the vertex is either a head or a tail.

Here is the specification for the Weighted DigraphADT. We have chosen to specify the digraph with weights because one of the observer functions that we introduce later is defined on weighted digraphs. An unweighted digraph can always be thought of as a weighted digraph in which all the weights are 1. We leave the specification for the Unweighted Digraph and the Labeled Digraph as exercises.

structure Digraph (of (Vertices, Edges))
      where   Vertices is a Set (of VertexType) and
                Edges is a Set (of <VertexType, VertexType, WeightType>)
interface
    Create $\rightarrow$ Digraph
    StoreVertex (Digraph, VertexType) $\rightarrow$ Digraph
    IsEmpty(Digraph) $\rightarrow$ Boolean
    DelVertex (Digraph, VertexType) $\rightarrow$ Digraph
    StoreEdge(Digraph, VertexType, VertexType, WeightType) $\rightarrow$ Digraph
    DelEdge(Digraph, VertexType, VertexType) $\rightarrow$ Digraph
    IsVertex(Digraph, VertexType) $\rightarrow$ Boolean
end

Because Vertices and Edges are sets, the Set ADT operations Create, Store, IsIn, Delete, IsEmpty, Members, and Card from Chapter 4 can be applied to them. Remember that the axioms for the Set ADT define a family of sets, one for each ItemType. ItemType for the set of vertices is VertexType; ItemType for the set of Edges is the ordered triple <VertexType, VertexType, WeightType>.

Because a digraph is an ordered pair of sets, we can express the digraph that is returned by each operation as the pair [Vertices, Edges]. Consequently, the notation can become quite complex, so we put the returned pairs of sets within square brackets. To express the semantics of deleting a vertex, we are going to need an additional axiom DeleteAll, which takes a set of edges and a vertex and removes all the edges for which the vertex is either a head or a tail.

DeleteAll(Edges, VertexType) $\rightarrow$ Edges

axioms for all v1, v2, v3, v4 in VertexType, w in WeightType, V(G) in Vertices, E(G) in Edges, and G in Digraph, let

Create = [Create(V(G)) , Create(E(G))]

StoreVertex (G, V$_1$) = [Store(V(G), V$_1$), E(G)]

StoreEdge(G, v1, v2, w) =
    IF IsVertex(V(G), v1) AND IsVertex(V(G), v2)
        THEN   [V(G), [Store(E(G), v1, v2, w)]]
        ELSE   Error

DelVertex(G, v1) = [Delete(V(G), v1), DeleteAll(E(G), v1)]

DeleteAll(Create, v1) = Create
DeleteAll(Store(E(G), v2, v3, w), v1) =
    IF (v2 = v1) OR (v3 = v1)
        THEN   DeleteAll(G, v1)
        ELSE   Store(DeleteAll(G, v1), v2, v3, w)
    END IF;

IsEmpty(G) = IsEmpty(V(G))

IsVertex(G, v1) = IsIn(V(G), i1)

In addition to the operations required to build a directed graph, there are several operations that we need when processing information represented in the graph structure. Therefore, we augment our DigraphADT with the following operations:

NumberOfVertices(Digraph)   → Integer
ListOfVertices(Digraph)   → List
FromEdges(Digraph, VertexType)   → Queue
where
    ItemType = VertexType (for the List)
    ItemType = Edges (for the Queue)

NumberOfVertices is an observer operation. ListOfVertices and FromEdges are iterators. ListOfVertices returns a list of vertices allowing us to iterate through the set of vertices, and FromEdges returns a queue of edges allowing us to iterate through the edges for which a specific vertex is a tail.

NumberOfVertices(Digraph) = Card(V(G))

ListOfVertices (Digraph, List) = Members(V(G), List)

FromEdges((V(G), Create), v1) = Create
FromEdges(StoreEdge(G, v2, v3, w), v1) =
    IF v1 = v2
        THEN   Enque(FromEdges(G, v1), v2, v3, w)
        ELSE   FromEdges(G, v1)
    END IF

All of the previous abstract data types that we have studied are structures into which we store information and from which we retrieve information. Each application needs the information organized and returned in the particular way in which the ADT provides it. Digraphs are different. Typically, general questions are asked about the information represented in a digraph. The answers are provided by established digraph algorithms.

Each of these algorithms provides a kind of observer function defined on the ADT Digraph. These observer functions are different from the ones we have used before, which provide auxiliary functions such as iterators. These observers actually apply an algorithm that processes the information represented in the digraph. Some important digraph algorithms (observer functions) for directed graphs are described below. In each case, the output type of the observer is any linear list, that has been specified previously as the ADT List. This output type is shown in parentheses beside the function.

Traversals (ADT List): Return a list of those vertices that may be encountered by using the edges of the digraph as a means of moving from one vertex to another. (List all the places I can get to in a direct flight.) Sometimes traversals are called searches.

Single-Source Shortest Path (ADT List): Return a list of vertices and costs that represents the minimum cost path from one vertex to each of the other vertices. (What is the cheapest way to get from here to all the other places represented in the digraph?)

Topological Sort (ADT List): Return a list of vertices in an acyclic directed graph such that, if the path from vertex$_i$ to vertex$_j$ exists in the digraph, then vertex$_i$ comes before vertex$_j$ in the list. (Give me a list of the subcontractors, ordered so that if subcontractors A and B are interrelated, and if A comes before B in the list, then A's work must be completed before B's can begin.)

Hamiltonian Circuit (ADT List): Return a list of all vertices that represents a cycle and contains each vertex exactly once, except that the cycle begins and ends at the same vertex. (Give me a list of the cities in my territory that I must visit without backtracking through a city I have already visited.)

Additional, frequently-used algorithms are covered in Chapter 11 in the context of undirected graphs.

Implementation

We could implement the ADT digraph exactly as it is specified, that is, as a pair of sets. Because we do not have a limit on the number of vertices or the number of edges, we would have to use the implicit method of implementing the sets, that is, keep a list of the vertices and a list of the edges. The size factor for Vertices is the number of vertices; the size factor for Edges is the number of edges. The operations needed to build and alter the digraph would be reasonable using this implementation, but several of the special digraph observer operations would require excessive times using this implementation. For example, a simple traversal would be O(Card(V(G))Card(E(G)) because we would have to search the list of edges to determine which vertex to visit next.

There are two classic ways of representing digraphs: an adjacency matrix and adjacency lists. Both of these implementations are better than keeping the digraph as a list of vertices and a list of edges.

An *adjacency matrix* is a square, two-dimensional array with one row and one column for each vertex in the directed graph. An entry in row i and column j is 1 if there is an edge from the vertex corresponding to row i to the vertex corresponding to column j, and is 0 otherwise. (If the directed graph is weighted, then the entry 1 is replaced by the weight.)

An *adjacency list* is a collection of lists of vertices in which each list contains those vertices (with weights, if applicable) that are adjacent from a specified vertex.

Adjacency Matrix

Because the definition of an adjacency matrix may seem rather abstract, we first consider an example, the graph of Figures 10.4 and 10.5. Earlier in the chapter, we specified this digraph as follows:

V(G3) = {Supermarket, Library, Clothing Store, Post Office, Police Station, Donut Shop, Drug Store}

E(G3) = {<Supermarket, Library>, <Library, Supermarket>,
<Library, Post Office>, <Post Office, Library>,
<Clothing Store, Supermarket>, <Supermarket, Clothing Store>,
<Supermarket, Police Station>, <Police Station, Supermarket>,
<Police Station, Clothing Store>, <Clothing Store, Police Station>,
<Police Station, Donut Shop>, <Donut Shop, Drug Store>,
<Drug Store, Post Office>, <Clothing Store, Donut Shop>,
<Post Office, Clothing Store>}

In considering an adjacency matrix for this directed graph, we first number the vertices based upon some ordering of the vertices. For this example, we might number the vertices as follows:

1. Supermarket
2. Library
3. Clothing Store
4. Post Office
5. Police Station
6. Donut Shop
7. Drug Store

With this numbering, we construct a matrix in an array (AdjArray) that specifies the edges of our digraph. Specifically, the first edge given above is <Supermarket, Library>. In our ordering, Supermarket was numbered 1 and Library was numbered 2, so we record this edge by making an entry in row 1 column 2 of our array, AdjArray[1,2]. In some applications, it may be enough simply to place a Boolean value True in this array position, indicating that an edge exists. However, as we shall see shortly, the adjacency matrix has additional significance if we place the number 1 in such entries.

Looking at our digraph, we observe that there is no edge from the Library (vertex 2) to the Clothing Store (vertex 3), so we place the value 0 in row 2, column 3 (AdjArray[2,3] = 0). Continuing our examination of the edges in the digraph, we find an edge from the Drug Store (vertex 7) to the Post Office (vertex 4), so AdjArray (7,4) = 1. On the other hand, there is no edge from the Post Office to the Drug Store, so AdjArray(4,7) = 0. Following this approach for the rest of the adjacency matrix gives the following result.

Columns

(Heads)

(To)

		[1]	[2]	[3]	[4]	[5]	[6]	[7]
	[1]	0	1	1	0	1	0	0
	[2]	1	0	0	1	0	0	0
Rows	[3]	1	0	0	0	1	0	0
(Tails)	[4]	0	1	1	0	0	0	0
(From)	[5]	1	0	1	0	0	1	0
	[6]	0	0	0	0	0	0	1
	[7]	0	0	0	1	0	0	0

As noted previously, one way of interpreting the entries in this matrix is to say that AdjArray[i,j] = 1 if there is an edge from vertex i to vertex j and AdjArray[i, j] = 0 if there is no such edge. From this perspective, 1 corresponds to True and 0 to False. Extending this perspective slightly in the case when a digraph is labeled, we might specify that AdjArray[Tail, Head] should contain the label (or weight) for each edge.

Theoretical Results

Another way of viewing the entries of an adjacency matrix is to note that each entry of the AdjArray indicates the number of paths of length 1 from one vertex to another. Any path of length 1 must be a path with a single edge, so such paths correspond exactly to the edges in a digraph. Thus, when AdjArray[i, j] is 1, we may conclude that there is exactly one path of length 1 from vertex i to vertex j. When AdjArray[i, j] is 0, no such paths exist.

With this observation concerning the adjacency matrix itself, it is natural to ask if the adjacency matrix also can help us find out about paths of other lengths between vertices. As a special case, we note that any adjacency matrix is square; that is, the number of rows equals the number of columns. Thus, it is always possible to multiply an adjacency matrix by itself. For example, suppose matrix A is the adjacency matrix from Figures 10.4 and 10.5, which we have already computed as

$$
A = \begin{vmatrix}
0 & 1 & 1 & 0 & 1 & 0 & 0 \\
1 & 0 & 0 & 1 & 0 & 0 & 0 \\
1 & 0 & 0 & 0 & 1 & 0 & 0 \\
0 & 1 & 1 & 0 & 0 & 0 & 0 \\
1 & 0 & 1 & 0 & 0 & 1 & 0 \\
0 & 0 & 0 & 0 & 0 & 0 & 1 \\
0 & 0 & 0 & 1 & 0 & 0 & 0
\end{vmatrix}
$$

From this, we may compute A*A, or A^2, as the following matrix:

$$A^2 = \begin{vmatrix} 3 & 0 & 1 & 1 & 1 & 1 & 0 \\ 0 & 2 & 2 & 0 & 1 & 0 & 0 \\ 1 & 1 & 2 & 0 & 1 & 1 & 0 \\ 2 & 0 & 0 & 1 & 1 & 0 & 0 \\ 1 & 1 & 1 & 0 & 2 & 0 & 1 \\ 0 & 0 & 0 & 1 & 0 & 0 & 0 \\ 0 & 1 & 1 & 0 & 0 & 0 & 0 \end{vmatrix}$$

Again, this is a square matrix with the same dimensions as A. Thus, if we want to, we can continue this multiplication to produce $A*A*A = A^3$, $A*A*A*A = A^4$, and so on. Stated recursively, $A^1 = A$, and $A^n = A*A^{n-1}$ for $n > 1$.

Powers of the Adjacency Matrix We now return to the question of counting paths of a specified length from one vertex to another. In our example from Figures 10.4 and 10.5, we may wonder how many paths of length 2 there are starting at the Post Office and ending at the Supermarket. Looking at the figures, we see that there are two: Post Office to Clothing Store to Supermarket and Post Office to Library to Supermarket. Similarly, we could ask how many paths of length 2 there are starting and ending at the Supermarket. In this situation, we would go from the Supermarket to somewhere else and back again. Looking at the figures again, we see that the intermediate point on the path could be the Library, the Clothing Store, or the Police Station, so there are three such paths.

With these results, we now note that the same entries occur in the matrix A^2 above, that is, in the square of the adjacency matrix. Specifically, the Post Office is vertex 4 and the Supermarket vertex 1, and A^2 [4, 1] is 2, the number of paths of length 2 from one vertex to the other. Similarly, A^2 [1,1] = 3, the number of paths of length 2 from the Supermarket (vertex 1) to itself.

The following result indicates that this situation is not an accident.

> *Theorem*: Let A be an adjacency matrix for a directed graph G with vertices V and edges E. Then, $A^k[i,j]$ gives the number of paths of length k from vertex i to vertex j.

The proof of this result uses mathematical induction and draws upon a careful counting argument together with the definition of matrix multiplication.

Proof. The proof proceeds by mathematical induction on the power k; that is, we first prove that the result is true when $k = 1$. Then we assume that we already know that the result is true for A^k and we prove that the result holds for A^{k+1}, where $k \geq 1$.

Base Case: $k = 1$.

$A^1 = A$, because this is what is meant by the first power of a matrix (or by the first power of any number), and we have already noted that the entries in an adjacency matrix A can be interpreted as the number of paths from one vertex to another. Thus, the result holds trivially for this base case.

Induction Case: Assume the result for A^k and prove that the result holds for A^{k+1}, where $k \geq 1$.

To get a path of length $k + 1$ from vertex i to vertex j, we first must go along a path of length 1 from vertex i to another vertex (say, vertex q) and then we must follow a path of length k from vertex q to our destination, vertex j. This routing is shown in the following figure.

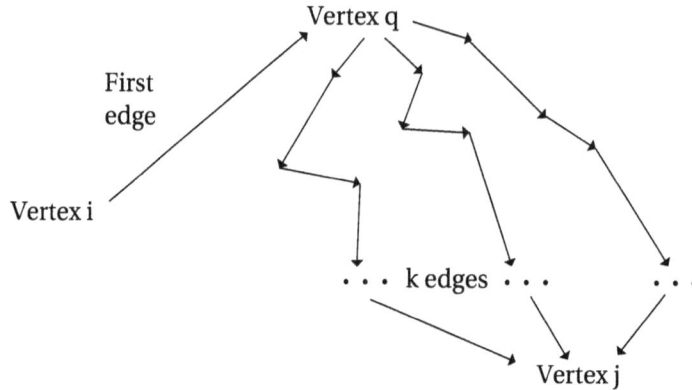

Overall length : k + 1 edges

Next, we count all such paths. For the first step, we pick any edge from vertex i to another vertex, q. Then, we can follow any of the paths of length k from vertex q to vertex j. By our induction hypothesis, we already know that $A^k[q, j]$ is the number of such paths from q to j. Thus, to find the total number of paths of length $k + 1$ from i to j, we simply need to add the appropriate number from each vertex q.

While this idea works fine, we need to be a little careful in our adding, because we can only count the number of paths from vertex q if there is an initial edge from vertex i to vertex q. As a practical matter, therefore, we need to compute the sum

$$\sum A^k[q, j]$$

where the sum is taken over all of those vertices q where there is an edge from i to q. While this sum is correct, it involves some tedium to compute, because we must pick only the relevant vertices q.

As an alternative approach to counting, we could sum over all vertices if we added a fudge factor f(i, q) to each term.

$$\sum f(i, q) * A^k[q, j]$$

Here, f(i, q) is a fudge factor; that is, we want f(i, q) = 1 if there is an edge from vertex i to vertex q, and 0 if not. With this additional factor, we can expand the sum to include all vertices. The vertices connected by edges to q are all counted (using the multiplicative factor 1), and the others are not counted (because f(i, q) is 0 in those cases).

In looking at this sum, however, we already have a name for our fudge factor f(i,q), because that was how we defined the adjacency matrix A! Specifically, A[i, q] is the value f(i, q). Therefore, we conclude that the number of paths from vertex i to vertex j is

$$\sum A[i, q]*A^k[q, j]$$

This is the exact definition of the entry in the ith row and jth column of the matrix product $A*A^k$, or A^{k+1}. To reiterate, the entry $A^{k+1}[i, j]$ is precisely the sum we seek for the number of paths of length k + 1 from vertex i to vertex j. This completes the proof of our theorem.

As a related result, let us consider what might happen if we add an edge from each vertex to itself. With this addition, the digraph of our small town might look like Figure 10.10. This new digraph sometimes is called an *augmented digraph*, a digraph obtained from directed (or undirected) digraph G by adding an edge from each vertex of G to itself.

With this augmented digraph, we can form a corresponding **augmented adjacency matrix**, M. In considering this matrix, all entries are the same as the previ-

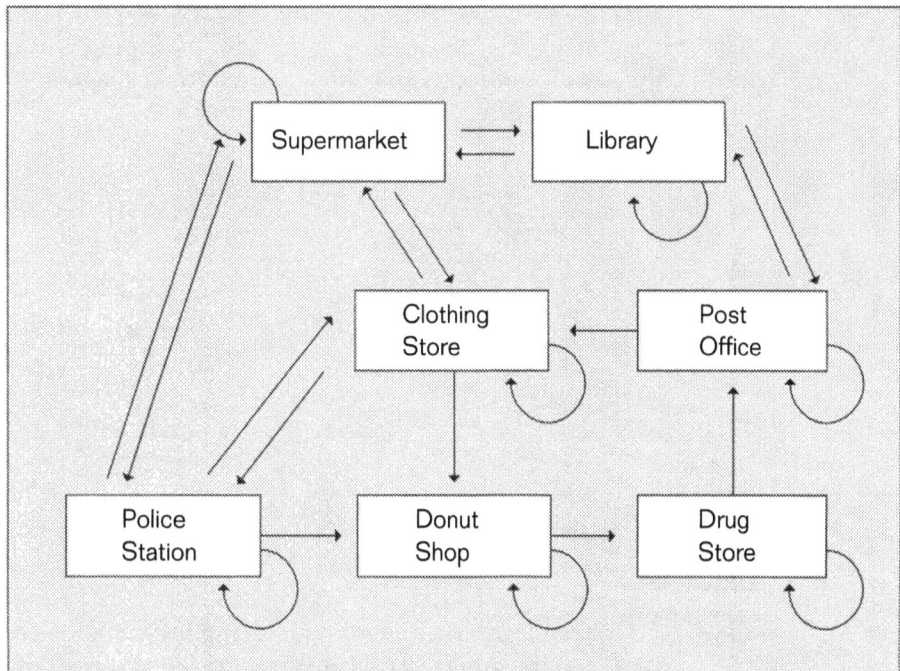

Figure 10.10 Layout of a Small Town Including Edges from Each Vertex to Itself

ous adjacency matrix, except now each vertex has exactly one edge from itself to itself. Thus, M[i,i] is 1 for each vertex i. In our example, therefore, the new matrix is

$$M = \begin{vmatrix} 1 & 1 & 1 & 0 & 1 & 0 & 0 \\ 1 & 1 & 0 & 1 & 0 & 0 & 0 \\ 1 & 0 & 1 & 0 & 1 & 0 & 0 \\ 0 & 1 & 1 & 1 & 0 & 0 & 0 \\ 1 & 0 & 1 & 0 & 1 & 1 & 0 \\ 0 & 0 & 0 & 0 & 0 & 1 & 1 \\ 0 & 0 & 0 & 1 & 0 & 0 & 1 \end{vmatrix}$$

which is just the matrix A shown earlier, with diagonal elements changed from 0 to 1.

> **Augmented adjacency matrix** Matrix obtained from the adjacency matrix for a digraph by changing the 0's on the diagonal to 1's.

Just like the adjacency matrix, this augmented adjacency matrix is square, with the number of rows and the number of columns equal to the number of vertices in the digraph. Thus, we can consider powers of this matrix, just as we did for the original adjacency matrix, and ask what interpretation we can give to the entries in this augmented matrix.

By our previous theorem, the entries of M^k give the precise number of paths from one vertex to another of length k in the augmented digraph. With this new augmented digraph, however, it is possible to follow an edge back to the same vertex where we began. Thus, if we have a path of length k in the augmented digraph, it is possible that some edges in the path do not move us from one vertex to another. Such a situation is shown in the following diagram.

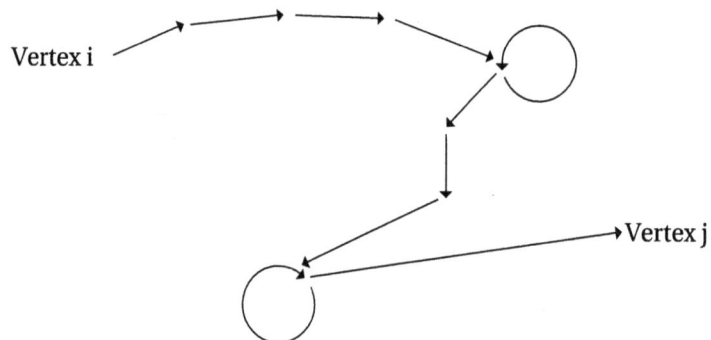

In this diagram, we have a path of length 10, although two of the edges simply leave us at the same place where we started. If we count edges that actually move us to separate vertices, then this path has only eight edges.

More generally, if we have a path of length k made out of edges in the augmented adjacency matrix, we can leave out the circles to obtain a path of the original digraph edges, although the resulting path might be shorter than length k.

Conversely, if we have any path of length k − 1, we can make it into a path of length k by adding a circular edge at any of the vertices on the path. In this way, one path of length k − 1 can lead to several paths of length k.

This discussion shows that several paths of length k can give rise to one path of, perhaps, shorter length based upon the original edges if we leave out any circular edges. If we count these different versions of the same path as being distinct from one another, our previous theorem indicates that the entry $M^k[i,j]$ specifies the number of paths of length k that exist from vertex i to vertex j. If we ignore circular edges, then this number tells us how many paths of length no longer than k are present from vertex i to vertex j, although this number includes the unintended circles. This gives us the following result.

> *Theorem*: Let M be an augmented adjacency matrix for a directed graph G with vertices V and edges E. Then $M^k[i,j]$ gives the number of paths of length ≤ k from vertex i to vertex j when the paths are counted appropriately.

Connectivity and the Adjacency Matrix   We conclude this discussion of the adjacency matrix by applying our previous theoretical results to the question of when a matrix is strongly connected. The definition of a strongly connected, directed graph states that there has to be a path from every vertex to every other vertex.

Let us now suppose that the digraph has n vertices and that we have any path from one vertex i to vertex j. Paths can amble around considerably, so they can be quite long, as illustrated in the following diagram.

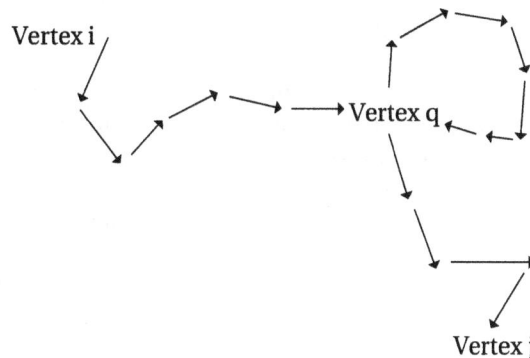

This path starts from vertex i, goes to vertex q, and then returns to vertex q before moving onward to vertex j. If we had wanted to be efficient in our movement from i to j, we could have removed the extra loop in this path that starts and ends at q. The result would have been a shorter path that still went from vertex i to vertex j. Of course, if other vertices had been repeated on this shorter path, we could have removed other loops to obtain a still shorter path.

The above process shows that if we have any path from vertex i to vertex j, we can use it to get a path where no vertex is repeated by simply removing loops that involve the same vertex multiple times. If there are n vertices altogether in our digraph and if there is also a path from vertex i to vertex j, then there must be a path containing no more than n vertices between i and j. Such paths contain no more than $n - 1$ edges.

Putting the various pieces of our discussion together, a directed graph is strongly connected if there is a path from every vertex to every other vertex, and we can always take such a path to contain, at most, $n - 1$ edges. Previously, we found that the number of such paths, appropriately counted, is given by $M^{n-1}[i,j]$. If this number is nonzero, therefore, there must be at least one path between the given vertices. If this number is zero, no such path exists. This gives us the following result.

> *Theorem*: Suppose a directed graph has n vertices, and let M be the augmented adjacency matrix of the graph. Then the digraph is strongly connected if and only if every entry of M^{n-1} is nonzero.

Adjacency matrices provide a simple representation of the edges of a digraph, and powers of the matrix provide information concerning paths from one vertex to another. Furthermore, when stored as two-dimensional arrays, programs can access this information very efficiently.

Adjacency Lists

Unfortunately, adjacency matrices also may have a significant drawback: for digraphs of any size, such matrices may be very large. For example, if a digraph has 100 vertices, then an adjacency matrix is a 100 by 100 table, with 10,000 entries. More generally, the adjacency matrix for a digraph with n vertices has dimensions n by n, and thus has n^2 entries. Therefore, the space required for an adjacency matrix can be considerable.

In many real applications, however, only a few edges are attached to each vertex. For example, on a road map, only a few roads connect to each city. On such digraphs, most entries in an adjacency matrix are 0, because edges rarely go from one vertex to many others. In Chapter 6, matrices with relatively few nonzero entries were called sparse matrices, and we considered how to store such matrices efficiently by focusing only upon the nonzero entries.

One simple format for representing such sparse matrices associates a list of adjacent vertices for each vertex in the digraph. Such a representation is called an *adjacency list*. The easiest way to implement this adjacency list is to have a one-dimensional array indexed by the vertices, where each array entry is a pointer to a list containing those vertices representing edges. Figure 10.11 shows the adjacency list representation of G6 from Figure 10.8.

In this figure, the edge <A, B> is represented as the entry B on A's list. More generally, we can tell if an edge <X, Y> exists by determining if the vertex Y appears on the list associated with vertex X.

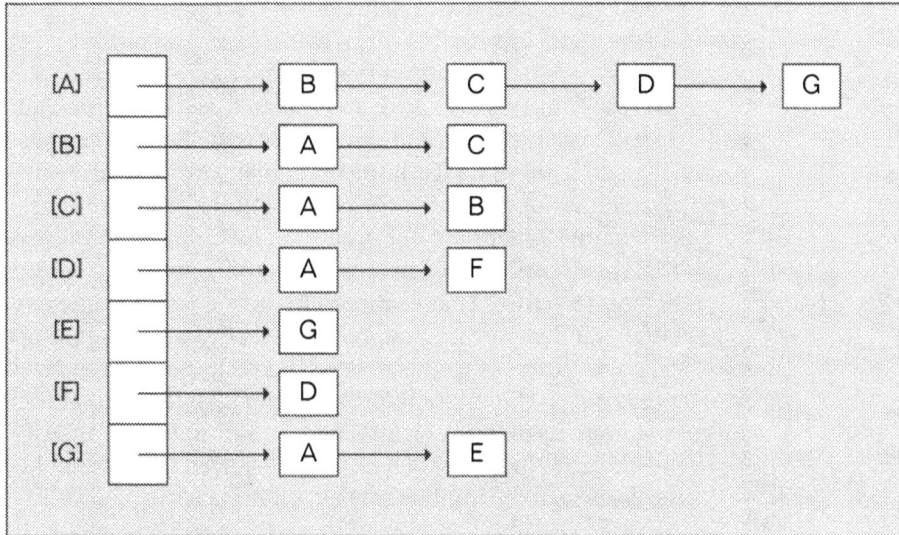

Figure 10.11 An Adjacency List for Digraph G6 from Figure 10.8.

Internal and External Names

At this point, we need to reemphasize the starting point for adjacency matrices. In particular, all of our work began with the numbering of the vertices of a digraph, so that we knew which vertices corresponded to which rows and columns. In working with adjacency lists, we could change this perspective by storing the full name of a vertex at each node of each list, but this approach would have at least two disadvantages: a string array for each edge in the digraph could consume a considerable amount of memory, and processing to compare strings could require a fair amount of time. A much more efficient approach would be to associate an ordinal value with each vertex, as we did with adjacency matrices.

For example, consider the cities in Digraph G9 from Figure 10.9. We could assign a number to each city in the order in which the cities were first mentioned. In this simple approach, the first vertex entered would be 1, the next vertex 2, and so on; that is, we could map each vertex into a number that represented the order in which it was introduced. We could call the vertex the **external name** and the ordinal representation the **internal name**.

> **External name** The input string representing the vertex.
>
> **Internal name** The ordinal number assigned to the vertex.

We need a support structure that can map the external name into the internal name. Fortunately, we already have just the right ADT coded and sitting in the program library! It is called a keyed table. The key is the external name, and the internal name is the associated value. We also need a table that maps the internal name into the external name. Why? Because the outputs from the observer functions need to be in terms of the external names. A keyed table works here as well. The key is the internal name, and the value is the external name. In fact, this keyed table also can represent the set of vertices. There is no need to have the external names in a separate list implementation of a set. We can simply substitute the keyed table operations for the corresponding set operations.

Figure 10.12 shows this process of mapping the vertices representing an edge from the external vertex names to internal names and inserting the edge into the digraph structure. That is, the user enters a vertex name as a string (the external name) and the string is mapped into an ordinal value for use within the digraph structure. When output is generated using the digraph structure, a vertex name comes out in the internal form and must go through another transformation to get back to its external form. When we look at the complexity of these operations, we see that these two keyed tables—KeyedTable1 and KeyedTable2 in Figure 10.12—need to be implemented in different ways.

Digraph Implementation Details

We wish to hide the implementation details from the user of the ADT Digraph so that our interface does not reflect these external/internal/external conversions or the structure being used. Thus, StoreVertex takes a string name as a parameter and uses the KeyedTable ADT to find a corresponding internal name. The axioms that we specified previously stated that the vertices used to specify an edge must be in the set of vertices or else an error occurs. Here, we choose to change those specifications to make them more general. If the vertices used to represent an edge are not in the set of vertices, we add them before storing the edge. Hence, a vertex can be inserted either explicitly or implicitly. You are asked to write the axioms for this version of StoreEdge in the exercises.

The user deletes a vertex from the set of vertices or an edge from the set of edges. If the user deletes a vertex from the set of vertices, the axioms specify that all edges associated with that vertex must be removed from the set of edges. Nowhere does the user need to know anything about the underlying structure being used.

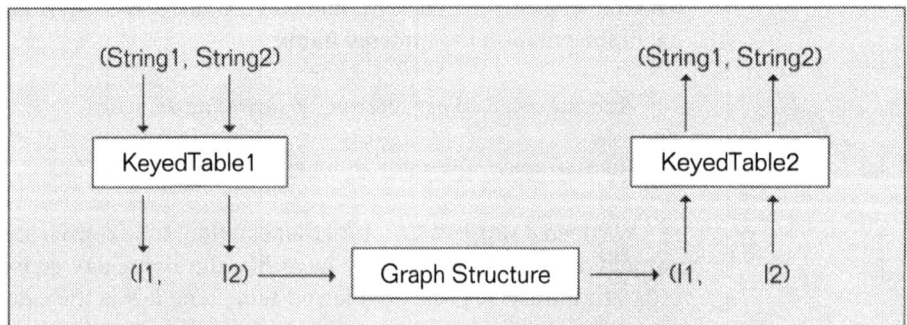

Figure 10.12 External/Internal/External Mapping of an Edge

We begin here by writing the implementation of the weighted Digraph ADT as defined previously with the enhanced StoreEdge operation. We later show how we can easily represent nondirected graphs in the same structure. However, this generality means that the Create operation is more complex than any other ADT we have looked at, because we must set the parameters (directed, undirected) and (weighted, unweighted), when a digraph is created. Because it is unlikely that a user needs more than one digraph at a time, we define DigraphType and the digraph structure itself within the implementation section of the module.

Interface Section

USES ADT Sorted List
 (* ItemType is Vertex. Operations used: Create, Insert, and Delete. *)
 (* Represents list of edges in adjacency list implementation. *)

USES ADT Queue
 (* ItemType is <vertex, vertex, weight> triple. Operations used: Create, *)
 (* Enqueue, and Dequeue. Represents list of edges, output from *)
 (* FromEdges. *)

TYPE
 StringType = Packed ARRAY [1..15] of Char;
 Vertex = StringType;

Create(Weighted, Directed: Boolean);
(* Post: G <> ⊥ *)
(*   IF Weighted, G is weighted, else nonweighted. *)
(*   IF Directed, G is directed, else undirected. *)

StoreVertex(Vertex: VertexType);
(* Pre: G <> ⊥ *)
(* Post: Vertex has been added to V(G) *)

IsEmpty: Boolean;
(* Pre: G <> ⊥ *)
(* Post: IsEmpty = V(G) = {} *)

IsVertex(Vertex: VertexType) : Boolean;
(* Pre: G <> ⊥ *)
(* Post: IsVertex = IsIn (V(G), Vertex) *)

NumberOfVertices(Vertex: VertexType) : Integer;
(* Pre: G <> ⊥ *)
(* Post: NumberOfVertices = Card (V(G)) *)

DelVertex(Vertex: VertexType)
(* Pre: G <> ⊥ *)
(* Post: NOT Vertex IN V(G) *)
(*   IF Vertex1 is any other vertex IN V(G), *)
(*   THEN (Vertex, Vertex1) NOT IN E(G) *)
(*   (Vertex1, Vertex) NOT IN E(G) *)

StoreEdge(Vertex1, Vertex2: VertexType, Weight: WeightType)
(* Pre: G ⬦ ⊥   *)
(* Post: IsIn (V(G), Vertex1)   *)
(*   IsIn (V(G), Vertex2)   *)
(*   IsIn (E(G), Vertex1, Vertex2, Weight)   *)

DelEdge(Vertex1, Vertex2: VertexType)
(* Pre: G ⬦ ⊥   *)
(* Post: NOT (Vertex1, Vertex2, Weight) in E(G)   *)

ListOfVertices(VAR List: SortedListType)
(* Pre: G ⬦ ⊥   *)
(* Post: Returns a sorted list of vertices.   *)

FromEdges(Tail: InternalType, VAR Queue: QueueType)
(* Pre: G ⬦ ⊥   *)
(* Post: Returns a queue of edges where Tail is the tail *)
(*   of the edge.   *)

The following algorithms apply to both the adjacency array and adjacency list implementations. The program implementing these algorithms should be optimized for one or the other. The algorithms assume a WeightType of Integer, and weights are initialized to 0 in the adjacency array. If the digraph is unweighted, we assign a weight of 1 to each edge. Note that the theoretical properties of the adjacency matrix that were discussed earlier do not apply if the cells in the matrix contain weights other than 1.

In the adjacency list representation, the list representing the edges contains a vertex represented by its internal name and a weight. While we list both ListOfVertices and FromEdges in our interface, we note that ListOfVertices is needed by users much more often than FromEdges. Thus, as a practical matter, the observer operation ListOfVertices is commonly found within digraph library operations, while FromEdges is much less common.

Because we are using several previously defined ADTs, we append the ADT name to the operation if there are duplicate names.

Implementation Section

USES ADT KeyedTable
    (* KeyType is Vertex; ValueType is Integer. Operations used: Create, Store *)
    (* IsEmpty, IsIn, Delete, Find, and ListOfKeys. Represents set of vertices. *)

USES ADT Queue
    (*ItemType is <index, index, weight>. Operations   *)
    (*used; Create, Enque, Deque, IsEmpty   *)

TYPE
    AdjacencyType = (* Type definition for an adjacency matrix or adjacency lists *)
    ImplementationType = (AdjArray, AdjLists);

```
DigraphType = RECORD
      Weighted: Boolean;
      Directed: Boolean
END RECORD;

CONST
    Implementation = (* either AdjArray or AdjLists *);
    MaxVertices = (* maximum size of vertex set needed for array implementation *)

VAR
    Digraph : DigraphType;
    ExternalToInternal: KeyedTable; (* SetOfVertices *);
    InternalToExternal: (* some implementation of a KeyedTable *)
    Adjacency: AdjacencyType;
    VertexNumber: Integer ; (* Variable to assign new number to each new vertex *)
    VertexCount: Integer ;    (* Number of vertices in current digraph *)
```

Create (Weighted, Directed: Boolean)

```
Digraph.Weighted ← Weighted
Digraph.Directed ← Directed
CreateTable (ExternalToInternal)
CreateTable (InternalToExternal)
VertexNumber ← 0
VertexCount ← 0
(* Initialize Adjacency Structure *)
CASE Implementation OF
    AdjArray:  FOR I ← 1 TO MaxVertices DO
                    FOR J ← 1 TO MaxVertices DO
                        Adjacency[I,J] ← 0
                    END FOR
                END FOR
    AdjLists:     FOR I ← 1 TO MaxVertices DO
                    List.Create(AdjLists[I])
                END FOR
END CASE
```

StoreVertex (Vertex: VertexType)

```
VertexNumber ← VertexNumber + 1
VertexCount ← VertexCount + 1
StoreTable(ExternalToInternal, Vertex, VertexNumber)
StoreTable(InternalToExternal, VertexNumber, Vertex)
```

Is Empty: Boolean

```
RETURN KeyedTable.IsEmpty(ExternalToInternal)
```

IsVertex (Vertex: VertexType)

```
RETURN KeyedTable.IsIn(ExternalToInternal, Vertex)
```

NumberOfVertices: Integer

```
RETURN VertexCount
```

DelVertex (Vertex: VertexType)

```
Find(ExternalToInternal, Vertex, I1)
KeyedTable.Delete(ExternalToInternal, Vertex)
KeyedTable.Delete(InternalToExternal, I1)
VertexCount ← VertexCount − 1
CASE Implementation OF
    AdjArray:       FOR Index ← 1 TO VertexNumber DO
                        Adjacency[Index, I1] ← 0
                        Adjacency[I1, Index] ← 0
                    END FOR
    AdjLists:       List.Create(Adjacency[I1])
                    FOR Index ← 1 TO VertexNumber DO
                        List.Delete(Adjacency[Index], I1)
                    END FOR
END CASE
```

Store Edge(Vertex1, Vertex2: VertexType, Weight: WeightType)

```
IF NOT KeyedTable.IsIn(ExternalToInternal, Vertex1)
    THEN
        VertexNumber ← VertexNumber + 1
        KeyedTable.Store(ExternalToInternal, Vertex1, VertexNumber)
        KeyedTable.Store(InternalToExternal, VertexNumber, Vertex1)
        I1 ← VertexNumber
    ELSE   KeyedTable.Find(ExternalToInternal, Vertex1, I1)
END IF
IF NOT KeyedTable.IsIn(ExternalToInternal, Vertex2)
    THEN
        VertexNumber ←VertexNumber + 1
        KeyedTable.Store(ExternalToInternal, Vertex2, VertexNumber)
        KeyedTable.Store(InternalToExternal, VertexNumber, Vertex2)
        I2 ← VertexNumber
    ELSE   KeyedTable.Find (ExternalToInternal, Vertex2, I2)
END IF
(* PlaceEdge(I1, I2, Weight) *)
CASE Implementation OF
    AdjArray:       Adjacency[I1, I2] ← Weight
    AdjLists:       List.Insert(Adjacency[I1], I2, Weight)
END CASE
```

Delete Edge (Vertex1, Vertex2: VertexType)

```
KeyedTable.Find(ExternalToInternal, Vertex1, I1)
KeyedTable.Find(ExternalToInternal, Vertex2, I2)
CASE Implementation OF
    AdjArray:    Adjacency[I1, I2] ← 0
    AdjLists:    Delete(Adjacency[I1], I2)
END CASE
```

From Edges (I1: InternalType, VAR Queue: QueueType)

In the array-based implementation, we traverse the row Adjacency[I1] enqueueing the edge where the weight is nonzero. In the list-based implementation, we traverse the list Adjacency(I1) enqueueing the edges. In Chapter 6 in the discussion on nonindexed lists, we said that an iterator was not provided because Head could be used. However, a direct implementation of the specifications results in a destructive Head operation. In our algorithm shown below, we assume that Head is destructive and make a copy of the list before we traverse it. In practice, you would probably implement a nondestructive iterator. Because ItemType for this list is an <index, weight> pair, we use functional notation to access the individual parts of ItemType: Index(Item) returns the index, and Weight(Item) returns the weight.

```
CASE Implementation OF
    AdjArray:     FOR Index ← 1 TO VertexNumber DO
                      IF Adjacency[I1, Index] <> 0
                          THEN
                              Enqueue (Queue, <I1, Index,
                                          Adjacency[I1, Index]>)
                          END IF
                      END FOR
    AdjLists:     TempList ← Adjacency[I1] (* copy list *)
                  WHILE NOT List.IsEmpty(TempList) DO
                      Item ← Head(TempList)
                      Enqueue(Queue, <I1, Index(Item), Weight(Item)>)
                      TempList ← Tail(TempList)
                  END WHILE
END CASE
```

ListOfVertices(VAR List: ListType)

Because the set of vertices is being represented in the ExternalToInternal KeyedTable, the operation ListOfKeys(ExternalToInternal) returns exactly what we want: a list of the vertices.

```
List ← ListOfKeys(ExternalToInternal)
```

Complexity of Operations to Build a Digraph

Each operation except for Create, NumberOfVertices, and IsVertex involves mapping the external name into the internal name. This mapping is done in a keyed table, so the order is the order of the implementation of the keyed table. We have examined a variety of structures that can be used to implement a keyed table. If there are n vertices in the digraph, the Find operation varies from best case O(1) and worst case O(n) in a hash table to best case O(log n) in a tree-based implementation. The IsEmpty operation may require a full examination of the keyed table or there may be a separate record of the number of items in the structure. In the former case, IsEmpty has O(MaxVertices), while in the latter case, IsEmpty has O(1). Because we do not need the inverse keyed table for the operations that build the digraph, we discuss its complexity when we discuss the complexity of the special digraph algorithms.

In discussing the complexity of the alternate implementations of the digraph, we do not include the time required to make the external/internal/external transformations.

Adjacency Array Implementation

The orders of the operations in the array implementation are the orders of the corresponding array operations. StoreEdge is O(1). Create is O(MaxVertices^2), because the entire array is initialized. (You are asked in the exercises to change the implementations of Create and InsertVertex so that InsertVertex initializes the appropriate row rather than having Create initialize all of the structure. This change, of course, changes the order of the operations.) IsEdge and DelEdge have bounded (actually constant) time complexity, O(1). DelVertex requires a traversal of a row and a column. Therefore, DelVertex is O(MaxVertices) or O(VertexNumber).

Adjacency Lists Implementation

The order of the operations here is based on the order of the implementation of the List used to hold the <index, weight> pairs. What is the size factor of the List in this application? The number of edges in the list. However, if n is the number of vertices, then the number of edges incident on a vertex is n in the worst case, so we can use n for the size factor in both implementations.

To create a digraph in the adjacency lists implementation, we must create a list for each of the possible vertices, giving us O(MaxVertices). If we assume an ADT List implementation that is O($\log_2$ n) to store and retrieve, we find that StoreEdge and DelEdge are O($\log_2$ n) operations. DelVertex requires that we search all lists of edges to find the edges where the vertex to be deleted is a head. With n lists of up to n entries each, this is O(n^2).

The complexity of the two implementations is summarized in Table 10.1. In the case of the adjacency lists implementation, the operations are based on a List implementation where the store and retrieve are $\log_2$ n operations.

Except for the Create operation, the array-based implementation seems better—and it *is* better if space is no problem. In fact, the adjacency lists are simply

Table 10.1. Complexity of Operations on ADT Digraph with n Vertices

Operation	AdjArray	AdjLists
StoreEdge	$O(1)$	$O(\log n)$
Create	$O(\text{MaxVertices}^2)$	$O(\text{MaxVertices})$
DelEdge	$O(1)$	$O(\log n)$
DelVertex	$O(n)$	Directed $O(n^2)$
		Non-Directed $O(n \log n)$

another sparse array implementation. The decision on which implementation to use should be based on the number of edges relative to the number of vertices.

Application: Dependency Graphs

The distinction between digraphs and other ADTs is important. Most applications using trees and lists of all kinds use the structure to store data that the application needs to access in a certain order. A digraph is a structure that represents data objects and the *relationships among them*. The nature of the objects and the relationships is in the mind of the user when V(G) and E(G) are defined. The importance of studying such relationships is illustrated in the notion of dependency graphs and their application to parallel computing.

Informally, a dependency graph shows which computations or steps in a program depend upon earlier results. Before we make this idea more precise, consider a computation that you may recall from elementary algebra.

Example: Solving $ax^2 + bx + c = 0$ Using the Quadratic Formula

From elementary algebra, you may recall that if we are given a, b, and c, then the solution to $ax^2 + bx + c = 0$ is given by the formula:

$$x_1 = \frac{-b + \sqrt{b^2 - 4ac}}{2a}, \qquad x_2 = \frac{-b - \sqrt{b^2 - 4ac}}{2a}$$

If we compute these two values within a program (assuming a is not 0), we might compute the square root, $-b$, and $2a$ independently and then combine them to give the desired results. Furthermore, to compute the square root, we need to compute b^2 and $4ac$ and perform a subtraction before applying the square root function. Of course, in a program based upon a high-level language, several of these steps might be done as part of the same statement. For instance,

SecondTerm ← sqrt(b∗b − 4∗a∗c)

At the machine level, each operation must be done as a separate step. In the following code, for example, we perform only one operation at a time, and we store one result in a temporary variable before going on to the next step.

```
MinusB ← −b;
BSquared ← b*b;
AC ← a*c;
FourAC ← 4*AC
Discriminant ← BSquared − FourAC;
SecondTerm ← sqrt( Discriminant);        (* Function call used here *)
Numerator1 ← MinusB + SecondTerm;
Numerator2 ← MinusB − SecondTerm;
Denominator ← 2*a;
X1 ← Numerator1 / Denominator;
X2 ← Numerator2 / Denominator;
```

Graphically, we can represent this flow of processing in a directed graph. In the digraph, each statement above corresponds to a vertex. Also, we draw an edge from one vertex (program statement) to another if the result of the first statement is used in the second. The digraph corresponding to our example is shown in Figure 10.13. In this figure, we have labeled each vertex with both the variable computed and the actual computation performed.

In this digraph, we first listed the initial values a, b, and c. Then we drew an edge from b to MinusB and BSquared because the value of b is used in computing −b and b*b. Similarly, we have edges from Denominator and Numerator1 to X1, because the value of X1 is computed from these two other values. The other vertices and edges are similarly identified. This idea generalizes to a dependency graph.

A *dependency graph* for a computation is a directed graph in which the vertices consist of each of the values computed in the computation and in which an edge is drawn from one computation to another if the result of the first is used in the computation of the second.

Dependency Graphs and Ability to Parallelize Computations

Once the dependency graph is formulated for a program or computation, we observe that two computations can be done independently or in parallel if there is no path from one to the other. For example, in Figure 10.13, Discriminant and Denominator are not connected by a path; we can either compute the Discriminant (b*b−4*a*c) before the Denominator (2*a), or vice versa. Furthermore, if we have two processors, one processor can compute one of these values while the second processor computes the other value. Similarly, once SecondTerm and MinusB are computed, we can compute Numerator1 and Numerator2 in either order or in parallel. Then, we can compute X1 and X2 in parallel.

This observation suggests the following way of transforming a traditional, sequential algorithm into a parallel one, taking advantage of multiple processors that might be available. First, draw a dependency graph based on each computation or program statement. Next, divide the required computations among vari-

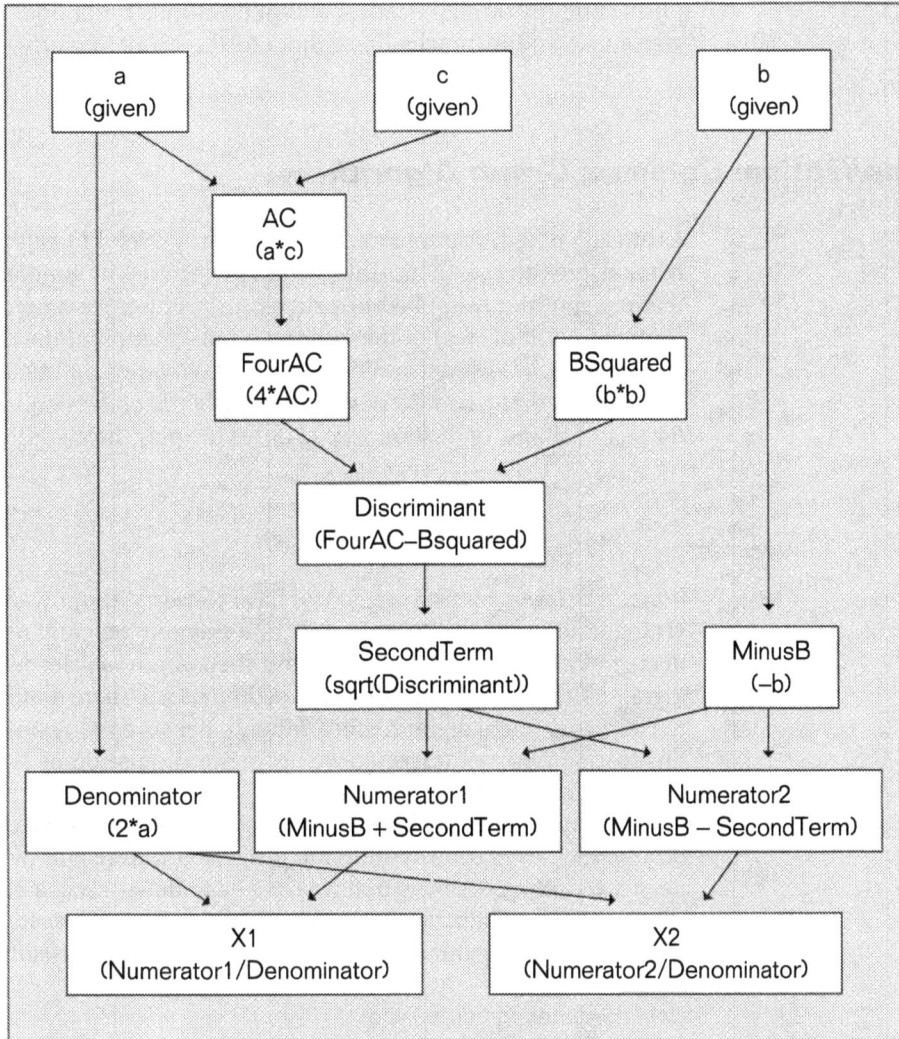

Figure 10.13   A Dependency Graph for the Computation of the Quadratic Formula

ous processors so that each value is determined only after its components are known as indicated by the dependency graph.

Many processors proceeding at once may allow a significant speedup of an overall algorithm if the dependency graph indicates that many vertices are independent of each other. On the other hand, if the dependency graph looks much like a linear list, then the computations must be done in a specific order, because each computation depends on the previous one. In such cases, the availability of multiple processors may not be helpful at all.

Note also that the process of forming a dependency graph and analyzing it for opportunities for parallelism can be automated, allowing a compiler to read a traditional program and generate parallel code—at least in certain cases. Such compilers can provide significant speedup of various traditional algorithms and programs using multi-processors without further work by a programmer.

Application: Common Graph Algorithms

As already noted, digraphs can be particularly useful in studying objects and the relationships among them. This section presents some general digraph algorithms that are commonly applied to a digraph structure. We describe these algorithms from the point of view of the internal representation of the objects and relationships, that is, as abstract vertices and edges. Whether a particular algorithm makes sense or not in the context of the meaning of the objects and their relationships is the responsibility of the user who chooses to apply the algorithm to the data.

Traversals

When we traverse a tree, we do not have to worry about whether or not we have visited a node before. There is only one way to reach any node, because the in-degree of any node is, at most, 1 and there are no cycles in a tree. In a general digraph, the in-degree of a node is not limited and there may be many cycles. This makes traversing a digraph more difficult. Because many operations on digraphs involve some sort of traversal, we begin our discussion of digraph algorithms by looking at traversals.

We traverse a digraph by following edges from one vertex to another. If a cycle occurs, we can end up visiting the same nodes over and over again forever. We need a way of recognizing that we have been down a particular path before. That is, we need the ability to mark a vertex as having been visited. Therefore, we assume the following three operations in the ensuing discussion.

```
UnMark(Vertex : InternalType);
(* Pre:     Vertex in V              *)
(* Post:    IsMarked(Vertex) is False    *)

Mark(Vertex : InternalType);
(* Pre:     Vertex in V              *)
(* Post:    IsMarked(Vertex) is True     *)

IsMarked(Vertex : InternalType) : Boolean
(* Pre:     Vertex in V              *)
(* Post:    IsMarked = (Mark(Vertex)     *)
(*          has been applied             *)
```

We use InternalType to represent the range 1..VertexNumber. Mark can be an array [1..MaxVertices] of Boolean or Mark can be a field associated with each vertex. The algorithms for these are left as an end-of-chapter exercise.

Depth-First Traversal

A depth-first traversal is a visitation of the vertices such that all descendants of a vertex are visited before the siblings of a vertex, where siblings of a vertex are those adjacent from the same vertex. This traversal requires a stack or recursion. We use Visit to stand for whatever processing is done on each vertex during the traversal. Visit often converts the internal name to the external name and writes out the external name.

Before we actually write the algorithm, we work through an example, performing a depth-first traversal beginning at H for the digraph shown in Figure 10.14.

For simplicity, we do not distinguish between internal and external names. To begin a depth-first traversal from vertex H, we put H on the stack first. Then we enter a loop that continues until the stack is empty. We pop H off the stack. It has not been marked, so we mark it, visit it, and put all of the vertices on the stack for which <H,_> is an edge. At this point, the stack contains (C, G).

We pop the stack, getting vertex C. C is not marked, so we mark it, visit it, and put all of the vertices on the stack for which <C,_> is an edge. At this point, the stack contains (A,D,H,G). So far, C and H have been visited.

We pop A off the stack. It has not been marked, so we mark it, visit it, and put F, C, and B on the stack, giving (B,C,F,D,H,G). We pop off B. It has not been marked, so we mark it, visit it, and put D on the stack, giving (D,C,F,D,H,G). C, H, A, and B have been visited.

We pop D off the stack. D has not been visited, so we mark it, visit it, and put G and B on the stack, giving (B,G,C,F,D,H,G). We pop B off the stack; it has been visited. We pop G off the stack; it has not been visited. We visit G, mark it, and put F on the stack. At this point, the stack is (F,C,F,D,H,G) and C, H, A, B, D, and G have been visited.

We pop F, which has not been visited. We visit F, mark it, and put E and A on the stack. The stack is now (A,E,C,F,D,H,G). A is popped off; it has been visited. E is popped off; it has not been visited before. E is visited and marked, and F is put on the stack. The stack is now (F,C,F,D,H,G). All of the vertices are marked now, so the stack is just emptied.

This traversal is not unique. In our example, we put the items on the stack in reverse alphabetical order because this seemed like a good way of doing it,

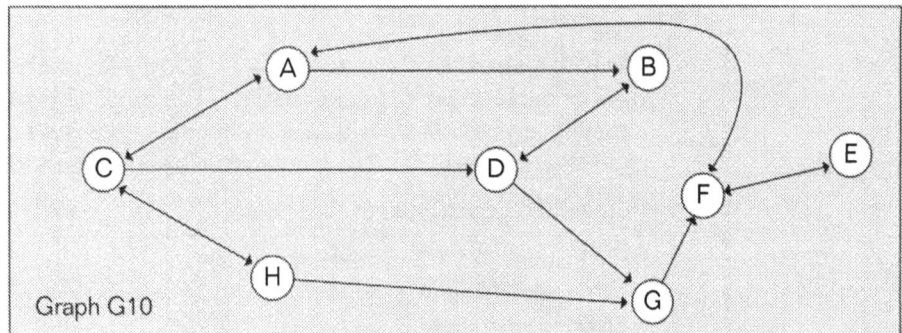

Figure 10.14   A Digraph to Illustrate Searching or Traversals

but they could have been put on the stack in any order. The point about a depth-first traversal is that you go as deep as possible before traversing another edge of the starting point. You might visit a vertex from another edge that also forms an edge with the starting point, but you are reaching that vertex through the other edge.

Although this algorithm can be coded directly, it is very inefficient because it puts unnecessary vertices on the stack. In fact, in a complete graph, there may be Card(E(V)) vertices on the stack. We can make the algorithm more efficient by putting a pointer to the queue of edges on the stack rather than to all the vertices themselves. The queue can then be implemented within the adjacency matrix or adjacency lists, thus not using any additional space.

DepthFirst (I1: VertexType)

```
Stack.Create(S)
Queue.Create(Q)
FOR Count ← 1 TO VertexNumber DO
    UnMark(Count)
END FOR
FromEdges(I1, Q)
WHILE NOT Queue.IsEmpty(Q)DO
    Deque(Q, Edge)
    I1 ← Head(Edge)
    IF NOT IsMarked(I1)
        THEN
            IF NOT Queue.IsEmpty(Q)
                THEN Push(S, Q)
            END IF
            Queue.Create(Q)
            Mark(I1)
            Visit(I1)
            FromEdges(I1, Q)
    END IF
    IF Queue.IsEmpty(Q) AND (NOT Stack.IsEmpty(S))
        THEN Pop(S, Q)
END WHILE
```

As with many algorithms involving a stack, an alternative version of this algorithm is possible where recursion replaces the stack. This version follows. Notice that the top level of the algorithm is not recursive, because the nodes must all be marked as not visited. Then the recursive part of the algorithm is called.

DepthFirst (I1: VertexType) (∗ alternate ∗)

```
FOR Count ← 1 TO VertexNumber DO
    UnMark(Count)
END FOR
Queue.Create (Q)
DepthFirstRecursive(I1)
```

DepthFirstRecursive (I1: VertexType)

```
Queue.Create(Q) Mark(I1)
FromEdges(I1, Q)
WHILE NOT IsEmpty(Q) DO
    Deque(Q, Edge)
    IF NOT IsMarked(Head(Edge))
        THEN DepthFirstRecursive(Head(Edge))
    END IF
END WHILE
```

Breadth-First Traversal

A breadth-first traversal visits the siblings of each vertex before it visits the descendants of the vertex. Using a queue to hold the next vertices to visit allows us to visit them in this order. A breadth-first traversal beginning at C of the digraph in the last example visits the nodes in the following order:

C H D A G B F E

C is visited, as well as C's children H, D, and A. Then H's child G is visited, D's child B is visited, and A's child F is visited. G has no children that have not been visited. Finally, B's child E is visited, and the traversal is complete.

Breadth First (I1: VertexType)

```
Queue.Create(Q)        (*Queue of vertices*)
Queue.Create(Q2)       (*Queue of edges*)
FOR Count ← 1 TO VertexCount DO
    UnMark(Count)
END FOR
Enque(Q, I1)
Mark(I1)
REPEAT
    Deque(Q, Tail);
    FromEdges(Tail, Q2)
    WHILE NOT IsEmpty(Q2) DO
        Deque(Q2, Edge)
        IF NOT IsMarked(Head(Edge))
            THEN
                Mark(Head(Edge))
                Enque(Q, Head(Edge))
            END IF
    END WHILE
UNTIL IsEmpty(Q)
```

In comparing the nonrecursive depth-first traversal and the breadth-first traversal, note that the steps of each are the same, with the stack of the depth-first algorithm replaced by a queue for the breadth-first version.

Depth-first and breadth-first traversals each have advantages and disadvantages. In breadth-first traversals, we first visit all vertices adjacent to the start, then all vertices of distance 2, then all at distance 3, and so on. Thus, if we keep track of which step placed a vertex on the queue, we can determine how close each vertex is from the start, following the path with the smallest number of edges. Breadth-first traversals, therefore, can be very useful in finding short paths, when they exist. In contrast, depth-first traversals go as far as they can in one direction before trying another route. Thus, in going from Minneapolis to its twin city, St. Paul, in Minnesota, the depth-first traversal might go through Los Angeles, Austin, Miami, and Boston if it started out to the west first and made poor choices of direction. The breadth-first traversals would find the direct path over the river to St. Paul very quickly.

Single-Source Shortest Path

This problem can be stated as follows: for a particular vertex I1, determine the minimum cost from I1 to all of the other vertices, where cost is defined as the sum of the weights on a path from one vertex to another. The digraph is positively weighted and can be either directed or undirected, although the problem is usually formulated for directed graphs. The solution is known as *Dijkstra's algorithm.*

The basic idea of the algorithm is to determine the minimum cost from I1 to one vertex at each iteration (call it I2), mark I2 as fixed, and recalculate the cost from I1 to each of the unfixed vertices going through I2. At each iteration, the vertex that becomes fixed is the unfixed vertex with the minimum cost.

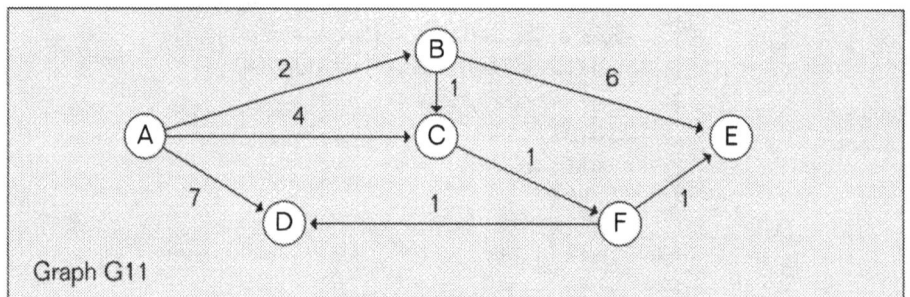

Graph G11

As an example, consider digraph G11 and suppose we want to find the smallest cost for travel from vertex A to each other vertex. In what follows, we use an asterisk to show that we have not yet found a cost to a particular vertex.

A to	B	C	D	E	F
Cost	2	4	7	*	*

The cost to B is the minimum, so B is fixed, and the costs to C, D, E, and F are recalculated through B. A to C through B costs 3, which is lower than the direct path from A to C. A to D through B does not exist. A to E through B costs 8. A to F does not exist. We indicate that a vertex is fixed by putting a box around it.

A to	B	C	D	E	F
Cost	2	3	7	8	*

The cost to C is the lowest of the nonfixed vertices, so we now fix C, and the other costs are recalculated through C. D and E cannot be reached through C directly. F can be reached through C; the cost is 4.

A to	B	C	D	E	F
Cost	2	3	7	8	4

The cost to F is the minimum among the unfixed vertices. We fix F and recalculate the costs to D and E, the unfixed vertices. A to E through F costs 5, and A to D through F costs 5.

A to	B	C	D	E	F
Cost	2	3	5	5	4

This time we have a tie. We can choose either, and we might decide to fix E. There is no path from A to D through E, so the cost to D, the only remaining vertex, is 5.

In following this algorithm rather than keeping a table, we let a priority queue (as defined in Chapter 5) do the work for us, where the weight or cost of an edge provides the priority.

We initialize the process by enqueueing all the edges in FromEdges(I1, Queue) into the priority queue (PQ). At each iteration, edges are served until an edge is found where Head(Edge) is not fixed. I2 becomes Head(Edge), the vertex to be fixed at this iteration; the cost from I1 to I2 is Weight(Edge). All outgoing edges from I2 where the other vertex has not been fixed are Enqueued, with Weight(Edge) added to each edge weight before the edge is Enqueued. The process continues until all the vertices have been fixed.

At each iteration, we print I2, the cost from I1 to I2, and the last vertex in the path from I1 to I2. At the end of the processing, this table of output contains the minimum cost from I1 to each of the other vertices and the path through which the minimum is obtained.

We use the term "fixing a vertex" when discussing this algorithm. The marking scheme we have been using works very well here. To fix a vertex I2, we Mark(I2).

To further clarify this approach, we hand-calculate the previous example, using the priority queue. We visualize the priority queue in the order in which items are enqueued. Serve returns the one with the highest priority. We initialize the priority queue (PQ) with all the out-edges from A.

PQ: (<A,B,2>, <A,C,4>, <A,D,7>)

The edge <A,B,2> is served. B is fixed and the out-edges from B are put on the priority queue with 2 added to the weight on each edge.

PQ: (<B,E,8>, <B,C,3>, <A,C,4>, <A,D,7>)

The edge <B,C,3> is served. C is fixed and the out-edges from C are put on the priority queue with 3 added to the weight on each edge.

PQ: (<C,F,4>, <B,E,8>, <A,C,4>, <A,D,7>)

Depending on how the implementation of the priority queue handles duplicates, we get either <C,F,4> or <A,C,4>. Let us assume that the priority queue is stable and we get <A,C,4>. Because C has already been served, we go on to the next edge, and <C,F,4> is served. The out-edges from F are put on the priority queue with 4 added to the weight on each edge.

PQ: (<F,D,5>, <F,E,5>, <B,E,8>, <A,D,7>)

The edge <F,E,5> is served. E is fixed. E has no unfixed out-edges. The edge <F,D,5> is now served and the process is finished. The remaining edges (<B,E,8> and <A,D,9>) on the priority queue are popped off and discarded. The algorithm with the edges printed is shown below.

SingleSourceShortestPath (I1: VertexType)

```
PQueue.Create(PQ)
Queue.Create(Q)
FOR Count ← 1 TO VertexCount DO
    UnMark(Count)
END FOR
PQueue.Enque(PQ, <I1, I1, 0>)
REPEAT
    Serve(PQ, Edge)
    IF NOT IsMarked(Head(Edge))
        THEN
            Cost ← Weight(Edge)
            I2 ← Head(Edge)
            Find(InternalToExternal, I2, Vertex)
            Find(InternalToExternal, Tail(Edge), Vertex2)
            Print(Vertex2, Vertex, Cost)
            Mark(I2)
            FromEdges(I2, Q)
```

```
                  WHILE NOT IsEmpty(Q) DO
                      Deque(Q, Edge)
                      IF NOT IsMarked(Head(Edge))
                          THEN
                                Weight(Edge) ← Weight(Edge) + Cost
                                PQueue.Enque(PQ, Edge)
                          END IF
                      END WHILE
              END IF
    UNTIL IsEmpty(PQ)
```

The output from the previous example would look like the following if Print put in the arrows and parentheses.

A → B (2)
B → C (3)
C → F (4)
F → E (5)
F → D (5)

Dijkstra's algorithm is an example of a general class of algorithms called **greedy algorithms**. A greedy algorithm proceeds through a series of steps where, at each step, we choose the best option. In other words, the best solution is obtained by choosing the best at each stage. In such solutions, being greedy pays off.

> **Greedy Algorithm** The best choice at each step leads to the best overall solution.

In Dijkstra's algorithm, each step involves choosing a remaining vertex of minimal distance from the vertices processed previously, and the vertex chosen is always the optimal one for the current collection of vertices. This choice of the optimal, short-term option is the motivation behind greedy algorithms. In the case of Dijkstra's algorithm, this choice of the optimal vertex for the current setting allows us to identify the shortest overall paths to all vertices; our choice is based upon the best path now, without regard for long-term consequences, but the result turns out to be the best overall as well. This use of tunnel vision to find the best in the long run is the major characteristic of greedy algorithms. Unfortunately, this approach solves only some types of problems, including the single-source shortest-path problem; we cannot ignore long-term consequences in trying to solve everything.

Topological Sort

A topological sort returns a linear ordering of vertices in which $vertex_i$ precedes $vertex_j$ if there exists a path from i to j in the digraph. Notice that this definition says nothing about the relationship of vertices in the ordering for which a path does not exist. A topological sort is defined only on a directed, acyclic graph. A directed, acyclic graph is often called a *DAG*.

The basic idea is to choose a vertex with no predecessors (in degree of 0), output the vertex, and remove the vertex from V(G), thus removing all of the edges from the vertex as well, and then to choose another vertex with no predecessors and repeat the process. This is another example of a greedy algorithm.

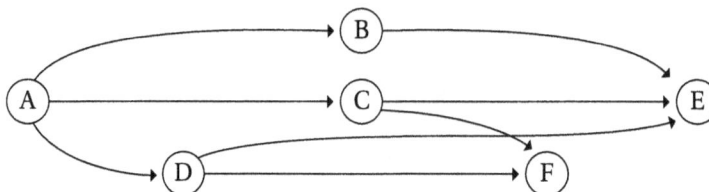

In this example, A has no predecessors, so A is printed and removed from the digraph.

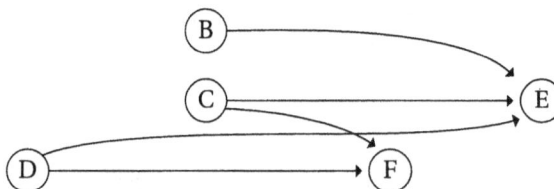

B, C, and D have no predecessors, so we can remove whichever one we choose. We choose to remove B.

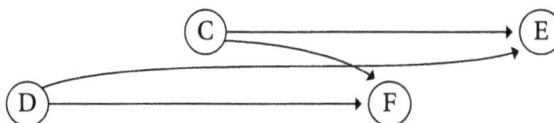

Now we remove C.

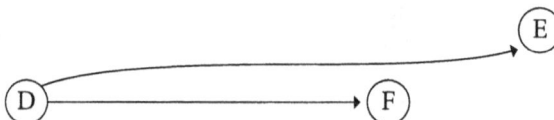

D and E have no predecessors, and we remove D.

E and F have no predecessors and can be removed in either order. We remove E first and then F. The topological order resulting from the order in which we removed the vertices is

A B C D E F

This order is not unique. A must be first, but B, C, or D could be second. B must be before E; C must be before E and F; and D must be before E and F.

This algorithm has one major problem—it destroys the digraph in the process. As an alternative, we wish to find an algorithm that simulates "removing the vertex" rather than actually doing so.

The key to the algorithm is the word *precedes*. If a vertex is adjacent from another vertex (is the Head of an edge), then it cannot be output until the Tail has been output. How can we tell that a vertex can be output? When it is not the Head of any edge in the digraph. How can we tell that it is not the Head of any edge? Keep a count of the in-degree of each vertex. When a vertex is output, reduce the in-degree count for each vertex adjacent from it. When the in-degree of a vertex is 0, it can be output and "removed."

We start, then, by calculating the in-degree of each vertex. There must be a vertex with in-degree of 0; otherwise, there would be a cycle. We output this vertex and adjust the in-degrees of all the vertices adjacent from it. What if there is more than one vertex with an in-degree of 0? The vertices can be output in any order; they have no predecessors. Make a list of them so that they can be processed systematically. Either a queue or a stack should do nicely. In the following algorithm, we use a queue.

TopologicalSort

```
Calculate InDegrees (InDegrees)
FOR Index ← 1 TO VertexCount DO
    IF InDegree[Index] = 0
        THEN   Enque(ReadyToPrintQ, Index)
    END IF
END FOR
REPEAT
    Deque(ReadyToPrintQ, I1)
    KeyTable.Find(InternalToExternal, I1, Vertex)
    Output Vertex
```

```
        WHILE NOT IsEmpty(Q) DO
            Deque(Q, Edge)
            Adjust InDegrees (Head(Edge), InDegree, ReadyToPrintQ))
        END WHILE
    UNTIL IsEmpty(ReadyToPrintQ)
```

CalculateInDegrees (Var InDegree: OneDArray)

The in-degree of a vertex in an array-based implementation is the sum of the edges in its column. In the list-based implementation, it is the number of times it appears in any of the other lists.

```
FOR Index ← 1 TO VertexNumber DO
    InDegree[Index] ← 0
END FOR
CASE Implementation OF
    AdjArray:        FOR Vertex ← 1 TO VertexNumber DO
                         FOR Index ← 1 TO VertexNumber DO
                             IF Adjacency[Index, Vertex] <> 0
                                 THEN InDegree[Vertex] ←
                                 InDegree[Vertex] + 1
                             END IF
                         END FOR
                     END FOR
    AdjLists:        FOR Index ← 1 TO VertexNumber DO
                         FOR Index2 ← 1 TO VertexNumber DO
                             IF List.IsIn(Adjacency[Index2], Index)
                                 THEN   InDegree[Index] ←
                                 InDegree[Index] + 1
                             END IF
                         END FOR
                     END FOR
END CASE
```

AdjustInDegrees (Vertex:VertexType, VAR InDegree:OneDArray, ReadyToPrintQ: Queue)

```
CASE Implementation OF
    AdjArray:        FOR Index ← 1 TO VertexNumber DO
                         IF Adjacency[Vertex, Index] <> 0
                             THEN
                                 InDegree[Index] ← InDegree[Index] − 1
                                 IF InDegree [Index] = 0
                                     THEN   Enque(ReadyToPrintQ, Index)
                                 END IF
                             END IF
                         END FOR
```

```
AdjLists:          FOR Index ← 1 TO VertexNumber DO
                     IF IsIn(Adjacency[Index], Vertex)
                        THEN
                           InDegree[Index] ← InDegree[Index] − 1
                           IF InDegree[Index] = 0
                              THEN   Enque(ReadyToPrintQ, Index)
                        END IF
                     END IF
                   END FOR
END CASE
```

We said that a topological sort is defined only on a directed acyclic graph, and we assumed the precondition that the digraph had no cycles. A slight change in our algorithm allows us to detect cycles as we go. We keep a count of how many vertices we have "removed" as we go along. If the queue ReadyToPrintQ is empty and not all of the vertices have been removed, the digraph contains a cycle.

Hamiltonian Circuit

You may have heard of this topic in the context of a related problem, the **traveling salesperson problem**, which asks, "What is the least expensive way that I can visit every city in my territory and end up where I started without going through any city more than once?" A **Hamiltonian circuit** does not consider the cost of such a trip, but simply describes one way that each city could be visited without going through any city more than once.

> **Hamiltonian Circuit** A simple cycle that contains all the vertices exactly once.
>
> **Traveling Salesperson Problem** A problem that seeks to find the Hamiltonian circuit of minimal cost.

Hamiltonian circuits may or may not exist. For example, a Hamiltonian circuit is not possible in an acyclic digraph or in a digraph in which any vertex has only one edge.

The following recursive algorithm finds a Hamiltonian circuit (if it exists) by building up a list of vertices representing the circuit. A Hamiltonian circuit has been found when the list contains all of the vertices and the vertex being examined is the first vertex on the list. Thus, we need to add an operation to our Unordered List ADT that allows us to access the first item on a list.

```
First(List)        → ItemType
First(Create) = Error
First(Store(L, il)) =
    If L = Create
        THEN il
        ELSE First (L)
    END IF
```

**Hamiltonian(VAR List: UnsortedList, VAR Finished: Boolean,
Vertex: VertexType)**

```
Queue.Create(Q)
IF Length(List) = VertexCount AND Vertex = First(List)
    THEN
        Finished ← True; (* List contains the vertices in the circuit. *)
    ELSE
        IF NOT List.IsIn(List, Vertex)
            THEN
                List.Store(List, Vertex)
                FromEdges(Vertex, Q)
                WHILE NOT Finished AND NOT IsEmpty(Q) DO
                    Deque(Q, Edge)
                    Hamiltonian(List, Finished, Head(Edge))
                END WHILE
                IF NOT Finished
                    THEN List.Delete(List, Vertex)
                END IF
        END IF
END IF
```

A brute force approach to the traveling salesperson problem is to determine all possible cycles that include each vertex exactly once (Hamiltonian circuits), calculate the cost of each, and select the cheapest. This approach requires a great many operations because we must consider all potential cycles. How many such cycles might there be in a digraph with n vertices? Pick any vertex to begin. Any of the remaining $n - 1$ vertices could be second in the cycle; any of the remaining $n - 2$ could be third; and so on. The total number of potential cycles is

$$(n - 1)*(n - 2)* \ldots *2*1 = n!$$

Because computing the cost of each cycle requires n operations, the total number of operations is n!.

To improve this solution, some refinements are clearly possible. For example, we could abandon a cycle when the accumulated cost is greater than the minimum cost up to that point. Even with such improvements, however, no known algorithm (utilizing only one processor) can solve this problem in polynomial time; that is, there are no known algorithms where the order is a polynomial in the number of vertices. We return to this issue in the next chapter.

Complexity of Application Algorithms

In a digraph with n vertices, FromEdges has O(n) in both the adjacency array implementation and the adjacency lists implementation. InternalToExternal is a keyed table that takes an ordinal value and maps it into its associated string. The best implementation for this keyed table is an array indexed by the internal name. Using this implementation, Find has $O(1)$.

Each of the application operations uses a traversal of the digraph in some way. Therefore, the complexity of the traversal is the lower bound for each operation. What is the complexity of the traversal? To answer that question, we must visit every vertex. We might be able to do that by following $n - 1$ edges, but then again, we might have to traverse every edge to visit all the vertices. Thus, the order of any traversal in a digraph is the number of edges. The upper bound for the number of edges is n^2, but a more precise figure is E, the exact number of edges in any particular digraph. Hence, the complexity of any traversal is $O(E)$.

The single-source, shortest-path algorithm is a slightly different kind of traversal because it begins at a particular vertex and the vertices must be visited in an order based on weights, but each of the edges may have to be examined. We have already discussed the complexity of the Hamiltonian circuit.

The topological sort is somewhat different, and we first consider the necessary preprocessing. The in-degree of each vertex, which has $O(n^2)$ in the adjacency array representation and $O(E)$ in the adjacency lists representation, must be calculated. The list of in-degrees must be searched for those with no predecessors ($O(n)$).

During the "removal process," a vertex is output ($O(1)$) and the in-degree of vertices adjacent from it are adjusted ($O(n)$). Because each vertex is output, this process is repeated n times. Thus, the order of the topological sort is

$$O(n^2) + O(n^2) = O(n^2)$$

in the adjacency array implementation and

$$O(E) + O(n^2) = O(n^2)$$

in the adjacency lists implementation.

SUMMARY

Mathematically, a digraph is composed of a set of objects and a set of edges, where the edges represent relationships among the objects. An edge is represented by a pair of vertices and a weight if the digraph is weighted. The set of vertices can be represented in an ADT KeyedTable, where the external name of the object is the key and the internal name is the value. Information concerning edges may be stored in a two-dimensional array called the adjacency matrix or in a sparse matrix representation called an adjacency list.

Powers of the adjacency matrix provide information concerning the number of paths of a given length from one vertex to another. Various algorithms provide additional information concerning digraphs.

Directed graphs arise naturally in many applications, including maps and dependency relationships.

EXERCISES

1. Define the following terms.

graph	adjacent to	depth-first traversal
directed graph	connected graph	breadth-first traversal
undirected graph	cycle	path length
complete graph	in-degree	minimum cost path length
adjacent from	out-degree	Hamiltonian circuit

Use the following graph for Exercises 2–6.

$G = (V,E)$
$V = \{A, B, C, D, E, F, G, H\}$
$E = \{<A,B>,<A,C>,<A,D>,<B,H>,<F,E>,<F,H>,<H,E>,<F,C>,<C,F>,<D,F>\}$

2. a. This graph is (directed, undirected) _____

   b. This graph is (complete, not complete) _____

   c. This graph is (strongly connected, not strongly connected) _____

3. a. Write the adjacency matrix T for this graph, based upon the alphabetical ordering of vertices given.

   b. Compute T^2 and T^3.

4. Draw the adjacency list representation for this graph.

5. a. Find all paths of length 2.

   b. Compare the number of paths from (a) with appropriate entries of matrices obtained in Exercise 3(b).

6. Form the augmented graph for the graph specified for Exercises 2–6, and answer Exercises 3 and 5 for this new graph.

In Exercises 7–15, consider the following as the adjacency matrix S for a weighted, directed graph. (*Note:* 0 means there is no edge.)

	A	B	C	D	E	F	G
A	0	10	6	4	0	7	0
B	10	0	9	0	11	0	18
C	6	9	0	1	1	0	0
D	4	0	1	0	1	2	0
E	0	11	1	1	0	0	14
F	7	0	0	2	0	0	15
G	0	18	0	0	14	15	0

7. Draw a picture of the graph represented by this adjacency matrix S without the weights.

8. Is this graph directed or undirected? Explain.

9. List the vertices in depth-first order beginning with vertex A. Process the S from left to right.

10. List the vertices in breadth-first order beginning with vertex A.

11. Find the shortest path from vertex D to each of the other vertices.

12. Compute S^2 and S^3.

13. Find the number of paths of length 3 that start from vertex D.

14. Form the augmented adjacency matrix associated with this graph.

15. a. Find the number of paths of length 3 that start from vertex D in this augmented graph.

    b. Explain how these paths relate to those in the original graph.

16. Determine the shortest path from vertex 1 to each of the other vertices in the following digraph.

    $V = \{1, 2, 3, 4, 5\}$
    $G = \{<1,2,10>, <1,5,40>, <2,4,100>, <2,3,60>, <2,5,20>,$
    $\quad <3,4,5>, <3,5,10>, <5,4,15>\}$

17. Refer to the digraph in Exercise 16 to do the following.

    a. List all the vertices adjacent from vertex 2.

    b. List all the vertices adjacent to vertex 2.

    c. List the vertices in topological order.

18. Consider the Courses and Prerequisites digraph from Figure 10.1.

    a. List the vertices obtained in a breadth-first traversal, beginning with Computer Science I. When you have a choice of which item to enqueue next, pick the one that comes first alphabetically.

    b. List the vertices obtained in a depth-first traversal, beginning with Computer Science I. Again, use alphabetical order to decide which vertices to use first.

    c. Apply the topological sort algorithm to this digraph or explain why it cannot be applied.

    d. Does this digraph contain a Hamiltonian circuit? Why or why not?

19. Repeat Exercise 18 for the digraph in Figure 10.4, where traversals start at the Police Station.

20. Consider the digraph in Figure 10.4 as a weighted digraph, where each edge has weight 1.

    a. Apply the single-source, shortest-path algorithm from vertex Police Station. In the case where two vertices yield the same weight, choose the one that comes first alphabetically in the algorithm.

    b. Compare your result in part (a) with the breadth-first traversal from Exercise 19(a). Explain any similarities or differences that you observe.

21. The digraph implementation in this chapter uses a variable VertexNumber to specify an internal name for each new vertex identified, and these numbers demonstrate the order in which vertices are specified.

    a. Why is it incorrect to implement the IsEmpty function by returning the result of the comparison (VertexNumber = 0)?

b. As vertices are added and deleted from a digraph, VertexNumber always increases in this computation of VertexNumber. What would happen to the various digraph operations if VertexNumber exceeded MaxVertices for either the adjacency matrix or adjacency lists implementation?

c. To avoid any difficulties identified in part (b), one programmer suggested that VertexNumber be decreased by 1 within DelVertex each time a vertex was deallocated. Thus, VertexNumber would give the number of vertices currently in the digraph. What difficulties might be introduced by such an approach?

d. Develop an approach for allocating internal vertex numbers that avoids the difficulties identified in parts (a), (b), and (c) of this exercise.

22. The text states that a complete, directed graph of N vertices has $N(N - 1)$ edges, while a complete, undirected graph of N vertices has $N(N - 1)/2$ edges. Justify each of these assertions.

23. The text observes that a binary tree is a directed, acyclic graph in which one vertex has in-degree 0, all other vertices have in-degree 1, and all vertices have out-degree 0, 1, or 2. Is the converse true? That is, suppose G is a directed, acyclic graph with the above constraints on the in-degrees and out-degrees of its vertices. Must such a digraph be a binary tree? Justify your answer either by giving a proof that the result must be true or by giving a counterexample to show that it is false.

24. Assume that a digraph has N vertices, and let A be its adjacency matrix. Each of the following questions asks for a Yes or No answer. In each case, if the answer is Yes, prove your result. If the answer is No, give a counterexample.

a. If A^{N-2} has some nonzero entries, must A^{N-1} have some zero entries?

b. If A^{N-1} has all nonzero entries, could A^N have any zero entries?

c. If A^{N-1} has all nonzero entries, is it possible for A^M to have any zero entries for any integer M larger than $N-1$?

25. The text suggests that the topological sort algorithm can be used to determine if a digraph contains cycles.

a. Modify the topological sort algorithm to determine if a digraph contains cycles.

b. Modify the breadth-first or depth-first traversal algorithms to determine if a digraph contains a cycle.

c. Determine how one might use powers of the adjacency matrix to determine if a digraph contains a cycle.

26. The following directed graph, called a *resource-allocation graph*, arises in the study of operating systems.

We consider each disk file, printer, keyboard, computer screen, or other computer device as a resource. Other resources might include memory partitions and communication ports. Suppose these resources are numbered $R_1, R_2, \ldots, R_n$.

A computer supports the running of various processes, and we number these $P_1, P_2, \ldots, P_m$. During its running, a process may request various resources that it needs for its work. For example, a process may need access to a disk file or a communication port. Such requests are handled by the operating system.

Within this framework, the resource-allocation graph is defined as follows: the vertices of the graph are the collection of resources plus the collection of processes. A directed edge is drawn from process P_i to resource R_j if P_i has been given R_j by the operating system. A directed edge is drawn from resource R_j to process P_i if P_i has requested R_j, but this request has not yet been granted.

a. Suppose processes 1, 2, and 3 need three files a, b, and c, and suppose further that process 1 has been granted file a, process 2 has been granted file b, and process 3 has been granted file c. Each process has requested the other files, but these requests remain outstanding because the operating system cannot allow more than one process to write on a file at once.

   Write the resource allocation graph for this situation.

Deadlock occurs within a computer if two processes each have some resources that others need in order to continue. For example, in part (a), process 1 has file a, which process 2 needs; and process 2 has file b, which process 1 needs. Thus, both processes are waiting for the other and processing cannot continue.

b. Suppose that only one process at a time can use a given resource. Explain why a cycle in the resource-allocation graph corresponds to a deadlock in which some processing is suspended indefinitely because at least two processes are waiting for the other.

c. Draw a graph to illustrate that a deadlock might involve an arbitrarily large number of processes. (In other words, n processes are deadlocked, but processing could be completed if any one of them were removed.)

d. Develop an algorithm that examines a resource-allocation graph for potential deadlocks.

27. How many Hamiltonian circuits exist on a complete digraph with n vertices? Justify your answer.

28. Write an algorithm that determines if a Hamiltonian circuit exists in a digraph.

In Exercises 29–34, determine the complexity of the specified operations, assuming there are N vertices and E edges. Assume that all edge operations are in terms of internal names.

29. Depth-first traversal

   _____ list of edges _____ adjacency matrix _____ adjacency lists

30. Breadth-first traversal

   _____ list of edges _____ adjacency matrix _____ adjacency lists

31. Topological sort

   _____ list of edges _____ adjacency matrix _____ adjacency lists

32. Single-source shortest path

   _____ list of edges _____ adjacency matrix _____ adjacency lists

33. Delete Vertex in a directed graph

   _____ list of edges _____ adjacency matrix _____ adjacency lists

34. Delete Edge

   _____ list of edges _____ adjacency matrix _____ adjacency lists

Give the complexity of the following operations, which deal with implementations of the symbol table that maps the external name into an internal name.

35. Insert Vertex (hash table used)

36. Insert Vertex (unsorted array)

37. Insert Vertex (sorted array)

38. Insert Vertex (sorted linked list)

39. Insert Vertex (unordered linked list)

40. Insert Vertex (binary search tree)

41. Insert Vertex (AVL tree)

42. Find Vertex (sorted array)

43. Find Vertex (sorted linked list)

44. Find Vertex (binary search tree)

45. Write the algorithms for marking a vertex. Use a Boolean array indexed from 1 to VertexNumber.

46. Specify the Unweighted Digraph ADT.

47. Specify the Labeled Digraph ADT.

48. Write the axioms for StoreEdge so that when a vertex is used to specify an edge that is not in V(G), the vertex is added to V(G) and then the edge is inserted.

49. Rewrite Create and StoreVertex so that the StoreVertex operation initializes where the edges associated with the vertex are to be represented.

Undirected Graphs and Complexity

Chapter 10 introduced the definition of a graph G as a mathematical object that contains a set of vertices and a set of edges connecting selected vertices. The chapter then focused upon directed graphs, in which an edge $<v_1, v_2>$ goes in a specified direction from vertex v_1 to vertex v_2. This chapter studies undirected graphs, in which each edge (v_1, v_2) goes in both directions between v_1 and v_2.

Following common usage, we use the term *graph* to mean *undirected graph* throughout this chapter.

A Computer-Networking Example

As a simple example of an undirected graph, consider a collection of computers as the vertices of a graph, and consider the communication channels between the machines as the edges. Of course, if the communication could flow in only one direction between machines, then the graph would be directed. But in this example, each wire allows two-way communication, and so the graph is undirected.

Communication between machines can involve specific costs. For example, we could measure the average time required to send a message of a standard size from one place to another, in which case the cost might be related to transmission speeds and processing delays due to hardware or operating systems. Costs might also involve monetary factors—for instance, if we were leasing wires from a communication company and were charged for each unit of data transmitted. Such circumstances give rise to weighted graphs, where the cost of transmission is given for each edge or communication channel. A simple example of such a graph is shown in Figure 11.1.

This graph, G1, shows eight machines, each of which has been given a specific name. Each machine is connected directly to three others through specific wires. The weights associated with each edge give the cost (for example, time delays, usage charges) for communication along each channel.

Many of the algorithms discussed for directed graphs apply here as well and provide interesting information. For example, in the graph in Figure 11.1, a breadth-

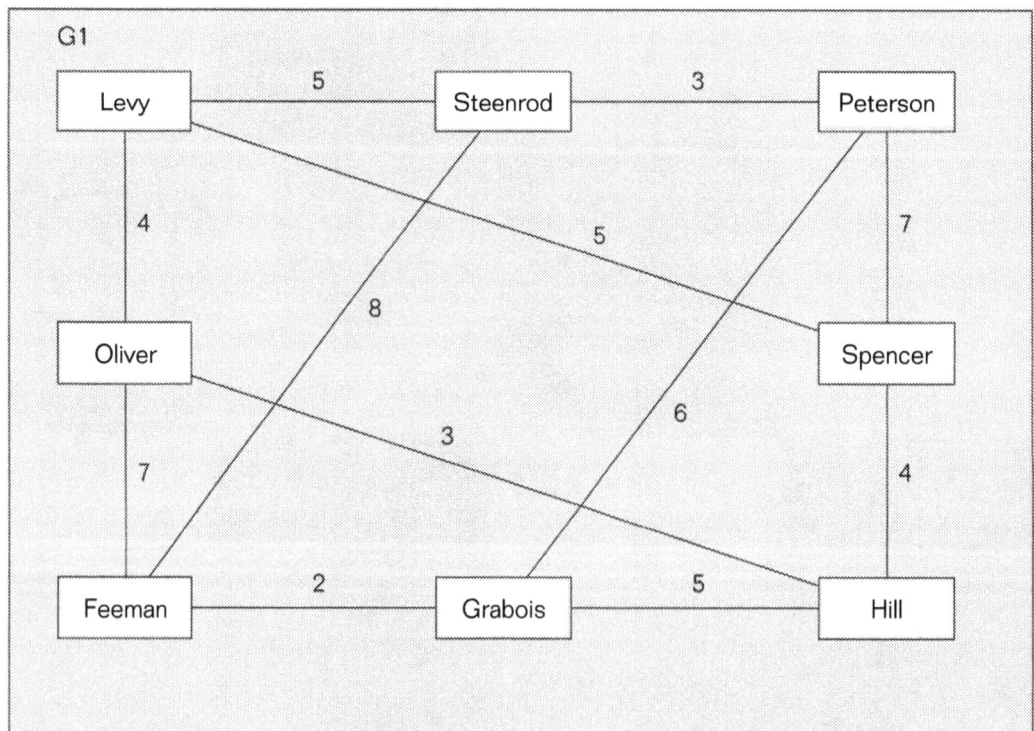

Figure 11.1 Computers and Communication Channels Between Them

first traversal from vertex Levy first identifies vertices that can be sent messages directly (Oliver, Spencer, Steenrod), and then determines that all other nodes in the graph can be sent messages with only one intermediate stage. More generally, a breadth-first traversal can be used to determine how to send a message from one machine to another with the smallest possible number of retransmissions.

In Figure 11.1, the single-source, shortest-path algorithm determines the least cost from one machine to each of the others. Thus, if cost counts the time delay involved in the transmission of a message from one machine to another, then the single-source, shortest-path algorithm indicates how to send a message in the fastest possible way between machines. Note that this path may be different than one obtained using a breadth-first traversal, because the breadth-first minimizes the number of retransmissions and does not consider the time delay for each transmission. If each retransmission involves the same delay, then the two algorithms should give similar results. If different machines have different capabilities, however, then the results may be quite different.

A Hamiltonian circuit in Figure 11.1 would specify a path that would allow a message to be passed from one machine to each of the others, going through each intermediate machine only once.

In contrast to the algorithms just discussed, the topological sort algorithm does not apply to undirected graphs. In Figure 11.1, messages can be sent in either direction along communication channels, and no vertex can be identified as being first, as would be required for a topological sort.

Specification

As with directed graphs, undirected graphs are determined by a set of vertices and a set of edges, and all of the operations of directed graphs also apply to undirected graphs. The axioms for graphs, therefore, are virtually identical to those for directed graphs. We have to be careful, however, to specify that any edge (v_1, v_2) from vertex v_1 to vertex v_2 goes in the other direction—from v_2 to v_1—as well.

Much of the value of undirected graphs comes from determining various relationships among vertices and edges within the graph, and many such results are provided by established graph algorithms. For example, the following two observer functions provide answers to commonly asked questions. In each case, the output type of the observer is in parentheses beside the function. We use ADT List to mean any linear list.

Connectivity (Boolean): Is the graph connected? (That is, can I get from any vertex to any other one?)

Minimum-Cost Spanning Tree (ADT List): Returns a list of edges, that specify a complete traversal, which minimizes a function of the values on the edges. (That is, what is the cheapest way to connect machines within a communication system? Note that this cheapest connection never contains redundant paths, because removing redundancy always lowers cost.)

In reviewing graph algorithms discussed previously, we can also consider how we might use parallelism to obtain results more quickly. For example, we can consider parallel versions of our traversal algorithms. While the availability of multiple processors normally does not change the specifications for the problems we want to solve, a parallel-processing environment can change the way we tackle problems.

Implementation

Because graphs are really directed graphs with all edges going in both directions between vertices, we can implement graphs using adjacency matrices or adjacency lists, as we did for directed graphs. An edge (v_i, v_j) connects the vertices v_i and v_j in both directions, so each edge is recorded as going from v_i to v_j and from v_j to v_i. For adjacency matrices, this two-directional quality of edges means that any matrix entry $A[i,j]$ for row i, column j is the same as the entry $A[j,i]$ in row j, column i. An n by n matrix A is said to be *symmetric* if $A[i,j] = A[j,i]$ for all i and j. Because edges in undirected graphs always go in both directions, adjacency matrices for graphs are always symmetric.

In mathematics, symmetric matrices are found to have some special properties. For example, if A is a symmetric matrix, then all powers of A (for example, A^2, $A^3, A^4, \ldots, A^n$) are also symmetric. All of these properties, therefore, apply to adjacency matrices for graphs.

In Chapter 10, we found that powers of the adjacency matrix correspond to the number of paths of a specific length from one vertex to another; the entry $A^k[i,j]$ gives the number of paths of length k from vertex v_i to vertex v_j. Because powers of symmetric matrices are symmetric, general mathematical theory indicates that $A^k[i,j] = A^k[j,i]$, so there must be the same number of paths from vertex v_i to vertex v_j as there are from vertex v_j to vertex v_i. With this in mind, you might wonder how we could obtain such paths from vertex v_j to vertex v_i. One simple approach uses the observation that given a path

$$v_i \rightarrow v_a \rightarrow v_b \rightarrow \ldots \rightarrow v_j$$

we can obtain a corresponding path from v_j to v_i by simply going backwards along the given path. In this way, every path from v_i to v_j gives rise to a corresponding path from v_j to v_i. Viewed in this way, it is hardly surprising that the number of paths of length k from v_j to v_i is the same as the number of paths of length k from v_j to v_i.

Adjacency lists for graphs have a similar symmetric property that, whenever vertex v_j appears on the list for vertex v_i, then vertex v_i also appears on the list for vertex v_j.

While implementations of adjacency matrices and lists must maintain these properties of symmetry, such details are all easily handled without further comment as part of the StoreEdge and DelEdge operations.

Application: Sequential Graph Algorithms

After developing algorithms to solve one problem, it is natural to ask if we might be able to solve other questions using similar approaches. For example, we already have written algorithms to traverse graphs, and from Chapter 4 we know several algorithms to process sets of vertices and edges. In this section, we apply several of these previous insights to the problems of connectivity, spanning trees, and minimum-cost spanning trees. As in Chapter 10, we describe each algorithm in terms of the internal representation of the objects and relationships, that is, as abstract vertices and edges. Internal names are translated into external ones within the specific applications.

Connectivity

Two related questions arise concerning graph connectivity:

1. Is a graph connected? In other words, is it possible to find a path from any vertex in a graph to any other vertex?

2. Are two specified vertices in the same connected component of a graph? In other words, is it possible to find a path from the first vertex to the second?

One way to approach both of these questions follows from the discussion of the adjacency matrix in Chapter 10. Specifically, suppose G is a graph with n vertices and M is the augmented adjacency matrix for G. In Chapter 10, we proved that G is connected if and only if every entry of M^{n-1} is nonzero. Furthermore, in considering two vertices v_i and v_j, we noted that if there is any path at all from v_i to v_j, then there must be a path of length no longer than $n - 1$. Chapter 10 also showed that if we count correctly, then $M^{n-1}[i,j]$ gives the number of paths no longer than this length.

These observations give rise to corresponding algorithms. The versions that follow assume that an application references only one graph and that information concerning that graph is stored within the Graph Module. Thus, references to the adjacency matrix are implicit within any reference to an operation on the graph. This follows the same approach used with the algorithms in Chapter 10. If an application were to utilize several graphs, then the application program would need to declare variables for each graph structure, and a graph parameter would be required for each graph operation.

Connected : Boolean

```
Compute Mⁿ⁻¹
NonZero ← True
I ← 1
WHILE NonZero AND I <= N DO
        J ← 1
        WHILE NonZero AND J <= N DO
                NonZero ← Mⁿ⁻¹[I,J]<>0
                J ← J + 1
        END WHILE
        I ← I + 1
END WHILE
RETURN NonZero
```

SameComponent (Vertex1, Vertex2: VertexType) : Boolean

```
Compute M^(n-1)
RETURN (M^(n-1)[Vertex1, Vertex2] <> 0)
```

While both of these algorithms are conceptually rather simple, both require the computation of M^{n-1}. Unfortunately, using a single processor, the natural algorithm to multiply two n by n matrices is $O(n^3)$. (There are three nested FOR loops. Each entry in the result is the sum of n products, and entries are arranged in n rows and n columns.) Therefore, computing M^{n-1} using $n - 2$ matrix multiplications would be $O(n^4)$. The exercises at the end of the chapter suggest a way of computing M^{n-1} with only $\log_2 n$ matrix multiplications, but this still yields an algorithm of $O(n^3 \log_2 n)$, which is unreasonably long. While this time complexity is discouragingly high, we see shortly that we can do much better if we have enough processors available.

An alternative approach to connectivity modifies the breadth-first or depth-first traversal described in Chapter 10. Here, we start with any vertex and determine if all the vertices have been visited. More specifically, during a traversal, we count the number of vertices visited. Then, when the traversal is completed, we can compare the count with the total number of vertices in the graph.

Connected : Boolean

```
Create(Q)
FOR Count ← 1 TO VertexCount DO
     UnMark(Count)
END FOR
Enque(Q, I1)
Mark (I1)
Count ← 0
REPEAT
    Deque(Q, Tail);
    FromEdges(Tail, Q2)
    WHILE NOT IsEmpty(Q2) DO
        Deque (Q2, I1)
        IF NOT IsMarked (I1)
            THEN
                    Mark (I1)
                    Count ← Count + 1
                    Enque(Q, I1)
        END IF
    END WHILE
UNTIL IsEmpty(Q)
RETURN (Count = VertexCount)
```

A similar approach to connectivity could be used to determine if two vertices are in the same component. Here, the traversal starts at one of the vertices, and processing stops as soon as the second vertex is found. Alternatively, if the traversal finishes without encountering the second vertex, then we conclude that the two vertices are in different components.

In yet another variation of connectivity algorithms, we can ask which vertices are connected to which other vertices. A *connected component* of a graph G is a maximal collection C of vertices and incident edges with paths from every vertex in C to all other vertices in C.

Thus, a connected component of graph G gives rise to a subgraph of G that is connected. Given G, we might be interested in a listing of the vertices in each of the components of G. For this, we first make a list of all vertices in the graph. Then we pick one vertex and begin a graph traversal from that point. Because all vertices in the traversal are connected, such vertices are in the same connected component. If we finish the traversal without processing all of the vertices, then we select another starting point and apply the traversal again. This process continues until all vertices in the graph are visited.

For this algorithm, we must obtain the list of vertices and be sure that each vertex has been reached. Again, we base our algorithm on a breadth-first traversal, although the depth-first traversal would work equally well.

While the concept of these searches applies nicely, a complication arises in practice because actual programs distinguish between internal and external names. For example, we cannot just use the internal names from 1 to VertexCount, because a vertex may have been deleted. Instead, we must use the keyed table ExternalToInternal to begin the process for each new connected component, and we use the InternalToExternal keyed table in order to print the appropriate vertex names.

Connected Components

```
ListOfVertices (List) (* gives list of vertices in the graph *)
Queue.Create (Que)
FOR Count ← 1 TO VertexCount DO
    UnMark(Count)
END FOR
WHILE NOT List.IsEmpty (List) DO
    KeyedTable.Find(InternalToExternal, Head(List), Vertex)
    Enque(Q, Vertex)
    Mark(Vertex)
    Print 'Beginning at'
    REPEAT
        Deque(Q, Tail);
        Print Vertex
        Delete (List, Tail)
        FromEdges (Tail, Q2)
        WHILE NOT Queue.IsEmpty (Q2) DO
            Deque (Q2, I1)
            IF NOT IsMarked (I1)
                THEN
                    Mark (I1)
                    Enque(Q, I1)
```

```
        END IF
      END WHILE
    UNTIL Queue.IsEmpty(Q)
  END WHILE
```

In contrast to the connectivity algorithms based upon matrix multiplication, the algorithms based upon traversals require only an examination of each vertex and edge. As noted in Chapter 10, details of these traversals depend upon various implementation choices, such as the use of adjacency matrices or lists. However, in each case, the analysis of this algorithm is similar.

Determining the computational complexity of this code requires some care. The analysis is clarified if we outline the main control structures of the code. For later reference, we have numbered the various lines of the code:

```
1   WHILE NOT List.IsEmpty (List) DO
2       Enque (Q, Vertex)
3       Mark(Vertex)
4       REPEAT
5           Deque (Q, Tail);
6           Delete (List, Tail)
7           FromEdges(Tail, Q2)
8           WHILE NOT Queue.IsEmpty(Q2) DO
9               Deque (Q2, I1)
10              IF NOT IsMarked (I1)
11                  THEN
12                      Mark(I1)
13                      Enque(Q, I1)
14              END IF
15          END WHILE
16      UNTIL Queue.IsEmpty(Q)
17  END WHILE
```

First, we consider the work of outermost WHILE loop and the REPEAT loop. Together, these loops examine each vertex in the graph. More specifically, vertices are placed on a queue before they are processed. Further, vertices are marked when they are placed on the queue, so that they can be placed upon the queue only once. If there are N vertices in the graph, these observations indicate that the statements within the REPEAT loop (lines 5–7) repeat exactly N times, and the beginning code (lines 2–3) repeats no more than N times. The Enque, Mark, and Deque operations all have O(1), so altogether the work involved with lines 2–3 and 5 has O(N).

Deletion from a list has 0(N) in line 6, and our previous observations indicate that this Delete operation is called N times. Thus, the total work for line 6 has O(N²).

FromEdges (line 7) identifies the edges from a particular vertex. Because line 7 is called for all N vertices, FromEdges is called N times, and it may process up to e edges, the number of edges in the graph. Altogether, line 7 may require O(max {N, e}) to process all vertices and edges. Sometimes this is written O(N + e).

Turning to the innermost WHILE loop, Q2 handles all edges for all vertices. IsEmpty and Deque have O(1), so the amount of work altogether for lines 8–9 again is O(N + e). Similarly, the total work for the evaluation of line 10 has O(N + e).

Finally, the body of the inner IF-THEN code (lines 11–14) involves two O(1) operations, and each of these are executed only when a vertex is not marked. As noted above, each vertex is processed only once, so altogether the work for lines 11–14 have O(N)*O(1) or O(N).

Putting all of these pieces together, the highest order work involves deletion from the list of vertices in line 6, and the entire algorithm has O(N²).

Spanning Trees

A *spanning tree* of a graph G is a connected subgraph of G that contains all of G's vertices but no cycles. Thus, a spanning tree may be viewed as a subgraph that is obtained by beginning with G and then removing edges until no cycles remain, while retaining the connectivity of G. Because spanning trees are connected, they are defined only on connected graphs or connected components of unconnected graphs.

Depth-First and Breadth-First

The edges represented in either a depth-first traversal or a breadth-first traversal form a spanning tree. Figures 11.2 and 11.3 show some spanning trees generated from Figure 11.1 using these traversals, starting from node Levy. At each node, an arbitrary choice is made concerning which node to visit next. Because these searches do not depend upon the weights associated with edges, these weights are not shown.

A review of Figures 11.2 and 11.3 may suggest why these subgraphs are said to span—namely, because the edges in a spanning tree tie all of the vertices together. The use of the term "tree" may or may not be clear, however, because these graphs may not look much like traditional trees with a root at the top. In order to obtain this more traditional look, suppose the vertices are objects held together by edges made of string. Now, consider what happens if you pick up a spanning tree by a vertex and allow the remaining vertices and edges to dangle downward. The resulting structure has the node you are holding as a root, and other vertices are in a hierarchical tree structure. Thus, while a spanning tree may not look familiar initially, it does represent the traditional tree structure.

Minimum Cost

The minimum-cost spanning tree is defined on a weighted, undirected, connected graph. A *minimum-cost spanning tree* is a spanning tree in which the sum of the weights on the edges is a minimum. Such a subgraph contains (NumberOf Vertices – 1) edges. (Why?)

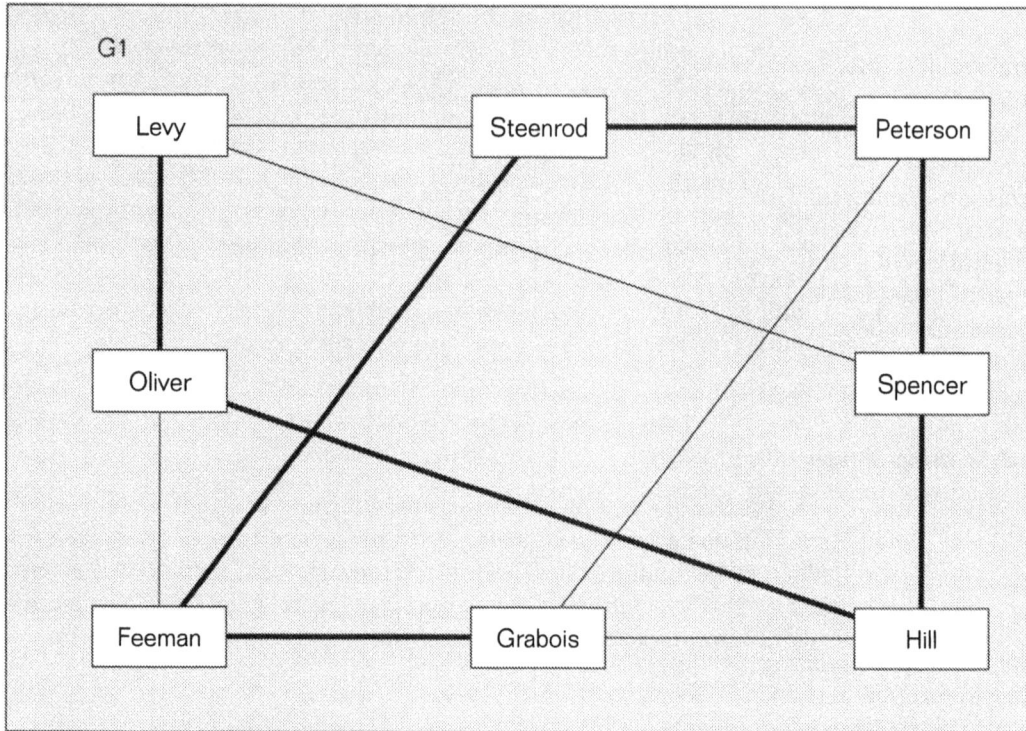

Figure 11.2 Spanning Tree Generated by a Depth-First Search (Tree edges are highlighted)

Several classic algorithms can be used to solve this problem. The best known is Kruskal's algorithm, which examines each edge in order by weight and adds the edge to the set if it does not cause a cycle. In fact, it uses the Union/Find algorithms to determine if a cycle exists. Each vertex starts out in a set by itself. If the Head and Tail of an edge are in different sets, the sets are joined and the edge goes into the spanning tree. If the Head and Tail are in the same set, the edge is not put in the spanning tree because adding the edge would cause a cycle. (Note that the constraint of the number of edges in the spanning tree excludes a cycle.) You are asked to implement this algorithm in the exercises.

The algorithm we present here is slightly different and is another example of a greedy algorithm. Recall that greedy algorithms are motivated by making short-term choices that seem optimal in some sense. The long-term result is then obtained by putting these short-term choices together.

Here, we implement a traversal of the graph in order of priority, using the marked property of a vertex to detect cycles. The items on the priority queue are weighted edges (Tail, Head, Weight). We use the notation Head(Edge) and Weight(Edge) to refer to the Head and Weight, respectively. Weight(Edge) is the priority. We initialize the process by putting the FromEdges from a vertex on the priority queue and marking the vertex. Any vertex suffices, so we are free to choose this starting point in any way we wish.

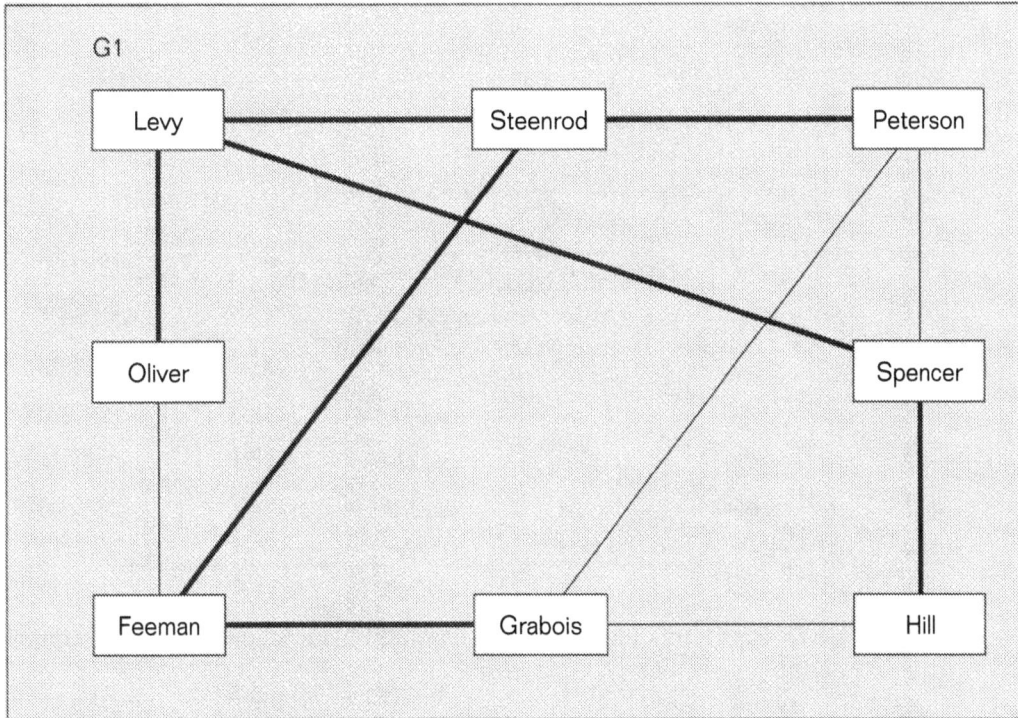

Figure 11.3   Spanning Tree Generated by a Breadth-First Search (Tree edges are highlighted)

When an edge is removed from the priority queue, it is discarded if Head(Edge) is marked because adding a marked edge causes a cycle. Otherwise, the edge is added to the spanning tree and all the edges adjacent from Head(Edge) are put on the priority queue. AddToSpanningTree refers to whatever we want to do to the edge—print it, perhaps.

Minimum-Cost Spanning Tree

```
Create(PQ)
Create(Queue)
FOR Count := 1 TO VertexCount DO
    UnMark(Count)
END FOR
Choose any vertex as vertex Vertex1
Mark(Vertex1)
FromEdges(Vertex1, Queue)
WHILE NOT IsEmpty(Queue) DO
    Dequeue(Queue, Edge)
    Enqueue(PQ, Edge)
END WHILE
```

```
REPEAT
    Serve(PQ, Edge)
    Vertex ← Head(Edge)
    IF NOT IsMarked(Vertex)
            THEN
                AddToSpanningTree(Edge)
                Mark(Vertex)
                FromEdges(Vertex, Queue)
                WHILE NOT IsEmpty(Queue) DO
                    Deque(Queue, Edge)
                    IF NOT IsMarked(Head(Edge))
                        THEN
                            Enque(PQ, Edge)
                        END IF
                END WHILE
        END IF
UNTIL Empty(PQ)
```

To clarify this algorithm, we hand simulate it to find the minimum-cost spanning tree for graph G2 in Figure 11.4.

We mark A and put all the edges for which A is the tail on the priority queue. When the loop is entered, the priority queue contains the edges(A,D,4), (A,C,1), and (A,B,3). The repeat loop is entered, and the edge (A,C,1) is served. C has not been marked, so the edge (A,C,1) is added to the spanning tree and C is marked. All the edges for which C is a tail and for which the head has not been marked are enqueued. The priority queue now holds (A,D,4), (A,B,3), (C,B,2), and (C,D,3).

The loop repeats, and (C,B,2) is served. B has not been marked, so the edge is added to the spanning tree and B is marked. The edges where B is the tail and where the head has not been marked are enqueued: (B,E,4) and (B,D,2).

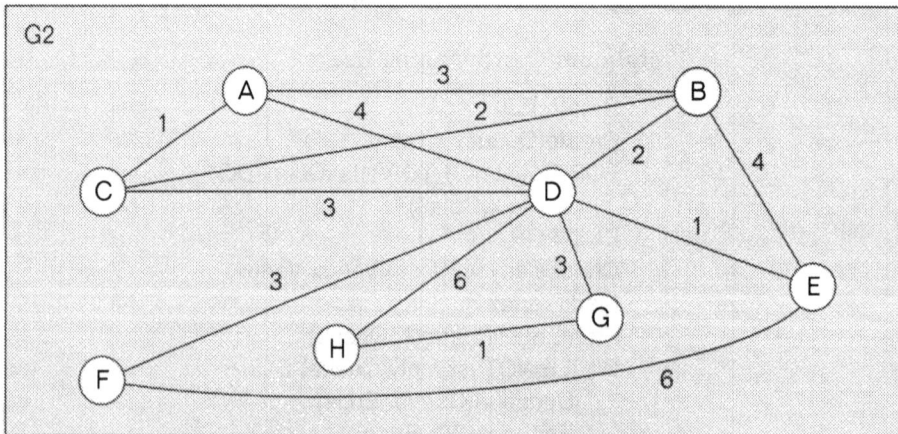

Figure 11.4 Weighted Graph

On the next iteration, (B,D,2) is served and added to the spanning tree, vertex D is marked, and the edges (D,E,1), (D,F,3), (D,H,6), and (D,G,3) are enqueued. On the next iteration, (D,E,1) is served and added to the spanning tree, vertex E is marked, and the edge (E,F,6) is enqueued. At this point, the priority queue holds (A,D,4), (A,B,3), (C,D,3), (B,E,4), (D,F,3), (D,H,6), (D,G,3), and (E,F,6).

On the next three iterations, the edges (A,B,3), (C,D,3), and (D,F,3) are served. The first two are discarded because the heads of the edges have been marked. (D,F,3) is processed, adding edge (F,E,6) to the priority queue. The edge (D,G,3) is then served and processed, adding edge (G,H,1) to the priority queue. This edge is immediately served and processed. Because all of the vertices have now been marked, the priority queue is now emptied.

The minimum-cost spanning tree is shown on the graph in Figure 11.5 as heavily shaded edges. Because we simulated the priority queue by hand, we arbitrarily chose an edge when there were duplicate weights (priorities). It is possible to have alternate minimum-cost spanning trees. Had we chosen different edges when duplicates occurred, the result might have been different. However, the sum of the weights would be the same in any alternate set of edges in a minimum-cost spanning tree.

Application: Parallel Graph Algorithms

We have discussed several classical algorithms for directed and undirected graphs in this chapter and the previous one, but in each case we assumed that we had only one processor available for the work. When several processors are available, it turns out that more efficient solutions are possible for each of the graph problems we have considered. Here, we present a few of these parallel algorithms in order to suggest some of the problem-solving approaches that can help us take advantage of multiple processors for handling graphs.

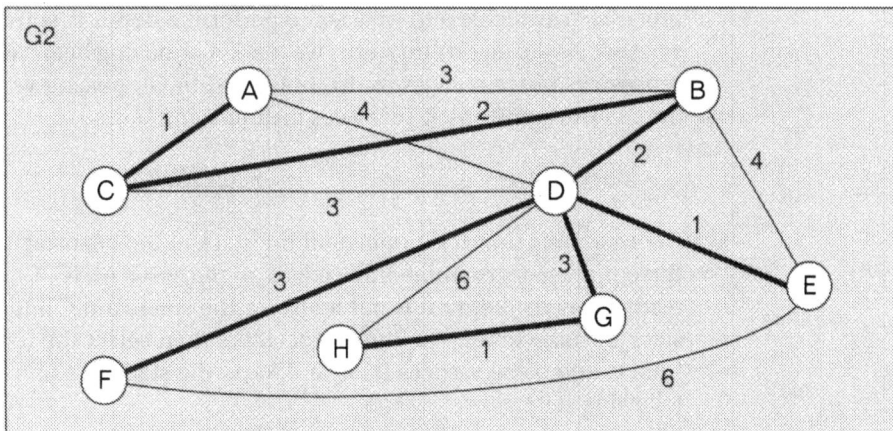

Figure 11.5 Minimum-Cost Spanning Tree

Parallel Graph Traversals

The sequential depth-first and breadth-first traversals have many similarities. In both cases, one begins with a graph and a designated starting vertex within that graph, and output takes the form of a printed or sequential list of vertices. During processing, each algorithm uses a secondary structure (a stack or a queue) to identify vertices that have not yet been processed. While the details of handling this secondary structure differ between a depth-first and a breadth-first approach, the basic algorithms share the following outline:

1. Specify that all vertices are unmarked.
2. Place initial vertex on a secondary structure (stack or queue).
3. Continue while the secondary structure is nonempty.
   a. Remove a vertex V from the secondary structure.
   b. If V is not marked,
      i.   Mark V.
      ii. Perform processing at V (print, add to output list, etc.).
      iii. For each edge (V, V2), if V2 has not been visited already, insert it into the secondary structure.

In the sequential traversals, only one vertex and one edge at a time can be processed in Step 3. With several processors, we have the potential to process several vertices or several edges at once.

As an example, consider a depth-first traversal in an environment where we have p processors that share a common memory. In this context, in processing a vertex V in Step 3(b)(iii), we can have each processor examine a different edge, thus processing p edges concurrently. When one processor finishes with an edge, that processor can process another edge from V, until all edges from V are processed. Once all of the edges from V are examined and the stack is updated, then another vertex is popped off of the stack and all p processors handle the edges from that next vertex.

As an example, consider the graph in Figure 11.6. Suppose we have three processors available and we wish to perform a depth-first traversal, beginning at vertex A. As the algorithm starts, we mark A as having been visited. Then the three processors process edges (A, B), (A,F), and (A,G), placing vertices B, F, and G on the stack in some order. This gives the following state:

Marked: A   Stack: G, F, B

Assuming that G is popped off the stack at the next stage, G is visited and the three processors examine three edges, perhaps (G, A), (G, C), and (G, F). A has already been visited, so it is not added to the stack, but C and F are placed on the stack in some order. The three processors then select the remaining three edges from G and place vertices H, K, and M on the stack in some order. This gives the following state:

Marked: A, G   Stack: M, K, H, F, C, F, B

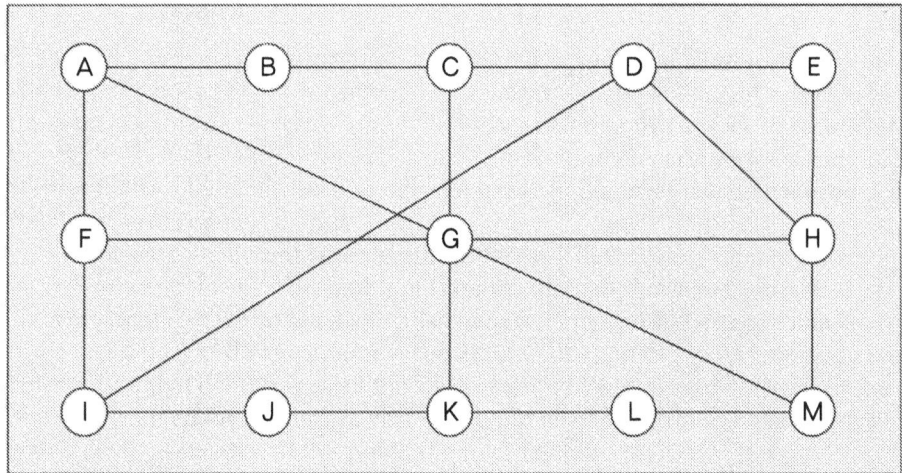

Figure 11.6 An Undirected Graph

Assuming that M is popped off the stack next, M is visited, and the three processors examine (M, G), (M, H), and (M, L), placing H and L on the stack as unmarked vertices. This gives the following state:

Output: A, G, M   Stack: L, H, K, H, F, C, F, B

Processing now may pop L off the stack, and L is visited. Because L has only two edges, (L, K) and (L, M), only two processors are used at this stage. K is placed on the stack, while M has already been marked and is not considered further. During this work, the third processor is idle, as there is no edge for it to process. The new state is:

Marked: A, G, M, L   Stack: K, H, K, H, F, C, F, B

Three processors are used again in processing edges from K. As G and L have both been visited previously, only vertex J is added to the stack at this stage. Processing edges from vertex J again requires only two processors for the two edges incident with J, and only I is placed on the stack. The new state is now:

Marked: A, G, M, L, K, J   Stack: I, H, K, H, F, C, F, B

Processing of edges from vertex I utilizes three processors, and vertices D and F are placed upon the stack. Similarly, processing vertex F requires three processors, but no items are placed upon the stack. Processing of vertex D utilizes three processors initially to examine edges (D, C), (D, E), and (D, H); C, E, and H are placed on the stack. In the next round, edge (D, I) is the only edge from D that has not yet been examined, so only one processor can be utilized at this stage. The new state is now:

Marked: A, G, M, L, K, J, I, F, D   Stack: C, E, H, H, K, H, F, C, F, B

In subsequent processing, the remaining edges are visited and marked. In some cases, vertices on the stack have already been marked. When they are popped off of the stack, they are not processed again, and the algorithm moves directly to the next vertex on the stack.

In this traversal, multiple processors can be used effectively to examine edges. Also, some parallelism is possible in updating the stack in parallel, although care must be taken to allow multiple updates. Typically, the coordination of multiple updates involves an order ($\log_2 p$) algorithm, because each processor must tell the others if it is incrementing the stack, and room must be left in the stack for each new entry. Such communication may be based upon the tree structure of communication described in Chapter 7.

While multiple processors can speed up this traversal, the example illustrates that the depth-first traversal cannot always utilize all of its processors effectively, because the amount of parallelism is limited by the number of edges incident on each vertex. This limitation is overcome more effectively in a parallel version of a breadth-first search, because multiple processors can be used to process several vertices from the secondary structure (that is, the queue) in parallel. Again, we illustrate this approach by using three processors to traverse the graph in Figure 11.6, beginning at vertex A.

Initially, A is the only vertex considered. Thus, one processor marks A, examines edges incident with A, and places vertices B, F, and G on the queue. In the next stage of processing, each processor selects one of these vertices, and B, F, and G are visited in parallel. The first processor handles B and places C on the queue. A second processor examines F and places I and G on the queue. (Because the third processor is considering G concurrently, the second processor may or may not know that G has already been visited. Thus, depending upon how updates are coordinated, G may or may not be placed upon the queue.) A third processor handles vertex G, adding vertices C, H, M, K, and perhaps F to the queue. As with the depth-first traversal, coordination is needed to allow multiple processors to update the queue concurrently. At the end of this work, if we assume that G and F are added to the queue, the resulting program state might be as follows:

Marked: A, B, F, G   Queue: C, I, G, C, H, K, M, F

Of course, the vertices could be placed on this queue in any order, as each processor could select edges and vertices in any order. Also, the lists from each processor could be merged in any order.

Given the order of vertices shown, the next stage of processing utilizes three processors to visit vertices C, I, and G. Again, this work proceeds independently. Processing vertex C adds vertex D to the queue. (B and G are not added, because they already are processed.) Similarly, processing I adds vertices J and D; processing G adds nothing to the queue.

Marked: A, B, F, G, C, I   Queue: C, H, K, M, F, D, J, D

In the next phase of processing, vertices C, H, and K are visited concurrently by the three processors, adding vertices D, E, M, L, and J to the queue. The new state might be as follows:

Marked: A, B, F, G, C, I, H, K   Queue: M, F, D, J, D, D, E, M, L, J

Subsequent processing proceeds similarly. Thus, in the next round, vertices M, F, and D are examined. The processor handling M determines that H and G are marked, but L is not. Processing F adds nothing to the queue, but processing D adds E.

Marked: A, B, F, G, C, I, H, K, M, D   Queue: J, D, D, E, M, L, J, L, E

Processing then continues until all of the vertices are marked. As with the depth-first parallel traversal, coordination is needed in the parallel breadth-first algorithm to allow multiple processors to update the queue concurrently. Additional coordination is needed in the examination and marking of a vertex as seen in the current example. Here, vertex D appears on the queue several times. If several processors started work on D at the same time, they might all determine that D had not been visited previously, and they all might process this vertex. To guard against such repeated processing of the same vertex, only one processor at a time may be allowed to test and update the "Marked" flag for a given vertex. In the study of operating systems, this limited allowable access for testing and updating a variable gives rise to the notion of a critical section. A *critical section* is a collection of variables or code segments that only can be accessed or executed by one processor at a time.

While the implementation of critical sections within a multiple-processor environment is beyond the scope of this text, the parallel breadth-first traversal illustrates that the notion of a critical section may arise whenever several processors try to access or update the same variable within a parallel algorithm.

Matrix Multiplication

In our discussion of determining the connectivity of a graph earlier in this chapter, we noted that a simple approach examines the matrix power A^{n-1} based on the adjacency matrix A of a graph with n vertices. Other algorithms also depend upon products of such matrices. Because the obvious, sequential multiplication algorithm has $O(n^3)$, however, this approach can be quite time-consuming. But with n^2 processors, matrix multiplication may be performed in $O(n)$.

In the multiplication of matrix A by matrix B, recall that entries in each row of A are multiplied by corresponding entries in each column of B. In our investigation of how to use multiple processors to help in this task, we begin by limiting our focus to multiplying A by just one column of B. For simplicity in this discussion, we assume a square matrix. The matrix product then has the following form:

$$
\begin{array}{ccccc}
A & * & B & = & \text{PRODUCT C}
\end{array}
$$

$$
\begin{pmatrix}
a_{11}\,a_{12} \ldots a_{1n} \\
a_{21}\,a_{22} \ldots a_{2n} \\
a_{31}\,a_{32} \ldots a_{3n} \\
a_{n1}\,a_{n2} \ldots a_{nn}
\end{pmatrix}
\begin{pmatrix}
b_1 \\
b_2 \\
b_3 \\
b_n
\end{pmatrix}
=
\begin{pmatrix}
a_{11}\,b_1 + a_{12}\,b_2 + \ldots a_{1n}b_n \\
a_{21}\,b_1 + a_{22}\,b_2 + \ldots a_{2n}b_n \\
a_{31}\,b_1 + a_{32}\,b_2 + \ldots a_{3n}b_n \\
a_{n1}\,b_1 + a_{n2}\,b_2 + \ldots a_{nn}b_n
\end{pmatrix}
$$

The result of this simplified product is a row of numbers in C, where each number is obtained by multiplying elements in a row of A with the B column. We obtain the result in each entry by accumulating a sum. In order to motivate how these computations may be done in parallel, we focus on the product C, and we rewrite the entries by shifting individual rows, as follows:

$$
\begin{array}{ccccccccc}
1 & 2 & 3 & 4 & & n & n+1 & n+2 & 2n-1
\end{array}
$$

$$
a_{11}\,b_1 + a_{12}\,b_2 + a_{13}\,b_3 + a_{14}\,b_4 \qquad + a_{1n}\,b_n
$$

$$
a_{21}\,b_1 + a_{22}\,b_2 + a_{23}\,b_3 + \ldots \qquad + a_{2n}\,b_n
$$

$$
a_{31}\,b_1 + a_{32}\,b_2 + \ldots \qquad\qquad + a_{3n}\,b_n
$$

$$
\cdot
$$
$$
\cdot
$$
$$
\cdot
$$

$$
a_{n1}\,b_1 + a_{n2}\,b_2 + a_{n3}\,b_3 + \ldots + a_{nn}\,b_n
$$

Within this format, we first focus on the computation concerning the number b_1. The number b_1 is multiplied by a_{11} in the first equation, a_{21} in the second equation, a_{31} in the third, and so forth. Similarly, b_2 is multiplied by a_{12} in the first equation, a_{22} in the second equation, and so forth.

If we follow this format from left to right, we also note that the work in each column involves different entries in both the A and B arrays. For example, column 3 includes the products $a_{13}\,b_3$, $a_{22}\,b_2$, and $a_{31}\,b_1$.

We now introduce parallelism into this computation by assigning a separate processor for multiplication involving b_1, another for multiplication by b_2, another for b_3, and so forth. These processors are connected in a row, and each processor passes the result of its work to the processor to its right. The resulting configuration is shown in the diagram on the next page.

Inputs from A matrix

| Col. 1 of A | Col. 2 of A | Col. 3 of A | | Col. n of A |

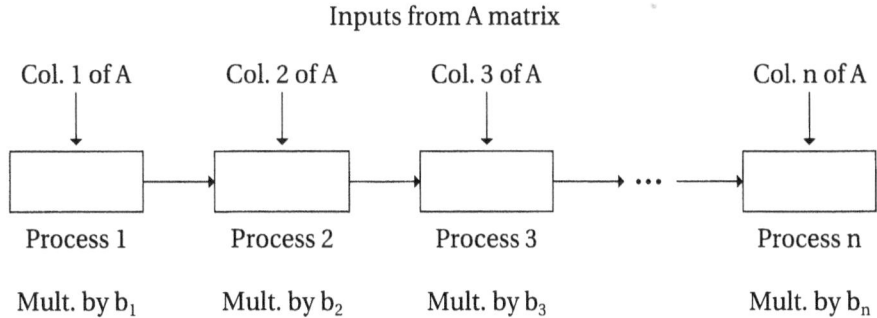

Process 1   Process 2   Process 3   Process n

Mult. by b_1 Mult. by b_2 Mult. by b_3 Mult. by b_n

Each of these processors follows the same basic algorithm, shown below:

Receive input from the processor on its left.
Multiply its B value by an input that gives an appropriate A value.
Add this product to the left input.
Send the result to the processor on the right.

Look back at the equations as they were rewritten. The labels on the columns can be interpreted as time increments. The columns represent which calculations can take place in parallel at each time increment.

In order to understand this approach more clearly, we trace the first several steps in the computation. Initially, process 1 receives a_{11} as input and multiplies it by b_1. This product is passed to process 2. This completes all computations in column 1 in the reformatted product described earlier.

The second time increment completes computations in column 2 in this reformatted product. Process 2 receives the value a_{12} as an external input. The entry a_{12} then is multiplied by b_2 (because this work takes place in process 2), and the result is added to the product $a_{11}b_1$ obtained previously from process 1. The result, $a_{11}b_1 + a_{12}b_2$, is passed along to process 3 for later use. During this same time increment, process 1 receives the value a_{21} as input, multiplies it by b_1, and passes the result along to the right.

The key to this approach is to enter the appropriate entries of the A matrix into the correct processor at the correct time. Because processing starts in the left processor, array entries cannot be given to processes on the right until work on a given row has worked its way through each of the previous processors. More precisely, the first entry of column 1 can start immediately at the first processor. The first entry of column 2, however, must wait one time unit, until processor 2 has received a value from processor 1. The third processor needs to wait yet another time unit before receiving the first entry of A's column 3, and so forth.

This timing is suggested in the following diagram, where inputs on the same line are given to processors at the same time.

Inputs from A matrix

Time:

Time				
4	a_{41}	a_{32}	a_{23}	a_{14}
3	a_{31}	a_{22}	a_{13}	
2	a_{21}	a_{12}		
1	a_{11}			

Processor 1	Processor 2	Processor 3	Processor n
Mult. by b_1	Mult. by b_2	Mult. by b_3	Mult. by b_n

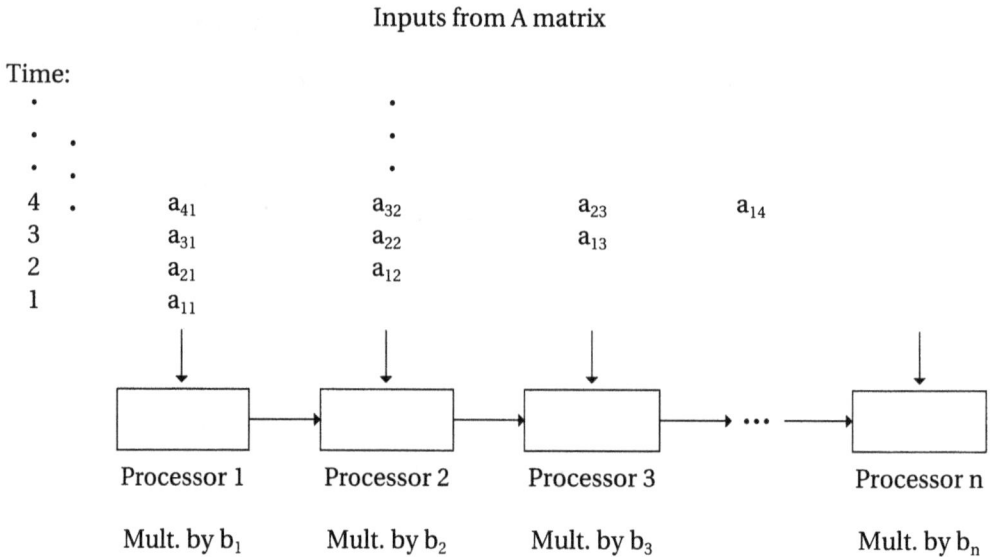

To finish this computation, we need to move each element of B to the appropriate processor. This can be done either by using the inputs on the top of the diagram directly or by entering the column entries of B along a separate input to the left of process 1 and transmitting the B entries to the right. Conceptually, direct access seems clearer. But in practice, the second approach is quite common. With this approach, process n outputs the successive entries of the product once it receives the required inputs from its left and from the last column of A.

The multiplication of a 3×3 and a 3×1 is shown below with the answer obtained by regular matrix multiplication.

$$\begin{pmatrix} 4 & 6 & 2 \\ 1 & 0 & 1 \\ 2 & 3 & 2 \end{pmatrix} \begin{pmatrix} 1 \\ 2 \\ 1 \end{pmatrix} = \begin{pmatrix} 18 \\ 2 \\ 10 \end{pmatrix}$$

We apply this algorithm to be sure we get the same answer. Recall that the processing in a column under each time iteration is done in parallel.

Time:	1	2	3	4	5	
	4×1	$+ \quad 6 \times 2$	$+ \quad 2 \times 1$			
		1×1	$+ \quad 0 \times 2$	$+ \quad 1 \times 1$		$= \begin{pmatrix} 18 \\ 2 \\ 10 \end{pmatrix}$
			2×1	$+ \quad 3 \times 2$	$+ \quad 2 \times 1$	

While this processing only handles the simple case in which B has one column, the same approach generalizes easily. If B has many columns, we simply duplicate a row of processors for each column of B. Each row of processors then performs the computations just described for a specific column of B. Such a configuration is shown below.

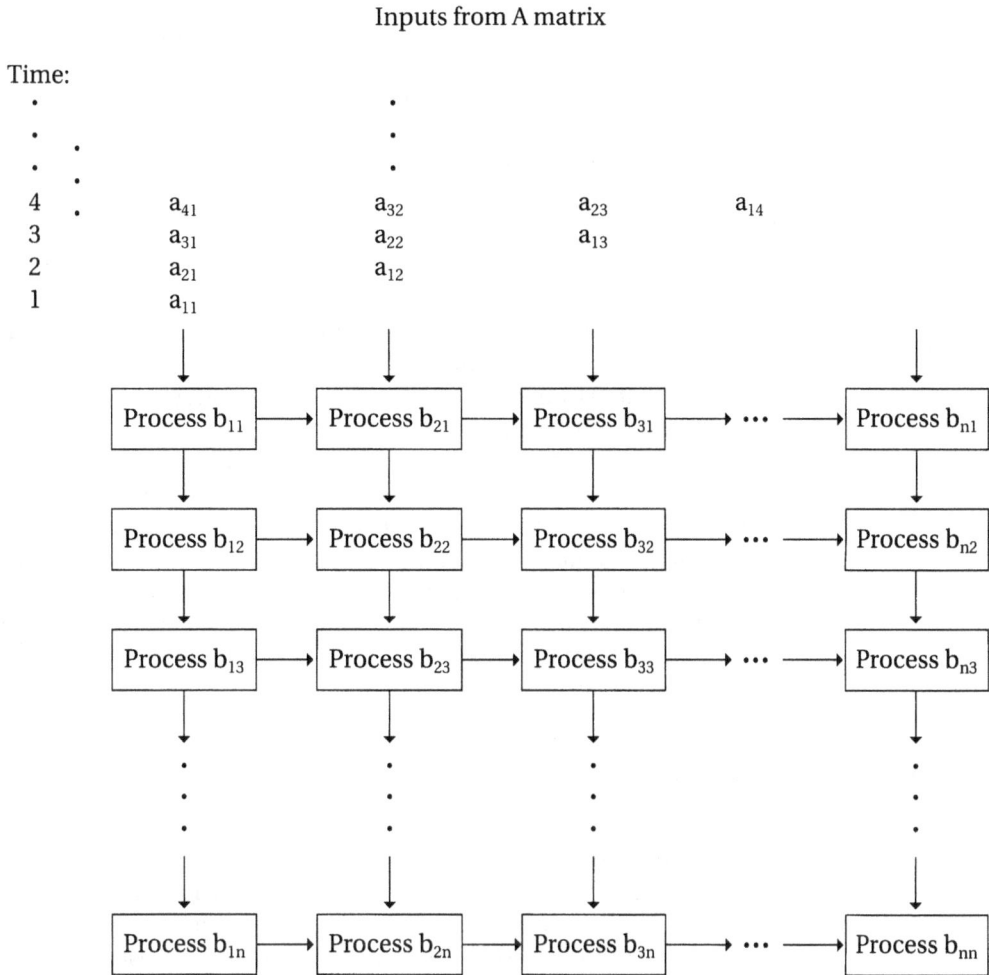

Inputs from A matrix

Time:

		•		
	•	•		
	•	•		
4	• a_{41}	a_{32}	a_{23}	a_{14}
3	a_{31}	a_{22}	a_{13}	
2	a_{21}	a_{12}		
1	a_{11}			

Process b_{11}	→	Process b_{21}	→	Process b_{31}	→ ⋯ →	Process b_{n1}
↓		↓		↓		↓
Process b_{12}	→	Process b_{22}	→	Process b_{32}	→ ⋯ →	Process b_{n2}
↓		↓		↓		↓
Process b_{13}	→	Process b_{23}	→	Process b_{33}	→ ⋯ →	Process b_{n3}
↓		↓		↓		↓
Process b_{1n}	→	Process b_{2n}	→	Process b_{3n}	→ ⋯ →	Process b_{nn}

In this diagram, each processor specializes in multiplications involving only one entry of B, and typically these values are entered from inputs at the left (not shown). Such a configuration of processors is called a *two-dimensional mesh of processors*. For the first row, processing proceeds as described for one column, with the values of A being input at the top with the time delays as discussed.

In reviewing the algorithm, the same time delays for the A values are needed in each row of processors. Thus, in this approach for matrix multiplication, once an A value is utilized in the first row, it is sent to the second row, then to the third row, and so on. The resulting algorithm for each processor then has the following slightly extended form.

Matrix Multiplication for Processor i, j

```
(* initialize processors with B array *)
Obtain B values (b_{i, j} through b_{n,j}) from processor on left.
Send any additional B values (b_{i+1, j} through b_{n,j}) to the processors on the right.
(* process A values, accumulate sums, and pass results to right *)
Receive input from the processor on its left.
Receive A value (a_{k, i}) from processor above.
Send this A value to processor below.
Multiply B value (b_{i, j}) by a_{k, i}.
Add this product to the left input.
Send the result to the processor on the right.
```

The resulting algorithm involves only the transmission of A values, B values, and partial sums through the rows or columns of the processors in the mesh. If A and B are both n by n matrices, then this transmission never requires more than n steps, and the resulting algorithm has $O(n)$.

The use of a mesh of processors, therefore, allows matrix multiplication to be done in $O(n)$, rather than $O(n^3)$ as expected from the definition of this multiplication. Computing the $(n - 1)$th power of a matrix then can be done in $O(n^2)$. (Actually, taking advantage of squaring operations, one can reduce this to $O(n \log_2 n)$ with only modest overhead. Further details are suggested in the exercises.)

This suggests that a mesh architecture allows us to solve questions of connectivity directly from the adjacency matrix in $O(n^2)$, rather than $O(n^4)$ as described for a single-processor environment.

Traveling Salesperson Problem

A rather different strategy for using parallelism may be illustrated in a parallel solution to the traveling salesperson problem. From Chapter 10, recall that a Hamiltonian circuit is a path that goes through all vertices of a graph exactly once, except that it starts and stops at the same vertex. The traveling salesperson problem then asks one to find a Hamiltonian circuit of least cost; that is, the sum of the weights of the edges in the circuit is to be a minimum. Chapter 10 described a solution to this problem by identifying all possible Hamiltonian circuits, computing the cost of each, and then taking the minimum. Unfortunately, Chapter 10 also showed that potentially we would have to check n! such circuits, so this algorithm had $O(n!)$. As n! becomes very large for even small values of n, this approach did not seem reasonable.

With enough processors, however, this approach can be viewed in a more positive light. Suppose that we have n! processors available for our work. Then we can assign a different Hamiltonian circuit to each processor and compute the cost of each circuit in parallel. In a graph of n vertices, such a circuit involves n edges, and we can compute the cost of the path in $O(n)$ by simply following the path edge-by-edge and adding the costs as we go.

To complete the work, we only have to find the minimum of these n! costs. To do this, suppose we arrange our processors in a balanced, binary tree. Then, to find a minimum, the processors at the leaves can report their costs to their parent processor. This parent can then find the minimum costs among its two children and itself, and report the result to its parent. This reporting algorithm yields the following algorithm for each processor, based at a node of a balanced, binary tree.

Receive cost from left and right children (if any).
Compare costs received with cost computed previously at this node.
Report minimum cost to parent.

If one wants to know the Hamiltonian circuit associated with this minimum cost, then this information can be added to each communication concerning cost.

In this approach, the minimum is found as soon as the communications reach the root of the tree, so the time required depends on the tree's height. From Chapter 7, we know that a balanced, binary tree of height h can contain $2^{h+1} - 1$ nodes. Thus, for a tree of n! nodes, we need height h, where $2^{h+1} - 1 = n!$, or h = $\log_2 (1 + n!) - 1$. Thus, h is approximately $\log_2 (n!)$.

Because $n! = n*(n - 1)*(n - 2)* \ldots 3*2*1$, we can conclude $n! < n*n*n* \ldots *n = n^n$. Thus, we can fit all of our processors in a tree of height h if h = $\log_2(n!)$ < $\log_2(n^n) = n \log_2 n$. Finding the minimum value in a tree is $O(h)$. Thus, we can find the minimum cost in no worse than $O(n \log_2 n)$ if we have enough processors configured appropriately in a tree.

Altogether, finding a minimum-cost Hamiltonian circuit requires first finding the cost of each potential circuit in parallel ($O(n)$) and then finding the minimum of these costs ($O(n \log_2 n)$), so the overall time of this algorithm is $O(n \log_2 n)$.

Computational Complexity

The parallel solution to the traveling salesperson problem illustrates a situation that arises with some frequency. We found a sequential algorithm that solves a problem, but this solution takes a great deal of time. For the traveling salesperson problem, our one-processor solution has order $O(n!)$. With sufficient processors, however, we found a parallel algorithm whose order is much more reasonable—in this case, $O(n \log_2 n)$.

We find this same situation in examining solutions to many other problems. Here is a listing of three such problems with the same property. In each case, we begin with a graph G with a set V of n vertices and a set E of edges.

Vertex cover problem: Given a positive integer $k \leq n$, can we find a subset S of k vertices, so that at least one end of every edge is in S? If we can, such a set S must have the property that if (v_1, v_2) is any edge in G, then either v_1 or v_2 (or both) must be in S. Such a subset S is called a *vertex cover* of G.

Graph k-colorability problem: Given a positive integer $k \leq n$, can we assign one of k colors to each vertex so that, whenever two vertices are connected by an edge, the vertices have different colors?

Degree-constrained spanning tree: Given a positive integer $2 \leq k \leq n$, is there a spanning tree in which no vertex has degree more than k?

We illustrate each of these problems by considering the graph in Figure 11.7.

In considering this graph, the set {A, C, D, G, H} and {B, C, E, F, H} are both vertex covers of size 5. (In the vertex cover problem, k = 5.) However, {A, C, G} is not a vertex cover, because (D, E) is an edge of the graph, but neither D or E is in the set {A, C, G}. (See Figure 11.8.) These remarks show that the vertex cover problem can be solved for k = 5 and that {A, C, G} does not solve the problem for k = 3. For a complete analysis for k = 3, we would have to determine whether some other subset of three vertices existed that would cover all edges of the graph. (We leave it for you to prove that this graph has no vertex cover with four or fewer vertices.) Of course, we can always add vertices to a vertex cover to obtain a larger vertex cover (for example, {A, B, C, D, G, H} is also a vertex cover, obtained by adding B to the first cover listed above). Thus, if we can solve the vertex cover problem for one value of k, we can also solve it for any larger value of k.

Turning to the graph k-colorability problem, suppose k = 3 in our example. We can conclude that the graph in Figure 11.7 is three-colorable by assigning the following coloring to the vertices:

Red: A, C, G

Yellow: B, D, H

Blue: E, F

In this list, we have used a total of three colors to paint all of the vertices, and vertices connected by edges always have different colors (see Figure 11.9). Furthermore, because we now have a coloring with three colors, we can certainly find colorings with more colors. For example, if we also have the color green, we could change E's color to green, and vertices connected by edges still would have different

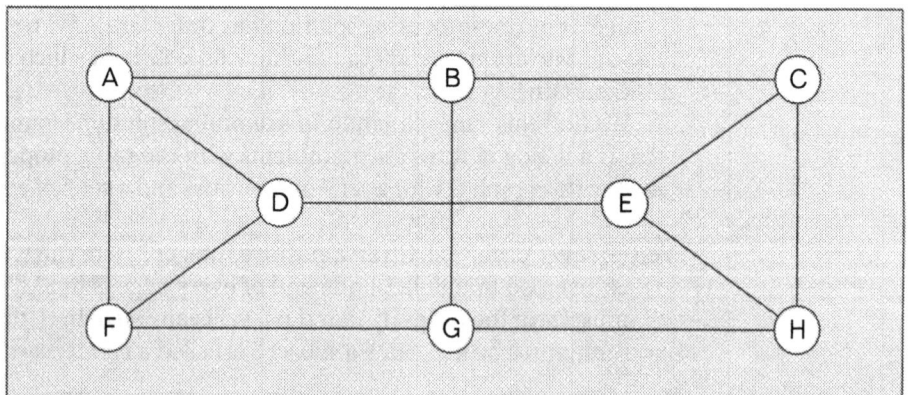

Figure 11.7 A Graph Example

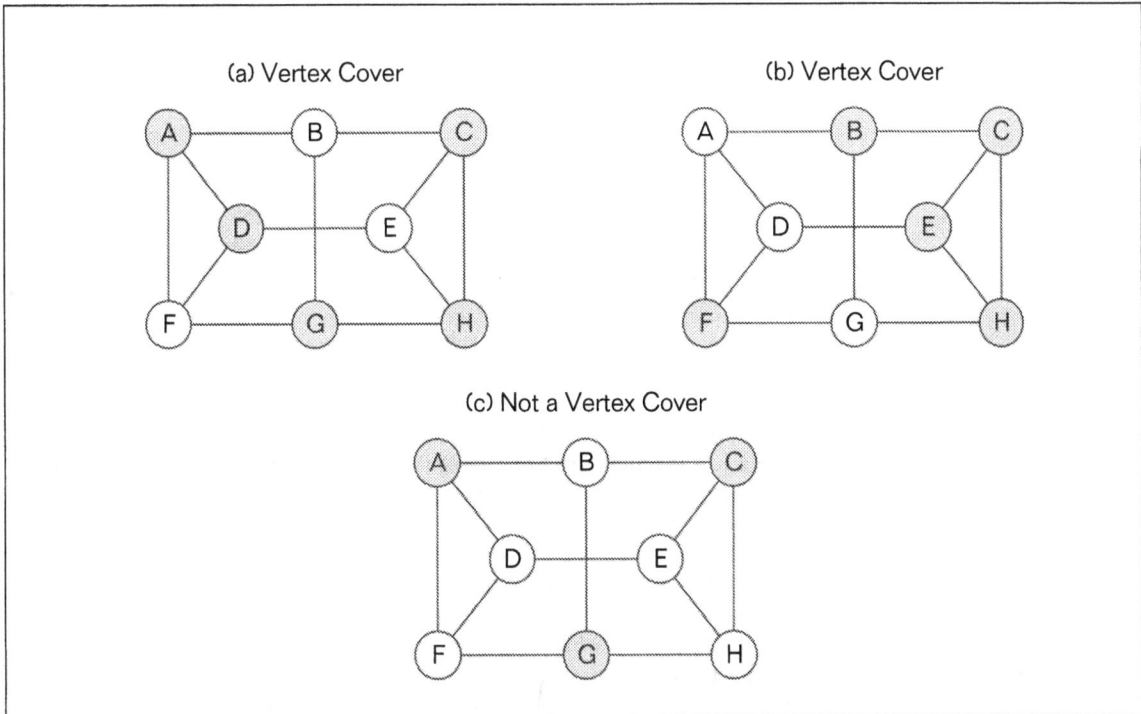

Figure 11.8 Examples of Vertex Covers

colors in each case. On the other hand, this graph is not two-colorable, because A, D, and F are all connected to each other and must all have different colors.

In considering spanning trees, we first note that any spanning tree for the graph in Figure 11.7 must have the property that the degree of each vertex is no more than 3, because in the graph itself all vertices have degree 3. At the other extreme, because any spanning tree is connected, some vertices must be linked to at least two others (unless the graph contains only one or two vertices). Thus, spanning trees can never have 1 as their maximum degree (at least, if the graph has at least three vertices). It is more difficult, however, to determine if the graph in Figure 11.7 has a spanning tree with maximum vertex degree 2. After some trial and error, such a tree can be found, as shown in Figure 11.10.

Although the details of these problems differ, the problems are similar in that each one asks whether there is a solution (cover, coloring, tree) with a particular property. A related question would ask us to produce an example of such a solution, if one existed. All of these problems can be tackled using a similar strategy. More specifically, we could generate all possible covers, colorings, or spanning trees, and determine if they had the desired properties. For example, given k, we could look at all subsets of k vertices and determine which, if any, covered all of the edges. In short, we could attempt an exhaustive search of all potential candidates to determine if any of them solve our problem.

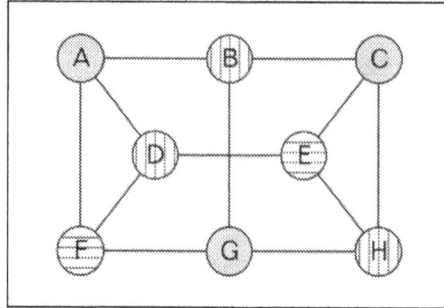

Figure 11.9 Graph Colored with Three Colors

As we saw in the solution to the traveling salesperson problem, in principle, such algorithms are straightforward. However, in practice, each of these algorithms can be extremely time-consuming. For example, for the k-colorability problem, suppose we have n vertices. Then we have to consider colorings where each of the n vertices is assigned each of k colors, and there are k^n such colorings. The number of potential choices for the other problems involves factorials. Thus, each of these algorithms may take an unreasonable amount of time, at least when only one processor is available.

With sufficient processors, however, an exhaustive search can be done reasonably quickly. In each case, we can assign a different potential solution to a separate processor, and it is easy to check to see if that potential solution solves the problem appropriately. For example, given a coloring of vertices, we check all edges in the graph to determine if there are any instances where both the head and the tail of an edge have the same color. Even if a graph has many edges, the worst case would involve searching all edges specified in an adjacency matrix, so such a check would be no worse than $O(n^2)$.

Once each potential solution has been checked, we only have to collect the answers to determine if any solution exists at all. As with our discussion of the traveling salesperson problem, this task can be accomplished by arranging

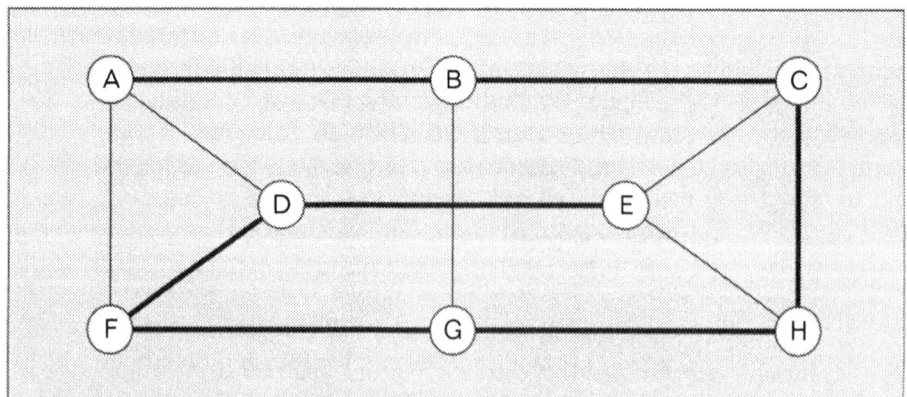

Figure 11.10 Spanning Tree with Maximum Vertex Degree 2

the many processors in a hierarchical tree structure and communicating the answers from each processor up the tree to the root. As before, the height of the tree determines the time required for this communication, and analysis similar to that which we have described earlier shows that such work for the graph k-colorability problem can be accomplished in $O(\log (k^n)) = O(n \log k)$. The computational complexity for the other algorithms is similar.

Classes P and NP

This discussion of solutions to various graph problems suggests that some problems may be solved by efficient algorithms when we have sufficient processors, but algorithms for these problems may not be very efficient when we have only one processor available. These examples motivate the following definitions, which help us classify problems.

A problem is said to be in **Class P** if it can be solved with one processor by an algorithm of complexity f(n), where f is a polynomial function of the size n of the problem's input. A problem is said to be in **Class NP** if it can be solved with a sufficiently large number of processors by an algorithm of complexity g(n), where g is a polynomial function of n, the size of the problem's input.

> **Class P Problems** Problems that can be solved with one processor in polynomial time.
>
> **Class NP Problems** Problems that can be solved in polynomial time with as many processors as desired.

In reviewing these definitions, we first note that most problems in this text are in Class P. For example, we have seen many algorithms to search or sort lists, and even the worst of these has complexity n^2, which is a (very simple) polynomial. Thus, the problems of sorting and searching in lists are in Class P.

Of course, saying that a problem is in Class P does not guarantee that every algorithm solving the problem is efficient; we can always make algorithms worse—for example, by adding loops that do little or nothing. Asserting that a problem is in Class P does, however, indicate that there is at least some polynomial-time algorithm, running on one processor, that solves the problem. Not all solutions to the problem need to be efficient, but some must be.

Next, we observe that any problem in Class P is also in Class NP. If we have a solution running on one processor, we can always run it on many processors by letting one machine do all of the work and ignoring all of the other machines. Thus, any algorithm of polynomial order for one processor is also an algorithm of polynomial order for many processors.

Our earlier discussion also suggests that some problems are clearly in Class NP, while we may not know if they are in Class P. For example, we have found solutions of $O(n \log_2 n)$ or $O(n^2)$ for the traveling salesperson problem, the vertex cover problem, the graph k-colorability problem, and the constrained-degree spanning tree problem. In each case, we have identified algorithms to solve these problems reasonably efficiently (that is, in polynomial time), *if* there are enough processors.

We know, therefore, that each of these problems is in Class NP. We have not, however, demonstrated any polynomial-time algorithms for these problems that utilize only one processor.

The classification of these problems, therefore, is not completely clear. This uncertainty concerning the classification of problems in Class P or Class NP turns out to be much more general than the specific examples we have just discussed. In fact, it is not known whether there are *any* problems in Class NP that are not in Class P. Many problems, known to be in Class NP, have no known polynomial-time algorithms with one processor. For all such problems, however, no one has been able to show that such single-processor algorithms *cannot* be found. Overall then, we know that Class P is contained in Class NP, but whether these two classes are different is open to research.

In investigating the relationship between Class NP and Class P, certain problems are found to be of special interest. In particular, some problems seem fundamental or basic, in that it is possible to translate all other problems of Class NP to any one of these basic problems.

A problem is said to be *NP-Hard* if all problems in Class NP can be reduced to it using a polynomial-time algorithm running on one processor. A problem is said to be *NP-Complete* if it is NP-hard and is also in Class NP.

To understand why NP-Hard and NP-Complete problems are studied, suppose we had an efficient algorithm to solve some NP-Hard problem. With such an algorithm, we then could solve any problem in Class NP using two steps:

Step 1. Reduce the problem in Class NP to the given NP-Hard problem using an algorithm of polynomial order. (The existence of such a reduction is guaranteed by knowing that our designated problem is NP-Hard.)

Step 2. Solve the designated NP-Hard problem.

If we had polynomial-order algorithms for both Steps 1 and 2, then the two steps together also could be done in polynomial time. This approach to problem solving is shown in Figure 11.11.

This outline indicates that if we could find an algorithm to solve any NP-Hard problem in polynomial time using one processor, then we would know how to solve all problems in Class NP with polynomial-time algorithms using one processor. Thus, finding any such solution to any NP-hard problem would demonstrate that Class P and Class NP were the same.

To take advantage of this approach, however, we first need to identify some NP-Complete problems. In one of the major advances in computer science, Stephen Cook identified the first such problem, called the *Satisfiability Problem*, in 1971.[1] This problem involves finding values for variables that make given Boolean expressions true. The interested reader may wish to consult texts on the theory of computation for additional details.

---

[1] S. A. Cook, "The complexity of theorem-proving procedures," *Proceedings of the Third Annual ACM Symposium on the Theory of Computing*, New York: Association for Computing Machinery, 1971, pp. 151–158.

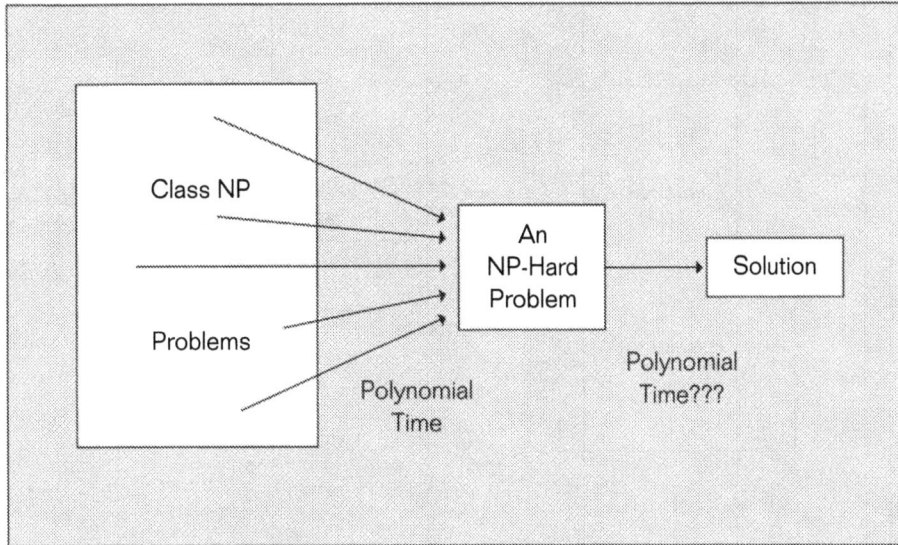

Figure 11.11   Solution of Problems in Class NP

Once the satisfiability problem is found to be NP-Complete, then a simpler strategy allows us to show that another problem S is also NP-Complete. We simply find a polynomial-time algorithm to translate the satisfiability problem to problem S. If we can find such a translation or reduction, then we can conclude that any problem in Class NP can be translated to our second problem in two steps:

Step 1. Translate the arbitrary problem to the satisfiability problem.

Step 2. Follow the translation of the satisfiability problem to S.

Combining these steps gives us a translation of any problem to problem S. A picture of this method of solving problems is shown in Figure 11.12.

Using this reduction technique, many problems have been proven to be NP-complete. For example, we can show that the traveling salesperson problem, the vertex cover problem, the graph k-colorability problem, and the constrained-degree spanning problem are all NP-complete. Already, we have shown that these problems are in Class NP. In each case, it has been shown that a known NP-complete problem can be reduced to each of these four problems.

More generally, in 1979, Michael Garey and David Johnson tabulated over 300 problems that were known to be NP-complete or NP-Hard.[2] That text also serves as an excellent resource for results and techniques related to such problems. While much additional work has been done on specific results since that book was written, the basic questions concerning the relationship between Class P and Class NP still remain.

---

[2] Michael R. Garey and David S. Johnson, *Computers and Intractability: A Guide to the Theory of NP-Completeness*, San Francisco: W. H. Freeman and Company, 1979.

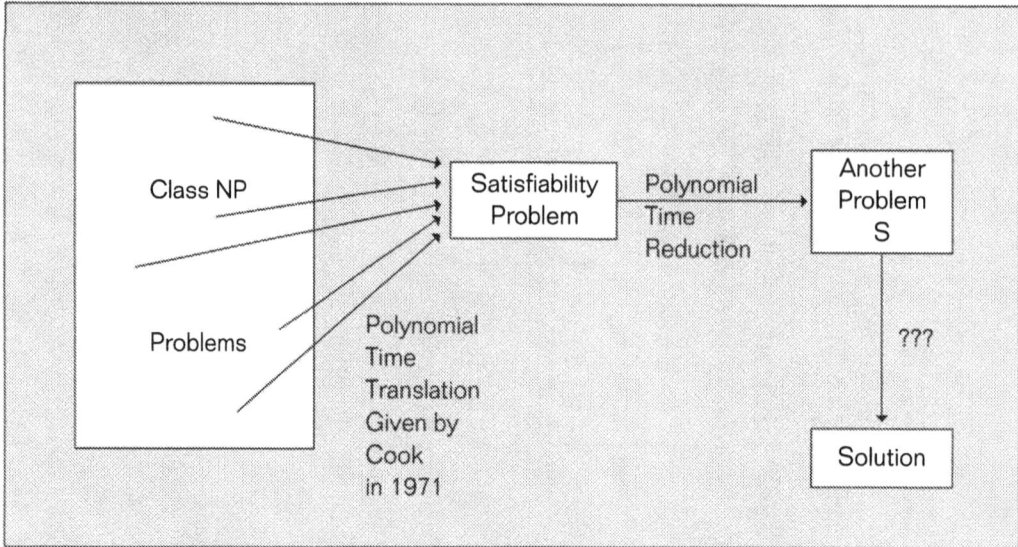

Figure 11.12 Solving All Class NP Problems by Reduction to the Satisfiability Problem and Then to Problem S

Tractable and Intractable Problems

While algorithms that run in polynomial time may take a long time to run, our experience writing code and running it indicates that such algorithms may at least be considered feasible. In contrast, way back in Table 2.1 in Chapter 2, we noted that algorithms of higher complexity (for example, factorial or exponential order) can take an extremely long time even on small data sets.

From this perspective, solutions to problems in Class P may be classified as feasible, and problems in Class NP may be considered almost feasible. For example, NP-complete problems may be solved in polynomial time if we have a sufficient number of processors, although the number of such processors may be extremely large. On the other hand, problems that cannot be solved in polynomial time, even with as many processors as we might want, can hardly be described as having reasonable solutions.

A problem is said to be **intractable** if it cannot be solved or if every algorithm used to solve the problem has complexity $h(n)$, where h is not bounded by a polynomial and where we allow the use of as many processors as desired. A problem is said to be **unsolvable** if no algorithms can be found to solve it.

> **Unsolvable Problems** Problems where no solution is possible.
>
> **Intractable Problems** Problems that have no algorithms that run in polynomial time, even when an unlimited number of processors are available. Unsolvable problems are also intractable.

A problem outside Class NP can be described as intractable. Furthermore, the definition in the preceding box identifies the following two ways in which a problem may fail to be in Class NP:

1. A problem may have solutions, but the solutions may require too much time.
2. A problem may have no solution at all.

Regular-Expression Non-Universality Problem

In order to state a problem that is known to have a solution requiring exponential order, we introduce the general notion of regular expressions, which provide a recursive specification of substrings. Initially, regular expressions are defined formally using recursion, but they also may be visualized as a type of graph. While much of our discussion here is motivated by the statement of an intractable problem, we also note that the more general subject of regular expressions has general theoretical significance for computer science and has specific practical use in the development of parsers and compilers. Due to space limitations here, we focus on a few main definitions and the formulation of a specific problem. We leave a more general discussion of the topic to other courses.

We begin by considering input symbols from the set {0, 1}, and we specify expressions that correspond to collections of strings. In fact, we consider two types of these expressions: *regular expressions* and *regular expressions with squaring.*[3] Regular expressions are built from the following four rules.

1. ϕ, {ϕ}, {0}, and {1} are allowable as regular expressions, where ϕ represents the empty set (or a set containing no strings).
2. If A and B are regular expressions, so is A + B, which represents the union of strings in A and B.
3. If A and B are regular expressions, so is AB, which represents the collection of strings that are formed by taking a string in A followed by a string in B.
4. If A is a regular expression, then we define A^i recursively for i ≥ 0, with $A^0 = \phi$ and $A^i = A^{i-1}A$. With this notation, if A is a regular expression, then so is A^*, where A^* represents the union

$$A^* = \bigcup_{i=0}^{\infty} A^i$$

A fifth definition gives rise to the term "regular expressions *with squaring.*"

5. If A is a regular expression with squaring, then so is the set $A^2 = \{x\,x$ so that x is in A}, the set of all strings obtained by concatenating each string of A with itself.

---

[3] This discussion of regular expressions with squaring is taken from "Computer Science 2: Principles of Software Engineering, Data Types, and Algorithms" by Henry M. Walker, Scott, Foresman and Company, 1989, and is used by permission of the copyright holder.

To see how these rules might be applied, consider the expression {01}*. This expression can be built using the rules as follows. First, {0} and {1} are allowable regular expressions with squaring, by Rule 1. By Rule 3, therefore, {01} is also allowable. Finally, by Rule 4, {01}* is allowed.

Next, to interpret the expression {01}*, we identify which strings are included within this collection. Here, the symbol * means that we should take zero or more copies of the string 01 and put them together. The expression {01}*, therefore, includes the strings ϕ, 01, 0101, 010101, ... These strings include the null string plus all alternating sequences of 0's and 1's that start with 0 and end with 1.

As a second illustration of how these rules might be used, check that {0*1*}* is a legal regular expression (or a regular expression with squaring) and that this expression specifies all possible strings of 0's and 1's.

As a third example, consider the expression $\{0^2 + 1^2\}^2$. Here, 0^2 consists of the string 00. Similarly, 1^2 is the string 11. Thus, $\{0^2 + 1^2\}$ is the set of two strings, 00 and 11. To form $\{0^2 + 1^2\}^2$, we take each string in $\{0^2 + 1^2\}$ and concatenate it with itself. Applying this squaring operation to the strings 00 and 11, we get the strings 0000 and 1111. We conclude that $\{0^2 + 1^2\}^2$ is the set containing two strings, 0000 and 1111.

An alternative view may be obtained by visualizing regular expressions as a directed, labeled graph, where edges are allowed from a vertex to itself. (Unfortunately, this visualization process does not extend to the squaring operation.) The rules for constructing graphs parallel those for defining the regular expressions. Every such graph has one vertex designed as a starting point and one designated as an ending vertex. Edges are labeled by input strings or by the symbol ε, representing an empty string, although sometimes the symbol ε is not written explicitly. The four rules for constructing graphs follow. In these rules, valid strings for a regular expression correspond to paths through the graph from the designated start to the ending vertex.

1. The graphs in Figure 11.13 present the regular expressions ϕ, {ϕ}, {0}, and {1}, respectively. In this figure, the empty set corresponds to a string where no input leads from the starting point to the end. Similarly, an input of 0, 1, or the empty set leads from the starting vertex to the ending vertex, based upon the given input symbol.

The remaining rules specify how existing graphs can be placed together. For simplicity, the graph representing the regular expression A is shown here.

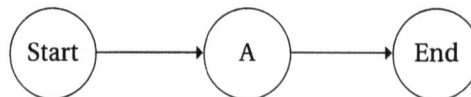

This notation shows the starting and ending vertices of A. The remaining vertices of A and the edges that connect those vertices are represented symbolically as the arrows to and from the starting and ending vertices.

Figure 11.13 Graphs for Regular Expressions

2. If A and B are graphs representing regular expressions, then the following is the graph for A + B.

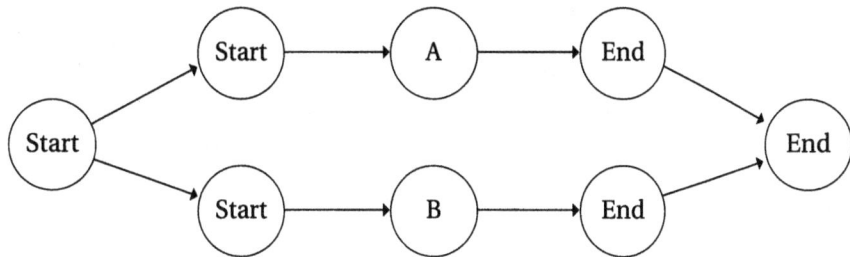

A string for the union A + B can be obtained as a valid string for A or as a valid string for B.

3. If A and B are graphs representing regular expressions, then the following represents the graph for AB.

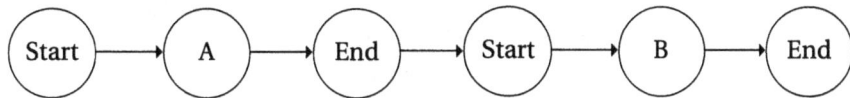

A string for the composition AB comes from a valid string for A followed by a valid string for B.

4. If A is a regular expression, the A* is associated with the following graph.

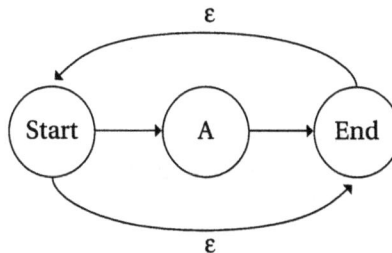

A* represents zero or more strings from A in succession, and this diagram allows all such strings. One can go directly from the starting vertex to the end (zero copies of A), one can take one string from A in going from start to the end, or one can loop back to obtain as many strings from A as desired.

To illustrate the use of these graph-construction rules, we return again to our examples on page 522. First, consider the expression, {01}*. The strings 0 and 1 have already been drawn. The string 01 then is given by the following graph.

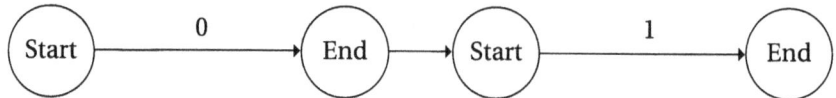

In order to move from the starting vertex at the left of this graph to the end at the right, we first must have an input 0 (to move one step right). Next, we can go to the middle vertex marked *Start* without further input. Finally, we need the input 1 to move to the far right.

From this graph, we allow movement from the initial start directly to the final ending vertex (to allow an empty input string), and we allow as many copies of 01 as desired with an arrow back. This gives the following graph.

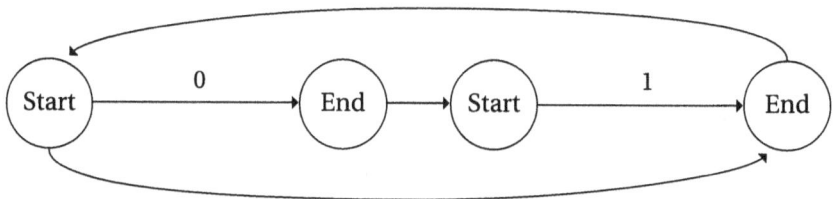

From this figure, we can obtain all strings of alternating 0's and 1's, beginning with 0 and ending with 1 by following all paths, beginning at the left vertex and ending at the last vertex on the right.

Similarly, our second string example, {0*1*}*, gives the following graph.

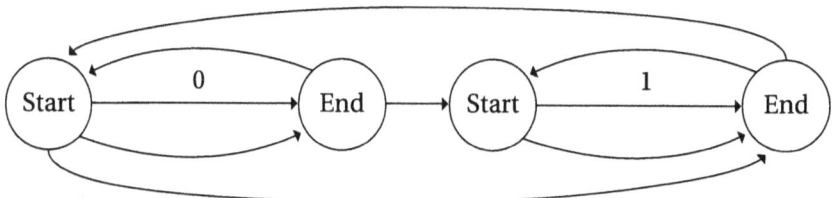

While these examples illustrate how we can translate from regular expressions to appropriate graphs, it also turns out that translation is possible from appropriate labeled graphs to regular expressions. Further discussion concerning the relationship between regular expressions and graphs is beyond the scope of this text. Additional information may be found in studies of deterministic finite automata (DFA). Beyond these theoretical results, it is also worthwhile to reiterate that such regular expressions and associated graphs have direct application in areas such as designing and implementing parsing algorithms and compilers.

With this notation and background, we now can state the following problem, called the *Regular Expression Non-Universality Problem*, which is of interest in both theoretical computer science and linguistic theory: *given a regular expression with squaring, determine whether that expression specifies all possible strings of 0's and 1's.* In examining this problem, some expressions are fairly easy to analyze, such as {01}* and {0*1*}* discussed above. In general, however, it is very difficult to determine whether all possible strings are included in a given regular expression with squaring. Specifically, Meyer and Stockmeyer have shown that any algorithm for solving this problem must have at least exponential order.[4] Thus, this regular-expression non-universality problem is known to be intractable.

The Halting Problem

The second type of intractable problem is one that contains no solutions at all. As an example, consider the *halting problem*, which asks if a program halts with a given input. In essence, this problem asks whether a specific algorithm becomes caught within an infinite loop for a given input.

One way to tackle this problem is to start the specified program running with the given input and wait to see what happens.[5] If the program stops, we know that the program is not caught in an infinite loop, and the answer to the question is obvious. If the program continues to run awhile, however, the answer may not be so clear. Certainly the program may be caught in an infinite loop and never halt. However, it is possible that the program eventually stops; you just have not waited long enough. Because you as a user cannot distinguish between the infinite loop and the program that is still executing, this algorithm of trying the program is not adequate for solving the halting problem.

In one of the most famous results in the field of computer science, Alan Turing proved in 1936 that no other general solution to the halting problem exists. Of course, it may be easy to tell if some programs halt; for example, a program with no loops must stop eventually, as each instruction is performed only once. Turing's result, however, states that no general algorithm can be applied to every program operating on any input. In effect, Turing showed that any potential solution to the halting problem that you might propose fails on at least some programs with some inputs. That is, he proved that every potential solution contains an

---

[4] Details of this work are presented in A. R. Meyer and L. J. Stockmeyer, "The equivalence problem for regular expressions with squaring requires exponential time," *Proceedings of the 13th Annual Symposium on Switching and Automata Theory*, Long Beach, CA: IEEE Computer Society, 1972, pp. 125–129.

[5] This discussion of the Halting Problem also is taken from "Computer Science 2: Principles of Software Engineering, Data Types, and Algorithms" by Henry M. Walker, Scott, Foresman and Company, 1989, and is used by permission of the copyright holder.

error. While a proof of this result is beyond the scope of this text, readers interested in more details are encouraged to examine a text on the theory of computing or on the limits of computing.[6]

Classification of Problems

Our discussion of the solvability of problems leads us to the classification of problems that is shown in Figure 11.14. Virtually all algorithms that we have discussed in previous chapters have had polynomial complexity, so they represent solutions to problems in Class P. Some problems described in this chapter have also been in Class P, as we have described polynomial-time algorithms for them as well. However, other algorithms in this chapter run in polynomial time only if we utilize a (possibly large) number of processors to perform the work. For example, the solution to the traveling salesperson problem is $O(n!)$ with one processor, but is $O(n \log_2 n)$ if we have many processors available. Such problems are in Class NP, but it is unknown currently whether such NP problems are also in Class P, that is, whether they also can be solved in polynomial time with a single processor. In Figure 11.14, therefore, we have drawn a dotted line between Classes P and NP, because it is possible that they represent exactly the same collection of problems.

In contrast to problems in Class P and Class NP, although the regular-expression non-universality Problem can be solved, no solution can be found with less than exponential-time complexity. The halting problem cannot be solved at all. Such problems are intractable.

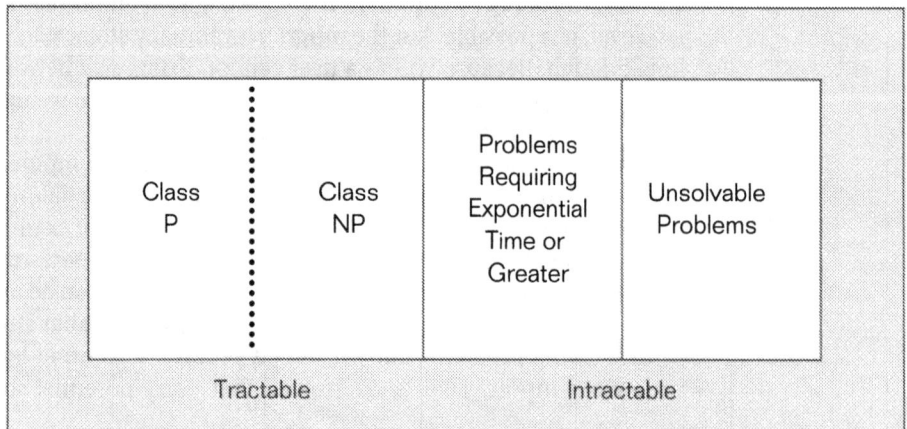

Class P		Class NP	Problems Requiring Exponential Time or Greater	Unsolvable Problems
Tractable			Intractable	

Figure 11.14 A Classification of Problems and Their Solutions

---

[6] See, for example, Henry M. Walker, *The Limits of Computing*, Jones and Bartlett, Boston, MA, 1994.

SUMMARY

Mathematically speaking, an undirected graph is a special case of a directed graph: edges in an undirected graph always connect vertices in both directions. From this perspective, many algorithms developed for digraphs also apply to undirected graphs. Graph traversals and shortest-path algorithms all can be used directly. On the other hand, some algorithms, such as a topological sort, require an acyclic graph, and such algorithms do not apply to undirected graphs.

Other algorithms apply specifically to undirected graphs. For example, questions of connectivity and the construction of spanning trees are much more natural when a graph is not directed.

All of these algorithms depend upon the same representations discussed in Chapter 10; either adjacency matrices or adjacency lists may be used.

Various parallel versions of algorithms also may be used to solve graph problems when multiple processors are available, and such algorithms can speed work up considerably.

Problems in Class P are those for which a known polynomial-time algorithm exists. Some problems, however, can only be solved in a reasonable amount of time when many processors are available. In contrast to problems in Class P, some problems in Class NP have no known polynomial-time solutions involving single processors, but reasonable algorithms are available that take advantage of multiprocessors.

Still other problems have no reasonable solutions at all. And, even though solutions to some of these problems exist, in some cases it is known that even the best solutions require at least exponential time. Other problems, such as the halting problem, have no solutions at all, and we can prove that any potential solution must contain errors. These observations indicate that while computers can be helpful in many ways, technological solutions are not always available for every problem. For example, there are no algorithms to determine if arbitrary programs halt.

EXERCISES

1. Define the following terms.

connected graph	intractable problem
spanning tree	NP-complete
minimum-cost spanning tree	NP-hard
regular expression	traveling salesperson problem
Class P	vertex cover problem
Class NP	graph k-colorability problem
tractable problem	degree-constrained spanning tree problem

2. a. If A is a symmetric n by n matrix, use the definition of matrix multiplication to show that all powers of A ($A^2, A^3, \ldots, A^n$) are also symmetric.

   b. If A and B are both symmetric n by n matrices, does it follow that the product AB is also symmetric? If your answer is yes, prove the result. If your answer is no, produce a counterexample.

3. The chapter outlines a variation of a breadth-first traversal to determine if two vertices are in the same connected component of a graph. Write the detailed code for this algorithm.

4. Yet another approach for determining connected components is based on set algorithms. Here, we begin by considering each vertex as part of its own, disjoint sets. Then, each edge allows us to connect or combine these disjoint sets, and we can continue this combination process until all edges are reviewed.

   In Chapter 4, we found that the union/find algorithm was particularly effective in allowing sets to be combined into larger pieces.

   a. Develop an algorithm to determine if two vertices are in the same connected component, based upon the union/find algorithm and the edges of a graph.

   b. Determine the efficiency of your algorithm.

   c. Suppose that the need to determine if two vertices were in the same connected component arose frequently in processing. How could you use your algorithm to minimize the average amount of processing needed over many requests?

5. The discussion of minimum-cost spanning trees at the beginning of the chapter gives a brief description of Kruskal's algorithm, using the union/find algorithm from Chapter 4. Write out the details for this algorithm, in pseudocode.

6. Show the state of the computation after each main step of the algorithm for a parallel, depth-first traversal using three processors for the graph in Figure 11.1. That is, after each step when up to three processors examine edges from a vertex, show the state of the stack and the list of vertices output.

7. Show the state of the computation after each main step of the algorithm for a parallel, breadth-first traversal using three processors for the graph in Figure 11.1. That is, after each step when up to three processors examine edges from a vertex, show the state of the queue and the list of vertices output.

8. Consider the graph in Figure 11.1 containing eight vertices, and consider an 8 by 8 mesh of processors.

   a. Write an adjacency matrix A for this graph, based upon ordering the vertices alphabetically.

   b. Assume that this mesh was used to compute A^2, and draw a diagram of the mesh. On the diagram, label which processor would handle which array element(s), identify which inputs would be sent where and in what order, and show the outputs that would be obtained.

   c. Write a paragraph describing the processing that would take place, based on your diagram from part (b).

9. Find a Hamiltonian circuit of least cost for the graph in Figure 11.1.

10. The text presents an informal description of the communication required among processors for a parallel, breadth-first traversal. Write out in detail the pseudocode for each processor for a parallel, breadth-first traversal of a graph, together with a statement of any initialization that might be required.

11. *Computing A^r where A is a real number or a matrix and where r is a positive integer.*

We illustrate an efficient algorithm for computing a power of a number or matrix with an example. Suppose we want to compute A^{51}. First, we write 51 in binary form: $51 = 110011$. Next, we observe that $A^{110011} = A^{(100000 + 10000 + 10 + 1)} = A^{100000}A^{10000}A^{10}A$, so we can compute A^{51} if we can compute $A^{32}A^{16}A^2A$. However, we can compute A^{32}, A^{16}, and A^2 by squaring: $A^2 = AA$, $A^4 = A^2A^2$, $A^8 = A^4A^4$, $A^{16} = A^8A^8$, and $A^{32} = A^{16}A^{16}$. Putting these pieces together, we may compute A^{51} by successive squaring to get A^2, A^4, A^8, A^{16}, and A^{32}, and by then multiplying the appropriate powers (A, A^2, A^{16}, A^{32}). Altogether, this requires five multiplications to obtain the powers (through A^{32}) and three more multiplications to put these pieces together). Hence, A^{51} can be computed in eight multiplications rather than 51.

a. Use the approach illustrated in this example to compute 2^{21}. (Show your steps.)

b. Following this approach, write the pseudocode for a formal algorithm to compute A^r, based upon the binary representation of the integer r.

c. Analyze your algorithm to prove it has complexity $O(\log_2 r)$.

Use the following graph for Exercises 12–18.

G = (V,E)
V = {A, B, C, D, E, F, G, H}
E = {(A,B) ,(A,D) ,(A,F) ,(B,F), (C,E),(C,H), (D,F),(E,G),(E,H)}

12. a. This graph is (directed, undirected) _____

b. This graph is (complete, not complete) _____

c. This graph is (connected, not connected) _____

13. Draw the adjacency matrix for this graph.

14. Draw the adjacency list representation for this graph.

15. List the connected components in depth-first order beginning with node A. (Visit the nodes in alphabetical order when there is a choice.)

16. Draw the spanning tree associated with the traversal in Exercise 15.

17. List the connected components in breadth-first order beginning with node F.

18. Draw the spanning tree associated with the traversal in Exercise 17.

Use the following graph for Exercises 19 and 20. (It is being represented by its adjacency matrix. A 0 means there is no edge.)

	A	B	C	D	E	F	G
A	0	10	6	4	0	7	0
B	10	0	9	0	11	0	18
C	6	9	0	1	1	0	0
D	4	0	1	0	1	2	0
E	0	11	1	1	0	0	14
F	7	0	0	2	0	0	15
G	0	18	0	0	14	15	0

19. List the edges in a spanning tree for a depth-first traversal beginning with vertex A. Process the adjacency matrix from left to right.

20. List the edges in a spanning tree for a breadth-first traversal beginning with vertex A.

21. Show the minimum-cost spanning tree for the following diagram.

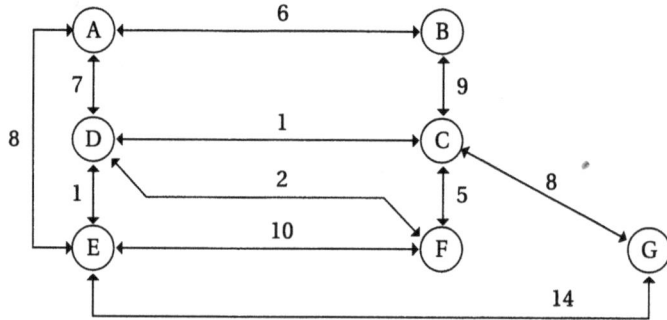

22. Show that the graph in Figure 11.5 has no vertex cover with four or fewer vertices.

23. The chapter describes a parallel algorithm to solve several NP-complete problems utilizing many processors. For each of the following problems, identify the number of processors that might be needed and the time-complexity of the parallel algorithm (including any required interprocessor communication).

   a. The vertex cover problem

   b. The graph k-colorability problem

   c. The constrained-degree spanning tree problem

24. Suppose a graph has N vertices and D edges. Determine the order of each of the following algorithms, assuming all edge operations are in terms of internal names.

   a. Determine if graph is connected using

      1. list of edges implementation.

      2. adjacency matrix implementation.

      3. adjacency lists implementation.

   b. Minimum-cost spanning tree (Kruskal's algorithm) using

      1. list of edges implementation.

      2. adjacency matrix implementation.

      3. adjacency lists implementation.

   c. Minimum-cost spanning tree (priority queue traversal) using

      1. list of edges implementation.

      2. adjacency matrix implementation.

      3. adjacency lists implementation.

25. Consider the houses in a community as vertices for a graph. For each house, we can consider the potential cost of running a sewer from one house to another as giving rise to weighted edges connecting vertices. Which algorithm might we use to connect all of the houses with sewer pipe for the lowest cost?

26. a. Show that the following are valid regular expressions with squaring, as defined in this chapter.

    $\{(0)^2 1^*\}$ $\qquad$ $(\{01, 10\})^2$ $\qquad$ $\{0^*, 1^*\}^*\{0\}$

    b. Describe which strings are defined by these expressions.

    c. Draw the graphs associated with these expressions.

27. The construction of graphs associated with regular expressions gave rise to directed graphs. Determine which of the following properties *must* hold for any such graphs, which *may* hold, and which *cannot* hold. In each case, justify your answer.

    a. There exists a path from the starting vertex to the ending vertex.

    b. There exists a path from the starting vertex to every other vertex.

    c. There exists a path from the ending vertex to every other vertex.

    d. The graph is acyclic.

    e. The topological sort algorithm can be applied to the graph.

    f. The graph has a Hamiltonian circuit.

28. a. Find an algorithm that runs in polynomial time to solve the traveling salesperson problem or another NP-complete problem.

    b. Consult with your instructor or another computer scientist concerning where your solution should be published.

29. Describe the significance of intractable problems such as the halting problem from the standpoint of computer science.

30. What social implications can you identify that might arise from the existence of intractable problems?

31. Rewrite the algorithm for DelVertex using adjacency lists for an undirected graph. Take advantage of the fact that given Adjacency[I1] you know where to look for the vertices for which the vertex being deleted is a head.

32. The chapter described ways to visualize regular expressions as graphs. In particular, each rule for constructing a regular expression translated to a rule for constructing graphs. It is tempting to try this same process for building a new graph based on the squaring operation. Although the text claimed that such a construction was not possible, what is wrong with the following graph construction?

    Rule 5: If A is a regular expression with squaring, then let the expression A^2 be represented by the following graph.

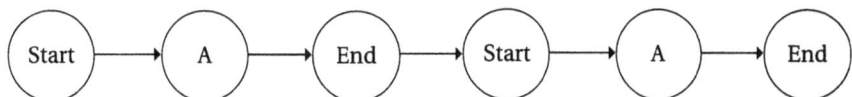

a. If A is a regular expression, does the above graph give rise to all strings that are included in A^2?

b. If A is a regular expression, does the above graph give rise to some strings that are not included in A^2?

In each case, justify your conclusion by giving either a proof or a counterexample.

Generalized Lists

12

In Chapter 1, we defined an unsorted, nonindexed linear list of data elements, and we expanded and refined this notion of lists in Chapter 6. In both discussions, lists contained a series of data elements, all of which had the same type. In this chapter, we extend the notion of a list even further. Generalized lists are defined recursively as lists in which the components can be single data elements or other generalized lists.

Generalized lists are particularly flexible and useful structures. We can use such lists to represent virtually all of the other ADTs introduced in this book. In addition, generalized lists provide the main data structure for several programming languages, such as LISP and Scheme. Other languages, such as T and Miranda, include lists and their operations as built-in capabilities. This widespread inclusion of generalized lists in many languages and environments attests the value of such lists in many applications.

In the application section, we examine how to read and write generalized lists and how to evaluate a program represented in a list.

The Translation of Several ADTs to Generalized Lists

Because generalized lists are lists whose components can be individual data elements or other generalized lists, such lists provide an extremely flexible way of organizing data, and many ADTs may be translated naturally to generalized list structures.

A KeyedTable ADT may be represented as a list of <key, information> pairs where the key is an atom and the information is another generalized list. For example, suppose we want to store the following course numbers and instructors in a keyed table.

CS1	Walker
CS2	Dale
CS3	Bruce
CS4	Moore
CS5	Walker
CS6	Stone

Here, we use the course number as the key, and we attach the instructor's name to the course he or she teaches. This gives rise to the pairs (CS1 Walker), (CS2 Dale), (CS3 Bruce), (CS4 Moore), (CS5 Walker), (CS6 Stone). If we think of each of these pairs as a list with two data elements, then overall we could describe the keyed table as a list of these six pairs, as follows:

((CS1 Walker) (CS2 Dale) (CS3 Bruce) (CS4 Moore) (CS5 Walker) (CS6 Stone))

If we represent a list as a header node followed by a series of component nodes, then this list might be pictured as follows.

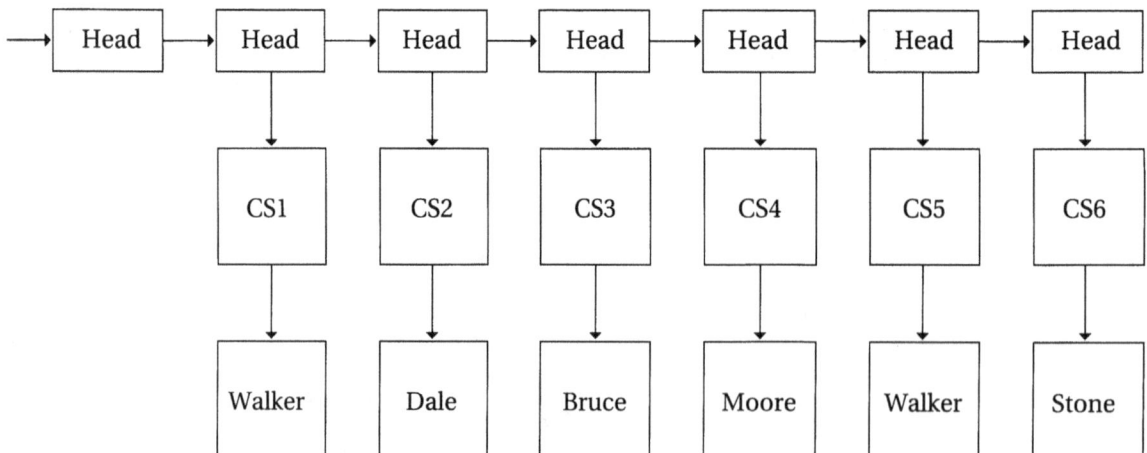

A one-dimensional array can be represented by a generalized list in at least two ways. One way is simply to link the array elements sequentially. Thus, to represent an array A[1], . . . , A[10], a first pointer would specify a node holding the data from A[1], and each later A[i] would be pointed to by the node for A[i − 1]. Here, the array index is not stored explicitly, but rather can be inferred by counting the nodes from the start of the list.

A second way of storing one-dimensional arrays within a generalized list stores (index, data element) pairs, following the discussion of arrays in Chapter 6. Thus, if the value 3.141592 is stored in A[1], then the pair (1 3.141592) is placed on the corresponding generalized list. This approach effectively treats a one-dimensional array as a keyed table, with subscripts as the keys.

A two-dimensional array can be thought of as a list of rows (or a list of columns). One of these rows can then be viewed as a list of elements, as just described for one-dimensional arrays. For example, consider the following two-dimensional array A[1..3, 1..5]:

```
3  1  4  1  5
9  2  6  5  3
5  8  9  7  9
```

Storing this array by rows, and using header nodes at the beginning of lists, we might get the following structure.

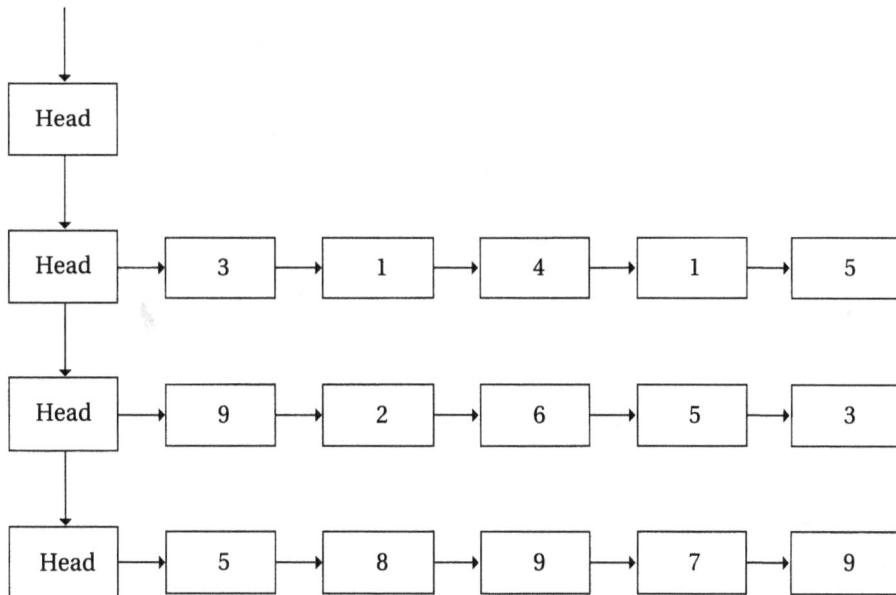

A tree structure can be stored as a generalized list in several ways. One way is to recursively list a root followed by its children. In this approach, an empty tree would be represented as the null list ( ). Next, a binary tree with only a root B might be written as the list containing the root B followed by empty subtrees. Such a generalized list might have the form (B ( ) ( )). Alternatively, we might decide to omit the explicit mention of empty subtrees, in which case this tree would be denoted by (B).

In this simplified notation, the tree with root B, left subtree A, and right subtree E would be written as (B (A) (E)). If E, in turn, were the root of a subtree with left node D and right node F, the resulting tree would be denoted by (B (A) (E (D) (F))). As a further example, the general tree in Chapter 7, Figure 7.1 could be written as:

(b (c) (d (g))   (e (h (m) (n)) (i))   (f (j) (k (o p q)) (l)))

This expression identifies a tree with b as root and with four subtrees of the root—namely, (c), (d (g)), (e (h (m) (n)) (i)), and (f (j) (k (o p q)) (l)). The first of these subtrees contains a single node, c. The second subtree contains d as root and has g as a node below d. The other subtrees of b contain 5 and 7 nodes, respectively. You should check that these subtrees correspond to the structure indicated in Figure 7.1.

Specification

A *generalized list* is a nonindexed linear list of zero or more data elements or generalized lists. Thus, a generalized list may be made up of a number of components, some of which are data elements and others of which are generalized lists. The literature on generalized lists usually refers to the data elements as *atoms*. Although we often think of an atom as being an indivisible data element such as a number or a letter, here an atom is an indivisible piece of data within the context of a particular problem. For example, an atom might be a fixed-length string of characters.

As with trees and graphs, we need to develop some vocabulary to use with generalized lists before we look at the specification and implementation algorithms. Because of the recursive nature of generalized lists, it is ambiguous to refer to the first element in the list. Do we want the first atom or the first atom in the first element if the first element is a list? (See what we mean?) To avoid this confusion, we refer to a generalized list as a list of components. Each component may be an atom or a list. Following our terminology for nonindexed linear lists, we use the terms Head and Tail to refer to parts of a generalized list. The *Head* is the first component in the generalized list, and the *Tail* is the list with the first component removed. These definitions are just like the operations Head and Tail that we defined for the ADT UnsortedList in Chapter 1. The only difference is that Head, when applied to a GeneralizedList, can return either an atom or a list. In either ADT, Tail always returns a (generalized) list.

Here is the formal specification for the GenList ADT.

type	ComponentType = (Atom, GenList)	
structure	GenList (of ComponentType)	
interface	Create	→ GenList
	IsEmpty(GenList)	→ Boolean
	WhichType(ComponentType)	→ ComponentType
	PutFirst(GenList, ComponentType)	→ GenList
	Head(GenList)	→ ComponentType
	Tail(GenList)	→ GenList

     end

     axioms   **for c in ComponentType, GL1, GL2 in GenList, let**

IsEmpty(Create) = True
IsEmpty(PutFirst(GL1,c)) = False

Head(Create) = Error
Head(PutFirst(GL1, c)) = c

Tail(Create) = Error
Tail(PutFirst(GL1, c)) = GL1

     end
end GenList

The axioms for these operations are identical to those for the UnsortedList ADT. The only difference is that the basic constructor is called PutFirst instead of Make. Because of the recursive nature of the GenList ADT, we need an iterator that allows us to list the atoms in the generalized list in a uniform manner. The following axioms make use of various operations for the UnsortedList ADT, as described in Chapter 1.

Augment Domains with ADT List

ListOfAtoms(GenList)   → UnsortedList
ListOfAtoms(Create)   → Create
ListOfAtoms(PutFirst(GL1, c)) =
    IF WhichType(c) = Atom
       THEN   Make(ListOfAtoms(GL1), c)
       ELSE   Concat(ListOfAtoms(GL1), ListOfAtoms(c))
    END IF

Implementation

Generalized lists may be conceptualized in several different ways, and the various views can lead to very different-looking structures. Therefore, we examine list usage using parenthesized notation and pictures of implementation structures before we turn to actual implementation algorithms.

Hierarchy of List Interpretations

As already stated earlier in this chapter, generalized lists can be expressed conveniently using parenthesized notation. Here, for consistency with other uses and applications, we adopt the general notation used in the LISP programming language. (The acronym LISP actually stands for LISt Processing.) In this notation, atoms are represented directly as letters or numbers. A list is constructed by placing parentheses around its components. The components themselves are separated by spaces. Atoms are lowercase letters or numbers. Names of lists begin with capital letters. Here are five list expressions. An operator in an expression is replaced by the component resulting from the operation.

L1 = (a (b c d) ())

L2 = ((x) L1)

L3 = (Head(L1) w Tail(L1))

L4 = (Head(L2) Head(Head(L2)) Tail(Head(L2))

L5 = (a b L5)

L1 is a list made up of three components. The first component is an atom, the second is a list made up of three atoms, and the third is the empty list. One approach to visualizing generalized lists uses a header node, following the earlier examples in this chapter. In this approach, each generalized list has a header node labeled *Head*.

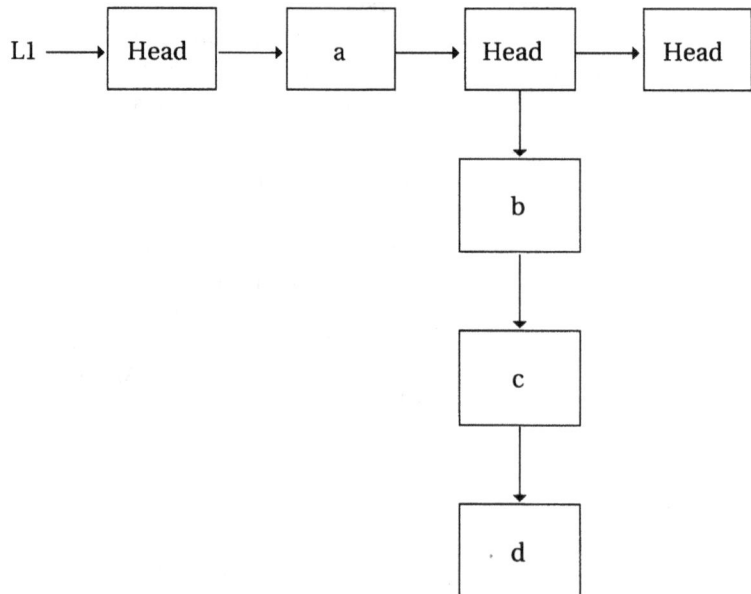

If, in addition, we want to include a label with a list for future reference, we can include that identifier in the Head node.

L2 is a list with two components. The first component is a list made up of one atom. The second component is the list L1. In the diagram, the reference to L1 is shown in the third header node.

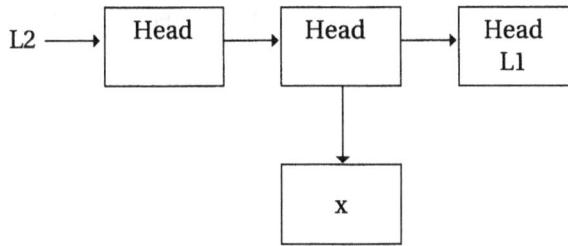

L3 is a list made up of three components. The first component is the head of L1, which is the atom a. The second component is the atom w. The third component is the tail of L1, which is the list made up of two components, the list (b c d) and the empty list.

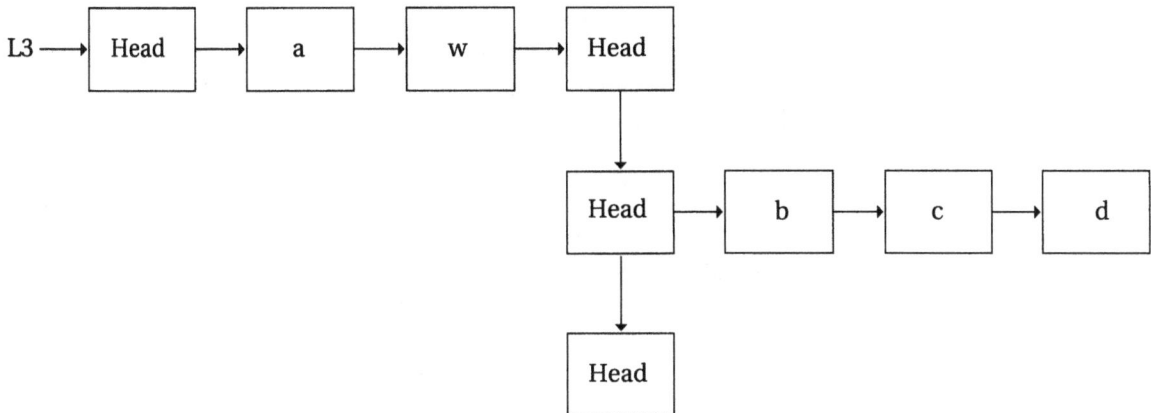

L4 is a list made up of three components. The first component is the head of L2, which is the list (x). The second component is the head of the head of L2, that is, the head of the list (x), which is the atom x. The third component is the tail of the head of L2, which is the tail of the list (x). The tail of a list with only one component is the empty list, just as the Tail of a one-item linear list is the empty list.

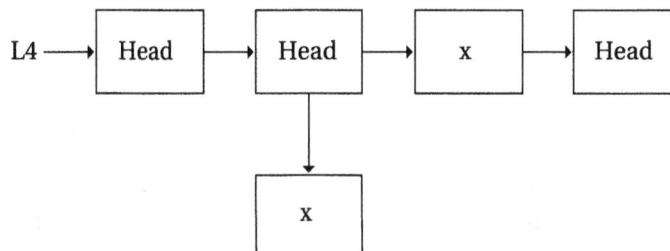

L5 is the list made up of three components, the atoms a and b and the list L5.

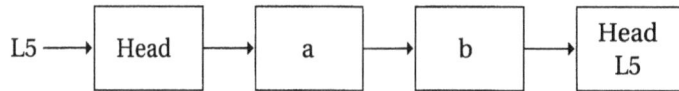

These five examples illustrate several very important issues concerning generalized lists. L1 references only atoms or lists with no names. This is easy to visualize and represents the simplest class of generalized lists, where no references are allowed to any other list.

In the case of L2, we visualized its second component as L1 rather than repeating the contents of the list L1. In L3, we repeated the list (b c d). Is the (b c d) in L3 the same list as in L1 or is it a copy? Is the L1 in L2 the exact same list or is it a copy? What about L5? It references itself. There is no way that we could copy or print the entire list L5. We would never finish. It is a recursive list. A recursive list is one that references itself or some other list that directly or indirectly references it.

These three cases represent classes of generalized lists in order of implementation complexity. The *referenced list* is the list whose name appears within another list. The *referencing list* is the list being created. More formally, the three classes of generalized lists are as follows:

1. Lists where no shared references are allowed.

2. Lists with shared references. The components of one list can be parts of another list. Listed below are two logical interpretations of lists of this type.

    a. *Static interpretation:* The current status of the referenced list is intended. The referenced list is copied into the referencing list.

    b. *Dynamic interpretation:* The list itself is intended. Any future changes in the referenced list should be reflected in the referencing list. The referenced list is represented by some sort of pointer.

3. Recursive lists. Lists that can directly or indirectly reference themselves.

Lists with No Shared Reference

The first class of generalized lists is one in which no shared references are allowed. That is, one list cannot reference another list. Atoms, however, can be repeated. One implementation of such lists uses a linked list with a header node, as described in the diagrams earlier in this chapter. While such implementations can work quite well, a simpler approach is possible, based upon the simple axioms for Head, Tail, and PutFirst. In this second approach, a list can be specified by indicating the head and tail of the list at each stage. This approach, which also demonstrates the representation of lists in the LISP programming language, considers every list node as a pair of pointers, with the first pointer indicating the location of the head of the list and the second pointer giving the location of the tail.

Figure 12.1 shows the representation of the NIL list in each of these three forms: the parenthesized notation, the header node format described earlier, and LISP's linked Head/Tail representation.

When representing a list containing one atom a, two forms are often used for the Head/Tail representation. Both forms are shown in Figure 12.2. Following the representations in LISP, every list node in a Head/Tail representation has a pointer to the head and to the tail. Therefore, if a list contains one element, the atom a, then the list should be represented using one list node, the head of which points to a and the tail of which is NIL. In practice, however, it is common to collapse the atom box with the head of the node. This simplifies diagrams considerably, and so is used in many textbooks and references. Throughout the rest of this chapter, we utilize this common, collapsed form for Head/Tail representations whenever possible. This often simplifies diagrams and allows our diagrams to parallel those commonly used in describing lists in LISP. In each case, we could get a more complete picture of the Head/Tail representation if we replaced the head of a Head/Tail node containing an atom with a pointer to a separate atom box.

Figure 12.3 presents two more list examples represented in each of the tree formats.

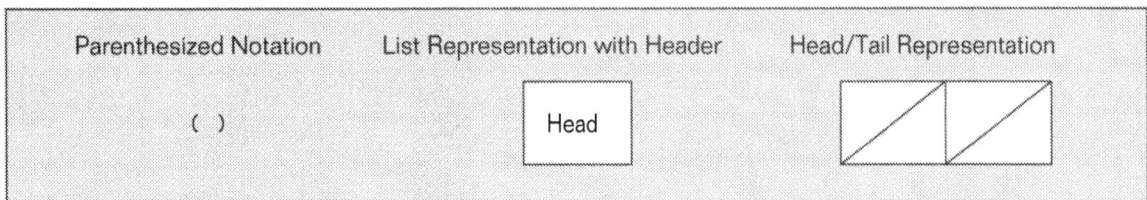

Figure 12.1 Representations of the NIL List

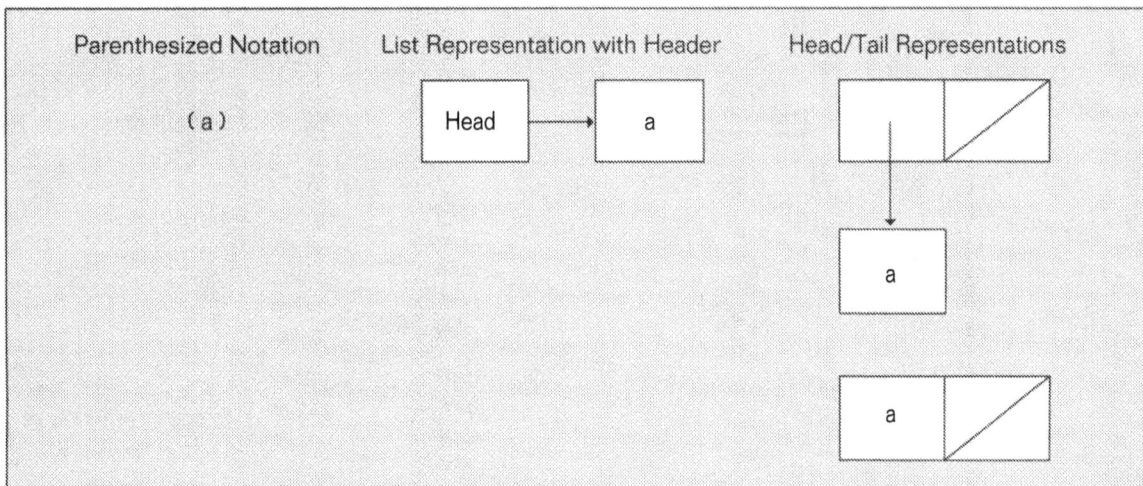

Figure 12.2 Representations of a List Containing One Element a

L1: (a b c)   Parenthesized Notation

L1 ⟶ | Head | ⟶ | a | ⟶ | b | ⟶ | c | List Representation with Header

L1 ⟶ | a | · | ⟶ | b | · | ⟶ | c | ╱ | Head/Tail Representation

L2: ((a) b (( )))   Parenthesized Notation

L2 ⟶ | Head | ⟶ | Head | ⟶ | b | ⟶ | Head | List Representation with Header
                         ↓   ↓
                       | a | | Head |

L2 ⟶ | · | · | ⟶ | b | · | ⟶ | ╱ | ╱ | Head/Tail Representation
        ↓   ↓
      | a | ╱ | | ╱ | ╱ |
                                       ↓
                                     | ╱ | ╱ |

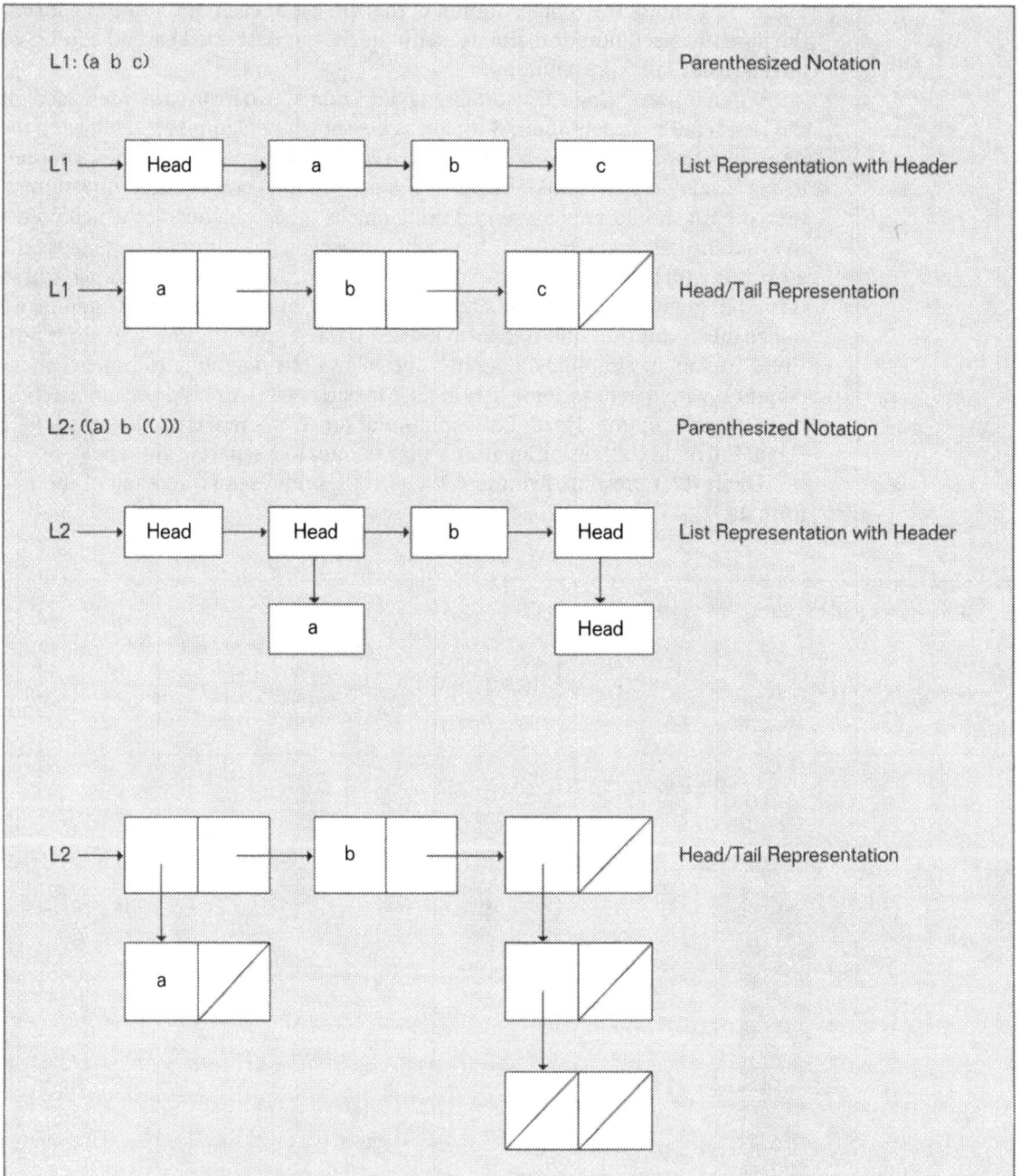

Figure 12.3 Three Representations of Lists with No Shared References

In this figure, L1 is a generalized list, all of whose components are atoms, so L1 is also an unsorted list as defined in Chapter 1. In the figure, the parenthesized notation simply indicates the three atoms on this list, and the linked list representation follows the familiar form using a header list. The Head/Tail representation follows from the axioms using the primitive constructor PutFirst. With these axioms, the list (a b c) is constructed from Create by adding c, b, and a in that order. Thus, the list constructed from the axioms is PutFirst (PutFirst (PutFirst (Create, c), b), a). In this form, PutFirst (Create, c) is given by the last node (on the right), and this forms the tail of the list starting with b. The resulting list (b c) is the tail of the list starting with a.

The description of L2 is somewhat more complex. L2 is a list with three components. The first and last components are lists, and the second component is the atom b. The first of these component lists is the list (a) with one component. This component follows the (familiar) format for lists with a header node or with a as head and a null list as tail. The third component of L2 is the list (()), which is a list containing the list () as its only component. Thus, this third component of L2 is a list with a header node or with a Head/Tail format. The head of this component also is a list (the null list) and the tail is null. These characteristics are shown in Figure 12.3.

Altogether, these examples illustrate several cases. We have both atoms and lists appearing in the first position of a node. There is no ambiguity when drawing pictures. When we convert our pictures to data types and implementation code, we must distinguish components that are lists from components that are atoms. In the following discussion, we focus upon the Head/Tail format just described, although many similar comments apply to the list with header representation as well.

The full Head/Tail representation contains two types of boxes, as shown in Figure 12.2. A list node contains two pointers, for the head and the tail of the list; an atom node or box contains specific data. Similarly, the collapsed Head/Tail representation uses one type of node, but the head can be either an atom or a pointer to a list. In either representation, we must be able to distinguish between atoms and list nodes. In practice, this can be done in any one of the ways listed below.

1. A separate tag field can be added to each node or to the head within a list node, to distinguish atoms from lists.

2. A separate table can be maintained, recording for each node whether the node is an atom or a list node.

3. All atoms can be stored in one part of memory, while all list nodes can be stored in another part of memory. The type of information specified by a pointer can then be inferred by inspecting the address given by the pointer.

Each of these approaches actually has been used in various implementations of lists. The first approach seems particularly natural if one is building an implementation from scratch, and shortly we examine this approach in more detail. The second approach is used in some current implementations, when such type tables are automatically maintained by the implementation language. (For example, LISP interpreters written in C++ may use separate tables, because C++ maintains type tables as part of its work.) The third approach was used in some early LISP versions where hardware considerations made it particularly efficient to treat a list node simply as two addresses, with no other fields. Here, a list node contained two addresses, and the nature of the node (atom or list node) was determined by checking which part of memory was being accessed.[1]

These notes reinforce a common theme in this text—namely, that ADTs may be implemented in a variety of ways. The choice of implementation often depends upon particular characteristics of an application or upon issues of time or space efficiency. We analyze the characteristics of several implementations of generalized lists at the end of this chapter. Before this analysis, however, it is helpful to consider how some implementation choices translate into pieces of code. In what follows, therefore, we implement two variations of the Head/Tail representation. Later in this chapter, we consider the full Head/Tail representation, where atoms and list nodes are considered different types of boxes.

In the rest of this section, we implement several operations using the collapsed Head/Tail representation, where the head of a list node holds either an atom or a pointer to a list. In order to distinguish between these two possibilities, we add a tag field to the head of each node. In what follows, some code is simplified somewhat if we package the head of a list (tag field plus atom or list pointer) together as a package, a record of ComponentType.

```
TYPE
    TypeOfComponent = (AtomType, GenList);
    NodePtr = ↑NodeType;

    ComponentType = RECORD
        CASE Kind: TypeOfComponent OF
            AtomType  : Atom  : Character;
            GenList   : List  : NodePtr
        END CASE
    END RECORD

    NodeType = RECORD
        Next          : NodePtr;      (* pointer to the tail *)
        Component     : ComponentType (* head of the list *)
    END RECORD

    GenListType = NodePtr
```

In this definition, it is worthwhile to note that NodeType contains a field that is a variant record. In case you have not studied such a type in detail before, we consider this notion carefully for a moment before continuing with our discussion of the implementation of the generalized list ADT operations.

Variant Records

Now suppose that Node is a variable of NodeType. This record specifies that Node has a Next field (Node.Next) and a Component field (Node.Component). The

---

[1] For more information on this third approach to implementing LISP lists, see John Allen, *Anatomy of LISP*, McGraw-Hill, 1978.

Component field, which is a variant record, has two fields: Component.Kind and either Component.Atom or Component.List. If the value of Component.Kind is AtomType, Node also has a field, Node.Component.Atom of type Character. On the other hand, if Component.Kind has the value GenList, then Node has a List field, Node.Component.List. In this example, the field Kind is called a *tag field*, and its value determines what other fields are defined.

When a compiler allocates space for a structure containing a variant record (or variant records), the compiler first determines the space required for all fields that are part of any variable of NodeType. In the example, every such variable has a Next field and a Kind tag field. Then the amount of space required for each variant is computed, and space is allocated for the largest of these variants. This common space for the variants is used by each of the variant alternatives. Thus, in our example, space might be allocated as follows:

Next	
Kind	
List	Atom

Here, a cell is allocated for Next and for Kind. In addition, a cell is allocated for the List field in case the Kind field has the value GenList. Because a character takes less space than a pointer, the Atom field uses part of the space for the List field when the Kind field has the value AtomType.

Details of Generalized List Operations

With this background, we now consider the details of a simple, collapsed Head/Tail implementation of the generalized list operations, following our earlier Type declarations. We make the assumption that the user has set the tag field properly on the parameter of ComponentType.

Create(VAR List: GenListType)

```
List ← NIL
```

PutFirst(VAR List: GenListType, Item: ComponentType)

```
New(Node)
Node↑.Component ← Item
Node↑.Next ← List
List ← Node
```

Head(List: GenListType) : ComponentType

```
RETURN List↑.Component
```

If the Head is a list, it cannot be made part of another list, or the constraint on no shared references would be broken. However, this is not the responsibility of the implementor of the ADT Operations. The implementor is responsible for guaranteeing the postcondition—namely, that the constraint not be violated by any of the ADT GeneralizedList operations. The application system that uses these operations guarantees the precondition that there are no shared references.

Tail(List: GenListType) : GenListType

```
RETURN List↑.Next
```

This brings up an interesting question. The tail of List now exists in two places: as Tail and as the tail of List. If the operation is executed as part of the statement

List ← Tail(List)

then the no-shared-lists constraint is not broken. If the operation is executed as part of the statement

List2 ← Tail(List)

then there is a problem. The *consistency* of the use of the operations within the three categories of generalized lists can be a major problem. However, this is not a problem we can solve while examining the algorithms. You, as future designers and implementors of software systems, however, must be aware of these types of issues.

ListOfAtoms(GenList: GenListType) : ListType

We can use one of our unsorted list primitives. Recall that we used the general Insert rather than Make for these implementations. Because Tail returns the list without the head, successive calls to Tail destroy the list. We certainly do not want the List operation to destroy its input, so we copy the list before traversing it.

```
Create(NewList)
TempList ← Copy(GenList)
MakeList(TempList, NewList)
RETURN NewList
```

MakeList(TempList: GenListType, VAR NewList: ListType)

```
IF NOT IsEmpty(TempList)
    THEN
        CASE Head(TempList).Kind OF
            Atom:       MakeList(Tail(TempList), NewList)
                        Insert(NewList, Head(TempList))
            GenList:    MakeList(Tail(TempList), NewList)
                        MakeList(Head(TempList), NewList)
                        NewList ← Concat(NewList. NewList)
        END CASE
END IF
```

Lists with Shared Reference

At the beginning of this implementation section, we drew tree-like diagrams of several lists to illustrate different classes of implementations of generalized lists. In the class of lists where shared references are allowed, there are two interpretations of what referencing a list within another list actually means. In one case, we copied the referenced list in the diagram, and in the other we just wrote the list name. Although this sounds purely like an implementation issue, it is not. This question reflects two different logical interpretations of what it means to reference a list within another list.

The first interpretation is that the reference is a *static reference*. In this interpretation, it is the state of the list at the time of the reference that is intended. The second interpretation is a *dynamic reference*, where it is the list itself that is intended, not the current instantiation. In this interpretation, any subsequent change to the list being referenced is reflected in the referencing list.

Both of these interpretations are valid. From a logical implementation point of view, referencing a list within another list could be interpreted in two ways: the referenced list could be copied into the new list or the referenced list could be represented by some sort of pointer to the list. The results are different in the two cases. The implementation structure should reflect the intended interpretation.

To illustrate this difference, consider the following three statements, which we assume are executed in sequence.

L1 = (a b (c d))

L2 = (x (y) L1)

L1 = Tail(L1)

If the static interpretation is used, L1 should be copied into L2. L2 is not changed by subsequent changes to L1. It remains

(x (y) (a b (c d)))

until the list L2 is explicitly changed.

If the dynamic interpretation is used, a pointer to L1 is inserted into L2. L2 is implicitly changed every time L1 is changed. Therefore, after redefining L1 as its own tail, L2 is now

(x (y) (b (c d)))

The atom a is no longer part of the list L2.

To summarize, the first interpretation is that L2 is the list made up of the atom x, the list (y), and the list L1 as it exists at the time that L2 is defined. Only an operation that takes L2 explicitly as an argument can change L2. The second interpretation is that L2 is the list made up of the atom x, the list (y), and the list L1 as it is at any point in time. A change to L1 automatically changes L2. The implementation must reflect the interpretation that is intended.

If a particular application needs both interpretations, then some convention must be adopted to indicate this. For example, Copy(L1) could be used to indicate that a copy is to be made. That is, given the following sequence of operations,

L1 = (a b (c d))

L21 = (x (y) Copy(L1))

L22 = (x (y) L1)

L1 = Tail(L1)

L22 would be changed by the redefinition of L1, but L21 would not be changed. In fact, L21 would be a completely independent list. It would have no memory that the third component was ever a list or part of another list. Because a copy of the referenced list is made in this interpretation, it is by far the easier of the two interpretations to implement, but it clearly takes more memory.

Implementation—Static Interpretation

Because the static interpretation of referencing lists within lists is the simpler one, we begin with it. As in the case of no shared references, an obvious logical structure to represent a component is a node designating the head and tail of a linked list. Figure 12.4 shows several examples of lists represented in this fashion using the static interpretation.

Any operation that changes L1 has no effect on any of the other lists. The algorithms to implement Create, Head, and Tail are exactly the same as those for the generalized lists with no shared reference.

Implementation—Dynamic Interpretation

In implementing generalized lists with dynamic shared reference, we again can consider whether we should use the Head/Tail representation illustrated earlier or linked lists with a header node. In order to gain insight into an appropriate selection, we consider some examples. Four lists are diagrammed in Figure 12.5 using the Head/Tail representation, where references are considered to be dynamic. The parenthesized representation is also shown.

Now suppose we set L1 to be equal to its own tail, thereby deleting the head. In the Head/Tail representation, L1 is referenced in four other places in the structure. Removing the first component, then, requires changing three other pointers. Furthermore, we have to keep track of everything pointing to L1 in order to locate these pointers that need changing. This seems very complicated.

Fortunately, the linked-list representation with a header node provides a simple way to resolve this complexity. When every list has a header node, the internal pointers to referenced lists can point to the header node. That way, changes to the list do not require changes to the internal pointers to the list. At first glance, it seems as if we are solving one problem and creating another; that is, operations on the first component in a list are easier but we are requiring an additional node

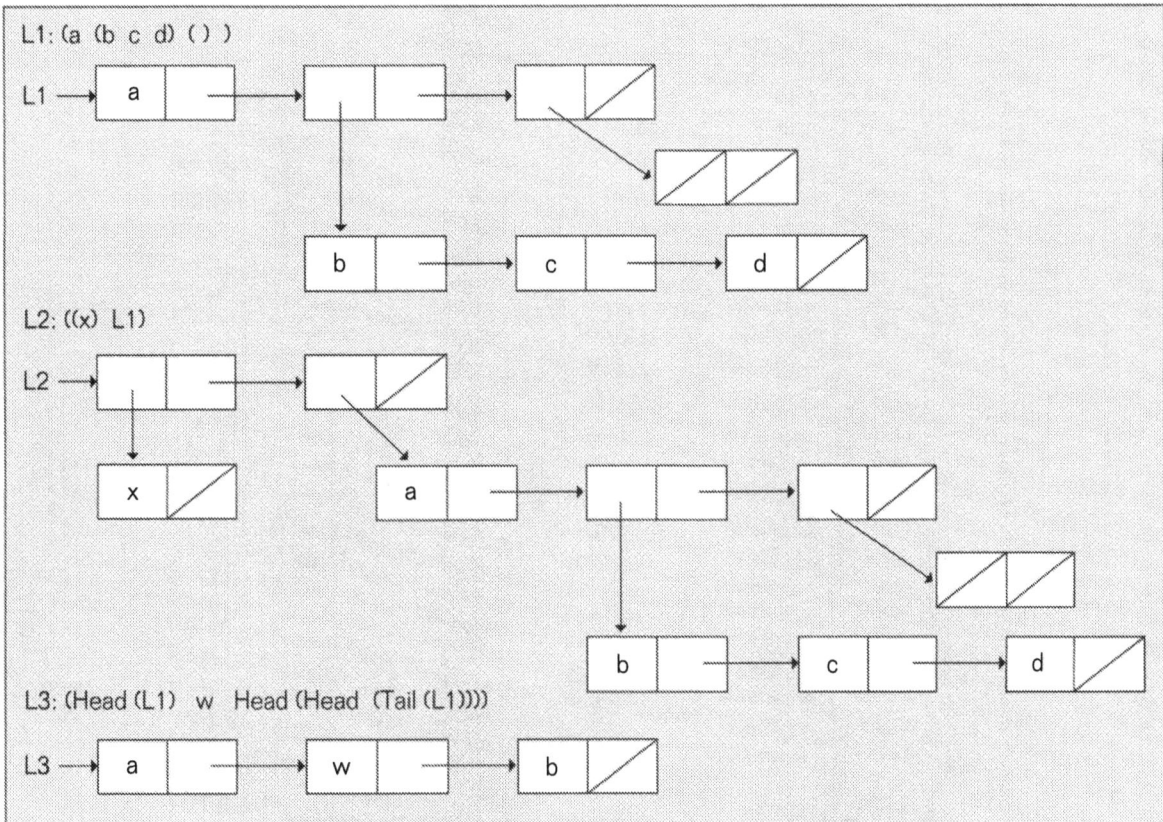

Figure 12.4 Linked Structure with (Static) Shared Reference

for each list. This header node, however, can be used to great advantage to keep track of how many references there are to the list. The count is called a *reference count*, and we can use it to determine when a list is no longer needed.

For example, in Figure 12.5, what would happen if one part of a program "decided" that L1 was no longer needed and disposed the pointer to L1? The lists L2, L3, and L4 would then contain references to nodes that did not exist! Note that disposing an external pointer to L1 is not the same as setting L1 to the empty list. Disposing the external pointer implies that L1 is no longer needed. In a system of generalized lists where one list is allowed to be part of one or more other lists, some scheme must be devised to determine when a list is truly no longer needed by any application or any part of the program.

With a count field in the header node, we can easily record how many references there are to the list. Whenever a list is referenced, the reference count is incremented. When a list is disposed, the reference count is decremented. When the reference count reaches zero, the list is actually disposed. We have more to say about this technique in Chapter 13.

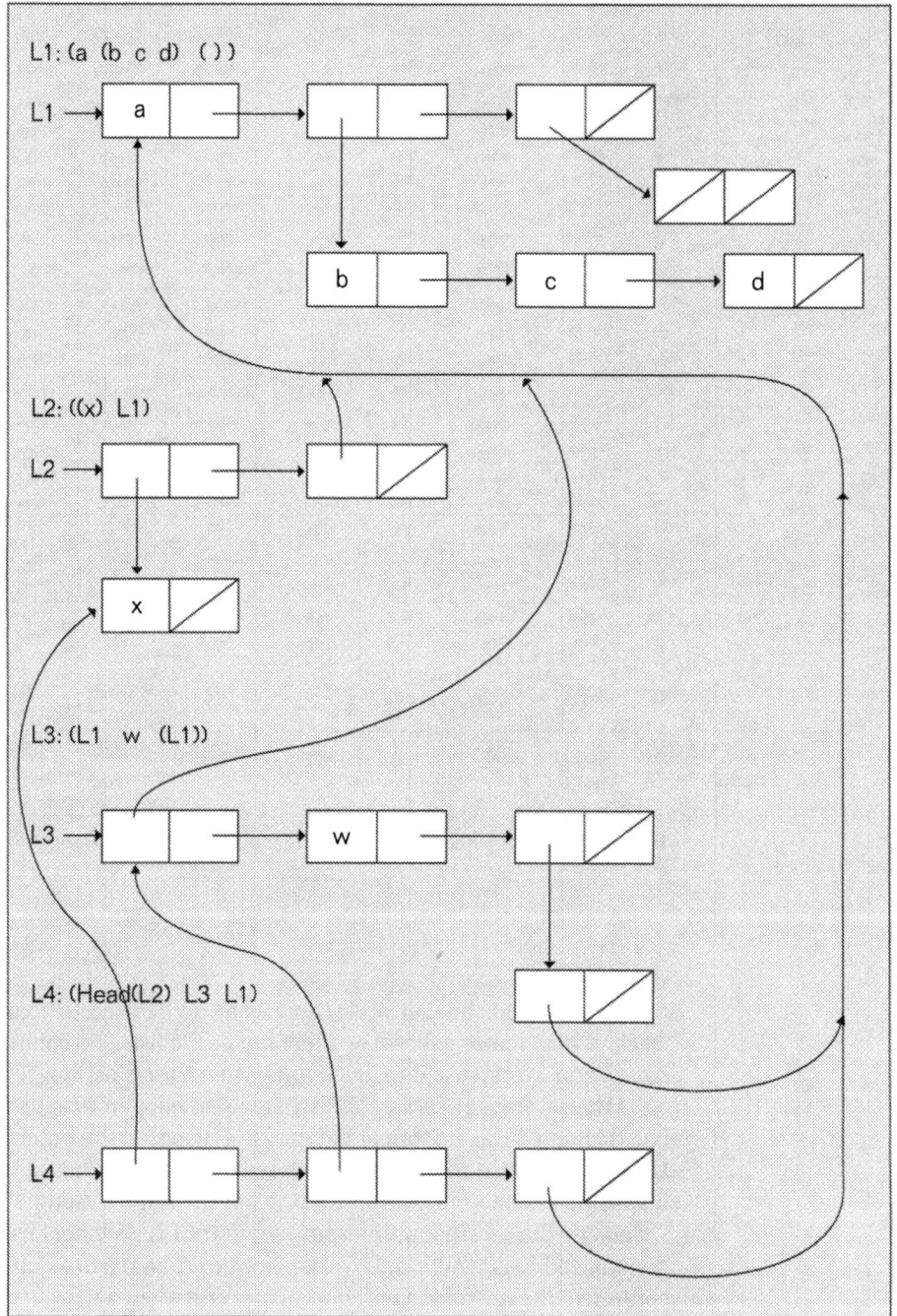

Figure 12.5 Linked Structure with (Dynamic) Shared Reference

With the use of headers, our implementation now must distinguish among three types of nodes: headers, atoms, and lists. We can accomplish this task by expanding the variant record structure described earlier in the chapter.

```
TYPE
    TypeOfComponent = (AtomType, GenList, Header);

    NodePtr = ↑NodeType;
    ComponentType = RECORD
        CASE Kind: TypeOfComponent OF
            AtomType : Atom    : Character;
            GenList  : List    : GenListType;
            Header   : RefCount : Integer
    END RECORD

    NodeType = RECORD
        Next            : NodePtr; (* next node in list *)
        Component       : ComponentType
    END RECORD

    GenListType = NodePtr
```

Header nodes have a special function. The first field of a header node contains the number of lists that reference this list. If no other list references this list, then this count is 1. Nodes that are tagged Atom or List have the same function as before; that is, they are actual components in the list. They are distinguished by whether the first field contains an atom or a pointer to another list. Figure 12.6 shows three lists with their header nodes.

We now consider the details of each of the operations for generalized lists, assuming a dynamic shared reference interpretation and using linked lists with headers for our implementation.

Create(VAR List: GenListType)

```
New(NewList)
NewList↑.Component.Kind ← Header
NewList↑.Component.RefCount ← 1
NewList↑.Next ← NIL
```

Head(VAR List: GenListType): ComponentType

The input to the Head operation must be a list, so the first node encountered is the header. The output argument from the Head operation is a component that may be an atom or a list. It is the component in the second node of the list. If the head is an atom, no further bookkeeping is necessary. If the head is a list, should the reference count for the header of the list be incremented? Rather than answering this question within the Head operation, we provide an IncRefCount utility for incrementing the count, and we let the application decide.

```
RETURN List↑.Next↑.Component
```

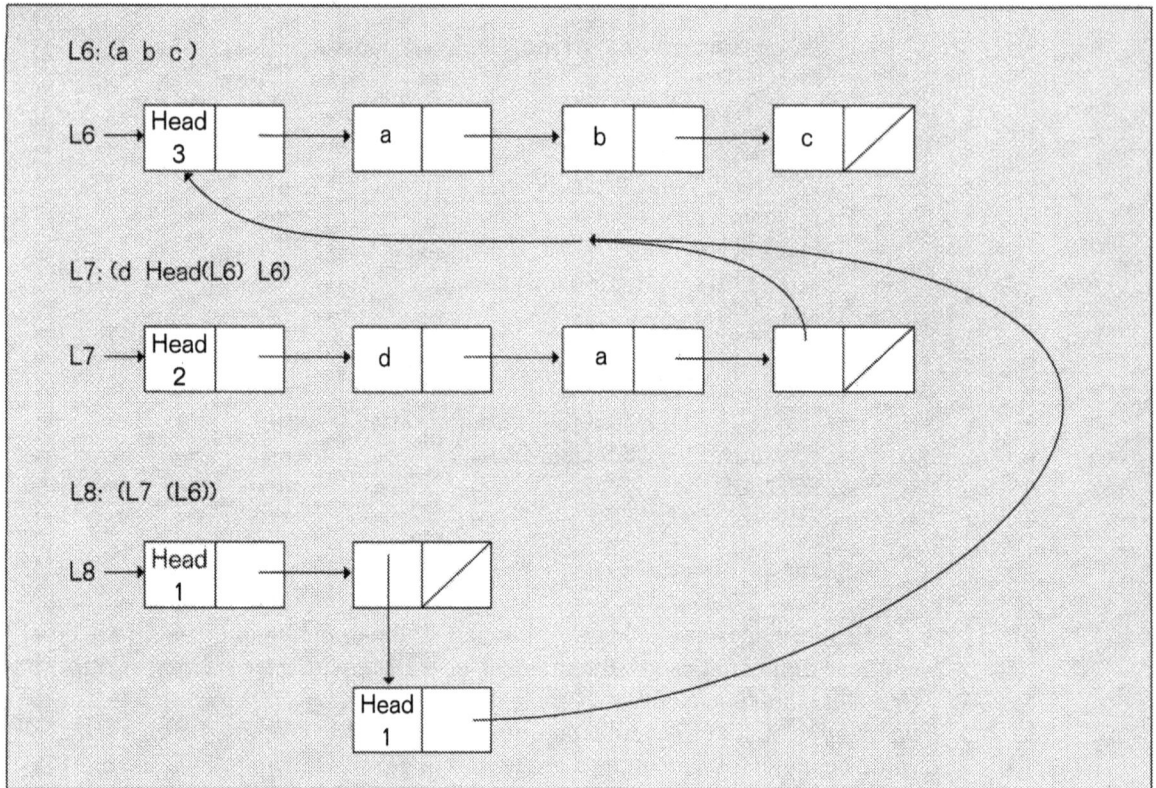

Figure 12.6 Linked Structure with Headers for Lists with (Dynamic) Shared Reference

IncRefCount(VARList: GenListType)

$$\text{List}\uparrow.\text{Component.RefCount} \leftarrow \text{List}\uparrow.\text{Component.RefCount} + 1$$

Tail(List: GenListType) : GenListType

The tail is a pointer to the rest of the list following the head. It is the Next field associated with the first component. Because the tail is by definition a list, should we insert a header with a reference count of 1? As in the case of the Head operation, the answer depends on what the application is going to do with the tail. We make the same compromise here and provide the utility InsertHeader.

$$\text{RETURN List}\uparrow.\text{Next}\uparrow.\text{Next}$$

InsertHeader(VAR List: GenListType)

```
New(NewNode)
NewNode↑.Next ← List
List ← NewNode
List↑.Component.Tag Header
List↑.Component.RefCount ← 1
```

PutFirst(VAR List: GenListType, Item: ComponentType)

```
New(Node)
Node↑.Component ← Item
Node↑.Next ← List↑.Next
List↑.Next ← Node
IF Item.Kind = GenList
    THEN Item.List↑.Component.RefCount
            ← Item.List↑.Component.RefCount + 1
END IF
```

ListOfAtoms(GenList: GenListType) : ListType

Because Head takes care of the Header node, this operation is exactly the same as in the static implementation.

Recursive Lists

Recursive lists are lists that are allowed to reference themselves either directly or indirectly. Figure 12.7 shows several examples of recursive lists. Note carefully the reference counts.

Clearly, a recursive structure must be implemented with some type of pointer. A problem occurs when we try to determine if a list is free to be returned to available space. Because the reference count includes the self-reference, this count is never zero even though the structure is not accessed by any other. This creates a situation where memory can be cluttered with structures that are not being used, but the system does not know it. We discuss this problem in more detail in Chapter 13.

The algorithms for the operations on a recursive structure do not differ from those that are allowed on a dynamic, shared-reference structure unless a traversal is involved. When traversing a recursive list, we need some way to stop. Otherwise, we would traverse forever! For example, within the ListOfAtoms algorithm, Make-List calls for traversing the top level of each list until all atoms are reached. If the top level is recursive, an atom may never be reached. We can resolve this problem using the same type of marking technique used for graph traversals.

Applications

Because generalized lists are extremely versatile, they are used in a wide variety of applications. In some cases, the applications take advantage of the main concepts of generalized lists without reference to the traditional ADT operations described earlier in this chapter. For example, this type of application might involve a trans-

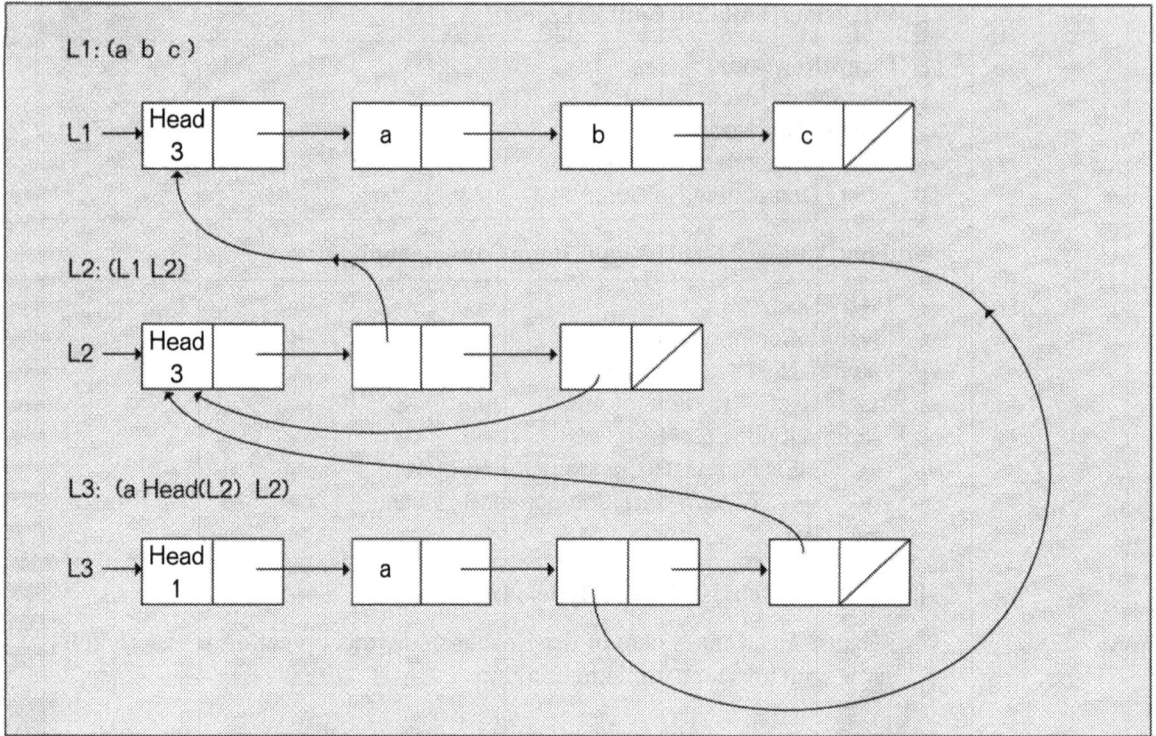

Figure 12.7 Linked Structure for Lists with Recursive Reference

fer operation, beginning with a generalized list as a string in parenthesized notation and translating it to a Head/Tail representation. A second example might take
an expression in Head/Tail form and evaluate it.

A second type of application utilizes generalized lists as an internal structure
within a programming language. For example, generalized lists are utilized in at
least two ways within the LISP language itself.

In still other types of applications, generalized lists form a natural structure for
the storage of needed information. For example, many expert systems maintain
lists of rules and data, and programs utilize this information to infer conclusions.

In this section, we study each of these types of applications. First, we build the
input and output routines to convert input strings to a Head/Tail form, and we
consider how to evaluate such expressions. Second, we review briefly two uses of
generalized lists within the LISP language itself. Third, we outline briefly some
common uses of generalized lists within expert system programs.

List Input, Output, and Evaluation

Until now, we have looked at how to build lists by constructing them from the bottom up, starting with an empty list and adding atoms or lists as the first component. Here, we examine reading a generalized list in parenthesized notation and
then printing a list in parenthesized notation. We then evaluate expressions represented in a generalized list where the heads of lists are operations that are to be
applied to the list represented in the tail.

Input

As noted earlier in this chapter, in this section we consider generalized lists to be implemented according to the full Head/Tail representation. Here, we distinguish between atom nodes and list nodes. In particular, rather than using a variant record, each node has three fields: Name, Head, and Tail. Atoms are represented by the value of the atom in the Name field and by NIL for both Head and Tail. The Name field for a list contains a special symbol, the word "List" or an asterisk. Figure 12.8 shows an atom and an empty list. Figure 12.9 compares a list using this structure with the structure used earlier in the chapter.

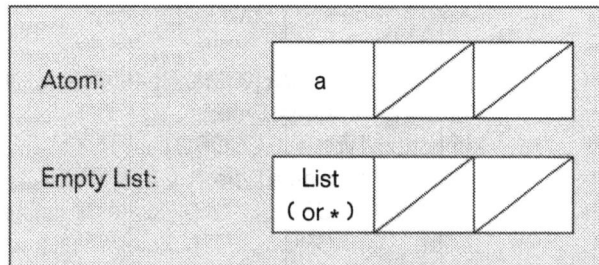

Figure 12.8   Alternate Node Representation

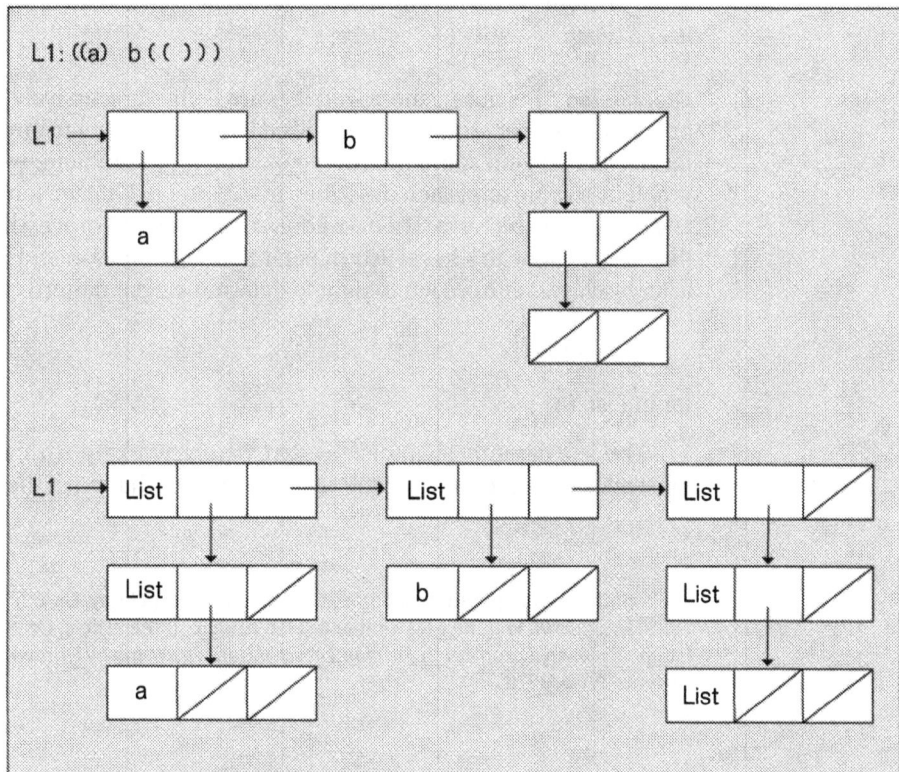

Figure 12.9   Comparison of Different Linked Structures

In the representation in Figure 12.6, a variant record is used. If the variant is an AtomType, then the component is an Atom. If the variant is a GenList, the component is a list. If the variant is a Header, the component is a header. In the revised representation we are introducing for this section, there are three fields in each node. The first is a Name field, the second is a pointer to the head, and the third is a pointer to the tail. If an atom is the head of a list, the Head field contains a pointer to the atom. In this problem, we do not need header nodes because we are not concerned with shared references.[2] The following declarations clarify our record structure.

```
(* To access MaxCharInAtom. *)
USES <module defining MaxCharInAtom>
TYPE
    NameType = ARRAY[0..MaxCharInAtom − 1] OF Character;
    CPtr = ↑ComponentType;
    ComponentType = RECORD
        Name  :  NameType;
        Head  :  CPtr;      (* Pointer to list head, if such exists *)
        Tail  :  CPtr       (* Pointer to list tail, if such exists *)
    END RECORD
```

For this problem, an atom is a string of uppercase characters. The Head and Tail fields of atoms are NIL. The asterisk (*) in the Name field designates a list. We call it a ListFlag.

Discussion   Because generalized lists are defined recursively as lists whose components are either atoms or generalized lists, it is natural to approach this problem recursively. To gain some intuition concerning the problem, we follow the general problem-solving approach described in Chapter 8. First we look at some examples and draw some pictures. Then we analyze the required processing in some detail; in this case, we look at several lists in parenthesized notation and examine them character by character from left to right to determine what patterns we can discern.

Example 1

Input List: (A)

The left parenthesis indicates that we are working with a list. Therefore, we must allocate a node and set the Name field to *. What must the component follow-

---

[2] This problem was posed as a student project in an article by Dr. Jeff Brumfield in the *ACM SIGCSE Bulletin*, Volume 17, Number 1, March 1985. In the article, Dr. Brumfield attributes the original idea to a problem in *Fundamentals of Data Structures* by Horowitz and Sahni, Computer Science Press, 1976.

ing a left parenthesis be? Either a list or an atom. In either case, it is the head of the list we just generated. In this case, it is an atom. Set head and tail to NIL. The next character is a right parenthesis. This indicates the end of a list. Which list? The last list we were processing. In this case, it is the end of the input. The tail, then, must be set to NIL. Which tail? The tail that goes with the last list we were processing.

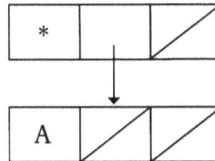

Example 2

Input List: **(A B)**

Again, the left parenthesis signals that a list node must be created. The character following the left parenthesis is the beginning of an atom. The symbol ending the atom (blank in this case) is not a right parenthesis, so what follows must be a tail. We must get a node, insert it in the tail of the current list, and then proceed to look for the head of this new list. The next character is an uppercase letter and is therefore the beginning of an atom. We must store this atom as the head of this new list. The next character is a right parenthesis. This means there is no tail for the current head, so it must be set to NIL.

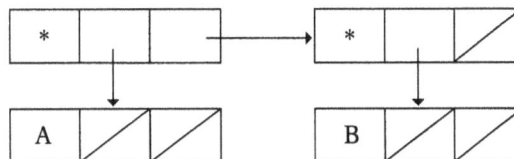

Example 3

Input List: **(( ))**

The left parenthesis signals a list. We set up a list node and proceed to get the head of the list. The next character is a left parenthesis, which signals a list. We set up a list node and proceed to get its head. The next character is a right parenthesis. The left parenthesis and right parenthesis bring up a special case. This is the empty list. This is the only case where a list node has NIL pointers for both head and tail.

Example 4

Input List: ((A) B (C))

    This is clearly a list. We set up a list node and get the head of the list. The head is itself a list, so we set up a list node and get the head. The head is an atom, so we construct an atom node with the Name field containing the atom A. The right parenthesis indicates the end of the list, so the tail of the node that has A as its head is set to NIL, and we back up. The node that had (A) as its head must now have its tail constructed. To construct a tail, we get a node for the tail to point to and then get the head of that node. The list constructed so far is as follows.

    The head of this new list is the atom B. The tail must now be constructed. The left parenthesis indicates that the next component is a list; that is, the head of the list is a list. For clarity, we draw the state of the list at the point where we have read the left parenthesis and are about to read the character C.

We now must get a node for the head to point to and mark it as a list. The next character is an atom. Therefore, the head of the new list must point to this atom. The closing parenthesis indicates that the tail of the list is NIL. The next right parenthesis indicates that the node above it has a tail that is NIL. The list is now complete.

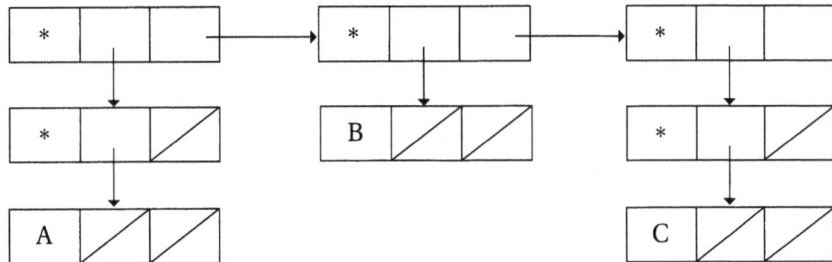

To summarize, this example has identified the following patterns.

1. The beginning left parenthesis signals that we are reading a list.
2. If we have a list, a list node should be initialized. The next component to be input is the head of this newly initialized list.
3. When getting the head, three things can happen:
    a. If the next input character is an uppercase character, an atom should be read and put into a node with NIL head and tail pointers.
    b. If the next input character is a right parenthesis, we have reached the end of a list. The only time this can happen when getting a head is when we have a null list.
    c. If the next input character is a left parenthesis, we must get a list.
4. When coming back from getting a head, if the next character is a right parenthesis, then we have finished that list.

Algorithm A recursive pattern is emerging. If a left parenthesis is encountered, we initialize a list and get its head. If an atom or a right parenthesis is encountered when getting a head, we have finished and can back up a level. A right parenthesis always signals the end of a list. This suggests that what we do depends on whether we are getting a list or getting a head. A first approximation to an algorithm is given below.

GetAList (VAR List: ComponentType)

```
New(List)
List↑.Name ← ListFlag
GetAHead(List↑.Head)
IF NextCharacter = RightParen
    THEN   List↑.Tail ← NIL
    ELSE   GetAList(List↑.Tail)
END IF
```

GetAHead (VAR List: ComponentType)

```
IF NextCharacter = LeftParen
    THEN  GetAList(List)
    ELSIF NextCharacter = RightParen
        THEN  RETURN    (* go back to calling level *)
        ELSE   (* must be an atom *)
            New(List)
            GetAtom(List↑.Name)
            List↑.Head ← NIL
            List↑.Tail ← NIL
END IF
```

As with many recursive solutions, the recursive procedures GetAList and GetAHead are rather simple, and we may think we have overlooked something. To check ourselves, we consider an algorithm walk-through with an example we used to design the algorithm, and we see what happens, making a note of any problems as they occur.

As we begin, we note that we have used the expression "next character" imprecisely in our discussion because it was clear what was meant. Because formal algorithms cannot tolerate such imprecision, we now define it to be the next character not yet read. In Pascal terms, the file buffer variable always points to this character. Ada and many versions of Modula-2 do not support this concept. (Because Modula-2 does not have a national or international standard, some versions may contain both Read and UnRead statements, which accomplish the same thing: looking at the next character and putting it back if that character is not what you were expecting.) In the Exercises, you are asked how to simulate the file buffer if your system does not support it.

We now work through our code, using the list (A B) as input.

Input List: (A B)

NextCharacter	Processing
(	**GetAList(List)**

A node (List↑) is allocated with the ListFlag in its Name field. GetListHead is called with the Head of this node as its parameter (L↑.Head).

| A | **GetAHead(List)   (List is previous List↑.Head)** |

Because the next character is an uppercase letter, a node (List↑) is allocated. GetAtom is called to input the characters that make up the atom into the Name field and to put NIL in the two pointer fields of List↑.

Problem: GetAtom must leave the input line positioned so that NextCharacter is the next atom of interest. We return from the call to GetAHead.

B   **GetAList following call to GetAHead**

The next character is not a right parenthesis, so GetAList is called to get the Tail of List.

B   **GetAList(List)   (List is previous List↑.Tail)**

A node (List↑) is allocated with the ListFlag in the Name field. GetAHead is called to input the head of this list (List↑.Head).

B   **GetAHead(List)   (List is previous List↑.Tail↑.Head)**

Because the next character is an atom (or the first character in an atom), List↑ is defined and GetAtom is called to define the Name field, and the pointer fields are set to NIL.

)   **GetAList(List)   following call to GetAHead**

The next character is a right parenthesis. List↑.Tail is set to NIL. This is the original List↑.Tail↑.Tail. This ends the original call to GetAList and the process is complete.

A subtle error surfaces if we look closely at our assumption about when the next character changes. GetAHead is called twice. The first time we assumed that NextCharacter changed; the second time we did not. Clearly, we cannot have it both ways. When the next character is the initial left parenthesis, we want to move beyond it as we call GetAHead. In every other occasion, we do not.

Notice that all other left parentheses are recognized in GetAHead. In GetAHead, we do want to move to the next character after the left parenthesis. The problem is that GetAList assumes that a left parenthesis occurred prior to the call to GetAList. This problem can be solved by making the original call not to GetAList, but to GetAHead. The opening left parenthesis is recognized and discarded, and GetAList is called to get the list.

Our algorithm recognizes that we can encounter a right parenthesis in both GetAList and GetAHead. The normal ending to the recursive process of getting a Head occurs when an atom is reached. The only other occasion is when we have a null list, which is signaled by a right parenthesis immediately following a left parenthesis. We know this has occurred when a right parenthesis is recognized in GetAHead. Therefore, when this happens, we must set the List to NIL and leave the right parenthesis for GetAList to recognize. This properly constructs the null list.

A Better Algorithm Before we rewrite our algorithm with these changes, we need to think about how we implement next character. In some instances when we query next character, we want to go on to the following character, and in some instances we do not. This depends on what the character is and at what point we look at it. In addition, if the next character is an uppercase letter, it is an atom (or the beginning of an atom). We have written the algorithms in terms of the next character being a left or right parenthesis with the atom being the ELSE branch to take care of this problem. How the atom is read has been hidden in GetAtom.

In considering these cases so far, we have been reading information character by character, but we want to think more abstractly. Looking more carefully at our processing, we are really dealing with two types of input atoms: parentheses (one character each) and atoms (up to MaxCharInAtom). It is not very elegant to treat these different elements as individual characters. Our input is logically in terms of markers (parentheses) and atoms. Our access to the input should be in these terms. Breaking an input line up into its logical units (called tokens) is called **lexical analysis**. This is always the first task of any language processor. In this case, we should have a procedure GetToken that returns a record containing the next token.

> **Lexical Analysis** Breaking up input into its logical units, called lexical units or tokens.

As noted earlier, the tokens in this problem serve two functions. The parentheses are used only as markers. An atom, in contrast, has its value stored within the structure of the lists. We not only need to know that it is an atom, but we need to know its value. Therefore, GetToken must return both the token and its type. The type is used in the control structure of the algorithms.

GetAList and GetAHead need a parameter move which controls whether a token is read or not.

```
(* To access MaxCharInAtom and EndString. *)
USES <module defining MaxCharInAtom and EndString>
TYPE
    NameType = ARRAY[0..MaxCharInAtom − 1] OF Character;

    TypeOfToken = (LeftParen, RightParen, Atom);

    TokenValue = RECORD
        TokenTag     :      TypeOfToken;
        CASE TypeOfToken OF
            LeftParen :      ();   (* No variant needed here *)
            RightParen:      ();
            Atom      :      (Value : NameType)
        END CASE
    END RECORD
```

With these declarations, we now can give updated and corrected implementations for our desired operations.

GetNextToken(VAR Token: TokenValue)

```
REPEAT                  (* Skip blanks. *)
    Read(Character)
UNTIL (Character <> Blank)
IF Character = '('
    THEN  TokenTag ← LeftParen
ELSIF Character = ')'
    THEN   TokenTag ← RightParen
    ELSE
        TokenTag ← Atom
        Count ← 0
        REPEAT
            Value[Count] ← Character
            Count ← Count + 1
            Read(Character)
        UNTIL (Character = Blank) OR (Character = ')' )
        IF Count < MaxCharInAtom    (* check for short atom *)
            THEN   Value[Count] ← EndString
        END IF
END IF
```

The algorithms for GetAList and GetAHead are rewritten, making use of Get-NextToken. Remember that the original call is to GetAHead rather than to GetAList.

Get AHead (VAR List: ComponentTypeMove: Boolean)

```
IF Move THEN GetNextToken(Token)
CASE Token.TokenTag
    LeftParen  :    GetAList(ListTrue)
    RightParen:    List ← NIL
    Atom       :    New(List)
                    List↑.Name ← Token.Value
                    List↑.Head ← NIL
                    List↑.Tail ← NIL
END CASE
```

GetAList (VAR List: ComponentType)

```
New(List)
List↑.Name ← ListFlag
GetAHead(List↑.Head)
IF Token.TokenTag = RightParen
    THEN
        List↑.Tail ← NIL
        GetNextToken(Token)
    ELSE   GetAList(List↑.TailFalse)
END IF
```

Because these procedures are mutually recursive and they both need Token, Token has to be either a variable global to the module or a parameter passed to all procedures. In practice, the use of the global variable within the module results in clearer, more efficient code.

Output

We have spent a great deal of time on the input routines because they represent many concepts, including mutual recursion. Basically, the output routines mirror the input routines, so they are presented below with no further discussion.

WriteHead (List: ComponentType)

```
IF List↑.Name <> ListFlag (* is an Atom*)
    THEN  WriteString(List↑.Name)
    ELSIF List↑.Head = NIL
        THEN   (* is the null list *)
            Write( '(' )
            Write( ')' )
        ELSE
            Write( '(' )
            WriteList(List.Tail)
END IF
```

WriteList (List: ComponentType)

```
WriteHead(List↑.Head)
IF List↑.Tail = NIL
    THEN   Write( ')' )
    ELSE
        Write(Blank)
        WriteList(List↑.Tail)
END IF
```

Expression Evaluation

The third part of this problem is to write a procedure to evaluate an expression represented as a generalized list where some of the atoms are names of functions. The following operations are to be evaluated.

Function	Argument(s)	Returns
HEAD	List	First component in List
TAIL	List	List with first component removed
CONS	Component, List	A list with Component as the head and
		List as the tail (same as PutFirst operation)
QUOTE	Component	Component

As an aside, we note that each of these names defines the corresponding operation in LISP. (For historical reasons, LISP also defines CAR and CDR as synonyms for HEAD and TAIL.)

As with our previous work with generalized lists, we begin our development of an evaluation algorithm by looking at some examples. Also, as a variation in our visualization of generalized lists, consider what happens when we rotate a simple list structure about 45 degrees clockwise.

List: ((A) B)

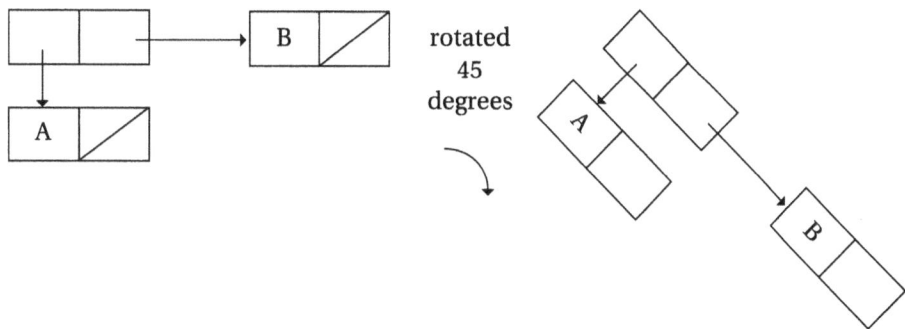

The resulting figure looks like a tree with the list node as root and the head and tail as children. This perspective of list nodes works whenever the Head/Tail representation is used. Because nodes have two pointers and no shared reference, we can represent them as roots of a tree with an asterisk (∗) and two pointers. The head pointer is to the left and the tail pointer is to the right. The atoms are all in the leaf nodes. As illustrated above, this method of representing the lists is equivalent to the other pictorial representation—just rotate the paper. While this revised way of visualizing lists is not strictly necessary, it may provide some additional insight as we try to develop algorithms.[3] In each of the following examples, we consider the tree structure for an input list, and we consider how we might evaluate it.

Input List: (QUOTE A)

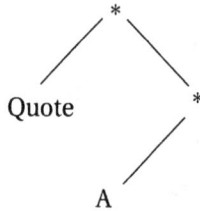

The result of evaluating this expression is the atom A. We can describe the action as follows: given a list, if the head of the list points to an atom Quote, we return the head of the tail of the list.

Input List: (TAIL (QUOTE (A B C)))

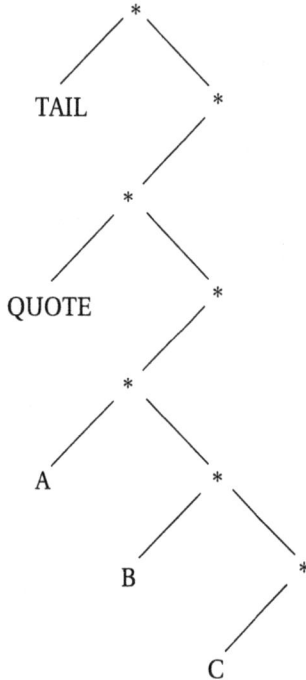

We do not want the tail containing the function QUOTE; we want the tail of the result of evaluating the function QUOTE. This means that we must evaluate the head of the tail of the list before we can evaluate the head of the list.

This suggests that, given a list L, we apply the function in L↑.Head to the result of evaluating the list L↑.Tail↑.Head.

---

[3] This way of visualizing the lists for this problem was suggested by Jeff Porter, a student during the semester in which we used this assignment.

Input List: (HEAD (TAIL (QUOTE (A B C))))

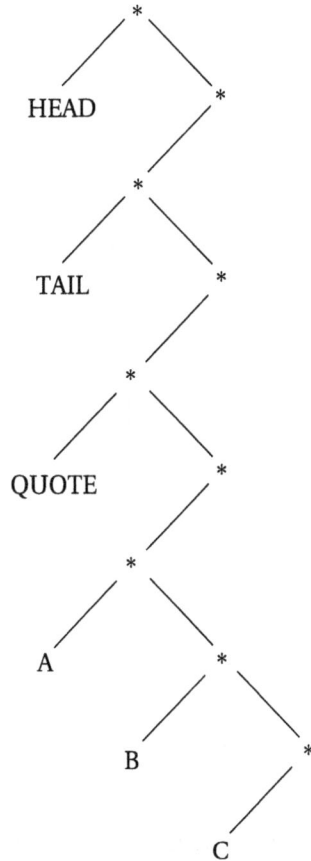

```
              *
            /   \
          /       \
    HEAD           *
                  /
                /
              *
            /   \
          /       \
    TAIL           *
                  /
                /
              *
            /   \
          /       \
   QUOTE           *
                  /
                /
              *
            /   \
          /       \
    A              *
                  /
                /
              B      *
                    /
                  /
                C
```

HEAD must be applied to the result of evaluating the component in the head of the tail. This is a list where the first component is the atom TAIL. TAIL must be applied to the result of evaluating the head of the tail. This is the list where QUOTE is the first component and the list (A B C) is the second component.

When we recognize QUOTE, we send back the head of the tail (A B C) to be evaluated by TAIL. The result (B C) is sent back to be evaluated by HEAD (atom B).

QUOTE tells us that we can stop going any farther in the list. We have the result to be passed back up to the previous level.

Input List: (CONS (QUOTE A) (QUOTE (B))

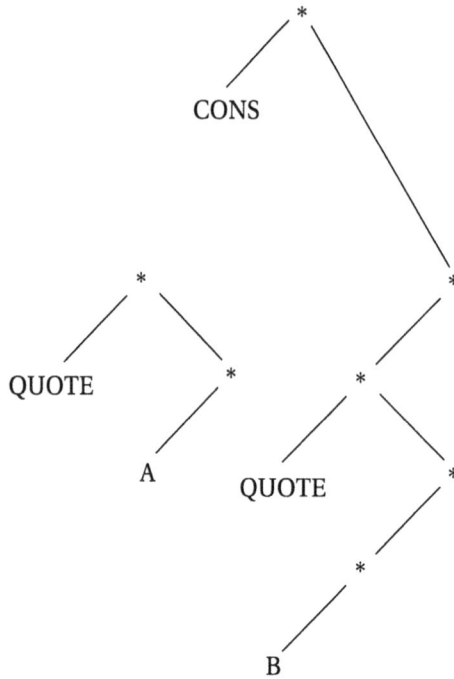

We need to apply the function in the head of the list to the result of evaluating the list in the head of the tail. The result is the atom A. CONS, however, is a binary function; that it, it needs two arguments.

Evaluating CONS, therefore, must wait until we evaluate the second argument, which is in the head of the tail of the tail of the list.

The result is a list with the first argument as the head and the second argument as the tail.

In each example, we have talked about the "head of the tail." The first component in any list L is in L↑.Head. The second component is in L↑.Tail↑.Head. Again, this looks like a recursive algorithm. Actually, we would be very surprised if an algorithm on a recursive structure were not recursive. The position of the functions and their arguments is summarized in Figure 12.10.

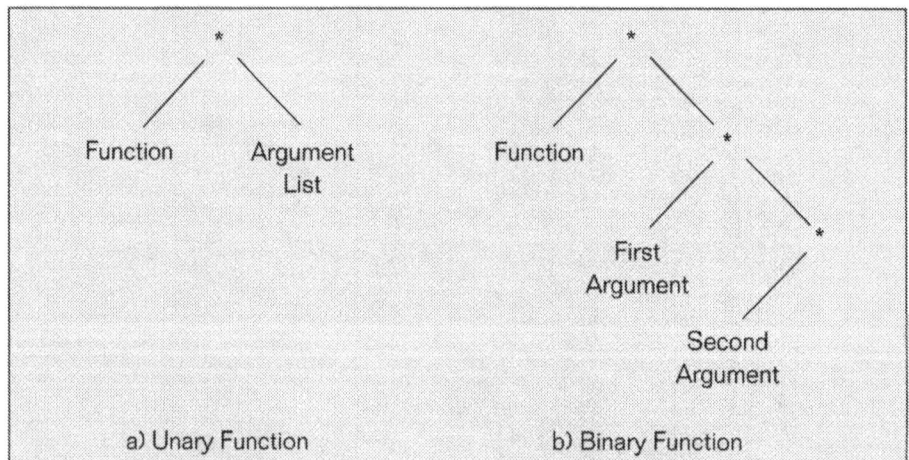

a) Unary Function   b) Binary Function

Figure 12.10. Position of a Function and Its Arguments in a List

In our input and output algorithms, we recursed until we recognized the end of a list. In the algorithm to evaluate a list expression, we move deeper into the structure until we find a QUOTE operation. When the head of a sublist is QUOTE, we return the tail of that sublist.

After we have evaluated QUOTE, we have a result on which the previous function can operate. In turn, the result from that function can be passed back up the chain to the previous level. The process stops when we recurse back to the original call. The result can then be printed with the WriteList procedure. We call this algorithm Eval because this is the term used in LISP to evaluate an expression.

Eval (L: ComponentType, VAR Result: ComponentType)

```
CASE Operation (L↑.Head↑.Name) OF
    QUOTE:     Result:= L↑.Tail ↑.Head;
    HEAD:      Eval (L↑.Tail↑.Head, Result);
               Result ← Result↑.Head
    TAIL:      Eval (L↑.Tail↑.Head, Result);
               Result ← Result↑.Tail
    CONS:      New (Result);
               Result↑.Name ← ListFlag;
               Eval (L↑.Tail↑.Head, Result↑.Head);
               Eval (L↑.Tail↑.Tail↑.Head, Result↑.Tail);
END CASE
```

Some Uses of Generalized Lists within LISP

In this chapter, we have already noted that LISP is a programming language that was developed for LISt Processing. Previous sections also have indicated that LISP supports generalized lists, and that much LISP processing involves inputting a parenthesized expression, representing the expression as a generalized list, applying EVAL to the list, and printing the result. This section describes two additional uses of generalized lists within LISP—namely, *property lists* and *association lists*.

Property Lists in LISP

We have already noted that generalized lists are sequences of components, where each component is either an atom or another generalized list. In LISP, the atomic building blocks can be numbers or identifiers (called *symbols*). (Some versions of LISP also consider strings and arrays to be atoms.)

Each symbol, in turn, is a data object that includes the print name of the object and other information that may be relevant to the processing that involves that symbol. In LISP, such information associated with each symbol is stored on a generalized list, called a *property list* or *plist*, for the symbol. Each symbol has its own unique plist. For example, if a program contains a symbol Donna, then within LISP there is a plist as follows:

PList for Donna

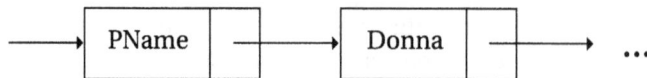

This plist indicates that if there is a need to print the symbol, then the data printed should be the string "Donna." Because any program may need to print the name of a symbol, every symbol has the *print name* or *pname*, and usually a programmer is not allowed to change this part of the list. Programmers are allowed, however, to add other properties to the plist in the form of pairs. Specifically, a programmer can designate the name of a property and the relevant information related to that property. For example, if a programmer wants to record the name of Donna's parents, then the pairs (Father Henry) and (Mother Theresa) might be added to Donna's plist.

PList for Donna

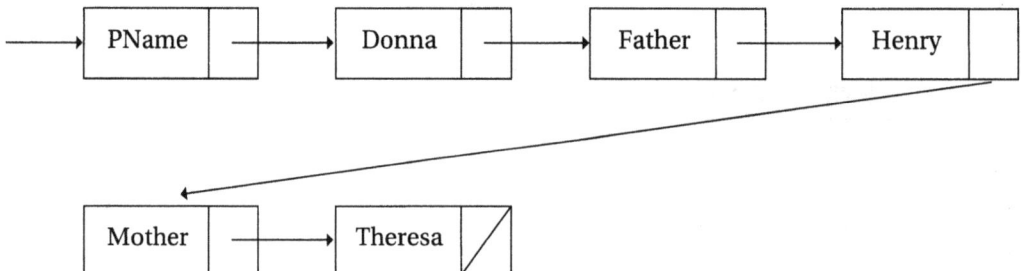

In constructing this list, the first part of the pair (for example, PName, Father, or Mother) is typically a symbol that is used for subsequent look-ups. The second part of the pair can be any value, including an atom or a generalized list. For example, if a programmer wants to store the class schedule for student Barbara as one property on the plist, then the first part of the property list for the symbol Barbara might have the following form.

PList for Barbara

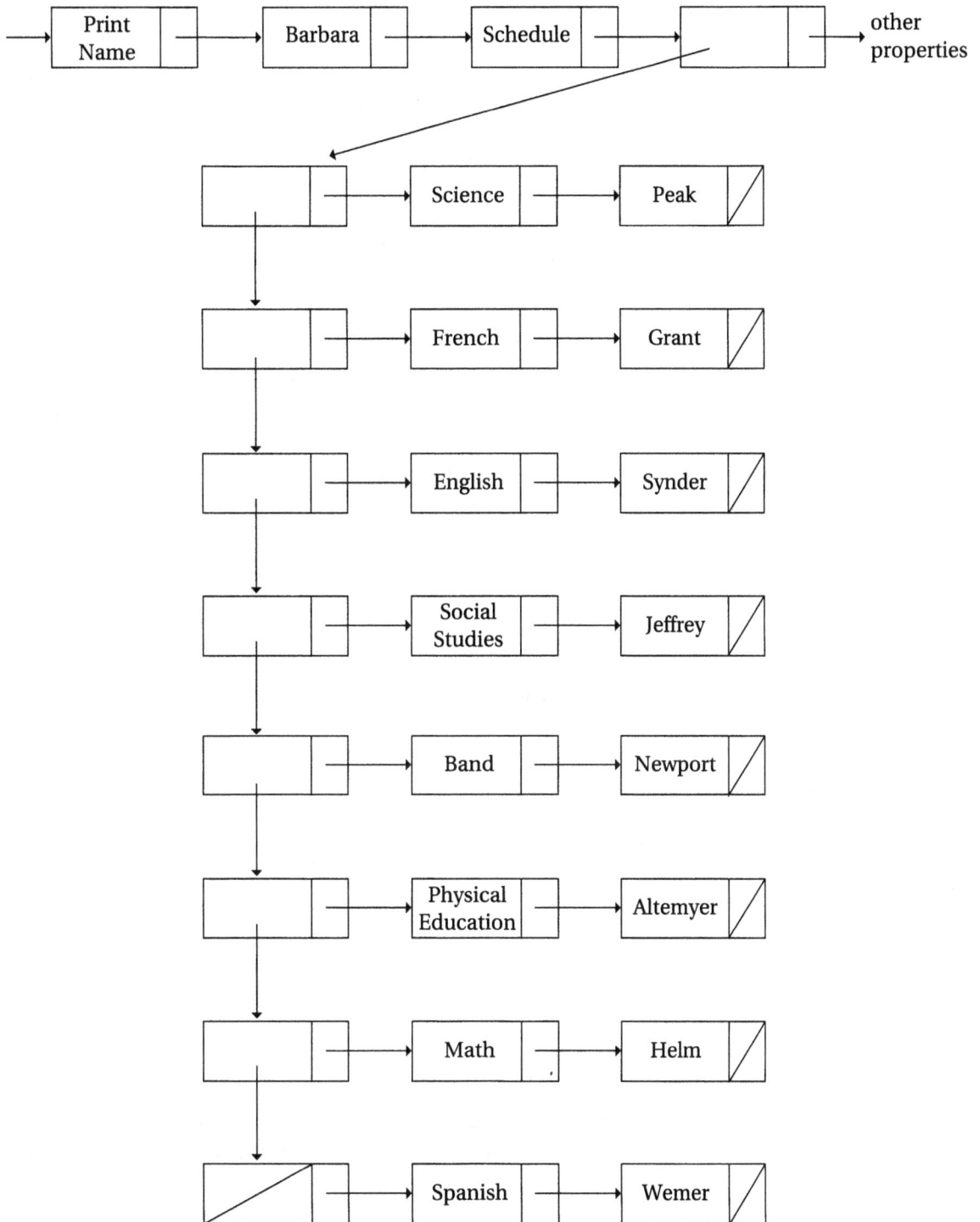

In this example, successive classes in Barbara's school day form an ordered linked list, with the subject name and teacher given for each period. While the plist in the example is lengthy, it illustrates the flexibility available within LISP property lists. More generally, plists have several important characteristics, listed here.

1. A plist contains an even number of components, where the odd-numbered components give the names of properties and the even-numbered components describe information related to those properties.

2. The name of a property serves as a key, and LISP provides information storage and retrieval by key.

3. Each key on the plist is unique. When one stores new information under a key, then the new data replace any earlier information that might have been stored under that key.

4. While LISP maintains some properties, such as pname, as part of its processing of any symbol, programmers may add or modify any other (key, information) pairs on the property list for any symbol.

While the capabilities and principles of property lists are always part of any LISP dialect, it should be noted that several implementations of symbols are possible, so some details of implementation may vary from one LISP dialect to another.

Association Lists in LISP

Association lists or *a-lists* in LISP also store pairs of information for easy retrieval. The standard reference for LISP describes these a-lists as follows:

> *An advantage of the a-list representation is that an a-list can be incrementally augmented simply by adding new entries to the front. Moreover, because the searching function* assoc *searches the a-list in order, new entries can "shadow" old entries. If an a-list is viewed as a mapping from keys to data, then the mapping can not only be augmented but also altered in a non-destructive manner by adding new entries to the front of the a-list.*[4]

As with property lists, association lists store and retrieve information in a (key, data) form, although several details are somewhat different. Listed below are the important characteristics of association lists.

1. Association lists are not directly related to symbols. Rather, a-lists have a separate existence, and programmers may create, modify, and use them independently of specific symbols.

2. A-lists allow the same key to be stored several times with different data. New information normally is added to the beginning of an a-list, and built-in search functions perform a linear search, starting at the front of the list.

3. Because a-lists always store pairs, they use a notation different from the standard list structure described throughout this chapter for generalized lists. In particu-

---

[4] Guy L. Steele, Jr., *Common LISP, The Language*, Burlington, MA: Digital Press, 1984, p. 279.

lar, while they use the same cell structure with two fields, neither field is considered a "next" field. For example, instead of storing the pair (A B) as a linked list

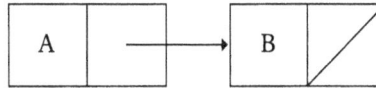

an a-list structure saves space by placing the A and the B in the same record.

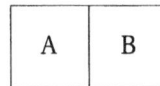

The result, denoted (A.B) in LISP, does not follow the normal format for a list structure, but it does support reasonably efficient data storage and retrieval. In this notation, the information listed above concerning Donna's parents would be in an a-list such as the following.

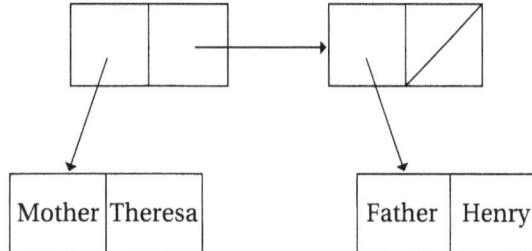

4. While this example shows both the key and the associated information as single symbols, LISP normally expects only the key to be an atom. The associated information could be any generalized list. (If the information is not an atom, then the second field of the above structure would be a pointer to the generalized list.)

While additional details of LISP are beyond the scope of this text, these examples of property and association lists illustrate that generalized lists are structures that may be useful not only to application programmers. Generalized lists also may be utilized within a programming language itself to store relevant information concerning symbols or other elements of a program.

Use of Generalized Lists Within Expert Systems

An expert system is a type of software package that utilizes rules in order to solve problems. For example, one such system uses various standardized test scores and high school transcript data to place students entering college into mathematics and computer science courses at an appropriate level.[5] In this context, rules describe what conclusions can be drawn under what circumstances. While the details are somewhat complicated, the following may suggest the nature of many such rules.

Rule 125:

If the student's Advanced Placement Math AB test score is at least 3,

Then there is suggestive evidence (0.7) that the student should be placed in Calculus II.

Rule 161:

If: 1) the student has taken at least two semesters of precalculus, and

2) the student had at least a C average in precalculus or in math overall, and

3) the student's standardized test scores (on the ACT or SAT) were at least fair,

Then it is definite (1.0) that the student should be placed in Calculus I or higher.

These rules also demonstrate a common characteristic of expert systems—namely, that conclusions may be made with varying levels of confidence. Rule 125 provides a tentative conclusion, while rule 161 is much more definite. More generally, a confidence factor of 1.0 implies certainty, 0.0 implies that no conclusion can be made at all, and −1.0 implies that the conclusion is definitely false.

While the details of such rules vary from one system to another, one such expert system coded the above rules as follows.

```
(rule125    (greateq* (VAL1 cntxt APBC) 3)
            (conclude cntxt TPLACE 133 tally 700))

(rule161    ($and  (greateq* (VAL1 cntxt SemofPcalc) 2)
                   ($or   (greateq* (VAL1 cntxt GRADES) 2.0)
                          (greateq* (VAL1 cntxt PCALCGRADES) 2.0))
                   ($or   (same cntxt stdscores high)
                          (same cntxt stdscores good)
                          (same cntxt stdscores fair)))
            (conclude cntxt TPLACE 131 tally 1000))
```

Here, the variable cntxt refers to the information for a specific student, and tally 700 or tally 1000 gives a confidence factor out of 1000. Also, 131 is the course number for Calculus I, while 133 is the course number for Calculus II. The meaning of the other terms generally reflect the English words.

---

[5] For more information on this expert system, see "An Expert System to Place Incoming Students in Mathematics and Computer Science Classes," by Vikram Subramaniam, Ivan Sykes, and Henry M. Walker, *Computer Science Education*, Volume 5, Number 2, 1994, pp. 137–148.

Such rules commonly combine several conditions as requirements for a particular conclusion. Within a database or program, it is natural to organize such rules as a single list in the format (rule-number (conditions) (conclusion)). The condition, in turn, often involves several parts or sublists.

Once these rules are determined, often by interviewing experts and by reviewing results, a program reads information about a specific student and then applies the rules to determine a likely placement. Such a program is called an *inference engine*, while the collection of rules is often called the *knowledge base*. Other common expert systems involve rules for such applications as identifying diseases, analyzing English sentences, or solving problems from physics textbooks.

All of these expert systems contain many rules that must be accessed efficiently. Furthermore, data must be collected for each student, individual, problem, or actual circumstance. Such information fits naturally into generalized lists, and expert systems rely upon such lists to a great extent.

This reliance upon generalized lists in many expert systems and other applications in the general field of artificial intelligence is one important reason why so many of these applications are written in the LISP programming language, which has generalized lists as its main data structure. (The rules listed above are taken from a LISP program without change. That program also stored student information on a p list associated with each student.) Other languages, such as T and Miranda, include lists and their operations as built-in capabilities. These languages provide the generalized list ADT operations as part of the language syntax, so a programmer can manipulate such lists directly. When a language does not have these capabilities built-in, then a programmer interested in such applications must implement the ADT operations, as discussed earlier in this chapter.

Analysis

Because generalized lists extend the concept of nonindexed linear lists, as described in previous chapters, the efficiency of many of the generalized list operations parallels that of the corresponding operation for simpler lists. For example, Make, Head, Tail, PutFirst, and IsEmpty all have $O(1)$ time complexity. In each case, the operation either examines a node (or atom), separates a node into its head or tail pieces, or combines two pieces to obtain a larger list.

Similarly, a search or the ListOfAtoms operation can require the processing of all parts of the list. Here, however, we must be careful to identify just what pieces are processed. For example, the list ((a b c)) contains just one component, but that component, in turn, contains three elements. Thus, the search for the atom c could involve looking within each component of each list and sublist. Overall, this could involve examining all atoms, regardless of how they were arranged within sublists. Similarly, the application of ListOfAtoms to the list (( ) ( ) ( ) ( )) would examine four components, only to find that each was empty. These examples suggest that any analysis of searches or ListOfAtoms must consider both the number of atoms and the number of null lists, counted recursively in all components. We can still say that a search or a listing of atoms has $O(n)$ as with simpler list structures, but here we must interpret n as the number of atoms plus the number of null lists (counted recursively throughout the structure).

Beyond these general observations of efficiency for the ADT operations, it is helpful to compare the three implementations described in this chapter. The linked list with header node implementation parallels our implementations of previous chapters most closely, and we have already observed that header nodes are useful when we want to maintain some general information about each list. For example, we noted that the header node may be used to store information about how many times a list is referenced. Similarly, we could store a count of the number of atoms or the number of components in a header node if such information would be helpful for an application.

In contrast, the Head/Tail representations of generalized lists do not have header nodes. While this can lengthen operations requiring reference counts or other summary information, the Head/Tail representation does not require an extra node as overhead when this information is not needed. Within this general approach, some additional differences can be noted between the full Head/Tail representation and the collapsed format. The full Head/Tail representation uses different types of boxes (records) for atoms and for list nodes. This allows both atoms and lists to exist independently. Furthermore, special information can be attached to atoms (or to list nodes) as desired. If a list node only may contain pointers, then the nodes can be relatively small even if the data associated with atoms are quite extensive. If a node can contain either a list or an atom, then care must be taken to select an appropriate size for this node so that it can include adequate information for any type of object. In a strongly typed language, such as Pascal, Modula-2, or Ada, nodes need to be variant records or records with fields of fixed size, and this size must be set carefully depending upon the application. In languages with more flexible typing, the sizes of nodes may be adjusted as needed.

Similar comments concerning the size of records apply to the collapsed Head/Tail representation of a generalized list. Here, atoms can be stored directly within nodes, and some additional node pointers from the full representation may not be needed. However, nodes still must be declared as appropriately sized to contain appropriate information about each atom. The collapsed Head/Tail representation has an additional difficulty: there is no way to represent a single atom, outside of a list. The atom cannot be put within a list node in this case, because the atom is being considered separate from any list. On the other hand, this collapsed Head/Tail representation accurately describes the common Head/Tail pictures of lists, where atoms are placed within the head. Coding from these pictures can be fairly straightforward.

SUMMARY

Generalized lists are indeed very general structures, whose components can be atoms or other lists. These very flexible structures can lead to various types of implementations. The simplest one is one in which the lists are independent. No list references another list, so the structures are easy to build.

The next level of complexity is one in which lists are allowed to reference other lists, but no recursive references are allowed. This reference can be viewed as either static or dynamic. If the reference is static, the list being referenced is copied. If the reference is dynamic, a pointer to the list being referenced is inserted.

The most complex structure is one where lists reference other lists and recursive references are allowed. Additional complexity arises in determining when a list is no longer needed. If recursion is not allowed, a scheme of reference counting can be used to keep track of when a list is in use. When the reference count of a list becomes zero, the nodes in the list can be freed. If recursion is allowed, this scheme fails because a recursive reference never allows the reference count to reach zero. We discuss these problems in more detail in Chapter 13.

Because generalized lists are very flexible structures, they may be used not only in applications but also within programming languages themselves to record information concerning symbols or other programming elements. For example, the main built-in data structure provided to the user in LISP is the generalized list. In addition, LISP also uses generalized lists to support its underlying structures such as property lists and association lists.

EXERCISES

1. The beginning of the chapter describes the translation of tree structures into generalized lists, and an example is given for the translation of Figure 7.1 in Chapter 7.

   a. Translate the tree structure in Figure 7.2 in Chapter 7 to a generalized list.

   b. Translate the multi-way tree in Figure 9.1 in Chapter 9 to a generalized list.

2. At the start of the chapter, the axioms for a generalized list are augmented to include an operation ListOfAtoms, which places all atoms on a generalized list onto a regular list.

   a. Apply these axioms to the generalized list ((a b c) (d (e (f)))).

   b. On the basis of the example in part (a), describe how the order of atoms on the generalized list L relates to the order of atoms on List(L). Justify your answer.

   c. Rewrite the axioms of ListOfAtoms so that its components have the opposite order.

3. Figure 12.3 shows the collapsed Head/Tail representation of two lists, where atoms are stored as the head of a list node. Redraw these lists in the expanded Head/Tail representation, where atoms are stored as a separate entity and where list nodes always contain two pointers, one to the head and one to the tail of the node.

4. Draw the storage structure for the following lists. Capital letters are names of lists and little letters are atoms. Header is used only if the list is named. The references among lists are assumed to be dynamic.

   a. p1 ← A(x (y z))

   b. p2 ← Z(() A A (a))

   c. p3 ← B(x (y) A Z W(x ((s)) B)

5. How many cells are freed in Exercise 4 when the following actions occur in sequence?

   a. Dispose (p1)

   b. Dispose (p2)

   c. Dispose (p3)

6. Redraw the storage structures in Exercise 4 where static references are used. (Delete the recursive reference in P3.)

    a. p1 ← A(x (y z))

    b. p2 ← Z(() A A (a))

    c. p3 ← B(x (y) A Z W(x ((s)))

7. Give the algorithm for disposing a general list when dynamic references are used.

8. Given the storage structure shown below,

    a. Are shared references allowed in the list? If so, are they static or dynamic?

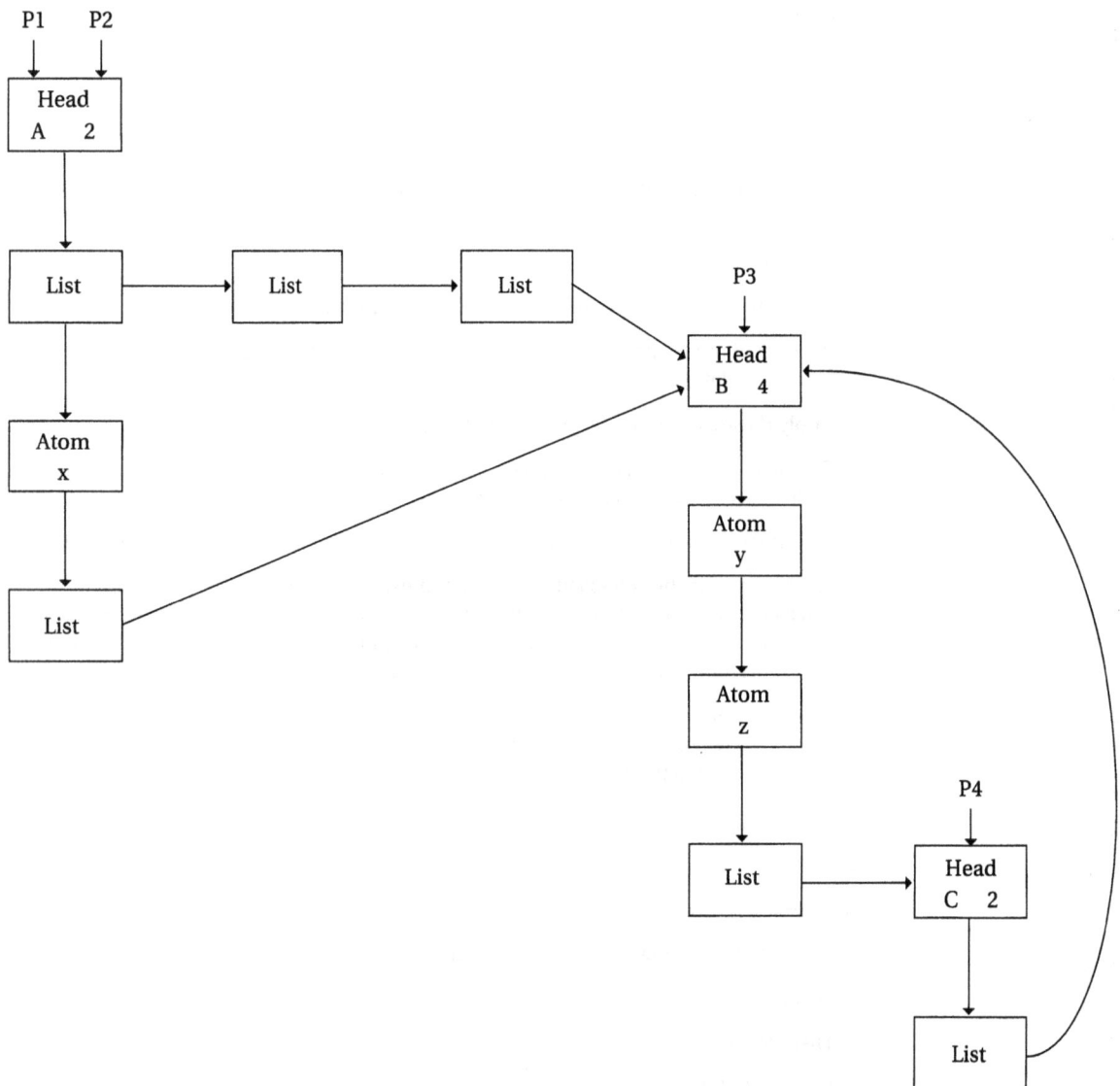

   b. Give the lists represented.

   c. How many more nodes are released at each stage of the following operations?

Operation	Nodes Released
Dispose (P1)	
Dispose (P2)	
Dispose (P3)	
Dispose (P4)	

9. Evaluate the following list expressions.

   a. CONS (HEAD (A B C)) (TAIL (Q R S)))

   b. CONS (HEAD ((A) B C)) (TAIL (Q R S)))

   c. CONS (HEAD (A B C)) (TAIL ((Q) R S)))

10. Suppose that L is a list containing more than one component.

   a. Simplify the expression (CONS (HEAD L) (TAIL L)).

   b. Justify your answer with an appropriate picture.

11. If A and B are atoms, does CONS (A B) represent a valid list? Explain.

12. List-processing languages, such as LISP and Scheme, have a function EVAL to evaluate lists. (In fact, in an interpretive environment, EVAL is implicitly called every time a user or programmer enters any line.) Furthermore, EVAL may appear within a list itself. For example, the expression

   (EVAL (QUOTE (HEAD (A B))))

applies EVAL to the list that is obtained from (QUOTE (HEAD (A B))). Because this latter list is the unevaluated list (HEAD (A B)), the result of the example is to apply EVAL to (HEAD (A B)), which gives the head of the (A B) list, or A.

Expand the EVAL function specified in the chapter to include an explicit call of EVAL within a list.

13. List-processing languages naturally represent arithmetic expressions as lists using prefix notation. Furthermore, operations such as addition (+) and multiplication (*) may be applied to as many values as are present within a list. For example, (+ 1 2 3) and (* 2 2 2 2) give the numbers 6 and 16, respectively. More complex arithmetic expressions, such as (+ 2 (* 3 4 5) (/ 6 2)), are considered generalized lists.

Modify GetToken and the input and output routines for generalized lists, as described in this chapter, to store general arithmetic expressions as generalized lists, where each node is a header node or contains a number or an arithmetic operation. Assume that all numbers are integers.

14. Revise the EVAL operator to evaluate the general arithmetic expressions read as generalized lists in the previous problem. In this exercise, you should assume that all numbers are integers, so division (/) gives a truncated result without remainder.

15. a. Identify three characteristics that distinguish property lists in LISP from association lists.

   b. Based upon your answer to part (a), give guidelines for when you would use each of these structures.

16. a. Code the algorithms for list input and output using the implementation involving a header node.

    b. Code the algorithms for list input and output using the collapsed Head/Tail representation.

17. Draw the generalized lists for Rules 126 and 161 from the placement expert system, using both Head/Tail representations and using the header node representation.

18. Write a procedure that counts the number of atoms in a generalized list.

19. Write a procedure that produces a copy of a generalized list (without destroying the original list).

20. Creating a list used two mutually recursive procedures. They can be combined into one by considering the generalized list to be an atom or a sequence of components.

21. Rewrite the algorithms to print a generalized list as one procedure.

22. The Eval algorithm assumes a correct expression. Add error checking to this algorithm.

Memory Management

13

In all of our discussions of abstract data types and their implementation alternatives, we have assumed that memory is handled correctly. If we need an array, we define its type and declare an array variable of that type. If we are building a linked structure, we issue a call to New and trust that the system returns a pointer to a variable of the proper type. Following the principles of abstraction and information hiding, we have taken for granted the fact that the compiler and the run-time support system of our language perform as advertised.

It is now time to move from the user's view of memory management and consider more closely the functions of a "Memory Manager," the environments in which these functions are applied, and how these functions might be implemented.

Functions of the Memory Manager

Simply put, the functions of a Memory Manager are twofold: to allocate and deallocate collections of contiguous storage locations (called *blocks* of storage).[1] The environment in which the Memory Manager operates dictates different strategies and different algorithms.

For example, an operating system in a multiprogramming environment allocates and deallocates blocks of storage for programs. A word processor (in conjunction with the operating system) allocates blocks for files. When a file is deleted, the blocks that the file occupied are made available for another file to use.

Compilers allocate storage for global program variables but do not deallocate them, because all storage assigned to a program usually is deallocated automatically when a program finishes. The run-time support systems for compilers like Pascal, Modula-2, and Ada that allow dynamic storage allocation for subprograms and declaration of variables at run time (referenced variables) have two Memory Managers, one that allocates and deallocates the storage for subprogram parameters and local variables and one that allocates and deallocates storage for dynamic variables. These two interact to determine when a program runs out of memory.

The collection of techniques that a Memory Manager uses can be classified by the types of blocks that are being allocated and deallocated. If the blocks that are being allocated and deallocated are all the same size, very simple schemes can be used. If the blocks are of varying sizes, the initial allocation is not difficult, but reallocating a block becomes a problem. We look in detail at both types of allocation.

Another factor that determines the techniques to be used is the determination of when a block is free to be reallocated. In most applications, a block is free to be used again when it is returned to the Memory Manager by the program (disposed). There are applications, however, where it is not known when a block is free to be used again; that is, the block may be returned by one part of a program but still be needed elsewhere. In this case, the Memory Manager must have a way of determining when a block is actually available for reallocation. This task can be simple or complex depending on the type of processing being done on the blocks. The problem of determining when a block is free was alluded to in Chapter 12.

In certain cases, the Memory Manager may receive a request for a block of storage that is larger than any block that is available for allocation. There may be smaller blocks available that can be collected into one larger block (coalesced) or memory may need to be reorganized (compacted). We look at these situations in detail in this chapter.

Interface with the Memory Manager

In the first 12 chapters of this book, our discussions focused on abstract data types, which provided a utility for the user. Here, our focus must change. The data

---

[1] Throughout this chapter, we use memory and storage interchangeably. Although memory is usually associated with internal storage, these algorithms apply to disk or any contiguous storage medium.

type must now be the *user* of the utility provided by the Memory Manager. Previously, an algorithm issued a call to New to get a block of storage and assumed that the run-time support system would Dispose of the block when it was no longer needed. Now, we are going to switch hats and become the Memory Manager. Our job is to *allocate blocks* of storage when a New is issued and *deallocate blocks* of storage when a Dispose is issued (by either the user or the run-time support system). (See Figure 13.1.)

Depending upon the application, a block of storage might be one bit, one byte, one word, or many words. For purposes of our discussion, a block is a contiguous collection of fixed-size units of storage. Each block is designated by the address of the first unit (the base address). If all the blocks are the same size, the number of units in a block is implicit. If the number of units in a block varies from request to request, then the number of units must be a parameter to the request for storage allocation and deallocation. The number of units in a block is called the *size* of the block.

Because this discussion is from the point of view of the Memory Manager, a **free block** is one that is under the control of the Memory Manager and available to be allocated, that is, an unallocated block. The Memory Manager allocates free blocks by giving the beginning address of the block to the user (the person or program requesting the block) and recording that the block has been allocated. The

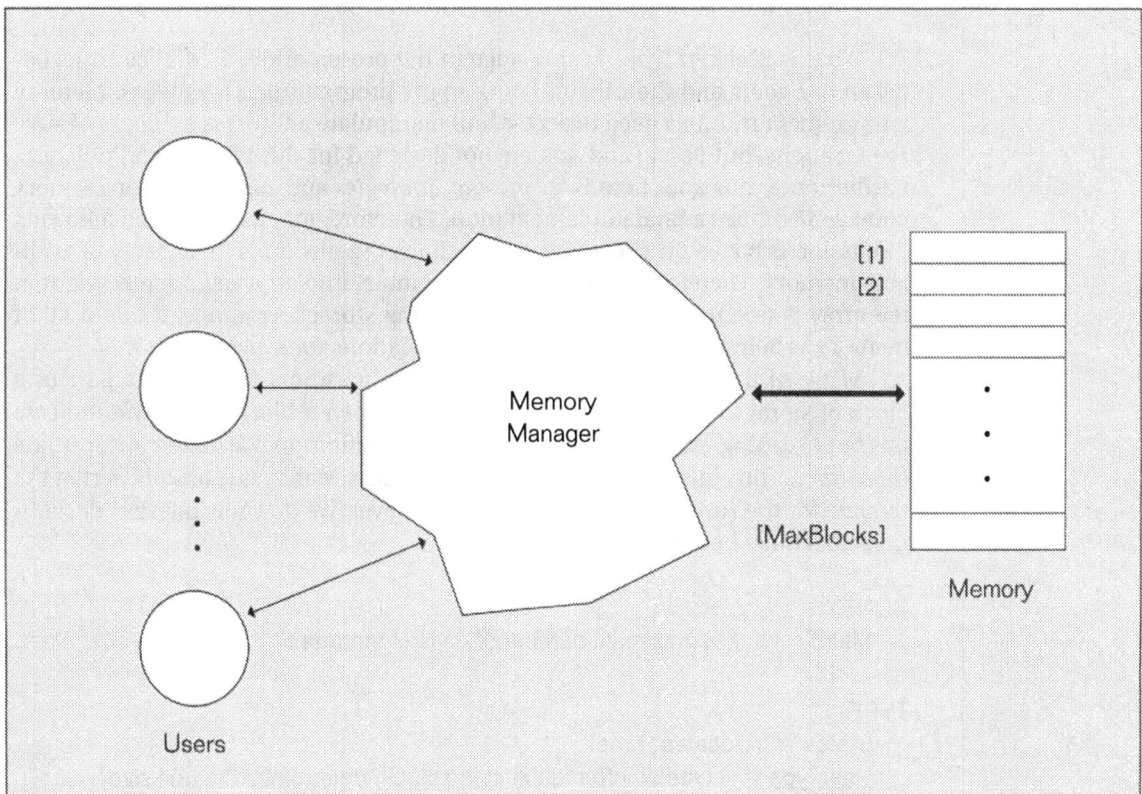

Figure 13.1 Model of Function of the Memory Manager

method of recording that a block has been allocated is usually implicit: the Memory Manager has a list of blocks that are free. If a block is not on the list, it is allocated.

> **Free Block** An unallocated block of storage that is under the control of the Memory Manager and free to be allocated.

When the user returns a block to the Memory Manager, it is deallocated. In most cases, the Memory Manager deallocates a block by putting the block on the list of free blocks. Here is the interface that we use throughout this chapter.

```
PROCEDURE Allocate(VAR BlockPtr: BlockPtrType, Size: Integer)
(* Post:    If there is a block of Size units, BlockPtr is the address    *)
(*          of the first unit in the block and the block is no longer     *)
(*          free; otherwise, ERROR.                                        *)

PROCEDURE Deallocate(BlockPtr: BlockPtrType, Size: Integer)
(* Pre:     Block of Size units beginning at BlockPtr was allocated.    *)
(* Post:    Block of Size units beginning at BlockPtr is now free.      *)
```

What is BlockPtrType? At this stage in the presentation, a conflict arises between our goals and the capabilities of many programming languages. Memory management routines need to access and manipulate addresses of blocks of storage locations, but Pascal and Ada are not designed for this type of manipulation. Furthermore, our goal here is to present *strategies* and *algorithms* for memory management, not a final implementation. Therefore, for simplicity, the following discussion is based on allocating and deallocating positions in an array of available memory. Therefore, BlockPtrType is an index into an array. Each element in the array is one unit. When actually allocating storage locations, think of all of memory as being one large array of storage locations (bits, bytes, or words).

Many of the allocation and deallocation algorithms need to use part of a block of storage for bookkeeping information when a block is free. We indicate this bookkeeping use by a CASE within the type definition. We do not encapsulate these operations in a module, because the Memory Manager is usually part of the module for the run-time support system. However, we do show relevant declarations that must be supplied, as shown below.

```
CONST
    MaxBlocks = < maximum number of units of storage >

TYPE
    Status = (Allocated, Free)
    UserType = < type of information in the block; determines the unit size >
    BlockPtrType = 0..MaxBlocks;
```

```
BlockType = RECORD
    CASE Status OF
        Allocated   : UserInfo : UserType
        Free        : <whatever information the Memory Manager needs>
    END RECORD;

MemoryType = ARRAY [1..MaxBlocks] OF BlockType
```

We begin examining the techniques for allocating and deallocating blocks of storage by looking at the simplest case first: fixed-sized blocks needed by only one user. In all of the following situations, the exception ERROR is set if a request for an allocation cannot be filled.

Fixed-Sized Blocks

The job of the Memory Manager is to allocate (hand out) a block of memory when it receives a request and to deallocate (make the block available for reuse) when the user indicates that the block is no longer needed. The Memory Manager's job is similar to that of the head waiter in a restaurant. The head waiter keeps track of which tables are free; the Memory Manager keeps track of which blocks of memory are free. The head waiter often organizes his or her work by keeping a list of free tables. This technique is often used by the Memory Manager as well. By tradition, the list of free memory blocks is called the *available space list*, and the external pointer to the list is called *Avail*.

The least complicated environment in which a Memory Manager can operate is one in which all of the blocks are the same size and there is only one user. The blocks of memory are linked together into a list. When a request for a block is received, the Memory Manager removes the first block, crosses it off the list, and returns it to the user. When a block of storage is returned, the Memory Manager puts it back on the list. Because all the blocks are the same size, the returned block can be put anywhere on the list. The structure that we used to implement a binary tree in Chapter 7 was a specific example of this type of memory management. The following algorithms for Allocate and Deallocate implement this scheme in a general fashion. Memory is linked as in the example in Chapter 7. We assume the following global declarations given in the last section.

Allocate(VAR BlockPtr: BlockPtrType)

```
IF Avail = 0
    THEN
        ERROR
    ELSE
        BlockPtr ← Avail
        Avail ← Memory[Avail].Next
END IF
```

Deallocate(BlockPtr: BlockPtrType)

```
Memory[BlockPtr].Next ← Avail
Avail ← BlockPtr
```

Initialize

We must initialize available space by linking all the nodes together.

```
FOR Counter ← 1 TO (MaxBlocks − 1) DO
    Memory[Counter].Next ← Counter + 1
END FOR
Memory[MaxBlocks].Next ← 0
Avail ← 1
```

The algorithm described above defines a pool of storage as an array of fixed-sized blocks that are linked together. Allocate returns an index into the array. The user accesses the block of storage by accessing Memory[BlockPtr].

Another variation of the same type of scheme is to have a Boolean flag in each block that is True if the block is free, and False otherwise. The Allocate procedure searches Memory looking for the first free block, sets the Boolean flag to False, and returns the index. Deallocate simply sets the Boolean flag to True. Still another variation is to not initialize memory by linking each block together, but simply to hand out blocks from memory as they are requested. When the last block has been allocated, future allocations come from Avail.

Complexity

The complexity of Allocate and Deallocate as shown has bounded time, O(1). Initialize, however, requires a traversal of the entire memory, giving a complexity of O(MaxBlocks). The exercises at the end of the chapter ask you to examine the complexity of the alternative suggested in the preceding paragraph.

Stack-Based Order (Fixed- or Mixed-Sized Blocks)

Allocation and deallocation of storage for subprogram calls follow the basic principle of a stack. All accesses to parameters and local variables are done through a global variable called the *stack pointer*. This stack pointer is adjusted by the Memory Manager each time a procedure is invoked (memory is allocated) or exited (memory is deallocated). The important point here is that when memory is deallocated, the system knows that it is the last memory allocated; that is, the last-in-first-out principle applies. Because this method of allocation and deallocation is such an important one, we look at the process in detail.

When a subprogram (procedure or function) is compiled, the compiler determines how much storage the subprogram requires for parameters, local variables, and temporary variables. This information is used to define an *activation record* (sometimes called *stack frame*) for the subprogram. The run-time support system puts this activation record on the stack each time the procedure or function is called. The code for the subprogram accesses its parameters and local variables by their relative positions in the activation record. The activation record also must contain its size and the address of the next instruction to be executed when the subprogram has finished its execution. For example, the following procedure needs an activation record with five positions.

PROCEDURE ProcessList(VAR List: ListType, Item: ItemType);
(* Post: List.Values[1].. List.Values[List.Length] is processed. *)

VAR Counter : Integer

The activation record for this procedure might look like this.

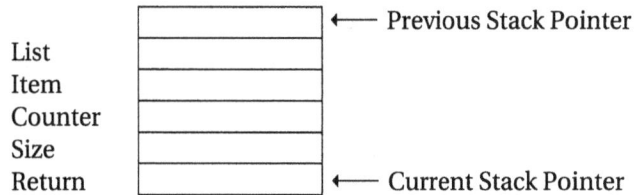

When the procedure is called, the address of the parameter List (a VAR parameter) is stored in the first place in the activation record and a copy of Item (a value parameter) is stored in the second place. Counter is a local variable; it gets a position in the activation record. Size and Return are information that the run-time support system needs. Size is the number of locations (storage units) in the activation record. The size of each activation record is needed in order for the stack pointer to be set properly when the procedure or function returns. Return is the address of the statement following the procedure or function call. The run-time support system supplies this address with each call. (In some languages, other information concerning a subprogram or its environment also may be stored in the activation record, but we do not consider this possibility in what follows.)

While it is common to use the expression "put the activation record on the stack," we must be careful not to be misled by this phrase. What actually happens is this: the current value of the stack pointer is incremented by the number of storage units needed for the activation record. For our example, if we assume that each parameter or local variable is the size of one storage unit, then the stack pointer would be incremented by five in this case. That is, the current stack pointer is five plus the address of the previous stack pointer.

All accesses by either the run-time support system or the code of a procedure or function are made through the stack pointer. In our example, the address of Return would be specified by the stack pointer; Size would be in the location obtained by subtracting 1 from the location stored in the stack pointer; Counter would be the location in the stack pointer minus 2; and so on. When a procedure or function finishes executing, the value designated by the stack pointer is decremented by the number of positions in the activation record (Size). Hence, in this situation, the job of the Memory Manager involves only incrementing and decrementing the stack pointer!

If one subprogram calls another, the most recently activated subprogram is on the top of the stack. If ProcessList calls Calculate (shown below), the stack looks as follows (the top of the stack is at the bottom of the figure).

FUNCTION Calculate (Item1, Item2: ItemType): ItemType;
VAR
    Temp: ItemType

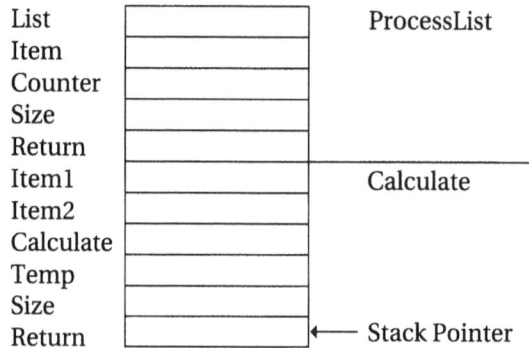

Complexity

Allocation requires that a value be added to the stack pointer. Deallocation requires that a value be subtracted from the stack pointer. Therefore, the complexity is bounded time (actually constant) for both allocation and deallocation. Because the block being allocated or deallocated contains its own size, this simple scheme is independent of the size of the blocks. They can all have one fixed size or they can have mixed sizes.

Mixed- (Variable-) Sized Blocks

The next step up in the complexity of the environment in which a Memory Manager works is illustrated by the generation and disposing of dynamic (referenced) variables. Not only are the blocks of different sizes, but they are allocated and deallocated in no set order. Of course, any particular program might have only one pointer type so that the blocks are fixed in size, but the Memory Manager must be programmed to handle the more general case. Pascal, Modula-2, and Ada call the area of memory from which storage is allocated for dynamic variables the *heap*. The word heap here is used in the generic sense. Memory is *not* organized as a partially ordered tree; in fact, it is not organized at all. Memory is considered just a "heap" of locations.

In order to have maximum flexibility, the heap is often in one end of memory and the stack for procedure and function calls is in the other. That is, memory is organized as follows.

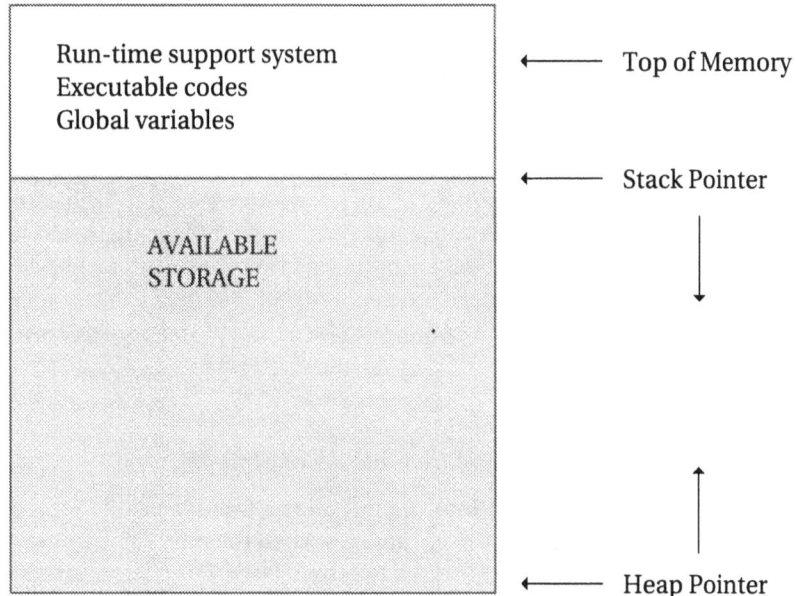

Run-time support system Executable codes Global variables	←——— Top of Memory
	←——— Stack Pointer
	↓
AVAILABLE STORAGE	
	↑
	←——— Heap Pointer

The stack pointer and the heap pointer move towards each other. A program runs out of memory only when the stack pointer and the heap pointer meet. The stack pointer moves up and down as storage is allocated and deallocated. What happens when storage assigned from the heap is deallocated? If a block that is deallocated just happens to be the last one allocated, the heap pointer can be adjusted. However, this situation is rather unusual, and the algorithms for the Memory Manager cannot count on this situation. Thus, like the fixed-size block case, the Memory Manager must keep a list of blocks that are returned.

Now the algorithm to allocate a block of storage becomes more complex. There is the heap pointer, which points to a block of storage available above it, and a list of blocks that are free between the heap pointer and the end of storage. To complicate matters, the blocks may vary in size. How is the list of available space kept? Is storage taken from above the heap pointer first and the list examined only if adjusting the heap pointer would make it meet the stack pointer? Various answers to these questions define alternative strategies for allocating and deallocating mixed-sized blocks of storage.

Heap management is an example of the type of memory management environment in which storage begins as one large block of MaxBlocks units on the available space list from which blocks of different sizes are allocated. When a block is deallocated, it is put on the available space list. Allocations and deallocations are for blocks of various sizes, and they occur in no particular order. We now look at various strategies for manipulating the list of available space under these constraints.

Available Space List

Each block of storage is specified by its beginning position and its length. The list of available space is initialized to contain one block, that is, all available storage. In the discussion of the heap, we talked about the heap pointer being at the end of storage and moving up. However, in the following discussion, we assume that available memory starts at location 1. In the fixed-size block example, we stored the available space links within the blocks themselves. Because storing the links within the blocks is not always feasible, we may need to keep the information on available blocks in a separate list. Before we examine allocation and deallocation strategies, we look at the placement of the available space list.

Avail Separate from Blocks of Storage

Keeping the information on the free blocks of storage separate from the blocks themselves has advantages when the individual units of storage are small and addresses and sizes are relatively large. For example, this separation of the available list and actual storage is helpful when we are storing strings. Each character requires only a byte of storage, while integers to record sizes and addresses typically require significantly more space.

```
TYPE
    UserType = < type of information in the block; determines the unit size >
    NodePointer = ↑AvailNode;

    AvailNode = RECORD
        BlockPtr   : BlockPtrType;      (* first position in block *)
        Size       : 1..MaxBlocks;      (* number of units in the block *)
        Next       : NodePointer        (* link to next AvailNode *)
    END RECORD;

    MemoryType = ARRAY [1..MaxBlock] OF UserType;
```

```
VAR
    Avail       : NodePointer;
    Memory      : MemoryType
```

Avail is the external pointer to the list of free blocks; Memory designates the array of storage from which we wish to allocate space. The nodes that make up the available space list are dynamically allocated; they are completely separate from the blocks of storage. That is, information about the blocks of storage is kept separately from the blocks themselves.

The initialization of the list of available space is the same no matter what allocation scheme is used: Avail is set to point to one block of memory beginning at position 1 with Size equal to MaxBlocks. Each position in the array is one unit of storage. For specificity, we assume that MaxBlocks is 1000. Also, we use the index 0 to indicate there are no additional blocks of free space on the available list. In the balance of this chapter, unallocated space is shaded.

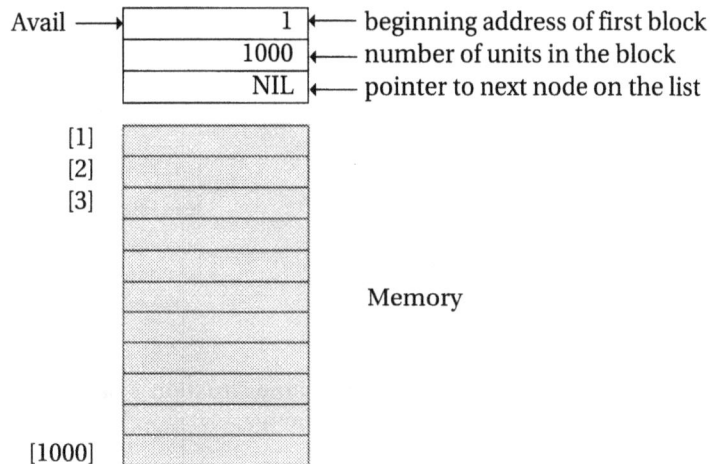

Avail ⟶ | 1 | ⟵ beginning address of first block
          | 1000 | ⟵ number of units in the block
          | NIL | ⟵ pointer to next node on the list

[1]
[2]
[3]

Memory

[1000]

To begin the process, suppose the Memory Manager receives a request for 80 units of storage. There is only one block on the available space list, so 80 positions are allocated. Does it matter whether we allocate the first 80 in the block or the last 80? If we allocate the last 80, only the Size has to be changed. The beginning address of the block remaining on the list is the same. Allocating the locations from the end of the block only saves changing one variable in this case. However, later we see that it also makes the processing easier when there are more nodes on the available space list.

In order to keep track of different blocks, we number the requests. Request 2 is for 70 units, Request 3 is for 120 units, Request 4 is for 225 units, and Request 5 is for 180 units. Memory now looks as follows.

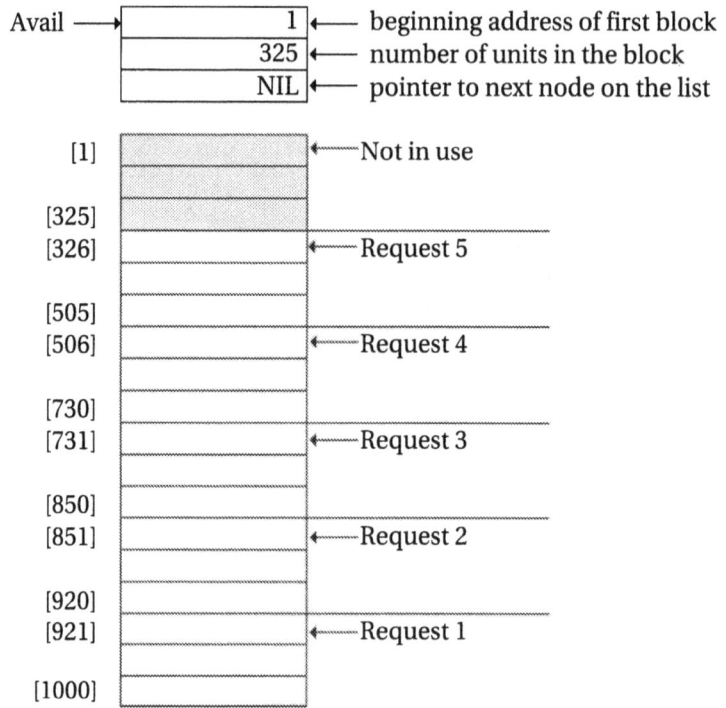

Now we look at the same situation where the list of available space is kept within the blocks of free storage.

Avail within Blocks of Storage

When items being stored are expected to be large, the blocks themselves can be used to record the desired information concerning a free list. In this setting, Avail records only the location of the first free space in memory, and the nodes in the list are the blocks themselves. The size and next fields are stored in the first part of each block.

In this approach, storage might look like the following after the requests in the previous section.

Avail: 1

[1]	325 ← Free (Size)
	0 (Next)
[325]	
[326]	← Request 5
[505]	
[506]	← Request 4
[730]	
[731]	← Request 3
[850]	
[851]	← Request 2
[920]	
[921]	← Request 1
[1000]	

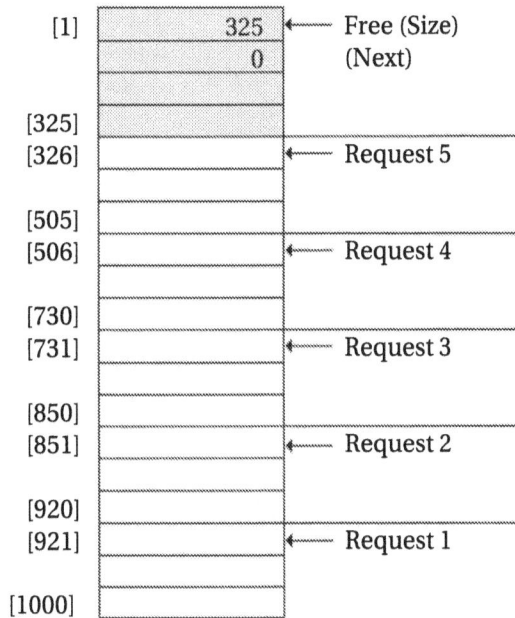

Allocation and Deallocation Strategies

If there is only one block of storage on the available space list, all of the allocation strategies work in the same way. Now, suppose that requests 1 and 2 return their 80 and 70 locations, respectively, giving us three blocks on the available space list. What happens now depends on the choice of strategy for allocating a block of storage. As we shall see, there are four different strategies for choosing which storage blocks to allocate when the Memory Manager receives a request: *first fit, best fit, next fit,* and *worst fit*. Each represents a different way of searching the available space list for a block of sufficient size.

In the *first fit* strategy, the available space list is kept as a simple linked list. When a request is received for a block of storage, Avail is scanned from the beginning. The first block on the list that is big enough to fill the request is allocated. When a block is returned, it is put on the list at one end or the other. Because it is easier to insert an item at the beginning of the list, this is usually where it goes. The following diagram shows the resulting position if request 1 returns its space first, followed by request 2. (In the balance of this discussion, we assume that the available space list is kept within the blocks.)

Avail: 851

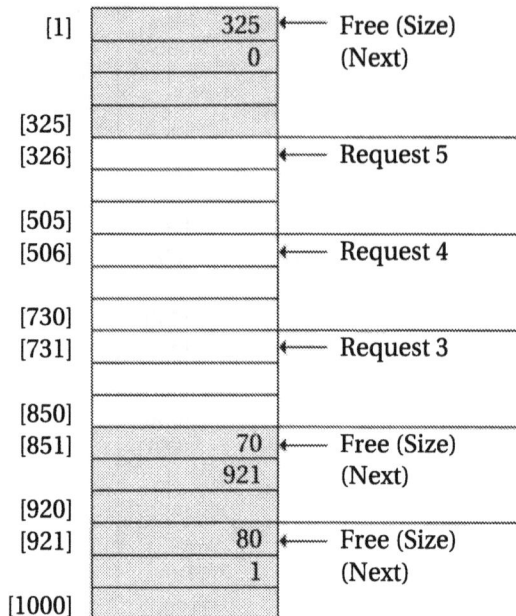

If the next request is for 200 and request 4 then returns its 225, the resulting picture is as follows.

Avail: 506

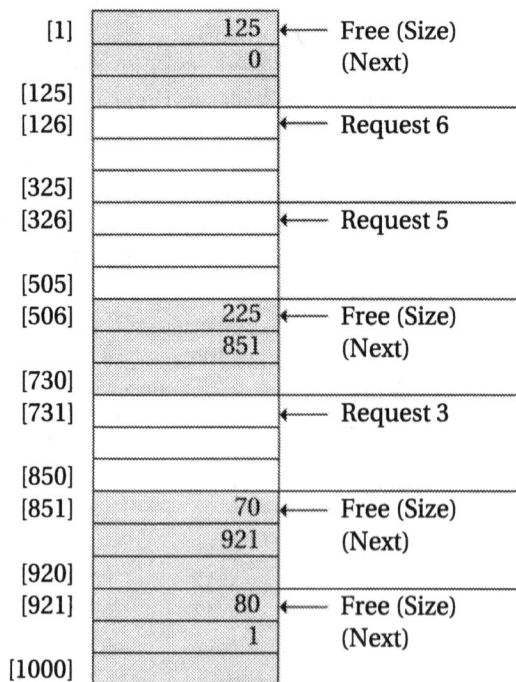

So far, each request has been large enough that only one free block has had adequate space to fill it. If there are two blocks large enough, which one do you use?[2]

Suppose the next request is for a block of size 125. Under the first fit strategy, positions 606 through 730 are assigned from the first block on the available space list, and the remaining 100 units in the block (positions 506–605) remain on the available space list. Notice that the last 125 units in the block are allocated so that the list of available space does not have to be changed. If we allocate the first 125 units, the pointer in the preceding block (Avail in this case) has to be changed to point to 631. Finding the preceding block in a list involves either traversing the list again or using more complicated code to keep track of both the current block and the previous block. Therefore, allocating from the end of the block is a better choice.

The *best fit* strategy scans the available space list for the block that is the closest fit to the requested block. Under the best fit allocation scheme, the block of size 125 (an exact fit) is assigned to fill the request for 125 units. The resulting two memory configurations are shown below.

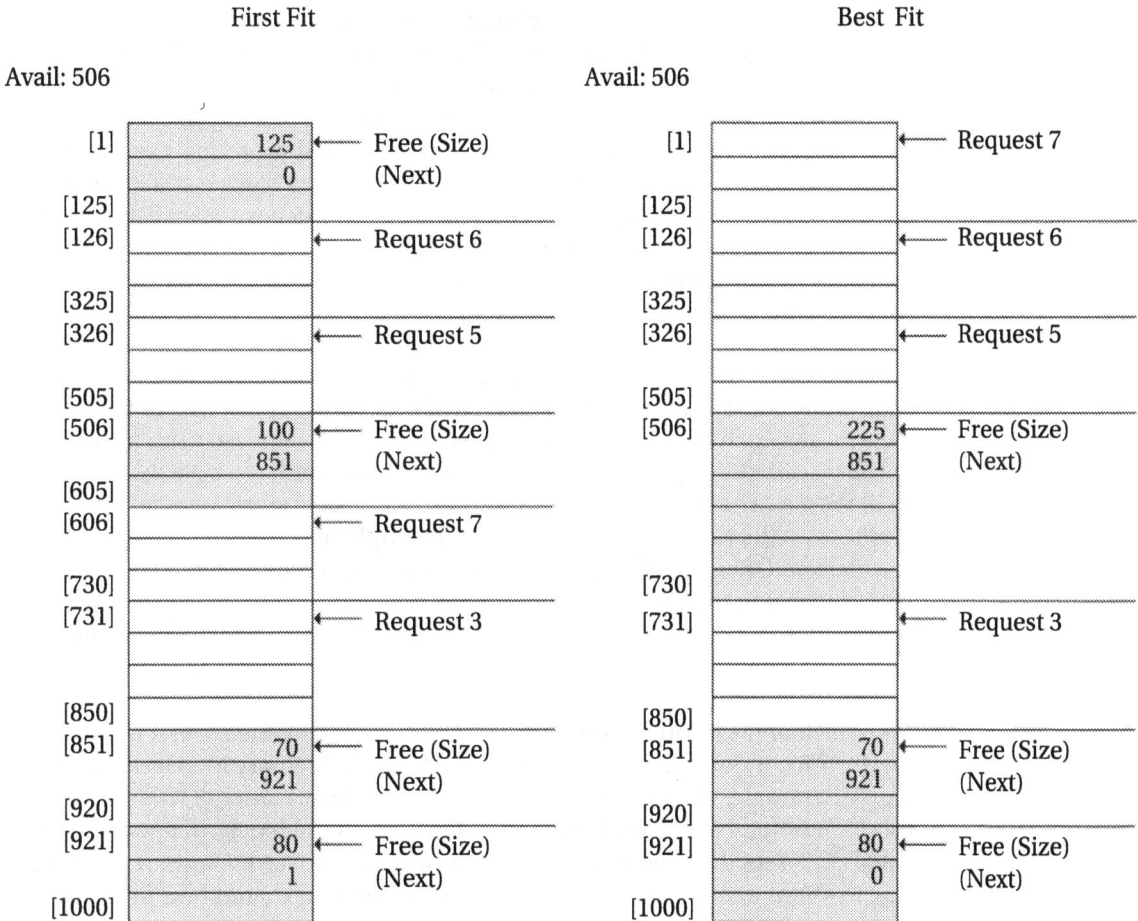

First Fit

Best Fit

Avail: 506

Avail: 506

First Fit		Best Fit	
[1]	125 ← Free (Size)	[1]	← Request 7
	0 (Next)		
[125]		[125]	
[126]	← Request 6	[126]	← Request 6
[325]		[325]	
[326]	← Request 5	[326]	← Request 5
[505]		[505]	
[506]	100 ← Free (Size)	[506]	225 ← Free (Size)
	851 (Next)		851 (Next)
[605]			
[606]	← Request 7		
[730]		[730]	
[731]	← Request 3	[731]	← Request 3
[850]		[850]	
[851]	70 ← Free (Size)	[851]	70 ← Free (Size)
	921 (Next)		921 (Next)
[920]		[920]	
[921]	80 ← Free (Size)	[921]	80 ← Free (Size)
	1 (Next)		0 (Next)
[1000]		[1000]	

---

[2] The answer to this question differentiates between the first fit strategy and the best fit strategy.

If there are N blocks on the available space list kept as an unsorted linked list, the order for an allocate operation is O(N) in both first fit and best fit. However, best fit requires a complete scan of the available space list, and first fit has to examine only N/2 blocks on the average. Best fit produces smaller leftover fragments when a block is split, thus better utilizing space. These two schemes represent the extreme ends of the spectrum. In between are two other strategies: *next fit* and *worst fit*.

When applying either first fit or best fit, the block on the available space list is not actually removed unless there is an exact fit. The positions that are allocated are taken from the end of the block and the Size is changed to reflect the number of positions (units) remaining in the block. This means that small blocks tend to cluster at the beginning of the available space list. The *next fit* strategy keeps the available space list as a circular list. Avail is left pointing to the block *immediately following* the block from which the last allocation was made. This speeds up the search of the available space list by effectively distributing the smaller fragments evenly throughout the list.

An alternative way to avoid examining very small blocks on the available space list is to decide not to keep a block that is below a certain size. That is, if the difference between what is requested and the size of the block from which storage is being allocated is within a certain limit, the entire block is allocated. This introduces another problem. The size of the block allocated is not the size that is requested. Who keeps track of the actual block size? When a block is deallocated, the size must be known. If this strategy is used by the Memory Manager, then the Memory Manager must be responsible for keeping track of the sizes of the allocated blocks as well as the free blocks. We discuss a way of doing this shortly when we look at the boundary tag system.

The fourth strategy is called the *worst fit* strategy. Here the available space list is kept ordered by block size with the largest block at the beginning of the list. All allocations come from the first block on the available space list. However, the block from which the units are taken must actually be removed from the list and the block with the remaining units must be inserted in order to keep the list sorted by block size. The list kept sorted by block size is just a priority queue, where the block size is the priority. Thus, the list can be implemented using a heap, making the allocate $O(\log_2 n)$. Of course, the deallocate becomes $O(\log_2 n)$ as well. The main advantage to this strategy, however, is not the $O(\log_2 n)$ allocate and deallocate but the fact that only one access is needed to determine whether or not the request can be fulfilled. If the largest block is not big enough to service the request, Allocate fails.

Which of these four strategies is the best? We cannot answer that question in the abstract. It depends on the context in which the Memory Manager is operating. For example, what is the ratio of deallocations to allocations? What is the distribution of the block sizes being requested? Are all the blocks of approximately equal size or do the sizes vary widely? If the available space list is short, a strategy that has O(n) allocation and O(1) deallocation (first, next, and best fit) is just as good (and maybe better) than a more complicated $O(\log_2 n)$ strategy (worst fit). We can say that next fit is better than first fit. They are equally simple to implement and have the same complexity for allocation and deallocation, but next fit avoids creating clusters of small blocks. Significant savings accrued for disk space allocation for PC-DOS 3.0 and MS-DOS 3.0 and higher when the first fit strategy was replaced with next fit.[3]

Fragmentation

After a series of allocations and deallocations, the original available storage is a mixture of blocks, some allocated and some free. Free blocks are spread (fragmented) throughout memory. This is called **fragmentation**. There may be enough free blocks to fill a request, but the locations may not be contiguous.

> **Fragmentation** The situation where available storage is broken into many noncontiguous pieces.

If a request for a block of storage cannot be filled, then memory compaction is an alternative. When memory is compacted, all allocated blocks are moved to the beginning of memory, and Avail is reinitialized to one block containing the rest of memory. In fact, memory compaction may be the only alternative; we discuss compaction later. There are, however, some intermediate steps that can be taken. In our example using the first fit strategy (page 595), consider what happens when a request for 140 units is received.

With the available list as shown, a request for 140 locations cannot be serviced *even though there are 140 free contiguous locations.* While there are 140 contiguous locations (actually 150: 851 – 1000), the available space list does not reflect this. This illustrates a problem associated with deallocating space. If a block being deallocated is contiguous to a block already on the available space list, the two blocks should be combined into one block. In our example, combining adjacent blocks into one block, called *coalescing,* would yield the following picture, where the two blocks at the upper end of memory are combined.

---

[3] G. Weissman, "Comparing Disk-Allocation Methods," *Byte 1987 Extra Edition: Inside IBM PCs.*

Avail: 506

[1]	125	← Free (Size)
	0	(Next)
[125]		
[126]		← Request 6
[325]		
[326]		← Request 5
[505]		
[506]	100	← Free (Size)
	851	(Next)
[605]		
[606]		← Request 7
[730]		
[731]		← Request 3
[850]		
[851]	150	← Free (Size)
		(Next)
	1	
[1000]		

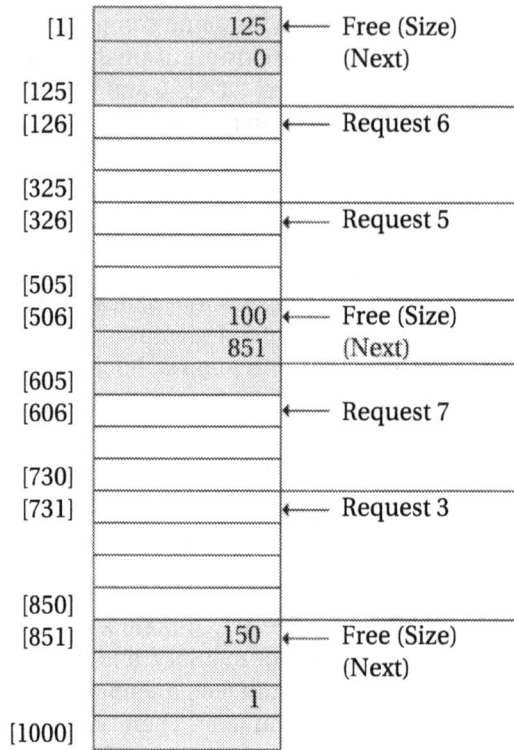

If the deallocation algorithm included coalescing, the request for 140 could be accommodated. This illustrates that it is desirable to keep contiguous locations together in a single block. The following discussion examines some ways of accomplishing this.

Coalescing

It is easy to determine if the space below the block being deallocated is free. The beginning address of a block plus its size gives the beginning address of the next block. This address can be calculated and the available space list can be scanned to see if a block with that beginning address is on the list.

Determining the address of the block above a given block may be done in at least two ways. The first way is to scan the entire available space list for the block whose beginning address is less than but closest to the beginning address of the block being deallocated. Once this block is determined, its size can be added to its beginning address to determine if the block being returned is immediately below it. The second way also moves along the available space list, adding the size of each block to its starting point to determine if this gives the address of the block being deallocated. Unfortunately, both of these approaches traverse the available list, an O(n) operation.

If the available space list is kept ordered by first position, the average search time can be cut in half. When a block is deallocated, the available space list is scanned for the insertion point. When the insertion point is found, the blocks before and after the block being deallocated can be examined to see if the blocks are contiguous, and if so, the blocks can be combined.

The simple deallocation scheme, which does not coalesce adjacent blocks, is very fast, O(1). If adjacent blocks are to be coalesced, keeping the available space list ordered to facilitate checking for empty neighbor blocks increases the order of complexity to O(n), where n is the number of blocks on the available space list. We now look at another technique for allocating and deallocating blocks of storage, which provides for easy coalescing of empty blocks but requires extra space in order to do so: the boundary tag method.

Boundary Tag System

The approach, known as the *boundary tag system*, is optimized for fast coalescing. In this scheme, the available space list is always kept within the blocks themselves.

Each block of storage has two positions at the beginning of each block and two positions at the end of each block that are dedicated to bookkeeping. These four positions are used by the Memory Manager to record the block size and whether the block is free or allocated. Furthermore, when a block is free, two additional locations are reserved in each block, so that the available space list can be implemented as a doubly linked list within the blocks themselves.

The list of available space is initialized to look as follows.

Avail: 1

[1]	1000	⟵ Block Size
[2]	Free	⟵ Free/Allocated Flag
[3]	0	⟵ Back link
[4]	0	⟵ Front link
[999]	Free	⟵ Free/Allocated Flag
[1000]	1000	⟵ Block Size

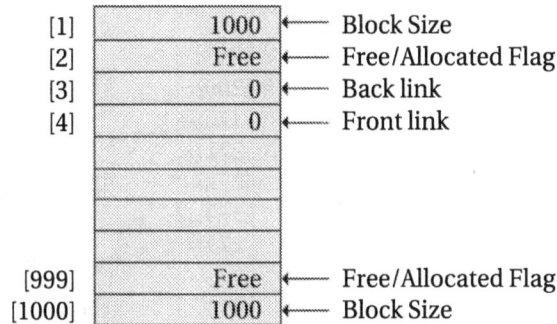

Now, suppose the Memory Manager receives the same sequence of requests that we considered at the beginning the previous example, namely:

Request 1:   80 locations

Request 2:   70 locations

Request 3:   120 locations

Request 4:   225 locations

Request 5:   180 locations

In the Boundary Tag system, we know that processing requires six additional storage locations for each free block of storage and four for each allocated block. For simplicity in the example, we assume that these needs have already been included within the sizes requested for each allocation. If this is not the case, then the Memory Manager has to add space to each request. Because the available

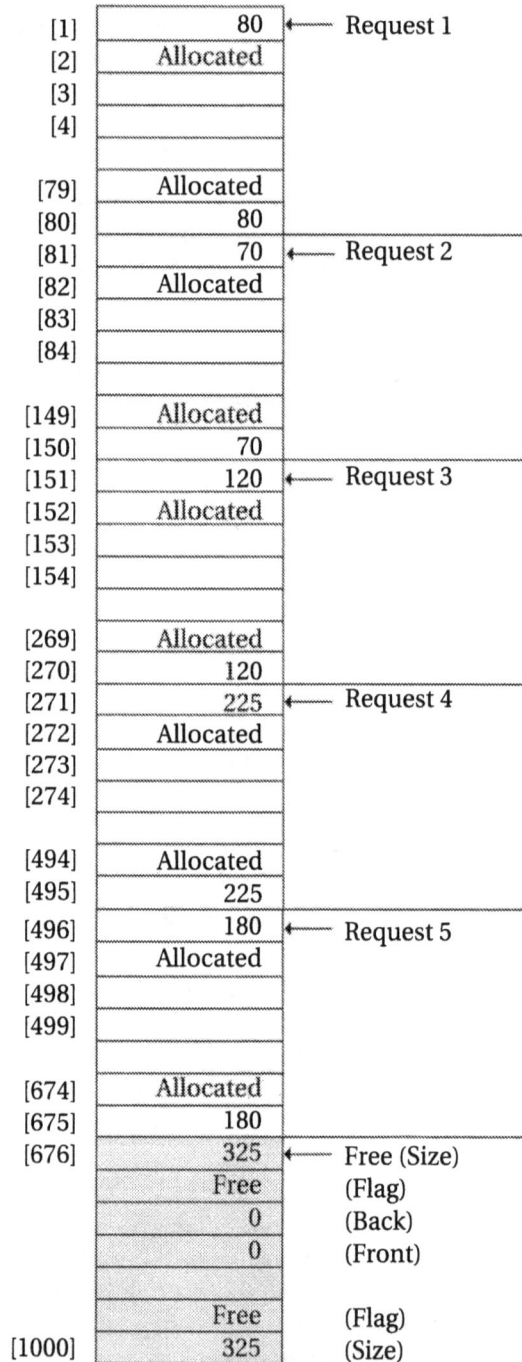

space list is doubly linked in this system, we can allocate from the beginning of a block without additional overhead to find the pointer to the block that is being split. We do so as a change. The resulting memory diagram would look as follows.

Avail: 676

[1]	80	←— Request 1
[2]	Allocated	
[3]		
[4]		
[79]	Allocated	
[80]	80	
[81]	70	←— Request 2
[82]	Allocated	
[83]		
[84]		
[149]	Allocated	
[150]	70	
[151]	120	←— Request 3
[152]	Allocated	
[153]		
[154]		
[269]	Allocated	
[270]	120	
[271]	225	←— Request 4
[272]	Allocated	
[273]		
[274]		
[494]	Allocated	
[495]	225	
[496]	180	←— Request 5
[497]	Allocated	
[498]		
[499]		
[674]	Allocated	
[675]	180	
[676]	325	←— Free (Size)
	Free	(Flag)
	0	(Back)
	0	(Front)
	Free	(Flag)
[1000]	325	(Size)

In this diagram, the first two locations and the last two locations within a job's block contain both the size of the block and a flag showing that the block is in use. The free block supplements this information with pointers to the previous and next items on the available list.

When the first request returns its space (locations 1 through 80), the Memory Manager can analyze the area directly before and after this freed space. In our example, there is no space before this newly freed area. Also, the Free/Allocated flag for the block after the one being returned (in location 82) shows that the following block is in use. Thus, no coalescing is possible, and the block is put on the available space list.

Avail: 1

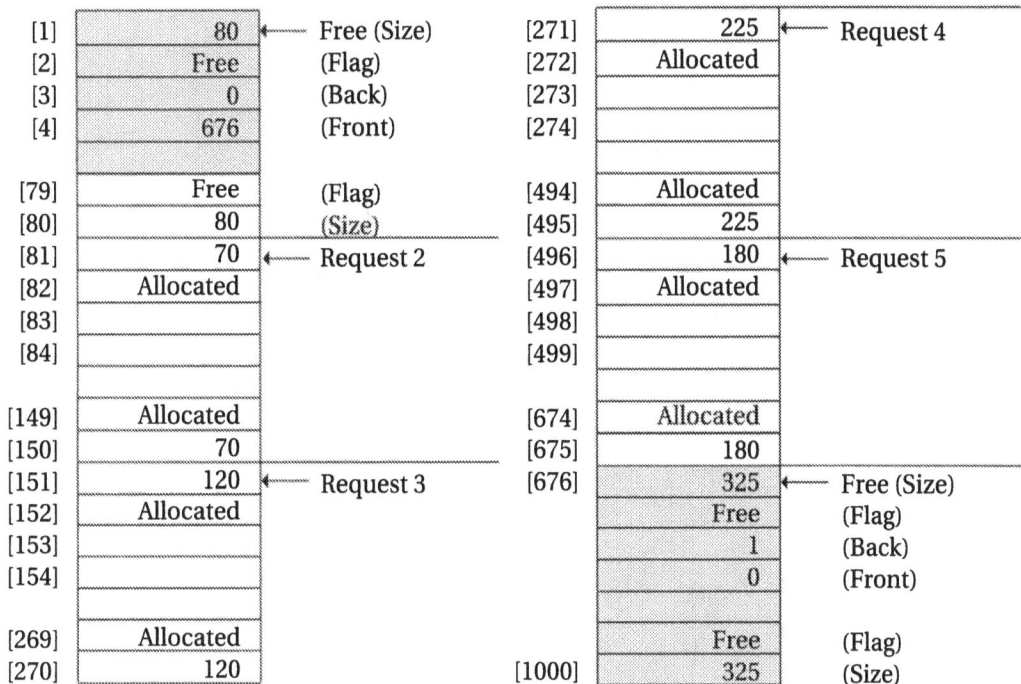

When Request 2 returns its locations, the Memory Manager can directly access the Free/Allocated flag for the block before and the block after the one being returned. The Free/Allocated flag for the block before the one being returned is in location 79 (the beginning of the block minus 2), and this shows that the previous block is free. The block being freed can then be coalesced with the free one above it. The resulting memory diagram is shown below.

Avail: 1

[1]	150	← Free (Size)		[271]	225	← Request 4
[2]	Free	(Flag)		[272]	Allocated	
[3]	0	(Back)		[273]		
[4]	676	(Front)		[274]		
[79]				[494]	Allocated	
[80]				[495]	225	
[81]				[496]	180	← Request 5
[82]				[497]	Allocated	
[83]				[498]		
[84]				[499]		
[149]	Free	(Flag)		[674]	Allocated	
[150]	150	(Size)		[675]	180	
[151]	120	← Request 3		[676]	325	← Free (Size)
[152]	Allocated				Free	(Flag)
[153]					1	(Back)
[154]					0	(Front)
[269]	Allocated				Free	(Flag)
[270]	120			[1000]	325	(Size)

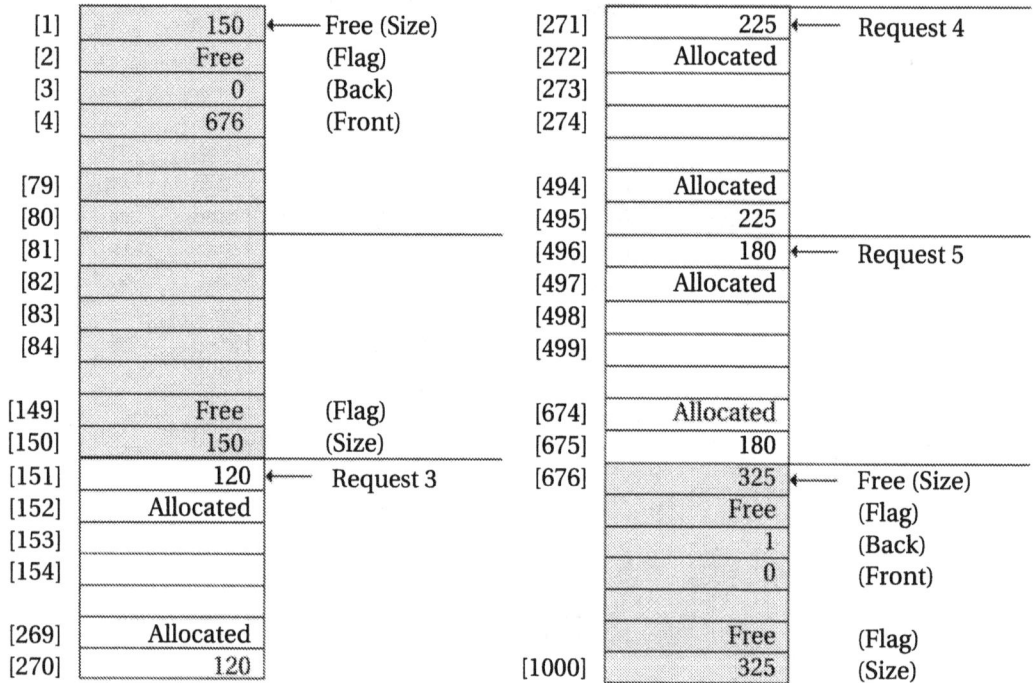

The available space list is kept as a doubly linked list to facilitate adjusting the list after coalescing takes place. When a block from the available space list is combined with a block below, only the length field of the block on the available space list must be adjusted. When a block from the available space list is combined with a block above, the previous block must also be adjusted—hence, the back link.

As another example, consider the following available space list. The list is depicted in linked form showing only the first four locations in each free block. (This list does not refer to the previous series of allocations and deallocations.)

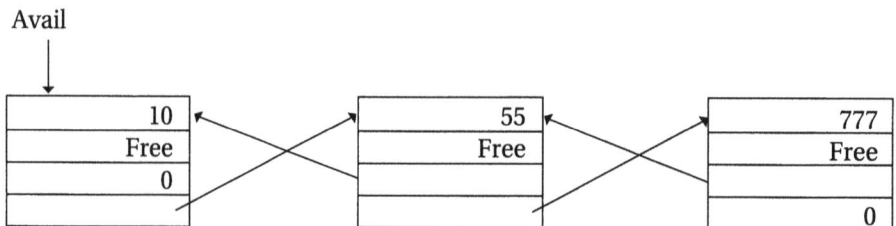

Avail

10	55	777
Free	Free	Free
0		
		0

Assume that a block of 15 locations is being returned that is contiguous to the second block on the available space. If the block being returned is below the block on the available space list, only the length field of the block already in the available space list needs to be changed. Of course, the size and Free/Allocated flag must be copied in the last two locations of the enlarged block.

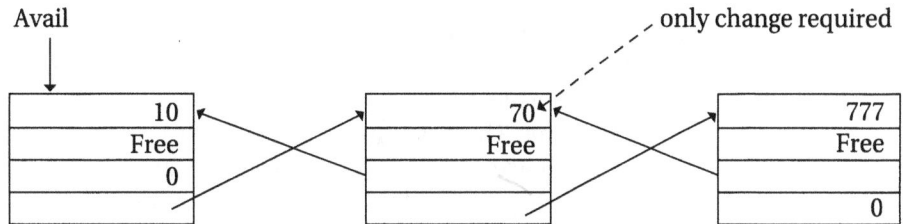

Avail

only change required

10	70	777
Free	Free	Free
0		
		0

However, if the block being returned is contiguous and above the block in the available space list, the block that points to the newly coalesced block must be changed. If the list is not linked in both directions, then the list has to be searched for the block pointing to the block that is being changed.

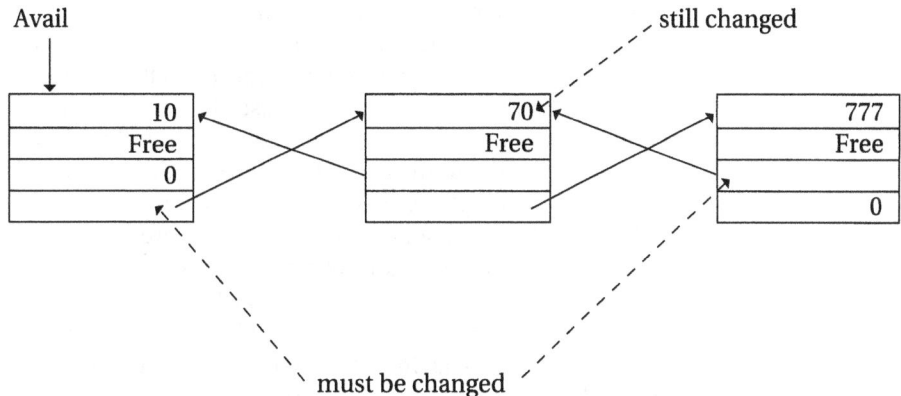

Avail

still changed

10	70	777
Free	Free	Free
0		
		0

must be changed

What have we gained with this more complex way of allocating and deallocating variable-sized blocks? Because the Free/Allocated flags in each block can be accessed directly to determine if a neighbor is free, the available space list does not have to be kept ordered. Therefore, deallocation has O(1) even though there is clearly more bookkeeping involved than a simple insert. The increase in time efficiency is gained at a loss of space efficiency. Four locations in each block are permanently reserved for bookkeeping information. If the blocks are quite large, this trade-off may be worth it. If the blocks being requested are small, it is probably not worth it.

Complexity The boundary tag system does not change the complexity of the allocation and deallocation algorithms. The strategy used to manipulate the available space list determines the order of allocation and deallocation. The advantage of the boundary tag system lies in O(1) coalescing.

Buddy Systems

In our earlier discussion of available space lists, we said that one way of avoiding searching through very small blocks is to allocate more space than is requested if the remaining block is too small to be of much use. This strategy creates **internal fragmentation**. There is unused storage, but it is not under the control of the Memory Manager because it has been allocated. In contrast, when the small blocks of storage are under the control of the Memory Manager the situation is called **external fragmentation**.

> **Internal Fragmentation** Fragmentation in which the unused storage is within an allocated block.
>
> **External Fragmentation** Fragmentation in which any unused blocks are in (free) storage and are under control of the Memory Manager.

There are allocation techniques that deliberately cause internal fragmentation in order to optimize coalescing. These techniques are known as *buddy systems*. In consecutive memory allocation (which we have been discussing), if a block of available space is split, the user is given the size requested and the remainder is put back on the available space list. In buddy systems, a block is split along predetermined lines. The two parts of the original block are called "buddies." A block can only be coalesced with its buddy.

The two most common buddy systems are binary buddies and Fibonacci buddies. In the binary buddy system, any block allocated must be a power of 2. The Fibonacci buddy system starts with a block whose size is a Fibonacci number and splits the block into the two preceding Fibonacci numbers.[4] Buddy systems are characterized by having an available space list for each possible block size. Because all blocks come in a predetermined set of sizes, the user is given the block size closest to (but larger than) the one requested.

Binary Buddy System

We have been allocating relatively small blocks. In the next example, for variety, we increase the size of the blocks, and we allocate blocks in 1K increments. Sup-

---

[4] The first two Fibonacci numbers are 0 and 1. Each successive Fibonacci number is the sum of the two preceding Fibonacci numbers.

pose the total memory available is 64K. Because the binary buddy system allocates blocks that are powers of two, we can have blocks of size 1K, 2K, 4K, 8K, 16K, 32K, and 64K, or 2^0K, 2^1K, 2^2K, 2^3K, 2^4K, 2^5K, and 2^6K. (Recall that 1K is 2^{10} locations.) We need seven available space lists, one for each possible block size. We use an array of available space lists, indexed by the exponent.

Available memory can be visualized as an array of 64 blocks of storage, each containing 2^{10} locations. Each block has a size field and a Free/Allocated flag. The available space lists are doubly linked, so a block on an available space list has a front and a back pointer. In fact, the blocks are very similar to those in the boundary tag scheme except that the information is not repeated at the end of the block. After initialization, the available space lists should look like the following where we refer to the first four locations in each block as the Size, Flag, Back, and Front fields, respectively.

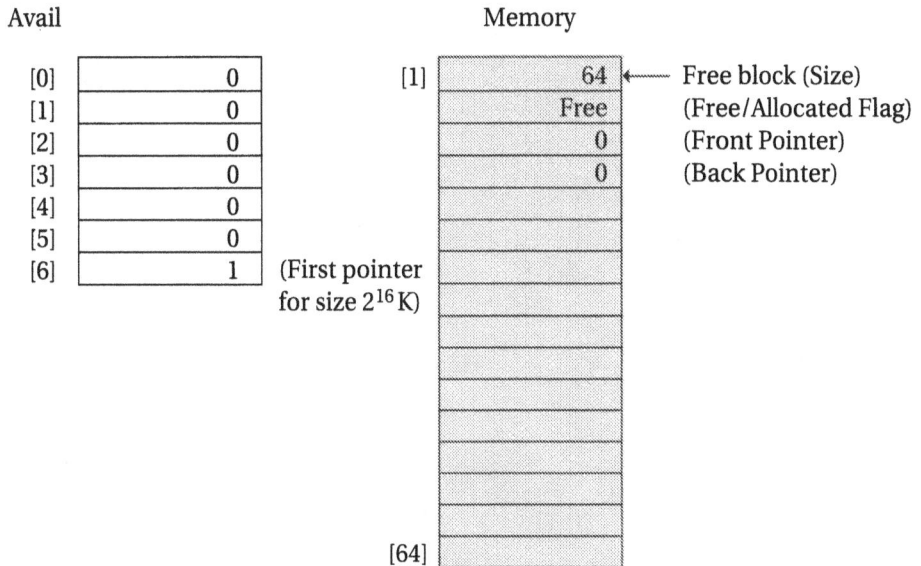

Avail   Memory

Index	Value	
[0]	0	
[1]	0	
[2]	0	
[3]	0	
[4]	0	
[5]	0	
[6]	1	(First pointer for size 2^{16} K)

Memory:

Index	Value	Label
[1]	64	← Free block (Size)
	Free	(Free/Allocated Flag)
	0	(Front Pointer)
	0	(Back Pointer)
[64]		

Note that block sizes are in terms of the number blocks of 2^{10}. The unit in this system is 1K. Before we look at the allocation and deallocation algorithms in detail, we look at what our data structures would look like after each of several requests.

As a change of pace, we use letters for requests. A requests 14, but because space is allocated in sizes that are powers of 2, A is given 16. As this is the first request, the initial block of storage is divided into two blocks of 32. These two blocks of 32 are binary buddies. The second block of 32 is put on Avail[5] and the first block is divided again into two blocks of 16. These two blocks of 16 are binary buddies. The second block of 16 is put on Avail[4], and the first block of 16 is given to the user.

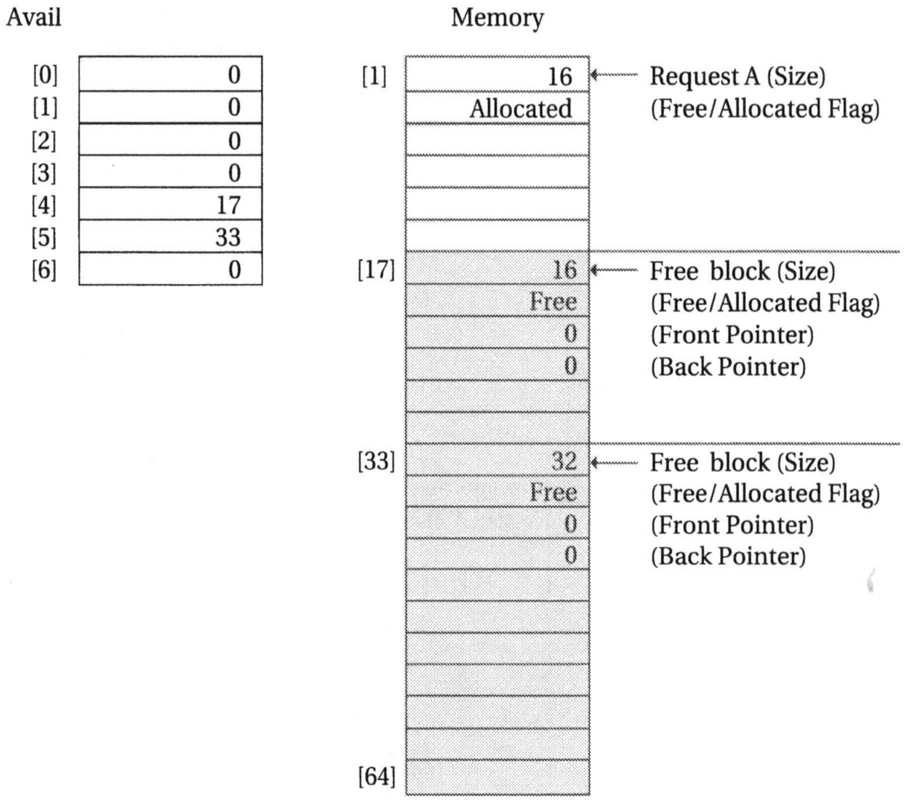

Avail

[0]	0
[1]	0
[2]	0
[3]	0
[4]	17
[5]	33
[6]	0

Memory

[1]	16	←——— Request A (Size)
	Allocated	(Free/Allocated Flag)
[17]	16	←——— Free block (Size)
	Free	(Free/Allocated Flag)
	0	(Front Pointer)
	0	(Back Pointer)
[33]	32	←——— Free block (Size)
	Free	(Free/Allocated Flag)
	0	(Front Pointer)
	0	(Back Pointer)
[64]		

B requests and is given 8, and the closest match is a block of size 16. This block is removed from Avail[4] and divided into two blocks of 8. The second one is put on Avail[3], and the first is returned to the user.

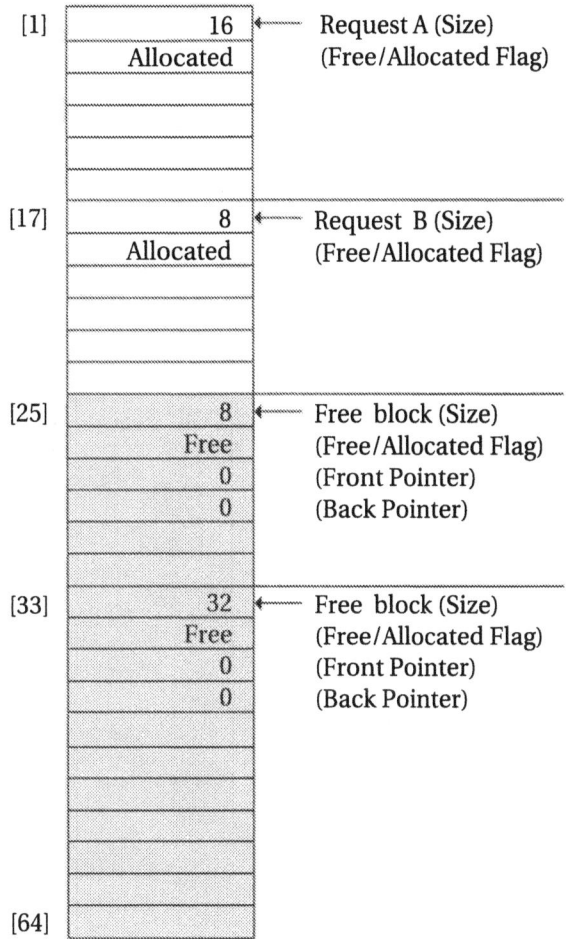

C requests 6 and is given 8. Avail[3] is not empty. A block is removed and allocated.

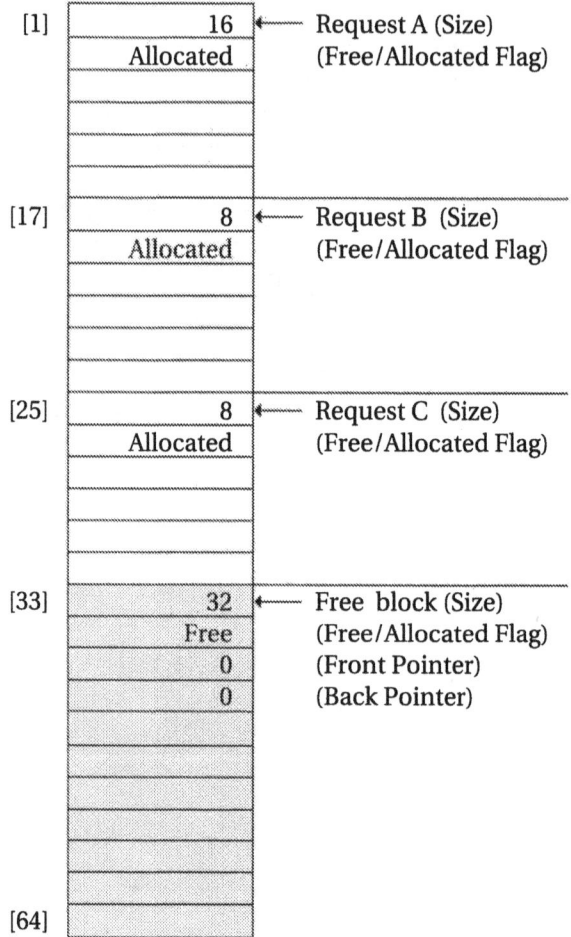

D requests and is given 16. Avail[4] is empty, but Avail[5] is not. A block is removed and divided into two parts. The second is put on Avail[4], and the first is allocated.

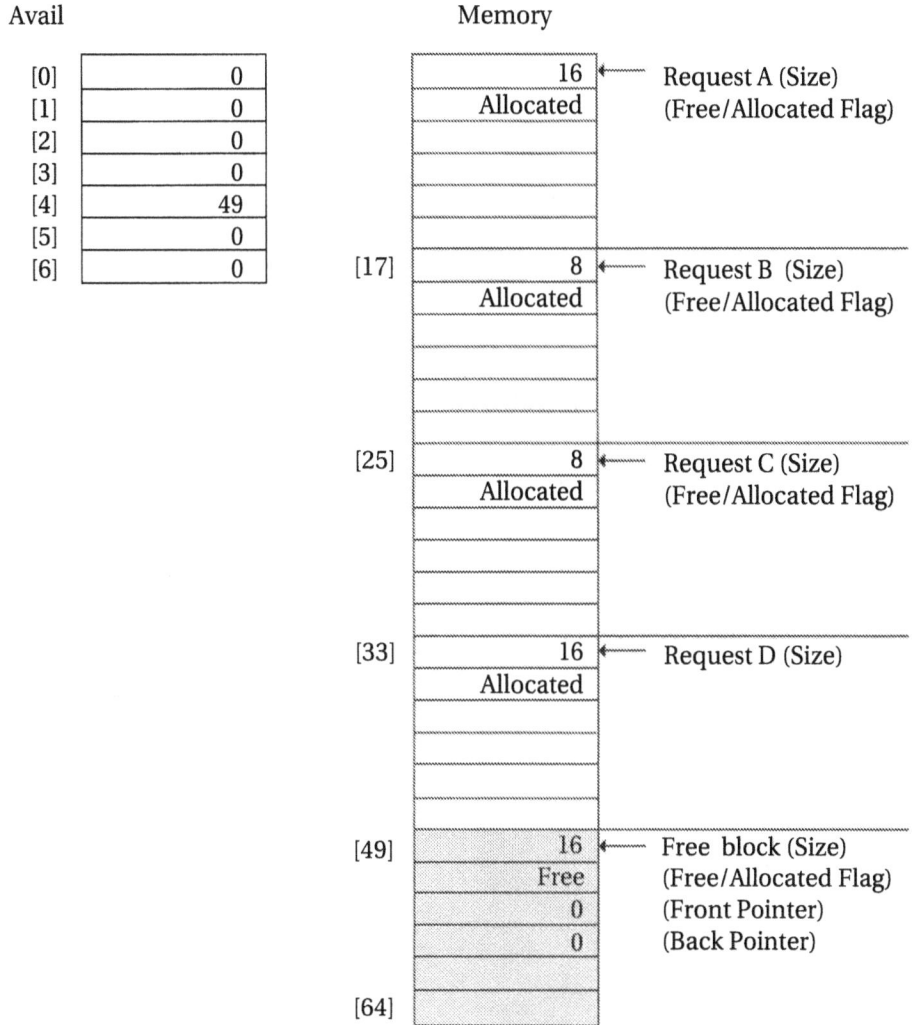

Avail

[0]	0
[1]	0
[2]	0
[3]	0
[4]	49
[5]	0
[6]	0

Memory

	16	Request A (Size)
	Allocated	(Free/Allocated Flag)
[17]	8	Request B (Size)
	Allocated	(Free/Allocated Flag)
[25]	8	Request C (Size)
	Allocated	(Free/Allocated Flag)
[33]	16	Request D (Size)
	Allocated	
[49]	16	Free block (Size)
	Free	(Free/Allocated Flag)
	0	(Front Pointer)
	0	(Back Pointer)
[64]		

E requests 5 and is given 8. Avail[3] is empty, but Avail[4] is not. A block is removed from Avail[4] and split. The first goes to the user; the second is put on Avail[3].

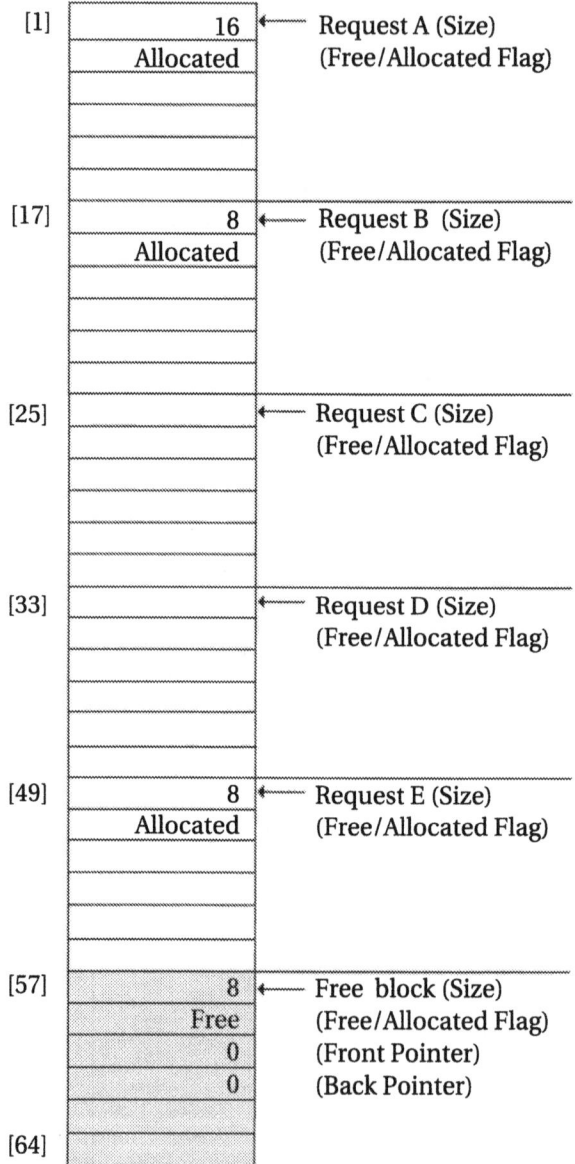

C returns its block of 8. A block can only coalesce with its buddy, that is, the block that it was combined with originally. The buddy of this block is not free, so no coalescing takes place. The block returned by C is inserted into Avail[3].

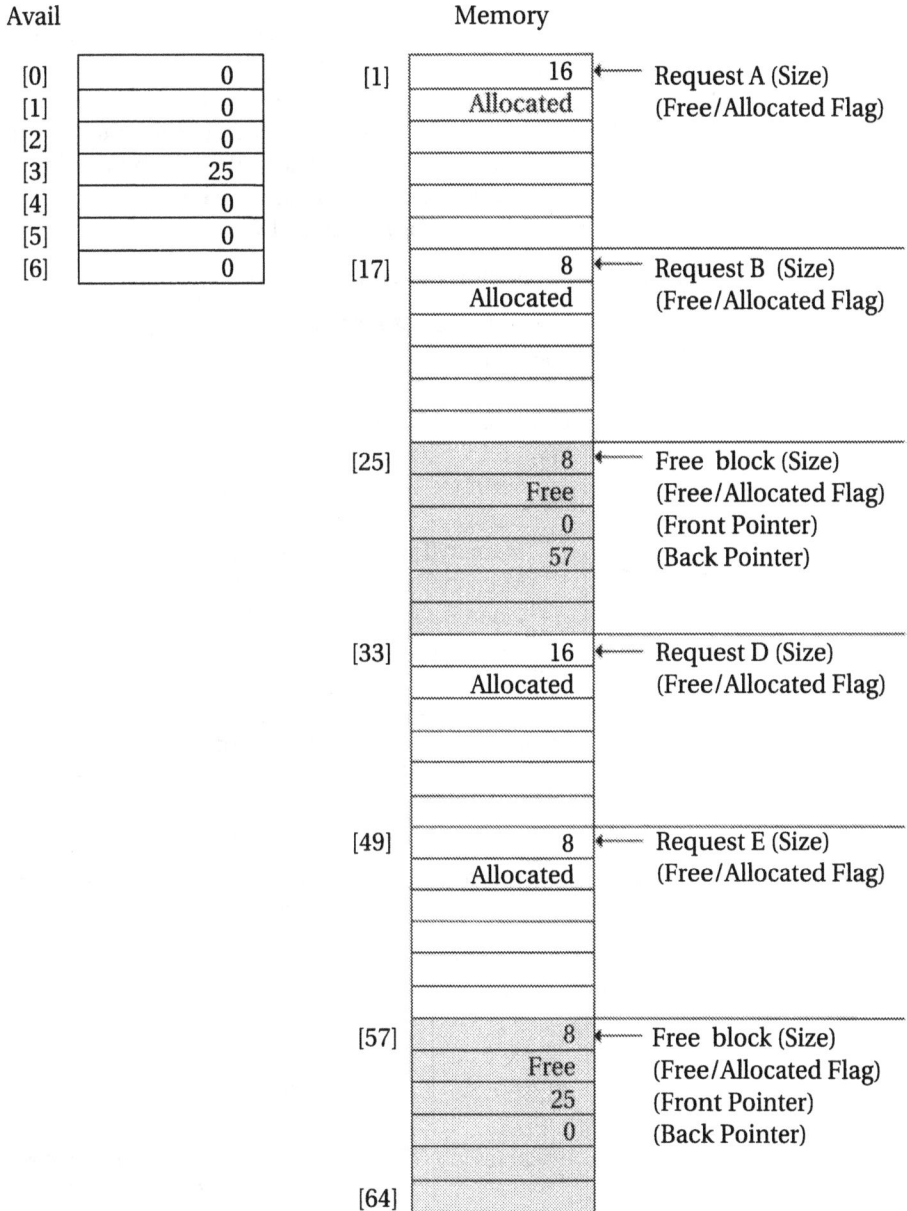

Avail

[0]	0
[1]	0
[2]	0
[3]	25
[4]	0
[5]	0
[6]	0

Memory

[1]	16	← Request A (Size)
	Allocated	(Free/Allocated Flag)
[17]	8	← Request B (Size)
	Allocated	(Free/Allocated Flag)
[25]	8	← Free block (Size)
	Free	(Free/Allocated Flag)
	0	(Front Pointer)
	57	(Back Pointer)
[33]	16	← Request D (Size)
	Allocated	(Free/Allocated Flag)
[49]	8	← Request E (Size)
	Allocated	(Free/Allocated Flag)
[57]	8	← Free block (Size)
	Free	(Free/Allocated Flag)
	25	(Front Pointer)
	0	(Back Pointer)
[64]		

Now that we understand how to apply the algorithm with paper and pencil, we write the algorithm for a computer implementation. When a request for storage is received, the correct sized block must be determined. We assume that

Size(Request) takes the actual size requested and returns a value i between 0 and 6, such that

$$2^{10+(i-1)} < \text{Request} \le 2^{10+i}$$

If Avail[i] is not empty, then this is the correct size and a block is allocated. If Avail[i] is empty, then the next larger size must be tried. If Avail[i + 1] is not empty, then a block is removed from this available list and split. One half goes on the available space list for blocks of that size (Avail[i]) and the other block is allocated to the user. If there are no blocks of size $2^{10+(i+1)}$, then we look for a block of $2^{10+(i+2)}$ and so forth. The algorithm for allocating a block follows. We assume that Size is in terms of our unit of memory, that is, 1K.

Allocate(VAR BlockPtr: BlockPtrType, Size : Integer)

```
Locate a block (i, Size, AvailableFlag)
IF AvailableFlag
    THEN
        Get a Block from Avail[i]
        WHILE i > Size
            NewSize ← Memory[Block].Size DIV 2
            Buddy ← NewSize + Block
            Memory[Buddy].Size ← NewSize
            Memory[Buddy].Flag ← Free
            Insert Buddy in Avail[i − 1]
            i ← i − 1
        END WHILE
        Memory[Block].Size ← Size
        Memory[Block].Flag ← Allocated
    ELSE (* whatever the Memory Manager does when there is no space *)
END IF
```

LocateBlock (VAR i : Integer, Size: Integer, VAR AvailableFlag: Boolean)

```
i ← Size
AvailableFlag ← False
REPEAT
    IF Avail[i] is empty
        THEN   i ← i + 1
        ELSE   AvailableFlag ← True
    END IF
UNTIL AvailableFlag OR i > LargestPowerOf2 (* 6 in our example *)
```

Next, we consider the deallocation of space. In our paper and pencil example, a block of 8 was returned. We saw that its buddy was not available, and we put it on the correct available space list. How can we directly access the buddy of a particular block? Each block is either an above buddy or a below buddy (or left buddy and right buddy if you prefer). If a block is an above buddy, then its buddy can be located by adding its beginning location to its size. If a buddy is a below buddy, then its buddy can be located by subtracting its size from its beginning location. The question, then, is how to tell whether a block is an above buddy or a below buddy.

To determine a pattern, we review our example. A block of size 64 is split into two blocks of 32. The above buddy begins at location 1 and the below buddy begins at location 33. The first block of 32 is split into two buddies of size 16, the first beginning at location 1 and the second beginning at location 17. The second block of 32 is split into two buddies of size 16, the first beginning at location 33 and the second beginning at location 49.

Notice that in each of these examples the location of the block divided by the size of the block is even for above buddies and odd for below buddies. This is not a coincidence. The determination of whether a block is an above buddy or a below buddy is a function of the beginning location of the block and the block's size. To summarize, divide the location of a block (index) by the size of the block. If the integer result is even, the block is an above (left) buddy. If the integer result is odd, the block is a below (right) buddy.

Deallocation(BlockPtr: BlockPtrType, Size : Integer)

```
REPEAT
    Coalesce ← False
    IF ODD((Block − 1) DIV Memory[Block].Size)
        THEN (* Buddy Is Above *)
                Buddy ← Block − Memory[Block].Size
                IF Memory[Buddy].Flag = Free AND
                    Memory[Block].Size = Memory[Buddy].Size
                    THEN
                        NewBlock ← Buddy
                        Coalesce ← True
                END IF
        ELSE (* Buddy Is Below *)
                Buddy ← Block + Memory[Block].Size
                IF Memory[Buddy].Flag = Free AND
                    Memory[Block].Size = Memory[Buddy].Size
                    THEN
                        NewBlock ← Block
                        Coalesce ← True
                END IF
        END IF
    IF Coalesce
        THEN
            Remove buddy from available space
            Block ← NewBlock
            Memory[Block].Size ← Memory[Block].Size * 2
        ELSE    Insert Block in Avail[Size(Memory[Block].Size)]
    END IF
UNTIL NOT Coalesce
```

RemoveFromAvail

Here is where the importance of having the available space lists doubly linked becomes apparent. We have the location of the block, but in order to remove it, the block *pointing to it* must be changed. If the blocks were not doubly linked, the entire list of available space would have to be traversed, looking for the block in order to remove it.

```
Memory[Memory[Buddy].Back].Front ← Memory[Buddy].Front
Memory[Memory[Buddy].Front].Back ← Memory[Buddy].Back
```

Complexity There are two size factors involved with the binary buddy algorithms: the number of available space lists (call it M) and the number of blocks (call it N). Allocate calls LocateBlock, which contains a loop bounded by the number of space lists (M). The loop in the body of Allocate is executed until a block of the appropriate size is found. In the worst case, 1K is requested and storage is all in one block, in which case the loop executes one less time than there are available space lists. All of the statements in the loop have O(1). Thus, Allocate has O(M).

Deallocate executes until no more coalescing is possible. The worst case here is when a block of 1K is returned. It coalesces with a block of 1K to become a block of 2K. The block coalesces with its buddy creating a block of 4K. This block, in turn, coalesces with its buddy, creating a block of 8K. Eventually, a block of 32K coalesces and storage is back in one block. How many times did this loop execute? M − 1 times. Therefore, Deallocation also has O(M). So, the order of allocating and deallocating in the binary buddy system is dependent only on the number of available space lists, not on how many blocks of storage there are.

Fibonacci Buddy System

As stated previously, the algorithms for Fibonacci buddies and binary buddies are very similar. Both allow only blocks of predetermined sizes, deliberately creating internal fragmentation to make coalescing easier. Both have an available space list for each of the predetermined block sizes. The advantage of the Fibonacci system is that it allows for a larger number of predefined block sizes within a given number of locations. The disadvantage of the Fibonacci system is twofold: first, to split or coalesce a block, the Fibonacci sequence must be known, and second, it is more complicated to determine whether you are an above buddy or a below buddy in the Fibonacci system.

There are two approaches to "knowing the Fibonacci sequence." The sequence can be stored or it can be calculated. Neither solution is difficult, but each requires additional overhead. Determining whether you are an above or a below buddy (alternatively, right or left) is more complex. This determination cannot be made from examining the beginning location and the size of the block. Information must be kept within the block itself. Therefore, each block must have a field in which to keep track of the number of times it is an above buddy. When this field is zero, the block is a below buddy. As in the binary buddy system, only blocks that have been split can be coalesced. We leave the detailed definition of the Fibonacci buddy algorithms as an exercise.

The characteristics of the buddy systems are summarized as follows.

1. Only blocks of predetermined sizes can be allocated, causing internal fragmentation.
2. There is an available space list for each block size.
3. Coalescing is only allowed with a split-buddy.

Garbage Collection

Garbage collection involves finding storage that is inaccessible from a program and making it available for allocation. In spite of this derogatory term, the unused storage is in no way "garbage." In fact, we go to great lengths to locate and retrieve it. A more descriptive term might be "inaccessible storage reclamation," or we might prefer to borrow the term "storage recycling" from environmentalists. Regardless of such preferences, however, tradition dictates that we use the terminology based on the wit of some computing pioneer from many years ago.

> **Garbage Collection** A technique that identifies inaccessible storage and makes it available for allocation.

In our discussion up to now, we have assumed that a block is free to be reallocated when it is returned to the Memory Manager (deallocated). There are cases when this is not true, however. Take, for example, the problem that can occur when there are several pointers pointing to a dynamically allocated variable NewBlock.

```
New(NewBlock)
Temp ← NewBlock
Dispose(Temp)
```

NewBlock still points to a block of storage, but that storage has been returned to the Memory Manager to reallocate. NewBlock is called a **dangling reference**. Dangling references are a problem for the run-time memory management functions of all programming languages that allow referenced variables.

> **Dangling Reference** A pointer to a block of storage that has been deallocated.

On the other side of the coin, there is the case where a block is rendered inaccessible by a series of statements and the Memory Manager is not aware of it.

```
New(NewBlock1)
New(NewBlock2)
NewBlock1 ← NewBlock2
```

The memory locations assigned to NewBlock1 are no longer accessible to the program. These locations have become **garbage**, but no harm is done unless the program runs out of memory. If it does, then a way of reclaiming this garbage must be employed.

> **Garbage** Allocated blocks of storage to which there is no access path from the program.

The problem of the dangling reference is more serious and there are two approaches to solve it. The first simply ignores all attempts to dispose storage. That is, the Memory Manager does nothing when a block of storage is disposed. This, of course, causes more garbage to accumulate. The second approach uses reference counts. Each time a pointer is set to reference a block of storage, a counter within the block is incremented. Each time a block of storage is disposed, the reference count is decremented. Only when the reference count for a block becomes zero is the block actually deallocated. This is very like the scheme described for lists in the last chapter, except that each node or block has a reference counter.

In some sense, any technique we use to keep track of storage not accessible by the program, whether allocated or unallocated, could be considered garbage collection. However, the term "garbage collection" normally refers to the case where the unused locations are unknown to the Memory Manager. When a request for a block of storage cannot be satisfied, the Memory Manager temporarily suspends the current program and invokes a routine to locate these inaccessible blocks and make them available.

Identifying Inaccessible Blocks

Identifying inaccessible blocks sounds like an impossible task. If a block is inaccessible, how can we identify it? We are identifying blocks *inaccessible to the program*. All blocks are accessible to the Memory Manager. We use an indirect technique to identify these blocks. We identify all blocks that are accessible by marking them, and by implication, blocks not marked are inaccessible.

All named variables within a program are directly accessible. All referenced variables are accessible if they can be reached from a named variable by following a chain of pointers. If a block cannot be accessed from any named variable in the program, then the program cannot access that block. Marking involves identifying each named variable in the program and any block that can be reached from it. Inaccessible storage is any block within memory that has not been marked. To implement marking, we must add a field, which we call Mark, to the overhead information of each block of storage. If Mark is False, the block has not been accessed. If Mark is True, the block can be accessed from the program.

The first step in marking is to make a pass through memory setting all the Mark fields to False. If all the blocks are the same size, this is easy to do. The algorithm is given below.

SetToFalse (* **fixed sized blocks** *)

```
Block.Address ← BeginningLocation
WHILE Block.Address <> EndingLocation DO
    Block.Mark ← False
    Block.Address ← Block.Address + FixedSize
END (* WHILE *)
```

If the blocks are of varying sizes and garbage collection is to be done, then each block must record its own size.

SetToFalse (* **Mixed-sized blocks** *)

```
Block.Address ← BeginningLocation
WHILE Block.Address <> EndingLocation DO
    Block.Mark ← False
    Block.Address ← Block.Address + Size(Block)
END (* WHILE *)
```

The second step in either case is to traverse all the lists in the program, setting the Mark field to True for each block that is accessed. After this traversal, we know which blocks are in use and which are free. Again, there are two cases dealing with the traversal algorithm. If the lists are all linear, they can be traversed with no additional overhead in terms of memory by simple recursion or the use of a stack. If the lists are not linear, the traversal algorithm is more complex. Each block must be marked, and if it contains pointer fields, the blocks to which the pointers point must be marked. The implication is that the Memory Manager must know where pointer variables reside within blocks. Alternatively, each pointer variable can be tagged in some way, and the Memory Manager can scan memory, looking for pointers.

To write a marking algorithm, the Memory Manager must know detailed information about the environment in which it is working. As an example, we present here the marking algorithm for the generalized lists described in Chapter 12. The unit is the generalized list node.

Marking

```
SetToFalse
Mark all named variables
For all lists MarkList (List)
Collect all unmarked blocks
```

MarkList(VAR: Node: NodeType)

```
IF Node <> NIL
    THEN
        IF NOT Node.Marked
            THEN
                Mark(Node)
                CASE Node↑.Component.Kind OF
                    AtomType,
                    Header     :    MarkList(Node↑.Next)
                    ListType   :    MarkList(Node↑.List)
                                    MarkList(Node↑.Next)
                END CASE
        END IF
END IF
```

There is a problem with this algorithm. Because we perform garbage collection when we are out of storage, we can question where the memory for recursion (or a stack) might be found. In fact, the Schorr-Waite algorithm makes use of the link fields in the lists themselves to hold the stack pointers and then restores the lists when the marking is finished. While it is a very clever, complex algorithm, we omit it here, as we believe it is beyond the scope of this text. Interested readers might consult some of the books in the bibliography.[5]

Making the Free Space Available

If we are dealing with fixed-sized blocks, all we have to do to make the blocks available is traverse memory putting all free blocks on Avail, the available space list. We can do the same with variable-sized blocks, but if we do, we still may not be able to service the request that triggered the garbage collection because of external fragmentation. When this happens, we must perform memory compaction.

Complexity

Notice that memory is being traversed in two ways: all blocks are marked sequentially from beginning to end, and all accessible blocks are visited, beginning with each named variable. If there are M blocks in memory and N of them are accessible, the complexity is a combination of M and N: O(M) to set all mark flags to False, O(N) to visit all accessible blocks, and O(M) to collect all unmarked blocks. Thus, the garbage collection algorithm is O(M + N). Because M is greater than N, we simply say O(M).

---

[5] For example, see A. Tenenbaum and M. Augenstein, *Data Structures Using Pascal*, 2nd edition, Prentice-Hall, 1986.

Memory Compaction

Memory compaction is performed by moving all accessible blocks to the beginning of memory. Memory compaction may be done in conjunction with garbage collection or in any situation where external fragmentation makes it impossible to fulfill a request for storage. This algorithm requires a list of all accessible blocks ordered by the block address. The first accessible block must be moved so that it begins at the first location in memory. The second accessible block must be moved so that it is adjacent to the first one. This process continues until all accessible blocks have been moved. This sounds simple enough, and it is if each block is self-contained, that is, if no block contains pointers to any other block.

Before we look at the compaction algorithm, be sure you understand the distinction between *coalescing blocks* of memory and *compacting memory*. Coalescing is the process of recognizing that two adjacent blocks of memory are free and combining them into one block. Compacting is the process of moving all blocks that are accessible to one end of memory, thus having memory divided into an allocated (and accessible) part and a free part. After compaction, there is only one block of free space, and it contains all of the available memory.

Both compacting and coalescing reduce the number of free blocks and increase the size of the free blocks. Compaction does this by reorganizing storage; coalescing does this by combining blocks on the available space list.

As a simple example of how compaction works, we consider the following diagram, which represents memory containing 60 blocks, 1–60. We assume that accessible blocks, which are highlighted in the following picture, are on a list ordered by block address for the Memory Manager to use.

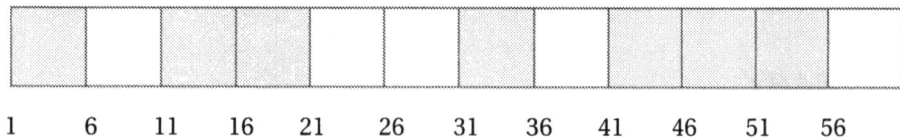

During memory compaction, blocks 1–5 remain where they are. Blocks 11–20 are moved to 6–15. Blocks 31–35 are moved to 16–20. Blocks 41–55 are moved to 21–35. Avail now points to free space containing 25 blocks beginning at block 36.

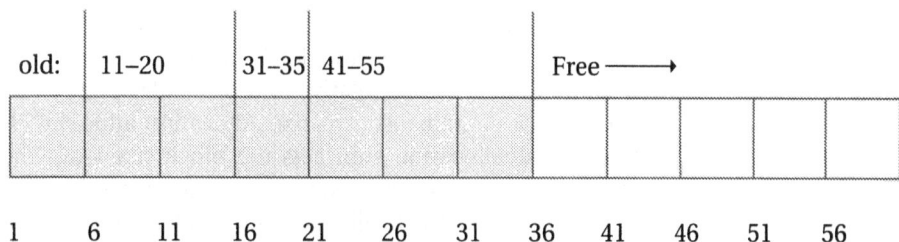

In the general case, a block may contain a pointer to another block of storage. We cannot just move accessible blocks, because the pointer would then point to the wrong block. In this case, we must make three passes through storage. The first pass determines where each block should be moved. The second pass goes through each accessible block and updates pointers to the new positions. The third pass actually moves (copies) the blocks. Using the previous example, here is what would happen at each of the three passes.

Pass 1:   The new addresses for each accessible block are determined.

Pass 2:   Anything pointing to a block between 10 and 19 would be adjusted by 5. Anything pointing to a block between 30 and 34 would be adjusted by 15. Anything pointing to a block between 40 and 54 would be adjusted by 20.

Pass 3:   Blocks 10 through 19 would be copied into blocks 5 through 14. Blocks 30 through 34 would be copied into blocks 15 through 19. Blocks 40 through 54 would be copied into blocks 20 through 34.

As in the case of marking, the Memory Manager must know where pointer variables exist in order to adjust them in the compaction algorithm.

Complexity

Memory compaction in the simple case requires one traversal of storage $O(M)$, and in the other case requires three traversals of $O(M)$. Because M is greater than or equal to N, the number of accessible blocks, the complexity reduces to $O(M)$. Does this mean that they are all equivalent? Of course not. It simply means that the size of memory is the dominant variable in each case.

SUMMARY

The role of the Memory Manager is to allocate and deallocate blocks of storage and take action if there is not enough storage to fill a request. The techniques used for each of these tasks vary depending on whether the blocks being manipulated are fixed-sized or variable-sized, whether allocations and deallocations come in a particular pattern (stack order), and whether the Memory Manager knows which blocks are inaccessible by the program.

Fixed-sized blocks can be allocated and deallocated by keeping the block pointers to free blocks on a simple linked list. Because the blocks are all the same size, one is as good as any other for each allocation. Therefore, both allocation and deallocation have $O(1)$.

Blocks that are allocated and deallocated in stack order are also easy to implement. Blocks are accessed relative to a particular place called the stack pointer, and each block contains its own size. Allocation adds the block size to the stack pointer, and deallocation subtracts the block size from the stack pointer. The complexity of allocation and deallocation is therefore $O(1)$.

Mixed-sized blocks are allocated and deallocated by keeping the information about each block (block pointer and size) on an available space list. The first fit strategy for manipulating the available space list allocates the first block encountered on the list that is large enough to fill the request. A block of the requested size is allocated, and the remainder of the original block remains on the available space list. The best fit strategy fills the request from the block that is closest to the size of the requested block. The next fit strategy implements the available space list as a circular list. The external pointer (Avail) is left pointing to the block immediately following the one from which the allocation is made. The worst fit strategy implements the available space list as a priority queue where block size is the priority (the largest block has the highest priority).

Regardless of which strategy is used for the available space list, fragmentation occurs. Fragmentation is the distribution of free (unallocated) blocks of storage throughout memory. Blocks that are physically adjacent may be on the available space as separate blocks. It is advantageous to have blocks be as large as possible, so contiguous blocks should be combined (coalesced). The boundary tag system, the binary buddy system, and the Fibonacci buddy system are three allocation and deallocation schemes that allow O(1P) coalescing when P is the number of available space lists.

If a request cannot be filled, the Memory Manager must try to find a block large enough by using several different techniques. If all allocated blocks are accessible, the Memory Manager can compact memory by moving all accessible blocks to one end of memory, leaving the rest of memory as one large block. If the Memory Manager does not know which blocks are accessible, garbage collection must be employed. Garbage collection is a technique that goes through memory and makes a list of all blocks inaccessible to the program. If the blocks are fixed-sized, no more needs to be done. If the blocks are mixed-sized, then memory compaction must be employed.

EXERCISES

1. Give two ways in which binary buddies and Fibonacci buddies are similar.

2. Give two ways in which binary buddies and Fibonacci buddies are different.

3. Distinguish between internal fragmentation and external fragmentation.

4. Fill in the following chart showing which kind of fragmentation each of the buddy systems can cause. Put an "X" if the buddy system can cause that kind of fragmentation.

	Internal	**External**
binary buddy	_____	_____
Fibonacci buddy	_____	_____
boundary tag buddy	_____	_____

5. Name the two factors that determine the complexity of the Memory Manager.

6. Why is it more complex to manage blocks of variable sizes than blocks of a single size?

7. Discuss the significance to the Memory Manager of allocations and deallocations being in stack order.

8. Define garbage collection.

9. Identify the two phases of garbage collection.

10. Define reference counts and discuss under what circumstances they should be used.

11. Define dangling reference.

12. Define recursive lists and discuss the implication for the Memory Manager.

13. a. List four strategies for sequential memory allocation.

   b. Discuss the relative merits of each of the four strategies.

14. The chapter shows how memory is configured using the first fit and best fit algorithms for the following sequence of events.

   Allocate: A 80
   Allocate: B 70
   Allocate: C 120
   Allocate: D 225
   Allocate: E 180
   Deallocate: A
   Deallocate: B
   Allocate: F 200
   Deallocate: D
   Allocate: G 125

   a. Show the configuration that would result from this sequence of requests using the next fit algorithm.

   b. Show the configuration that would result using the worst fit algorithm.

15. Assume a total of 64K memory allocations with a minimum of 1K allocated at one time, and consider the following sequence of events.

   Allocate: A 10
   Allocate: B 8
   Allocate: C 15
   Allocate: D 12
   Deallocate: A
   Allocate: E 11
   Deallocate: C
   Allocate: F 8
   Allocate: G 7
   Deallocate: D

   Suppose this sequence is performed by four common memory allocation algorithms: first-fit, next-fit, best-fit, and worst-fit. In each case, suppose the memory manager coalesces adjacent blocks of free memory, as prescribed by the various algorithms. Show the resulting allocation of memory and free space in each case, including complete information for each free list.

In Exercises 16 through 18, if a memory request cannot be met, assume the Memory Manager rejects the request and continues processing with the next request.

16. Using the binary buddy system, show what happens after the following allocations and deallocations. Use a total of 64K memory locations with a minimum of 1K. Show the available space lists after each operation.

   a. allocate 8K, 16K, 18K, 12K, 8K

   b. deallocate 16K, second 8K allocated, first 8K allocated

17. Using the Fibonacci buddy system, show what happens after the following allocations and deallocations. Use a total of 55K memory locations with a minimum of 1K. Show the available space lists after each operation.

   a. allocate 8K, 16K, 18K, 8K

   b. deallocate 16K, first 8K allocated

18. Using the boundary tag buddy system, show what happens after the following allocations and deallocations. Use a total of 64K memory locations with a minimum of 1K. Show the available space list after each operation.

   a. allocate 8K, 16K, 18K, 8K

   b. deallocate 16K, first 8K allocated

19. Give the algorithm for coalescing in the Fibonacci buddy system.

20. Give the algorithm for coalescing in the boundary tag system.

21. Given the following list of available space, show which block would be allocated for the given requests using the strategy indicated. The requests shown are sequential. <12,3> would be a block of 3 starting at position 12.

$$\text{Avail} \longrightarrow \text{<12,5>} \longrightarrow \text{<24,7>} \longrightarrow \text{<30,4>}$$

Requested	First Fit	Best Fit	Next Fit
Block of 4	<____,____>	<____,____>	<____,____>
Block of 1	<____,____>	<____,____>	<____,____>

Use the following allocations and deallocations for Exercises 22–25. The original block of memory contains 100 locations. The allocations are sequential. Do not coalesce adjacent fill blocks.

   Allocate 15
   Allocate 10
   Allocate 50
   Deallocate 10
   Deallocate 15
   Allocate 5

22. Draw the available space list assuming that the worst fit strategy is used.

23. Draw the available space list assuming that the next fit strategy is used.

24. Draw the available space list assuming that the best fit strategy is used.

25. Draw the available space list assuming that the first fit strategy is used.

26. Discuss the problems involved with coalescing after each deallocation (no multiple references allowed).

27. List several solutions to the problems discussed in Exercise 27.

28. Define memory compaction and discuss the circumstances under which it should be done.

29. Outline a scheme for memory compaction when there are no inter-block references.

30. Give the algorithm for memory compaction when there are inter-block references.

Suppose there are N items on the available space list. Give the order of the algorithms in Exercises 31–43. If there is more than one reasonable answer, discuss the alternatives.

31. Allocate where the next fit strategy is being used.

32. Allocate where the first fit strategy is being used.

33. Allocate where the best fit strategy is being used.

34. Allocate where the worst fit strategy is being used.

35. Deallocate to go with next fit strategy.

36. Deallocate to go with first fit strategy.

37. Deallocate to go with best fit strategy.

38. Deallocate to go with worst fit strategy.

39. Allocate where the binary buddy system is being used.

40. Allocate where the boundary tag system is being used.

41. Deallocate where the binary buddy system is being used.

42. Deallocate where the boundary tag buddy system is being used. (Available space is linked in only one direction.)

43. Deallocate where the boundary tag buddy system is being used. (Available space is doubly linked.)

44. In Chapter 12, Exercise 5(c), how many more cells would be freed after garbage collection?

45. In Chapter 12, Exercise 8(c), how many more cells would be freed after garbage collection?

46. Outline the algorithm for fixed-sized block allocation and deallocation where flags are used.

47. What is the complexity of the algorithms in Exercise 46?

48. Outline the algorithm for fixed-sized block allocation and deallocation where blocks are taken from memory sequentially until the last block is allocated and future requests are taken from Avail.

49. What is the complexity of the algorithms in Exercise 48?

Appendix A

Abstract Models

Stack ADT

To show another example of an abstract model specification, we define the abstract data type stack using another underlying model, a *set*. (The axiomatic specifications for the set abstract data type set are given in Chapter 4.) The ADT set may seem a strange model because the Set ADT is unstructured and the Stack ADT is semi-structured; Pop returns the item that has been in the stack the least amount of time. To introduce the structure necessary, we make the elements of the set ordered pairs, where the first member of the pair is the item to be put on the stack and the second member of the pair is the time that the element is entered on the stack.

Definitions: e, f, g, . . . are elements to be put on the stack S

$$S = \{<e,t_e>, <f, t_f>, <g, t_g>, \dots \}$$

where

t_e is the time of insertion of $<e, t_e>$ into S

Because successive Push operations are called at different times, it follows that whenever two distinct elements $<e, t_e>$, $<f, t_f>$ are on a stack S, their time stamps t_e and t_f are different. In particular, if we push the same data element on a stack twice, then the data values e and f may be the same but the time stamps t_e and t_f will be different.

Underlying Model: The Set
Operations

Create(VAR S : Stack)
Pre: True
Post: S = {}

Push(VAR S : Stack; i : Item)
Pre: $S' <> \perp$
Post: $S = S' \cup \{<i, t_i>\}$

Pop(VAR S : Stack)
Pre: $(S' <> \perp)$ AND $(S' <> \{\})$
Post: $S = S' - \{<i, t_i>\}$ where $<i, t_i> \in S$ satisfies the property
that $t_i \geq t_f$ for all $<f, t_f> \in S$

Top(S : Stack) : Item
Pre: (S' <> ⊥) AND (S' <> {})
Post: Top = i where <i, t$_i$> ∈ S satisfies the property
      that t$_i$ ≥ t$_f$ for all <f, t$_f$> ∈ S

IsEmpty(S : Stack) : Boolean
Pre: S' <> ⊥
Post: IsEmpty = (S = {})

The LIFO property is described by the postcondition of the Pop operation. It states that the time associated with the element i is greater than the time associated with any element left in the set. The time associated with an element is called the *time stamp* of the element.

Notice that the precondition for Create is not the same in the two examples. The precondition for Create in the example in Chapter 1 is that the input stack is undefined. The precondition for Create here is True, indicating that there are no assumptions about the input stack.

Each user of the Stack ADT written in accordance with the specification in the first example is responsible for determining if the stack already exists and not calling Create if it does. A user of the Stack ADT written in accordance with the second specification does not have to make such a test. There are no preconditions which he or she must guarantee. The implementor of the package written for the second specification must write the code for Create so that it works regardless of whether the stack already exists.

We made these preconditions different to make the point that a formal specification defines expected behavior. A formal specification is a contract between the user and the implementor of the data type. The writer of the formal specification—the contract—is responsible for determining what the behavior should be. The implementor is responsible for guaranteeing that behavior.

In the first example, the specification states that the input stack does not already exist—that it is undefined. In the second example, the specification states that no assumptions can be made as to whether the stack already exists.

Set ADT

The set is easy to specify using an abstract model because we can use the mathematical set as our underlying model. We use the following notation.

Underlying Model: The Set
Notation: S'   set on entry to the operation
            S   set on exit from the operation

Operations:
   Create(VAR S : SetType)
   Post: S = {}

Store(VAR S : SetType; Item : ItemType)
Pre: S' <> ⊥
Post: S = S' ∪ {Item}

IsEmpty(S : SetType) : Boolean
Pre: S' <> ⊥
Post: IsEmpty = (S' = {})

Card(S : SetType) : Integer
Pre: S' <> ⊥
Post: Card = |S'|

IsIn(S : SetType; Item : ItemType) : Boolean
Pre: S' <> ⊥
Post: IsIn = (Item ∈ S')

Delete(VAR S : SetType; Item : ItemType)
Pre: S' <>⊥
Post: S = S' − {Item}

Difference(S, T : SetType; VAR Result : SetType)
Pre: S', T' <> ⊥
Post: Result = S' − T'

Union(S, T : SetType; VAR Result : SetType)
Pre: S', T' <> ⊥
Post: Result = S' ∪ T'

Intersection(S, T : SetType; VAR Result : SetType)
Pre: S', T' <> ⊥
Post: Result = S'∩ T'

IsSubset(S, T: SetType) : Boolean
Pre: S', T' <> ⊥
Post: IsSubset = S' ⊆ T'

Members(S : SetType; VAR List : UnsortedList)
Pre: S' <> ⊥ AND IsEmpty(List')
Post: Item ∈ List if and only if Item ∈ S'

Keyed Table ADT

Underlying Model: The Set
Notation: KT'   keyed table on entry to the operation
       KT   keyed table on exit from the operation
   Value(Key)   Value in pair <Key, Value>

Operations:

Create(VAR KT: KeyedTable)
Post: KT <> ⊥

Store(VAR KT: KeyedTable; Key : KeyType; Value : ValueType)
Pre: KT' <> ⊥
Post: KT = KT' ∪ {<Key, Value>}

Delete(VAR KT: KeyedTable; Key : KeyType)
Pre: KT' <> ⊥
Post: KT = KT' − {<Key, Value(Key)>}

IsEmpty(KT : KeyedTable) : Boolean
Pre: KT' <> ⊥
Post: IsEmpty = (KT' = {})

IsIn(KT : KeyedTable; Key : KeyType) : Boolean
Pre: KT' <> ⊥
Post: IsIn = (<Key, Value(Key)> ∈ KT')

Find(KT : KeyedTable; Key: KeyType; VAR Value : ValueType)
Pre: <Key, Key(Value)> ∈ KT'
Post: Value = Value(Key)

FIFO Queue ADT

We use both the unsorted list and the set as underlying models to compare and contrast the specification of the FIFO queue with that of the stack.

Underlying Model: Unsorted List

Notation:	Q	a queue (a list)
	Q'	the queue Q prior to the last operation
	i	element of the queue (list)
	(i)	one-tem list
	()	empty list
	//	concatenation
	Head(Q)	first item in the list
	Tail(Q)	all but the first item
	⊥	undefined

If the queue Q is the formal parameter for the operation, Q' refers to the queue on input to an operation and Q refers to the queue on output from the operation.

Operations:

Create(VAR Q : Queue)
Post: Q = ()

Enq(VAR Q : Queue; i : ItemType)
Pre: Q' <> ⊥
Post: Q = Q'// (i)

Deq(VAR Q : Queue)
Pre: (Q' <> ⊥) AND NOT (Q' = ())
Post: Q = Tail(Q')

First(Q : Queue) : ItemType
Pre: (Q' <> ⊥) AND NOT (Q' = ())
Post: First = Head(Q)

IsEmpty(Q : Queue) : Boolean
Pre: Q' <> ⊥
Post: IsEmpty = (Q = ())

The specifications for the stack and the queue are identical (except for the names) in all cases except the Enq and Push. The post conditions for Push and Enq are

$$S = (i) \text{ // } S' \quad \text{and} \quad Q = Q' \text{ // } (i).$$

Push and Pop specify that an item is inserted on the left and the designated item is the left-most item. Enq and Deq specify that an item is inserted at the right and the designated item is the left-most item. Because the ADT Unsorted List is a linear data type, this visualization expresses the properties of LIFO and FIFO in a linear fashion.

Underlying Model: The Set

To specify the designated item, we make the elements of the set ordered pairs, in which the first member of the pair is the item to be put on the queue and the second member of the pair is the time that the element is entered on the queue.

Definitions: e, f, g, . . . are elements to be put on the stack

$$Q = \{<e, t_e>, <f, t_f>, <g, t_g>, \ldots\}$$

where t_e is the time of insertion of $<e, t_e>$ into Q

If elements e and f are two (not necessarily distinct) data values on the queue Q, then the time stamps t_e and t_f must be different. Thus, $<e, t_e>$ and $<f, t_f>$ must be different pairs.

Operations:
Create(VAR Q : Queue)
Pre: True
Post: Q = {}

Enq(VAR Q : Queue; i : ItemType)
Pre: Q'<> $\perp$
Post: Q = Q' $\cup$ {<i, t_i>}

Deq(VAR Q : Queue)
Pre: (Q' <> $\perp$) AND (Q' <> {})
Post: Q = Q' − {<i, t_i>} where <i, t_i>$\in$ Q satisfies the property
                 that $t_i \leq t_f$ for all <f, t_f> $\in$ Q

First(Q : Queue) : ItemType
Pre: (Q' <> $\perp$) AND (Q' <> {})
Post: First = i where <i, t_i>$\in$ Q satisfies the property
                that $t_i \leq t_f$ for all <f, t_f> $\in$ Q

IsEmpty(Q : Queue) : Boolean
Pre: Q' <> $\perp$
Post: IsEmpty = (Q = {})

This specification uses the concept of a time stamp to indicate the designated item: the designated item is the one with the earliest time stamp. Here, the Push and Enq operations are identical but the Pop and Deq are not. Pop returns the item with the latest time stamp.

ADT Priority Queue

The ADT Unsorted List cannot be used as the underlying model for specifying a priority queue. We must have a way of specifying that the designated item is the item with the highest priority. We can use the set as the underlying model provided that no duplicate <item, priority> pairs exist. Another alternative would be use the bag as the underlying model. Serve and Next are shown below. All of the other operations are specified exactly as the stack and queue with <i1, p1> replacing <i, t_i>.

Serve(VAR PQ : PQueue)
Pre: (PQ' <> $\perp$) AND (PQ' <> {})
Post: PQ = PQ' − {<i1, p1>} where <i1, p1> $\in$ PQ' satisfies the property
                 that p2 $\leq$ p1 for all <i2, p2> $\in$ PQ

Next(PQ : PQueue) : ItemType
Pre: (PQ' <> $\perp$) AND (PQ' <> {})
Post: Next = i1 where <i1, p1> $\in$ PQ' satisfies the property
                 that p2 < p1 for all <i2, p2> $\in$ PQ

Appendix B

Interactive Algebraic Specifications: Using the Mathematica Programming Language

Introduction

Learning to read and create abstract specifications is an important skill in computer science, although it takes practice to understand more complicated axioms. While learning to use this formal tool in Dr. Dale's class, I found that the *Mathematica* program (available at many universities on Macintosh, IBM PC, and UNIX machines) offers an interactive programming environment well suited as a "playroom" for these specifications.

The great part is that specifications can be entered into *Mathematica* almost exactly as they appear in this book! The syntax understood by *Mathematica* is very similar to that described in Chapter 1 and throughout the text, so you can enter and test some of the more complicated specifications, such as B-Trees and graphs, and you can test the semantics of your own ADTs.

Many people have problems with the heavily recursive nature of these specifications and are often unable to predict the results of axioms (other than by guessing from the name: "Delete", "Push", and so forth). By working with this environment, thinking recursively will become as easy as pie! This skill is important and can be fun as well.

I'll start with the simple stack example from Chapter 1, first entering the specification and then playing with it. A knowledge of the *Mathematica* programming language is not necessary, as I'll be using only a very small subset of its rich capabilities.

Input to *Mathematica* is shown as **sans-serif bold** font. When the *Mathematica* kernal returns a result, a regular sans-serif font is used. To "send" one or more lines of input to the kernal, type Shift-Enter.

A First Example

When we create an axiomatic specification, we are specifying an abstract data type (ADT). From Chapter 1, an ADT is a triple (D, F, A) where D is the set of data types involved, F is the set of operations, or formal syntax of function names, and A is the set of rules representing the semantics of our ADT. In *Mathematica*, these three sets are specified very logically. First, specify D, then F, then A. There is a different syntax for specifying each of these sets. Specifying the data types is very easy. Note that comments in *Mathematica* are like Pascal's (* .. *). Simply name the types, one per line:

```
(* Data Types *)
stack
st_item
boolean
```

Now let's specify set F by showing the formal function names. We don't need to specify arguments. Note that function names are enclosed in brackets, and that we specify constant values here too (True and False for the Boolean data type):

(* Set F *)
{True, False}
{create}
{push}
{pop}
{top}
{isempty}

Now for the fun part: Set A. Here we see some syntax differences, such as '[' and ']' instead of '(' and ')'. Also, note that variable names in the argument list of each axiom (such as s for stack, i for item, and so forth) are appended with an underscore. For now, just remember to add the underscore.

(* Axioms for stack *)

isempty [create] := True
isempty [push [s_, i_]] := False

top [create] := error
top [push [s_, i_]] := i

pop [create] := error
pop [push [s_, i_]] := s

After typing these in, Shift-Enter loads the specification into the *Mathematica* kernel, and we can begin interactive use. I'll call our stack FS and push, pop, top, and isempty all the way home! I'll be sure to illustrate all conditions. Note that we are using *Mathematica* as a functional language here, and we must assign the results of statements to FS. Otherwise, they just go to the console.

FS = create   **(* just made an empty stack *)**
create

isempty [FS]
true

pop [FS]   **(* should give an error, right? *)**
error

FS = push [FS, "A"]   **(* characters must be in quotes *)**
push [create, A]

FS = push [FS, "B"]
push [push [create, A], B]

Wow, now we're getting somewhere!

FS = push [FS, "C"]
push [push [push [create, A], B], C]

top [FS]
C

FS = pop [FS]
push [push [create, A], B]

top [FS]
B

Note that you can print FS at any time:

FS
push [push [create, A], B]

Let's remove one more item:

pop [FS]
push [create, A]

FS
push [push [create, A], B]

Hey! B is still on the stack, because I didn't assign the results of the pop to FS. Try again:

FS = pop [FS]
push [create, A]

FS
push [create, A]

Yes! Predictable = Good!

Recursive Axioms

Hopefully that was informative, but not very interesting. By entering a more complicated specification, such as the Set, we can see recursion in action and introduce the conditional control structure (good ol' "If").

Please note one important point. The stack ADT above, and the set ADT below, have at least one axiom name in common: IsEmpty. For simplicity, I will not change the name, but if you have entered several ADTs into *Mathematica* and are enjoying playing with them all at once, you will run into name conflicts. So, really it is best to give your ADT specification axioms unique names, such as Stack_IsEmpty or Set_IsEmpty, to prevent confusing you and *Mathematica*.

```
(* Data Types for Set ADT *)
set
boolean
itemtype

(* Function names *)
{True, False}
{create}
{store}                    (* base constructor *)
{add}                      (* checks for duplicates *)
{isempty}
{card}
{isin}
{delete}

(* Axioms! *)
create

isempty { create } := True
isempty [ store [ s_, i_ ] ] := False

(* here is our first look at recursion *)
card [ create ] := 0
card [ store [ s_, i1_ ] ] := 1 + card [ s ]

(* and here is our first look at Mathematica's *)
(* "If" statement. Note the "==" tests for equality *)
isin [ create, i1_ ] := False
isin [ store [ s_, i2_ ], i1_ ] :=
      If [ i1 == i2,
              True, (* then part *)
              isin [ s, i1 ] (* else part *)
        ]

delete [ create, i1_] := create delete [ store [ s_, i2_ ], i1_] :=
      If [ i1 == i2,
              s,
              store [ delete [ s, i1 ], i2 ]
        ]

add [ s_, i1_ ] :=
      If [ isin [ s, i1 ],
              s,
              store [ s, i1 ]
        ]
```

The observant reader should note that the "add" axiom is not in the text. *Mathematica* requires that the base constructor have no axioms at all, a concept with which the text agrees. However, it is necessary to ensure that no duplicate elements appear in the set, so the text includes a "mini-rule" for Store, which simply calls IsIn. Any "mini-rules" should be put into an axiom such as "add," if you want to use the specification in *Mathematica*.

Entering the romper room, we use strings as our data type. How about a candy machine with virtual morsels?

SnackBox = create   **(* gotta start somewhere *)**
create

SnackBox = add [SnackBox, "Sticky"]
store [create, Sticky]

SnackBox = add [SnackBox, "Chompo"]
store [store [create, Sticky], Chompo]

SnackBox = add [SnackBox, "Sneaky"]
store [store [store [create, Sticky], Chompo], Sneaky]

Let's try adding a duplicate, and see if we can sneak by!

SnackBox = add [SnackBox, "Chompo"]
store [store [store [create, Sticky], Chompo], Sneaky]

I guess not! Well, we should have three morsels.

card [SnackBox]
3

isempty [SnackBox]
False

isin [SnackBox, "Gummster"]
False

isin [SnackBox, "Sticky"]
True

SnackBox = delete [SnackBox, "Sticky"]
store [store [create, Chompo], Sneaky]

card [SnackBox]
2

Good, our Set ADT works. You've now seen all the *Mathematica* syntax you need to do this sort of thing. There is one built-in function that might come in handy. "Trace" gives you a printout of the steps *Mathematica* took to transform your expression from one form to another. Be warned that this command can produce a lot of output! But it helps to understand the recursion going on. Let's try it with Card on our SnackBox:

(* Syntax of Trace[ ] is Trace[expr], where expr is *)
(* any Mathematica expression *)

Trace [card [SnackBox]]

```
{ {SnackBox, store [ store [ create, "Chompo" ], "Sneaky" ]},
    card [ store [ store [ create, "Chompo" ], "Sneaky" ] ],
    1 + card [ store [ create, "Chompo" ] ],
    {card [ store [ create, "Chompo" ] ], 1 + card [ create ],
     {card [ create ], 0}, 1 + 0, 0 + 1, 1},
    1 + 1,
 2}
```

The output is not pretty, but it shows the mundane mechanical work going on under the recursion.

Let's add some traditional set operations. Union is easy:

```
(* Add the name set of function names *)
{union}
(* Axiom *)
union [ create, t_ ] := t
union [ store [ s_, i1_ ], t_ ] := add [ union [ s, t ], i1 ]
```

Notice again, I used "add" to keep duplicates out. Intersection is more complicated:

```
(* Add to set F *)
{intersection}
(* Axiom *)
intersection [ create, t_ ] := create
intersection [ store [ s_, i1_ ], t_ ] :=
    If [ isin [ t, i1 ],
            add [ intersection [ s, t ], i1 ],
            intersection [ s, t ]
    ]
```

We can test our axioms with another candy machine: SweetBin.

```
SnackBox
store [ store [create, Chompo ], Sneaky ]
SweetBin = create;
SweetBin = add [ SweetBin, "Chompo" ];
SweetBin = add [ SweetBin, "Gaggy" ];
SweetBin = add [ SweetBin, "Choco" ]
store [ store [ store [ create, Chompo ], Gaggy ], Choco ]
union [ create, SweetBin ]
store [ store [ store [ create, Chompo ], Gaggy ], Choco ]
union [ SnackBox, SweetBin ]
store [ store [ store [ store [ create, Chompo ], Gaggy ], Choco ], Sneaky ]
```

This might be a good place to mention another *Mathematica* function. Print[x] writes the value of x on a new line at the console. Print returns nothing, and the output is merely a side effect. Because our candy inventory is getting large, we should create an iterator that prints all the items in a set. However, this is merely a convenience function and not part of the ADT. Note that parentheses surround multiple statements and that semicolons separate them, as in Pascal.

```
(* No need to add the name to set F, since this is not *)
(* part of the ADT *)
printset [ create ] := Print [ "." ]
printset [ store [ t_, i1_ ] ] := ( Print [ i1 ]; printset [ t ] )
```

Okay, now we can go on. Let's do that last union again, but we'll pass the set returned by union to printset. This is a real joy of functional programming!

```
printset [ union [ SnackBox, SweetBin ] ]
Sneaky
Choco
Gaggy
Chompo

intersection [ create, SnackBox ]
create
intersection [ SnackBox, SweetBin ]
store [ create, "Chompo" ]
```

Only one item? Let's check the inventories of our machines:

```
printset [ SnackBox ]
Sneaky
Chompo

printset[SweetBin]
Choco
Gaggy
Chompo
```

Okay, intersection works properly.

Binary Search Tree

The binary search tree, as specified in Chapter 7, has a fairly complicated Delete operation, so let's enter these axioms. Notice the MaxEl axiom, which is a "utility" axiom for Delete.

```
(* Data Types for Binary Search Tree *)
bstree
bstreeitem
boolean
```

```
(* Function names *)
{True, False}
{create}
{make}
{lefttree}
{righttree}
{item}
{isempty}
{insert}
{delete}
{maxel}

(* Axioms for tree *)

(* These are easy *)
lefttree [ create ] := error
lefttree [ make [ bt1_, i1_, bt2_ ] ] := bt1
righttree [ create ] := error
righttree [ make [ bt1_, i1_, bt2_ ] ] := bt2
item [ create ] := error
item [ make [ bt1_, i1_, bt2_ ] ] := i1

isempty [ create ] := True
isempty [ make [ bt1_, i1_, bt2_ ] ] := False

insert [ create, i1_ ] := make [ create, i1, create ]
insert [ make [ bst1_, i2_, bst2_ ], i1_ ] :=
        If [ i1 < i2,
                make [ insert [ bst1, i1 ], i2, bst2 ],
                make [ bst1, i2, insert [ bst2, i1 ] ]
           ]

(* MaxEl is not really for users of the ADT, but for *)
(* the delete axiom *)
maxel [ create ] := error
maxel [ make [bst1_, i1_, bst2_ ] ] :=
        If [ isempty [ bst2 ],
                i1,
                maxel [ bst2 ]
           ]

(* delete is fairly complicated, but Chapter 7 walks *)
(* through it very carefully *)
```

```
delete [ create, i1_ ] := create
delete [ make [ bst1_, i2_, bst2_ ], i1_ ] :=
        If [ i1 == i2,
                If [ isempty [ bst1 ],
                        bst2,
                        If [ isempty [ bst2 ],
                                bst1,
                                make [ delete [ bst1, maxel [ bst1 ] ],
                                        maxel [ bst1 ], bst2 ]
                                ]
                        ],
                If [ il < i2,
                        make [ delete [ bst1, i1 ], i2, bst2 ],
                        make [ bst1, i2, delete [ bst2, i1 ] ]
                        ]
                ]
        ]
```

That delete makes my eyes water, but the case of two nonempty child nodes must be adressed. Let's create a tree of integers. In *Mathematica,* we could set the ==, <, and > operators for other data types as well.

```
b = create
create
b = insert [ b, 5 ]
make [ create, 5, create ]
b = insert [ b, 3 ];
b = insert [ b, 4 ];
b = insert [ b, 1 ];
b = insert [ b, 17 ];
b = insert [ b, 10 ]
make [ make [ make [ create, 1, create ], 3,

        make [ create, 4, create ] ], 5,

        make [ make [ create, 10, create ], 17, create ] ]
```

The data structure gets large quickly! (In terms of text generated, not "size," that is.) So it's time for a standard traversal function. I'm sure we could write this in our sleep! We use the *Mathematica* keyword "Null" in the base rule to specify that nothing happens.

```
inorder [ create ] := Null
inorder [ make [ bst1_, i1_, bst2_ ] ] :=

        (       inorder [ bst1 ];
                Print [ i1 ];
                inorder [ bst2 ] )
```

Note the parentheses for multiple statements.

inorder [b]
1
3
4
5
10
17

b = delete [b, 5]
make [make [make [create, 1, create], 3, create], 4,

   make [make [create, 10, create], 17, create]]

inorder [delete [b,3]]
1
4
10
17

Can stacks of sets of queues of trees be far behind?

Graphs: An Extended Example

I find graphs very exciting. Modeling relationships between cities, people, and so on, and then performing query operations on them . . . now that's computing! But graphs require a bit more work than other ADTs, because they need support structures. Let's enter the basic graph axioms, then talk about the supports needed for a depth-first traversal:

(* ADT Graph *)
graph
vertex
weight
boolean
(* F *)
True,False

store	**(* graph vertex vertex weight − > graph *)**
{addtog}	**(* graph vertex vertex weight − > graph *)** **(* use this axiom rather than store to *)** **(* add elements to the graph, as that it *)** **(* keeps duplicates out *)**
{ndaddtog}	**(* graph vertex vertex weight − > graph *)** **(* use ndaddtog to add elements to an** **undirected *)** **(* graph. Convenience routine *)**

{deledge}   (* graph vertex vertex − > graph *)
{delvertex}   (* graph vertex − > graph *)
{isempty}   (* graph − > boolean *)
{isthere}   (* graph vertex vertex − > boolean *)
{getweight}   (* graph vertex vertex − > weight *)

(* Axioms *)

isempty [create] := True
isempty [store [g_, v1_, v2_, w_]] := False

deledge [create, v1_, v2_,] := create
deledge [store [g_, v3_, v4_, w_], v1_, v2_] :=
       If [(v3 == v1) && (v4 == v2),
            g,
            store [deledge [g, v1, v2], v3, v4, w]
       ]

delvertex [create, v1_] := create
delvertex [store [g_, v3_, v4_, w_], v1_] :=
       If [(v3 == v1) || (v4 == v1),
            delvertex [g, v1],
            store [delvertex [g, v1], v3, v4, w]
       ]

isthere [create, v1_, v2_] := False
isthere [store [g_, v3_, v4_, w_], v1_, v2_] :=
       If [(v3 == v1) && (v4 == v2),
            True,
            isthere [g, v1, v2]
       ]

getweight [create, v1_, v2_] := error
getweight [store [g_, v3_, v4_, w_], v1_, v2_] :=
       If [(v3 == v1) && (v4 == v2),
            w,
            getweight [g, v1, v2]
       ]

addtog [g_, v1_, v2_, w_] :=
       If [isthere [g, v1, v2],
            g,
            store [g, v1, v2, w]
       ]

ndaddtog [g_, v1_, v2_, w_] :=
       If [(isthere [g, v1, v2]) || (isthere [g, v2, v1]),
            g,
            addtog [addtog [g, v2, v1, w], v1, v2, w]
       ]

Let's go ahead and create our example graph now. We'll use it in our queries later. Our graph will model some cities in Texas. Please excuse the small town of Gatesville, but I went to high school there! Our graph is undirected, so we add connections with ndaddtog to save typing. Weight represents the approximate number of hours to get from one city to another.

```
texas = create;
texas = ndaddtog [ texas, "Austin", "Gatesville", 2 ];
texas = ndaddtog [ texas, "Gatesville", "Dallas", 2.5 ];
texas = ndaddtog [ texas, "Gatesville", "El Paso", 9.5 ];
texas = ndaddtog [ texas, "Austin", "Dallas", 3 ];
texas = ndaddtog [ texas, "Austin", "San Antonio", 1.5 ];
texas = ndaddtog [ texas, "Dallas", "Houston", 4.5 ]
```

```
store [ store [ store [ store [ store [store [
    store [ store [ store [ store [ store [
    store [ create, "Gatesville", "Austin", 2 ],
    "Austin", "Gatesville", 2 ],
    "Dallas", "Gatesville", 2.5 ],
    "Gatesville", "Dallas", 2.5 ],
    "El Paso", "Gatesville", 9.5 ],
    "Gatesville", "El Paso", 9.5 ],
    "Dallas", "Austin", 3 ],
    "Austin", "Dallas", 3 ],
    "San Antonio", "Austin", 1.5 ],
    "Austin", "San Antonio", 1.5 ],
    "Houston", "Dallas", 4.5 ]
    "Dallas", "Houston", 4.5 ]
```

What a mess! But it's all there. Now, how about writing a depth-first search routine? We can start from any vertex in the graph and visit all other connected vertices, printing them to the screen. Let's ignore weight.

What do we need? We need the UnMark, Mark, and IsMarked routines from Chapter 10. We also need the FromEdges axiom that returns a Queue of edges connected to a vertex. We need a queue ADT, which is easy. I've printed this at the end of this appendix. Assuming our Queue has been entered, here is FromEdges:

```
{fromedges}                 (* graph vertex − > queue *)

fromedges [ create, v1_ ] := create
fromedges [ store [ g_, v3_, v4_, w_ ], v1_ ] :=
    If [ v1 == v3,
            enque [ fromedges [ g, v1 ], v4 ],
            fromedges [ g, v1 ]
    ]
```

A quick test of fromedges reveals:

fromedges [texas, "Austin"]
enque [enque [enque [create, Gatesville], Dallas],
    San Antonio]

As for the Marked routines, we can use our Set ADT from above. This makes things very simple:

(* Global MarkSet serves as the "array" of visited vertices *)

unmarkall [ ] := MarkSet = create
unmark [v_] := MarkSet = delete [MarkSet, v]
mark [v_] := MarkSet = add [MarkSet, v]
ismarked [v_] := isin [MarkSet, v]

Now for DepthFirst. As indicated in the text, there are several ways to do this. I'll write the recursive solution, although a nonrecursive solution using our Stack from the first example would work as well. I'll write this as two routines; depthfirst[graph,vertex] clears the MarkSet "array," prints the first vertex, and calls depthf2, which does the actual work. Study these carefully. Note the "While" loop. Also note the "Module" routine, which allows functions to have local variables.

```
depthfirst [ g_, v3_ ] := (unmarkall [ ]; Print [ v3 ]; depthf2 [ g, v3 ] )

depthf2 [ g_, v3_ ] := Module [ {q, tmp},
        (
        mark [ v3 ];
        q = fromedges [ g, v3 ];
        While [ ! emptyqueue [ q ],
                (
                tmp = first [ q ]; q = deque [ q ];
                If [ ! ismarked [ tmp ],
                        (Print [ tmp ];
                        depthf2 [ g, tmp ])
                        Null ];
                );]
        )]
```

Okay, let's try it:

depthfirst [texas, "Austin"]
Austin
Gatesville
Dallas
Houston
El Paso
San Antonio

depthfirst [texas, "El Paso"]
El Paso
Gatesville
Austin
Dallas
Houston
San Antonio

Yes! As an exercise, you should create the spanning tree algorithms and Dijkstra's algorithm. You'll need to enter the priority-queue axioms . . . but oh, the joy you'll have!

Conclusion

I've illustrated only a very small subset of the *Mathematica* programming language. With a little reading, you could learn to create three-dimensional graphical displays for your trees and graphs, or use many of the built-in functions to accomplish this goal. This kind of interactive environment for testing algorithms and specifications is very useful.

Mathematica supports "packages," which are much like units in Turbo Pascal. Using these units allows you to package your abstract specifications neatly. A package that contains all the ADTs entered is available by ftp from ftp.cs.utexas.edu in /pub/ndale/adts/abspecs.in

Michael Vincent Stanton
Student—UT Austin
email: mvs@cs.utexas.edu

Internal Appendix: Queue ADT

```
(* Data types for Queue ADT *)
queue
boolean
queueitem

(* Function names *)
{True, False}
{create}
{enque}        (* queue queueitem − > queue *)
{deque}        (* queue − > queue *)
{first}        (* queue − > queueitem *)
{emptyqueue}   (* queue − > boolean *)

(* Axioms *)
deque [ create ] := error
deque [ enque [ q_, i_ ] ] :=
     If [ emptyqueue [ q ],
              q,
              enque [ deque [ q ], i ]
         ]

first [ create ] := error
first [ enque [ q_, i_ ] ] :=
     If [ emptyqueue [ q ]
              i,
              first [ q ]
         ]

emptyqueue [ create ] := True
emptyqueue [ enque [ q_, i_ ] ] := False
```

Partial Bibliography

Aho, Alfred V., John E. Hopcroft, and Jeffery D. Ullman. *The Design and Analysis of Computer Algorithms*. Addison-Wesley, 1974.

———. *Data Structures and Algorithms*. Addison-Wesley, 1983.

Allen, John. *Anatomy of Lisp*. McGraw-Hill, 1978.

Baase, Sara. *Computer Algorithms: Introduction to Design and Analysis*, 2d ed. Addison-Wesley, 1988.

Bogart, Kenneth P. *Introductory Combinatorics*. Pitman, Boston, 1983.

Booch, Grady. *Software Components with Ada*. Benjamin/Cummings, 1986.

Bradley, James. *Introduction to Discrete Mathematics*. Addison-Wesley, 1988.

Brumfield, Jeff. *ACM SIGCSE Bulletin* 17, no. 1 (March 1985).

Carriero, N., and D. Gelernter. "How to Write Parallel Programs: A Guide to the Perplexed." *ACM Computing Surveys* 21, no. 3 (Sept. 1989).

———. *How to Write Parallel Programs: A First Course*. M.I.T. Press, 1990.

Cichelli, J. "Minimal Perfect Hash Functions Made Simple." *Communications of the ACM* 23, no. 1 (January 1980).

Comer, D. "The Ubiquitous B-Tree." *Computing Surveys* 11 (1979): 121–137.

Cook, S. A. "The Complexity of Theorem-Proving Procedures," *Proceedings of the Third Annual ACM Symposium of the Theory of Computing*, 151–158. New York: Association for Computing Machinery, 1971.

Cormen, Thomas H., Charles E. Leiserson, and Ronald L. Rivest. *Introduction to Algorithms*. M.I.T. Press, Cambridge, MA/McGraw-Hill, New York, 1990.

Dale, Nell, and Susan Lilly. *Pascal Plus Data Structures, Algorithms, and Advanced Programming*. Fourth ed. D. C. Heath, 1995.

Dale, Nell, and Henry M. Walker. "A Classification of Data Types." *Journal of Computer Science Education* 3, no. 3 (1992): 223–232.

Dale, Nell, and Chip Weems. *Introduction to Turbo Pascal and Software Design*. D. C. Heath, 1995.

Garvey, Michael R., and David S. Johnson. *Computers and Intractability: A Guide to the Theory of NP-Completeness*. W. H. Freeman and Company, San Francisco, 1979.

Gersting, Judith L. *Mathematical structures for computer science*. W. H. Freeman, New York, 1987.

Horowitz, Ellis, and Sartaj Sahni. *Data Structures in Pascal*, Computer Science Press, 1990.

Ja'Ja', Joseph. *An Introduction to Parallel Algorithms*. Addison-Wesley, 1992.

Knuth, Donald E. *The Art of Computer Programming*. Vol. 1, *Fundamental Algorithms*. Addison-Wesley, 1968.

———. *The Art of Computer Programming*. Vol. 3, *Sorting and Searching*. Addison-Wesley, 1973.

Knuth, Donald E., J. Morris, Jr., and V. R. Pratt. "Fast Pattern Matching in Strings." *SIAM Journal on Computing* 6, no. 2: 323–350.

Larson, P. "Dynamic Hash Tables." *Communications of the ACM*. 31, no. 4 (April 1988).

Lewis, H. R., L. Denenberg. *Data Structures and Their Algorithms*. HarperCollins, 1991.

Liao, A. M., "Self-Adjusting Data Structures." *Dr. Dobb's Journal*. February 1990.

Liskov, Barbara, and Jon Guttag. *Abstraction and Specification in Program Development*. The MIT Press, 1986.

Maeder, R. E. *Programming in Mathematica*, 2d ed. Redwood City, CA: Addison-Wesley, 1991.

Martin, James J. *Data Types and Data Structures*. Prentice-Hall International Series in Computer Science, 1986.

Meyer, A. R., and L. J. Stockmeyer. "The Equivalence Problem for Regular Expressions with Squaring Requires Exponential Time." *Proceedings of the 13th Annual Symposium on Switching and Automata Theory*, 125–129. Long Beach, CA: IEEE Computer Society, 1972.

Naps, Thomas L. *Introduction to Data Structures and Algorithm Analysis*. West Publishing Company, 1992.

Pratt, Terrence. *Programming Languages: Design and Implementation*. Prentice-Hall, 1984.

Quinn, Michael J. *Parallel Computing Theory and Practice*, 2d ed. McGraw-Hill, Inc., 1994.

Rosen, Kenneth H. *Discrete Mathematics and its Applications*. Random House, New York, 1988.

Smith, Harry E. *Data Structures: Form and Function.* Harcourt, Brace, Jovanovich, 1987.

Steele, Guy L., Jr. *Common LISP, the Language.* Digital Press, Burlington, MA, 1984.

Strassen, Volker. "Gaussian Elimination is Not Optimal." *Numerische Mathematik* 13 (1969): 354–356.

Subramaniam, Vikram, Ivan Sykes, and Henry M. Walker. "An Expert System to Place Incoming Students in Mathematics and Computer Science Classes," *Journal of Computer Science Education* 5, no. 2 (1994): 137–148.

Svatos, R. *A Study of Global Rebalancing Algorithms for Threaded Binary Search Trees.* M.S. Thesis, Tulane University, 1988.

Tenenbaum, Arron M., and Moshe J. Augenstein. *Data Structures Using Pascal.* Prentice-Hall, 1986.

Walker, Henry M. *Computer Science 2: Principles of Software Engineering, Data Types, and Algorithms.* Scott, Foresman and Company, 1989.

———. *The Limits of Computing.* Jones and Bartlett, 1994.

Weiss, Mark Allen. *Data Structures and Algorithm Analysis in Ada.* Benjamin/Cummings, 1993.

Weissman, G. "Comparing Disk-Allocation Methods." *Byte 1987 Extra Edition: Inside IBM PCs*, 1987.

Winograd, Shmuel. "On the Number of Multiplications Necessary to Compute Certain Functions." *Journal of Pure and Applied Math* 23 (1970): 165–179.

Wolfram, S. *Mathematica: A System for Doing Mathematics by Computer,* 2d ed. Redwood City, CA: Addison-Wesley, 1991.

Wood, Derick. *Data Structures, Algorithms, and Performance.* Addison-Wesley, 1993.

Wulf, William A., Mary Shaw, Paul N. Hilfinger, and Lawrence Flon. *Fundamental Structures of Computer Science.* Addison-Wesley, 1981.

Glossary

abstraction   Remembering the what, ignoring the how

abstract model   A formal mechanism for specifying an abstract data type where the operations on the domain *d* are described in terms of operations on another data type

accessible type   A data type that can be accessed by the user program

activation record   A record that contains all the information necessary for a subprogram to execute; stored on the run-time stack by the run-time support system

acyclic graph   A graph that contains no cycles

adjacency list   A collection of lists of vertices associated with a graph in which each list contains those vertices (with weights, if applicable) that are adjacent from a specified vertex

adjacency matrix   A square, two-dimensional array with one row and one column for each vertex in a directed graph, in which an entry in row i and column j is 1 if there is an edge from the vertex corresponding to row i to the vertex corresponding to column j and which is 0 otherwise. In an undirected graph, a 1 is placed in both row i, column j and row j, column i if there is an edge between the vertices corresponding to rows i and j, and both entries are 0 otherwise

adjacent from   If <vertex1, vertex2> is an edge of a graph, then vertex2 is adjacent from vertex1

adjacent to   If <vertex1, vertex2> is an edge of a graph, then vertex1 is adjacent to vertex2

ADTs (abstract data types)   Classes of objects whose logical behavior is defined by a set of values and a set of operations

agenda parallelism   An algorithmic approach to parallelism that organizes work into a logical network or graph of tasks

alist   *See* association lists

allocate storage   Make a block of storage available to a user program

ancestor   A node that comes before another node in a path

array   An ADT of a designated size in which storage and retrieval is based upon one or more indices

association list   A LISP list that stores pairs of information for easy retrieval

atom   An indivisible piece of data within the context of a particular problem

augmented adjacency matrix   A square, two-dimensional array formed from the adjacency matrix associated with a graph by placing the value 1 in each diagonal entry in the array

avail   External pointer to the available space list

available space list   List of free space in main memory

average case analysis   Analysis that considers some average amount of work

AVL trees   Binary search trees in which every node is height balanced

axiomatic (algebraic) specifications   A formal mechanism for *completely* specifying an abstract data type; the operations are defined in terms of themselves

balanced merge   The merge phase of an external sort (K files) in which K/2 files are used for input and K/2 files are used for output on each merge pass

balanced trees   Binary search trees that grow naturally until they get out of balance and must be rebalanced

base address plus offset   A technique for storing and accessing items in arrays and records in which the base address is where the first item is stored. Each item accessed by taking this base address, subtracting 1, and adding the value of the index

best case analysis   Time analysis that assumes the data required the least amount of work from the code

best fit strategy   A strategy for handling the available space list that allocates memory from the block that is closest to (but greater than or equal to) the size requested

Big-O notation   A notation for expressing time complexity using a formal approximation

binary buddy system   A buddy system in which allowable block sizes are powers of two

binary search tree   A binary tree with the following search property: the values in a node's left subtree are less than the value in the node, and the values in a node's right subtree are greater than or equal to the value in the node

binary tree   A tree in which the maximum degree of any node is two

bit vector   An implementation (of sets) that maps each item in the component type to a Boolean flag

blocks   Collections of contiguous memory locations

boundary tag system A memory management scheme for handling variable-size blocks that allows O(1) coalescing

bounded data type A data type in which the number of items that can be stored in an instance of the data type is limited

bounded order or complexity Time complexity is bounded by a constant; O(1) in Big-O notation

breadth-first spanning tree The spanning tree made up of the edges in a breadth-first traversal

breadth-first traversal A traversal in which all of the siblings of a node are visited before the children of a node

B-tree An M-way search tree in which all leaves are on the same level, insertions are made in the leaf nodes, all nodes have at most M children, all nodes (except the root) have at least [M/2] nonempty children, and the number of keys is one less than the number of children

B+-tree An index tree with B-tree properties

bucket Stores a fixed number of items (usually one) in a hash table

buddy systems Memory allocation techniques that deliberately cause internal fragmentation to optimize coalescing

child node A node in a tree is the child of node B if the subtree with root B is made up of node B together with subtrees T_1, T_n, and if A is the root of one of the subtrees T_i (for some i)

class NP Problems that can be solved in polynomial time with as many processors as desired

class P Problems that can be solved with one processor in polynomial time

closed hash table Buckets contain the items themselves; resolve overflow by looking (probing) for a free spot; also called closed hashing

coalescing Combining two contiguous memory blocks into one block

collision Two keys hash into the same bucket (index position)

complete binary tree A binary tree that is either full or full through the maximum level minus one, and the nodes on the last level are as far to the left as possible

complete graph A graph that contains the maximum number of edges

connected component A maximal collection C of vertices and incident edges, so that there exist paths from every vertex in C to all other vertices in C

connected graph An undirected graph where a path exists between each pair of vertices

critical section A collection of variables or code segments, that only one processor is allowed to access or execute at a time

cubic complexity Time complexity is bounded by the size measure cubed; $O(n^3)$ in Big-O notation

cycle A path of at least two distinct edges starting and ending at the same vertex

dangling reference A pointer to a block of storage that has been deallocated

data abstraction Separation of the logical properties of data from the implementation details

data-parallel programming Several processors execute the same instructions in lock-step on different data sets

data structures The implementation of an ADT

deallocate storage Take storage from a user and make it available for allocating to another user

decision tree A tree that represents the execution of a program with branches for each choice or decision that must be made

degree-constrained spanning tree A spanning tree in which no vertex has degree more than k, given a positive integer $2 \leq k \leq n$

degree of a node in a tree The number of non-NIL children in a node

degree of a tree The maximum degree of a node in a tree

dependency graph A directed graph for a computation whose vertices consist of each of the values computed and where an edge is drawn from one computation to another if the result of the first is used in the computation of the second

depth-first spanning tree The spanning tree made up of the edges from a depth-first traversal

depth-first traversal A traversal of a graph in which all of the descendants of a node are visited before the siblings of a node

depth of a node *See* level of a node

descendant A node that follows another node in a path

digraph An abbreviation for a directed graph

Dijkstra's algorithm An algorithm for solving the single-source shortest-path problem

directed edge An ordered pair <n_1, n_2> of nodes; a designated pair of digraph vertices

directed graph   A graph where edges have a specified direction

directed path   A sequence of directed edges, $e_1, e_2, \ldots, e_n$, where the node at the end of one edge serves as the beginning of the next edge

disjoint graphs   Graphs that have no vertices in common

domain name   The logical name for a computing system attached to the Internet

dynamic binary search trees   Binary search trees for which nothing is known about the tree data and whose nodes may change over time

dynamic keyed tables   Keyed tables where there is no information on the distribution of the keys

dynamic shared reference   Shared reference in which the referenced list is interpreted to refer to its current and future instantiation

edge   *See* directed edge and undirected edge

efficiency of a parallel algorithm   Let $T(n)$ be the shortest time required to solve a problem involving n data items using a single processor, and let $T_p(n)$ be the time required to solve the same problem with p processors. Then the efficiency $E_p(n)$ of the parallel algorithm is $T(n)/(pT_p(n))$

empty tree   A tree with no nodes

encapsulate   To bind definitions, declarations, and code into a separately compilable, named collection and make the collection available while keeping the implementation details inaccessible

encapsulation   Implementation of information hiding. The use of a programming language feature that provides mechanisms (1) to separately compile named collections of definitions, declarations, and code, and (2) to make the structure described inaccessible and the details of the operations invisible while making the named collection available; a programming mechanism that enforces information hiding

Ethernet address   A 48-bit address that is built into each actual machine or Ethernet board

exception   A built-in language mechanism for handling unusual processing conditions such as errors

expert system   A type of software package that utilizes rules in order to solve problems

explicit set representation   Time and space are proportional to the size of the universe set

exponential complexity   Time complexity is bounded by a constant raised to the power of the size measure; $O(2^n)$, $O(3^n)$, and so on in Big-O notation

extended binary search tree   A binary search tree where NIL pointers are replaced failure boxes

external fragmentation   Fragmentation in which the blocks are in (free) storage

external name   An input string representing a vertex in a graph or, more generally, representing an object in an ADT

external nodes   *See* failure boxes

external path length   The sum of the path lengths from the root to all the external nodes in a tree

external sorting   Sorting undertaken when the collection of N records (to be sorted) is too large to fit into main memory

failure boxes   Boxes drawn to replace NIL pointers in a tree

failure links   Index positions used in the Knuth-Morris-Pratt pattern matching algorithm to determine where in a string pattern to resume a searching after a match has failed

Fibonacci buddy system   A buddy system where the allowable block sizes are the values in the Fibonacci sequence

Fibonacci numbers   The first two Fibonacci numbers are 0 and 1; each successive Fibonacci number is the sum of the two preceding Fibonacci numbers

first fit strategy   A strategy for handling the available space list that allocates memory from the first block that is large enough

fragmentation   The situation where available storage is broken in many noncontiguous pieces

free block   An unallocated block of storage under the control of the Memory Manager; it is free to be allocated

full binary tree   A binary tree where all of the leaves are on the same level and that level has the maximum number of leaves

garbage   Allocated blocks of storage to which there is no access path from the program

garbage collection   Identifying inaccessible storage and making it available for allocation

generalized list   A nonindexed linear list of zero or more data elements or generalized lists; recursively defined list where the components can be single data elements or another generalized list

generic data types   Data types where the operations are defined, but the types of the items being manipulated are not; the set of operations is defined, but the set of values is not

graph   A usually nonempty set of vertices and a set of edges

graph k-colorability problem   Given a positive integer $k \leq n$, assign one of k colors to each vertex, so that whenever two vertices are connected by an edge, then the vertices have different colors

greedy algorithm   An algorithm in which the best choice at each step leads to the best overall solution

Halting Problem   Does a program halt with a given input?

Hamiltonian circuit   A simple cycle that contains all the vertices in a graph exactly once

hash function   A function that maps a key into the range 0..MaxTable − 1; the result is used as an index into a hash table

hash table   An array [0..MaxTable − 1] of buckets

head of an edge   The second vertex listed in the pair <vertex, vertex>

head of a list   The first component in a list

heap (binary tree)   A binary tree with both the shape property and the value property

heap (memory)   An area of memory from which dynamic variables are allocated

height   The length of the path from the root to a node on the lowest level

height-balanced (at node S in tree T)   The heights of the left and right subtrees of S differ by no more than 1

Huffman algorithm   An algorithm that generates variable length codes with the prefix property

hypercube   A configuration of 2^n processors, where certain processors are connected to others on the basis of a mathematical model of n-dimensional space

implementation section (of a module)   The portion of the module that contains the code for the operations described in the interface section

implicit set representation   Items in a set are stored explicitly. Other items (not stored) are implicitly not in the set

in-degree   The number of vertices adjacent *to* a vertex

indexed linear list   An ADT in which the data objects are placed in a logical order and where storage and retrieval of the objects is based upon an index value

index tree   A multiway search tree in which the pointers in the internal nodes point to other index nodes; the pointers in the leaf nodes are not NIL, but rather point to where the information associated with each key is stored on disk

information hiding   Use of programming techniques that hide the implementation details of data or actions from other parts of a program

in-order list   A list that contains the in-order list of the left-most subtree, the root, and the in-order list of each of the other subtrees from left to right

insertion search path   The path from the root to a newly inserted node, following the simple binary-search-tree insertion algorithm

interface section (of a module)   The visible portion of the module; the part that describes what the user of the module needs to know

internal fragmentation   Fragmentation in which the unused storage is within an allocated block

internal name   The ordinal value assigned to a vertex in a graph or, more generally, to an object in an ADT

internal nodes   Nodes within the tree itself; not external nodes

internal path length   The sum of all the path lengths from the root to internal nodes in a tree

internal sorting   Sorting in which the collection of N records (to be sorted) can fit in main memory at one time

Internet protocol number (IP number)   A 32-bit address assigned to a machine on the Internet

intractable   Problems that have no algorithms that run in polynomial time, even when an unlimited number of processors are available; unsolvable problems also are intractable

keyed table   An unordered data type made up of a collection of <key, information> pairs

Knuth-Morris-Pratt Pattern-Matching Algorithm   A string pattern-matching algorithm that specifies where a search should resume following a partial, but unsuccessful, match

Kruskal's algorithm   An algorithm for finding the minimum-cost spanning tree

labeled graph   A directed or undirected graph, where *information* is attached to either the vertices or the edges

leaf node   A tree node with no children

length of a path   The number of edges in the path

level of a node   The length of the directed path to that node

lexical analysis   Breaking up the input into its logical units called lexical units or tokens

linear complexity   Time complexity is bounded by constant times the size measure; O(n) in Big-O notation

linear probing   A collision resolution technique that examines each successive location until one is found or the original bucket is accessed again

LISP (LISt Processing)   A programming language in which the list is the major data structure

loading density   The number of items stored in a closed table divided by the number of places in the table

logarithmic complexity   Time complexity is bounded by the log of the size measure; $O(\log_2 n)$ in Big-O notation

macro analysis   An analysis that ignores machine-dependent issues and focuses upon the processing of large data sets

matrix factoring algorithm   An algorithm that determines the optimal way to group matrices for successive multiplication

memory compaction   The process of moving all blocks that are accessible to one end of memory, thus having memory divided into an allocated (and accessible) and a free part

Memory Manager   Software whose function is to allocate and to deallocate collections of contiguous storage locations

merge pass   The merging of a complete set of runs from one set of files to another

message passing   A mechanism used by processors to synchronize their activities by sending information back and forth

micro analysis   An analysis based on the specific details of an implementation on a given machine

minimum-cost spanning tree   A spanning tree in which the sum of the weights on the edges is a minimum

module   A named collection of definitions, declarations, and code that are stored and compiled separately; called a unit in Pascal, a module in Modula-2, and a package in Ada

multidimensional array   An ADT of a designated size in which storage and retrieval is based upon two or more indices

multiway search trees   Multiway trees in which the search property holds for each subtree

multiway trees   Trees in which one or more logically unrelated data items are stored in a node

next fit strategy   A strategy for handling the available space list that uses the first-fit strategy but keeps the list as a circular list with the external pointer pointing to the block immediately following the block from which storage was allocated for the previous request

n log n complexity   Time complexity is bounded by the size measure times the log of the size measure; $O(n \log_2 n)$ in Big-O notation

nonindexed linear list   An ADT in which the data objects are placed in a logical order but where storage and retrieval of the objects depends upon the relative location of objects (e.g., first, last, next) rather than an index value

NP-complete   A problem that is in class NP and is NP-hard

NP-hard   A problem to which all problems in class NP can be reduced using a polynomial-time algorithm running on one processor

one-dimensional array   An ADT of a designated size in which storage and retrieval is based upon a single index

opaque types   Only the name of the data type is visible; access to variables of opaque types must be through operations defined in the interface module that defines the type name

open hash table   Buckets contain pointers to a list of synonyms; also called open hashing

optimal binary search tree   A binary search tree in which the weighted internal and external path lengths are minimized

order of an algorithm   If an algorithm requires T(n) steps to process n pieces of data, then the algorithm has order g(n) if there are constants c and N_0 so that $|T(n)| \leq c\,|g(n)|$ for all $n \geq N_0$

order of a function   Function f(n) has order g(n) if there are constants c and N_0 so that $|f(n)| \leq c\,|g(n)|$ for all $n \geq N_0$

out-degree   The number of vertices adjacent *from* a vertex

overflow   Collision occurs and there is no room for the new item in the bucket; collision and overflow are synonymous when the bucket size is one

package (Ada) *See* module

path A sequence of edges, $e_1, e_2, \ldots, e_n$, where the head of one edge is the tail of the next edge

path length The number of edges in the path

pipelining Processors are arranged in tandem, where each contributes one part to an overall computation

pivot node The last unbalanced node passed before reaching the insertion point; if all nodes visited are balanced, no pivot node is designated

plist *See* property list

polynomial complexity Time complexity is bounded by a function that is a polynomial in the size measure

polyphase merge The merge phase of an external sort (K files) in which one file is used for output and $K - 1$ files are used for input on each merge pass

postorder list A list that contains the postorder subtrees of the root from left to right, followed by the root

prefix property No shorter code duplicates the beginning of a longer code

preorder list A list that contains the root, followed by the preorder nodes of the subtrees of the root from left to right

priority queue data type A semi-structured data type composed of <priority, information> pairs; the designated item in the one with the highest priority

private types The type description is visible but access to variables of the type must be through the operations defined in the interface module

procedural abstraction Separation of the logical properties of an action from the implementation details

procedural languages Programming languages based on the von Neuman model; also called imperative languages; use sequential execution, variables, and assignment statements with mechanisms for grouping code in procedures or functions

process A logical computational unit

processor A hardware device with its own processing capabilities. In a multi-tasking environment, one processor may be capable of running several processes

property list A data object in LISP that includes the print name of the symbol and other information that may be relevant to processing involving that symbol

public type A type defined in the interface section of a module and available for access by all

quadratic complexity Time complexity is bounded by the size measure raised to the second power; $O(n^2)$ in Big-O notation

quadratic probing A collision resolution technique that examines locations until one is found or the original bucket is accessed again using the formula $((\text{Hash(Key1)}) \pm i^2) \text{ MOD MaxTable}$

queue A semi-structured data type where the designated item is the one that has been in the structure the longest time

rank of v in B The number of elements of the sorted list B that are less than or equal to v; written rank (v, b)

record An unordered data type composed of a collection of <field, value> pairs; the fields are known in advance

recursive rewrite rules Rules used to rewrite an expression where the same term appears on both sides of the rule

red/black trees A binary tree structure representation of the nodes of a 2-3-4 tree

reduced form An expression consisting of only the basic constructors

reference count A record of the number of times a list is referenced by another list

referenced list A list whose name appears within another list

referencing list A list that is being created and references another list

regular expression A recursively-defined sequence of symbols, beginning with basic symbols (usually 0, 1, and the empty set) and allowing the operations of union, concatenation, and a star (∗) construction

Regular Expression Non-Universality Problem The problem of determining whether regular expressions with squaring represent all possible strings of 0's and 1's

regular expression with squaring A recursively-defined sequence of symbols, allowing all operations of regular expressions together with a rule to square or duplicate specific strings

rehashing A collision resolution technique that uses a series of hash functions Hash1(Key1), Hash2(Key1), ... until a free space is found or it is determined that the table is full

replacement selection An algorithm for generating variable-length initial runs for an external sort using a priority queue

result parallelism An algorithmic approach to parallelism that focuses on the desired results; each processor is responsible for calculating a specific result

root, rooted tree A tree is defined recursively as: a set of zero objects in a tree, called the empty tree or the null tree; if $T_1, T_2, \ldots, T_n$ are n trees for $n \geq 0$ and R is an object, called a node, then the set T containing R and the trees $T_1, T_2, \ldots, T_n$ is a tree; within T, R is called the root of T and $T_1, T_2, \ldots, T_n$ are called subtrees

run A sorted sequence of M records

sequence A (usually) unbounded indexed linear list where the position of a value is bound to an index only temporarily and may be changed by a subsequent insert or delete operation

set An unstructured data type that models the mathematical construct

shape property (heap) An organization of nodes within a binary tree in which the tree is either (1) full or (2) full to the next-to-the-lowest level and with all leaves on the lowest level as far as possible to the left

shared memory Global memory shared (or accessible) by more than one processor

shared reference The situation in which one list is allowed to reference another list

siblings Nodes in a tree that have the same parent

simple path A path where all the vertices are different except possibly the first and the last

single-source shortest path An algorithm that computes the minimum cost between one vertex and all the other vertices

software engineering The development and application of careful methodologies to the writing of software

sorted list A linear, structured, nonindexed list where the items are kept ordered

sorting Arranging a collection of N records in ascending (or descending) order of the value of the key field in each record

spanning tree A connected subgraph of G that contains all of G's vertices but contains no cycles

sparse matrix A matrix with relatively few nonzero elements

specialist parallelism An algorithmic approach to parallelism that focuses on the specialized tasks to be done; each processor is responsible for a certain type of special work

specification A formal statement of what operations or ADTs are supposed to do, without indicating how they are to be implemented

speedup Let $T(n)$ be the shortest time required to solve a problem involving n data items using a single processor, and let $T_p(n)$ be the time required to solve the same problem with p processors. Then the speedup $S_p(n)$ is $T(n)/T_p(n)$

stack A semi-ordered data type where the designated item is the one that has been in the structure the least amount of time

stack pointer Pointer to the top of the run-time stack where activation records are stored; managed by the run-time support system of a programming language

static binary search trees Binary search trees for which the tree data are known in advance and the tree structure does not change

static keyed tables The keys are known in advance

static shared reference Shared reference in which the referenced list is interpreted as its current instantiation

string A sequence of characters

strongly connected graph A directed graph where a path exists from each vertex to each other vertex

subgraph of G A graph G′ where the vertices and edges in G′ are also in G; that is, V(G′) C V(G) and E(G′) C E(G)

subtree A tree whose nodes and edges constitute a part of another tree

symbol table A keyed table in which the key is an identifier in a programming language and the information consists of data about the identifier that the compiler uses

synchronous processing Multiple processors apply the same program in lockstep to multiple data sets

synonyms Keys that hash to the same bucket

tail of an edge The first vertex in the <vertex, vertex> pair

tail of a list The list with the first component removed

task *See* process

terminal node *See* leaf node

threads In-order pointers that replace the NIL pointers in a tree

topological sort An ordering of the vertices in an acyclic digraph such that if an edge exists between two vertices in the graph, the tail vertex appears in the ordering before the head vertex

transparent types   The description of the type is known; component variables of that type can be accessed directly by the user

traveling salesperson problem   A problem that seeks to find a Hamiltonian circuit of minimal cost

traversal of a graph   A systematic visit to all of the vertices in a graph

tree   *See* rooted tree

truncated rank of v in B   The number of elements of the sorted list B that are less than v; trank (v, B)

two-dimensional mesh of processors   A configuration of processors in a parallel processing environment

2-3 tree   A multiway search tree where each node contains one or two data values and there is always one more child than data values; insertions are made in the leaves

2-3-4 trees   Multiway search trees where each node has zero, two, three, or four children and where all leaves and null pointers are at the same level

type1 rotation   A single rotation (either to the left or right) used to rebalance an AVL tree

type2 rotation   A double rotation (either left-right or right-left) used to rebalance an AVL tree

unbounded data type   A data type in which there are no limits on the number of items that can be stored in an instance of the data type; a designated pair of graph vertices

undirected edge   An unordered pair (n_1, n_2) of nodes

undirected graph   *See* graph

union/find algorithms   Algorithms for operations union and find on mutually disjoint sets

unit (Pascal)   *See* module

unsolvable   Problems for which no solution is possible

unsorted list   A linear, structured, nonindexed list where the items are not kept ordered

value property (heap)   A property of binary trees in which the value of any node in the tree has equal or higher value than any node in either its left subtree or its right subtree

vertex cover problem   Given a positive integer $k \leq n$, find a subset S of k vertices, so that at least one end of every edge is in S

visible type   The definition of the data type can be seen by the user

weighted external path   The sum of each path length to an external node times the weight of the external node

weighted graph   A labeled graph where the information is numeric

weighted internal path   The sum of each path length to an internal node times the weight of the internal node

worst-case analysis   Analysis that assumes the data always require the most work possible

worst-fit strategy   A strategy for handling the available space list that allocates memory from the largest block

Answers to Selected Exercises

Chapter 1

1. **structure** Stack (of ItemType)
   interface Create → _Stack_____
   Push(Stack, ItemType) → _Stack_____
   Pop(Stack) → _Stack_____
   Top(Stack) → _ItemType_____
   IsEmpty(Stack) → _Boolean_____
   axioms for all S in Stack, i1 in ItemType, let
   IsEmpty(Create) = True
   IsEmpty(Push(S, i1)) = False
   Pop(Create) = Error
   Pop(Push(S,i1)) = S
   Top(Create) = Error
   Top(Push(S, i1)) = i1

2. Push(Push(Push(Push(Push(Create, 'r'), 'q'), 'd'), 'b'), 'a')

4. **axioms** **for all Cookie1 and Cookie2 in CookieType, Jar in CookieJar, let**
   Eat(Create, Cookie2) = Error
   Eat(PutIn(Jar, Cookie1), Cookie2) =
       IF Cookie1 = Cookie2
          THEN   Jar
          ELSE   PutIn(Eat(Jar, Cookie2), Cookie1)
       END IF

6. No. There was the possibility of having duplicate items in the Jar.

10. Axioms for the Concat, IsIn, and Length functions of the ADT UnsortedList using Head and Tail to decompose the list.

    Concat(L1,Create) = L1
    Concat(L1, L2) =
        Make(Concat(Tail(L1), L2), Head(L1))

    IsIn(Create, i1) = False
    IsIn(L1, i1) =
        IF Head(L1) = i1
           THEN   True
           ELSE   IsIn(Tail(L1), i1)
        END IF

    Length(Create) = 0
    Length(L1) = 1 + Length(Tail(L1))

12. The Stack implementation given in the text actually implements most UnsortedList axioms if the names of the operations are changed: Push becomes Make, Top becomes Head, Pop becomes Tail. IsEmpty remains the same. Only a new Delete procedure is needed. The Delete for the case where the most recent copy is removed (if present) follows.

```
PROCEDURE Delete (VAR List: ListType; Item: ItemType)
(* Most recent occurrence of Item is removed. *)
VAR
    Ptr , Back: ListType;
    Removed : Boolean;
BEGIN
    Ptr : ← List;
    Back : ← NIL;
    Removed: ← False;
    WHILE Ptr <> NIL AND NOT Removed DO
        IF Ptr↑.Data = Item
            THEN
                IF Back = NIL
                    THEN    List ← Ptr↑.Next
                    ELSE    Back.Next ← Ptr↑.Next
                END IF
                Dispose(Ptr);
                Removed ← True
            ELSE
                Back ← Ptr;
                Ptr ← Ptr↑.Next
        END IF
    END WHILE
END;
```

If the list is empty, it is returned unchanged. If the list is not empty and Item is not in the list, the list is returned unchanged. This verifies Delete(Create, i) = Create. Because the mapping puts each new item at the front of the list and this code searches the list from the front, the most recent copy of Item is found and removed. The items on the list that do not match Item are left unchanged. This verifies the general case.

Chapter 2

1. Both Micro and Macro Analysis examine an algorithm's running time. Micro Analysis is based on the specific details of an implementation on a given machine. Macro Analysis ignores machine-dependent issues and focuses upon the processing of large data sets.

4. a. Index might be kept as a variable with the machine code mirroring the Pascal code, or Index might be kept in a register with all operations involving it carried out in the register. A similar comment applies to the variables Found and Length.

   If a machine instruction is available to increment a register value by 1, then the statement Index := Index + 1 might be performed in a single machine instruction. If Index is stored in main memory, then the value 1 might be stored in the machine instruction itself, in a register, or in main memory. Storage in the machine instruction itself requires no additional processing beyond decoding the machine instruction. The other options require successively more time to obtain desired values.

   If a machine instruction is available to give the results of a negative Boolean test (NOT Found), then that part of the Boolean evaluation could be done in one step. If not, then this work might proceed in two steps: (1) test Found, and (2) negate the result.

b. The directions specify that a = 1, b = 1, and m = 2. These constants are retained for the following discussion of the general case.

Suppose all variables are kept in registers (except for the List array) after the loop intialization. The reference List[Index] may be done in one machine instruction if the base address of List is stored in a register and if the machine allows indirect addressing. In this scenario, the worst case for the amount of work for the code would be as follows:

Initialization: Assignment Found, Index: 2m

Loop

   Exit condition tried (Length+1) times: (Length+1) * 2b

     one test (Index <= Length), one combined instruction for AND NOT

   Loop body executed Length times: Length * (m + b + a)

     Memory access for List[Index], register addition/assignment

     (If item not found, then one less addition, but Found accessed)

The total amount of work, therefore, is 2m + 2b + Length(a + 3b + m). The best case would be where list is empty (2m + 2b) or the Item is in the first position in the array: 2m + 2b + a + 3b + m. The average case would be where Length/2 items are examined; the worst case is where all Length items are examined.

c. The algorithm has $O(n)$ and therefore also $O(n^2)$ and $O(3n^2)$.

d. The constants m, b, and a are in time units. Let N_0 be the constant 2m + 2b. Then 2m + 2b $\leq$ n for all n $\geq N_0$. Also, (a + 3b + m)n $\leq$ (a + 3b + m)n for all n. Adding the two inequalities, we obtain 2m + 2b + (a + 3b + m)n $\leq$ (a + 3b + m + 1)n for all n $\geq N_0$. If we let c be the constant (a + 3b + m + 1), we have shown 2m + 2b + (a + 3b + m)n $\leq$ cn for all n $\geq N_0$ as required.

Cn $\leq n^2$ for all n $\geq$ C. Combining this with the previous inequality for n larger than both C and N_0, we obtain 2m + 2b + (a + 3b + m)n $\leq n^2$ for all n $\geq N_1$ where N_1 is the maximum of C and N_0. Thus 2m + 2b + (a + 3b + m)n also has $O(n^2)$. Because $n^2 \leq 3n^2$ for all n, it also follows that 2m + 2b + (a + 3b + m)n $\leq 3n^2$ for all n $\geq N_1$ for the N_1 defined earlier. Thus, 2m + 2b + (a + 3b + m)n is $O(n^2)$ as well.

e. Because part d was done with general constants a, b, and m, the analysis holds for all timings, and the algorithm always has $O(n)$ and therefore also $O(n^2)$ and $O(3n^2)$.

6.

	O(1)	O(N)	O(5N)	O(N²)	O(N³)
10,000	no	yes	yes	yes	yes
N	no	no	no	yes	yes
5*N	no	no	no	yes	yes
N²	no	no	no	no	yes

Note: When the blank is filled with N^2, the number of steps is approximately computed by the formula

$$\sum_{J=1}^{N} \left(\sum_{I=1}^{J^2} 1 \right) = \sum_{J=1}^{N} J^2 = N(N + 1)(2N + 1)/6$$

7. Suppose a FOR loop requires time X for initialization and time Y each time through its execution for incrementing the control variable and for exit-condition testing. Suppose the assignment of an initial value to a variable requires time Z, the increment of a variable takes time A, and the comparison of values takes time B.

a. In the worst case, we have the following:

> Initialization: Assignment: Z
> Outer loop: Initialization: X + loop iteration N*Y
> Inner loop: Repeated N times: Initialization X + loop iteration NY + test NB +
> incrementing NA

This is a total of $Z + X + NY + N(X + NY + NB + NA) = Z + X + NY + N^2(Y + B + A)$.

This has $O(N^2)$, as follows.

> $Z + X \leq N^2$ for $N \geq Z + X$ (as long as $Z + X$ is positive).
> $NY \leq N^2$ for $N \geq Y$.
> $N^2(Y + B + A) \leq N^2(Y + B + A)$ for all N.

Adding $Z + X + NY + N^2(Y + B + A) \leq N^2(2 + Y + B + A)$ for all positive N greater than both Y and $Z + X$. Letting $c = 2 + Y + B + A$ and letting N_0 be a positive integer greater than both Y and $Z + X$, we have $Z + X + NY + N^2(Y + B + A) \leq cN^2$ for all $N \leq N_0$, as required.

d. The analysis is similar to that of part a, except that the inner loop is done I times. The amount of work, therefore, is $Z + X + N^2Y + N^2X + (Y + B + A)$ (number of times inner loop executed).

The inner loop is first done once (with $I = 1$), then twice, then three times, and so on, until I reaches N*N.

The amount of work becomes

$$Z + X + N^2Y + N^2X + \sum_{I=1}^{N \cdot N} I (Y + B + A)$$

The last sum is slightly tricky: A standard formula (from most discrete mathematics books) shows that $1 + 2 + \ldots + K$ is $K(K + 1)/2$. Here, K is N*N and we multiply each term in the sum by $(Y + B + A)$. Thus, the above summation term is $(Y + B + A)$ $(N*N(N*N + 1))/6$ and the actual amount of work is $Z + X + N^2Y + N^2X + (Y + B + A)$ $(N*N(N*N + 1))/6$. Within this sum, the highest order term is N^4 and this expression has $O(N^4)$. The formal proof of this order parallels the proof for part a, using N^4 instead of N^2 on the right-hand side of each inequality.

9. Let $N_0 = 1$ and $c = 1$. Then trivially $f(n) \leq c f(n)$ for all $n \geq N_0$. By the definition of order, it follows that $f(n) \in O(f(n))$.

10. a. Normally, the symbol $=$ means that the two elements in question are the same. For example, the statement $X = 5$ means that X represents a numeric value and that value is the number 5. Further, if also $Y = X$, then by transitivity we can conclude that Y also has the value 5 (i.e., $Y = 5$ is also true). The notation $f(n) = O(g(n))$ does not follow this normal convention and transitivity does not hold. For example, in this notation, $n = O(n^2)$ and $n^2 = O(n^2)$, but it is not true that $n = n^2$.

b. The notation $O(g(n))$ represents a collection of functions and the statement that "$f(n)$ has order $O(g(n))$" means that $f(n)$ is one of the functions in the collection $O(g(n))$. The statement "$f(n)$ ε $O(g(n))$" expresses this meaning using conventional mathematical set notation.

11. a. Suppose $g(n) = 1$ if n is odd and $g(n) = 2$ if n is even. Then $g(n)$ has $O(1)$ as it is bounded by the number 2. However, $g(n)$ is not constant.

b. Let $f(n) = | \sin(n\pi/2)|$ and let $g(n) = | \cos(n\pi/2) |$. $f(n)$ is 0 for even n, while $g(n)$ is 0 for odd n. Both are 1 otherwise. Thus, neither function is bounded by a constant times the other.

c. Both functions given in b are bounded by the constant 1, so both have $O(1)$.

14. Consider another mapping where the Data[1] corresponds to the head of the list and Data[Length] is the last element.

   a. Make(L, i) maps to moving L[i] to L[i + 1] for i going from 1 to Length. Length is incremented, and i is stored in L[1]. Head(L) returns L[1]. Tail(L) returns L[2]..L[Length].

   b. The specifications do not have to be changed because they do not affect implementation.

   c. The Make is O(Length) because L[i]..L[Length] must be moved to L[i + 1].. L[Length + 1].

17. a. n! (n-factorial) permutations are possible.

   b. Each of n! permutations may be checked for order (an order n operation), so the overall algorithm has O(n*n!).

   c. 10 elements should take about 12,000 seconds (3.3 hours), while 20 elements should take 1.6×10^{15} seconds (1.87×10^{11} days or 511,820,000 years).

19. a. Big-O notation for each of the operations on the list.

Create initializes the list.
Insert puts the item on the list.
Delete removes the item with the highest value.
IsEmpty returns True if the list is empty; False otherwise.
Length returns the number of items in the list.

	Array Based		Linked List		B.S.T.	
	Sorted*	*UnSorted*	*Sorted***	*Unsorted*	*Balanced*	*Unbalanced*
Create	_O(1)_	_O(1)_	_O(1)_	_O(1)_	_O(1)	O(1)
Insert	_O(N)_	_O(1)_	_O(N)_	_O(1)_	_O(logN)	O(N)
Delete	_O(1)_	_O(N)_	_O(1)_	_O(N)_	_O(logN)	O(N)
IsEmpty	_O(1)_	_O(1)_	_O(1)_	_O(1)_	_O(1)	O(1)
Length ***	_O(1)_	_O(1)_	_O(N)_	_O(N)_	_O(1)	O(1)

* List is maintained sorted in ascending order by value.
** List is maintained sorted in descending order by value.
*** The array and binary search tree implementations have a length field; the linked list implementations do not.

   b. The algorithm used is the one given in the text.

Chapter 3

1. Standard Pascal has full evaluation. Turbo Pascal uses partial evaluation with a compiler option that allows for full evaluation. C, C^{++}, and Modula 2 use partial evaluation. Ada provides two separate operators for AND and OR, one with partial evaluation and one with full evaluation.

2. The generic data types that allow the user to define the types in a separate module do not allow for more than one instance of the data type in a program. If another instance is needed, the data type module can be duplicated with a different name. All references to the operations would then have to be prefaced with the module name.

3. *Interface Section DataDefn;*
(* Defines ItemType for ListOfItem module *)
TYPE
    ItemType = 0.0..100.0
END

5. *Interface Section DataDefn;*
(* Defines ItemType for SortedList module *)
TYPE
    CompareType = (Less, Equal, Greater)

    [NameType = Array[1..15] of CHAR;
    ItemType = RECORD
        FirstName,
        LastName : [NameType;
        (* whatever else is needed *)
    END RECORD;

FUNCTION Compare(Item1, Item2: ItemType) : CompareType;
(* Pre: Item1 and Item2 have valid data in the name fields.   *)
(* Post:Compare returns Less if the name in Item1 comes before the name in   *)
(*   Item2; Equal if the names are identical; and Greater otherwise.   *)

Implementation Section DataDefn;
FUNCTION Compare(Item1, Item2: ItemType) : CompareType;
BEGIN
    IF Item1.LastName < Item2.LastName
        THEN Return Less
    ELSIF Item1.LastName > Item2.LastName
        THEN Return Greater
    ELSIF Item1.FirstName < Item2.FirstName
        THEN Return Less
    ELSIF Item1.FirstName > Item2.FirstName
        THEN Return Greater
    ELSE Return Equal
END

6. a. In result parallelism, each part of a building would be identified (e.g., foundation, each exterior wall, each interior wall, heating and cooling vents, plumbing, wiring, and so forth). A construction team would be assigned to work on each part. Each team would be responsible for its building segment. In some cases, a team might not be able to start until another team was finished (e.g., the walls cannot be built until the foundation is laid). In this case, the team just waits for prerequisite work to be completed.

   Note: This approach is employed in barn raising, where neighbors meet to help a friend construct a barn. Typically, the workers divide into groups to work on individual walls of the barn. These walls are then raised together and assembled to form the exterior walls of the barn.

   b. In specialist parallelism, specific skills are identified and individuals specialize in these different areas. Thus, there may be bricklayers, electricians, woodworkers, plumbers, plasterers, painters, and so forth. As work progresses, each person contributes his or her trade. Initially, those able to perform excavation work dig a hole for the foundation; others may be idle. Next, bricklayers may become involved. Once part of the foundation is poured, electricians and plumbers may begin installing their special systems.

Note: This approach is sometimes observed in the building of large structures, where one crew begins the foundation in one area and then moves to a second area, then to a third, and so forth. Once the foundation in the first area is done, a second crew begins work on that area—perhaps installing a superstructure. When the superstructure is done in the first area, this second crew moves to the foundation in a second area, just completed by the foundation crew. After the superstructure, other crews may add electrical and mechanical systems. Next, walls are installed and finished; windows may then be put in place. Thus, at a point during the construction, the foundation crew may be working in one area, the superstructure crew in a second, the electrical/mechanical systems crew in a third, the wall-finishing crew in a fourth, and so forth.

c. Reviewing either the result or specialist approach, a list of tasks may be established of all work that might be needed in the construction of the building. With this master list, a crew of generalists is employed, where each individual is able to do whatever work might be needed (excavation, brick laying, electricial systems, plumbing, woodworking, wall finishing, and so forth). Each individual is assigned a task at the start of the list. Then, when the task is done, the individual moves on the the next item on the list.

Note: This approach is common when a family undertakes a project. Each person may have the same general level of skill, and each person pitches in to help as needed.

7. a. Basketball team: specialist parallelism—each person specializes in a certain position—there may even be specialization within a position (e.g., the forward on the left may behave differently and may focus upon different shots from a forward who normally is on the right of the court).

b. Track team: result parallelism—each runner does the same thing, with the best time being used for the final result.

c. Motor racing: specialist parallelism—each person has a specialty.

d. Golf team: result specialism—as with track team described above.

e. Baseball team: agenda parallelism—each player may be at any position, as needed.

11. One way to process work on one processor would be to simulate the work being done on p processors—that is, doing the work of the p processors sequentially. If this approach is followed, the time $T(n)$ would be the sum of the times for each individual processor or p times $T_p(n)$. In this case, speedup would be $T(n)/T_p(n) = pT_p(n)/T_p(n) = p$. Furthermore, this time $T(n)$ for one processor does not reflect any overhead required for parallel processing. If some such overhead were required for p processors but could be eliminated with a one-processor implementation, then $T(n)$ would be smaller and efficiency would be less than p.

14. If two programs request memory at the same time, they might be given the same memory locations. The programs might be reading and writing into the same locations causing errors in both programs.

If two users are given simultaneous access to the same disk file(s), problems identical to the bank problem can occur.

A printer cannot print two files at the same time. Some mechanism must be established to order the requests. Otherwise, the lines of the two files might end up being mixed together on the printed output!

Chapter 4

1. *Universe set:* The set containing every item in the component or base type.
   Empty set: The set with no items.
   Power set: The set of all subsets.
   Subset: A is a subset of B if every item in A is also in B.
   Proper subset: A is a proper subset of B if A is a subset of B and B contains at least one item that is not in A.
   Cardinality of a set: The number of items in a set.
   Component type of a set: The type of the items in the set.

3. The carrier domain is Set. The auxiliary domains are Boolean and ItemType.

6. The bit vector implementation assigns one bit to every member of the component type. A member of the component type is in the set if the bit is set to True; the component is not in the set if the bit is set to False.

11. Because the complexity of the bit vector operations is constant time, this implementation is preferable if the cardinality of the universe set is small enough. If the only operations are Union and Find and the sets are mutually disjoint, the Union/Find implementation is preferable. The complexity of Union is O(1) and the complexity of Find is O(N). However, the weighting rule and collapsing rule reduce the constant. The scheme is designed to optimize operations that begin with a collection of N sets and end with one set. If the component type is large and the full range of set operations is required, the list representation is the only possible scheme.

13. Intersection, Union, and IsSubset in O(N) time.

Intersection(Set1, Set2: SetType, VAR Set3: SetType)

```
CreateL(Set3)
Members(Set3, List1)
Members(Set3, List2)
IF NOT List.IsEmpty(List1) AND NOT List.IsEmpty(List2)
  THEN
     Item1 ← Head(List1)
     List1 ← Tail(List1)
     Item1 ← Head(List2)
     List2 ← Tail(List2)
     LOOP
       CASE Compare(Item1, Item2) OF
         LessThan  :  IF List.IsEmpty(List1)
                         THEN   EXIT
                         ELSE
                            Item1 ← Head(List1)
                            List1 ← Tail(List1)
                         END IF
         Equal     :  Store(Set3, Item1)
                      IF NOT List.IsEmpty(List1) AND NOT
                            List.IsEmpty(List2)
```

```
                              THEN
                                  Item1 ← Head(List1)
                                  List1 ← Tail(List1)
                                  Item2 ← Head(List2)
                                  List2 ← Tail(List2)
                              ELSE EXIT
                              END IF
            GreaterThan :  IF IsEmpty(List2)
                              THEN   EXIT
                              ELSE
                                  Item2 ← Head(List2)
                                  List2 ← Tail(List2)
                              END IF
        END CASE
     END LOOP
   END IF
```

Union(Set1, Set2: SetType, VAR Set3: SetType)

```
    CreateL(Set3)
    Members(Set3, List1)
    Members(Set3, List2)
    IF NOT List.IsEmpty(List1) AND NOT List.IsEmpty(List2)
      THEN
        Item1 ← Head(List1)
        List1 ← Tail(List1)
        Item1 ← Head(List2)
        List2 ← Tail(List2)
        LOOP
          CASE Compare(Item1, Item2) OF
            LessThan  :  Store(Set3, Item1)
                         IF List.IsEmpty(List1)
                            THEN   EXIT
                            ELSE
                                Item1 ← Head(List1)
                                List1 ← Tail(List1)
                         END IF
            Equal     :  Store(Set3, Item1)
                         IF NOT List.IsEmpty(List1) AND NOT
                            List.IsEmpty(List2)
                            THEN
                                Item1 ← Head(List1)
                                List1 ← Tail(List1)
                                Item2 ← Head(List2)
                                List2 ← Tail(List2)
                            ELSE   EXIT
                         END IF
```

```
            GreaterThan : Store(Set3, Item2)
                          IF List.IsEmpty(List2)
                              THEN   EXIT
                              ELSE
                                  Item2 ← Head(List2)
                                  List2 ← Tail(List2)
                          END IF
         END CASE
       END LOOP
   END IF
   WHILE NOT List.IsEmpty(List1) DO
     Item1 ← Head(List1)
     List1 ← Tail(List1)
     Store (Set3, Item1)
   END WHILE
   WHILE NOT List.IsEmpty(List2) DO
     Item1 ← Head(List2)
     List1 ← Tail(List2)
     Store (Set3, Item2)
   END WHILE
```

IsSubset(Set1, Set2: SetType) : Boolean

```
   Members(Set3, List1)
   Members(Set3, List2)
   Subset ← True
   IF NOT List.IsEmpty(List1) AND NOT List.IsEmpty(List2)
     THEN
         Item1 ← Head(List1)
         List1 ← Tail(List1)
         Item1 ← Head(List2)
         List2 ← Tail(List2)
         LOOP
           CASE Compare(Item1, Item2) OF
             LessThan    :  Subset ← False
                            EXIT
             Equal       :  IF NOT List.IsEmpty(List1) AND NOT
                                   List.IsEmpty(List2)
                              THEN
                                  Item1 ← Head(List1)
                                  List1 ← Tail(List1)
                                  Item2 ← Head(List2)
                                  List2 ← Tail(List2)
                              ELSE   EXIT
                            END IF
             GreaterThan :  IF List.IsEmpty(List2)
                              THEN
                                  Subset ← False
                                  EXIT
```

```
                        ELSE
                           Item2 ← Head(List2)
                           List2 ← Tail(List2)
                        END IF
              END CASE
            END LOOP
          END IF
          IF List.IsEmpty(List2) AND NOT List.IsEmpty(List1)
            THEN   Subset ← False
          END IF
          RETURN Subset
```

18. O(N)

19. O(N²) loop through unordered linked list (O(N))
       look up in ordered list (O(logN))
       insert into ordered list (O(N))

O(NlogN) loop through unordered linked list (O(N))
       look up in ordered list (O(logN))
       insert into unordered list (O(1))
sort resulting list (O(NlogN))
   ==> O(NlogN) + O(NlogN)

20. O(N)

24. Work in parallel down the ordered lists O(N)
Any item in linked list not in the array is inserted O(N)
    ===> O(N²)

26. Axioms for the operation ProperSubset.
    ProperSubset(SetType, SetType) → Boolean
    ProperSubset(Create, T) =
      IF IsEmpty(T)
        THEN   False
        ELSE   True
      END IF

    ProperSubset(Store(S, i1), T) =
    IF NOT IsIn(T, i1)
      THEN   False
      ELSE   ProperSubset(S, Delete(T, i1))
    END IF

29. Replace(KeyedTable, KeyType, ValueType) → KeyedTable. If the key is in the table, value replaces the original value. If the key is not in the table, the table is unchanged.

    axiom   For k1, k2 in KeyType, v1, v2 in ValueType, KT in KeyedTable, let
    Replace(Create, k2, v2) = Create
    Replace(Store(KT, k1, v1), k2, v2)
      IF k1 = k2
        THEN   Store(KT, k1, v2)
        ELSE   Store(Replace(KT, k2, v2), k1, v1)
      END IF

30. Write an algorithm for a hash function that divides an eight-digit number into four groups of two and sums the groups. The result is MOD MaxTable.

Hash(Number) : Integer

```
RightTwoDigits ← Number MOD 100
Number ← Number DIV 100
NextTwoDigits ← Number MOD 100
Number ← Number DIV 100
ThirdTwoDigits ← Number MOD 100
Number ← Number DIV 100
Hash ← (RightTwoDigits + NextTwoDigits +ThirdTwoDigits + Number) MOD
       MaxTable
```

Chapter 5

2. Enque(Enque(Enque(Enque(Enque(Create, a),b),d),q),r)

5. The state of the queue after the following series of operations.

P1 ← Create	P1 = Create
P2 ← Enque(P1, 1)	Enque(Create, 1)
P3 ← Enque(P2, 2)	Enque(Enque(Create, 1), 2)
P4 ← Enque(P3, 0)	Enque(Enque(Enque(Create, 1), 2), 0)
Q1 ← Create	Q1 = Create
Q2 ← Enque(Q1, 6)	Enque(Create, 6)
Q3 ← Enque(Q2, 7)	Enque(Enque(Create, 6), 7)
Q4 ← Guess(P4, Q3)	Guess(Enque(P3, 0), Q3)
	Enque(Guess(P3,Q3), 0)
	Enque(Guess(Enque(P2, 2),Q3), 0)
	Enque(Enque(Guess(P2,Q3), 2), 0)
	Enque(Enque(Guess(Enque(P1, 1),Q3), 2), 0)
	Enque(Enque(Enque(Guess(P1, Q3), 1), 2), 0)
	Enque(Enque(Enque(Guess(Create,Q3), 1), 2), 0)
	Enque(Enque(Enque(Q3, 1), 2), 0)

6. output: 6 7 1 2 0

8. Given a file of 500 records, a run size of 10, and 8 files, the status of each merge pass is as follows:

500 records with a run size of 10 gives 50 runs

Initial Distribution of Runs
       Left[0] 1 5 ... 45 49
       Left[1] 2 6 ... 46 50
       Left[2] 3 7 ... 47
       Left[3] 4 8 ... 48

First Merge Pass
       Right[0] (1–4)   (17–20) (33–36) (49–50)
       Right[1] (5–8)   (21–24) (37–40)
       Right[2] (9–12)   (25–28) (41–44)
       Right[3] (13–16)   (29–32) (45–48)

Second Merge Pass
        Left[0]   (1–16)
        Left[1]   (17–32)
        Left[2]   (33–48)
        Left[3]   (49–50)

Third Merge Pass
        Right[0] (1–50)

12. Distribution of runs for a polyphase merge of 17 runs with 4 files.

F1	F2	F3	F4
1	0	0	0
0	1	1	1
1	0	2	2
3	2	0	4
7	6	4	0

14. Suppose that a priority queue was used to store strings of bounded length and termi-
nated by a null character (as is done in C). The copying of a string must proceed char-
acter-by-character until a null is encountered. While the time required for such
copying depends upon the number of characters in the string, the time is bounded by
the maximum length of the string. A similar situation is found when strings are stored
as a record, containing the length of the string and an array of a maximum length containing characters. In each case, copying the string has bounded, but not constant,
time.

17. Run 1: 1 3 4 4 6 7 8 10 11
    Run 2: 2 2 3

18. a. If the original file is already sorted, one run is generated.
    b. If the original file is sorted in reverse order, the same number of runs is generated as
       would be if replacement selection were not being used. That is, ceiling function of
       file size divided by the queue size.
    c. If the original file is in unknown order, the number of runs lies between 1 and the
       maximum where replacement is not used. The expected run size is twice the size of
       the queue.

Chapter 6

2. A fifth parameter MaxElements could be added to the Create function.

    Create(MaxElements, IndexType, IndexType, IndexType, IndexType)   → Array
    Create(Max, i1, i2, i3, i4) =
        IF (i2 − i1 + 1) * (i4 − i3 + 1) > Max
            THEN   Error

3. The relevant formulas are

$$\sum_{D=1}^{N} D = N(N+1)/2 \qquad \sum_{D=1}^{N} D^2 = N(N+1)(2N+1)/6$$

With these formulas:

$$\text{TotalWork} = \sum_{D=2}^{N} D\,(N - D + 1) = \sum_{D=1}^{N} (D(N+1) - D^2) \ - N$$

$$= (N+1) \sum_{D=1}^{N} D - \sum_{D=1}^{N} D^2 \ - N$$

$$= (N+1)*N(N+1)/2 - N(N+1)(2N+1)/6 - N$$
$$= (N^3 + 2N^2 + N)/2 - (2N^3 + 3N^2 + N)/6 - N$$
$$= (3N^3 + 6N^2 + 3N)/6 - (2N^3 + 3N^2 + N)/6 - 6N/6$$
$$= (N^3 + 3N^2 - 4N)/6$$
$$= N^3/6 + N^2/2 - 2N/3$$

8. rank (3, A) = 2   trank (3, A) = 1
   rank (6, A) = 4   trank (6, A) = 4
   rank (9, A) = 6   trank (9, A) = 5

10. L1 ← Create   Create
    L2 ← Store(L1, 1, a)   Store(Create,1,a)
    L3 ← Store(L2, 2, x)   Store(Store(Create,1,a),2,x)
    L4 ← Store(L3, 3, b)   Store(Store(Store(Create,1,a,),2,x),3,b)
    R ← Retrieve(L4, 3)   Retrieve(Store(L3,3,b),3)
                    3 = 3, returns b
    L5 ← Insert(L4, 2, q)   Insert(Store(L3,3,b),2,q)
                    3 > 2, Store(Insert(L3,2,q),4,b)
                      Store(Insert(Store(L2,2,x),2,q),4,b)
                    2 = 2, Store(Store(Store(L2,2,q),3,x),4,b)

11. **structure**   UnsortedList (of ItemType)

interface	Create	→ UnsortedList
	Make(UnsortedList, ItemType)	→ UnsortedList
	Last(UnsortedList)	→ ItemType
	Leader(UnsortedList)	→ UnsortedList
	Concat(UnsortedList, UnsortedList)	→ UnsortedList
	IsEmpty(UnsortedList)	→ Boolean
	Length(UnsortedList)	→ Integer

     end

     axioms   **for all L1, L2 in UnsortedList, i in ItemType, let**
    IsEmpty(Create) = True
    IsEmpty(Make(L1, i)) = False
    Last(Create) = Error
    Last(Make(L1, i)) = i
    Leader(Create) = Error
    Leader(Make(L1, i)) = L1
    Length(Create) = 0
    Length(Make(L1, i)) = 1 + Length(L1)
    Concat(L1, Create) = L1
    Concat(L1, Make(L2, i)) = Make(Concat(L1, L2), i)

12. Pascal version

```
PROCEDURE PrintFacMatrices(Min : TwoDArrayType; i, j : Integer);

VAR
    k : Integer;
BEGIN
 IF i = j
    THEN (* factor of 1 *)
      BEGIN
        Write('M');
        Write(i)
      END
    ELSE
      BEGIN
        Write('(');
        k := Min[i,j].k;
        PrintFacMatrices(Min, i, k);
        Write('*');
        PrintFacMatrices(Min, k + 1, j);
        Write(')');
      END
END;
```

13. ((A*[B*(C*D)))*(E*F))

16. Single, sorted list of triples.

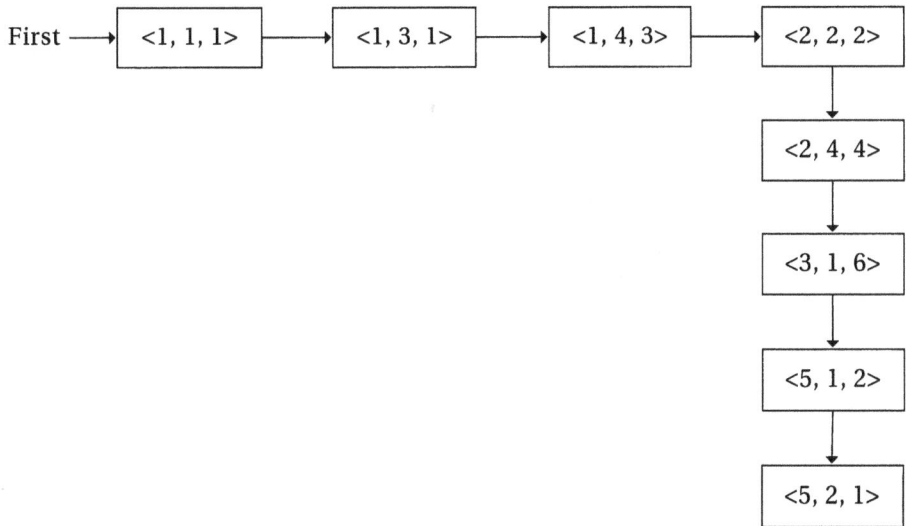

Single, sorted list of triples, with additional row pointers.

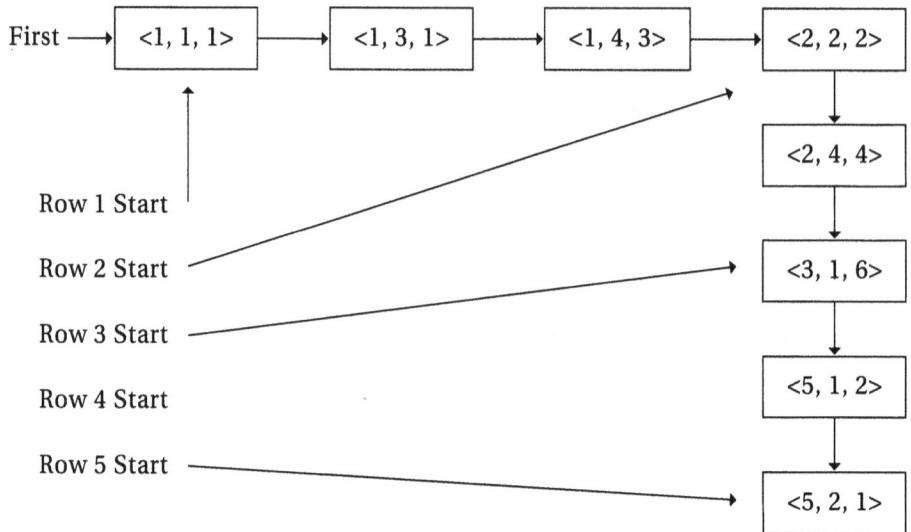

First → | <1, 1, 1> | → | <1, 3, 1> | → | <1, 4, 3> | → | <2, 2, 2> |

| <2, 4, 4> |

Row 1 Start

Row 2 Start → | <3, 1, 6> |

Row 3 Start

Row 4 Start → | <5, 1, 2> |

Row 5 Start → | <5, 2, 1> |

Sorted list of pairs, with row pointers.

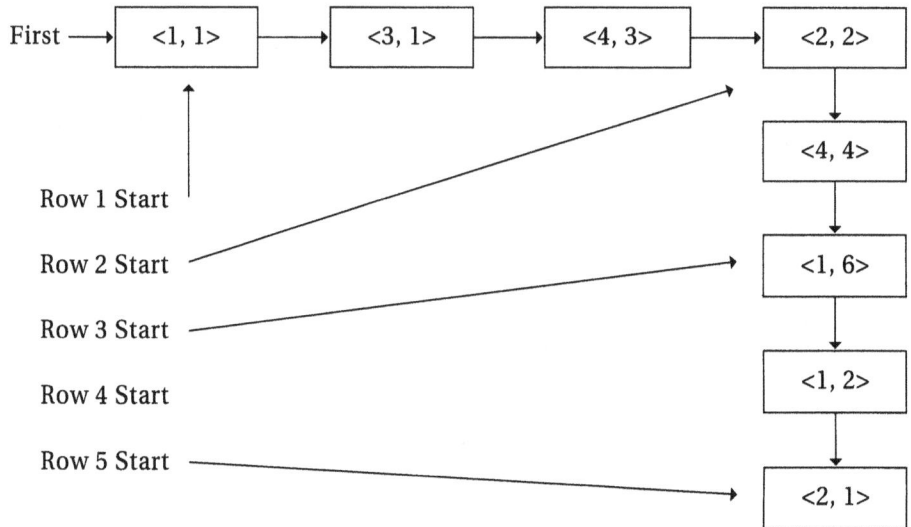

First → | <1, 1> | → | <3, 1> | → | <4, 3> | → | <2, 2> |

| <4, 4> |

Row 1 Start

Row 2 Start → | <1, 6> |

Row 3 Start

Row 4 Start → | <1, 2> |

Row 5 Start → | <2, 1> |

Separate, sorted lists of pairs or triples, with a separate list for each row.

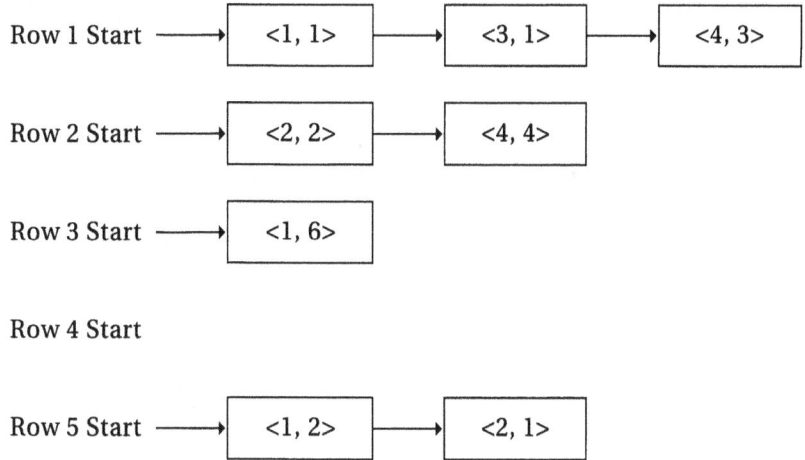

Row 1 Start ⟶ | <1, 1> | ⟶ | <3, 1> | ⟶ | <4, 3> |

Row 2 Start ⟶ | <2, 2> | ⟶ | <4, 4> |

Row 3 Start ⟶ | <1, 6> |

Row 4 Start

Row 5 Start ⟶ | <1, 2> | ⟶ | <2, 1> |

Pairs or triples stored in lists both by row and by column, with first pointers stored in arrays.

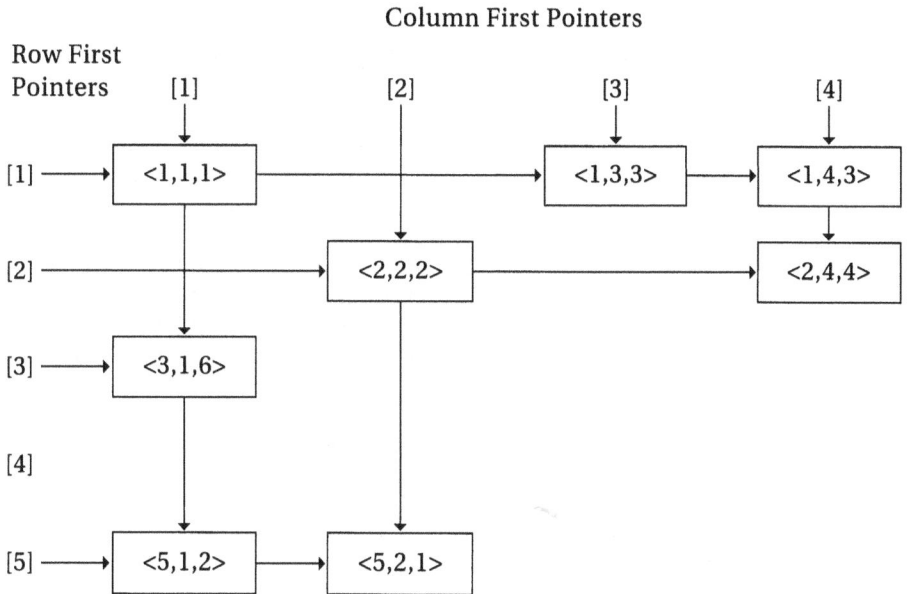

Column First Pointers

Row First Pointers	[1]	[2]	[3]	[4]
[1] ⟶	<1,1,1>		<1,3,3>	<1,4,3>
[2] ⟶		<2,2,2>		<2,4,4>
[3] ⟶	<3,1,6>			
[4]				
[5] ⟶	<5,1,2>	<5,2,1>		

Pairs or triples stored in lists both by row and by column, with first pointers stored in linked lists.

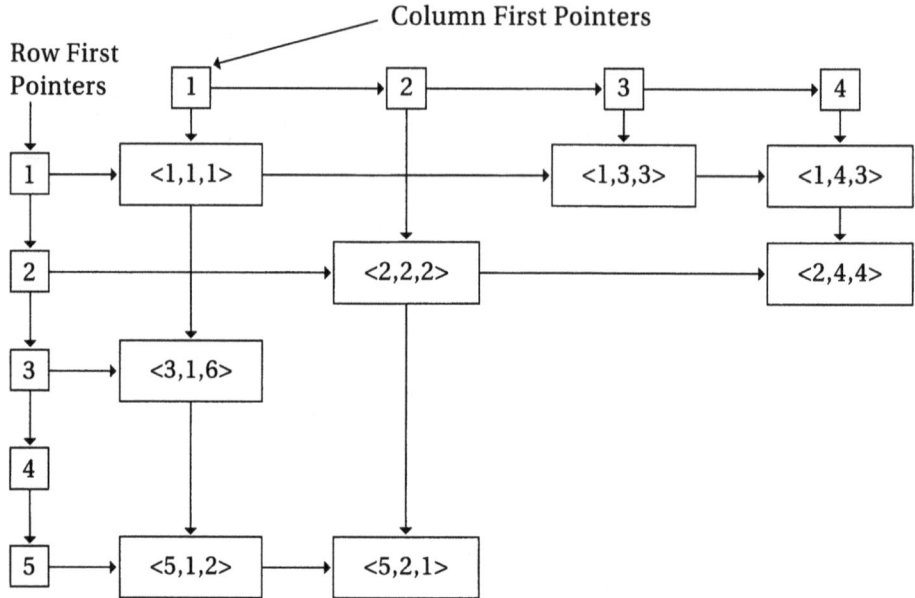

20. Copy(Sequence) → Sequence
    Copy(Create) = Create
    Copy(Store(S, v1, i1)) = Store(Copy(S), v1, i1)

26. The axioms given here for IsSubSequence keep matching until an unequal pair is found. When this occurs, the search begins again with the substring, including the unmatched item and the target string (the string without the unmatched item). For example, if S1 = (a, b, c, a, d, b) and S2 = (a, c), then the axioms would work as follows:

	IsSubSequence(S1, S2)	IsSubSequence(Insert(S1, a), Insert(S2, a))
a = a:	IsSubSequence(S1, S2)	IsSubSequence(Insert(S1, b), Insert(S2, c))
b <> c:	IsSubSequence(S1, Insert(S2, c))	IsSubSequence(Insert(S1, c), Insert(S2, c))
c = c:	IsSubSequence(S1, S2)	IsSubSequence(Insert(S1, a), Create)
		True

These axioms specify that the characters in a subsequence do not have to be consecutive.

27. Store(Store(Store(Store(Store(Create, c), e, d, a, b).

28. S: Append(Store(Store(Store(Create, 1, a), 2, b), 3, c), d)
    Append(Store(S, 3, c), d)
    SubStr(S, 1, 2) =   SubString(Append(S, d), 1, 2)   2 < 4
    SubStr(S, 1, 2) =   SubString(Append(S, c), 1, 2)   2 < 3
    SubStr(S, 1, 2) =   Substring(Append(S, b), 1, 2)   2 = 2
    Append(SubSstr(S, 1, 1), b) =   Append(SubStr(Append(S, a), 1, 1), b)   1 = 1
    Append(Append(SubStr(S, 1, 0), a), b) =   Append(Append(SubStr(Create, 1, 0), a), b)
    Append(Append(Create), a), b)

Chapter 7

1. Leaf: a node with no children (out-degree 0)
   Degree: the number of children (edges incident to (or from) a vertex)
   Sibling: nodes that share a common parent
   Ancestor, Descendant: if there is a directed path from node a to node b in a tree, then node a is said to be an ancestor of b, and b is a descendant of a
   Level: the distance between the node and the root
   Full tree: a tree in which all of the leaves are on the same level and every nonleaf node has two children
   Complete tree: a tree that is either full or full through the next-to-last level, with the leaves on the last level as far left as possible

2. a. $2^{n+1} - 1$
   b. 2^i

4. **structure**   bTree (of ItemType)
   interface   Create   → bTree
                   Make (bTree, ItemType, bTree)   → bTree
                   lChild(bTree)   → bTree
                   rChild(bTree)   → bTree
                   Root (bTree)   → ItemType
                   Insert(bTree, ItemType)   → bTree
                   Find (bTree, ItemType)   → Boolean
   end
   axioms   for all l, r in bTree, i, i1, and i2 in ItemType, let
     lChild (Create) = Error
     lChild (Make(l,i,r)) = l
     rChild (Create) = Error
     rChild (Make(l,i,r)) = r
     Root (Create) = Error
     Root (Make(l,i,r)) = i
     Insert (Create, i1) = Make(Create, i1, Create)
     Insert (Make(l,i2,r), i1) =
       IF i1<i2
         THEN
           Make(Insert(l, i1), i2, r)
         ELSE
           Make(l, i2, Insert(r, i1))
     Find (Create,i1) = False
     Find (Make(l,i2,r), i1) =
       IF i1 = i2
         THEN   True
         ELSE IF i1< i2
           THEN
             Find (l, i1)
           ELSE
             Find (r, i1)
   end

5. PostOrd (bTree)   → queue
   PreOrd (bTree)   → queue
   InOrd (bTree)   → queue

axioms   **for all l,r in bTree, i in Item, let**
  PostOrd (Create) = Create
  PostOrd (Make(l,i,r)) =
    Append(Append(PostOrd(l), PostOrd(r)), Enque(Create,i))
  or
    Enque(Append(PostOrd(l), PostOrd(r)), i)

  PreOrd (Create) = Create
  PreOrd (Make(l,i,r)) =
    Append(Append(Enque(Create, i), PreOrd(l)), PreOrd(r))

  InOrd (Create) = Create
  InOrd (Make(l,i,r)) =
    Append(Append(InOrd(l), Enque(Create,i)), InOrd(r))

7.

Insert(Node, Parent : NotePtr)

```
IF Node.Info < Parent.Info
  THEN
     SetLeftThread(Node, Left(Parent))
     SetRightThread(Node, Parent)
     SetLeft(Parent) to Node
  ELSE
     SetRightThread(Node, Right(Parent))
     SetLeftThread(Node, Parent)
     SetRight(Parent) to Node
```

10. One problem of the linked representation of any binary tree is that much space is wasted in null pointers. One way to use this space is to replace the null point with pointers to other nodes in the tree. These pointers are called threads, and the resulting tree is called a threaded binary tree. Specifically, a null left link at a node is replaced by a pointer to its immediate in-order predecessor. A null right link at a node is replaced by a pointer to its immediate in-order successor. Two Boolean fields are added to each node to distinguish between threads and regular pointers. As a result, no additional stack is needed to find the immediate successor (or predecessor) of an arbitrary node in a threaded binary tree.

12. Find the immediate predecessor of Node:

```
IF Left (Node) is a thread
  THEN
     Predecessor ← Left (Node)
  ELSE
     Temp ← Left (Node)
     WHILE Right (Temp) is NOT a thread
        Temp ← Right (Temp)
     Predecessor ← Temp
END IF
```

14.

Header

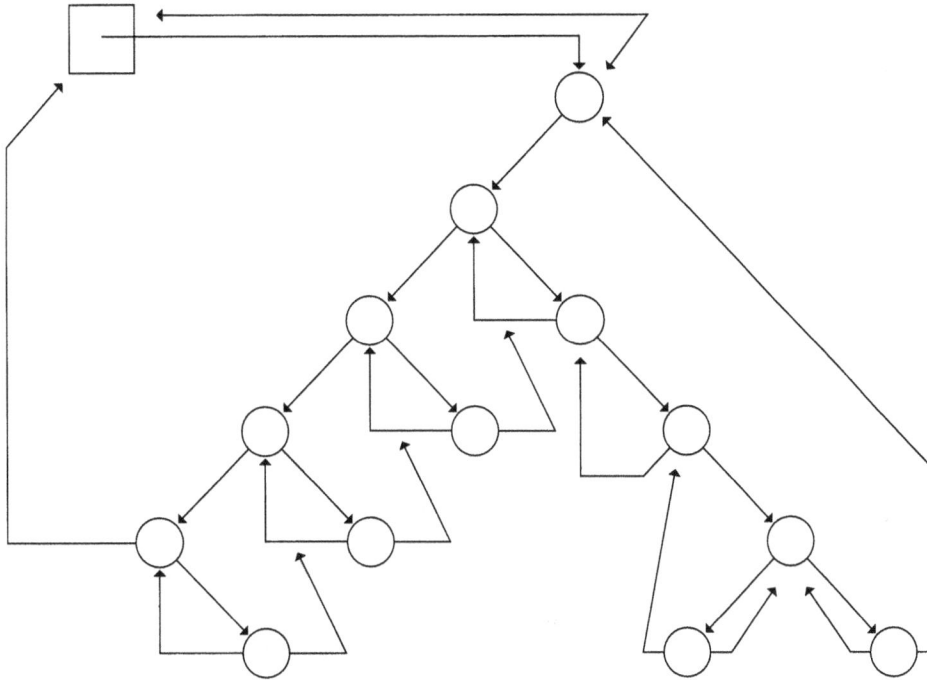

18.

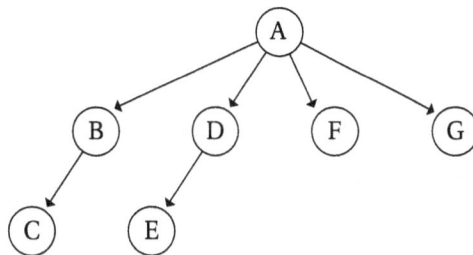

19. Next right sibling in the original tree.

20. Left-most child in the original tree.

29. We keep a module variable MaxNodes that is adjusted by Insert and Delete, which contains the maximum number of nodes in a full tree with the same number of levels as currently in the heap. Rather than insert recursively, we use an iterative algorithm that adjusts the maximum number of nodes each time it moves right or left.

Full (Index: HeapNodes): Boolean;

TempMax is initialized to MaxNodes before first call to Full and kept current.

If the subtree beginning at AHeap.Heap[NodeIndex} is full, True is returned; False is returned otherwise. This function accesses the global variable TempMax, which gives the maximum number of nodes for the subtree of a given height.

```
Full ← AHeap.Length >= TempMax + TempMax DIV 2 + Index
```

Insert (VAR AHeap: HeapType, Item: ItemType)

A careful examination of the general axiom for insert shows that the OR condition takes care of the case where the initial tree is full. A tree cannot be full and one of its subtrees not full. We can set a Boolean flag for this case rather than call Full at each level.

```
TempMax ← MaxNodes
NodeIndex ← 1
TreeFull ← AHeap.Length = MaxNodes
WHILE NodeIndex < AHeap.Length DO
   NodeIndex ← NodeIndex*2
   IF NOT Full(NodeIndex) OR TreeFull
      THEN (* go left *)
        IF Item > AHeap.Heap[NodeIndex]
           THEN Swap(Item, AHeap.Heap[NodeIndex])
        END IF;
      ELSE (* go right *)
        NodeIndex ← NodeIndex + 1
        IF Item > AHeap.Heap[NodeIndex]
           THEN Swap(Item, AHeap.Heap[NodeIndex])
        END IF;
   END IF
   TempMax ← TempMax DIV 2
END WHILE
AHeap.Length ← AHeap.Length + 1
AHeap.Heap[AHeap.Length] ← Item
IF TreeFull (* level is added *)
   THEN MaxNodes ← MaxNodes*2 + 1
END IF
```

32. Merge(Create, L2) = L2
    Merge(L1, Create) = L1
    Merge(Make(L1, i1), Make(L2, i2)) =
       IF i1 < i2
         THEN
           Make(Merge(L1, Make(L2, i2)), i1)
         ELSE
           Make(Merge(Make(L1, i1), L2), i2)

Chapter 8

1. We assume a binary tree in which a single record is stored at each node of the tree. A binary search tree is constructed so that if node b is the left child of any node a, then the key of every descendant of b (including b itself) is less than the key of a. On the other hand, if node b is the right child of node a, then the key of every descendant of b is greater than or equal to the key of a.

3. a.

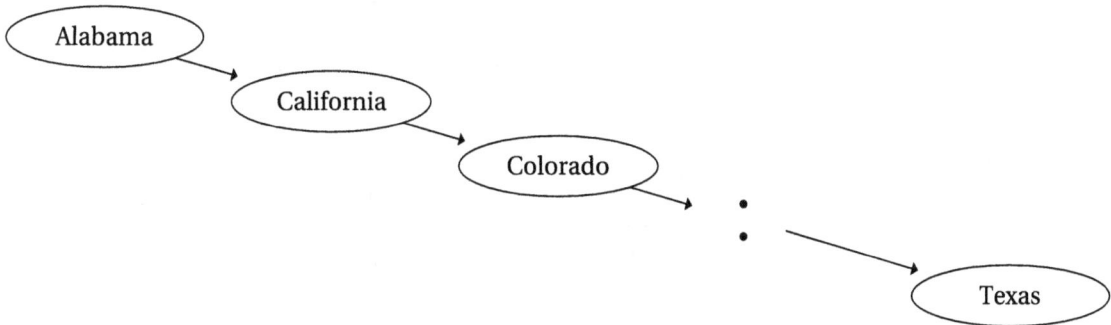

b. $(1 + 2 + 3 + \ldots + 12)/12 = 78/12 = 6.57$

5. a.

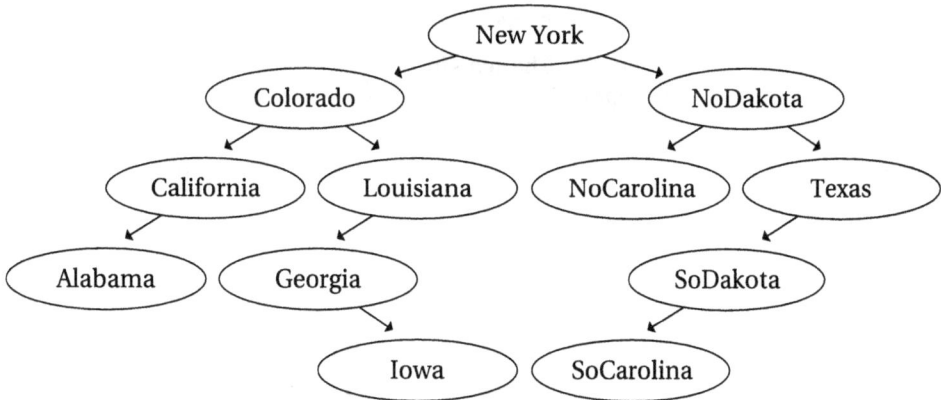

b. $(1 + 2*2 + 3*4 + 4*3 + 5*2)/12 = 3.25$

6. Extended tree for Exercise 5.

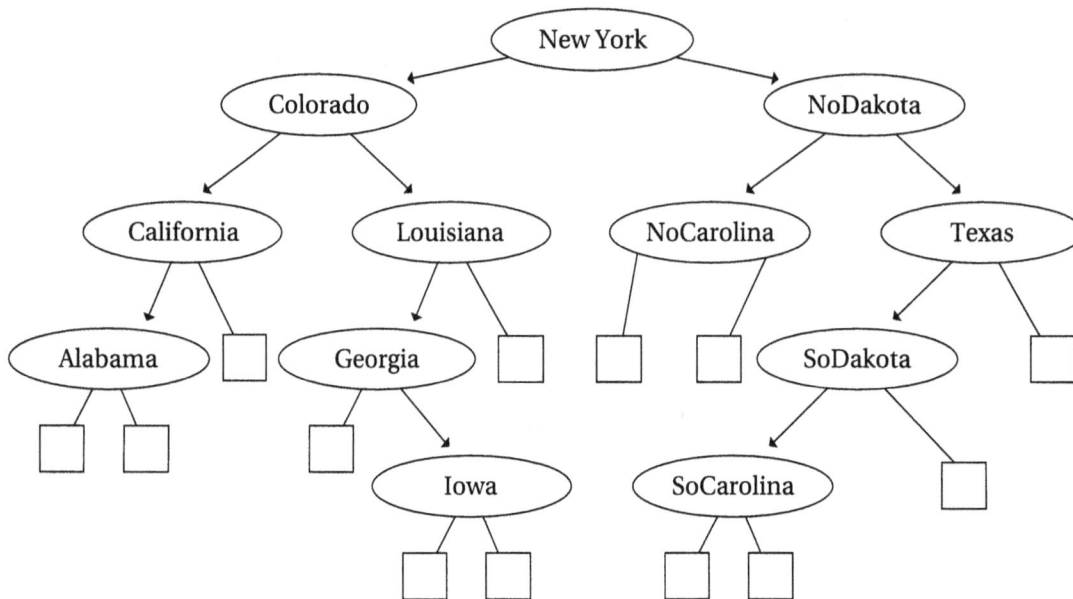

7. $I = 1 * 2 + 2 * 4 + 3 * 5$ $= 25$

    $E = 3 * 3 + 4 * 10$ $= 49$

    $I = 1 * 2 + 2 * 4 + 3 * 3 + 4 * 2$ $= 27$

    $E = 3 * 5 + 4 * 4 + 5 * 4$ $= 51$

10. *Static BST:* The items in the tree and their distribution as known. The contents and shape do not change.

   Dynamic BST: The items in the tree and their distribution are unknown. The contents and shape of the tree are constantly changing.

11. $[1 * 3 + 2 * (2 + 7) + 3 * (3 + 2 + 1 + 3) + 4 * (1 + 5 + 2) + 5 * (7 + 4)]/12 = 11.25$

14.

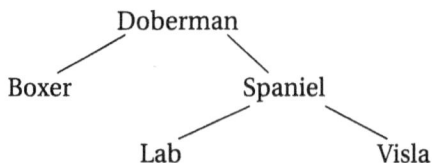

18. An AVL tree is a binary search tree in which for every node the heights of the left and right subtrees differ by no more than 1.

19.

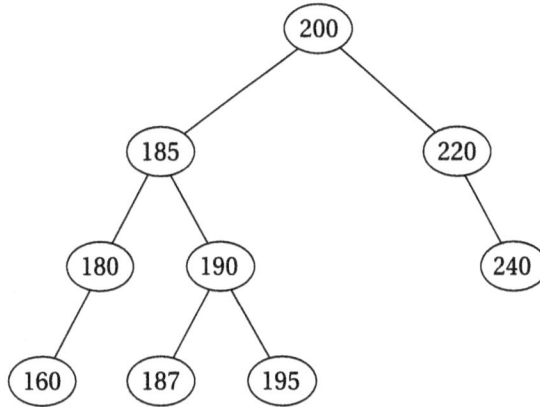

27. a. H
    b.

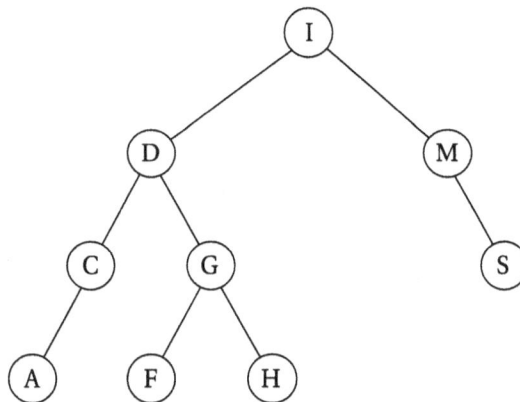

28. N is the number of the items in consideration. Forest is the list of extended binary trees with weights in their nodes.

```
FOR Count going from 1 to N − 1 DO
    Get a node (T)
    Get a tree with minimum weight from Forest (T1)
    Remove T1 from Forest
    Left (T) ← T1
```

> Get a tree with minimum weight from Forest (T2)
> Remove T2 from Forest
> Right (T) ← T2
> Weight (T) ← Weight (T1) + Weight (T2)
> Insert T into Forest
> END FOR

29.

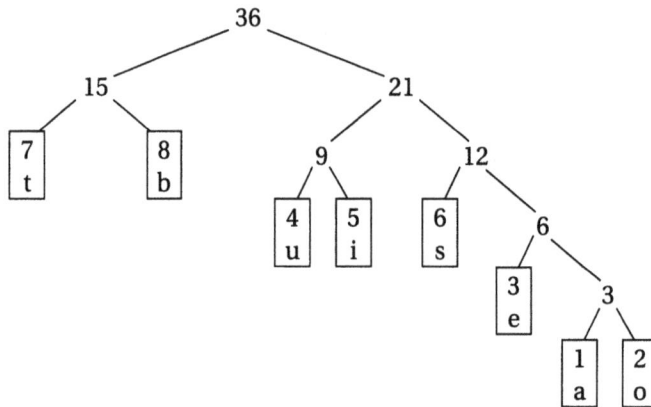

30.
t	00	s	110
b	01	e	1110
u	100	a	11110
i	101	o	11111

31. 01111000101001011101111011010100101110

32. bitbetbatboo

33. None of the shorter codes duplicates the beginning of the longer codes.

Chapter 9

1. In addition to the search property, a 2/3 tree has the following properties:

   All leaf nodes are at the same level;
   There must be at least one value in each node; and
   All values are inserted into leaf nodes.

2. A B-tree is an M-way search tree with the following properties:

   The root node has at least 2 children;
   All nodes other than the root node have at least $\lceil M/2 \rceil$ children;
   All nodes have at most M children;
   All failure nodes are at the same level; and
   The number of keys is one less than the number of children.

3. A B-tree is a multiway search tree where the insertion and deletion algorithms keep the search tree balanced with respect to structure and to the distribution of keys over the structure.

4. A B+-tree is a B-tree where the nonleaf nodes are used purely for indexing. Each key that is in the nonleaf nodes is repeated in a leaf node. The pointers in the nonleaf nodes all point to nodes in the tree. The pointers in the leaf nodes point to where the information associated with the keys can be found.

7. The middle subtree must be null, because any data item in this subtree must be both greater than or equal to the first value in the node and less than the second value in the node. If these values are equal, no data value could meet these requirements.

15. a.

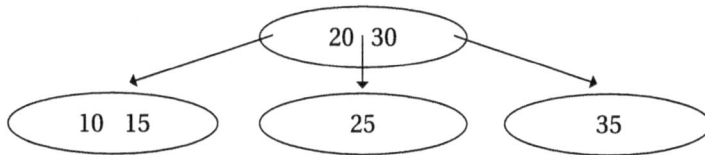

b.

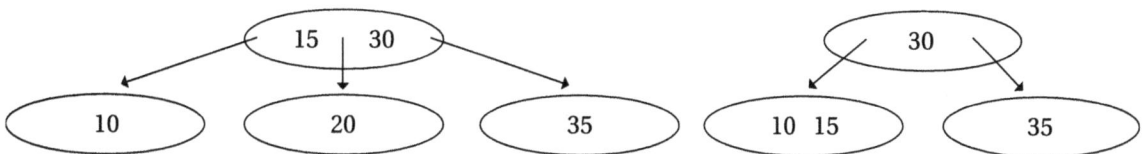

21.

Insertion (VAR Tree: TreeType, Key: KeyType)

```
Insert(Tree, Key, Split, MiddleKey, NewNode)
IF Split
    Get NewNode
    Left-most child ← Tree
    Next child ← NewNode
    First Key ← MiddleKey
END IF
```

Insert(VAR Tree: TreeType, Key: KeyType, Split: Boolean,

   MiddleKey: KeyType, NewNode: NodeType)

```
IF Tree is a leaf
    THEN
        IF Number of keys < M − 1
            THEN
                Insert Key
                Split ← False
            ELSE
                Get NewNode
                Leave (M − 1)/2 + 1 keys in Tree
                Move (M − 1)/2 keys to NewNode
                MiddleKey ← Middle Value
                Split ← True
        END IF
    ELSE
        Find Path(NextTree)
        Insertion(NextTree, Key, Split, MiddleVaue, NewNode)
        IF Split
            THEN
                IF Number of keys in Tree < M − 1
                    THEN
                        Insert Key w/pointer
                        Split ← False
                    ELSE
                        Get NewNode
                        Leave (M − 1)/2 keys in Tree
                        Move (M − 1)/2 keys to NewNode
                        MiddleKey ← Middle Value
                        Split ← True
                END IF
        END IF
END IF
```

DeleteKey (Tree: TreeType, Key: KeyType)

```
Delete(NIL, Tree, Key)
    IF Tree has only a Left Pointer
        THEN
            Tree ← Left Pointer
    END IF
```

Delete (Parent, Tree, Key)

```
IF Tree is a leaf
   THEN
      Remove key
      IF Tree contains < M/2 − 1 keys
         THEN
            PatchUp(Parent, Tree)
         ELSE
            Find Path(NextTree)
            Delete(Tree, NextTree, Key)
            IF Tree contains < M/2 − 1 keys
               THEN
                  PatchUp(Parent, Tree)
            END IF
      END IF
END IF
```

PatchUp (Parent, Node: NodeType)

```
IF Right Sibling exists AND has ≥ IM/2I − 1 keys
   THEN
      Borrow from Right(Parent, Node, Right)
   ELSE
      IF Left Sibling exists AND has ≥ IM/2I − 1 keys
         THEN
            Borrow from Left(Parent, Node, Left)
         ELSE
            IF Right Sibling exists
               THEN
                  Coalesce(Parent, Node, Right)
               ELSE
                  Coalesce(Parent, Left, Node)
            END IF
      END IF
END IF
```

Coalesce (Parent, Node1, Node2: NodeType)

```
Move Keys from Node2 into Node1
Remove Separator and Node1 pointer from Parent
```

BorrowFromRight (Node, Right: NodeType)

```
MoveKey LeftMostKey of Right
Move MoveKey to Node
Replace Separator in Parent with MoveKey
```

BorrowFromLeft (Node, Left: NodeType)

```
Move RightMostKey of Left to Node
Replace Separator in Parent with RightMostKey in Left
```

Chapter 10

2. directed, not complete, not strongly connected

3. a.

	A	B	C	D	E	F	G	H
A	0	1	1	1	0	0	0	0
B	0	0	0	0	0	0	0	1
C	0	0	0	0	0	1	0	0
D	0	0	0	0	0	1	0	0
E	0	0	0	0	0	0	0	0
F	0	0	1	0	1	0	0	1
G	0	0	0	0	0	0	0	0
H	0	0	0	0	1	0	0	0

Squared

	A	B	C	D	E	F	G	H
A	0	0	0	0	0	2	0	1
B	0	0	0	0	1	0	0	0
C	0	0	1	0	1	0	0	1
D	0	0	1	0	1	0	0	1
E	0	0	0	0	0	0	0	0
F	0	0	0	0	1	1	0	0
G	0	0	0	0	0	0	0	0
H	0	0	0	0	0	0	0	0

Cubed

	A	B	C	D	E	F	G	H
A	0	0	2	0	3	0	0	2
B	0	0	0	0	0	0	0	0
C	0	0	0	0	1	1	0	0
D	0	0	0	0	1	1	0	0
E	0	0	0	0	0	0	0	0
F	0	0	1	0	1	0	0	1
G	0	0	0	0	0	0	0	0
H	0	0	0	0	0	0	0	0

4.

[A] ⟶ B ⟶ C ⟶ D

[B] ⟶ H

[C] ⟶ F

[D] ⟶ F

[E]

[F] ⟶ C ⟶ E ⟶ H

[G]

[H] ⟶ E

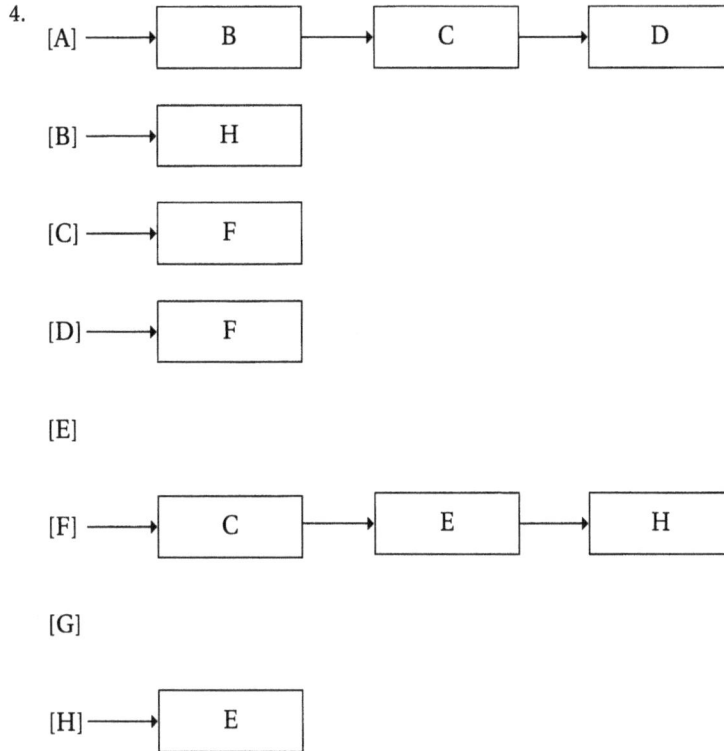

5. a. There are twelve paths of length 2:

A, B, H   A, C, F   A, D, F   B, H, E   C, F, E   C, F, C
C, F, H   D, F, C   D, F, E   D, F, H   F, C, F   F, H, E

There are fourteen paths of length 3:

A, B, H, E   A, C, F, C   A, C, F, E   A, C, F, H   A, D, F, C
A, D, F, E   A, D, F, H   C, F, C, F   C, F, H, E   D, F, C, F
D, F, H, E   F, C, F, C   F, C, F, E   F, C, F, H

b. In the squared adjacency matrix, [A, F] contains 2. This means that there are two paths of length 2 that begin with A and end with F. An examination of those listed in part a shows this to be the case. This pattern is true for each nonzero slot in the squared adjacency matrix.

    In the cubed adjacency matrix, [A, C] contains 2. This means that there are two paths of length 3 beginning with A and ending with C. An examination of those listed in part a shows this to be the case. This pattern is true for each nonzero slot in the cubed adjacency matrix.

7.

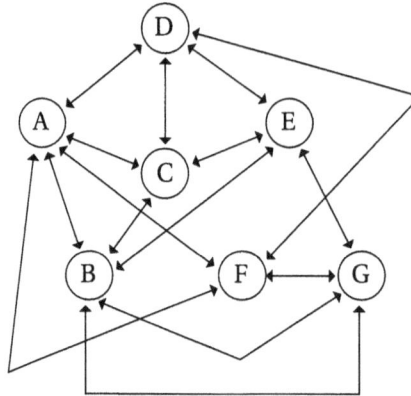

8. We know that it is directed because of the statement before Exercise 7. However, we cannot tell from the adjacency matrix itself. If the matix is not symmetric, we know that it is directed. If the matrix is symmetric, the graph could be directed or undirected.

9. A B C E E G F

10. A B C D F E G

16. $1 \rightarrow 2$ (cost 10)

     $1 \rightarrow 2 \rightarrow 5$ (cost 30)

     $1 \rightarrow 2 \rightarrow 5 \rightarrow 4$ (cost 45)

     $1 \rightarrow 2 \rightarrow 3$ (cost 70)

17. a. 4, 3, 5
    b. 1
    c. 1, 2, 3, 5, 4

18. a. Computer Science I, Computer Science II, Computer Organization, Theory of Computation, Algorithms & Data Types, Operating Systems, Compiler Design, Programming Languages
    b. Computer Science I, Computer Science II, Computer Organization, Algorithms & Data Types, Programming Languages, Compiler Design, Operating Systems, Theory of Computation
    c. Calculus I, Calculus II, Computer Science I, Computer Science II, Discrete Mathematics, Computer Organization, Algorithms & Data Types, Operating Systems, Programming Languages, Theory of Computation, Compiler Design
    d. A Hamiltonian Circuit does not exist, as there is no edge into Computer Science I (or into Calculus I).

21. a. If VertexNumber = 0, IsEmpty is True. However, IsEmpty can be true when VertexNumber <> 0, because VertexNumber is incremented when each new vertex is entered but is not decremented.
    b. If VertexNumber exceeds MaxVertices, the program must halt. The implementation of ADT KeyedTable may check for this problem and raise an ERROR. If not, the StoreEdge crashes because no check exists for this error condition.

c. This scheme gives the proper number of vertices, but the correspondence between the external name and the internal name of the vertices is destroyed.

d. When a vertex is deleted, its internal name should be put on a list of free names. New internal names should be assigned from this list first. VertexNumber should be increased only when the list of names is empty. If VertexNumber minus the number of items in the list of free names is 0, IsEmpty is true.

24. a. A^{N-1} could be all zero. For example, suppose a graph has N vertices $\{1, 2, \ldots, N\}$ with vertex i connected to vertex $i + 1$ by a directed edge for $i = 1, 2, \ldots, N - 2$. A^{N-2} is nonzero, as there is a path of length $N - 2$ from vertex 1 to vertex $N - 1$. However, because it is the longest path in the graph, there is no path of length $N - 1$. Hence $A^{N-1} = 0$ for this graph.

b. A^N cannot have any zero entries. The proof follows.

Any entry $A^N[i,j]$ gives the number of paths from vertex i to vertex j. If all entries of A^{N-1} are nonzero, then there is a path from vertex i to vertex j of length $N - 1$. Let vertex k be the first vertex after vertex i along this path. By construction, there is an edge from vertex i to vertex k. Next, $A^{N-1}[k,j]$ is nonzero by hypotheses, so there must be a path of length $N - 1$ from vertex k to vertex j. Putting these pieces together, we can construct a path of length N from vertex i to vertex j (first go to vertex k in one step, then go from k to j in $N - 1$ steps). As $A^N[i,j]$ counts the number of paths from vertex i to vertex j of length N, this matrix entry must be at least one. Therefore, this entry cannot be zero, and we conclude no entry of A^N can be zero.

c. No entries of A^M can be zero. The argument for part b can be extended by mathematical induction to any $M \geq N$.

26. a.

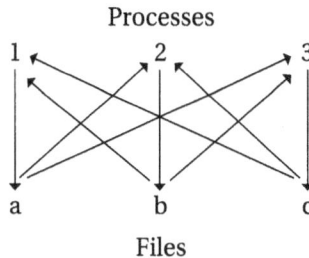

Processes

a   b   c

Files

b. Suppose there is a cycle in the resource allocation graph, and a process P on this cycle. In considering the cycle, there must be an edge from some resource R to P. However, the edge to R on the cycle indicates that R has been allocated to some other process S. Since only one process can use a resource at any given time, P cannot continue until S releases R. Similarly, S must be waiting for another resource, which is held by another process. Following the cycle through all processes, none of the identified processes can continue as each is waiting for another resource. Each resource, in turn, is held by one of these same processes. In short, no process can continue until other work is done, but no other relevant work can be done—a situation described as a deadlock.

c. Label processes $P_1, P_2, \ldots, P_N$ and label resources $R_1, R_2, \ldots, R_N$. Suppose each process P_i has been allocated resources R_i and suppose each process also requests the next resource (in other words, P_1 requests R_2, P_2 requests $R_3, \ldots, P_{N-1}$ requests R_N and P_N requests R_1. This gives a cycle involving each of the N processes.

Processes

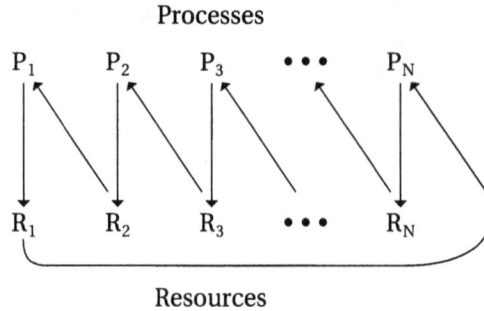

Resources

d. From part b, an algorithm that detects cycles in a resource-allocation graph can conclude that a potential deadlock may occur. While many such algorithms exist, one would compute successive powers of the adjacency matrix and examine entries on the diagonal. For any cycle, there would be a path from a vertex to itself, which would be reflected as a nonzero entry on the diagonal. As a second approach, any path without a cycle could not be of length N for a graph of N vertices. Thus, if a graph is acyclic, then the Nth power of its adjacency matrix would have to be 0. In contrast, graphs containing cycles have paths of any length, so the Nth power of the adjacency matrix would contain nonzero entries. A third such algorithm would perform a search similar to that discussed for finding Hamiltonian circuits, although the search would look for cycles containing fewer than N vertices.

27. On a complete digraph, start at any vertex. A Hamiltonian circuit could go to any $N - 1$ vertices. The circuit would then go to any of the remaining $N - 2$ vertices, then to any of the remaining $N - 3$ vertices, and so forth. The total number of such circuits, therefore, is $(N - 1)(N - 2)(N - 3) \ldots 2 * 1 = (N - 1)!$.

29. $O(N*E)$ $O(N^2)$ $O(E)$

30. $O(N*E)$ $O(N^2)$ $O(E)$

31. $O(N*E)$ $O(N^2)$ $O(N^2)$

34. $O(E)$ $O(1)$ $O(N)$

35. $O(1)$ average case $O(N)$ worst case

38. $O(N)$

41. $O(\log N)$

43. $O(N)$

45. Supporting structure:

```
TYPE
   MarkedArray = ARRAY[1.. MaxVertices] OF Boolean;
VAR
   Mark: MarkedArray;

PROCEDURE UnMark(Vertex: InternalType);
(* Pre: Vertix In V *)
(* Post: Mark(Vertex) is False *)
```

```
BEGIN
   Mark[Vertex] ←False
END;

PROCEDURE Mark(Vertex: InternalType);
(* Pre: Vertex In V *)
(* Post: Mark(Vertex) is True *)
BEGIN
   Mark[Vertex] ←True
END;

FUNCTION IsMarked(Vertex: InternalType) : Boolean;
(* Pre: Vertex in V *)
(* Post: IsMarked = Mark(Vertex) *)
BEGIN
   RETURN Mark[Vertex]
END;
```

48. StoreEdge(G, v1, v2, w) = [Store(Store(V(G), v1, v2), Store(E(G), v1, v2, w)]

Chapter 11

2. a. Proof that A^2 is symmetric. We show entries $A^2[i,j]$ and $A^2[j,i]$ are equal, given that A is symmetric.

$$A^2[i,j] = \sum_{k=1}^{N} A_{ik}A_{kj} \quad \text{by the definition of matrix multiplication}$$

$$= \sum_{k=1}^{N} A_{ki}A_{jk} \quad \text{since A is given to be symmetric}$$

$$= \sum_{k=1}^{N} A_{jk}A_{ki} \quad \text{since multiplication of real numbers is commutative}$$

$$= A^2[j,i] \quad \text{by the definition of matrix multiplication}$$

The other powers are shown to be symmetric using mathematical induction.
   Suppose A^r is known to be symmetric. We show A^{r+1} is also symmetric by showing entries [i,j] and [j,i] are equal.

$$A^{r+1}[i,j] = A*A^r[i,j] \qquad \text{by the definition of the r + 1st power of A and the associativity of matrix multiplication}$$

$$= \sum_{k=1}^{N} A_{ik}A^r_{kj} \qquad \text{by the definition of matrix multiplication}$$

$$= \sum_{k=1}^{N} A_{ki}A^r_{jk} \qquad \text{since A is given to be symmetric and } A^r \text{ is symmetric by the induction hypothesis}$$

$$= \sum_{k=1}^{N} A^r_{jk}A_{ki} \qquad \text{since multiplication of real numbers is commutative}$$

$$= A^r*A[j,i] \qquad \text{by the definition of matrix multiplication}$$

$$= A^{r+1}[j,i] \qquad \text{by the definition of the r + 1st power of A and the associativity of matrix multiplication}$$

b. AB need not be symmetric, as illustrated in the following example:

$$\begin{pmatrix} 1 & 2 \\ 2 & 1 \end{pmatrix} * \begin{pmatrix} 3 & 4 \\ 4 & 5 \end{pmatrix} = \begin{pmatrix} 11 & 14 \\ 10 & 13 \end{pmatrix}$$

A	B	AB
Symmetric		Not Symmetric

6. Parallel, depth-first traversal of Figure 11.1, beginning with vertex "Levy"

Start: Visited: None

     Stack: Levy

Step 1: Visited: Levy

     Stack: Oliver, Spencer, Steenrod

Step 2: Visited: Levy, Oliver

     Stack: Feeman, Hill, Spencer, Steenrod

Step 3: Visited: Levy, Oliver, Feeman

     Stack: Grabois, Steenrod, Hill, Spencer, Steenrod

Step 4: Visited: Grabois, Levy, Oliver, Feeman

     Stack: Hill, Peterson, Steenrod, Hill, Spencer, Steenrod

Step 5: Visited: Hill, Grabois, Levy, Oliver, Feeman

     Stack: Spencer, Peterson, Steenrod, Hill, Spencer, Steenrod

Step 6: Visited: Spencer, Hill, Grabois, Levy, Oliver, Feeman

     Stack: Peterson, Peterson, Steenrod, Hill, Spencer, Steenrod

Step 7: Visited: Peterson, Spencer, Hill, Grabois, Levy, Oliver, Feeman

     Stack: Steenrod, Peterson, Steenrod, Hill, Spencer, Steenrod

Step 8: Visited: Steenrod, Peterson, Spencer, Hill, Grabois, Levy, Oliver, Feeman

     Stack: Peterson, Steenrod, Hill, Spencer, Steenrod

Subsequent steps 9–13: One vertex popped off stack after each step.

8. a. The adjacency matrix A follows, with rows labeled and numbered and with columns having corresponding numbers.

(Row Number)	1	2	3	4	5	6	7	8
1. Feeman	0	2	0	0	7	0	0	8
2. Grabois	2	0	5	0	0	6	0	0
3. Hill	0	5	0	0	3	0	4	0
4. Levy	0	0	0	0	4	0	5	5
5. Oliver	7	0	3	4	0	0	0	0
6. Peterson	0	6	0	0	0	0	7	3
7. Spencer	0	0	4	5	0	7	0	0
8. Steenrod	8	0	0	5	0	3	0	0

b. In the following diagram, each processor specializes on one element of the array A. Processors are labeled by their position in the array and by the value they will process.

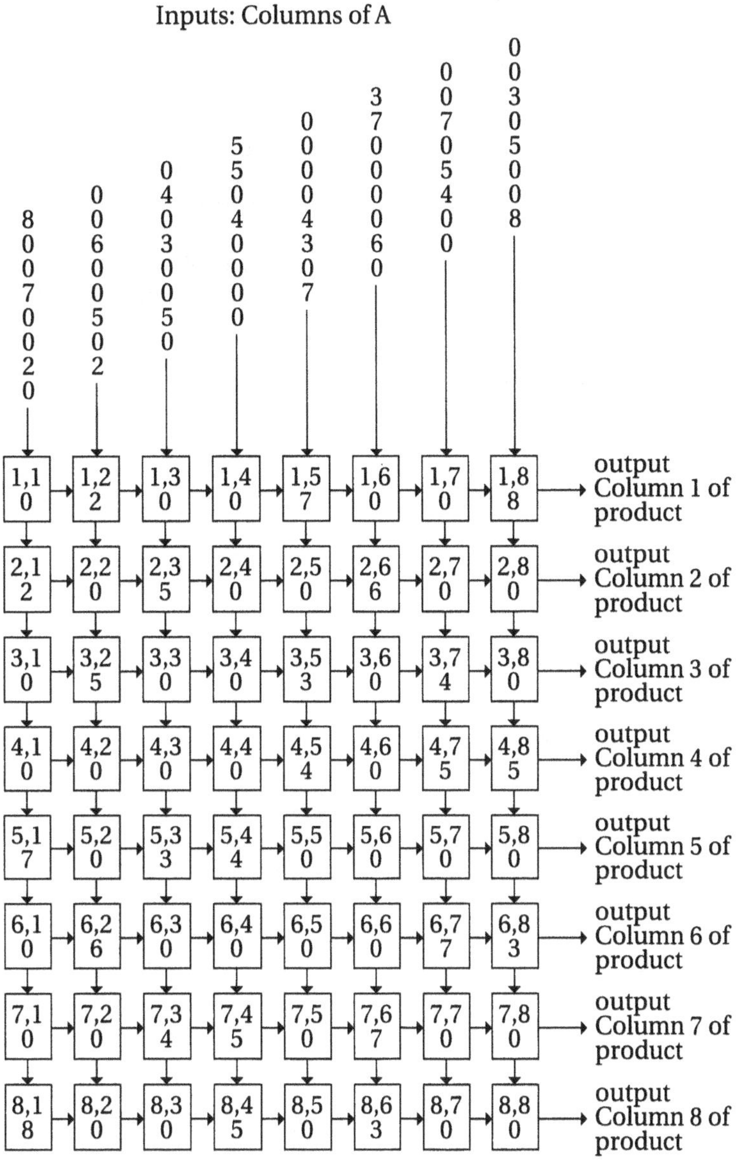

Inputs: Columns of A

Input columns (top to bottom):

- Column 1: 8 0 0 7 0 0 2 0
- Column 2: 0 0 6 0 0 5 0 2
- Column 3: 0 4 3 0 0 5 0
- Column 4: 5 5 0 4 0 0 0
- Column 5: 0 0 0 4 3 0 7
- Column 6: 3 7 0 0 0 6 0
- Column 7: 0 0 7 0 5 4 0
- Column 8: 0 0 3 0 5 0 0 8

Processor grid (each cell: position / value):

1,1 0	1,2 2	1,3 0	1,4 0	1,5 7	1,6 0	1,7 0	1,8 8	→ output Column 1 of product
2,1 2	2,2 0	2,3 5	2,4 0	2,5 0	2,6 6	2,7 0	2,8 0	→ output Column 2 of product
3,1 0	3,2 5	3,3 0	3,4 0	3,5 3	3,6 0	3,7 4	3,8 0	→ output Column 3 of product
4,1 0	4,2 0	4,3 0	4,4 0	4,5 4	4,6 0	4,7 5	4,8 5	→ output Column 4 of product
5,1 7	5,2 0	5,3 3	5,4 4	5,5 0	5,6 0	5,7 0	5,8 0	→ output Column 5 of product
6,1 0	6,2 6	6,3 0	6,4 0	6,5 0	6,6 0	6,7 7	6,8 3	→ output Column 6 of product
7,1 0	7,2 0	7,3 4	7,4 5	7,5 0	7,6 7	7,7 0	7,8 0	→ output Column 7 of product
8,1 8	8,2 0	8,3 0	8,4 5	8,5 0	8,6 3	8,7 0	8,8 0	→ output Column 8 of product

c. In the diagram, each processor takes a value received from the input above it, multiplies that value by the value at the node, adds the resulting product from the value received from the left processor, and sends the sum obtained to the right. Values at the top represent the rows of A, arranged in columns. Timing proceeds with A[1,1] being entered first into the first (upper left) cell of the processor mesh. Next A[1,2] is input to processor [1,1], while A[2,1] is entered into processor [1,2]. Subsequent rows of A are entered as columns, with each row starting one time until later than the previous one. This staggered start is illustrated by the alignment of the values at the top of the diagram.

9. a. There are six distinct Hamiltonian circuits:

   Levy-Steenrod-Peterson-Spencer-Hill-Grabois-Feeman-Oliver-Levy   Cost: 37
   Levy-Steenrod-Feeman-Grabois-Peterson-Spencer-Hill-Oliver-Levy   Cost: 39
   Levy-Spencer-Hill-Grabois-Peterson-Steenrod-Feeman-Oliver-Levy   Cost: 42
   Levy-Spencer-Peterson-Steenrod-Feeman-Grabois-Hill-Oliver-Levy   Cost: 37
   Levy-Steenrod-Feeman-Oliver-Hill-Grabois-Peterson-Spencer-Levy   Cost: 46
   Levy-Steenrod-Peterson-Grabois-Feeman-Oliver-Hill-Spencer-Levy   Cost: 35

   b. Clearly the last of these Hamiltonian circuits has the least cost.

12. undirected, not complete, not connected

13.

	A	B	C	D	E	F	G	H
A	0	1	0	1	0	1	0	0
B	1	0	0	0	0	1	0	0
C	0	0	0	0	1	0	0	1
D	1	0	0	0	0	1	0	0
E	0	0	1	0	0	0	1	1
F	1	1	0	1	0	0	0	0
G	0	0	0	0	1	1	0	0
H	0	0	1	0	0	1	0	0

14.

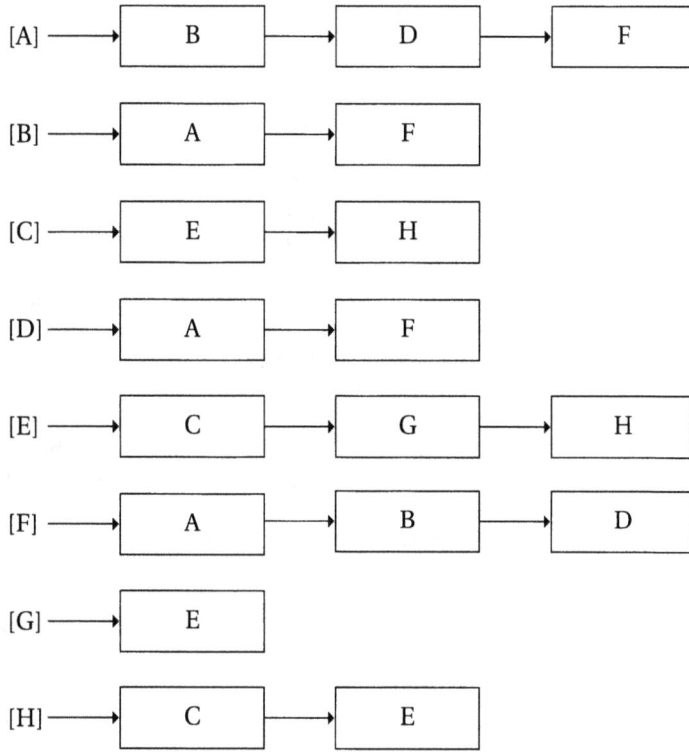

[A] →	B	D	F
[B] →	A	F	
[C] →	E	H	
[D] →	A	F	
[E] →	C	G	H
[F] →	A	B	D
[G] →	E		
[H] →	C	E	

15. A B F D

    C E G H

16.

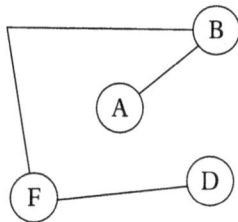
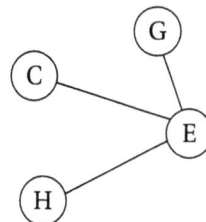

19. A B C D E G F

21. (A, B, 6), (A, D, 7), (D, C, 1), (C, G, 8), (D, F, 2), (D, E, 1)

25. Minimum cost spanning tree

27. a. Must hold: The construction of each step of the graph connects the starting and end-
        ing vertices. Thus at each stage, this property remains.
    b. Must hold: Same justification as part a.
    c. May hold: If A* is represented in the diagram, then edges are included that connect
        the ending vertex to the starting one. From part b, there is always a path from the
        start to all other vertices. Thus, in the representation of A*, a path leads from the end
        to the start and then to any other vertex desired. In contrast, the graph for {01} shows
        that some graphs may not have paths from the end to any other vertex. We conclude
        that some graphs have the desired property, while others do not.
    d. May hold: The examples in part c illustrate one case (A*) where the graph may be
        cyclic and another case {01} where no cycles exist.
    e. May hold: The topological sort applies to acyclic graphs. By part d, such graphs may
        or may not be acyclic.
    f. May hold: To have a Hamiltonian circuit, there must be an outward edge from
        every vertex. In particular, the ending vertex must have such an outward edge, a cir-
        cumstance that arises only when the graph has the form A*. Focusing on A*, the
        Hamiltonian circuit would have to go from End to Start, through A, and back to the
        end. Thus, the vertices of A must be on a line that follows a simple path from A's start
        to end; the path cannot contain duplicate vertices. Such paths are possible, as shown
        in the diagram for {01}* in the text. On the other hand, any use of the "or" construc-
        tion eliminates this possibility. For example the graph for {(0 + 1)}* contains no
        Hamiltonian circuit.

28. Any correct solution would have considerable significance and should be published
    quickly.

30. The existence of intractable problems implies that society cannot rely upon technology
    to solve all of the world's problems. Of course, technology can be helpful in many ways.
    However, one cannot assume that solutions always exist. In particular, managers and
    politicans should resist the temptation to plunge into expensive or critical technical

solutions without first determining if there is reason to believe that the problem has a tractable solution. For example, a politician may decide to allocate a large sum of money to support the solution of the Halting Problem, because that might seem politically popular. Such expenditures, however, cannot produce the desired result.

As a more concrete example, much discussion of the Strategic Defense Initiative (SDI) in the 1980s centered upon the desirability of a comprehensive defense shield. Many computer scientists believed, however, that the development of such a system was a problem that could not be solved. In such circumstances, politicans need to consider both technical possibility and political desirability. (For more information on such problems, see Henry M. Walker, *The Limits of Computing*, Jones and Bartlett, Boston, 1994, or David Bellin and Gary Chapman, *Computers in Battle—Will They Work*, Harcourt Brace Jovanovich, 1987.)

32. a. The diagram includes all strings in A^2. The proof follows.
    Let a be a string in A. We must show aa is represented in the given diagram. Since a is in A, there is a path through the graph

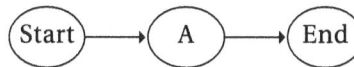

    that corresponds to string a. If we follow that path through each half of the diagram given in the figure, the resulting path represents aa, as required.
    b. The diagram given may produce additional strings. For example, suppose $A = \{0, 1\}$. In that case, $A^2 = \{00,11\}$. However, in the diagram, the string 0 gives one path through A and 1 gives rise to another such path. If we follow the first of these paths in the first half of the given diagram and the second path in the second half, then we have a path representing 01 that should not be included in A^2.

Chapter 12

2. a. (f e d c b a)
   b. The order of the elements on List (L) are reversed from those on L (with the parentheses removed), because components on L are processed by the axioms as they are identified and placed at the tail of the resulting list.
   c. Only the third axiom of List need be changed, reversing the order of elements listed in the Concat operation:

   List (PutFirst (GL1, c)) =
       IF WhichType(c) = Atom
           THEN   Make(List(GL1), c)
           ELSE   Concat (List(c), List(Gl1))
       END IF

4. In the following diagrams, we use the Head/Tail representation of lists with headers, as described in the text.

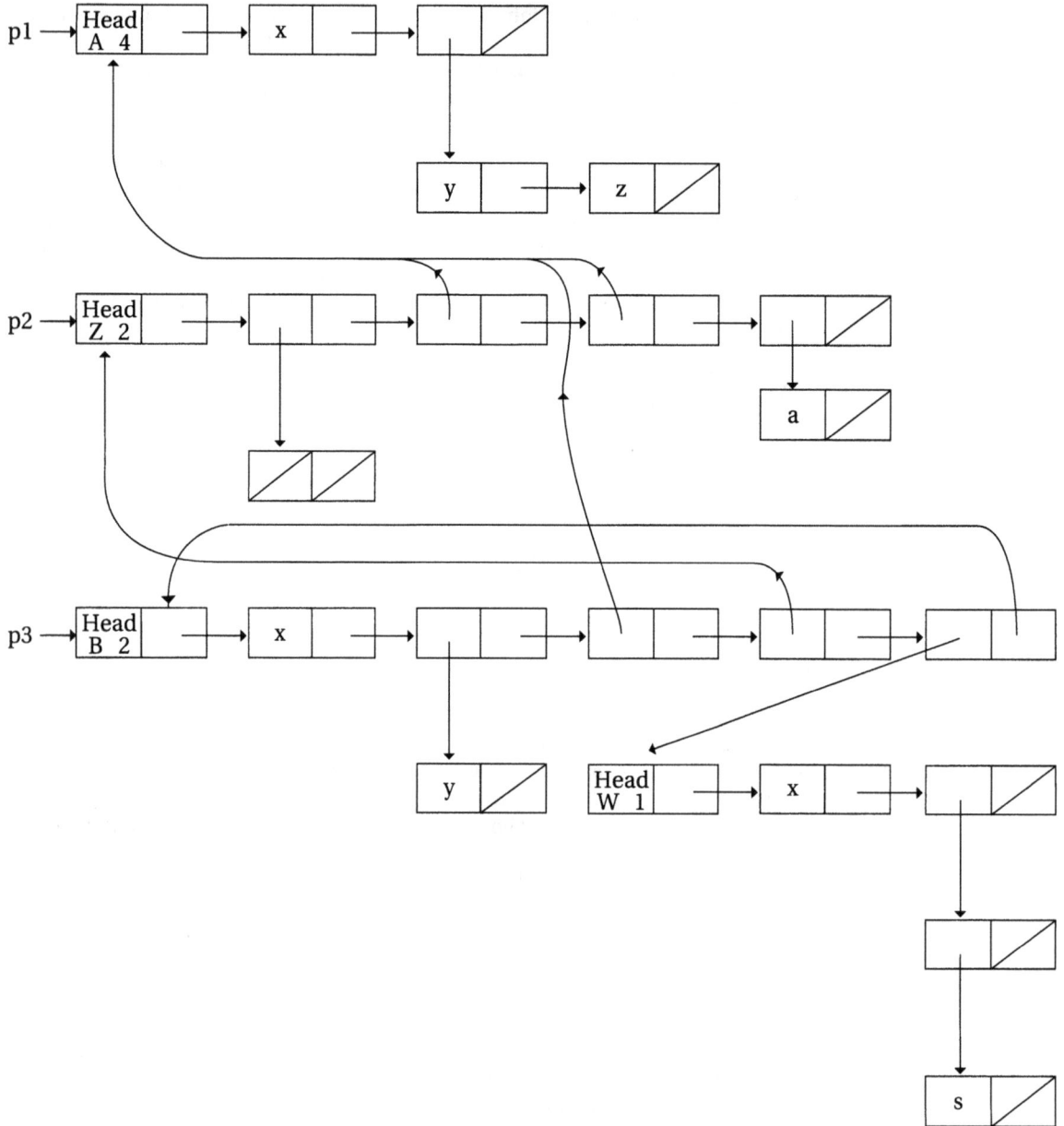

5. a. 0
   b. 0
   c. 0

6.

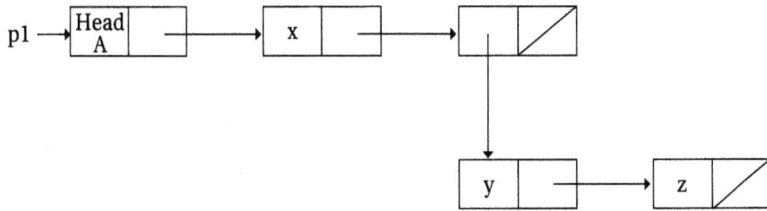

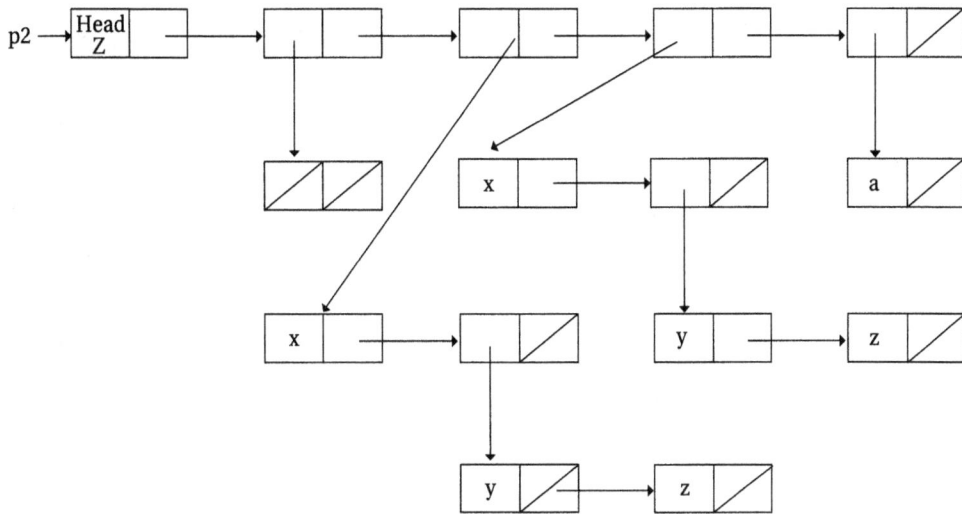

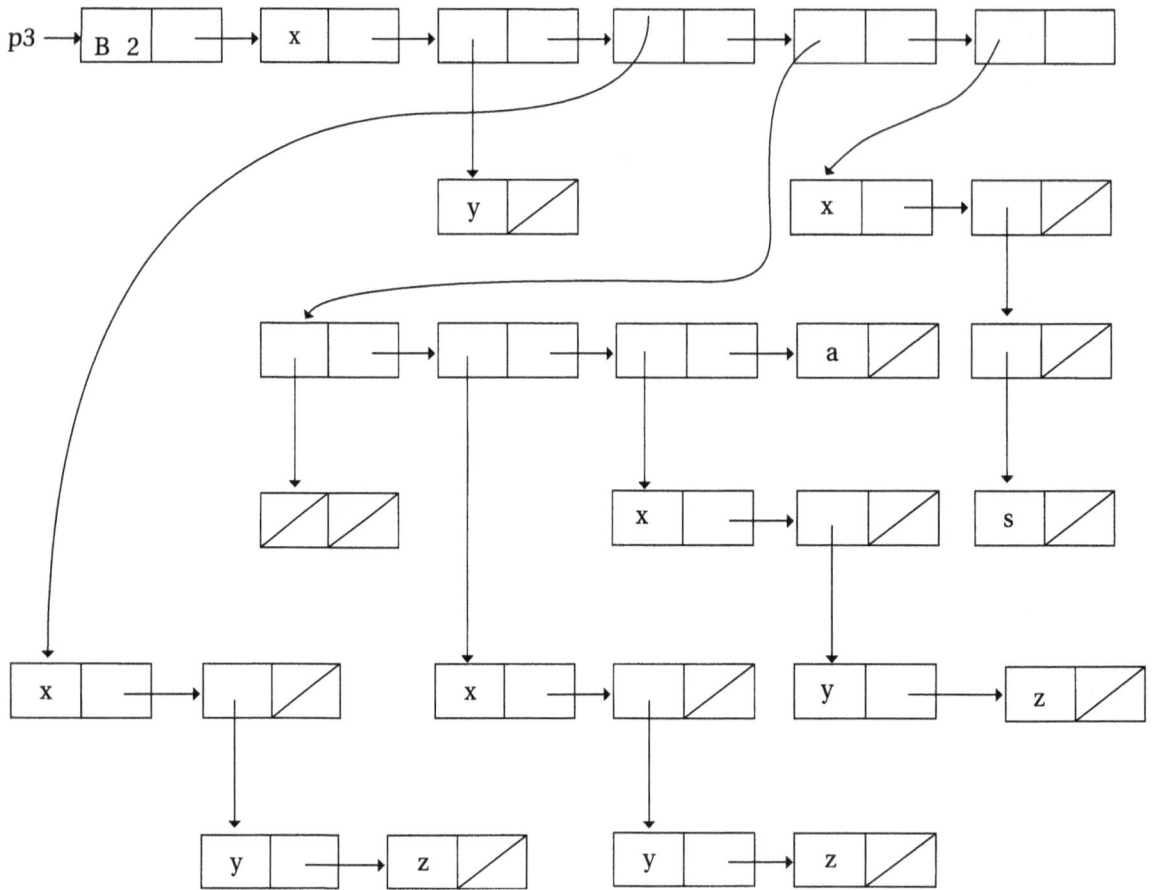

7.

DisposeGList (GList: GenListType)

```
Dismantle ← True
IF Tag(GList) = Header
   THEN
      RefCount(GList) ← RefCount(GList) − 1
      IF RefCount(GList) is NOT 0
         THENsDismantle ← Ffalse
      END IF
END IF
```

```
IF Dismantle
   THEN
      WHILE GList is NOT null DO
         IF Tag(GList) = List
            THEN   DisposeGList (ListComponent(GList))
         END IF
         Temp ← GList
         GList ←NextComponent(GList)
         Dispose (Temp)
      END WHILE
END IF
```

9. a. (A R S)
   b. ((A) R S)
   c. (A R S)

10. a. (CONS (HeadL)(Tail L)) simplifies to L.
    b. In the following picture, the head of list L is called H.

List L

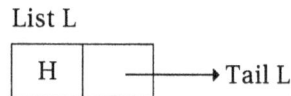

The CONS operation applied to H and (Tail L) produces a new cell, with H as head and with (Tail L) as its tail. This is precisely the representation of the list L itself.

11. In a valid list, the head of the first cell points to the head of the list, and the tail of the first cell is a pointer to the rest of the list, as illustrated in the figure for Exercise 10(b). In particular, the second half of the cell must be a pointer. In constructing CONS(A, B), the second half of the cell designates B, which is an atom. Thus, the second half of the cell cannot be a pointer, as required for a list structure. Note: In LISP, (CONS A B) is designated using a dot notation: (A . B).

15. a. (1) Property lists are connected to symbols, while association lists need not take this form. (2) Property lists allow only one instance of a key on a list, while association lists allow several. (3) Property lists typically keep all properties and their attributes on a single linked list, while association lists maintain a list of pairs, where each pair is stored in a separate record.
    b. Property lists are useful when information is to be kept for each symbol, while association lists can be accessed through various sources.
       Association lists can be useful when a new value for a key may supersede another value temporarily, but where the old value may be needed later. Property lists provide only one authoritative value for each key.

17. The generalized list structure for rule 125 follows:

Header Representation

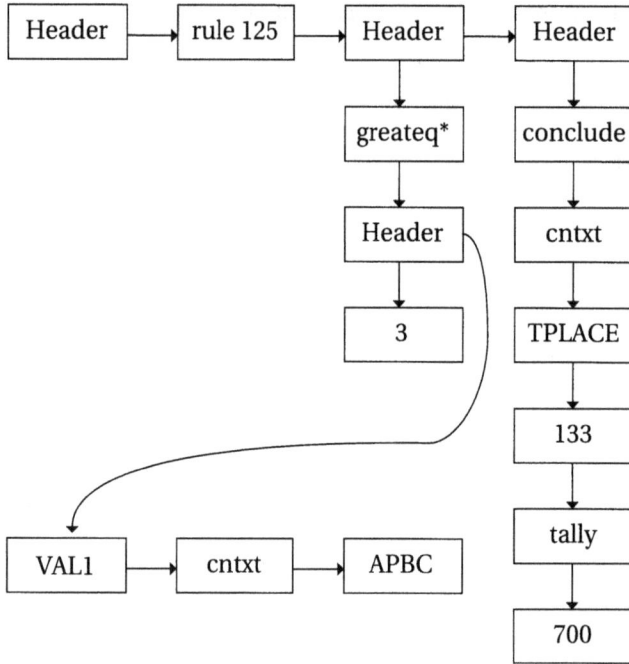

Head/Tail Representation

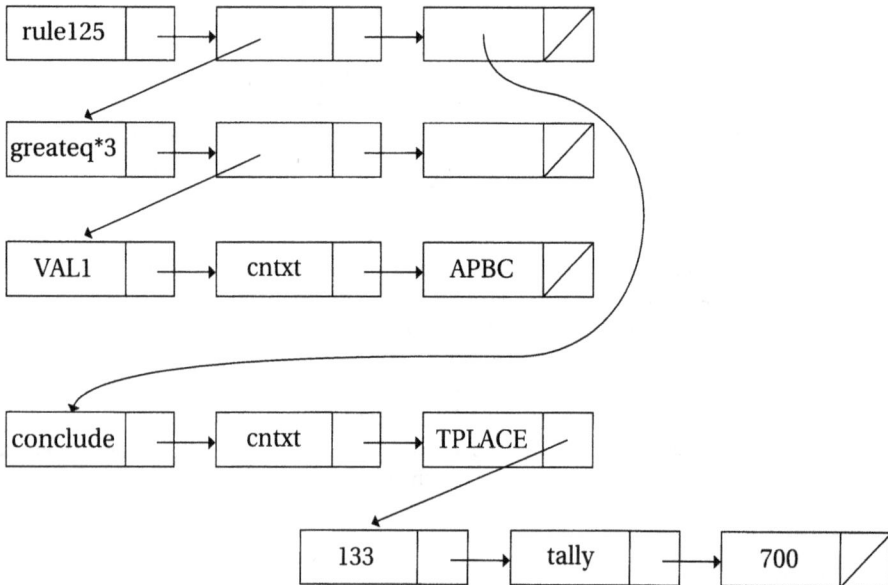

Chapter 13

1. Two ways that binary buddies and Fibonacci buddies are similar: (1) Block sizes are predetermined; and (2) a list of available space is maintained for each block size.

2. Two ways that binary buddies and Fibonacci buddies are different: (1) Blocks are of size a power of 2 in a binary buddy system; block sizes coincide with the Fibonacci sequence in a Fibonacci buddy system. (2) The algorithm for computing the address of the buddy is more complex in a Fibonacci buddy system.

6. If the block size is a constant, we can immediately tell whether the request can be satisfied, and it does not matter which block is given. Thus, allocation is O(1). The returned block may be placed anywhere in the available space list. Deallocation is always O(1). When the blocks are not the same size, allocation and deallocation range from O(log N) to O(N) depending on the strategy used to handle the available space list.

9. Garbage collection is locating unused space and making it available for allocation.

12. Recursive lists are lists that reference themselves. There is no simple way to determine when recursive lists may be physically erased. It is no longer possible to return all free nodes to the available space pool when they become free. Thus, when recursive lists are used, it is possible to run out of available space even though not all nodes are in use.

13. a. Four strategies for sequential memory allocation:

   First fit—the first block on the available space list that is big enough to service the request is used.
   Best fit—the closest fit to the requested block on the available space list is used.
   Next fit—the available space list is circular. The external pointer points to the block immediately following the block from which the last allocation was made. When a request is received, the first block that is big enough to service the request is used.
   Worst fit—the largest block on the available space list is used.

   b. The relative merits of each of the four strategies for sequential memory allocation:

   First fit—algorithms are straightforward. Deallocation can be made O(1) if the list is unsorted.
   Best fit— produces smaller left-over fragments when a block is split, thus better utilizing space.
   Next fit—speeds up the search of the available space list by distributing the smaller fragments evenly throughout the list.
   Worst fit—makes it easy to determine if the request can be serviced O(1).

19.

```
REPEAT
  Coalesce ← False
  CASE LocationOfBuddy (Block)
  BuddyIsBelow :
    Buddy ← Block +  Memory[Block].Size
    IF Memory[Buddy].Flag = Free
      THEN
        NewBlock ← Block
      Coalesce ← T\rueE
    END IF
  BuddyIsAbove :
    Buddy ← Block − Memory[Block].Size
    IF Memory[Buddy].Flag = Free
      THEN
        NewBlock ← Buddy
        Coalesce ← True
      END IF
  END CASE
  IF Coalesce
    THEN
      Remove Buddy from available space
      Block ← NewBlock
      Memory[Block].Size ← Memory[Block].Size*2
    ELSE Insert Block in Avail[log(Memory[Block].Size)]
    END IF
UNTIL NOT Coalesce
```

21. Assume that the first four locations of each block contain the block size, the Allocated/Free flag, and front and back pointers. Also, assume that the last two locations contain the flag and the size. (These assumptions follow those in the text.) Also, assume each "book-keeping" field takes 1 unit of memory.

```
BlockAbove ← Block − Memory[Block − 1]
BlockBelow ←Block + Memory[Block]
EndOfBlockBelow ←BlockBelow + Memory[BlockBelow]
IF (Memory[Block − 2] = Allocated) AND (Memory[BlockBelow + 1] = Allocated)
   THEN
      Memory[Block + 1] ←Free
      Memory[BlockBelow − 2] ←Free
      Memory[BlockBelow − 1] ←Memory[Block]
      Memory[Block + 3] ←null
      Memory[Block + 2] ←Avail
      Memory[Avail + 3] ←Block
      Avail ←Block
   ELSIF (Memory[Block − 2] = Free) AND
     (Memory[BlockBelow + 1] = Allocated)
      THEN
         Memory[BlockAbove] ←Memory[BlockAbove] + Memory[Block]
         Memory[BlockBelow − 1] ←Memory[BlockAbove]
         Memory[BlockBelow − 2] ←Free
   ELSIF (Memory[Block − 2] = Allocated) AND
     (Memory[BlockBelow + 1] = Free)
      THEN
         Memory[Memory[BlockBelow + 3] + 2] ←Block
         Memory[Memory[BlockBelow + 2] + 3] ←Block
         Memory[Block + 3] ←Memory[BlockBelow + 3]
         Memory[Block + 2] ←Memory[BlockBelow + 2]
         Memory[Block] ←Memory[Block] + Memory[BlockBelow]
         Memory[EndOfBlockBelow − 1] ←Memory[Block]
         Memory[EndOfBlockBelow − 2] ←Free
   ELSE
         Memory[Memory[BlockBelow + 3] + 2] ←Memory[BlockBelow + 2]
         Memory[Memory[BlockBelow + 2] + 3] ←Memory[BlockBelow + 3]
         Memory[BlockAbove] ←Memory[BlockAbove] + Memory[Block] +
                              Memory[BlockBelow]
         Memory[EndOfBlockBelow − 1] ←Memory[BlockAbove]
         Memory[EndOfBlockBelow − 2] ←Free
END IF
```

23. Available space list if the worst fit strategy is being used; list is not ordered.

Initial status	< 1, 100>
After allocating 15	<1, 85>
After allocating 10	<1, 75>
After allocating 50	<1, 25>
After deallocating 10	<76, 10> → <1, 25>

After deallocating 15	< 86, 15> → <76, 10> → <1, 25>
After allocating 5	< 86, 15> → <76, 10> → <1, 20>

25. Available space list if the best fit strategy is being used.

Initial status	< 1, 100>
After allocating 15	<1, 85>
After allocating 10	<1, 75>
After allocating 50	<1, 25>
After deallocating 10	<76, 10> → <1, 25>
After deallocating 15	< 86, 15> → <76, 10> → <1, 25>
After allocating 5	< 86, 15> → <76, 5> → <1, 25>

29. Memory compaction is the reallocation of storage resulting in a partitioning of memory into two contiguous blocks (one used, the other free). With increasing use of the memory space, the size of free nodes tends to become ever smaller. While the total amount of memory available may still be fairly large, it is impossible to meet requests for all but the smallest of nodes. Under such circumstances, it is necessary to reallocate the storage of the nodes in use so that the free portion of memory forms a contiguous block.

30. Scan memory from beginning to end, relocating nodes in use so that they form a contiguous block at one end of memory.

32. O(N)

34. O(N)

36. O(1)

41. O(N)

42. O(1)

43. O(1)

44. O(N)

45. 24

46. 6

Index

www.ingramcontent.com/pod-product-compliance
Lightning Source LLC
Chambersburg PA
CBHW080339220326
41598CB00030B/4546